Forty-eighth issue

yearbook of american and canadian churches 1980

Constant H. Jacquet, Jr., Editor

Prepared and edited in the Office of Research. Evaluation and Planning of the National Council of the Churches of Christ in the U.S.A., 475 Riverside Drive, New York, NY 10027

Published and distributed by Abingdon

Nashville

PREVIOUS ISSUES

Year of *Publication*	*Title*	*Editor*
1916	Federal Council Year Book	H. K. Carroll
1917	Federal Council Year Book	H. K. Carroll
1918	Yearbook of the Churches	C. F. Armitage
1919	Yearbook of the Churches	C. F. Armitage
1920	Yearbook of the Churches	S. R. Warburton
1922	Yearbook of the Churches	E. O. Watson
1923	Yearbook of the Churches	E. O. Watson
1925	Yearbook of the Churches	E. O. Watson
1927	The Handbook of the Churches	B. S. Winchester
1931	The New Handbook of the Churches	Charles Steizle
1933	Yearbook of American Churches	H. C. Weber
1935	Yearbook of American Churches	H. C. Weber
1937	Yearbook of American Churches	H. C. Weber
1939	Yearbook of American Churches	H. C. Weber
1941	Yearbook of American Churches	B. Y. Landis
1943	Yearbook of American Churches	B. Y. Landis
1945	Yearbook of American Churches	B. Y. Landis
1947	Yearbook of American Churches	B. Y. Landis, G. F. Ketcham
1949	Yearbook of American Churches	G. F. Ketcham
1951	Yearbook of American Churches	G. F. Ketcham
1952	Yearbook of American Churches	B. Y. Landis
1953	Yearbook of American Churches	B. Y. Landis
1954	Yearbook of American Churches (Edition for 1955)	B. Y. Landis
1955	Yearbook of American Churches (Edition for 1956)	B. Y. Landis
1956	Yearbook of American Churches (Edition for 1957)	B. Y. Landis
1957	Yearbook of American Churches (Edition for 1958)	B. Y. Landis
1958	Yearbook of American Churches (Edition for 1959)	B. Y. Landis
1959	Yearbook of American Churches (Edition for 1960)	B. Y. Landis
1960	Yearbook of American Churches (Edition for 1961)	B. Y. Landis
1961	Yearbook of American Churches (Edition for 1962)	B. Y. Landis
1963	Yearbook of American Churches (Edition for 1963)	B. Y. Landis
1964	Yearbook of American Churches (Edition for 1964)	B. Y. Landis
1965	Yearbook of American Churches (Edition for 1965)	B. Y. Landis
1966	Yearbook of American Churches (Edition for 1966)	C. H. Jacquet
1967	Yearbook of American Churches (Edition for 1967)	L. B. Whitman
1968	Yearbook of American Churches (Edition for 1968)	L. B. Whitman
1969	Yearbook of American Churches (Edition for 1969)	C. H. Jacquet
1970	Yearbook of American Churches (Edition for 1970)	C. H. Jacquet
1971	Yearbook of American Churches (Edition for 1971)	C. H. Jacquet
1972	Yearbook of American Churches (Edition for 1972)	C. H. Jacquet
1973	Yearbook of American and Canadian Churches	C. H. Jacquet
1974	Yearbook of American and Canadian Churches	C. H. Jacquet
1975	Yearbook of American and Canadian Churches	C. H. Jacquet
1976	Yearbook of American and Canadian Churches	C. H. Jacquet
1977	Yearbook of American and Canadian Churches	C. H. Jacquet
1978	Yearbook of American and Canadian Churches	C. H. Jacquet
1979	Yearbook of American and Canadian Churches	C. H. Jacquet

Printed in the United States of America
ISBN 0-687-46634-2
Library of Congress catalog card number: 16-5726

INTRODUCTION

This edition of the **Yearbook of American and Canadian Churches** is the 48th in a series that stretches back to 1916. A listing of years of publication, title, and editor appears on page ii.

In any work of this complexity, the cooperation of many hundreds of people in both Canada and the United States is essential not only in terms of supplying information on their organizations but also in correcting directory forms, filling out statistical reports, and providing special articles. Many informants have sent in valuable information on the existence of significant religious bodies heretofore omitted or about certain errors of commission, which has helped to make the **Yearbook** more reliable. Since the **Yearbook** became a bi-national volume in 1972, the editor has worked with an Advisory Committee for the **Yearbook of American and Canadian Churches** which meets in Toronto annually. This committee has been very helpful in keeping the editor apprised of significant religious developments in Canada which need to be recorded here. To all those people who have helped to produce this annual compilation, the editor is most grateful.

When this book is published, the neat, orderly pages and crispness of form are impressive. Yet much painstaking work goes into standardizing the material returned by hundreds of people, typing statistical tables, correcting copy, proofreading, keeping records, and doing other necessary tasks connected with transforming the not so orderly raw materials received into the finished product. Mrs. Alice Jones, editorial assistant in the Office of Research, Evaluation and Planning, National Council of Churches, has performed the above tasks superbly and, with the publication of this edition, has helped produce ten **Yearbooks**. For all this effort, the editor wishes to thank Mrs. Jones. Her work is essential to the production of the **Yearbook**.

Practically all the material in this edition of the **Yearbook** has been brought up to date since last year and the annual changes are quite extensive. Directories which have not been updated are identified by the symbol (†). Statistics in the 1980 **Yearbook of American and Canadian Churches** are defined as "current" if they are for the years 1978 or 1979. "Non-current" statistics are for the year 1977, or earlier. Statistics carry the date of reporting in most tables. On page iv, following, there is a "Guide for the User of Church Statistics" to which the user of the **Yearbook** is especially referred. It provides some important qualifications relating to denominational statistics and their use.

There being no established legal definitions for churches, clergy or religion, these concepts are always subjective. The constitutional separation of church and state has left religious organizations basically free from guidance, classification and regulation. Religious bodies, though incorporated legally in a state in the U.S. or a province in Canada, determine their own institutions, doctrines and standards of conduct.

Religious life in the United States and Canada is quite complex. The dynamic nature of these two nations, the patterns of immigration, the exchange of ideas and movements across the border, religious liberty and political freedom, and the high degree of affluence provide conditions supporting the development of religious organizations. In recent years, this has led to the formation of a bewildering diversity of sects and cults primarily in the United States but also in Canada, numbering in the thousands, some of which have received considerable attention in the news media and have been studied in detail by scholars. These sects and cults are generally characterized by small size, organizational instability, and bizarre and sometimes controversial beliefs and practices. Most of them are led by charismatic personalities who provide a sense of belonging and security to special segments of the population in quest for spiritual identity. Although important as social and religious phenomena, these groups are difficult to communicate with, record or classify. We do not attempt to list these bodies in the **Yearbook**.

What we do attempt to describe and record are the major religious bodies and institutions in the United States and Canada having the great majority of churches, clergy and membership. The editor will be grateful for knowledge of any significant omissions that fall within the categories now covered in the various directory sections in this volume.

What religious bodies are included in each edition of the **Yearbook** must, for reasons stated above, be an editorial matter based upon subjective criteria to some extent, and exclusion from the **Yearbook** should not necessarily be interpreted by readers as an adverse reflection on the nature, purpose, or reputation of any religious body.

Constant H. Jacquet, Jr.
Editor

A GUIDE FOR THE USER OF CHURCH STATISTICS

This guide is placed in a prominent position in each edition of the **Yearbook** to emphasize the fact that church statistics, like those of many other groups, vary greatly in quality and reliability. Therefore, necessary qualifications concerning them must be stated clearly and without reservation.

The **Yearbook of American and Canadian Churches** this year reports data from 222 U.S. religious bodies in Section III; Statistical and Historical Section. Of these, 111 bodies report current data; that is, data for the years 1979 or 1978. Current data, comprising 50.0 percent of all reports, account for 87.6 percent of recorded membership. Concerning denominations gathering statistics, some computerize data and have an accurate bank of information on cards or tape. Perhaps the largest group of denominations still gather statistics by conventional hand tabulation methods. Quite a few bodies are still operating on the basis of "educated guesses" in many statistical areas.

In addition to the general observations above, four major qualifications should be made about church statistics:

1) Church statistics are always incomplete, and they pass through many hands, some skilled and some not so skilled, and come up through many channels in church bureaucratic structures.

2) Church statistics are not always comparable. Definitions of membership, and of other important categories, vary from denomination to denomination. Jewish statistics are estimates of the number of individuals in households where one or more Jews reside, and, therefore, include non-Jews living in these households as the result of intermarriage. The total number of persons in Jewish households is estimated to be 8 pecent larger than the number of Jewish persons residing in these households. It should be noted that estimates of Jews has nothing to do with membership in synagogues. Roman Catholics and some Protestant bodies count all baptized persons, including children, as members. Most Protestant bodies include only "adults," usually 13 years of age and older, as members.

3) Church statistical data reported in the **Yearbook** are not for a single year. Not only do the reporting years differ from denomination to denomination, but some bodies do not report regularly. Therefore, the reports based on data for the year 1977 or earlier are "non-current" reports. Attempts to combine current and non-current data for purposes of interpretation or projection will lead to difficulties.

4) Many of the more important types of statistical data are simply not available for a large group of denominations. Records on church attendance are rarely kept, and there are no socio-economic data generally available. Statistics of participation by members in church activities and programs do not exist.

Statistics form an important part of church life and are necessary for the sound development of planning and program. Therefore, strong efforts should be made in each denomination to upgrade the quality of its church statistics. Interdenominational cooperation leading toward standardization of categories and sharing of techniques it is hoped, will continue to grow. New ways of adapting data gathered by the U.S. Bureau of the Census to church needs and programs must be discovered and utilized. The use of survey methods to obtain valuable socio-religious information about American religious life should be encouraged and expanded.

CONTENTS

1
A CALENDAR FOR CHURCH USE

1980–1981–1982–1983

The following calendar lists the dates of religious observances in the Protestant, Orthodox, Roman Catholic, and Jewish religious bodies. In addition, certain other special dates frequently recognized by religious bodies are included.

	1980	1981	1982	1983
1st Sunday in Advent	Nov 30	Nov 29	Nov 28	Nov 27
1st Day of Hanukkah	Dec 3	Dec 21	Dec 11	Dec 1
2nd Sunday in Advent	Dec 7	Dec 6	Dec 5	Dec 4
3rd Sunday in Advent	Dec 14	Dec 13	Dec 12	Dec 11
4th Sunday in Advent (Sunday before Christmas)	Dec 21	Dec 20	Dec 19	Dec 18
Christmas	Dec 25	Dec 25	Dec 25	Dec 25
First Sunday after Christmas	Dec 28	Dec 27	Dec 26	Dec 30
New Year's Eve (Watch Night)	Dec 31	Dec 31	Dec 31	Dec 31
New Year's Day	Jan 1	Jan 1	Jan 1	Jan 1
Twelfth Night: Epiphany Eve	Jan 5	Jan 5	Jan 5	Jan 5
The Epiphany	Jan 6	Jan 6	Jan 6	Jan 6
1st Sunday after the Epiphany	Jan 13	Jan 11	Jan 10	Jan 9
2nd Sunday after the Epiphany (Missionary Day)	Jan 20	Jan 18	Jan 17	Jan 16
Week of Prayer for Christian Unity	Jan 18 to 25	Jan 18 to 25	Jan 18 to 25	Jan 18 to 25
3rd Sunday after the Epiphany	Jan 27	Jan 25	Jan 24	Jan 23
4th Sunday after the Epiphany	Feb 3	Feb 1	Jan 31	Jan 30
Presentation of Jesus in the Temple	Feb 2	Feb 2	Feb 2	Feb 2
5th Sunday after the Epiphany	Feb 10	Feb 8	Feb 7	Feb 6
6th Sunday after the Epiphany	Feb 17	Feb 15	Feb 14	Feb 13
Brotherhood Week	Feb 17 to 24	Feb 15 to 22	Feb 14 to 21	Feb 13 to 20
7th Sunday after the Epiphany	———	Feb 22	Feb 21	———
8th Sunday after the Epiphany	———	Mar 1	———	———
9th Sunday after the Epiphany	———	———	———	———
Last Sunday after the Epiphany (See also Aug. 6)	Feb 17	Mar 1	Feb 21	Feb 13
Ash Wednesday	Feb 20	Mar 4	Feb 24	Feb 16
World Day of Prayer	Mar 7	Mar 6	Mar 5	Mar 4
1st Sunday in Lent	Feb 24	Mar 8	Feb 28	Feb 20
2nd Sunday in Lent	Mar 2	Mar 15	Mar 7	Feb 27
3rd Sunday in Lent	Mar 9	Mar 22	Mar 14	Mar 6
Purim	Mar 2	Mar 20	Mar 9	Feb 27
4th Sunday in Lent	Mar 16	Mar 29	Mar 21	Mar 13
The Annunciation	Mar 25	Mar 25	Mar 25	Mar 25
5th Sunday in Lent	Mar 23	Apr 5	Mar 28	Mar 20
Holy Week	Mar 30 to Apr 5	Apr 12 to Apr 18	Apr 4 to 10	Mar 27 to Apr 2
Palm Sunday (Passion Sunday)	Mar 30	Apr 12	Apr 4	Mar 27
Maundy Thursday	Apr 3	Apr 16	Apr 8	Mar 31
Good Friday	Apr 4	Apr 17	Apr 9	Apr 1
Easter Eve	Apr 5	Apr 18	Apr 10	Apr 2
Easter (Western)	Apr 6	Apr 19	Apr 11	Apr 3
Easter (Orthodox)	Apr 6	Apr 26	Apr 18	May 8

A CALENDAR FOR CHURCH USE

	1980	1981	1982	1983
2nd Sunday of Easter	Apr 13	Apr 26	Apr 18	Apr 10
3rd Sunday of Easter	Apr 20	May 3	Apr 25	Apr 17
1st Day of Passover	Apr 1	Apr 19	Apr 8	Mar 29
4th Sunday of Easter	Apr 27	May 10	May 2	Apr 24
5th Sunday of Easter	May 4	May 17	May 9	May 1
May Fellowship Day	May 2	May 1	May 7	May 6
Rural Life Sunday (Rogation Sunday, 6th Sunday of Easter)	May 11	May 24	May 16	May 8
National Family Week	May 4 to 11	May 3 to 10	May 2 to 9	May 1 to 8
Festival of the Christian Home (Mother's Day)	May 11	May 10	May 9	May 8
Ascension Day	May 15	May 28	May 20	May 12
7th Sunday of Easter	May 18	May 31	May 23	May 15
1st Day of Shavuot	May 21	June 8	May 28	May 18
Whitsunday (Pentecost)	May 25	June 7	May 30	May 22
Trinity Sunday	June 1	June 14	June 6	May 29
2nd Sunday after Pentecost	June 8	June 21	June 13	June 5
Children's Sunday	June 8	June 14	June 13	June 12
3rd Sunday after Pentecost	June 15	June 28	June 20	June 12
4th Sunday after Pentecost	June 22	July 5	June 27	June 19
5th Sunday after Pentecost	June 29	July 12	July 4	June 26
Father's Day	June 15	June 21	June 20	June 19
St. Jean Baptiste Day (French Canada)	June 24	June 24	June 24	June 24
6th Sunday after Pentecost	July 6	July 19	July 11	July 3
7th Sunday after Pentecost	July 13	July 26	July 18	July 10
8th Sunday after Pentecost	July 20	Aug 2	July 25	July 17
9th Sunday after Pentecost	July 27	Aug 9	Aug 1	July 24
The Transfiguration (Also last Sunday after the Epiphany)	Aug 6	Aug 6	Aug 6	Aug 6
10th Sunday after Pentecost	Aug 3	Aug 16	Aug 8	July 31
11th Sunday after Pentecost	Aug 10	Aug 23	Aug 15	Aug 7
12th Sunday after Pentecost	Aug 17	Aug 30	Aug 22	Aug 14
Labor Sunday	Aug 31	Sept 6	Sept 5	Sept 4
Labor Day	Sept 1	Sept 7	Sept 6	Sept 5
13th Sunday after Pentecost	Aug 24	Sept 6	Aug 29	Aug 21
14th Sunday after Pentecost	Aug 31	Sept 13	Sept 5	Aug 28
15th Sunday after Pentecost	Sept 7	Sept 20	Sept 12	Sept 4
1st Day of Rosh Hashanah	Sept 11	Sept 29	Sept 18	Sept 8
16th Sunday after Pentecost	Sept 14	Sept 27	Sept 19	Sept 11
17th Sunday after Pentecost	Sept 21	Oct 4	Sept 26	Sept 18
Yom Kippur	Sept 20	Oct 8	Sept 27	Sept 17
1st Day of Sukkot	Sept 25	Oct 13	Oct 2	Sept 22
18th Sunday after Pentecost	Sept 28	Oct 11	Oct 3	Sept 25
19th Sunday after Pentecost	Oct 5	Oct 18	Oct 10	Oct 2
Christian Education Emphases	a week in September			
20th Sunday after Pentecost	Oct 12	Oct 25	Oct 17	Oct 9
Shemini Atzeret	Oct 2	Oct 20	Oct 9	Sept 29
World Communion Sunday	Oct 5	Oct 4	Oct 3	Oct 2
Laity Sunday	Oct 12	Oct 11	Oct 10	Oct 9
Simhat Torah	Oct 3	Oct 21	Oct 10	Sept 30
Thanksgiving Day (Canada)	Oct 13	Oct 12	Oct 11	Oct 10
21st Sunday after Pentecost	Oct 19	Nov 1	Oct 24	Oct 16
Reformation Sunday	Oct 26	Oct 25	Oct 31	Oct 30
Reformation Day	Oct 31	Oct 31	Oct 31	Oct 31

	1980	1981	1982	1983
22nd Sunday after Pentecost	Oct 26	Nov 8	Oct 31	Oct 23
All Saints' Day	Nov 1	Nov 1	Nov 1	Nov 1
All Soul's Day	Nov 2	Nov 2	Nov 2	Nov 2
World Community Day	Nov 7	Nov 6	Nov 5	Nov 4
23rd Sunday after Pentecost	Nov 2	Nov 15	Nov 7	Oct 30
24th Sunday after Pentecost	Nov 9	Nov 22	Nov 14	Nov 6
25th Sunday after Pentecost	Nov 16	——	Nov 21	Nov 13
26th Sunday after Pentecost	Nov 23	——	——	Nov 20
27th Sunday after Pentecost	——	——	——	——
28th Sunday after Pentecost	——	——	——	——
Stewardship Day	Nov 9	Nov 8	Nov 14	Nov 13
Bible Sunday	Nov 23	Nov 15	Nov 21	Nov 20
Thanksgiving Sunday (U.S.)	Nov 23	Nov 22	Nov 21	Nov 20
Thanksgiving Day (U.S.)	Nov 27	Nov 26	Nov 25	Nov 24

A TABLE OF DATES AHEAD

The following table indicates when Easter and other important festival days occur during the next few years. It also indicates the number of Sundays after the Epiphany and after Pentecost for each year of the period. Easter may come as early as March 22 or as late as April 25, thus bringing a wide variation in the number of Sundays included in certain of the Christian seasons.

Year	Sundays after the Epiphany	Ash Wednesday	Western Easter	Orthodox Easter	Whitsunday	Sundays after Pentecost	First Sunday in Advent
1980	6	Feb 20	Apr 6	Apr 6	May 25	26	Nov 30
1981	8	Mar 4	Apr 19	Apr 26	June 7	24	Nov 29
1982	7	Feb 24	Apr 11	Apr 18	May 30	25	Nov 28
1983	6	Feb 16	Apr 3	May 8	May 22	26	Nov 27

II
DIRECTORIES

1. UNITED STATES COOPERATIVE ORGANIZATIONS, NATIONAL

NATIONAL COUNCIL OF THE CHURCHES OF CHRIST IN THE UNITED STATES OF AMERICA

The National Council of the Churches of Christ in the United States of America is a cooperative agency of Christian communions seeking to fulfill the unity and mission to which God calls them. The member communions, responding to the gospel revealed in the Scriptures, confess Jesus, the incarnate Son of God, as Savior and Lord. Relying on the transforming power of the Holy Spirit, the Council works to bring churches into a life-giving fellowship and into common witness, study, and action to the glory of God and in service to all creation.

Semi-Annual Meetings of the Governing Board
Indianapolis, IN, May 7-9, 1980
New York, NY, November 6-8, 1980

Offices at 475 Riverside Dr., New York, NY 10027
except as stated below.
Tel. (212) 870-2200

GENERAL OFFICERS

President, Rev. M. William Howard
General Secretary, Claire Randall
Vice-Presidents, Rev. Tracey K. Jones; Dorothy J. Marple; Bishop Maximos of Diokleia
Treasurer, Julia Piper
Recording Secretary, Bishop Chester A. Kirkendoll
Vice-Presidents for Program, Rev. George Telford (Church and Society); Rev. Howard Ham (Education and Ministry); Rev. Oscar McCloud (Overseas Ministries); Sonia Francis (Communication Comm.); Rev. Jeanne Audrey Powers (Faith and Order); Rev. Lewis H. Lancaster, Jr. (Regional and Local Ecumenism); Rev. Robert Richardson (Stewardship); Rev. Eunice Velez (Justice, Liberation, and Human Fulfillment)

ELECTED STAFF OFFICES OF THE GENERAL SECRETARY

Gen. Sec., Claire Randall
Assoc. Gen. Sec., James A. Hamilton
Asst. Gen. Sec. for the Ofc. of the Gen. Sec., Rev. Arleon L. Kelley
Dir. of the Washington Office, James A. Hamilton, 110 Maryland Ave., NE, Washington, DC 20002. Tel. (202) 544-2350. Assoc. Dir., Jane Leiper; Asst. Dir., Mary Anderson Cooper
Coordinator for Hunger Concerns, Rev. Louis L. Knowles

DIVISION OF CHURCH AND SOCIETY

Assoc. Gen. Sec. for Church and Society, Kenyon Burke
Staff Assoc. for International Affairs, Alice Wimer
Staff Assoc. for Religious and Civil Liberty, Rev. Dean M. Kelley
Staff Assoc. for Domestic Hunger and Poverty, Mary Ellen Lloyd
Staff Assoc. for Racial Justice Concerns, ———
Staff Assoc. for Economic & Social Justice, Chris Cowap
Staff Assoc. for Justice for Women, Rev. Joan M. Martin
Co-Dirs. Child and Family Justice Project, Rev. Eileen W. Lindner; Rev. Richard L. Killmer
Exec. Dir., Proj. for Incarcerated Veterans, Louise Ransom

Related Movements Sponsored by DCS

Dir. *Delta Ministry,* Owen H. Brooks, P.O. Box 457, Greenville, MS 38701. Tel. (601) 334-4587
Dir., *Interfaith Center on Corporate Responsibility,* Timothy H. Smith
Dir., *National Farm Worker Ministry,* Rev. Wayne C. Hartmire, 1430 Olympic Blvd., Ste. 501, Los Angeles, CA 90015. Tel. (213) 386-8130.

DIVISION OF EDUCATION AND MINISTRY

Assoc. Gen. Sec. for Education and Ministry, Emily V. Gibbes
Exec. Asst. for Finance, Kathleen Wroe
Dir., Geneva Point Center, Rev. Harry Widman, Star Rt. 62, Box 469, Center Harbor, NH 03226, Tel. (603) 253-4366 (summer); or P. O. Box 905, Wolfeboro, NH 03894, Tel. (603) 569-1606

Program Committee, Education for Christian Life and Mission

Exec. Dir., Rev. J. Blaine Fister
Staff Assoc., Commission on Education for Mission, and

Exec. Dir., Friendship Press, Rev. Ward L. Kaiser
Man. Ed., Friendship Press, Linda J. Ferm
Business and Promotion Mgr., Friendship Press, Wells Drorbaugh, Jr.
Staff Administrator, Committee Uniform Lessons, Rev. J. Blaine Fister
Dir. Adult Education/Leadership Dev., Rev. J. Blaine Fister
Dir., Black and Multi Ethnic Christian Education Resources Center, Joseph V. Nash
Dir., Commission on Family Ministries and Human Sexuality, Rev. G. William Sheek
Dir., Learning Needs, Vacation, Leisure and Outdoor Education, Ima Jean Kidd
Staff Assoc., Youth Ministry/Human Relations Trng./Public Education Concerns, Dorothy R. Savage

Program Committee, Education in the Society

Exec., Rev. Robert Parsonage
Assoc. Exec., ———
United Board for College Development, 159 Forrest Ave., N.E., Rm. 514, Atlanta, GA 30303. Tel. (404) 659-6331 (The following can be reached at the above address.)
Dir., Rev. Charles C. Turner

Program Committee, Professional Church Leadership

Exec., Rev. James W. Gunn

DIVISION OF OVERSEAS MINISTRIES

Assoc. Gen. Sec. for Overseas Ministries, Rev. Eugene L. Stockwell
Assoc. Sec., Rev. Paul F. McCleary
Interpretation & Promotion:
Dir., Rev. Larry D. Hollon
Finance and Adm., Dir., James E. Styer

Functional Offices

Agricultural Missions:
Dir., Rev. J. Benton Rhoades;
Dir. for Nutrition and Rural Community Edu., Therese Drummond
Dir. for Agronomic Services, Osbert Liburd
Associated Mission Medical Office, Dir., John D. Frame, M.D.
Church World Service:
Exec. Dir., Rev. Paul F. McCleary;
Asst. to CWS Dir. for Development, ———
Asst. to the CWS Dir. for Emergency Response, Stanley Mitton
Dir., West Coast Office, CWS, Hugh Wire, 111A Fairmont Ave., Oakland, CA 94611. Tel. (415) 465-5733
Material Resources,
Dir., Rev. John W. Schauer, Jr.
Immigration and Refugees,
Dir., Nancy L. Nicalo
Family Life and Population Programs
Dir., Iluminada R. Rodriguez
CWS/LWR Rep. for Development Planning, Rev. Paul L. Minear
CWS/Elkhart
Mailing Address, CWS, Elkhart, IN 46515 Tel. (219) 264-3102:
Nat'l Dir., Rev. Ronald Stenning;
Dir. Fin. Management, Rev. John Metzler Jr.;
Dir. Field Services, Rev. Lila E. McCray;
Human Rights, Dir. Rev. William L. Wipfler
Intermedia
Dir., Rev. David W. Bridell
Dir. for Adult Basic Ed., Sr. Kristen McNamara
Dir. for Writer Trng. & Print Media, Marion Van Horne
Internat'l Congregations & Lay Ministry,
Dir., Rev. John R. Collins
Leadership Development, Dir., John W. Backer
Overseas Personnel, Dir., Rev. Paul W. Yount Jr.

Geographic Offices

Africa, Dir., Rev. Robert C. S. Powell; Assoc. Dir., Willis H. Logan
East Asia & the Pacific:
Dir., Rev. Edwin M. Luidens;
China Program, Dir., Rev. Franklin J. Woo;
Japan and Hong Kong Program,
Dir., Rev. Robert W. Northrup;
Central America, Mexico and the Caribbean, Dir., Rev. Ruben Lores
South America, Dir. Rev. Joel Gajardo
Middle East: Dir. J. Richard Butler
Europe, Rev. Eugene L. Stockwell
Southern Asia, Dir., Kirk Alliman

COMMUNICATION COMMISSION

Asst. Gen. Sec. for Communication, Rev. William F. Fore
Exec. Dir. for Broadcasting, Rev. D. Williams McClurken
Dir., for Media Resources, Rev. David W. Pomeroy
Dir., Placement and Distribution, Lois J. Anderson

COMMISSION ON FAITH AND ORDER

Asst. Gen. Sec. for Faith and Order, ———
Assoc. Exec. Dir., Sr. Ann Patrick Ware

COMMISSION ON REGIONAL AND LOCAL ECUMENISM

Asst. Gen. Sec. for Regional and Local Ecumenism, Rev. Joan B. Campbell
Assoc. Exec. Dir. and Spcl. Asst. to Gen. Sec. for Christian/Jewish Rel., ———

COMMISSION ON STEWARDSHIP

Asst. Gen. Sec. for Stewardship, Rev. Nordan C. Murphy
Staff Assoc. for Interpretation and Promotion, Bertie Meeker

COMMISSION ON JUSTICE, LIBERATION, AND HUMAN FULFILLMENT

Asst. Gen. Sec. for Justice, Liberation, and Human Fulfillment, Rev. Jovelino P. Ramos

OFFICE OF RESEARCH, EVALUATION, AND PLANNING

Asst. Gen. Sec. for Research, Evaluation and Planning, Peggy L. Shriver
Staff Assoc. Information Services, Constant H. Jacquet, Jr.

OFFICE OF FINANCE AND SERVICES

Asst. Gen. Sec. for Finance and Services, and Asst. Treas, NCC, Robert N. Galloway

Department of Financial Development

Exec. Dir., ——

Department of Financial Management

Exec. Dir., Anne Krupsky
Assoc. Exec. Dir., Marion Perdiz

Department of Business Services

Exec. Dir., Dorothy L. Weeks
Asst. Exec. Dir., Mary McAllister
Dir., Office Services, Ann K. Davis

Department of Publication Services

Exec. Dir., Frederick W. Reed
Mgr., Letter Shop Operations, Lists and Mailing, ——
Dir., Business Opns., ——

OFFICE OF PERSONNEL

Asst. Gen. Sec. for Personnel, Emilio F. Carrillo, Jr.
Dir. of Personnel Operations, Lynn R. Best

OFFICE OF NEWS AND INFORMATION

Exec. Dir. of News and Information, J. Warren Day
Dir., Newspaper Services, David E. Osborne
Dir., Special Services, Faith Pomponio
Dir., Ecumedia News Service and Broadcast News, L. Franklin Devine

Constituent Bodies of the National Council

African Methodist Episcopal Church
African Methodist Episcopal Zion Church
American Baptist Churches in the U.S.A.
The Antiochian Orthodox Christian Archdiocese of North America
Armenian Church of America, Diocese of the (including Diocese of California)
Christian Church (Disciples of Christ)
Christian Methodist Episcopal Church
Church of the Brethren
The Coptic Orthodox Church
The Episcopal Church
Friends United Meeting
General Convention, the Swedenborgian Church
Greek Orthodox Archdiocese of North and South America
Hungarian Reformed Church in America
Lutheran Church in America
Moravian Church in America
National Baptist Convention of America
National Baptist Convention, U.S.A., Inc.
National Council of Community Churches
Orthodox Church in America
Philadelphia Yearly Meeting of the Religious Society of Friends
Polish National Catholic Church of America
The Presbyterian Church in the United States
Progressive National Baptist Convention, Inc.
Reformed Church in America
Russian Orthodox Church in the U.S.A. Patriarchal Parishes of the
Serbian Eastern Orthodox Church for the U.S.A. and Canada
Syrian Orthodox Church of Antioch
Ukrainian Orthodox Church in America
United Church of Christ
The United Methodist Church
The United Presbyterian Church in the United States of America

American Bible Society

Founded in 1816, the American Bible Society has been governed for more than a century and a half by a board of distinguished Christian laity. They see to it that the Society is operated efficiently, economically and strictly in accordance with its stated purpose of distributing the Holy Scriptures without doctrinal note or comment. Soon after its founding, the Society's program expanded from distribution in the United States to worldwide outreach. Presently the ABS cooperates with the United Bible Societies in global coordination of Scripture translation, production, and distribution.

Through the labors of diligent scholars and the efforts of skilled translators, at least one book of the Bible has been translated and published by various Christian organizations in more than 1,600 languages and dialects.

To meet the need for Scriptures in current texts and formats, the American Bible Society has produced the Word on tapes, records, and cassettes and has provided the Scriptures in a wide variety of formats and designs. These include brightly illustrated Scripture Selections and Portions, paperback editions—all designed to serve the churches in their total work and witness to the Gospel. As a result, Scripture distribution has increased dramatically. In 1978 ABS distribution in the United States was over 127 million. Overseas, the ABS cooperated with the United Bible Societies in more than 150 nations and territories. Total distribution of all the Bible Societies was over 503 million Scriptures.

Support of the Bible Society's far-flung mission is provided by concerned Christian individuals, congregations, and denominations.

Offices:
National Headquarters: 1865 Broadway, New York, NY 10023. Tel. (212) 581-7400

OFFICERS

Pres., Edmund F. Wagner
Vice-Pres., Coleman Burke
Gen. Secs., Alice E. Ball; Rev. John D. Erickson
Treas., Charles W. Baas
Exec. Officers: Rev. Edward A. Cline (National Distribution); Lorraine A. Kupper (Ways and Means); Charles Nelson (Finance); Rev. Eugene A. Nida (Translations); Russell J. Preston (Production and Supply); John Reimer (General Administration); Earl F. Schneider (Finance); Rev. Gilbert Darlington, Rev. Laton E. Holmgren, Rev. Eric M. North, and Rev. Robert T. Taylor (Consultants)
Departmental Officers: George Amann (Production and Supply); Rev. J. Milton Bell (Ways and Means); Rev. Arthur C. Borden (Ways and Means); Rev. Robert G.

Bratcher (Translations); Henry Bucher (Finance); Mary Cooke (Ways and Means); John A. Duguid (Ways and Means); Elizabeth J. Eisenhart (Library); Petra Greenfield (Finance); Arthur Kollmer (Finance); Clifford P. Macdonald (Ways and Means); Robert J. Maynes (Finance); Rev. Barclay M. Newman (Translations); Rev. Ivan H. Nothdurft (Library); Rev. Heber F. Peacock (Translations); Vartan Sahagian (Overseas); Edith M. Soffel (Finance); Rev. John A. Thompson (Translations); Michael J. Valentine (Finance); Richard C. Walter (Finance); William C. Wonderly (Translations)

PERIODICAL

Bible Society Record (m), 1865 Broadway, New York, NY 10023, Clifford P. Macdonald, Ed.

American Tract Society

The American Tract Society is a nonprofit, nonsectarian, interdenominational organization, instituted in 1825 through the merger of most of the then-existing tract societies. As one of the earliest religious publishing bodies in the United States, ATS has pioneered in the publishing of Christian books, booklets, and leaflets. The volume of distribution has risen to more than 31 million pieces of literature annually.

Office: P. O. Box 402008, Garland (Dallas), TX 75040. Tel. (214) 276-9408

OFFICERS

Chpsn, Dr. W. Theodore Taylor
Vice Chpsn., Oscar Bakke
Pres., Dr. S. E. Slocum, Jr.
Sec., Edgar L. Bensen
Treas., A. J. Widman

The Associated Church Press

The Associated Church Press was organized in 1916. Its member publications include major Protestant and Orthodox groups in the U.S. and Canada. There are also Catholic members. It is a professional religious journalistic group seeking to promote better understanding among editors, raise standards, represent the interests of the religious press to the governments in the western hemisphere. It sponsors seminars, conventions, workshops for editors, staff people, business members.

Pres., J. Martin Bailey, 1840 Interchurch Center, 475 Riverside Dr., New York, NY 10027
Exec. Sec., Donald F. Hetzler, P.O. Box 306, Geneva, IL 60134. Tel. (312) 232-1055
Treas., James M. Wall, 407 South Dearborn, Chicago, IL 60605

The Associated Gospel Churches

Organized in 1939, The Associated Gospel Churches is primarily a service agency for fundamental denominations, colleges, seminaries, and missions. It also provides fellowship for Bible-believing independent churches, various Christian workers, missionaries, chaplains, laymen, and students.

One of the chief functions of AGC is to endorse chaplain applicants from the various denominations it represents, a clientele of over 3,000,000. It is recognized by the U.S. Department of Defense and espouses the cause of national defense.

AGC devotes considerable effort toward gaining proper recognition for fundamental colleges, seminaries, and Bible Institutes. It was one of the founders of The American Association of Christian Schools of Higher Learning.

Associated Gospel Churches believes in the sovereignty of the local church, believes in the doctrines of the historic Christian faith, and practices separation from the apostasy.

Office: 1919 Beech St., Pittsburgh, PA 15221. Tel. (412) 241-7656

OFFICERS

Pres. and Chmn., Commission on Chaplains, Dr. W. O. H. Garman
Vice-Pres., and Co-Chmn., Commission on Chaplains, Chaplain (LTC) Ivan E. Speight
Sec.-Treas., Dale E. Walker
Vice-Chmn., Commission on Chaplains and Field Sec., Donald N. Martin

Association of Statisticians of American Religious Bodies

This Association was organized in 1934 and grew out of personal consultations held by representatives from The Yearbook of American Churches, The National (now Official) Catholic Directory, the Jewish Statistical Bureau, and The Methodist (now The United Methodist) Church.

ASARB has a variety of purposes: to bring together those officially and professionally responsible for gathering, compiling, and publishing denominational statistics; to provide a forum for the exchange of ideas and sharing of problems in statistical methods and procedure; and to seek such standardization as may be possible in religious statistical data.

OFFICERS

Pres., Paul M. Deeth, United Church of Canada, 85 St. Clair Ave., E., Toronto, Ontario M4T 1M8
Vice-Pres.'s, B. W. Lanpher, Christian and Missionary Alliance, Box C, Nyack, NY 10960; John P. O'Hara, Lutheran Church—Missouri Synod, 500 N. Broadway, St. Louis, MO 63102
Sec.-Treas., Edward A. Rauff, Lutheran Council/USA, 360 Park Ave. South, New York, NY 10010, Tel. (212) 532-6350

Christian Holiness Association

The Association is a coordinating agency of those religious bodies that hold the Wesleyan-Arminian theological view. It was organized in 1867.

Central Office: 7 Lawrence Ave., Stanhope, NJ 07879
112th Annual Convention, Ridgecrest Baptist Center, Ridgecrest, NC

OFFICERS

Pres., Dr. Dennis Kinlaw, Wilmore, KY
Exec. Dir., Rev. Darius L. Salter, 7 Lawrence Ave., Stanhope, NJ 07874

AFFILIATED ORGANIZATIONS

Bible Holiness Movement
Brethren in Christ Church
Churches of Christ in Christian Union
Evangelical Christian Church
Evangelical Church of North America
Evangelical Friends Alliance
Evangelical Methodist Church
Free Methodist Church of North America
The Canadian Holiness Federation
The Church of the Nazarene
The Salvation Army
The Salvation Army in Canada
United Brethren in Christ Church (Sandusky Conference)
The Wesleyan Church

COOPERATING ORGANIZATIONS

Methodist Protestant Church
Primitive Methodist Church
The Congregational Methodist Church
The Church of God (Anderson)
The Missionary Church

A Christian Ministry in the National Parks

The Ministry is an independent movement providing interdenominational religious services in 65 National Parks, Monuments, and Recreation Areas. For 20 years it was administered in the National Council of Churches. On January 1, 1972, it became an independent movement representing over 40 denominations, 60 local park committees, over 300 theological seminaries, and 16 separate religious organizations.

Office: 222½ E. 49th St., New York, NY 10017. Tel. (212) 758-3450

OFFICER

Dir., Dr. Warren W. Ost

PERIODICAL

Parkbound (annual), Warren W. Ost, Ed.

Church Women United in the U.S.A.

Church Women United in the U.S.A. is an ecumenical lay movement providing Protestant, Orthodox, and Roman Catholic and other Christian women with programs and channels of involvement in church, civic, and national affairs, CWU has some 2,000 units formally organized in communities located in all 50 states and the District of Columbia.

Office: 475 Riverside Dr., Room 806, New York, NY 10027. Tel. (212) 870-2347

OFFICERS

Pres., The Rev. Mary Louise Rowand, Dallas, TX
Deputy Vice-Pres., Thelma Davidson Adair, New York, NY
Vice Pres. for Cultivation, Dorothy G. Barnard, St. Louis, MO
Sec., Betsy A. Garland, Warwick, RI
Treas., Cora C. Sparrowk, Ione, CA
Regional Vice Pres.'s: Kathryn S. Gramley, Greensboro, NC (Southeastern); Vivian S. Hampers, Grand Rapids, MI (Central); Carol M. Kolsti, Austin, TX (South Central); Louise C. Leonard, Urbana, IL (East Central); Mirian M. Malonson, Seattle, WA (Northwestern); Miriam F. Phillips, West Medford, MA (Northeastern); Elsie E. Randolph, Silver Spring, MD (Mid-Atlantic); Beclee Newcomer Wilson, Piedmont, CA (Southwestern).

STAFF

Gen. Dir., Martha Edens
Assoc., Gen. Dir., Ruth M. Woodcock
Dir. of Financial Dev., Nan Cox
Adm. Services, Anne D. Martin
Citizen Action, Emma Darnell
Communications and Interpretation, Virginia Baron, Maria Martinez
Cultivation, Louise Weeks
International Community, Dorothy C. Wagner
Metropolitan Program, Elizabeth Haselden and Katie Booth
UN Affairs, Edna McCallion
WICS Liaison, Katie Booth
Faith-Life and Empowerment of Women, Gail D. Hinand

PERIODICAL

The Church Woman (6/yr.)
Lead Time (6/yr.)

Consultation on Church Union

Officially constituted in 1962, the Consultation on Church Union is a venture in reconciliation of ten American communions which has been authorized to explore the formation of a united church truly catholic, truly evangelical, and truly reformed. In 1979 the participating churches were African Methodist Episcopal Church, African Methodist Episcopal Zion Church, Christian Church (Disciples of Christ), Christian Methodist Episcopal Church, The Episcopal Church, National Council of Community Churches, The Presbyterian Church in the United States, United Church of Christ, The United Methodist Church, The United Presbyterian Church in the U.S.A.

SECRETARIAT

Address: 228 Alexander St., Princeton, NJ 08540. Tel. (609) 921-7866
Gen. Sec., Rev. Dr. Gerald F. Moede
Assoc. Gen. Sec., Rev. John E. Brandon
Asst. Gen. Sec. for Adm., Mrs. Doris B. Pettebone

GENERAL ORGANIZATION

The *Plenary Meeting,* which normally meets every eighteen months to two years, is composed of ten delegates and ten associate delegates from each of the participating churches. Included also are observer-consultants from over twenty other churches, other union negotiations, and conciliar bodies.

The *Executive Committee* is composed of the president, two representatives from each of the participating churches, and the secretariat.

The *Secretariat* are the full-time executive staff members at the national offices in Princeton.

Various *commissions* and *committees* are periodically set up to fulfill certain assignments. (1979 commissions include Commission on Generating Communities, Commission on Interim Eucharistic Fellowship, Commission on Governance, Theology Commission, Commission on Worship.) Special emphasis is also being given to a Women's Task Force and a Task Force of Persons with Disabilities.

OFFICERS

Pres., Rev. Dr. Rachel Henderlite, 4800 Valley Oak Dr., Austin, TX 78731
Vice-Pres., Bishop Arthur Marshall, Jr., Ben Hill Sta., P. O. Box 41138, Atlanta, GA 30331

Sec., Rev. Dr. Albert M. Pennybacker, University Christian Church, 2720 University Dr., Fort Worth, TX 76109

REPRESENTATIVES FROM PARTICIPATING CHURCHES

African Methodist Episcopal Church, Bishop Vinton R. Anderson, 2685 Halleck Dr., Columbus, OH 43209; Bishop Richard A. Hildebrand, 29 Bala Ave., Ste. 222, Bala Cynwyd, PA 19004

African Methodist Episcopal Zion Church, Bishop J. Clinton Hoggard, 1100 W. 42nd St., Indianapolis, IN 46206; Bishop Arthur Marshall, Jr., AME Zion Church, Ben Hill Sta., P. O. Box 41138, Atlanta, GA 30331

Christian Church (Disciples of Christ), Rev. Dr. Paul A. Crow, Jr., P. O. Box 1986, Indianapolis, IN 46206; Rev. Dr. Albert M. Pennybacker, University Christian Church, 2720 University Dr., Ft. Worth, TX 76109

Christian Methodist Episcopal Church, Bishop E. P. Murchison, Paul Brown Bldg., Rm. 762, 818 Olive St., St. Louis, MO 63136; Bishop Caesar D. Coleman, 2320 Sutter St., Dallas, TX 75216

The Episcopal Church, Rt. Rev. John M. Krumm, 412 Sycamore St., Cincinnati, OH 45202; Dr. Cynthia Wedel, Goodwin House, 4800 Fillmore Ave., Apt. 832, Alexandria, VA 22311

National Council of Community Churches, Rev. Joe V. Hotchkiss, 89 Wilson Bridge Rd., Worthington, OH 43085; Rev. E. Weldon Keckley, Bethany Union Church, 1750 W. 103rd St., Chicago, IL 60643

The Presbyterian Church in the United States, Rev. Dr. William A. Benfield, Jr., First Presbyterian Church, 16 Broad St., Charleston, WV 25301; Rev. Robert B. Smith, Drawer 2438, Midland, TX 79702

United Church of Christ, Rev. Dr. William K. Laurie, 41 Crosswell Rd., Columbus, OH 43214; Mrs. Louise Wallace, 5340 Belinder Rd., Shawnee Mission, KS 66206

The United Methodist Church, Rev. Dr. Robert W. Huston, 475 Riverside Dr., Rm. 1300, New York, NY 10027; Bishop Edward G. Carroll, 581 Boylston St., Boston, MA 02116

The United Presbyterian Church in the United States of America, Mrs. Lois H. Stair, 401 N.E. 19th Ave., Apt. 74, Deerfield Beach, FL 33441; Mr. William P. Thompson, 475 Riverside Dr., New York, NY 10027

PUBLICATIONS

In Quest of a Church of Christ Uniting; An Emerging Theological Consensus (1976)

A Plan of Union for the Church of Christ Uniting (1970)

An Order of Worship for the Proclamation of the Word of God and the Celebration of the Lord's Supper

An Order for the Celebration of Holy Baptism, with Commentary

Digest of the 14th Plenary Meeting

Official Record of the 13th Plenary Meeting

A Lectionary.

Guidelines and Steps for Interim Eucharistic Fellowship

Congregations Uniting for Mission

Generating Communities: A Way Ahead in Church Union

Word Bread Cup (Guidelines for ecumenical worship)

In Common (occasional newsletter)

In Community (occasional newsletter)

The Evangelical Church Alliance

The Evangelical Church Alliance was incorporated in 1928 in Missouri as The World's Faith Missionary Association and was later known as The Fundamental Ministerial Association. The title Evangelical Church Alliance was adopted in 1958.

ECA (1) licenses and ordains ministers who are qualified and provides them with credentials from a recognized ecclesiastical body; (2) provides through the Bible Extension Institute, courses of study to those who have not had seminary or Bible school training; (3) provides an organization for autonomous churches so they may have communion and association with one another; (4) provides an organization where members can find companionship through correspondence, Regional Conventions, and general conventions; (5) cooperates with churches in finding new pastors when vacancies occur in their pulpits.

ECA is an interdenominational, nonsectarian, Fundamentalist organization. Total ordained and licensed clergy members—1,132.

Headquarters: Rev. Glen E. Seaborg, Exec. Sec., 1273 Cardinal Dr., P.O. Box 9, Bradley, IL 60915

International Convention: Annual, next meeting, July, 1980, Huntington College, Huntington, IN

OFFICERS

Pres., Dr. Charles Wesley Ewing, 321 W. Harrison St., Royal Oak, MI 48067

1st Vice-Pres., Rev. John H. Bishop, 162 Grandview Ave., S., Newport, KY 41071

2nd Vice-Pres., Rev. Albert L. Harlan, 602 South Bay Front, Balboa Island, CA 92662

Exec.-Sec., Rev. Glen E. Seaborg, P. O. Box 9, Bradley, IL 60915

PERIODICAL

The Evangelical Church Alliance Evangel, P.O. Box 9, Bradley, IL 60915

Evangelical Press Association

An organization of editors and publishers of Christian periodicals.

OFFICERS

Pres., Robert V. Myers, The ARETE Journal, 402 River Bluff Rd., Elgin, IL 60120

Vice-Pres., Jerry B. Jenkins, Moody Monthly, 2101 W. Howard St., Chicago, IL 60645

Sec., Viola Blake, Decision, 1300 Harmon Pl., Minneapolis, MN 55403

Treas., Norman B. Rohrer, Quill-O' the Wisp, P. O. Box 707, La Canada, CA 91011

Exec. Sec. and Dir. E. P. News, Gary Warner, P.O. Box 4550, Overland Park, KS 66204. Tel. (913) 381-2017

General Commission on Chaplains and Armed Forces Personnel

The Commission is an incorporated civilian agency maintained by 41 affiliated and associated bodies. Since 1917 it has been a permanent conference on standards and support for the chaplaincy and the religious programs for armed forces personnel and hospitalized veterans.

Office: Ste. 310, 5100 Wisconsin Ave., NW, Washington, DC 20016. Tel. (202) 686-1857

OFFICERS

Chpsn., James C. Lont

Vice-Chpsn., Charles L. Burgreen

Sec., Earl VanDerVeer

Treas., Francis Jameson

Dir., Edward I. Swanson

Assoc. Dir., Norman G. Folkers

PERIODICAL

Chaplaincy (q), Norman G. Folkers, Chaplaincy Letter (m), Norman G. Folkers, Ed.

International Christian Youth Exchange

Eleven denominational agencies are sponsors of ICYE, which was formed in 1957 to continue the student exchange program previously administered by the Brethren Service Commission of the Church of the Brethren.

The U.S. Committee works in cooperation with national committees in sixteen other countries and the Federation of National Committees for ICYE, which has headquarters in Berlin, Federal Republic of Germany. ICYE sponsors the exchange of young people between nations as a means of international and ecumenical education in order to further commitment to and responsibility for reconciliation, justice, and peace. Exchangees 16-24 years of age spend one year in another country and participate in family, school, church service projects and community life. Exchanges for American youth going abroad and for overseas youth coming to the U.S. are sponsored by local churches and/or community groups.

Office: 74 Trinity Pl., Rm. 610, New York, NY 10006. Tel. (212) 349-3053.

OFFICERS

Exec. Dir., William D. Jones
Asst. Dir., Edwin H. Gargert

International Society of Christian Endeavor

Christian Endeavor is an international, interracial, and interdenominational youth movement in evangelical Protestant churches. It unites its members for greater Christian growth and service under the motto "For Christ and the Church." The first society was formed by Francis E. Clark in Portland, Maine, February 2, 1881.

The movement spread rapidly and, in 1885, the United Society of Christian Endeavor was organized. In 1927 the name was changed to the International Society of Christian Endeavor, to include Canada and Mexico. The World's Union was organized in 1895. The movement has thousands of societies in local churches, for all age groups. Worldwide there are societies and unions in approximately 75 nations and island groups, with over two million members.

Office: 1221 E. Broad St., P.O. Box 1110, Columbus, OH 43216. Tel. (614) 253-8541.

OFFICERS

Pres., Mr. Lavern Billig
Gen. Sec., Rev. Charles W. Barner
Exec. Sec., Rev. David G. Jackson

PERIODICAL

The Christian Endeavor World (q) 1221 E. Broad St., P.O. Box 1110, Columbus, OH 43216, Frances M. Becker, Actg. Ed.

Joint Strategy and Action Committee

This is a national ecumenical agency created by several denominational home mission and program agencies. Through the JSAC system, agencies collaborate with each other about issues, develop strategy options, screen project requests, and work on joint actions. JSAC has a series of national staff coalitions which work as Strategy/Screening Task Forces, Work Groups, or Committees.

National Office: 475 Riverside Dr., Rm. 1700-A, New York, NY 10027. Tel. (212) 870-3105

OFFICERS

Pres., Rev. Donald H. Larsen, Lutheran Council, USA
Vice-Pres., Dr. W. H. Vernon Smith, Program Agency, United Presbyterian Church
Sec., Dr. Henry W. Quinius, Jr. Presbyterian Church in the U.S.
Treas., Rev. William A. Norgren, Episcopal Church
Coord. Chpsn., Rev. Kinmoth W. Jefferson, Nat'l Division, Bd. of Global Ministries, United Methodist Church
Exec. Dir., Rev. John C. DeBoer

MEMBER DENOMINATIONAL AGENCIES

American Baptist Churches
American Lutheran Church
Church of God (Anderson)
Church of the Brethren
Cumberland Presbyterian Church
The Episcopal Church
Lutheran Church in America
Lutheran Church—Missouri Synod
Presbyterian Church in the U.S.
Progressive National Baptist Convention
Reformed Church in America
Southern Baptist Convention
United Church of Christ
United Church of Canada
United Methodist Church
United Presbyterian Church, U.S.A.

COOPERATING DENOMINATIONAL AGENCIES

African Methodist Episcopal Church
African Methodist Episcopal Zion Church
American Friends Service Committee
American Jewish Committee
Associate Reformed Presbyterian Church
Christian Church (Disciples of Christ)
Christian Reformed Church
Church Women United
Leadership Conference of Women Religious
Mennonite Central Committee
Unitarian-Universalist Church
United States Catholic Conference

PERIODICAL

Grapevine (10 times a year), Ms. Dorothy Lara-Braud

The Liturgical Conference

Founded in 1940 by a group of Benedictines. The Liturgical Conference is an independent, interconfessional, international association of persons concerned about liturgical renewal and meaningful worship. The Liturgical Conference is known chiefly, for its periodicals, books, audio-visual materials, and its sponsorship of regional and local workshops on worship-related concerns in cooperation with various church groups.

Headquarters: 810 Rhode Island Ave., N.E., Washington, DC 20018. Tel. (202) 529-7400

OFFICERS

Pres., Sr. Mary Collins, O.S.B.
Vice-Pres., Rev. Gerard S. Sloyan
Sec., Rev. Richard Vosko
Treas., Sr. Mary Charles Bryce, O.S.B.
Exec. Dir., Rev. Joseph A. Wysocki

PERIODICALS

Liturgy (bi-m), Marianne Sawicki, Ed.
Living Worship (10/yr.) Marianne Sawicki, Ed.
Homily Service (m), Marianne Sawicki, Ed.

The Lord's Day Alliance of the United States

The Lord's Day Alliance of the United States has served the church and nation for ninety years. It was founded in 1888 in Washington, D.C. and is the only national organization the sole purpose of which is the preservation and cultivation of Sunday, the Lord's Day, as a day of rest and worship. The Alliance also seeks to safeguard a Day of Common Rest for all people regardless of their faith. Its Board of Managers is composed of representatives from twenty-three denominations.

It serves as an information bureau, publishes a magazine *Sunday,* furnishes speakers and a variety of materials such as pamphlets, posters, radio spot announcements, decals, books, cassettes, news releases, articles for magazines and TV programs, and a new 15-minute motion picture.

Office: Ste. 107/2930 Flowers Road, South, Atlanta, GA 30341

OFFICERS

Exec. Dir. and Ed., Dr. James P. Wesberry
Pres., Dr. Charles A. Platt
Vice-Pres., Dr. Andrew R. Bird, Jr.
Sec., Rev. Donald R. Pepper
Treas., Mr. E. Larry Edison

PERIODICAL

Sunday (q), Dr. James P. Wesberry, Ed.

Lutheran Council in the U.S.A.

The Lutheran Council in the U.S.A. succeeded the National Lutheran Council January 1, 1967, as a cooperative agency of the major U.S. Lutheran church bodies. In addition to The Lutheran Church—Missouri Synod, which had not been a member of the NLC, participating churches are The American Lutheran Church, the Lutheran Church in America and the Association of Evangelical Lutheran Churches, the latter having been accepted as a participating body in 1978. With its authority derived from the participating bodies it serves, the council seeks to effect a threefold objective: (a) further the witness, work, and interests of the Lutheran Church; (b) achieve theological consensus among Lutherans; (c) provide a means of cooperation and coordination of efforts for more effective, efficient service in six major areas: theological studies, education, mission, welfare, public relations, and service to military personnel.

Headquarters: 360 Park Ave. So., New York, NY 10010. Tel. (212) 532-6350

Other Offices: 475 L'Enfant Plaza S.W., Ste., 2720 West Bldg., Washington, DC 20024. Tel. (202) 484-3950; 35 East Wacker Dr., Ste. 1847, Chicago, IL 60601. Tel. (312) 726-3791

OFFICERS

Pres., Dr. Herbert A. Mueller
Vice-Pres., Mrs. J. Leon Haines
Sec., Rev. Fred K. Bernlohr
Treas., Mr. Walter C. Sundberg
Gen. Sec., Dr. John R. Houck
Dir. of Business and Finance, Mr. Walter A. Jensen
Div. of Campus Ministry and Educational Services, Rev. Reuben C. Baerwald
Div. of Mission and Ministry, Rev. Ronald H. Larsen
Div. of Service to Military Personnel, Rev. Magnus P. Lutness
Div. of Theological Studies, Dr. Joseph A. Burgess
Office of Communication and Interpretation, Mr. Robert E. A. Lee
Office for Governmental Affairs, Dr. Charles V. Bergstrom
Office of Research, Planning and Development, ———

PERIODICALS

Circle (8/yr), Audrey Neff Hiney, Ed.
DEScription (10/yr), J. Victor Hahn, Ed.
Focus on Public Affairs (20/yr), Lita B. Johnson, Ed.
Interchange (11/yr), Benjamin A. Bankson, Ed.
In Step (6/yr), Benjamin A. Bankson, Ed.
Lutheran Scouter (q), Ralph Dinger, Ed.
Media Alert (m), Clement W. K. Lee, Ed.

The Mennonite Central Committee

The Mennonite Central Committee is the relief and service agency of North American Mennonite and Brethren in Christ Churches. Representatives from 17 Mennonite groups make up the MCC, which meets annually in January to review its program and to guide future outreach. Founded in 1920, MCC administers and participates in programs of agricultural and economic development, education, medicine, self-help, relief, peace, and disaster service. MCC has 742 volunteers serving in 42 countries in Africa, Asia, Europe, South America, and North America.

Contributions from North American Mennonite and Brethren in Christ churches provide the largest part of MCC's support. Other sources of financial support include the contributed earnings of volunteers, grants from private and government agencies, and contributions from Mennonite churches abroad. The total income in 1977, including material aid contributions, amounted to $10,805,335.

In the projects it undertakes, MCC tries to strengthen local communities by working in cooperation with local churches. Many personnel are placed with other agencies, including missions. Programs are planned with sensitivity to locally felt needs.

International headquarters: 21 S. 12th St., Akron, PA 17501. Tel. (717) 859-1151
Canadian office: 201-1483 Pembina Hwy., Winnipeg, Manitoba R3T 2C8

OFFICER

Exec. Secs., William T. Snyder; (Canada) J. M. Klassen

National Association of Ecumenical Staff

This is the successor organization, to the Association of Council Secretaries, which was founded in 1940. The name change was made in 1971.

NAES is an association of professional staff in ecumenical services. It was established to provide creative relationships among them, and to encourage mutual support and personal and professional growth. This is accomplished through training programs, through exchange and discussion of common concerns at conferences, and through the publication of the journal.

Headquarters: Room 870, 475 Riverside Dr., New York, NY 10027. Tel. (212) 870-2157
Annual Meeting: June 25-30, 1979

OFFICERS

Pres., Dr. W. Lee Hicks, 239 Fourth Ave., Pittsburgh, PA 15222. Tel. (412) 281-1515
Vice-Pres., Ms. Dorothy Berry, 4125 Gage Center Dr., Topeka, KS 66604
Sec., Rev. Charles Dorsey, 900 S. Arlington Ave., Harrisburg, PA 17109
Treas., Rev. Clark Lobenstine, 1419 V St., N.W., Washington, DC 20009

PERIODICAL

On Location (bi-m), Rm. 870, 475 Riverside Dr. New York, NY 10027.

†The National Association of Evangelicals

The National Association of Evangelicals had its beginning on April 7-9, 1942, when 150 evangelical leaders met in St. Louis, Mo., to launch a movement to bring Christians together in united action.

Since then, NAE has provided a means of "cooperation without compromise" among Bible-believing Christians. This fellowship is based upon a statement of faith that is descriptive of the true evangelical.

The NAE represents 35 complete denominations and has within its membership individual churches from at least 30 other groups, including Bible colleges, Christian schools, seminaries, ministerial fellowships, and evangelistic organizations, as well as individual Christians. Actual membership numbers above three million.

GENERAL ORGANIZATION

Headquarters: 350 S. Main Place, P. O. Box 28, Wheaton, IL 60187. Tel. (312) 665-0500
Office of Public Affairs: 1430 K St., N.W., Washington, DC 20005

OFFICERS

Pres., Dr. Carl Lundquist, 3900 Bethel Dr., St. Paul, MN 55112
1st Vice-Pres., Bishop Floyd J. Williams, P.O. Box 12609, Oklahoma City, OK 73112
2nd Vice-Pres., Rev. Arthur E. Gay, Jr., 1330 S. Courtland Ave., Park Ridge, IL 60068
Sec., Dr. D. Howard Elliott, 2007 Crest Dr., Topeka, KS 66604
Treas., Mr. Paul Steiner, 1825 Florida Dr. Ft. Wayne, IN 46805

STAFF

Exec. Dir., Dr. Billy A. Melvin
Sec. of Public Affairs, Mr. Robert P. Dugan
Dir. of Field Services, Dr. R. Gordon Bacon
Dir. of Information, Mr. Harold B. Smith
Dir. of Business Adm., Mr. Darrell L. Fulton
Natl. Field Rep., Rev. Darrel Anderson

COMMISSIONS AND AFFILIATES

Commissions: Commission on Chaplains, Commission on Higher Education, Evangelical Churchmen Commission, Evangelical Social Action Commission, Evangelism and Home Missions Association, Stewardship Commission, Women's Fellowship Commission, World Relief Commission
Affiliates: American Assn. of Evangelical Students, Evangelical Foreign Missions Assn., National Assn. of Christian Schools, National Religious Broadcasters, National Sunday School Assn.

PERIODICAL

United Evangelical Action (q), 350 S. Main Place, Wheaton, IL 60187, Dr. Billy A. Melvin, Exec. Ed.

MEMBER DENOMINATIONS

Assemblies of God
Baptist General Conference
Brethren Church (Ashland, Ohio)
Brethren in Christ
Christian Catholic Church (Evangelical Protestant)
Christian Church of North America
Christian and Missionary Alliance
Christian Union
Church of God (Cleveland, Tenn.)
Church of the United Brethren in Christ
Churches of Christ in Christian Union
Conservative Congregational Christian Conference
Elim Fellowship
Evangelical Church of North America
Evangelical Congregational Church
Evangelical Free Church of America
Evangelical Friends Alliance
Evangelical Mennonite Brethren Church
Evangelical Mennonite Church
Evangelical Methodist Church
Free-Baptized Holiness Church of God of the Americas
Free Methodist Church

Full Gospel Pentecostal Assn.
Greater Emmanuel Apostolic Faith Tabernacles, Inc.
International Church of the Foursquare Gospel
International Pentecostal Church of Christ
Mennonite Brethren Church
Midwest Congregational Christian Fellowship
Missionary Church
Open Bible Standard Churches
Pentecostal Church of God of America
Pentecostal Evangelical Church
Pentecostal Holiness Church
Primitive Methodist Church
Reformed Presbyterian Church of North America
Wesleyan Church

National Conference of Christians and Jews

The National Conference of Christians and Jews (NCCJ) is a non-profit human relations organization engaged in a nationwide program of intergroup education to eliminate prejudice and discrimination. Founded in 1928, the NCCJ works to build bridges of understanding among all groups, to bring the forces of enlightenment and education to bear upon racial and religious prejudice, and to achieve implementation of the moral law: giving to others the same rights and respect we desire for ourselves. It enlists all those who, without compromise of conscience or of their distinctive commitments, work to build better relationships among persons of all religious, races and nationalities. The NCCJ has 70 regional offices across the country staffed by approximately 200 people. Three hundred members comprise the National Board of Trustees and from that group there is a 19-member Executive Board. Each of the regional offices has its own local board of trustees, with the total throughout the nation reaching 3,500. The National Board of Trustees meets once annually.

Headquarters: 43 West 57th St. New York, NY 10019. Tel. (212) 688-7530

OFFICER

Pres., Dr. David Hyatt

National Council of Young Men's Christian Associations of the USA

A worldwide organization begun in London, England, in 1844, the first YMCA in the U.S. was established at Boston, Mass., in 1851.

The Young Men's Christian Associations of the United States of America is "in its essential genius, the worldwide fellowship united by a common loyalty to Jesus Christ for the purpose of developing Christian personality and building a Christian society."

The policies of the "Y" are guided by men and women from the fields of commerce, labor, the professions and youth committed to the above statement of purpose.

Specific goals adopted for the 1979-84 period include elimination of personal and institutional racism; changing the conditions that foster alienation, delinquency, and crime; reducing health problems by strengthening physical and mental health; strengthening family structures by enhancing relationships and improving communication; joining people from other countries in building international understanding and world peace.

There are approximately ten million members in 1,803 autonomous Associations. Over 39 per cent women, the membership includes men, women, boys and girls of all races, religious and nonreligious persuasions.

Corporate Name: National Board of Young Men's Christian Associations.

Office: 291 Broadway, New York, NY 10007. Tel. (212) 374-2000

OFFICERS

Pres., James O. Plinton, Jr.
Chpsn., Dr. Elija M. Hicks, Jr.
Exec. Dir., Dr. Robert W. Harlan
Treas, N. Conover English

National Interfaith Coalition on Aging, Inc.

The National Interfaith Coalition on Aging (NICA) is composed of national level representatives from the Roman Catholic, Jewish and Protestant faiths and of several associate and reciprocal organizations concerned about problems which face our nation's aging population. NICA grew out of a conference held in 1972 to make a vital response to the 1971 White House Conference on Aging.

Primary objectives of NICA are: to identify and give priority to those programs and services for the aging which best may be implemented through the resources of the nation's religious sector; to vitalize and develop the role of the church and synagogue with respect to their responsibility in improving the quality of life for the aging; to stimulate cooperative and coordinated action between the nation's religious sector and national secular private and public organizations and agencies whose programs and services relate to the welfare and dignity of older persons; to encourage the aging to continue giving to society from the wealth of their experiences and to remain active participants in community life.

NICA serves as a resource and training agency for its constituents. Current efforts are focussed on Gerontology in the religious educaton and training field, specially in seminary training.

Office: 298 South Hull St., P.O. Box 1924, Athens, GA 30603. Tel. (404) 353-1331

OFFICERS

Pres., Lt. Col. Mary E. Verner
Vice Pres., Miss. Betty J. Letzig (Protestant); Rabbi Sanford Seltzer (Jewish); Bro. Joseph Berg (Roman Catholic)
Sec., Dr. Grover Hartman
Treas., Rev. Earl N. Kragnes
Exec. Dir., Thomas C. Cook, Jr., P. O. Box 1924, Athens, GA 30603. Tel. (404) 353-1331

National Interreligious Service Board for Conscientious Objectors

NISBCO, formed in 1940, is a nonprofit service organization sponsored by a broad coalition of national religious groups. NISBCO responds to the needs of conscientious objectors by: providing information on how to register and document one's convictions as a conscientious objector; providing professional counseling for those who are working through convictions of conscientious objection and training religious CO counselors; alerting citizens to the latest developments in the drive to bring back registration and the draft and the efforts to institute compulsory national service; aiding COs in the armed forces who seek noncombatant transfer or discharge; maintaining an extensive referral service to local counseling agencies in all areas of the country, and to attorneys who can aid those in need of legal counsel; acting as a national resource center for those interested in CO/peace witness of all religious bodies in the United States: encouraging citizens through articles, speaking engagements, and NISBCO publications, to decide for themselves what they believe about participation in war based upon the dictates of their own consciences.

Office: Washington Bldg., Rm. 550, 15th and New York Ave., N.W., Washington, DC 20005. Tel. (202) 393-4868

OFFICERS

Chpsn., Charles Boyer, 1451 Dundee Ave., Elgin, IL 60120
Exec. Dir., Warren W. Hoover

PERIODICAL

The Reporter for Conscience' Sake (m)

North American Academy of Ecumenists

Organized in 1967, the stated purpose of the NAAE is: "to inform, relate, and encourage men and women professionally engaged in the study, teaching, and other practice of ecumenism."

Headquarters: c/o Rev. Thaddeus Horgan, S.A., Graymoor Ecumenical Institute, Garrison, NY 10524

OFFICERS

Pres., William J. Boney
Vice-Pres., ———
Sec.-Treas., Rev. Thaddeus Horgan, S.A.
M'ship Sec., R. L. Turnipseed

PERIODICAL

Journal of Ecumenical Studies (q), Temple University, Philadelphia, PA 19122, Leonard Swidler, Ed. (This periodical is affiliated with the Academy.)

North American Baptist Fellowship

Organized in 1966, the North American Baptist Fellowship is a voluntary organization of Baptist Conventions in Canada, the United States, and Mexico, functioning as a regional body within the Baptist World Alliance. Its objectives are: (a) to promote fellowship and cooperation among Baptists in North America, and (b) to further the aims and objectives of the Baptist World Alliance so far as these affect the life of the Baptist churches in North America. Its membership, however, is not identical with the North American membership of the Baptist World Alliance.

Church membership of the Fellowship bodies is over 19 million.

The NABF assembles representatives of the member bodies once a year for exchange of information and views in such fields as evangelism and education, missions, stewardship promotion, laymen's activities, and theological education. It conducts occasional consultations for denominational leaders on such subjects as church extension. It encourages cooperation at the city and county level where churches of more than one member group are located.

Headquarters: 1628 Sixteenth St., NW, Washington, DC 20009. Tel. (202) 265-5027.

EXECUTIVE OFFICERS

Chpsn., Rev. Fred Bullen, P.O. Box 1298, Brantford, Ontario N3T 5T6
Vice-Chpsn., Lee Satterfield, P.O. Box 509. Altavista, VA 24517
Sec. and Staff Exec., Dr. Charles F. Wills (Assoc. Sec. Baptist World Alliance), 1628 Sixteenth St., N.W., Washington, DC 20009
Treas., Fred B. Rhodes (Treas., Baptist World Alliance), 3101 N. Peary St., Arlington, VA 22207
Representing the Baptist World Alliance:
David Y. K. Wong, 73 Waterloo Rd. (1st Fl.) Kowloon, Hong Kong; Dr. Robert S. Denny, Gen. Sec. Baptist World Alliance, 1628 Sixteenth St., N.W., Washington, DC 20009

MEMBER BODIES

American Baptist Churches in the U.S.A.
Baptist Federation of Canada
General Association of General Baptists
National Baptist Convention of America
National Baptist Convention of Mexico
Progressive National Baptist Convention, Inc.
Seventh Day Baptist General Conference
North American Baptist Conference
Southern Baptist Convention

Pentecostal Fellowship of North America

Organized at Des Moines, Iowa, in October, 1948 shortly after the first World Conference of Pentecostal Believers was held in Zurich, Switzerland, in May, 1947, The PFNA has the following objectives: 1) to provide a vehicle of expression and coordination of efforts in matters common to all member bodies including missionary and evangelistic effort; 2) to demonstrate to the world the essential unity of Spirit-baptized believers; 3) to provide services to its constituents to facilitate world evangelism; 4) to encourage the principles of comity for the nurture of the body of Christ, endeavoring to keep the unity of the Spirit until we all come to the unity of the faith.

The PFNA has local chapters in communities where churches of the member groups are located, and fellowship rallies are held. On the national level, representatives of the member bodies are assembled for studies and exchange of views in the fields of home missions, foreign missions, and youth.

EXECUTIVE OFFICERS

Chpsn., Dr. M. E. Nicholls, 1100 Glendale Blvd., Los Angeles, CA 90026
1st Vice-Chpsn., Rev. Frank W. Smith, 2020 Bell Ave., Des Moines, Iowa 50315
2nd Vice-Chpsn., Rev. Jerome Ealden, P. O. Boc 157, Jellico, TN 37762
Sec., Rev. Robert Taitinger, 10 Overlea Blvd., Toronto, Ontario M4S 1A5
Treas., Rev. Carlton Spencer, Lima, NY 14485

PERIODICAL

P.F.N.A. News (q), 1445 Boonville Ave., Springfield, MO 65802

MEMBER GROUPS

Anchor Bay Evangelistic Association
Assemblies of God
Carolina Evangelistic Association
Christian Church of North America
Church of God of Apostolic Faith
Church of God (Cleveland, Tenn.)
Church of God, Mountain Assembly
Congregational Holiness Church
Elim Fellowship
Emmanuel Holiness Church
Free Gospel Church, Inc.

Free Will Baptist (Pentecostal Faith)
International Church of the Foursquare Gospel
International Pentecostal Church of Christ
Italian Pentecostal Church of Canada
Open Bible Standard Churches, Inc.
Pentecostal Assemblies of Canada
Pentecostal Assemblies of Newfoundland
Pentecostal Church of God
Pentecostal Free-Will Baptist
Pentecostal Holiness Church
Pentecostal Holiness Church of Canada

Religion in American Life, Inc.

Religion in American Life (RIAL) is a cooperative program of 50 major national religious groups (Catholic, Eastern Orthodox, Jewish, Protestant) which enables them to reach the American public through the advertising media. Every year since 1949 RIAL has been one of the major campaigns of The Advertising Council. This relationship results in as much as $32 million dollars' worth of space and time conributed in a single year by the media. Its advertising is produced without charge by a volunteer agency (Compton Advertising, Inc.) and its production and administration costs, funded by both business and religious groups, stresses the importance of religion in daily life as an essential extension of the worshipping community.

Office: 815 Second Ave., New York, NY 10017. Tel. (212) 607-5033

OFFICERS

Natl. Chpsn., J. Paul Lyet
Chpsn. of Bd., Rabbi Joseph B. Glaser
Treas., Mr. H. Peers Brewer
Sec., Archbishop Torkom Manoogian

STAFF

Pres., Dr. David W. Gockley
Vice Pres., Dr. David C. Brown
Dir., Program, ———
Asst. Treas., Anne Podmol

PERIODICAL

The Bulletin, 815 Second Ave., New York, NY 10017

Religion Newswriters Association

Founded in 1949, the RNA is a professional association of religion news editors and reporters on secular daily and weekly newspapers, news services, and news magazines. It sponsors three annual contests for excellence in religion news coverage in the secular press. Annual meetings during a major religious convocation.

OFFICERS

Pres., Majorie Hyer, Washington Post, Washington, DC 2005
1st Vice-Pres., Ben Kaufman, Enquirer, Cincinnati OH 45201
2nd Vice-Pres., Russell Chandler, L.A. Times, Los Angeles, CA 90053
Treas., Louis Moore, Houston Chronicle, Houston TX 77002
Sec., ———

PERIODICAL

News Letter, 475 Riverside Dr., New York, NY 10027, Martha Man, Ed.

The Religious Public Relations Council, Inc.

The Religious Public Relations Council, Inc., is an organization whose purposes are to establish, raise and maintain high standards of public relations and communication to the end that religious faith and life may be advanced; and to promote fellowship, counseling, and exchange of ideas among its members.

Now an interfaith non-profit professional association, the Council originally was founded as the Religious Publicity Council on November 27, 1929, in Washington, D.C. There were 29 charter members, representing seven denominations, the Federal Council of Churches, and four church-related agencies. In 1967 it opened its membership to qualified people of all Christian communions. In 1970, its membership was opened to all religious faiths.

Today RPRC has over 800 members in 12 chapters, as well as over 100 members-at-large in 28 states and Canada and six nations overseas.

The Council conducts an annual convention, sponsors two awards programs: one for secular journalism and broadcasting; the other, awards of excellence in nine categories for its own members; and each year has a week-long continuing education program.

Office: 475 Riverside Dr., Rm. 1031, New York, NY 10027. Tel. (212) 870-2014

OFFICERS

Pres., Sue Couch, Dir. of Information Services, Public Media Division, United Methodist Communicatons, 1525 McGavock St., Nashville, TN 37203
Vice-Pres., Thomas J. Brannon, Dir. of Public Relations, Genl. Bd. of South Carolina Baptist Convention, 907 Richland St., Columbia, SC 29201
Exec. Sec., Marvin C. Wilbur, Asst. Dir., United Presbyterian Foundation, 475 Riverside Dr., Rm. 1031, New York, NY 10027

PERIODICALS

Counselor (q), 475 Riverside Dr., New York, NY 10027, Dr. Marvin C. Wilbur, Ed.
Mediakit (bi-m), 475 Riverside Dr., New York, NY 10027

Standing Conference of Canonical Orthodox Bishops in the Americas

This body was established in 1960 to achieve cooperation among the various Eastern Orthodox Churches in the U.S.A. The Conference is "a voluntary association of the Bishops in the Americas established . . . to serve as an agency to centralize and coordinate the mission of the Church. It acts as a clearing house to focus the efforts of the Church on common concerns and to avoid duplication and overlapping of services and agencies. Special departments are devoted to campus work, Christian education, military and other chaplaincies, regional clergy fellowships, and ecumenical relations."

Office: 8-10 East 79th St., New York, NY 10021. Tel. (212) 628-2500

OFFICER

Chpsn., Most Rev. Archbishop Iakovos
Sec., Bishop Dimitry
Asst. Sec., Rev. Paul Schneirla

MEMBER CHURCHES

Albanian Orthodox Diocese of America
American Carpatho-Russian Orthodox Greek Catholic Church

Antiochian Orthodox Christian Archdiocese of New York and All North America
Bulgarian Eastern Orthodox Church
Greek Orthodox Archdiocese of North and South America
Orthodox Church in America
Romanian Orthodox Church in America
Serbian Orthodox Church for the U.S.A. and Canada
Ukrainian Orthodox Church of America
Ukrainian Autocephalic Orthodox Church in Exile

Young Women's Christian Association of the United States of America

The first YWCA of the U.S.A. group, known as the Ladies' Christian Association, appeared in 1858 in New York City, after the worldwide membership movement began in London, England, 1855. Today, it serves more than 2 million members and program participants.

The National Board unites into an effective continuing organization the autonomous member Associations for furthering the purpose of the National Association, which states:

"The Young Women's Christian Association of the United States of America, a movement rooted in the Christian faith as known in Jesus and nourished by the resources of that faith, seeks to respond to the barrier-breaking love of God in this day.

"The Association draws together into responsible membership women and girls of diverse experiences and faiths, that their lives may be open to new understanding and deeper relationships and that together they may join in the struggle for peace and justice, freedom and dignity for all people."

The National Board also represents Associations of the United States in the World YWCA.

NATIONAL BOARD

Office: 600 Lexington Ave., New York, NY 10022. Tel. (212) 753-4700

OFFICERS

Pres., Jewel Freeman Graham (Mrs. Paul N.)
Sec., Jacqueline Ferron Delahunt
Exec. Dir., Sara-Alyce P. Wright (Mrs. Emmett)

Youth for Christ, USA

Founded in 1945, the purpose of YFC is to participate in the body of Christ in responsible evangelism of youth, presenting them with the person, work and teachings of Christ and discipling them into the church.

Locally controlled YFC programs serve in 160 cities and metropolitan areas of the U.S.

YFC's Campus Life Club program involves teens who attend approximately 1,200 high schools in the United States. YFC's highly trained staff now numbers over 900. In addition, approximately 3,800 part-time and volunteer staff supplement the full-time staff. Youth Guidance, a ministry for nonschool-oriented youth includes group homes, court referrals, institutional services, and neighborhood ministries. The year-round conference and camping program involves approximately 30,000 young people each year. A family oriented ministry designed to enrich individuals and church family education programs is carried on through Family Forum, a daily 5 minute radio program on 130 stations and through Family Concern, a seminar ministry. A literature ministry includes Campus Life Books and Magazine, Family Concerns publicatons, and materials to aid church youth ministries. Independent, indigenous YFC organizatons also work in 54 countries overseas.

GENERAL ORGANIZATION

Headquarters: 360 S. Main Place, Carol Stream, IL 60187. Pres. Jay Kesler
International Organization: Box 77, 1211 Geneva 11, Switzerland. Pres., Dr. Sam Wolgemuth; Gen. Dir., Jim Groen
Canadian Organization: 306 Rexdale Blvd., Unit 3, Rexdale, Ontario M9W 1R6

PERIODICAL

Campus Life (m), P.O. Box 419, Wheaton, IL 60187. Don Lomangino, Publ.

2. CANADIAN COOPERATIVE ORGANIZATIONS, NATIONAL

This directory of Canadian Cooperative Organizations attempts to list major organizations working interdenominationally on a national basis. The editor of the **Yearbook of American and Canadian Churches** would appreciate receiving information on any significant organizations not now included. Those directories not reviewed for this edition carry the symbol (+) in front of them

The Canadian Council of Churches

The Canadian Council of Churches was organized in 1944. Its basic purpose is to provide the churches with an agency for conference and consultation and for such common planning and common action as they desire to undertake. It encourages ecumenical understanding and action throughout Canada through local councils of churches. It also relates to the World Council of Churches and other agencies serving the worldwide ecumenical movement.

The Council has a Triennial Assembly which is the basic governing body, a General Board which meets semiannually, and an Executive Committee. Program is administered through three commissions—Faith and Order, Canadian Affairs, and World Concerns.

40 St. Clair Ave. E., Toronto, Ontario M4T 1M9 Tel. (416) 921-4152

OFFICERS AND STAFF

Pres., Mrs. Heather Johnston
Vice-Pres., Rev. Canon D David Tatchell; Rev. Alan McIntosh
Treas., Mr. J. W. Glendinning, C.A.
Gen. Sec., Rev. Dr. Donald W. Anderson
Assoc. Secs., Rev. Tadashi Mitsui; Rev. Roger Cann; Ms. Gabrielle Lacelle

AFFILIATED INSTITUTION

Ecumenical Forum of Canada, 11 Madison Ave., Toronto, Ontario M5R 2S2. Dir., Arturo Chacun; Assoc. Dir., Sr. Veronica O'Reilly, C.S.J.

MEMBER CHURCHES

The Anglican Church of Canada
The Armenian Church of America—Diocese of Canada
Baptist Federation of Canada
Christian Church (Disciples of Christ)
Coptic Orthodox Church of Canada
Greek Orthodox Archdiocese of North and South America—9th District (Canada and Alaska)
Lutheran Church in America—Canada Section
Presbyterian Church in Canada
Reformed Church in America—Classis of Ontario
Religious Society of Friends—Canada Yearly Meeting
Salvation Army—Canada and Bermuda
United Church of Canada

Canadian Bible Society

As early as 1805 the British and Foreign Bible Society was at work in Canada. The Canadian Bible Society Branch at Truro, N.S., has been functioning continually since 1810. In 1904, the various auxiliaries of the British and Foreign Bible Society in Canada joined together to form the Canadian Bible Society.

Presently, the Canadian Bible Society has 19 districts and 4,000 branches. It holds an annual meeting of its Board which consists of two or more representatives of each district plus members appointed by the General Board of the CBS. There is also a meeting of its district secretaries annually.

In 1978, the CBS distributed over eight million Scriptures in 82 languages in Canada and provided over $1.4 million for the translation, publication and distribution of the Scriptures in some 150 other countries.

Headquarters: Ste. 200, 1835 Yonge St., Toronto, Ontario M4S 1Y1. Tel. (416) 482-3081

OFFICER

Gen. Sec., Rev. Dr. Kenneth G. McMillan

Canadian Council of Christians and Jews

The Canadian Council of Christians and Jews is an organization which builds bridges of understanding between Canadians. It strives to span the chasm of prejudice and discrimination by team effort. Its techniques of effecting social change are dialog, conciliation and education. The CCCJ believes that there exists in any community in Canada the reservoirs of good will, the mediating skills, and the enlightened self-interest which make accommodation to change and the creation of social justice possible.

The CCCJ was established in Toronto in 1947 by a group of prominent business, civic and religious leaders.

National Office: 49 Front St., E., Toronto, Ontario M5E 1B3. Tel. (416) 364-3101

STAFF

Pres., Dr. Victor Goldbloom
Dir. of Programs, Tom O'Leary
Dir. of Adm. and Fin., William G. Mercer
Student Exchange Coordinator, Dennis Flack
Public Information Coordinator, Jeanne Kotick
Christian-Jewish Dialogue Coordinator, ______

PERIODICAL

Newletter on Intergroup Relations (m), Kerry Knoll, Ed.

Canadian Tract Society

The Canadian Tract Society was organized in 1970 as an independent publisher of gospel leaflets to provide Canadian churches and individual Christians with quality materials in proclaiming the gospel through the printed page. It is affiliated with the American Tract Society, which encouraged its formation and assisted in its founding. The CTS is a nonprofit international service ministry.

Address: Box 203, Port Credit P.O., Mississauga, Ontario L5G 4L7

OFFICERS

Pres., Stanley D. Mackey
Exec. Sec., Robert J. Burns

The Church Council on Justice and Corrections

The Church Council on Justice and Corrections is an ecumenical body of church leaders from various centers across Canada, actively involved in the field of criminal justice, representing eleven major denominations. Its objective is to assist the Church's ministry in this field by promoting a more just and humane criminal justice system in Canada.

The Council consults with the Law Reform Commission in moral and theological matters and has produced a series of study papers to respond to these issues. Already completed are: William Klassen's *Release to Those in Prison*, Roger Hutchinson's *Religion Morality and Law in*

Modern Society, and Patrick Keran's *Religion and Culture in Canada.* Also available are: Tom Neufeld's *Guilt and Humanness and Terence R. Anderson's The Ethics of the Use of Recently Developed Mind/Behaviour Control Mechanisms By and On Convicted Criminals.* To be published in late 1979 are: *The Ministry of the Church in Canada's Penitentiaries* by Peter Hartgerink and *A Cultural Look at Native People and the Canadian Justice System* by Menno Wiebe and a statement *A Christian View of the Canadian Criminal Justice System.*

A major congregation packet of education resources has been bilingually produced and distributed to more than 10,000 churches for study and action. These materials are an integral part of the Council's National Community education Program, known as *Alternatives.* Its aim is to promote a greater understanding and public accountability of Canada's criminal justice system through study and participation by the community. *Alternatives* is an on-going project. Audio-visual materials have been prepared and new materials are being made available such as aids to *Court Watching, A Flow Chart of Alternatives to the Current Criminal Justice System,* and *Religious Volunteers* as well as *Training Kits* for school teachers and pupils.

Office: 200 Davignon Blvd., Cowansville, Quebec J2K 1N9
Tel. (514) 263-2000

OFFICERS

Pres., Mr. Frank P. Miller
Exec. Dir., Rev. J. D. McCord

Evangelical Fellowship of Canada

The Fellowship was formed in 1964. Presently there are 9 denominations, 30 organizations, and individual members totaling 300,000.

Its purposes are threefold: "Fellowship in the gospel" (Phil. 1:5). "the defence and confirmation of the gospel" (Phil. 1:7), and "the furtherance of the gospel" (Phil. 1:12).

The Fellowship believes the Holy Scriptures, as originally given, are infallible and that salvation through the Lord Jesus Christ is by faith apart from works.

In national and regional conventions the Fellowship urges Christians to live exemplary lives and to openly challenge the evils and injustices of society. It encourages cooperation with various agencies in Canada and overseas that are sensitive to man's social and spiritual needs.

Office: 512 McNicoll St., Willowdale, Ontario M2H 2E1. Tel. (416) 497-4796
Mailing Address: P.O. Box 8800, Sta. B, Willowdale, Ontario M2K 2R6

OFFICERS

Pres., Rev. Charles Yates
Vice Pres., Rev. William Newell; Mr. Keith Price
Treas., Rev. Claude Horton
Sec., Rev. Brian Stiller
Chpsn., Communications Commission, Rev. Allan Shantz
Chpsn., Christian Education Commission, Bishop Harvey Sider
Chpsn., Social Action Commission, Rev. Aire Van Eek
Chpsn., World Wide Mission & Evangelism Commission, Rev. William Tyler
Chpsn., Personnel and Nominating Committee, Rev. Robert Argue

Inter-Church Consultative Committee on Development and Relief (ICCDR)

The Inter-Church Consultative Committee on Development and Relief (ICCDR) was organized in October, 1971 to assist churches to work together in the fields of relief, development, and development education, consulting together and exchanging useful information.

ICCDR is made up of representatives from Christian Churches and Inter-Church Projects. Representatives include church titular heads; general or executive secretaries of churches, and of the Canadian Council of Churches and the Canadian Conference of Catholic Bishops; staff members or representatives from the fields of development, relief, social services and inter-church projects.

OFFICERS

Chpsn., Rev. Dennis Murphy, 90 Parent Ave., Ottawa, Ontario K1N 7B1. Tel. (613) 236-9461
Sec., Rev. Rodger Talbot, 50 Wynford Dr., Don Mills, Ontario M3C 1J7. Tel. (416) 441-1111

MEMBER CHURCHES

The Anglican Church of Canada
The Canadian Council of Churches
The Christian Church (Disciples of Christ)
The Lutheran Church in America-Canada Section
The Roman Catholic Church (CCCB)
The Presbyterian Church in Canada (CCDP)
The United Church of Canada

Inter-Church Communications

It is the cooperative grouping of communication units of Anglican, Baptist, Lutheran, Presbyterian, Roman Catholic, and United churches. Initiated in 1959 for broadcast training purposes, it was known as Interchurch Broadcasting until it was broadened in 1974.

It conducts workshops in production and media education, writes briefs to the government on various aspects of the media in Canada, produces television programs for national networks, distributes radio and television programs produced in Canada and elsewhere, does research in various areas of media such as cable TV and children's TV, acts as advisor to both church and community groups on questions related to the media.

In its television work Inter-Church Communications is identified as Religious Television Associates.

Office: Berkeley Studio, 315 Queen St., E. Toronto, Ontario M5A 1S7. Tel. (416) 366-9221

OFFICERS

Chpsn., Rev. W. Lowe
Sec., Rev. Frank Brisbin
Exec. Producer, Rev. Des McCalmont

Inter-Church Fund for International Development (ICFID)

This coalition began in October, 1974 and has the following purposes: 1) to increase the capacity of participating churches to respond quickly and effectively to development needs by (a) working toward mutual responsibility among all participating groups, (b) by working toward the goal of shared decision-making and accountability; 2) to encourage the planning and decision-making capacity of the churches and N.G.O.'s in developing countries; 3) to act on behalf of the participating Canadian churches as a receiving agency for development funds from government or other agencies for overseas programs.

Office: 71 Bronson Ave., Ottawa, Ontario KIR 6G6. Tel. (613) 232-7124

OFFICER

Exec. Sec., ______

MEMBER CHURCHES

The Anglican Church of Canada
The Lutheran Church in America-Canada Section

The Presbyterian Church in Canada
The Roman Catholic Church
The United Church of Canada

Inter-Varsity Christian Fellowship of Canada

Inter-Varsity Christian Fellowship is a non-profit, interdenominational Canadian student movement centering on the witness to Jesus Christ in campus communities: universities, high schools, teachers' colleges, and through a Canada-wide Pioneer camping programme. IVCF was officially formed in 1928-29 through the enthusiastic efforts of the late Dr. Howard Guinness, whose arrival from Britain challenged students to follow the example of the Inter-Varsity Fellowship from which he came, in organising themselves in prayer and Bible Study fellowship groups. Inter-Varsity has always been a student-initiated movement, emphasizing and developing leadership on the campus to call Christians to outreach, challenging other students to a personal faith in Jesus Christ, and study of the Bible as God's revealed truth within a fellowship of believers. A strong stress has been placed on missionary activity, and the triennial conference held at Urbana, Ill. (jointly sponsored by US and Canadian IVCF) has been a means of challenging many young people to service in Christian vocation. Inter-Varsity works closely with, and is a strong believer in, the work of local and national churches.

Headquarters: 745 Mount Pleasant Rd., Toronto, Ontario M4S 2N5. Tel. (416) 487-3431

OFFICERS

Gen. Dir., Rev. A. Donald MacLeod
Dir. of Finance and Admin., Reginald E. Gaskin

The Lord's Day Alliance of Canada

A secular organization devoted to achieving for Canada. Sunday as a national common day of rest and leisure.

The Alliance produces its publications *Sound About Sunday* and *Update* and furnishes speakers when requested.

Office: P. O. Box 457, Islington, Ontario M9A 4X4. Tel. (416) 489-4374

OFFICER

Actg. Gen. Sec., Les Kingdon

Lutheran Council in Canada

The Lutheran Council in Canada was organized in 1967 and is a cooperative venture of the Evangelical Lutheran Church of Canada, the Lutheran Church in America-Canada Section, and the Lutheran Church-Canada.

The Council has two divisions: theology; mission and ministry. Its activities include theological studies, communications, mission planning, co-ordinative service and national liaison in social ministry, campus ministry, chaplaincy, and scout activity. It acts in Canada for the Lutheran World Federation and participates in world development education efforts.

Office: 500-365 Hargrave St., Winnipeg, Manitoba R3B 2K3. Tel. (204) 942-0096

OFFICERS

Exec. Dir., Walter A. Schultz
Exec. Sec., Theology, Rev. Norman J. Threinen
Exec. Sec., Mission and Ministry, Rev. Leon C. Gilbertson

Mennonite Central Committee (Canada)

Mennonite Central Committee (Canada) was organized in 1964 to continue the work which several regional Canadian inter-Mennonite agencies had been doing in relief, service, immigration, and peace. All but a few of the smaller Mennonite groups in Canada belong to MCC (Canada).

MCC (Canada) is closely related to the international MCC organization which has its headquarters in Akron, Pennsylvania, and which administers all overseas development and relief projects. MCC (Canada) contributed $3,899,028 for this international ministry in 1978. Additionally, 290 Canadian volunteers were serving one to three year terms in MCC'S program at home and abroad during that same period.

The MCC (Canada) office in Winnipeg administers all voluntary projects located in Canada. Domestic programs of Voluntary Service, S.A.L.T. (Serve and Learn Together), Native Concerns, Peace and Social Concerns, Food Bank, Ottawa Office, Offender Ministries and immigration are all part of MCC's Canadian ministry. Whenever it undertakes a project, MCC attempts to relate to the church or churches in the area; it attempts in this way to support and undergird the local church.

Office: 201-1483 Pembina Hwy., Winnipeg, Manitoba R3T 2C8. Tel. (204) 475-3550

OFFICER

Exec. Sec., J.M. Klassen

Student Christian Movement of Canada

The Student Christian Movement of Canada was formed in 1921 from the student arm of the YMCA. It has its roots in the Social Gospel movements of the late nineteenth and early twentieth centuries. Throughout its long and varied history, the SCM in Canada has sought to relate the Christian faith to the living realities of the social and political context of each student generation.

The present priorities are built around the need to form more and stronger critical Christian communities on Canadian campuses within which individuals may develop their social and political analyses and experience spiritual growth.

The Student Christian Movement of Canada is affiliated with the World Student Christian Federation.

Office: 736 Bathurst St., Toronto, Ontario M5S 2R4. Tel. (416) 534-1352

Women's Interchurch Council of Canada

An ecumenical movement through which Christians may express their unity by prayer, fellowship, study, action. The purpose is: to enable Christian women across Canada to live in love and fellowship so that all people may find fullness of life in Christ. It sponsors the World Day of Prayer and the Fellowship of the Least Coin in Canada, as well as the Shawls of Solidarity Human Rights Project and the Canadian Prayer Booklet. Membership is composed of four representatives from each participating denomination which confesses Jesus Christ as Lord and Saviour, and one representative from related organizations invited by the Council.

Office: 77 Charles St., W., Toronto, Ontario M5S 1K5 Tel. (416) 922-6177

OFFICERS

Pres., Mrs. Margaret Elliott
Gen. Sec., Mrs. Lottie Franklin-Hearne

Young Men's Christian Association in Canada

The first YMCA in Canada was established in Montreal, November 25, 1851, the declared purpose being "the improvement of the spiritual and mental condition of young men." Toronto and Halifax followed in 1853. At the 125th anniversary of the Canadian movement (1976), YMCAs were found in 75 cities from St. John's, Newfoundland to Victoria, B.C., with programs for intellectual, spiritual, and physical development of all Canadians.

Originally forming a single movement with the YMCAs in the United States, the Canadian Associations formed their own National Council in 1912. However, the international outreach (assisting in the establishment of YMCA movements in Latin America, Asia, and Africa) was administered jointly with the YMCA in the U.S. through an International Committee until 1970, when an agreement recognized the Canadian YMCA's independent service abroad. Today many "partnership Programs" exist between the Canadian Associations and YMCAs in developing countries.

National Council of YMCAs of Canada: 2160 Yonge St., Toronto, Ontario M4S 2A9. Tel. (416) 485-9447

OFFICERS

Pres., Henry F. Davis
Gen. Sec., Rix G. Rogers
Dir., Int'l Aff., Richard A. Patten

Young Women's Christian Association of Canada

The first local Association was founded in Saint John, N.B., in 1870; the National Headquarters in 1894. Program and services (e.g., leadership development, housing) are provided in the 59 locals across Canada (no YWCA in P.E.I.). Of this number 30 are YMCA-YWCAs. Approximately a half million people are members of and/or participate in programs offered by the Association.

Office: 571 Jarvis St., Toronto, Ontario M4Y 2J1. Tel (416) 921-2117

OFFICERS

Pres., Mrs. Ann Northcote
Exec. Dir., Miss Ann Henders

3. RELIGIOUS BODIES IN THE UNITED STATES

Introduction

The following is a series of directories of United States religious bodies arranged alphabetically by official name. Individual denominational directories have been corrected by the religious bodies themselves. Those directories which have not been updated for this edition of the **Yearbook** by denominational officials carry the symbol (†) in front of the title of denomination.

Generally speaking, each directory listing follows the following organization: a historical or doctrinal statement: a brief statement of current statistics (data for 1979 or 1978), if any; information on general organization; officers; other organizations; and major periodicals.

More complete statistics will be found in the Statistical and Historical Section of this **Yearbook** in the table on Current and Non-Current Statistics and also in the table entitled "Some Statistics of Church Finances."

A listing of religious bodies by family groups (e.g., Baptists, Lutheran) is found at the end of this directory.

A recently published work by Dr. J. Gordon Melton entitled *A Directory of Religious Bodies in the United States,* New York, Garland Publishing Co., 1977 lists 1,275 "primary" religious bodies currently functioning in the United States. The title, address and principal publication is supplied. There is a typology for classification of these primary religious bodies which are then listed by family groups.

Advent Christian Church

A branch of the original Adventist group, composed of ministers and churches which withdrew from the American Millennial Association between 1854 and 1860, as a result of controversy over the question of immortality. As a corollary to their belief in conditional immortality, the group also held to the utter extinction of the wicked after the judgment. The General Conference was organized in 1860. In 1964 Life and Advent Union merged with this body.

Churches: 381 Inclusive Membership: 31,324 Sunday or Sabbath Schools: 330 Total Enrollment: 22,872 Ordained Clergy: 503

GENERAL ORGANIZATION

General Conference: triennial

Office: P.O. Box 23152, Charlotte, NC 28212, Rev. Adrian B. Shepard, Exec. Vice-Pres. Tel. (704) 545-6161

Organizations and periodicals are all at this address unless otherwise noted.

OFFICERS

Pres., Rev. Joe Tom Tate, 138 W. 17th St., Jacksonville, FL 32206

Sec., Rev. Joyce K. Thomas, 7820 Biltmore Dr., Miramar, FL 33023

Appalachian Vice-Pres., Rev. Glennon Balser, Rt. 1 Box 742, Charlotte, NC 28212

Central Vice-Pres., Rev. Dwight Carpenter, 333 Fourth St., Baraboo, WI 53931

Eastern Vice-Pres., Rev. Leon Horne, Jr., County Rd., West Wareham, MA 02576

Southern Vice-Pres., Carlyle Beasley, 107 E. Crestview Dr., Smithfield, NC 27577

Western Vice-Pres., Mr. Barron Knectel, 2231 S.E. Mesa Dr., Santa Ana, CA 92707

The Woman's Home & Foreign Mission Society: Pres., Mrs. Harry Pitts, 6213 Elmer Ave., N. Holly, CA 91606

PERIODICALS

The Advent Christian Witness (m), Rev. C. William Bailey, Cedar Park Estate #27, Rt. 6, Concord, NC 28025

Advent Christian News (bi-w), Rev. C. William Bailey, Ed.

Advent Christian Missions (m), Rev. J. E. Hickel, Ed.

Maranatha (q), Rev. C. William Bailey, Ed.

African Methodist Episcopal Church

This church began in 1787 in Philadelphia when persons in St. George's Methodist Episcopal Church withdrew as a protest against color segregation. In 1816 the denomination was started, led by Rev. Richard Allen, who had been ordained deacon by Bishop Asbury, and who was ordained elder and elected and consecrated bishop.

Churches: 3,050 Inclusive Membership: 1,970,000 Sunday or Sabbath Schools: 2,550 Total Enrollment: 105,250 Ordained Clergy: 3,938

GENERAL ORGANIZATION

General Conference: quadrennial (Next meeting, 3rd Wednesday, June 1980)

General Board, Annual Meeting 3rd Monday each year, June

Council of Bishops, Annually meeting 3rd Wednesday each year, February

OFFICERS

Senior Bishop, H. Thomas Primm, 1002 Kirkwood Ave., Nashville, TN 37203

Gen. Sec., A.M.E. Church, Dr. Richard Allen Chappelle, Sr., P.O. Box 183, St. Louis, MO 63166

Pres., Council of Bishops, Frederick H. Talbot, 2 Clieveden Ave., Kingston 6 Jamaica, W.I.

Sec. Council of Bishops, Bishop H. Hartford Brookins, 4908 Crenshaw Blvd., Los Angeles, CA 90008

Pres. General Board, Hubert Nelson Robinson, 7220 N. Illinois St., Indianapolis, IN 46260

Sec. General Board, Dr. Richard Allen Chappelle, Sr., P.O. Box 183, St. Louis, MO 63166

Treas., A.M.E. Church, Dr. Joseph C. McKinney, 2311 "M" St., N.W., Washington, DC 20037

Historiographer, Dr. Howard D. Gregg, 531 New Jersey Ave., Atlantic City, NJ 08401

Pres. Judical Council, Dr, Luna I. Mishoe, Delaware State College, Dover, DE 19901

DEPARTMENTS

Missions: Dr. John W. P. Collier, Jr., 475 Riverside Dr., Rm. 1926, New York, NY 10027

Church Extension: Dr. Hercules Miles, Sec.-Treas., 3526 Dodier, St. Louis, MO 63107

Christian Education: Dr. Andrew White, Sec., 500 8th Ave., S., Nashville, TN 37203

Evangelism: Dr. G. H. J. Thibodeaux, Dir., 1150 Portland Ave., Shreveport, LA 71103

Publications: Dr. Henry A. Belin, Jr., Sec.-Treas., 500 8th Ave., S., Nashville, TN 37203

Pension: Dr. J. M. Granberry , Sec.-Treas., 500 8th Ave., S., Nashville, TN 37203

Minimum Salary: Dr. Ezra M. Johnson, 280 Hernando St., Memphis, TN 38126

Lay Organization: Mr. J. D. Williams, Connectional Pres., 3232 E. 30th St., Kansas City, MO 64124
Women's Missionary Society: Ms. Mary E. Frizzell, Pres., 2311 "M" St., N.W., Washington, DC 20037
Religious Literature Department: Dr. Therion E. Cobbs, Editor-in-Chief, 500 8th Avenue, S. Nashville, TN 37203

PERIODICALS

A.M.E. Christian Recorder: Dr. Robert H. Reid, Ed., 500 8th Ave., S., Nashville TN 37203
A.M.E. Review: Dr. William D. Johnson, Ed., 468 Lincoln Dr., N.W., Atlanta, GA 30318
Voice of Missions: Dr. John W. P. Collier, Jr., Ed., 475 Riverside Dr., Rm. 1920, New York, NY 10027
Women's Missionary Magazine: Dr. Hattie Witt Greene, Ed., 1023 N. 5th St., Birmingham, AL 35204
Secret Chamber: Dr. G. H. J. Thibodeaux, Ed., 1150 Portland Ave., Shreveport, LA 71103

BISHOPS IN THE U.S.A.

First District: Richard Allen Hildebrand, 29 Bala Ave., Suite 222, Bala Cynwyd, PA 19004
Second District: Henry W. Murph, 1221 Massachusetts Ave., N.W., Ste. C, Washington, DC 20005
Third District: Vinton R. Anderson, 2685 Halleck Dr., Columbus, OH 43209
Fourth District: Hubert N. Robinson, 7220 N. Illinois St., Indianapolis, IN 46260
Fifth District: H. Hartford Brookins, 4908 Creshaw Blvd., Los Angeles, CA 90008
Sixth District: H. I. Bearden, 208 Auburn Ave., N.E., Atlanta, GA 30303
Seventh District: Frank M. Reid, Jr., 2522 Barhamville Road, Columbia, SC 29204
Eighth District: Frank C. Cummings, 2138 St. Bernard Ave., New Orleans, LA 70119
Ninth District: Phillip R. Cousin, 1000 Bessemer Rd., W., Birmingham, AL 35228
Tenth District: John H. Adams, 2812 Kendall La., Waco, TX 76705
Eleventh District: Samuel S. Morris, 915 Old Grove Manor, Jacksonville, FL 32207
Twelfth District: Fred C. James, 6514 Sherry Dr., Little Rock AR 72204
Thirteenth District: H. Thomas Primm, 1002 Kirkwood Ave., Nashville, TN 37203
Retired Bishops:
- O. L. Sherman, 2525 Chester, Little Rock, AR 72206
- D. Ward Nichols, 2295 Seventh Ave., New York, NY 10030
- I. H. Bonner, 2015 Stewart St., Camden, SC 29020
- Ernest L. Hickman, 120 Oakcrest Dr., S.W., Atlanta, GA 30311
- Harrison J. Bryant, 4000 Bedford Rd., Baltimore, MD 21207

African Methodist Episcopal Zion Church

The A.M.E. Zion Church is an independent body, having withdrawn from the John Street Methodist Church of New York City in 1796. The first bishop was James Varick.

Churches: 6,020 Inclusive Membership: 1,093,001 Sunday or Sabbath Schools: 6,018 Total Enrollment: 168,149 Ordained Clergy: 6,689

AFRICAN METHODIST EPISCOPAL ZION CHURCH

GENERAL ORGANIZATION

General Conference: Quadrennial (Next Meeting, May, 1980)

OFFICERS

Pres., Board of Bishops, Bishop Alfred G. Dunston, Jr., P.O. Box 19788, Philadelphia, PA 19143
Sec., Board of Bishops, Bishop Charles H. Foggie, 1200 Windermere Dr., Pittsburgh, PA 15218
Asst. Sec., Bishop John H. Miller, 6211 Red Bird Ct., Dallas, TX 75232
Treas., ———

OTHER AGENCIES

Gen. Sec.-Aud., Herman L. Anderson, P.O. Box 32843, Charlotte, NC 28232
Fin. Sec., Ms. Madie L. Simpson, P.O. Box 31005, Charlotte, NC 28231
A.M.E. Zion Publishing House: Mr. Lem Long, Jr., General Mgr., P.O. Box 30714, Charlotte, NC 28230
Dept. of Overseas Missions: Rev. Harold A. L. Clement. Sec.-Treas, 475 Riverside Dr., Ste. 1910, New York, NY 10027
Dept. of Home Missions, Pensions, and Relief: Rev. Jewett Walker, Sec.-Treas., P.O. Box 30846, Charlotte, NC 28201
Dept. of Christian Education: Rev. G. L. Blackwell, Sec., 128 E. 58th St., Chicago, IL 60637
Dept. of Church School Literature: Rev. Louis J. Baptiste, Ed., 3022 Depaul Ct., Charlotte, NC 28216
Dept. of Church Extension: Mr. Lem Long, Jr., Sec.-Treas., P. O. Box 31005, Charlotte, NC 28231
Dept. of Evangelism: Rev. J. Dallas Jenkins, Sr., Dir., 4550 Laurel Dr., Dayton, OH 45417
Dept. of Public Relations: Gregory R. Smith, Dir., 344 Hawthrone Terr., Mt. Vernon, NY 10550
Dept. of Public Health: Samuel C. Coleman, M.D., Dir., 128 Grove St., Hot Springs National Park, AR 71901
Woman's Home and Overseas Missionary Society: Gen Pres., Mrs. Alcestis Coleman, 120-19 Nashville Blvd., St. Albans, NY 11412; Exec. Sec., Mrs. Lonia Gill, 2864 Whistler St., Whistler, AL 36612; Treas., Mrs. Farris Williams, 3507 8th St., Tuscaloosa, AL 35401

PERIODICALS

Star of Zion (w), Rev. M. B. Robinson, Ed., P.O. Box 31005, Charlotte, NC 28230
Quarterly Review (q), ———.
Missionary Seer. Rev. Harold A. L. Clement, Ed., 475 Riverside Dr., Ste. 1910, New York NY 10027
Church School Herald (q), Rev. Louis J. Baptiste, Ed., 3022 Depaul Ct., Charlotte, NC 28216

BISHOPS

First Episcopal Area: ———
Second Episcopal Area: Bishop William Milton Smith, 3753 Springhill Ave., Mobile, AL 36608
Third Episcopal Area: Bishop William Alexander Hilliard, 690 Chicago Blvd., Detroit, MI 48202
Fourth Episcopal Area: Bishop Alfred Gilbert Dunston, Jr., P.O. Box 19788, Philadelphia, PA 19143
Fifth Episcopal Area: Bishop Charles Herbert Foggie, 1200 Windemere Dr., Pittsburgh, PA 15218
Sixth Episcopal Area: Bishop James Clinton Hoggard, 6401 Sunset La., Indianapolis, IN 46260
Seventh Episcopal Area: Bishop James W. Wactor, 709 Edgehill Rd., Fayetteville, NC 28302
Eighth Episcopal Area: Bishop Clinton R. Coleman, 3513 Ellamont Rd., Baltimore, MD 21215
Ninth Episcopal Area: Bishop Arthur Marshall, Jr., P.O. Box 41138, Ben Hill Sta., Atlanta, GA 30331

Tenth Episcopal Area: Bishop John H. Miller, 6211 Red Bird Ct., Dallas, TX 75232
Eleventh Episcopal Area: Bishop George J. Leake, 220 W. 10th St., Charlotte, NC 28208
Twelfth Episcopal Area: Bishop Ruben L. Speaks, 304 Pennsylvania Ave., Roosevelt, NY 11575
Retired:
Bishop William Andrew Stewart, 2314 20th St., N. W., Washington, DC 20009
Bishop Felix Sylvester Anderson, 741 S. 44th St., Louisville, KY 40211

The African Orthodox Church

The African Orthodox Church was instituted in 1921 by Archbishop George Alexander McGuire as a unit of those churches of Christ adhering to the orthodox confession of faith.

GENERAL ORGANIZATION

Headquarters: 122 W. 129 St., New York, NY 10027. Tel. (212) 662-0894

OFFICERS

Primate Most Rev. William R. Miller
Chancellor, Bishop G. Duncan Hinkson
Gen. Sec., Rev. Percival Evans
Fin. Sec., Rev. Canon Angel Vargas
Treas., William W. Selkridge
Rector, Very Rev. Canon Vincent Waterman

Albanian Orthodox Archdiocese in America

A Diocese of the autocephalous Orthodox Church in America, ministering to the Albanians in the United States of America. Established in 1908 by Metropolitan Fan S. Noli.
Churches: 16 Inclusive Membership: 40,000 Sunday or Sabbath Schools: 15 Total Enrollment: 1,400 Ordained Clergy: 25

OFFICERS

Primate, Most Rev. Metropolitan Theodosius 523 E. Broadway, South Boston, MA 02127. Tel. (617) 268-1275; Archdiocesan Chancery, Tel. (617) 698-3366
Bishop-Elect, Rt. Rev. Mark Forsberg, 529 E. Broadway Boston, MA 02127. Tel. (617) 268-1275
Chancellor, Rev. Arthur E. Liolin, 60 Antwerp St., East Milton, MA 02186. Tel. (617) 698-3366
Lay Chpsn., Ronald V. Nasson, 26 Enfield St., Jamaica Plain, MA 02130. Tel. (617) 522-8418
Gen. Sec., V. Rev. Spero L. Page, 1 Coombs Rd., Worcester MA 01602. Tel. (617) 791-4009

PERIODICAL

The Vineyard (Vreshta), (q), Metropolitan Fan S. Noli, Memorial Library, 529 East Broadway, South Boston, MA 02127

Albanian Orthodox Diocese of America

This Diocese was organized in 1950 as a canonical body administering to the Albanian faithful. It is under the ecclesiastical jurisdiction of the Ecumenical Patriarchate of Constantinople (Istanbul).

Churches: 10 Inclusive Membership: 5,250 Sunday or Sabbath Schools: 2 Total Enrollment: 130 Ordained Clergy: 4

GENERAL ORGANIZATION

Headquarters: 54 Burroughs St., Jamaica Plain, MA 02130. Tel. (617) 524-0477

OFFICER

Diocese Council: Pres., His Grace Bishop Mark (Lipa)

PERIODICAL

The True Light (m), P.O. Box 18162, Sta. A, Boston, MA 02118

Amana Church Society

Begun as the Community of True Inspiration in Hessen, Germany, in 1714. The group emigrated to America because of persecution in 1844, settling near Buffalo, N.Y., at Ebenezer. The Society then moved to Amana, Iowa, in 1854. The group is located in seven villages and is the only inspirationist movement of its kind in the world. Membership is placed at 1,500, living in communal society until 1932 and now reorganized. The Elders conduct church services.

GENERAL ORGANIZATION

Board of Trustees

OFFICERS

Pres., Charles L. Selzer, Homestead, IA 52236
Vice-Pres., Harry A. Geiger, Amana, IA 52203
Sec., Martin Roemig, Amana, IA 52203
Treas, Henry Schiff, Amana, IA 52203

American Baptist Association

A fellowship of regular and independent missionary Baptist churches distributed throughout the United States, with their greatest strength in the South. Their national fellowship was formed in 1905.

Churches: 5,000 Inclusive Membership: 1,500,000 Sunday or Sabbath Schools: 5,000 Total Enrollment: 800,000 Ordained Clergy: 5,425

GENERAL ORGANIZATION

American Baptist Association Headquarters: 4605 N. State Line Ave., Texarkana, TX 755011. Tel. (214) 792-2783

OFFICERS

Pres., Dr. Vernon L. Barr, 1917 Shortal Dr., Dallas, TX 75217
Vice-Pres.'s, W. A. Dillard, P.O. Box 176, Benton, AR 72015
D. S. Madden, 2011 Random Dr., Anaheim, CA 92804
Ray O. Brooks, 1706 Longview Dr., Henderson, TX 75652
Rec. Clks., W. E. Norris, 970 Louisiana, Sullivan, MO 63080 Gene Smith, 1208 W. 35th St., Pine Bluff, AR 71601
Parliamentarian, Dr. Roy M. Reed, P.O. Box 848, Bellflower, CA 90706
Bus. Mgr., Publications, Dr. J. B. Powers, Box 1828, Texarkana, AR 75501
Ed.-in-Chief Publications, O. H. Griffith, Box 502, Texarkana, TX 75501
Dir. Meeting Arrangements, Dr. Jack Dean, 3509 Mabank La., Bowie, MD 20715
Promotion Dir., Raymond J. Lewis, P.O. Box 901, Texarkana, TX 75501
Missionary-Treas., Kenneth Bazar, P. O. Box 1050, Texarkana, TX 75501

PERIODICALS

Missionary Baptist Searchlight (s-m), Box 663, Little Rock, AR 72203
Baptist Monitor (s-m), Box 591, Henderson, TX 75652
The Missionary (m), Box 5116, Nashville, TN 37206

The Baptist Anchor (s-m), Box 1641, Lakeland, FL 33802
The Missionary Baptist News, Box 123, Minden, LA 71055
Baptist Sentinel, Box 848, Bellflower, CA 90706
The Baptist World, Box 525 Mabelvale, AR 72103
The Baptist Review, Box 287, Marlow, OK 23055
Illinois Missionary Baptist, 2101 Washington Rd., Washington, IL 61571

American Baptist Churches in the U.S.A.

Originally known as the Northern Baptist Convention, this body of Baptist churches changed the name to American Baptist Convention in 1950 with a commitment to "hold the name in trust for all Christians of like faith and mind who desire to bear witness to the historical Baptist convictions in a framework of cooperative Protestantism."

In 1972 American Baptist Churches in the U.S.A. was adopted as the new name. Although national missionary organizational developments began in 1814 with the establishment of the American Baptist Foreign Mission Society and continued with the organization of the American Baptist Publication Society in 1824 and the American Baptist Home Mission Society in 1832, the general denominational body was not formed until 1907. American Baptist work at the local level dates back to the organization by Roger Williams of the First Baptist Church in Providence, R. I. in 1638.

Convention: Biennial
Headquarters: Valley Forge Pa. 19481 Tel. (215) 768-2000

OFFICERS

Pres., Rev. William F. Keucher
Vice-Pres., Mrs. Elizabeth L. Haselden
Gen. Sec., Rev. Robert C. Campbell
Assoc. Gen. Secs.: Rev. William K. Cober, Rev. Chester J. Jump, Jr., Rev. William T. McKee, Rev. Dean R. Wright

GENERAL ORGANIZATION

Office of the General Secretary: Gen. Sec., Rev. Robert C. Campbell; Research and Planning; Exec. Dir., Rev. Richard K. Gladden; Ecumenical Relations: Ecumenical Officer, Mrs. Pearl L. McNeil; Treasurer's Office: Treas., Rev. Newton E. Woodbury, Dir. of Acct., Donald W. Brown; Office of National Operations: Deputy, Rev. Martha M. Barr; Office of Regional Operations: Deputy, Rev. Harrison E. Williams; Office of World Mission Support: Exec. Dir., Rev. Ralph R. Rott; Assoc. Dirs., Rev. A. Q. Van Benschoten, Jr., Rev. Raymond Weigum; Dir. Field Actvs., Mrs. Patricia Merchant; Dir. A. B. Films, Rev. Ronald E. Schlosser; Fund of Renewal, Ntl. Dir., Rev. Ralph R. Rott.

REGION/STATE/CITY ORGANIZATIONS:

Central Region, American Baptist Churches of, Rev. Robert H. Roberts, Box 4105, Topeka, KS 66604 (Kansas and Oklahoma)
Chicago Baptist Associaton, Rev. William E. Nelson, 59 E. Van Buren, Ste. 257 Chicago 60605
Cleveland Baptist Association, Rev. Stanley P. Borden, 2246 Euclid Avenue, Cleveland 44115
Connecticut, American Baptist Churches of, Rev. Orlando L. Tibbetts, 100 Bloomfield Ave., Hartford 06105
District of Columbia Baptist Convention, Rev. James A. Langley, 1628 16th St., NW, 20009
Great Rivers Region, American Baptist Churches of the, Rev. J. Ralph Beaty, P.O. Box 3786, Springfield, IL 62708 (Illinois & Missouri)
Indiana Baptist Convention, Rev. Dallas J. West, 1350 North Delaware St., Indianapolis 46202
Indianapolis Baptist Association, Rev. L. Eugene Ton, 1350 N. Delaware St., Indianapolis 46202
Los Angeles Baptist City Mission Society, Rev. Arnold S. Boal, 427 W. Fifth St., Los Angeles, 90013
Maine, American Baptist Churches of, Rev. James A. Dillon, 107 Winthrop St., Augusta 04330
Massachusetts, American Baptist Churches of, Rev. Roscoe C. Robison, 88 Tremont St., Room 500, Boston 02108
Metropolitan New York, American Baptist Churches of Rev. Carl E. Flemister, 225 Park Ave. S., New York, NY 10003
Michigan, American Baptist Churches of, Robert E. McQuaid (Interim), 4610 S. Hagadorn Rd., East Lansing MI 48823
Mid-American Baptist Churches, Rev. Telfer L. Epp, 2913 Ingersoll Ave., Des Moines 50312 (Iowa & Minnesota)
Monroe Association, American Baptist churches of the, Rev. Hugh O. Morton, 175 Genesee St., Rochester 14611 (Rochester & vicinity)
Nebraska, American Baptist Churches of, Rev. Heinz H. Grabia, 6404 Maple St., Omaha 68104
New Hampshire, American Baptist Churches of, Rev. Robert W. Williams, P.O. Box 796, Concord 03301
New Jersey, American Baptist Churches of, Rev. George D. Younger, 161 Freeway Dr. E., East Orange, 07018
New York State, American Baptist Churches of, Rev. Arthur L. Whitaker, 3049 E. Genesee St., Syracuse 13224
North Dakota Baptist State Convention, Chester M. Bowman, 1524 S. Summit Ave., Sioux Falls, SD 57105
Niagara Frontier, American Baptist Churches of the, Rev. William D. Scott, 1272 Delaware Ave., Buffalo, N.Y. 14209 (Buffalo & vicinity)
Northwest, American Baptist Churches of, Rev. E. Wayne Roberts, 321 First Ave. W., Seattle, 98119, (Alaska, Idaho, Montana, Utah, Washington)
Ohio Baptist Convention, Rev. John A. Sundquist, P.O. Box 376, Granville 43023
Oregon, American Baptist Churches of, Rev. Glenn E. Camper, 0245 SW Bancroft St., Portland 97201
Pacific Southwest, American Baptist Churches of the, Rev. W. Lowell Fairley, 816 S. Figueroa St., Los Angeles, 90017 (Arizona, Baja, Southern California, So. Nevada & Hawaii)
Pennsylvania & Delaware, American Baptist Churches of, Rev. R. Eugene Crow, American Baptist Churches USA, Room C-127, Valley Forge 19481
Philadelphia Baptist Association, Rev. William L. Johnston, 1701 Arch St., Rm. 417, Philadelphia 19103
Pittsburgh Baptist Association, Rev. Carlton B. Goodwin, 507 Investment Building, 239 Fourth Ave., Pittsburgh 15222
Puerto Rico, Baptist Churches of, Rev. Jose Norat-Rodriquez, Mayaguez #21, Hato Rey, PR 00917
Rhode Island, American Baptist Churches of, Rev. W. Eugene Motter, 2 Stimson Ave., Providence, 02906
Rocky Mountains, American Baptist Churches of, Rev. James Havens, 1344 Pennsylvania St., Denver 80203 (Colorado, Wyoming & New Mexico)
South Dakota Baptist Convention, Chester M. Bowman 1524 South Summit Ave., Sioux Falls 57105
South, American Baptist Churches of the, Rev. Walter L. Parrish, II, 244 Citizens Trust Bldg., 75 Piedmont Ave., NE, Atlanta, GA 30303 (Alabama, Arkansas, Florida, Georgia, Kentucky, Louisiana, Maryland, Mississippi, North Carolina, Oklahoma, South Carolina, Tennessee, Texas, Virginia)
Vermont Baptist State Convention, Rev. Paul T. Losh, 19 Orchard Terrace, Burlington 05401
West, American Baptist Churches of, Rev. Robert D. Rasmussen, P.O. Box 23204, Oakland 94623 (Northern California, Northern Nevada)
West Virginia Baptist Convention, Rev. Douglas W. Hill, P.O. Box 1019, Parkersburg 26101.
Wisconsin Baptist State Convention, Rev. Chris E. Lawson, 15330 W. Watertown Plank Rd., Elm Grove, 53122

Board of Educational Ministries (incorporated as the American Baptist Board of Education and Publication) including Judson Press and Judson Book Stores. Office: Valley Forge, PA 19481. Exec. Dir., Rev. William T. McKee; Deputy Exec. Dir./Treas., Paul V. Moore; Assoc. Exec. Sec./Program, Rev. Grant W. Hanson; Divisional Dirs.: Christian Higher Education, Ms. Shirley M. Jones; Church Education, Rev. Grant W. Hanson; Publishing and Business, Rev. Frank T. Hoadley; Communication, Philip Jenks, Officers of the Board: Pres., Eric J. Stettner; Vice-Pres., Elmer Young, Jr. Rec. Sec., Rev. Grant W. Hanson

American Baptist Assembly (National Training Center) Green Lake, WI 54941. Exec. Dir., Rev. Roger W. Getz; Exec. Dir., BEM, Rev. William T. McKee; Dir. of Development/Promotion, ———; Dir. and Scheduling, Rev. Lawrence H. Janssen; Director of Finance, L. B. Standifer III; Officers of the Board; Pres. Harry E. Coulter; Vice-Pres., Ms. F. Mildred Thurston; Treas., William E. Jarvis; Rec. Sec., Mrs. Warren A. Harvey.

American Baptist Historical Society (Archives and History); Dir., Rev. William H. Brackney, 1106 S. Goodman St., Rochester, NY 14620; Pres., Dr. Charles H. Stuart

American Baptist Men: Exec. Dir., W. Burton Andrews, Valley Forge, PA 19481; Pres., Charles R. Browning

American Baptist Women: Exec. Dir., Mrs. Doris Anne Younger, Valley Forge, PA 19481; Pres., Mrs. Richard Ogrean

Commission on the Ministry: Exec. Dir., Rev. Paul O. Madsen

Board of International Ministries (incorporated as American Baptist Foreign Mission Society). Office: Valley Forge, PA 19481. Pres., Henry R. Roose; Vice-Pres, Mrs. Reino A. Jarvi; Exec. Dir., Rev. Chester J. Jump, Jr.; Assoc. Exec. Dir., Ms. Alice M. Giffin; Budget Dir., Rev. Lloyd G. James; Treas. & Bus. Mgr., William E. Jarvis. Overseas Division: Sec., Ms. Alice M. Giffin; Assoc. Sec. (Sec. for Planning), Rev. Russell E. Brown; Area Secretaries: Africa (Zaire & Nigeria) & Thailand, Rev. Robert G. Johnson; East Asia (Japan, Okinawa, Hong Kong, Philippines, Singapore), Rev. Russell E. Brown; Southern Asia (Nepal, Bangladesh, North East India, Bengal-Orissa-Bihar, South India, Burma), Rev. Raymond W. Beaver; Europe & Middle East, Ms. Alice M. Giffin; Latin America (Mexico, El Salvador, Nicaragua, Haiti), Rev. Victor M. Mercado; Assoc. Areas Secs.: Recruitment & Personnel, Rev. Richard G. Beers; Tours & Scholarships, Ms. Edythe M. McCarty. Overseas Prog. Assoc., Mrs. Louise A. Paw. Public Relations Division: Sec., Rev. Hugh W. Smith; Admin. Associates, Ms. Eleanor Menke (Church Relations); Rev. Dean R. Kirkwood, (Interpretation); Mrs. Jeannette S. Stuart (White Cross). Business and Finance Division: Treas. & Bus. Mgr., William E. Jarvis; Assoc. Treas. & Assoc. Sec., Walter C. Konrath; Chief Accountant, Austin B. Windle; Financial Analyst, Ms. Mary H. Leypoldt; Sec. of Estate Planning, Rev. Lorenz R. Michelson.

Board of National Ministries (incorporated as The American Baptist Home Mission Society and Woman's American Baptist Home Mission Society). Office: Valley Forge, PA 19481. Pres., Mrs. Margaret L. Prine; Vice-Pres., Rev. Charlton G. Christenson; Exec. Dir., Rev. William K. Cober; Rec. Sec., Rev. Richard M. Jones; Assoc. Exec. Dir's., Rev. Atha J. Baugh & Rev. Richard Jones; Mgr., Adm. Support Unit, Rev. Atha J. Baugh; Mgr., Church & Community Development Unit, Ms. Ernestine R. Galloway; Mgr., Direct & Contract Services Units, Rev. John A. Barker; Mgr. Individual & Corp. Responsibility Unit, Rev. Phyllip A. Henry; Mgr., Personal & Public Witness Unit, Rev. Emmett V. Johnson; Mgr., Program Support Unit, Rev. Richard M. Jones; Evangelism Dir., Rev. Emmett V. Johnson; Treas., Horace E. Gale.

The Ministers and Missionaries Benefit Board: Office: 475 Riverside Dr., New York, NY 10027: Pres., Rev. E. Spencer Parsons; Vice-Pres., 229 S. 18th St., Rittenhouse Square, Philadelphia, PA 19103 Huggins & Company, 1401 Walnut St., Philadelphia, PA 19102; Exec. Dir., Rev. Dean R. Wright; Assoc. Dir., Ms. Miriam R. Corbett; Treas., Rev. Gordon E. Smith; Rec. Sec. & Mortgage Officer, Frank L. Taylor; Regional Dir., East, Rev. Richard Arnesman; Regional Dir., West, Rev. Terry L. Burch

Ministers Council: Office: Valley Forge, PA 19481. Pres., Rev. James L. Pratt; Vice-Pres.'s (New England), Rev. Craig A. Collemer; (Mid-Atlantic), Rev. Robert F. Spencer; (South), Rev. G. Daniel Jones: (Great Lakes), Rev. Kathryn W. Baker; (Central), Rev. Walter B. Pulliam; (Western), Rev. Berkeley Ormond; Sec., Rev. Lamont Satterly; Treas., Rev. Hazel A. Roper; Exec. Dir., Rev. Charles N. Forsberg.

PERIODICALS

American Baptist (m), Valley Forge, PA 19481. Philip Jenks, Ed.

The Baptist Leader (m), Valley Forge, PA 19481, Rev. Vincie Alessi, Ed.

The Secret Place (q), Valley Forge, PA 19481. Rev. Vincie Alessi and Rev. Herschell H. Richmond, Eds.

Foundations (q), Rochester, NY 14620. Rev. Joseph R. Sweeny, Ed.

The American Carpatho-Russian Orthodox Greek Catholic Church

The American Carpatho-Russian Orthodox Greek Catholic Church is a self-governing diocese that is in communion with the Ecumenical Partriarchate of Constantinople. The late Patriarch Benjamin I, in an official Patriarchal Document listed as No. 1379 and dated September 19, 1938, canonized the Diocese in the name of the Orthodox Church of Christ.

GENERAL ORGANIZATION

Sobor: triennial (Next Sobor 1979)

Headquarters: Johnstown, PA 15906. Tel. (814) 536-4207

OFFICERS

Bishop: His Excellency, The Most Rev. John R. Martin, 312 Garfield St. Johnstown, PA 15906

Vicar General: Rt. Rev. Mitred Peter E. Molchany, 903 Ann St., Homestead, PA 15120

Chancellor: Very Rev. Msgr. John Yurcisin, 249 Butler Ave., Johnstown, PA 15906

Treas.: Very Rev. Michael Slovesko, R.D. 2, Box 6, Windber, PA 15963

PERIODICAL

Cerkovny Vistnik—Church Messenger (bi-w), 127 Chandler Ave., Johnstown, PA 19506, Rev. James S. Dutko, Ed.

The American Catholic Church, Archdiocese of New York

This body derives its orders from the Syrian Church of Antioch, commonly called the Jacobite Apostolic Church. Its doctrines are, with few exceptions, those held by the Old Catholic Church in Europe.

OFFICERS

Primate, Most Rev. James Francis Augustine Lashley, 457 W. 144th St., New York, NY 10031, Archbishop Sidney Ferguson, 116 W. 133rd St., New York, NY 10030; Archbishop Joel N. Ashby, 2032-34, Creston Ave., Bronx, NY 10453; Archbishop W. G. Almeida

The American Catholic Church (Syro-Antiochean)

This body derives its orders from the Syrian Patriarch of Antioch, formerly called the Jacobite Apostolic Church. Organized in 1915, it is Catholic in worship and discipline and uses Roman Catholic liturgy in the administration of the seven Sacraments. The church is, however, a self-governed American body.

Churches: 3 Inclusive Membership: 501 Sunday or Sabbath Schools: 2 Total Enrollment: 148 Ordained Clergy: 8

GENERAL ORGANIZATION

OFFICERS

Pres., The Most Rev. Archbishop H. Francis Wilkie; St. Mary Magdalene Catholic Church, 189 Lenox Ave., New York NY 10026. Tel. (212) 662-7188

Sec. Gen., Treas., Rev. Ronald St. John Wood, 2100 Beekman Pl., Brooklyn, NY 11225. Tel. (212) 462-8905

American Evangelical Christian Churches

Founded in 1944, the A.E.C.C. functions as a denominational body with interdoctrinal views incorporating into its ecclesiastical position both the Calvinistic and Arminian doctrines. Its churches operate under the name of Community Churches, American Bible Churches, and Evangelical Christian Churches. The Church has its own missionary home and Bible training school.

Headquarters: Pineland, FL 33945

OFFICERS

Mod., Dr. G. W. Hyatt, Waterfront Dr., Pineland FL 33945

Sec., Dr. Ben Morgan, 64 South St., Southport, IN 46227

The American Lutheran Church

This body was organized during a constituting convention at Minneapolis, Minn., April 22-24, 1960. It combined the following three church bodies: American Lutheran Church (ALC). The Evangelical Lutheran Church (ELC), and United Evangelical Lutheran Church (UELC).

The union brought together, for the first time this century, major Lutheran church bodies of different national heritage—German (ALC), Norwegian (ELC), Danish (UELC), National offices of the new church were established beginning January 1, 1961, at Columbus, Ohio, and UELC at Blair, Neb., were discontinued.

On February 1, 1963, the Lutheran Free Church (LFC) merged with The American Lutheran Church.

Churches: 4,837 Inclusive Membership; 2,377,235 Sunday or Sabbath Schools: 4,544. Total Enrollment: 625,660 Ordained Clergy: 6,789

GENERAL ORGANIZATION

Convention: biennial (Next meeting, Minneapolis, MN, October 1-7, 1980)

National Offices: 422 S. 5th St., Minneapolis, MN 55415. Tel. (612) 330-3100

GENERAL OFFICERS

Gen. Pres., Rev. Dr. David W. Preus
Vice-Pres., Rev. Dr. Frederick W. Meuser
Gen. Sec., Dr. Arnold R. Mickelson

DIVISIONS

Board for Life and Mission in the Congregation: Chpsn., Mrs. Marian Nickleson; Exec. Dir., Rev. Dr. Paul A. Hanson

Board for Service and Mission in America: Chpsn., Rev. Robert L. Otterstad; Acting Dir., Rev. Melvin A. Bucka

Board for World Mission and Inter-Church Cooperation; Chpsn., Rev. Herman A. Larsen; Dir., Rev. Dr. Morris A. Sorenson, Jr.

Board for Theological Education and Ministry: Chpsn., Rev. Dr. John V. Halvorson; Dir., Rev. Dr. Walter R. Wietzke

Board for College and University Services: Chpsn., Rev. Dennis V. Griffin; Dir., Dr. Ronald Matthias

SERVICE BOARDS

Board of Trustees: Chpsn., Mr. Frank R. Jennings; Exec. Sec., Rev. Dr. George S. Schultz

Board of Pensions: Chpsn., Mr. Richard O. Gregerson; Exec. Sec., Rev. Henry F. Treptow

Board of Publication: Chpsn., Mr. Richard Moe; Exec. Sec., Dr. Albert E. Anderson

ADMINISTRATIVE OFFICES

Office of Communication and Mission Support; Dir., Rev. Dr. John W. Bachman

Office of Research and Analysis: Dir., Dr. Carl F. Reuss

Office of Support to Ministries: Dir., Rev. Dr. Roger W. Fjeld

Office of the ALC Foundation: Dir., Rev. Roger E. Swenson

AUXILIARIES

American Lutheran Church Women: Pres., Mrs. Elaine Donaldson; Exec. Dir., Ms. Julie Stine

Luther League: Pres., Dana A. Wheeler; Exec. Dir., Rev. Richard J. Beckmen

PERIODICAL

(Published at 426 S. 5th St., Minneapolis, MN 55415)

The Lutheran Standard (bi-m), Rev. Lowell G. Almen, Ed.

American Rescue Workers

A movement formed in 1896 as an evangelistic home-missionary and non-sectarian church, military in form of organization.

ANGLICAN ORTHODOX CHURCH

Churches: 15 Inclusive Membership: 2,140 Sunday or Sabbath Schools; 18 Total Enrollment: 2,894 Ordained Clergy: 43

GENERAL ORGANIZATION

Council: annual

Headquarters: 2827 Frankford Ave., Philadelphia, PA 19134

Commander-In-Chief, General Paul Martin; Vice-Pres., Lt. Gen. Donald Mank (Chief of Staff); Natl. Sec., Col. George Gossett

PERIODICAL

The Rescue Herald (q) P. O. Box 22, Williamsport, PA 17701, Lt. Col. Charles Dederick, Ed.

The Anglican Orthodox Church

This body was founded on November 16, 1963, in Statesville, North Carolina, by the Most Rev. James P. Dees who is the Presiding Bishop. The church holds to 39 Articles of Religion, the 1928 Prayerbook, the King James Version of the Bible, and basic Anglican traditions and church government.

GENERAL ORGANIZATION

General Convention: Biennial (Next meeting, 1980)

OFFICER

Presiding Bishop, The Most Rev. James Parker Dees, 323 E. Walnut St., Statesville, NC 28677. Tel. (704) 873-8365

The Antiochian Orthodox Christian Archdiocese of North America

Formed in 1975 as a result of a merger of two former Archdioceses: namely, The Antiochian Orthodox Christian Archdiocese of New York and All North America (formerly the Syrian Antiochian Orthodox Archdiocese of New York and N.A.) and the Antiochian Orthodox Archdiocese of Toledo, Ohio and Dependencies in N.A. This Archdiocese is under the jurisdiction of the Patriarch of Antioch.

GENERAL ORGANIZATION

General Convention: annual.

Headquarters: 358 Mountain Rd., Englewood, NJ 07631. Tel. (201) 871-1355

OFFICERS

Metropolitan Archbishop, Metropolitan Philip (Saleba) Archbishop Michael Shaheen, 2656 Pemberton Dr., Toledo OH 43606. Tel. (419) 535-1390

PERIODICAL

The Word (m), V. Rev. G. S. Corey, 3400 Dawson St., Pittsburgh, PA 15213

Apostolic Christian Church (Nazarean)

This body was formed in America by an immigration from various European nations, from a movement begun by Rev. S. H. Froehlich, a Swiss pastor, whose followers are still found in Switzerland and Central Europe.

OFFICERS

Apostolic Christian Church Foundation, P.O. Box 151, Tremont, IL 61568, Gen. Sec., Walter H. Meyer, P.O. Box 151, Tremont, IL 61568. Tel. (309) 925-3551

Apostolic Christian Churches of America

This body was founded in Aargan, Switzerland in 1830 by S. H. Froelick. Around 1847, Benedict Weyeneth was sent to America as the first elder (Bishop) to establish churches.

The Apostolic Christian Churches are a holiness body with a very informal organization in the U.S.

CORRESPONDENT

Elder Roy L. Sauder, 3528 N. Linden Lane, Peoria, IL 61604. Tel. (309) 685-0113

The Apostolic Faith

This body organized in 1907 in Portland, Oregon, is a trinitarian fundamental evangelistic organization. It is Presbyterian in form of government and embraces original Wesleyan teaching of holiness and the Baptism of the Holy Ghost.

Churches: 45 Inclusive Membership: 4,100 Sunday or Sabbath Schools: 44 Total Enrollment: 6,800 Ordained Clergy: 75

GENERAL ORGANIZATION

Convention: annual (July)

Headquarters: SE 52nd & Duke St., Portland, OR 97206 Tel. (503) 222-9761

OFFICER

Gen. Overseer, Rev. Loyce C. Carver; 2 N.W. Sixth Ave., Portland, OR 97209

PERIODICAL

The Light of Hope (bi-m), S.E. 52nd & Duke St., Portland, OR 97206 (503) 222-9761. Rev. Loyce C. Carver, Ed.

Apostolic Lutheran Church of America

A Finnish body, organized in 1872, under the name of Solomon Korteniemi Lutheran Society. In 1929 the body was incorporated as the Finnish Apostolic Lutheran Church of America. In 1962 the name was changed as above.

GENERAL ORGANIZATION

Meets annually in June

OFFICERS

Pres., Rev. George Wilson, New York Mills, MN 56567
Sec., James Johnson, R. 2, Box 99, L'Anse, MI 49946

Treas., Rev. Richard Barney, Chassell, MI 49916
Statistician, Edwin Reini, Rt. 1, Box 415, Rindge, NH 03461

PERIODICAL

Christian Monthly (m), Apostolic Lutheran Book Concern, Rt. 1, Box 150, New York Mills, MN 56567, Mr. Alvar Helmes, Ed., Rt. 2, Box 293, Rockford, MN 55373

Apostolic Overcoming Holy Church of God

A Negro body incorporated in Alabama in 1919. It is evangelistic in purpose and emphasizes sanctification, holiness, and divine healing.

OFFICERS

Bishop Jasper Roby, 514 10th Ave., W., Birmingham, AL 35204
Bishop C. R. Harris, 2612 E. 93rd St. Chicago, IL 60617
Bishop G. W. Ayers, 1717 Arlington Blvd., El Cerrito, CA 94530
Bishop L. M. Bell, 2000 Pio Nono Ave., Macon, GA 31206
Bishop R. F. Sheriff, 6126 S. Carpenter St., Chicago, IL 60621
Bishop E. D. Moore, 1540 E. 70th St., Cleveland, Oh 44103
Bishop Gabriel Crutcher, 526 E. Bethune St. Detroit, MI 48202
Bishop F. Lamar, 292 Marion St., Brooklyn, NY 11233
Sec., Mrs. Juanita R. Arrington, 909 Jasper Rd. West, Birmingham, Al 35204
Asst. Sec., R. N. Jackson, 1707 Vancouver Dr., Dayton, OH 45406

Armenian Apostolic Church of America

Widespread movement of the Armenian people over the centuries caused the development of two seats of religious jurisdiction of the Armenian Apostolic Church in the World: the See of Etchmiadzin, now in Soviet Armenia, and the See of Cilicia, in Lebanon.

In America, the Armenian Church functioned under the jurisdiction of the Etchmiadzin See from 1887 to 1933, when a division occurred within the American diocese over the condition of the church in Soviet Armenia. One group chose to remain independent until 1957, when the Holy See of Cilicia agreed to accept them under its jurisdiction.

Despite the existence of two dioceses in North America, the Armenian Church has always functioned as one church in dogma and liturgy.

GENERAL ORGANIZATION

National Representative Assembly: annual
Headquarters: 138 E. 39 St., New York, NY 10016. Tel. (212) 689-7810

OFFICERS

Prelate, Eastern Prelacy, Bishop Mesrob Ashjian, 138 E. 39th St., New York, NY 10016. Tel. (212) 689-7810
Prelate, Western Prelacy, Very Rev. Yeprem Tabakian, 4401 Russell Ave., Los Angeles, CA 90026
Chpsn., Karnig Pilgian

Armenian Church of America, Diocese of the (Including Diocese of California)

The Armenian Apostolic Church was founded at the foot of the biblical mountain of Ararat in the ancient land of Armenia. Saints Thaddeus and Bartholomew preached Christianity in this ancient land. In 301 the historic Mother Church of Etchmiadzin was built by Saint Gregory the Illuminator, the first Catholicos of All Armenians. This cathedral still stands and serves as the center of the Armenian Church. A branch of this Church was established in North America in 1889 by the then Catholicos of All Armenians, Khrimian Hairig. Armenian immigrants built the first Armenian church in the new world in Worcester, Massachusetts, under the jurisdiction of Holy Etchmiadzin.

In 1927, as a result of the growth of the communities in California, the churches and the parishes there were formed into a separate Western Diocese under the jurisdiction of Holy Etchmiadzin, Armenia. In 1933 a few parishes seceded from the Armenian Church Diocese of America and in 1958 were formed into an illicit diocese, keeping, however, its oneness in dogma and liturgy.

The Armenian Apostolic Church, under the jurisdiction of Holy Etchmiadzin, also includes the Armenian Patriarchate of Jerusalem and the Armenian Patriarchate of Constantinople.

Churches: 57 Inclusive Membership: 326,500 Sunday or Sabbath Schools: 57 Total Enrollment: 7,000 Ordained Clergy: 60

GENERAL ORGANIZATION

Eastern Diocese of the Armenian Church of North America (excluding California)
Diocesan Assembly: Annual
Diocesan offices: St. Vartan Cathedral, 630 Second Ave., New York, NY 10016. Tel. (212) 686-0710

OFFICERS

Primate, His Eminence the Most Rev. Archbishop Torkom Manoogian, 630 Second Ave., New York, NY 10016
Vicar Gen., V. Rev. Fr. Houssig Bagdasian, 202 W. Mount Pleasant, Livingston, NJ 07039
Chpsn., Diocesan Council, The Hon, John Najarian, 986 Hartford Ave., Johnston, RI 02919
Sec., Diocesan Council V. Rev. Arshen Aivazian, 8500 Verree Road, Philadelphia, PA 19111
Canon Sacrist, St. Vartan Cathedral, Very Rev. Khajag Barsamian, 630 Second Ave., New York, NY 10016

Western Diocese
Diocesan Assembly: Annual
Diocesan offices: 1201 N. Vine St., Hollywood, CA 90038. Tel. (213) 466-5265

OFFICERS

Primate, Most Rev. Archbishop Vatche Hovsepian, 1201 N. Vine St., Hollywood, CA 90038, Tel. (213) 466-5265
Chrpsn., Diocesan Council, John Bozajian, 55-35 W. 64th St., Los Angeles, CA 90056
Sec., Diocesan Council, Father Moushegh Tashjian 275 Olympia Way, San Francisco, CA 94131

PERIODICALS FOR BOTH DIOCESES

The Armenian Church (q), 630 Second Ave., New York, NY 10016
Hayastanyaitz Yegeghetzy (q), in Armenian, 630 Second Ave., New York, NY 10016
Keghart (q) in English, 630 Second Ave., New York, NY 10016

Assemblies of God

The Assemblies of God is the largest and fastest growing of the Pentecostal groups which stemmed from the revivals at the turn of this century. An evangelical missionary fellowship, it is composed of self-governing churches which constitute 55 districts and seven foreign language districts. Congregations are located in every state of the U.S. and 101 countries of the world. The founding meeting was in Hot Springs, Arkansas, April 2-12, 1914.

Churches: 9,410 Inclusive Membership: 1,293,394 Sunday or Sabbath Schools: 9,410 Total Enrollment: 1,293,394 Ordained Clergy: 14,415

GENERAL ORGANIZATION

General Council: biennial, (August)

International Headquarters: 1445 Boonville Ave., Springfield, MO 65802. Tel. (417) 862-2781

EXECUTIVE PRESBYTERY

The 13-member Executive Presbytery includes the following:

Gen. Supt: Thomas F. Zimmerman; Asst. Supt.: G. Raymond Carlson

Gen. Sec.: Joseph R. Flower

Gen. Treas.: Raymond H. Hudson

Exec. Dir., Foreign Missions: J. Philip Hogan Great Lakes: Richard W. Dortch, P.O. Box 225, Carlinville, IL 62626; Gulf: James E. Hamill, P.O. Box 11267, Memphis, TN 38111; North Central: Roy Wead, Trinity Bible College, Ellendale, ND 58436; Northeast: R. D. E. Smith, Colvin Sta., P.O. Box 1, Syracuse, NY 13205; Northwest: N. D. Davidson, P.O. Box 9038, Salem, OR 97305; South Central: Paul Lowenberg, 1009 S. Broadway, Wichita, KS 67211; Southeast: J. Foy Johnson, P. O. Drawer C, Lakeland, FL 33802; Southwest: Dwight H. McLaughlin, 2500 Kent Dr., Bakersfield, CA 93306

INTERNATIONAL HEADQUARTERS

All departmental offices are at Assemblies of God International Headquarters, 1445 Boonville Ave., Springfield, MO 65802

General Superintendent's Office Administration: Gen. Supt., Thomas F. Zimmerman

Spiritual Life-Evangelism: Coord., C. W. Denton, MAPS Coord., Lamar Headley; MAPS Rep., Evan Paul; Natl. Evangelists Rep., Robert M. Abbott, Conference and Convention Coord., John V. Ohlin

Personnel: Mgr., Ray F. Roepke

General Services: Administrator, Jimmy Dunn

Research: Sec., Verna Flower

General Secretary's Office Administration: Gen. Sec., Joseph R. Flower; Secretariat Supervisor, Linda Reece

Division of the Treasury: Gen. Treasurer, Raymond H. Hudson

Stewardship Dept., Deferred Gifts and Trusts Dept.: Sec., Mel DeVries; Deferred Giving and Trusts Regional Consultants, Glenn Renick, Jr., Ray Loven, Paul Spence, Jesse Hannah

Finance Dept.: Administrator of Accounting Services, J. Lester Willemetz

Dept. of Benevolences: Sec., Stanley V. Michael; Representative and Promotions Coord., Edwin Eliason

Division of Christian Education, Natl. Dir., Hardy W. Steinberg

Church School Literature Dept.: Ed., Charles W. Ford; Assoc. Ed., Gary Leggett; Adult Ed., Kenneth D. Barney; Youth Ed. ———, Elementary Ed., John Maempa; Pre-school Ed., Edith Denton; Special Assignments Ed., James Erdman

Department of Education: Sec., Thomas M. Loven; Dean of Extension Edu., Russell Wisehart

Division of Church Ministries: Natl. Dir., Silas Gaither

Men's Dept.: Sec., Paul McGarvey; Action Crusades Coord., Wildon Colbaugh; Light-for-the-Lost Sec., Dwain Jones; Royal Rangers Nat'l. Cdr., Johnnie Barnes; Promotional and Training Coord., Paul E. Stanek, Jr.

Music Dept.: Sec., L. B. Larsen; Music Productions Ed., David Scott; Promotions Ed., Connie Sowell

Sunday School Department: Sec., Ronald Held; Rep. & Adm. Spec., David Torgerson; Adult and Family Life Spec., Larry Summers; Youth Spec., Ronald McManus; Elementary Spec., Ronald W. Clark; Preschool Spec., and Boys and Girls Missionary Crusades Coord., Sandra Askew; Research & Field Services Coord., George Edgerly; Growth & Outreach Consultant, Mike Hamilton; Publications Ed., Sylvia Lee; Media and Production Coord., Dale Shumaker

Women's Ministries Dept.: Sec., Elva Hoover; Publications Coord., Charlotte Schumitsch; Auxiliaries Coord., Jenell Ogg; WM Representative, Linda Upton; Trng. Coord., Joanne Ohlin

Youth Dept.: Sec., H. H. DeMent; Campus Ministries Rep., David Gable; College Ministries Training Coord., Dennis Gaylor; AIM Rep., Jim L. McCorkle; Promotions Coord., Carol Ball; Supervisor of Publications, Carol Ball; Speed-the-Light Rep., Brenton Osgood; The Youth Leader Ed., Glen Ellard; Special Assignment Ed., Roberta Bonnicci; Bible Quiz & Teen Talent Coord., Terry Carter

Division of Communications: Natl. Dir., Leland Shultz

Advance Magazine: Ed., Gwen Jones

Audio-Visual Services; Rep., Melvin Snyder

Office of Information: Sec., Juleen Turnage; Coord. of District/Church Relations, Mel Surface

Radio and Television Dept.; Sec.; Dan Betzer; Publ. Dir., Ronald Rowden; Revivaltime Choir Dir., Cyril McLellan; Revivaltime Prog. Dir., Don Upton; Revivaltime Speaker, Dan Betzer; Radio Field Rep., Jewell E. Tucker

Pentecostal Evangel Magazine: Ed., Robert C. Cunningham; Man. Ed., Richard G. Champion; News Ed., Ann Floyd

Division of Foreign Missions: Exec. Dir., J. Philip Hogan; Adm. Asst., Joseph Kilpatrick

Foreign Field Dirs.: Africa, Morris Williams; Eurasia, Charles E. Greenaway; Far East, Wesley R. Hurst; Latin America & West Indies, Loren Triplett; Fin. Sec./Systems Analyst, Dewey Hatley; Pub. Ed., Joyce Booze; Sec. of Missionary Personnel, Ronald Iwasko; Sec. of Missions Support, G. Edward Nelson, Jr.; Vida Publishers Mgr., David T. Scott; Missionary Service Coord., Juanita Evans; Deputation Sec., Norman Correll

Division of Home Missions: Natl. Dir., T. E. Gannon; Office Mgr., Frank Smith; Promotions Ed., Ruth Lyon

Special Ministries Dept.: Spec. Min. Coord., Paul R. Markstrom; Teen Challenge Rep., Frank M. Reynolds; Deaf and Blind Min. Rep., James E. Banks; Spcl. Reps., American Indian, John McPherson; Gypsy, Patrick McLane; Hawaii, Earl E. Blythe

New Church Evangelism Sec. Clarence E. Lambert, Chaplaincy Dept.: Chpsn., Comm. on Chaplains, T. E. Gannon; Chaplains Dept. Sec. Col. Earl E. Waugh; Institutional and Industrial Chaplaincy Rep., Paul R. Markstrom

Division of Publication (Gospel Publishing House): Natl. Dir., William Eastlake

PERIODICALS

All Assemblies of God periodicals are produced by the Gospel Publishing House, 1445 Boonville Ave., Springfield, MO 65802
Advance, (m), Gwen Jones, Ed.
Assemblies of God Home Missions (bi-m), Ruth Lyon, Ed.
At Ease (bi-m), T. E. Cannon, Ed.
CAM (Campus Ambassador Magazine), (bi-m), Dennis Gaylor, Ed.
Caring, (8/yr.) Ed Eliason, Ed.
Children's Church (q), James Erdman, Ed.
God's Word for Today, (q), Kenneth Barney, Ed.
High Adventure, (q), Johnnie Barnes, Ed.
Light & Heavy (q), Carol Ball, Ed.
Missionettes Memos, (q), Jenell Ogg, Ed.
Paraclete, (q), Hardy W. Steinberg, Ed.
Pentecostal Evangel, (w), Robert C. Cunningham, Ed.
Sunday School Counselor, (m), ———
Woman's Touch (bi-m) Elva Hoover, Ed.
The Youth Leader (m), Glen Ellard, Ed.

Associate Reformed Presbyterian Church (General Synod)

The remaining Synod (changed in 1935 to General Synod) of the former Associate Reformed Church which originated through a union of the American elements of the Associate Church and the Reformed Church of Scotland in 1782.

Churches: 158 Inclusive Membership: 32,139 Sunday or Sabbath Schools: 147 Total Enrollment: 15,566 Ordained Clergy: 170

GENERAL ORGANIZATION

General Synod: Annual, June.

OFFICERS

Moderator, Rev. Clyde T. McCants, P.O. Box 395, Due West, SC 29639
Principal Clk., Rev. C. Ronald Beard, 12005 S. Beltine, Columbia, SC 29205

AGENCIES AND INSTITUTIONS

Associate Reformed Presbyterian Center, One Cleveland St., Greenville, SC 29601.Tel. 803-232-8298. Dir., Mr. Ed. Hogan. (Headquarters for the following):
Associate Reformed Presbyterian Foundation, Inc.
Associate Reformed Presbyterian Retirement Plan
Office of Christian Education, Dir., Rev. Jerry R. Wolff
Office of Church Extension, Rev. W. C. Lauderdale
Office of Synod's Treasurer, Treas., Mr. W. M. Kennedy
Office of Secretary of Foreign Missions, Sec., Mr. John E. Mariner

PERIODICAL

The Associate Reformed Presbyterian, Rev. Zeb C. William, Ed.

Bahá'í Faith

Bahá'ís are followers of Bahá'u'lláh (1817-1892), whose religion upholds the basic principles of the oneness of mankind, progressive revelation, and the unity of religions.

The Bahá'í administrative order consists of local communities, each with local assemblies, elective national assemblies, and a spiritual and administrative world center at Haifa, Israel. There are 130 National Assemblies.

Within continental United States there are more than 1,400 Local Spiritual Assemblies and members in over 7,000 cities and towns.

GENERAL ORGANIZATION

National Spiritual Assembly, Headquarters: 536 Sheridan Rd., Wilmette, IL 60091. Tel. (312) 256-4400

OFFICERS

Chpsn., Judge James Nelson; Sec., Glenford Mitchell, 112 Linden Ave., Wilmette, IL 60091

Baptist General Conference

This body has operated as a Conference since 1879; its first church was organized in 1852: It has a ministry through 752 churches and six boards of operation.

Churches: 772 Inclusive Membership: 131,000 Sunday or Sabbath Schools: 772 Total Enrollment: 118,310 Ordained clergy: 1,002

GENERAL ORGANIZATION

General Conference: annual (June)
Headquarters: 1233 Central St., Evanston, IL 60201. Tel. (312) 328-8500

OFFICERS

Gen. Sec., Dr. Warren R. Magnuson, 1233 Central St., Evanston, IL 60201

OTHER ORGANIZATIONS

Board of Trustees: Exec. Sec., Dr. Warren R. Magnuson
Board of Home Missions: Sec., Rev. Clifford E. Anderson
Board of World Missions: Sec., Dr. Virgil A. Olson
Board of Communication: Sec., Mr. Jerry R. Turner
Board of Christian Education: Sec., Dr. L. Ted Johnson,
Board of Regents: Sec., Dr. Carl H. Lindquist, 3900 Bethel Dr., St. Paul, MN 55112

PERIODICAL

The Standard (m), 1233 Central St., Evanston, IL 60201, Dr. Donald Anderson, Ed.

Baptist Missionary Association of America

A group of regular Baptist churches organized in associational capacity in May, 1950, in Little Rock, Ark. as North American Baptist Association. Name changed in 1969 to Baptist Missionary Association of America. There are several state and numerous local associations of cooperating churches. In theology these churches are evangelical, missionary, fundamental, and in the main premillennial.

Churches: 1,487 Inclusive Membership: 219,697 Sunday or Sabbath Schools: 1,487 Total Enrollment: 96,785 Ordained Clergy: 3,125

GENERAL ORGANIZATION

The Association meets annually (in April). Next meeting: Little Rock, AR, April 21-23, 1980

PRESIDING OFFICERS

Pres., Rev. Jack R. Courtney, 6901 S. Shartel, Oklahoma City, OK 73139

Vice-Pres.'s, Rev. Gordon Renshaw, 402 S. Hervey, Hope, AR 71801, Rev. James V. Schoenrock, 3827 62nd Dr., Lubbock, TX 79413

Rec. Secs.: Rev. Ralph Cottrell, P.O. Box 2866 Texarkana, AR 75501; Rev. O. D. Christian P. O. Box 923, Fairfield, TX 75840 and G. H. Gordon, P.O. Box 6591, Jackson, MS 39212

DEPARTMENTS

Missions: Gen. Sec., Rev. Craig Branham, 721 Main St., Little Rock, AR 72201

Publications: Mgr. T. O. Tollett, 712 Main St., Little Rock, AR 72201; Ed.-in-Chief, Rev. Larry Silvey 1319 Magnolia, Texarkana, TX 75501

Christian Education: Baptist Missionary Association Theological Seminary, Seminary Heights, Jacksonville, TX 75766, Dr. John W. Duggar, Pres., Philip R. Bryan, Dean.

Baptist News Service: Dir., Dr. Leon Gaylor, P. O. Box 97, Jacksonville, TX 75766; Asst., James C. Blaylock, P. O. Box 97, Jacksonville, TX 75766

Radio/Television: Rev. Paul Bearfield, Dir., P. O. Box 6, Conway, AR 72032

Armed Forces Chaplaincy: Exec. Dir., William Charles Pruitt Jr., P.O. Box 912, Jacksonville, TX 75766

National Association of Baptist Students; John Steelman, BH, College Station, TX 77840

OTHER ORGANIZATIONS

Baptist Missionary Association Brotherhood: Pres., Andy Schalchlin, P.O. Box 59, CBC Station, Conway, AR 72032

National Women's Missionary Auxiliary: Pres., Mrs. Bert Jones, 2911 Old Mobile Hwy., Pascagoula, MS 39567

Baptist Missionary Association of America Assembly and Encampment: Mgr. of Daniel Springs Encampment, Rev. Eugene Gauntt, P. O. Box 398, Gary, TX 75643

PERIODICALS

The Advancer (m), 712 Main St., Little Rock, AR 72201, Larry Slivey, Ed.

The Gleaner (m), 721 Main St., Little Rock; AR 72201, Craig Branham, Ed.

Baptist Progress (w), P.O. Box 4205, Dallas, TX 75208, Danny Pope, Ed.

Baptist Trumpet (w), P.O. Box 9502, Little Rock, AR 72209, David Tidwell, Ed.

Mississippi Baptist (s-m), P.O. Box 639, Gautier, MS 39533. Rev. D. J. Brown, Ed.

Missouri Missionary Baptist (s-m), P.O. Box 571, Arnold, MO 63010 Rev. Harry Darst, Ed.

Louisiana Baptist Builder (m), P. O. Box 1126, Denham Springs, LA 70726. Rev. Leroy Mayfield, Ed.

Oklahoma Baptist (m), P. O. Box 727, Ada, OK 74820, Buster Hayes, Ed.

Baptist Herald (m), 718 Euclid Ave., Galena, KS 66739. Rev. Gerald Kellar, Ed.

Alabama Baptist Banner (m) 2564 Woodruff St., Mobile, AL 36607. Rev. J. R. Beasley, Ed.

Golden State Baptist (m), 4040 Cherry, Visalia, CA 93277, Wayne Holland, Ed.

The Advocate, (m) 2793 Lydia St., Jacksonville, FL 32205, Curtis E. Ganey, Ed.

Illinois and Indiana Missionary Baptist (m), 1401 14th St., Silvis, IL 61282. Rev. Leo P. Wilson, Ed.

Midwest Missionary Baptist (m), 2002 Romona Ave., Portage, MI 49081 J.E. Hoffman, Ed.

Beachy Amish Mennonite Churches

This group originates mostly from the Old Order Amish Mennonite Church.

Two congregations had been formed as early as 1927, but the others have all been organized since 1938.

Worship is held in meeting houses. Nearly all have Sunday schools, most congregations have prayer meetings, and many have Christian day schools. They sponsor evangelical missions at home and abroad; a monthly magazine, *Calvary Messenger*, as an evangelical and doctrinal witness; and Calvary Bible School, twelve weeks each winter, for an in-depth study of the Word of God to better equip their youth for Christian service.

Churches: 75 Inclusive Membership: 4,762 Sunday or Sabbath Schools: N. R. Total Enrollment: N. R. Ordained Clergy: 200

INFORMATION

Ervin N. Hershberger, R. D. 1, Meyersdale, PA 15552. Tel. (814) 662-6227

Berean Fundamental Church

Founded, 1934, in Denver, Colorado, this body emphasizes conservative Protestant doctrines.

GENERAL ORGANIZATION

Headquarters: North Platte, NB 69101. Tel. (308) 582-4516

Church Council meets annually.

OFFICERS

Pres., Rev. Carl M. Goltz, P.O. Box 863, Scottsbluff, NB 69361

Vice-Pres., Rev. Glenn H. Adams, P.O. Box 806, Olathe, KS 66061

Sec.-Treas., Rev. Earnest H. Skoog, P.O. Box 628, North Platte, NB 69101

PERIODICAL

Berean Digest (m), Box 549, No. Platte, NB 69101, Rev. Ivan E. Olsen, Ed.

†Bethel Ministerial Association, Inc.

Originally the Evangelistic Ministerial Alliance, founded in Evansville, Indiana, May 1934, later became Bethel Baptist Assembly, then incorporated under the laws of the State of Indiana, March 16, 1960.

GENERAL ORGANIZATION

General Conference: quarterly.

Headquarters: Box 5353. Evansville, IN 47715. Tel. (812) 422-0431

OFFICERS

Chpsn., W. Bruce Badger, 511 W. Cedar, LeRoy, IL 61752

Vice-Chpsn., Donald C. Etnier, Box 546, Decatur, IL 62522

Sec.-Treas., Norman Etnier, 1110 E. Curtis, Decatur, IL 62526

The Bible Church of Christ, Inc.

The Bible Church of Christ was founded on March 1, 1961 by Bishop Roy Bryant, Sr. Since that time, the Church has grown to include congregations in the U.S. and

Africa. The church is trinitarian and accepts the Bible as the divinely inspired Word of God. Its doctrine includes miracles of healing and the baptism of the Holy Ghost.

Churches: 5 Inclusive Membership: 2,300 Sunday or Sabbath Schools: 5 Total Enrollment: 719 Ordained Clergy: 17

GENERAL ORGANIZATION

General Meeting: annual (March)
Headquarters: 1358 Morris Ave., Bronx, NY 10456. Tel. (212) 588-2284

OFFICERS

Pres., Bishop Roy Bryant, Sr., 3033 Gunther Ave., Bronx, NY 10469. Tel. (212) 379-8080
Vice-Pres., Elder Roy Bryant, Jr., 34 Tuxedo Rd., Montclair, NJ 07042. Tel. (201) 746-0063
Sec., Sissieretta Bryant
Treas, Elder Artie Burney

EXECUTIVE TRUSTEE BOARD

Chpsn., Leon T. Mims, 1358 Morris Ave.,Bronx, NY 10456. Tel. (212) 588-2284
Vice-Chpsn., Peggy Rawls, 100 W. 2nd St., Mount Vernon, NY 10550. Tel. (914) 664-4602

OTHER ORGANIZATIONS

Foreign Missions: Pres., Elder Anita Robinson
Home Missions: Pres., Rev. Betty Gilliard; Co-Pres., Lucille Crawley
Sunday Schools: Gen. Supt., Evangelist Alice Jones
Public Relations: Dir., Elder Leon Harris
Youth: Pres., Lynette Harris, Vice-Pres., Carlos Foster
Minister of Music: Leon T. Mims
Evangelism: Natl. Dir: Evangelist Elizabeth Price, 1358 Morris Ave., Bronx, NY 10456. (Delaware Area): Rev. Diane Cooper, Diamond Acre, Dagsboro, DE 19939. (North Carolina Area): Elder Everett Thomas, Rt. 4 Box 102, Snowhill, NC 28580. (Monticello Area): Deacon Jesse Alston, 104 Waverly Ave., Monticello, NY 12701
Bible School: Pres., Dr. Roy Bryant, 1358 Morris Ave., Bronx, NY 10456. Tel. (212) 588-2284.

PERIODICAL

The Voice (q), 1358 Morris Ave., Bronx, NY 10456. Tel. (212) 588-2284. Montrose Bushrod, Ed.

Bible Protestant Church

The Bible Protestant Church is the continuing Eastern Conference of the Methodist Protestant Church. Name changed to Bible Protestant Church at 30th Annual Session held at Westville, N. J., September 26-30, 1940. Original date of incorporation and granting of charter, September 1914; present body still operating under same certificate of incorporation with corporate name changed.

Churches: 36 Inclusive membership: 2,077 Sunday or Sabbath Schools: 36 Total Enrollment: 3,505 Ordained Clergy: 58

GENERAL ORGANIZATION

Headquarters: R.D. 1 Box 12, Port Jervis, NY 12771

OFFICERS

Pres., Rev. Joseph E. Zearfaus, R.D. 1 Box 415, Monroeville, NJ 08343
Vice-Pres., Rev Ronald Shaffer, 106 Wabash Ave., Linwood, NJ 08221
Exec. Sec., Rev. Marshall Weatherby, R.D. Box 12, Port Jervis, 12771
Sec., Rev. A. Glenn Doughty, 134 Delsea Dr., Westville, NJ 08093
Asst. Sec., Rev. J. Jeffery Lyon, 528 Austin Ave., Barrington, NJ 08007
Treas. & Conference Hist., Rev. F. Leon Taggart, RD#1, Box 4, Port Jervis, NY 12771

Bible Way Church of Our Lord Jesus Christ World Wide, Inc.

This body was organized in 1957 in the Pentecostal tradition for the purpose of accelerating evangelistic and foreign missionary commitment and to effect a greater degree of collective leadership than was found in the body in which they had previously participated.

The doctrine is the same as that of the Church of Our Lord Jesus Christ of the Apostolic Faith, Inc. of which some of the churches and clergy were formerly members.

GENERAL ORGANIZATION

Headquarters: 1100 New Jersey Ave., N.W., Washington, DC 20001

OFFICERS

Presiding Bishop, Smallwood E. Williams, 4720 16th St., N.W., Washington, DC 20011
Gen. Sec., Bishop Christal T. Hairston, 16 Fells St., Richmond, VA 23222

PERIODICALS

The Bible Way News Voice (bi-m), Washington, DC

Brethren Church (Ashland, Ohio)

It was organized by progressive-minded German Baptist Brethren in 1882. They reaffirmed the teaching of the original founder of the Brethren movement, Alexander Mack, and returned to congregational government.

Churches: 122 Inclusive Membership: 15,082 Sunday or Sabbath Schools: 122 Total Enrollment: 8,234 Ordained Clergy: 160

GENERAL ORGANIZATION

General Conference: annual (August)
Headquarters: 524 College Ave., Ashland, OH 44805. Tel. (419) 289-3698
Exec. Sec. of the Central Council: Smith F. Rose, 641 Sandusky St., Ashland, OH 44805

OFFICERS

Mod., William Kerner, 8840 St. Joe Rd., Ft. Wayne, IN 46815
Mod. Elect., Brian Moore, 23292 Ardmore Trail, South Bend, IN 46628
Sec., Fred Horn, Sr., 23087 Ardmore Trail, South Bend, IN 46628
Treas., George Snyder, 600 Country Club, La., Ashland, OH 44805
Statistician, Larry Baker, 1127 Byron Dr., South Bend, IN 46614

BOARDS

The Brethren Publishing Company, 524 College Ave., Ashland, OH 44805. Exec. Dir., John Rowsey
The Missionary Board, 530 College Ave., Ashland, OH 44805

BRETHREN IN CHRIST CHURCH

Gen. Sec., M. Virgil Ingraham
The Benevolent Board, 524 College Ave., Ashland, OH 44805
The Board of Christian Education, Dir., Charles Beekley, 524 College Ave., Ashland, OH 44805

Brethren in Christ Church

The Brethren in Christ Church was founded in Lancaster County, Pa. in about the year 1778 and was an outgrowth of the religious awakening which occurred in that area during the latter part of the eighteenth century. This group became known as "River Brethren" because of their original location near the Susquehanna River. The name "Brethren in Christ" was officially adopted in 1863. In theology they are evangelical, Arminian, holiness, and premillennial.

GENERAL ORGANIZATION

General Conference: biennial

OFFICERS

Mod., Bishop Alvin J. Book, 10 Nittany Dr., Mechanicsburg, PA 17055
Gen. Conf. Sec., Dr. Arthur M. Climenhaga, 1093 T.R. 1704, Rt. 4, Ashland, OH 44805

OTHER ORGANIZATIONS

Board of Administration: Chpsn., Bishop Alvin J. Book, 10 Nittany Dr., Mechanicsburg, PA 17055; Sec., Dr. Arthur M. Climenhaga, 1093 T.R. 1704, Rt. 4, Ashland, OH 44805; Treas, Ray M. Musser, 911 W. Arrow Hwy., Upland, CA 91786
Board of Christian Education: Chpsn., W. Lloyd Hogg, R. 3, Stoufville, Ontario, Canada LOH 1LO; Sec., Warren L. Hoffman, Navaho BIC Mission, Star Rt. 4, Box 6000, Bloomfield NM 87413; Treas., J. Ralph Wenger, 8847 Holly St., Alta Loma, CA 91701
E. V. Publishing House: Evangel Press, Erwin W. Thomas, Nappanee, IN 46550
Ministerial Credentials Bd.: Chpsn., Dr. Owen Alderfer, 26 Leawood Ave., Ashland, OH 44805; Sec., Marion J. Heisey, Bloomfield, NM 87413
Schools and Colleges: Chpsn., John E. Zercher, R.R. 1, Nappanee, IN 46550; Sec., Wayne H. Schiedel, R. 2, Petersburg, Ontario, Canada
Board for Missions: Chpsn., Erwin Thomas, 301 N. Elm St., Nappanee, IN 46550; Sec., Roger Sider, 1432 Clover St., Rochester, NY 14610; Treas., Charles F. Frey, Rt. 2, Conestoga, PA 17516; Exec. Sec., J. Wilmer Heisey, Missions Office, 48½ S. Market St., Box 149, Elizabethtown, PA 17022
Board of Benevolence: Chpsn., Dale Allison, Box 68, Refton, PA 17568; Sec., Millard Herr, 10304 E. 19th St., Cucamonga, CA 91730; Treas., Musser Martin, Box 242, Mt. Gretna, PA 17064

PERIODICAL

Evangelical Vistor (bi-w), Nappanee, IN 46550, John E. Zercher, Ed.

Buddhist Churches of America

Founded in 1899, organized in 1914 as the Buddhist Mission of North America, this body was incorporated in 1942 under the present name and represents the Jodo Shinshu Sect of Buddhism in this country. It is a school of Buddhism which believes in salvation by faith in the Wisdom and Compassion of Amida Buddha.

GENERAL ORGANIZATION

Conference: annual (February)
Headquarters: 1710 Octavia St., San Francisco, CA 94109

OFFICERS

Bishop, Rt. Rev. Kenryu Tsuji, Exec. Sec., Rev. K. Fujinaga
Director, Buddhist Education: Rev. Toshio Murakami
Director, Sunday School Dept.: ———

OTHER ORGANIZATIONS

Western Adult Buddhist League: Pres., Yosh Kojimoto, National Young Buddhist Association: Pres., Marshall Kido
National Buddhist Women's Association: Pres., Toshie Yamaguchi
Federation of Western Buddhist Sunday School Teachers, Pres., Katy Taoka

Bulgarian Eastern Orthodox Church (Diocese of N. & S. America and Australia)

Bulgarian immigration to the United States and Canada started around the turn of the century, and the first Bulgarian Orthodox church was built in 1907 in Madison, Illinois. In 1938, the Holy Synod of the Bulgarian E. O. Church established the diocese here as an Episcopate, and Bishop Andrey was sent as diocesan Bishop. In 1947, the diocese was officially incorporated in New York State and Bishop Andrey became the first elected Metropolitan.

By a decision of the Holy Synod in 1972, the Bulgarian Eastern Orthodox Church was divided into the New York and Akron Dioceses.

OFFICERS

New York Diocese, Bishop Joseph, Metropolitan, 312 W. 101 St., New York, NY 10025. Tel. (212) 749-5992
Akron Diocese, Bishop Dometian, Administrator, 1953 Stockbridge Rd., Akron, OH 44313

Christ Catholic Church

The church is a catholic communion established in 1968 to minister to the growing number of people seeking an experiential relationship with God, and who desire to make a total commitment of their lives to him. The church is catholic in faith and tradition and its orders are recognized as valid by catholics of every tradition.

Churches: 7 Inclusive Membership: 1,365 Sunday or Sabbath Schools: 3 Total Enrollment: 98 Ordained Clergy: 12

GENERAL ORGANIZATION

Synod: annual. Next meeting, July, 1980

OFFICERS

Presiding Bishop, The Most Reverend Karl Pruter, 1744 W. Devon Ave., Chicago, IL 60660. Tel. (312) 465-7578

†Christadelphians

A body organized in 1844, accepting the Bible as the divinely inspired word of God; believing in the personal return of Christ to earth to establish the Kingdom of God; the resurrection from the dead; opposed to war; spiritual rebirth requiring belief and immersion in the name of Jesus; a godly walk in this life.

NO GENERAL ORGANIZATION

Co-Minister, H. P. Zilmer, 1002 Webster Lane, Des Plaines, IL 60016

The Christian and Missionary Alliance

An evangelical, evangelistic, and missionary movement, organized by Rev. A. B. Simpson, in New York, in 1887. It stresses "the deeper Christian life and consecration to the Lord's service."

Churches: 1,290 Inclusive Membership: 158,218 Sunday or Sabbath Schools: 1,188 Total Enrollment: 155,631 Ordained Clergy 1,529

GENERAL ORGANIZATION

Council: annual (May)
Headquarters: 350 N. Highland Ave., Nyack; NY 10960. Tel. (914) 353-0750

OFFICERS

Pres., Louis L. King
Vice-Pres., Paul Alford
Sec., Robert W. Battles
Vice-Pres. of Fin./Treas., Merlin C. Feather
Vice-Pres. of North American Ministries, Robert T. Henry
Vice-Pres. of Overseas Ministries, David L. Rambo
Vice-Pres. of Gen. Services, Gordon M. Cathey

PERIODICAL

Alliance Witness, 350 N. Highland Ave., Nyack, NY 10960 H. R. Cowles, Ed.

Christian Catholic Church (Evangelical-Protestant)

Church founded in 1896 in Chicago, IL. In 1901 the church opened the city of Zion, Illinois as its home and headquarters. Theologically, the church is rooted in evangelical orthodoxy. The Scriptures are accepted as the rule of faith and practice. Other doctrines call for belief in the necessity of repentance for sin and personal trust in Christ for salvation, baptism by triune immersion, and tithing as a practical method of Christian stewardship. The church teaches the Second Coming of Christ.

Churches: 6 Inclusive Membership 2,500 Sunday or Sabbath School: 6 Total Enrollment: 1,325 Ordained Clergy: 19

GENERAL ORGANIZATION

Convocation: annual (end of September) Headquarters: Dowie Memorial Dr., Zion, IL 60099. Tel. (312) 746-1411

OFFICER

Gen. Overseer, Roger W. Ottersen

PERIODICAL

Leaves of Healing (m), Dowie Memorial Dr., Zion, IL 60099, Roger W. Ottersen, Ed.-in-Chief

Christian Church (Disciples of Christ)

Started on the American frontier at the beginning of the 19th century as a movement to unify Christians, this body drew its major inspiration from Thomas and Alexander Campbell in western Pennsylvania and Barton W. Stone in Kentucky. Developing separately for a quarter of a century, the "Disciples," under Alexander Campbell and the "Christians," led by Stone, merged in Lexington, Kentucky, in 1832.

Churches: 4,347 Inclusive Membership: 1,231,817 Sunday or Sabbath Schools: 4,347 Total Enrollment: 368,624 Ordained Clergy: 6,635

GENERAL ORGANIZATION

General Assembly, biennial
General Office: 222 S. Downey Ave., Box 1986, Indianapolis, IN 46206. Tel. (317) 353-1491

OFFICERS

Gen. Minister and Pres., Kenneth L. Teegarden
Mod., Judge James A. Noe, 8250 S.E. 61st St., Mercer Island, WA 98040
1st Vice-Mod., Samuel W. Hylton, Jr., 4950 Fountain Ave., St. Louis, MO 63113
2nd Vice-Mod., Joy L. Greer, 6904 Burton St., Little Rock, AR 72204
Exec. Sec. Emeritus, Gaines M. Cook, R 1 Box 39-D, Black Mountain, NC 28711
Gen. Minister and Pres. Emeritus, A. Dale Fiers, 236 Inlet Way, Palm Beach Shores, FL 33404
Parliamentarian, Robert E. Kirkman, 2019 Baringer Ave., Louisville, KY 40204

GENERAL OFFICE STAFF

Gen. Minister and Pres., Kenneth L. Teegarden
Deputy Gen. Minister and Pres., Howard E. Dentler
Adm. Asst., Glenda I. Berkshire
Asst. to the Gen. Minister and Pres., William K. Fox
Dir. Office of Res., Walter R. Giffin
Deputy Gen. Minister and Pres., John O. Humbert
Legal Counsel, Wade D. Rubick
Dir. Office of Communication, Robert L. Friendly

ADMINISTRATIVE UNITS

Board of Church Extension: 110 S. Downey Ave., Box 7030, Indianapolis, IN 46207. Tel. (317) 356-6333. Pres., Elect., Harold R. Watkins
Christian Board of Publication (Bethany Press): Box 179, 2640 Pine, St. Louis, MO 63166. Tel. (314) 371-6900. Pres., W. A. Welsh
Christian Church Foundation: 222 S. Downey Ave., Box 1986, Indianapolis, IN 46206 Tel. (317) 353-1491, Acting Pres., James R. Reed
Christian Church Services, Inc. 222 S. Downey Ave., Box 1986, Indianapolis, IN 46206. Tel. (317) 353-1491, Pres. Howard E. Dentler
Christmount Christian Assembly, Inc.: Route 1, P.O. Box 38-E, Black Mountain, NC 28711. Tel. (704) 669-8977. Exec. Dir., Melba B. Banks
Church Finance Council, Inc.: 222 S. Downey Ave., Box 1986 Indianapolis, IN 46206. Tel. (317) 353-1491. Pres., Jean Woolfolk
Council on Christian Unity: 222 S. Downey Ave., Box 1986, Indianapolis, IN 46206 Tel. (317) 353-1491. Pres., Paul A. Crow, Jr.
Disciples of Christ Historical Society, 1101 19th Ave. S., Nashville, TN 37212. Tel. (615) 327-1444. Pres., Roland K. Huff
Disciples Peace Fellowship: 222 S. Downey Ave., Box 1986 Indianapolis, IN 46206. Tel. (317) 353-1491 Pres., C. Edward Weisheimer
Division of Higher Education: 119 N. Jefferson Ave., St. Louis, MO 63103. Tel. (314) 371-2050. Pres., D. Duane Cummins

CHRISTIAN CHURCH (DISCIPLES OF CHRIST)

Division of Homeland Ministries: 222 S. Downey Ave., Box 1986, Indianapolis, IN 46206. Tel. (317) 353-1491. Pres., Kenneth A. Kuntz

Division of Overseas Ministries: 222 S. Downey Ave., Box 1986, Indianapolis, IN 46206. Tel. (317) 353-1491. Pres., Robert A. Thomas

European Evangelistic Society: Box 268, Aurora, IL 60507, Pres., Robert W. Shaw

National Benevolent Association: 115 N. Jefferson Ave., St. Louis, MO 63103. Tel. (314) 531-1470. Pres. William T. Gibble

National City Christian Church Corporation: Thomas Circle, Washington, DC 20005. Tel. (202) 232-0323. Pres. A. Dale Fiers

National Evangelistic Association: 222 S. Downey Ave., Box 1986, Indianapolis, IN 46206. Tel. (317) 353-1491. Pres., Mrs. Bettie C. Griffith

Pension Fund: 700 Test Bldg., 54 Monument Circle, 14th at Massachusetts Ave., NW, Indianapolis, IN 46204. Tel. (317) 634-4504. Pres., William M. Smith

The United Christian Missionary Society: 222 S. Downey Ave., Box 1986, Indianapolis, IN 46206. Tel. (317) 353-1491. Pres., Robert A. Thomas

REGIONAL UNITS OF THE CHURCH

Alabama-Northwest Florida: Christian Church (Disciples of Christ) in Alabama-Northwest Florida, 1336 Montgomery Hwy., S., Box 20037, Birmingham, AL 35216. Tel. (205) 823-5647. Carl R. Flock, Regional Minister

Arizona: Christian Church (Disciples of Christ) in Arizona., 10 E. Roanoke, Rm. 26, Phoenix 85004. Tel. (602) 265-0531. Bruce L. Jones, Regional Minister

Arkansas: The Christian Church (Disciples of Christ) in Arkansas, Regional Minister, 6100 Queensboro Dr., P.O. Box 9739, Little Rock 72219. Tel. (501) 562-6053. James W. Rainwater, Regional Exec. Minister

California North-Nevada: The Christian Church (Disciples of Christ) of Northern California-Nevada, 111-A Fairmount Ave., Oakland 94611. Tel. (415) 839-3550, Karl Irvin, Jr., Regional Minister—President.

Capital Area: Christian Church (Disciples of Christ)—Capital Area, 8901 Connecticut Ave., Chevy Chase, MD 20015. Tel. (301) 654-7794. Richard L. Taylor, Regional Minister

Central Rocky Mountain Region: Christian Church (Disciples of Christ) Central Rocky Mountain Region, 2599 S. Lincoln St., Denver CO 80210. Tel. (303) 744-6194. Walter J. Lantz, Regional Exec. Minister

Florida: Christian Church (Disciples of Christ) in Florida, 122 E. Colonial, Ste. 205, Orlando, FL 32801. Tel. (305) 843-4652 Jimmie L. Gentle, Regional Minister

Georgia: Christian Church (Disciples of Christ) in Georgia, Inc., 2370 Vineville Ave., Macon 31204. Tel. (912) 743-8649. E. Lyle Harvey, Regional Minister

Idaho-South: Christian Church of South Idaho (Disciples of Christ), 2803 N. Cole Rd., Ste. H, Boise 83704. Tel. (208) 375-7274. H. Glenn Warner, Regional Minister

Illinois-Wisconsin: Christian Church (Disciples of Christ) in Illinois and Wisconsin, 1011 N. Main St., Bloomington IL 61701. Tel. (309) 828-6293. L. E. Pitman, Regional Minister

Indiana: Christian Church (Disciples of Christ) in Indiana, 1100 W. 42nd St., Indianapolis 46208. Tel. (317) 926-6051. John R. Compton, Regional Minister

Kansas: Christian Church in Kansas, 1010 Gage, Topeka 66604. Tel. (913) 273-1381, Lloyd G. Cox, Regional Minister

Kentucky: Christian Church (Disciples of Christ) in Kentucky, 190 Market St., Box 1418 Lexington 40591. Tel. (606) 254-2732. James A. Moak, General Minister

Louisiana: Christian Church (Disciples of Christ) in Louisiana, 316 Eola Dr., Alexandria 71301. Tel. (318) 443-0304. William E. Wright, Regional Minister

Michigan: Christian Church (Disciples of Christ) Michigan Region, 2820 Covington Ct., Lansing 48912. Tel. (517) 372-3220. Earle B. Van Slyck, Regional Minister

Mid-America Region: Christian Church (Disciples of Christ) of Mid-America, Hwy. 54 S., Box 1087, Jefferson City, MO 65101. Tel. (314) 636-8149. Warren F. Chrisman, Minister-President

Mississippi: Christian Church (Disciples of Christ), in Mississippi, 1619 N. West St., Jackson 39202. Tel. (601) 352-6774. William E. McKnight, Regional Minister

Montana: Christian Church (Disciples of Christ) of Montana, 1025 Central Ave., N., Great Falls 59401. Tel. (406) 452-7404. D. Franklin Kohl, Regional Minister

Nebraska: Christian Church in Nebraska (Disciples of Christ), 1268 S. 20th St., Lincoln 68502. Tel. (402) 432-0359. Robert M. Hall, Regional Minister

North Carolina: Christian Church (Disciples of Christ), in North Carolina, 509 W. Lee St., Box 521, Wilson 27893. Tel. (919) 291-4047. Charles E. Dietze, Regional Minister

Northeastern Region: Northeastern Association of Christian Churches (Disciples of Christ), 1272 Delaware Ave., Buffalo, NY 14209. Tel. (716) 882-4793. Charles F. Lamb, Regional Minister

Northwest Region: The Northwest Regional Christian Church (Disciples of Christ), 720 14th Ave. E., Seattle, WA 98112. Tel. (206) 323-8383, Robert C. Brock, Regional Minister and Pres.

Ohio: The Christian Church in Ohio (Disciples of Christ) 17119 Madison Ave., Cleveland 44107. Tel. (216) 221-8600. Herald B. Monroe, Regional Pastor and Pres.

Oklahoma: Christian Church (Disciples of Christ) in Oklahoma, 301 N.W. 36th St., Oklahoma City 73118. Tel. (405) 528-3577. Eugene N. Frazier, Regional Minister

Oregon: Christian Church (Disciples of Christ) in Oregon, 0245 S.W. Bancroft St., Portland 97201. Tel. (503) 226-7648, Mark K. Reid, Regional Minister

Pacific Southwest Region: Christian Church (Disciples of Christ) of the Pacific Southwest Region, 3126 Los Feliz Blvd., Los Angeles, CA 90039. Tel. (213) 665-5126. Charles A. Malotte, Regional Pastor

Pennsylvania: Christian Church (Disciples of Christ) in Pennsylvania, 727 Penn Ave., Pittsburgh 15221. Tel. (412) 731-7000. Dwight L. French, Regional Minister

South Carolina: Christian Church (Disciples of Christ) in South Carolina, 829 Savannah Hwy., Rm. 201, Box 31458, Charleston 29407. Tel. (803) 556-2971. David T. Brooks, Regional Minister

Southwest Region: Christian Church (Disciples of Christ) in the Southwest, 2909 Lubbock Ave., Fort Worth, TX 76109. Tel. (817) 926-4687. Harrell A. Rea, Exec. Minister

Tennessee: Christian Church (Disciples of Christ) in Tennessee, 3700 Richland Ave., Nashville 37205. Tel. (615) 269-3409. Allen S. Estill, Regional Minister

Upper Midwest Region: Christian Church (Disciples of Christ) in the Upper Midwest, 3300 University Ave., Box 1024, Des Moines, IA 50311. Tel. (515) 255-3168. Howard B. Goodrich; Jr., Regional Minister

Utah: Christian Church of Utah (Disciples of Christ), 2308 N. Cole Rd., Ste. H, Boise, ID 83704. Tel. (208) 375-7274. H. Glenn Warner, Regional Minister

Virginia: The Christian Church (Disciples of Christ) in Virginia, 2200 Monument Ave., Richmond 23220. Tel. (804) 353-5561. Lewis A. McPherren, Regional Minister

West Virginia: Christian Church (Disciples of Christ) in West Virginia. Rt. 5, Box 167, Parkersburg 26101. Tel. (304) 428-1681. Charles E. Crank, Jr., Regional Minister

Canada: All-Canada Committee of the Christian Church (Disciples of Christ), 39 Arkell Rd., RR 2, Guelph, Ontario N1H 6H8. Tel. (519) 823-5190. Robert K. Leland, Exec. Minister

PERIODICALS

The Disciple (bi-w), Box 179, St. Louis, MO 63166, James L. Merrell, Ed.

Vanguard (church planning), 222 S. Downey Ave., Box 1986, Indianapolis, IN 46206. Kenneth A. Kuntz, Ed.-in-Chief

Christian Church of North America, General Council

Incorporated 1948 in Pittsburgh, Pa.; earlier the body was known as Italian Christian Churches, Unorganized. The first General Council was conducted in 1927 in the city of Niagara Falls, New York.

Churches: 101 Inclusive Membership: 12,000 Sunday or Sabbath Schools: 101 Total Enrollment: 10,500 Ordained Clergy: 145

GENERAL ORGANIZATION

General Council: meets annually (September).
Headquarters: 1818 State St., Sharon, PA 16146

OFFICERS

Board of General Overseers:

Gen. Overseer, Rev. Carmine Saginario, P.O. Box 124, Breezewood, PA 15533

Asst. Gen. Overseers: Rev. Joseph Fiorentino, 440 Lexington St., Woburn, MA 01801; Rev. Joseph Borda, 195 E. Northampton, Wilkes Barre, PA 18702; Rev. Joseph Demola, 324 Stanley Ave., Staten Island, NY 10301; Rev. Emanuel Greco, 245 Exeter St., Brooklyn, NY 11235

Gen. Sec.-Treas., Rev. Richard A. Tedesco, P.O. Box 801, Sharon, PA 16146

Evangelism Dept.: Dir., Rev. John Del Turco, 305 Avery Ave., Syracuse, NY 13204

Foreign and Home Missions Dept.: Dir., Rev. Guy Bongiovanni, P.O. Box 801, Sharon, PA 16146

Institutions, Benevolences & Fellowships Dept.: Carmine Reigle, P.O. Box 644, Niles, OH 44446

Youth, Education & Sunday School Dept., Rev. James Demola, P.O. Box 157, Mullica Hill, NJ 08062

Publications Dept.; Rev. Frank Bongiovanni, 543-25th St., Niagara Falls, NY 14301

Faith, Order & Credential Dept., Rev. Joseph Demola, Dir, 324 Stanley Ave., Staten Island, NY 10301

PERIODICALS

Il Faro (m), P.O. Box 66, Herkimer, NY 13350. Rev. Guido Scalzi, Ed.

Vista (m) P.O. Box 136, Blairstown, NJ 07825. Rev. Charles Maves, Ed.

Christian Churches and Churches of Christ

The fellowship, whose churches were always strictly congregational in polity, has its origin in the American movement to "restore the New Testament church in doctrine, ordinances and life" initiated by Thomas and Alexander Campbell, Walter Scott and Barton W. Stone in the early years of the nineteenth century.

Churches: 5,535 Inclusive Membership: 1,054,266 Sunday or Sabbath Schools: N.R. Total Enrollment: N.R. Ordained Clergy: 7,689

NO GENERAL ORGANIZATION

CONVENTIONS

North American Christian Convention (founded 1927), 3533 Epley Rd., Cincinnati, OH 45239. NACC mailing address: Box 39456 Cincinnati, OH 45231

National Missionary Convention (founded 1947), Box 177, Kempton, IN 46049

PERIODICALS

Christian Standard (w), 8121 Hamilton Ave., Cincinnati, OH 45231, Sam E. Stone, Ed.

Restoration Herald (m), 5664 Cheviot Rd., Cincinnati, OH 45329. H. Sherwood Evans, Ed.

Directory of the Ministry (a), 1525 Cherry Rd., Springfield, IL 62704. Ralph D. McLean, Ed.

Horizons (bi-w), Box 177, Kempton, IN 46049. Richard L. Bourne, Ed.

The Christian Congregation, Inc.

Original incorporation, March 10, 1887; revised incorporation, October 29, 1898. The New Commandment, John 13:34-35, is the bond of fellowship in creative ethical activism. This denomination provides ministerial affiliation for independent clergymen.

Churches: 1,133 Inclusive Membership: 81,604 Sunday or Sabbath Schools: 1,031 Total Enrollment: 47,525 Ordained Clergy: 1,144

OFFICER

Gen. Supt., Rev. Ora Wilbert Eads, 804 W. Hemlock St., LaFollette, TN 37766

Christian Methodist Episcopal Church

In 1870 the General Conference of the M.E. Church, South, approved the request of its colored membership for the formation of their conferences into a separate ecclesiastical body, which became the Colored Methodist Episcopal Church.

At its General Conference in Memphis, Tenn., May 1954, it was overwhelmingly voted to change the name of the Colored Methodist Episcopal Church to the Christian Methodist Episcopal Church. This became the official name on January 3, 1956.

GENERAL ORGANIZATION

General Conference: quadrennial. (Next meeting in 1982)

OFFICER

Sec., Rev. N. Charles Thomas, P.O. Box 74, Memphis, TN 38101

OTHER ORGANIZATIONS

General Board of Missions: Chpsn., Bishop Joseph C. Coles, Jr., 2780 Collier Dr., NW, Atlanta, GA 30018. Gen. Sec., Rev. Lymell Carter, 4210 Belgrade, Houston, TX 77045

General Board of Christian Education: Chpsn., Bishop James L. Cummings, 5517 W. 63rd St., Los Angeles, CA 90056; Gen. Sec., Dr. W. R. Johnson, Jr., Board of Christian Education, 1474 Humber St., Memphis, TN 38101

General Board of Publication Services: Chpsn., Bishop J. Madison Exum, 654 E. Frank Ave., Memphis, TN 38101; Gen. Sec., Rev. E. Lynn Brown, P.O. Box 2018, Memphis, TN 38106

General Board of Fiscal Services: Chpsn., Bishop J. A. Johnson, Jr., 109 Holycomb Dr., Shreveport, LA 71103; Gen. Sec., Dr. O. T. Peeples, P.O. Box 1704, Memphis TN 38101

General Board of Personnel: Chpsn., Bishop C. D. Colemen, 2330 Sutter St., Dallas, TX 75216; Gen. Sec., Rev. N. Charles Thomas, P.O. Box 74, Memphis, TN 38101

General Board of Evangelism: Chpsn., Bishop C. A. Kirkendoll, 308 10th Ave., W., Birmingham, AL 35204; Gen. Sec., Rev. Anzo Montgomery, 17626 Scottsdale Blvd., Shaker Heights, OH 44120

General Board of Lay Activities: Chpsn., Bishop Nathaniel L. Linsey, 6524 16th St., N.W., Washington, DC 20012; Gen. Sec., I. Carlton Faulk, 1222 Rose St., Berkeley, CA 94702

Woman's Missionary Council: Pres., Mrs. Pauline Grant, 723 E. Upsal St., Philadelphia, PA 19119; Patron Bishop, Bishop Elisha P. Murchison, 11470 Northway, St., Louis, MO 63136

PERIODICALS

Christian Index (w), P. O. Box 665, Memphis, TN 38101, Rev. Othal H. Lakley, Ed.

Eastern Index (bi-m), 501 "N" St., N.W., Washington, DC 20001, Rev. Gene Williams, Ed.

Missionary Messenger, 730 Marechaneil St., Memphis, TN 38114. Mrs. Mattie I. Suttles, Ed.

Western Index, 971 E. 43rd St., Los Angeles, CA 90011, Rev. W. H. Graves, Ed.

BISHOPS

First District:
Bishop J. Madison Exum, 564 Frank Ave., Memphis, TN 38101. Tel. (901) 942-9336

Second District:
Bishop P. Randolph Shy, 6322 Elwynne Dr., Cincinnati, OH 45236. Tel. (513) 984-6825

Third District:
Bishop E. P. Murchison, 11470 Northway, St. Louis, MO 63136. Tel. (314) 741-5837

Fourth District:
Bishop J. A. Johnson, Jr., 109 Holcomb Dr., Shreveport, LA 71103. Tel. (318) 222-6284

Fifth District:
Bishop C. A. Kirkendoll, 308 10th Ave., W., Birmingham, AL. Tel. (205) 252-3541

Sixth District:
Bishop Joseph C. Coles, Jr., 2780 Collier Dr., Atlanta, GA 30018. Tel. (404) 752-7800

Seventh District:
Bishop Nathaniel L. Linsey, 6524 16th St., N.W., Washington, DC 20012. Tel. (202) 828-8070

Eighth District:
Bishop C. D. Coleman, 2330 Sutter St., Dallas, TX 75216. Tel. (214) 942-5781

Ninth District:
Bishop James L. Cummings, 5517 W. 63rd St., Los Angeles, CA 90056. Tel. (213) 649-1704

Christian Nation Church U.S.A.

Organized in 1895, at Marion, Ohio, as a group of "equality evangelists," who later formed the Christian Nation Church, semi-congregational in government; emphasizes evangelism. Reincorporated as Christian Nation Church U.S.A., 1961.

GENERAL ORGANIZATION

Congress: annual

OFFICERS

Gen. Overseer, Rev. Harvey Monjar, Box 142, South Lebanon, OH 45065

Asst. Overseer, Rev. A. R. Lusk, Box 3, Fanrock, WV 24834

Gen. Sec., Walter F. Clark, 345 Cedar Dr., Loveland, OH 45140

Christian Reformed Church in North America

The Christian Reformed Church represents the historic faith of Protestantism. Founded in the United States in 1857, it asserts its belief in the Bible as the inspired Word of God, and is creedally united in the Belgic Confession (1561), the Heidelberg Catechism (1563), and the Canons of Dort (1618-19). (Note: For total statistics for this body see also those listed under the Christian Reformed Church in North America in Directory 4, Religious Bodies in Canada, which follows.)

Churches: 623 Inclusive Membership: 211,302 Sunday or Sabbath Schools: N.R. Total Enrollment: N.R. Ordained Clergy: 950

GENERAL ORGANIZATION

Synod: annual (June)

OFFICERS

Stat. Clk., Rev. William P. Brink, Office Address: 2850 Kalamazoo Ave. S.E., Grand Rapids, MI 49560. Tel. (616) 241-1691

Denominational Financial Coord., Anthony Vroon, 2850 Kalamazoo Ave., SE Grand Rapids, MI 49560

Synodical Treas., Lester Ippel, 1452 Cornell S.E., Grand Rapids, MI 49506

OTHER ORGANIZATIONS

The Back to God Hour: Dir., Dr. Joel H. Nederhood, International Headquarters: 655 W. College Dr., Palos Heights, IL 60463

Board for Christain Reformed World Missions: Exec. Sec., Dr. Eugene Rubingh, 2850 Kalamazoo Ave., S.E., Grand Rapids, MI 49560

Christian Reformed Board of Home Missions: Exec. Sec., Rev. John G. Van Ryn, 2850, Kalamazoo Ave., S.E., Grand Rapids, MI 49560

Christian Reformed Board of Publications: Exec. Dir., A. James Heynen, 2850 Kalamazoo Ave., S.E., Grand Rapids, MI 49560

Christian Reformed World Relief Committee: Exec. Dir., John De Haan, 2850 Kalamazoo Ave., S.E. Grand Rapids, MI 49560

Ministers' Pension Fund, Adm., Garret C. Van de Riet, 2850 Kalamazoo Ave., S.E., Grand Rapids, MI 49560

PERIODICALS

The Banner (w), 2850 Kalamazoo Ave. S.E., Grand Rapids, MI 49560, Dr. Lester Dekoster, Ed.

De Wachter (w), 2850 Kalamazoo Ave. SE, Grand Rapids, MI 49560, Rev. W. Haverkamp, Ed.

Christian Union

Organized in 1864 in Columbus, Ohio. It stresses the oneness of the Church with Christ as its only head. The Bible is the only rule of faith and practice and good fruits the only condition of fellowship. Each local church governs itself.

GENERAL ORGANIZATION

General Council: triennial. (Next meeting, 1980)
Home Office: P.O. Box 38, Excelsior Springs, MO 64024

OFFICERS

Pres., Rev. Lawrence Rhoads, Box 31, Otway, OH 45657
Vice-Pres., Rev. Joe Redmond, Rt. 2, Box 115, Hennessey, OK 73742
Sec., Robert Uhrig, 961 Egypt Pike, Chillicothe, OH 45601
Asst. Sec., Rev. Earl W. Mitchell, 618 Henrie, Excelsior Springs, MO 64024
Treas., Rev. Hearold McElwee, 311 E. Fourth St., Indianola, IN 50125

PERIODICAL

Christian Union Witness (m), P.O. Box 38, Excelsior Springs, MO 64024, Rev. Jack Eggers, Ed.

Church of Christ

Organized April 6, 1830, at Fayette, New York, by Joseph Smith and five others; in 1831 Independence, Missouri, was designated as headquarters.

GENERAL ORGANIZATION

General Conference: annual
Headquarters: Temple Lot, Independence, MO

OFFICERS

Sec. of the Council of Twelve, Apostle William A. Sheldon, 1011 Cottage, Independence, MO 64050. Tel. (816) 833-3995
Gen. Bus. Mgr., Bishop C. LeRoy Wheaton Jr., P.O. Box 472, Independence, MO 64051
General Recorder, Tony Grzincic, 3231 Reynolds, Independence, MO 64055

PERIODICAL

Zion's Advocate, P.O. Box 472, Independence, MO 64051, Elder Kenneth J. Smith, 209 S. Crysler, Independence, MO 64050

Church of Christ, Scientist

A church founded by Mary Baker Eddy in 1879 to reinstate the healing power of primitive Christianity. Christian Science theology describes divine healing as scientifically based on underlying spiritual reality and law. The denomination is represented by The Mother Church, The First Church of Christ, Scientist, in Boston, Massachusetts, and its approximately 3,000 branches throughout the world.

GENERAL ORGANIZATION

Board of Directors, Headquarters: Christian Science Church
Center, Boston, MA 02115

OFFICERS

Bd. of Dirs., DeWitt John, Harvey W. Wood, Jean Stark Hebenstreit, Hal M. Friesen, Michael B. Thorneloe
Pres., Ada Reynolds Jandron
Treas., Marc Engeler
Clk., Robert H. Mitchell
First Reader, Bryan G. Pope
Second Reader, Virginia N. Chancey

OTHER ORGANIZATIONS

Board of Education: Teaches a class of 30 pupils once in 3 years for the purpose of providing authorized teachers of Christian Science
Board of Lectureship: Made up of 35 to 40 members, delivers free lectures worldwide
Committee on Publication: Corrects in a Christian manner impositions on the public in regard to Christian Science and injustices to Christian Scientists
Trustees Under the Will of Mary Baker Eddy: Owns and publishes Mrs. Eddy's writings. Publishing Society: Publishes or sells the authorized literature of Christian Science

PERIODICALS

The Christian Science Monitor (d) (w), Boston, MA
The Christian Science Journal (m), Boston, MA
Christian Science Sentinel (w), Boston, MA
Christian Science Quarterly (q), Boston, MA
The Herald of Christian Science (m), in French, German, Portuguese, Spanish; (q), in Danish, Dutch, Greek, Indonesian, Italian, Japanese, Norwegian, Swedish, and Braille

Church of Daniel's Band

A body Methodistic in form and evangelistic in spirit, organized in Michigan in 1893.

GENERAL ORGANIZATION

Conference: annual

OFFICERS

Pres., Rev. Wesley C. Hoggard, Rt. 2, Midland, MI 48640
Vice-Pres., Rev. Bryan Shook, Rt. 2, Beaverton, MI 48612
Sec.-Treas., Rev. Marie Berry, Rt. 9, Midland, MI 48640

The Church of God

Inaugurated by Bishop A. J. Tomlinson, who served as General Overseer, 1903 to 1943, and from which many groups of the Pentecostal and Holiness Movement stemmed. Bishop Homer A. Tomlinson served as General Overseer, 1943 to 1968. Episcopal in administration, evangelical in doctrines of justification by faith, sanctification as a second work of grace, and of the baptism of the Holy Ghost, speaking with other tongues, miracles of healing.

Churches: 2,035 Inclusive Membership: 75,890 Sunday or Sabbath Schools: 2,025 Total Enrollment: 96,500 Ordained Clergy: 2,737

CHURCH OF GOD (ANDERSON, IND.)

GENERAL ORGANIZATION

National Assembly, U.S.A.: annual, Cape Girardeau, MO
National Headquarters: U.S.A. 2504 Arrow Wood Dr., SE, Huntsville, AL 35803. Tel. (205) 881-9629

OFFICERS

Gen. Overseer and Bishop, Voy M. Bullen; Gen. Sec., and Treas., Betty Bullen
Church of God Publishing House, 2504 Arrow Wood Dr., SE, Huntsville, AL 35803
Bus: Mgr., ———

CHURCH AUXILIARIES

Address: 2504 Arrow Wood Dr., SE, Huntsville AL 35803
Assembly Band Movement: Gen. Sec., Bishop James F. Ray
Women's Missionary Band: Gen. Sec., Mary Alice Bell
Theocratic Bands: Gen. Sec., Rev. Ted Carr
Victory Leader's Band, Youth: Gen. Sec., Allen Abshire
Sunday Schools: Pres., Eddie Davidson
National Sunday School Superintendent: Eddie Davidson
Administration for Highway and Hedge Campaign: Earnest Hoover

PERIODICALS

The Church of God (s-m), 2504 Arrow Wood Dr., SE, Huntsville, AL 35803
Forward With Christ (m), 144 Fifth Ave., New York, NY 10011. Christopher Economou, Ed.
The Church of God Quarterly (q), 2504 Arrow Wood Dr., SE, Huntsville, AL 35803; Deacon Eddie Davidson, Ed.

Church of God (Anderson, Ind.)

This body is one of the largest of the groups which have taken the name "Church of God." Its headquarters are at Anderson, Ind. It originated about 1880 and emphasizes Christian unity.

Churches: 2,264 Inclusive Membership: 173,753 Sunday or Sabbath Schools: 2,239 Total Enrollment: 234,274 Ordained Clergy: 2,924

GENERAL ORGANIZATION

General Assembly: annual. Chpsn., Paul L. Hart, 4602 Parks Ave., La Mesa, CA 92041

EXECUTIVE COUNCIL

Box 2420, Anderson, IN 46011. Tel. (317) 642-0256. Exec. Sec., Paul A. Tanner
Dir. of World Service, David L. Lawson
Dir. of Church Service, Roscoe Snowden

OTHER ORGANIZATIONS

Board of Christian Education: Exec. Sec.-Treas., Donald A. Courtney, Box 2458, Anderson, IN 46011
Board of Church Extension and Home Missions: Exec. Pres.-Treas., Marvin J. Hartman, Box 2069, Anderson, IN 46011
Foreign Missionary Board: Exec. Sec.-Treas., Donald Johnson, Box 2498, Anderson, IN 46011
Women of the Church of God: Exec. Sec.-Treas., Nellie Snowden, Box 2328, Anderson, IN 46011
Board of Pensions: Exec. Sec.-Treas., Harold A. Conrad, Box 2299, Anderson, IN 46011
Mass Communications Board: Dir., Maurice Berquist, Box 2007, Anderson, IN 46011
Warner Press, Inc.: Pres., Donald Noffsinger, Box 2499, Anderson, IN 46011

PERIODICALS

Vital Christianity (bi-w), Box 2499, Anderson, IN 46011, Arlo F. Newell, Ed.
Church of God Missions (m), Box 2337, Anderson, IN 46011, Dondeena Caldwell, Ed.

†Church of God by Faith

Founded 1919, in Jacksonville Heights, Florida, by Elder John Bright. This body believes the word of God as interpreted by Jesus Christ to be the only hope of salvation, and Jesus Christ the only mediator for man.

GENERAL ORGANIZATION

General Assembly: meets every August, October, December
Headquarters: 3220 Haines St., Jacksonville, FL 32206

OFFICERS

Bishop, Elder Willie W. Matthews, 125 Holman St., Ozark, AL 36360
Exec. Sec., Elder James F. McKnight, Rt. 10 Box 26, Gainesville, FL 32601
Treas., Elder C. M. Fogle, 813 So. Delaney Ave., Avon Park, FL 33825
Ruling Elders: Elder John Robinson, 300 Essex Dr., Ft. Pierce, FL 33450; Elder Theodore Brown, 93 Girard Pl, Newark, NJ 07108
Ass't. Exec. Sec., Elder George Matthews, 8834 Camphor Dr., Jacksonville, FL 32208

PERIODICAL

The Spiritual Guide (m), 3125 Franklin St., Jacksonville, FL 32206, Aaron Matthews, Jr., Ed.

Church of God (Cleveland, Tenn.)

America's oldest Pentecostal Church began in 1886 as an outgrowth of the holiness revival under the name Christian Union. Reorganized in 1902 as the Holiness Church and in 1907 the church adopted the name Church of God. Its doctrine is fundamental and Pentecostal; it maintains a centralized form of government and an evangelistic and missionary program.

Churches: 4,847 Inclusive Membership: 392,551 Sunday or Sabbath Schools: 4,778 Total Enrollment: 373,501 Ordained Clergy: 9,095

GENERAL ORGANIZATION

General Assembly: biennial (Next meeting, August 1980)
General Offices, Keith St. at 25th NW, Cleveland, TN 37311. Tel. (615) 472-3361

OFFICERS

Gen. Overseer, Ray H. Hughes
Asst. Gen. Overseers, Frank Culpepper, T. L. Lowery, Floyd J. Timmerman
Gen. Sec.-Treas., E. C. Thomas

OTHER ORGANIZATIONS

World Missions: Gen. Dir., Robert White
Youth and C. E.: Gen. Dir. Floyd Carey
Publishing House: Publisher, O. C. McCane

Public Relations: Dir., Lewis J. Willis
Television and Radio Minister: Carl H. Richardson
Evangelism: Dir., Raymond Crowley
Education: Dir., Robert Fisher
Women's Auxiliary: Pres., Mrs. Ray H. Hughes

PERIODICALS

Church of God Evangel (bi-w), O. W. Polen, Ed.
Lighted Pathway (m), Hoyt Stone, Ed.
Leadership (q), James Humbertson, Ed.
Campus Call (m), R. Lamar Vest, Ed.
Sow (q), Robert White
Flame (q), Raymond Crowley, Ed.
The Willing Worker (m), Mrs. Ray H. Hughes, Ed.
Christian Challenge Literature (w), Hoyt Stone, Ed.

Church of God General Conference (Oregon, Ill.)

A number of churches holding premillennial Adventist views organized Churches of God in Christ Jesus in 1888. In 1921, a permanent Conference was organized with the name Church of God of the Abrahamic Faith. The corporate name is Church of God General Conference, Oregon, Illinois.

Churches: 132 Inclusive Membership: 7,550 Sunday or Sabbath Schools: 135 Total Enrollment: 9,510 Ordained Clergy: 119

GENERAL ORGANIZATION

General Conference: annual (August)
Headquarters: Oregon, IL 61061. Tel. (815) 732-7991

OFFICERS

Chpsn., William D. Lawrence, 32 E. Marshall, Phoenix, AZ 85012
Vice-Chpsn., Harold Doan, 19802 Windjammer Lane, Huntington, Beach, CA 92658
Sec., Joe James, Rt. 1 Buck Dr., Piedmont, SC 29673
Treas., Russell Magaw, 11388 Root Rd., Columbia Station, OH 44028
Exec. Dir., S. O. Ross, Box 100, Oregon, IL 61061

OTHER ORGANIZATIONS

Berean Youth Department, Oregon, IL: Dir., Hugh Harman
General Sunday School Department, Oregon, IL: Dir., David Krogh
Evangelism and Missions Board, Oregon, IL 61061: Supt. and Chpsn., Rachel Carr, 70 Pine Dr., Lake Havasu City, AZ 86403; Foreign Board: Chpsn, Mardy Lawrence, 32 E. Marshall Phoenix, AZ 85012; Home Board: Chpsn., Kent H. Ross, Box 8182, Grand Rapids, MI 49508

PERIODICALS

The Restitution Herald (m), Box 100, Oregon, IL, David Krogh, Ed.
Church of God Progress Journal (m), Box 100, Oregon, IL 61061, David Krogh, Ed.
Challenge Magazine (bi-m), Box 100, Oregon, IL 61061, Hugh Marman, Ed.

The Church of God in Christ

Organized in Arkansas in 1895 by Charles Harrison Mason and incorporated in 1897.

GENERAL ORGANIZATION

International Convocation: annual (November)
International Headquarters: 938 Mason St., Memphis, TN 38126. Tel. (901) 774-7770

GENERAL BOARD

Presiding Bishop, Bishop J. O. Patterson, 1774 S. Parkway, E., Memphis, TN 37114
1st Asst. Presiding Bishop, Bishop O. M. Kelly, 1020 Grand Concourse, Bronx, NY 10451
2nd Asst. Bishop, Bishop L. H. Ford, 9401 King Dr., Chicago, IL 60619
Gen. Sec., Bishop G. R. Ross, 815 Calmar Ave., Oakland, CA 94610
Treas., Bishop W. B. Odom, 2886 Forest St., Denver, CO 80207
Fin. Sec., Elder S. Y. Burnett, 234 Bement Ave., Staten Island, NY 11310

Bishop L. R. Anderson, 265 Ranch Trail W., Amherst, NY 14221
Bishop J. H. White, 2236 Penniston St., New Orleans, LA 70115
Bishop J. S. Bailey, 3230 Cambridge, Detroit, MI 48221
Bishop J. A. Blake, 2192 Harrison Ave., San Diego, CA 92113
Bishop F. D. Washington, 1328 President St., Brooklyn, NY 11213
Bishop J. D. Husband, 1096 Hobson St., SW, Atlanta, GA 30310
Bishop C. L. Anderson, 20485 Mendota, Detroit, MI 48221
Bishop Jacob Cohen, 3120 NW 48th Terrace, NW, Miami, FL 33142

OTHER ORGANIZATIONS

Bishop's Council, Chpsn., Bishop J. H. Sherman, P.O. Box 329, Charlotte, NC 28201
Bd. of Trustees, Chpsn., Elder, R. L. Jones, 118 River Forest, Flint, MI 48504
Elders' Council, Chpsn., Elder A. D. Baxter, 31 Modena Lane, Coatesville, PA 19380
Bd. of Publications, Chpsn., Elder Roy L. H. Winbush, 235 Walter St., Lafayette LA 70501
Women's Department, International Supervisor, Dr. Mattie McGlothen, 412 Stanford Ave., Richmond, CA 94801
Bd. of Education, Pres., Elder Woodrow W. Hicks, 843 S. 21st St., Maywood, IL 60525
Bd. of Home and Foreign Missions, Elder C. L. Moody, 2413 Leet St., Evanston, IL 60202
Bd. of Evangelism, Pres., Bishop L. C. Page, 1716 Victoria Ave., S., Los Angeles, CA 90019
Youth Congress, Pres., Bishop William James, 2132 Glenwood Ave., Toledo, OH 43620
International Sunday School Convention, Pres., Bishop C. W. Williams, 270 Division St., Derby, CT 06418
International Music Department, Pres., Mrs. Mattie Moss Clark, 18246 Sorrento St., Detroit, MI 48235
Dept. of Public Relations, Dir., Bishop W. L. Porter, 1235 E. Parkway, S., Memphis, TN 38114
Charles Harrison Mason Foundation, Dir., Mrs. Julia Mason Atkins, 1940 S. Parkway E., Memphis, TN 38114
Church of God in Christ Bookstore, Mgr., Mrs. Geraldine Miller, 1598 Buntyn St., Memphis, TN 38114

PERIODICALS

Whole Truth, 67 Tennyson, Highland Park, MI 48203. Elder James L. Whitehead, Jr., Ed.
Sunday School Literature, Publishing House, Church of God in Christ, 272 S. Main St., Memphis, TN 38103. Elder Roy L. H. Winbush, Ed.
Y.P.W.W. Topics, 67 Tennyson, Highland Park, MI 48203. Elder James L. Whitehead, Jr., Ed.
Sunshine Band topics, 648 Pearl St., Benton Harbor, MI 49022. Mrs. Mildred Wells, Ed.

Purity Guide, P.O. Box 1526, Gary, IN 46407, Mrs. Pearl McCullom, Ed.
International Directory, 930 Mason St., Memphis, TN 38126.

†The Church of God in Christ, International

Organized in 1969 in Kansas City, Missouri, by fourteen bishops of the Church of God in Christ of Memphis, Tennessee. The doctrine is the same, but the separation came because of disagreement over polity and governmental authority. The Church is Wesleyan in theology (two works of grace) but stresses the experience of full baptism of the Holy Ghost with the initial evidence of speaking with other tongues as the spirit gives utterance.

GENERAL ORGANIZATION

The General Assembly: annual
The Spring Conference: annual
College of Bishops: April and August
Headquarters: 170 Adelphi St., Brooklyn, NY 11025

OFFICERS

Presiding Bishop: The Rt. Rev. Carl E. Williams, Sr., 170 Adelphia St., Brooklyn, NY 11205
Vice Presiding Bishop, The Rt. Rev. A. J. Jones, Sr., 638 W. 35th St., Norfolk, VA 23508
Sec.-Gen. Treas., The Rt. Rev. David J. Billings, III, 315 Clinton Ave., Brooklyn, NY 11205
National Supervisor-Womens' Dept., Dr. Louise Norris, 210 Elmwood Ave., Bridgeport, CT 06605
President of the Youth Department, Evangelist Joyce Taylor, 151 N. Elliott Walk, Brooklyn, NY 11205
National Superintendent of Sunday Schools, Rev. Ronald L. Figueroa, 433 Macon St., Brooklyn, NY 11233
President of Music Department, Elder J. C. White; Co-Pres., Bro. Carl Williams, Jr., 295 Clinton Ave., Brooklyn, NY 11238
Chpsns. of the Board of Elders, Rev. Early C. Oliver, 1750 Revenall Ave., Orlando FL 32805; Dr. Lugenia Kilpatrick
Chpsns. of the Board of Bishops, Bishop A. J. Jones, 638 West 35th St., Norfolk, VA 23508; Rev. Anthony Monks
Exec. Sec., Sr. Janet Napper, 995 Myrtle Ave., Brooklyn, NY 11206
1st Special Assistant to Presiding Bishop, Bishop Charles Minor 423 Blake Ave., #1E, Brooklyn, NY 11212
National Scholarship Committee Housing Chpsn., Elder Eric Figueroa, 433 Macon St., Brooklyn, NY 11233

Church of God in Christ (Mennonite)

A section of the Mennonite body organized in 1859, in Ohio, for the reestablishment of the order and discipline of the Church.

Churches: 85 Inclusive Membership: 7,400 Sunday or Sabbath Schools: N.R. Total Ordained Clergy : N.R.

GENERAL ORGANIZATION

Headquarters: 420 N. Wedel St., Moundridge, KS 67107. Tel. (316) 345-2532

OFFICER

Conf. Mod., Norman Koehn, 105 Sylvia, Victoria, TX 77901

PERIODICAL

Messenger of Truth (bi-w), Box 188, Goltry, OK 73739 Reuben Koehn, Ed.

The Church of God of Prophecy

Organized August 19, 1886, by Elder Richard Spurling at Barney Creek Meeting House, Monroe County, Tenn. and reorganized May 15, 1902, with R. G. Spurling as pastor, at Camp Creek, Cherokee County, N.C.

In June, 1903, A. J. Tomlinson and four others were added to the membership and A. J. Tomlinson was selected as pastor. In January, 1906, the First Assembly was held in the Murphy home, Cherokee County, N.C., with A. J. Tomlinson as moderator and clerk. This dual office he continued to hold until the title was changed to General Overseer in the Fifth Assembly in 1910. Although it was understood that they were operating as the Church of God, it was in the Second Assembly held at Union Grove, Bradley County, Tenn., in 1907, that the name Church of God was formally adopted by the Assembly and entered into the records.

The Church of God continued to grow and operate with the same doctrine and government in spite of some early persecutions and disruptions. Foreign mission work of the Church of God spread from country to country and membership grew in the U.S.

A. J. Tomlinson continued as General Overseer until his death in 1943, and his son, M. A. Tomlinson, was chosen to succeed him and continues to this day.

By 1950 several organizations were using the Church of God as their name and confusion arose regarding property, mail, and banking. After several trying experiences with these problems, the Church began using, in May, 1952, the name Church of God of Prophecy for secular purposes only.

The doctrine is fundamental, conservative, and evangelical, stressing justification by faith, sanctification as a second work of grace, speaking in tongues as the initial evidence of being filled with the Holy Ghost, divine healing, and the second coming of Christ. The government is central and theocratic.

GENERAL ORGANIZATION

General Assembly: annual
World Headquarters: Bible Place, Cleveland, TN 37311. Tel. (615) 472-4511

OFFICERS

Gen. Overseer, Milton A. Thomlinson
Exec. Comm.: Gen. Overseer, Gen. Treas., Bus. Mgr. W.W.P.H.

GENERAL APPOINTEES

Field Secs., M. T. Linkous, Jacob Monijo, E. L. Jones
Gen. Treas., Leonard F. Kendrick
Publ. Rel., Bill J. White
Asst. Publ. and Bus. Mgr. of White Wing Publishing House, Henry Oneal
Asst. Ed., Billy Murray
Dir. of Evang., D. Elwood Matthews
Assembly Band Movement Sec., Eugene Weakley
Sunday School Sec., Caroline S. Ledbetter
Victory Leaders Sec., Terry L. Mahan
Women Missionary Band Sec., Elva Howard
Church of Prophecy Marker Assoc. Sec. & Fields of the Wood Mgr., Charles S. Pennington
Sunday School Literature Ed., Richard E. Davis
World Mission Sec., Adrian L. Varlack
Mission Reps., Bobby R. Snow, Roy D. Mixon, Paul Torres, Alvin Moss
World Language Sec., Felix R. Garcia
Bible Training Inst. Supt., Ray C. Wynn
Communications Bus. Mgr., Thomas Duncan
Communications Spanish Minister, Jose O. Reyes
Minister of Music, Verlin D. Thornton
Ministerial Aid Dir., Perry E. Gillum

PERIODICALS

Published by the White Wing Publishing House and Press, Keith St., Cleveland, TN 37311
White Wing Messenger, (bi-m)
Happy Harvester (m)

The Church of God of the Mountain Assembly, Inc.

Founded in 1906 by J. H. Parks, S. N. Bryant, Thomas Moses, and Andrew J. Silcox.

GENERAL ORGANIZATION

Headquarters and General Offices: Florence Ave., Jellico, TN 37762. Tel. (615) 424-8260. General Assembly, annually in August

OFFICERS

Gen. Overseer, Rev. Jerome Walden, Box 157, Jellico, TN 37762
First Asst. Gen. Overseer, Rev. K. E. Massingill, Box 157, Jellico, TN 37762
Second Asst. Gen. Overseer, Rev. J. E. Prewitt, P.O. Box 288, Goshen, OH 45122
Gen. Sec.-Treas., Rev. James L. Cox, Jr., Box 157, Jellico, TN 37762

PERIODICAL

The Gospel Herald (m), P.O. Box 288, Goshin, OH 45122, Rev. Dennis A. McClanahan, Ed.

†The Church of God (7th Day)

Organization traced from Old and New Testament times. Reorganized at a convention held at Salem, West Virginia, in November 1933. The tithe system is used to pay the ministry.

GENERAL ORGANIZATION

Apostolic Council: meets bi-yearly, in Salem, WV (on the second Sunday in January and the second Sunday in July)
Headquarters: 79 Water St., Salem, WV 26426 (Box 328)

OFFICERS

Apostolic Council, made up of Twelve Apostles, 70 Prophets (Elders)
Seven Financial Stewards
Overseers of different countries and districts. Eph. 2:20, 4:11

PERIODICAL

The Advocate of Truth (s-m), Sabbath Sunday School Lessons (q) The Advocate of Truth Press, Inc., Box 328, Salem, WV 26426, Chris W. Royer, Ed.

The Church of God (Seventh Day), Denver, Colo.

This body observes the seventh day as the Sabbath; believes in the imminent, personal, and visible return of Jesus; and that the earth will be the eternal abode of the righteous.

GENERAL ORGANIZATION

General Conference: biennial (Next meeting, 1981)
Headquarters: 330 W. 152nd Ave., P.O. Box 33677, Denver, CO 80233. Tel. (303) 452-7973

OFFICERS

Chpsn., Wm. Robert Coulter
Sec.-Treas., David M. Kauer
Spring Vale Academy: Principal, Kenneth Moldenhauer
Faithful Youth Challengers: Dir., Steve Kurtright, Houston, TX
Bible Advocate Press: Mgr., LeRoy Dais
Media Outreach Services: Dir., John Roina
National Women's Assoc., Pres., Mrs. Dorthy Keim, 506 E Osage, McAlester, OK 74501
Publishing: (Bible Advocate Press, Denver, CO 80201). LeRoy Dais, Mgr.
Ministerial Training Center: Dir., Jerry Griffin, Denver, CO

PERIODICALS

The Bible Advocate (m), Denver, CO 80201, Floyd A. Turner, Ed.
Aim (m), Denver, CO 80201, Mrs. Gail Rincker, Ed.
The Harvest Field Messenger (bi-m), Denver, CO 80201, Floyd A. Turner, Ed.
Women's Association News Digest (WAND) (q) Box 33677, Denver, CO 80233, Mrs. Donna Griffin, Ed.
Footprints (bi-m), Denver, CO 80201, Gina Tolbert, Ed.

Church of God (Which He Purchased with His Own Blood)

This body was organized in 1953 in Oklahoma City, Okla. by William Jordan Fizer after his excommunication from the Church of the Living God over doctrinal disagreements relating to the Lord's Supper. The first annual convention was held in Oklahoma City, November 19-21, 1954.

The Church of God (W.H.P.W.H.O.B.) believes that water is not the element to be used in the Lord's Supper but rather grape juice and unleavened bread. The Lord's Supper is observed every Sunday.

This body is non-Pentecostal and rejects speaking in tongues. Its doctrine holds that the Holy Ghost is given to those who obey the Lord. Foot washing is observed as an act of humility. Baptism must be administered in the name of the Father, Son, and Holy Ghost. The Church of God believes that it is the Body of Christ, and its members are urged to lead consecrated lives unspotted from the world. Tobacco and strong drinks are condemned. Divine healing is an article of faith, but not to the exclusion of doctors.

Churches: 8 Inclusive Membership: 747 Sunday or Sabbath Schools: 7 Enrollment: 180 Ordained Clergy: 8

GENERAL ORGANIZATION

Convention: Annual, ending on the fourth Sunday in October.
Headquarters: 1628 N.E. 50th, Oklahoma City, OK 73111. Tel. (405) 427-8264

OFFICERS

Chief Bishop, William J. Fizer, 1907 N.E. Grand Blvd., Oklahoma City, OK 73111
Gen. Sec. and Treas., Alsie May Fizer
Asst. Treas., Bishop Isaac Freeman, 1809 Peachtree St., Oklahoma City, OK 73121
Overseers: J. W. Johnson, R.1, Box 214, Choctaw, OK 73020; F. McElwee, 509 E. 47th Pl., N., Tulsa, OK 74126; M. Roberson, Rt. 2, Box 214, Mounds, OK 74047

PERODICAL

Gospel News (m), William J. Fizer, Ed.

†The Church of Illumination

Organized in 1908 for the express purpose of establishing congregations at large, offering a spiritual, esoteric, philosophic interpretation of the vital biblical teachings, thereby satisfying the inner spiritual needs of those seeking spiritual truth, yet permitting them to remain in, or return to, their former church membership.

GENERAL ORGANIZATION

The Assemblage: annual
Headquarters: "Beverly Hall," Clymer Rd., Quakertown, PA 18951

OFFICERS

Dir., Rev. Emerson M. Clymer

The Church of Jesus Christ (Bickertonites)

Organized 1862 at Green Oak, Pennsylvania, by William Bickerton, who obeyed the Restored Gospel under Sidney Rigdon's following in 1845.

Churches: 60 Inclusive Membership: 2,551 Sunday or Sabbath Schools: 60 Total Enrollment: 5,250 Ordained Clergy: 234

GENERAL ORGANIZATION

General Conference: annual (April)
Headquarters: Sixth & Lincoln Sts., Monongahela, PA 15063. Tel. (412) 258-9923

OFFICERS

Pres., Dominic Thomas, 6010 Barrie, Dearborn, MI 48126
First Counselor, Nicholas Pietrangelo, 24106 Meadow Bridge Dr., Mt. Clemens, MI 48043
Second Counselor, V. James Lovalvo, 5769 Pleasant Ave., Fresno, CA 93711
Exec. Sec., Paul Palmieri, 319 Pine Dr., Aliquippa, PA 15001

PERIODICAL

The Gospel News (m), Sixth & Lincoln Sts., Monogahela, PA 15063, Ken Staley, Ed.

The Church of Jesus Christ of Latter-day Saints

Organized April 6, 1830, at Fayette, New York, by Joseph Smith. Members consider the bible, Book of Mormon, Doctrine and Covenants, and the Pearl of Great Price to be the word of God. Their belief is summed up in thirteen Articles of Faith written by Joseph Smith. Membership is worldwide.

Churches: 6,272 Inclusive Membership: 2,592,000 Sunday or Sabbath Schools: 6,270 Total Enrollment 2,380,000 Ordained Clergy: 21,536

GENERAL ORGANIZATION

General Conference sessions, April and October, Salt Lake City, Utah
Headquarters: 50 East North Temple St., Salt Lake City, UT 84111

OFFICERS

Pres., Spencer W. Kimball
1st Presidency: Spencer W. Kimball, Nathan Eldon Tanner, and Marion G. Romney
The Quorum of the Twelve: Ezra Taft Benson, Mark E. Petersen, James E. Faust, LeGrand Richards, Elder Howard W. Hunter, Gordon B. Hinckley, Thomas S. Monson, Boyd K. Packer, Marvin J. Ashton, Bruce R. McConkie, and L. Tom Perry, David B. Haight
Patriarch to the Church: Eldred G. Smith
The First Quorum of the Seventy:
Presidents: Franklin D. Richards, Wm. Grant Bangerter, J. Thomas Fyans., A. Theodore Tuttle, Neal A. Maxwell, Marion D. Hanks, Paul H. Dunn
Additional Members: Sterling W. Sill, Henry D. Taylor, Alvin R. Dyer, Franklin D. Richards, Theodore M. Burton, Bernard P. Brockbank, James A. Cullimore, Marion D. Hanks, Joseph Anderson, William H. Bennett, John H. Vandenberg, Robert L. Simpson, O. Leslie Stone, James E. Faust, J. Thomas Fyans, Neal A. Maxwell, William Grant Bangerter, Robert D. Hales, Adney Y. Komatsu, and Joseph B. Werthlin; S. Dilworth Young, Elder Gene R. Cook, A. Theodore Tuttle, Paul H. Dunn, Hartman Rector, Jr., Loren C. Dunn, and Rex D. Pinegar, Elder Charles A. Didier, William R. Bradford, George P. Lee, Carlos E. Asay, M. Ballard Jr., John H. Groberg, Jacob de Jager, Vaughn J. Featherstone, Dean L. Larsen, Royden G. Derrick, Robert E. Wells, G. Homer Durham, James M. Paramore and Richard G. Scott, Hugh W. Pinnock, F. Enzio Busche, Yoshihiko Kikuchi, Ronald E. Poelman, Derek A. Cuthbert, Robert L. Backman, Rex C. Reeve, Sr., F. Burton Howard, Teddy E. Brewerton, Jack H. Goaslind, Jr.
Presiding Bishopric: Victor L. Brown, H. Burke Peterson, and J. Richard Clarke
Church Historian and Recorder: Leonard J. Arrington

AUXILIARY ORGANIZATIONS

The Relief Society of the Church of Jesus Christ of Latter-day Saints: Gen. Pres., Barbara Bradshaw Smith
Sunday Schools: Gen. Pres., Russell M. Nelson.
Young Women: Gen. Pres., Elaine Cannon
Primary Association: Gen. Pres., Naomi Maxfield Shumway
Genealogical Society of The Church of Jesus Christ of Latter-day Saints: Pres., J. Thomas Fyans
Board of Education: Commissioner of Education, Jeffrey B. Holland

PERIODICALS

Deseret News (d), Salt Lake City, UT, Gordon B. Hinckley, Pres.
The Ensign of The Church of Jesus Christ of Latter-day Saints (m), Salt Lake City, UT, Jay M. Todd, Man. Ed.
New Era (m), Salt Lake City, UT, Brian K. Kelly, Man. Ed.
Friend (m), Salt Lake City, UT, Lucile C. Reading Man. Ed.

Church of Our Lord Jesus Christ of the Apostolic Faith, Inc.

This Church as an organized body was founded by Bishop R. C. Lawson in Columbus, Ohio, and moved to New York City in 1919. It is founded upon the teachings of the Apostles and Prophets, Jesus Christ being its chief cornerstone.

GENERAL ORGANIZATION

National Convocation: annual (August)
Headquarters: 2081 7th Ave., New York, NY 10027. Tel. (212) 866-1700

OFFICERS

Senior Apostle, Bishop W. L. Bonner; Apostle, Bishop H. D. Jones; Apostle, Bishop J. P. Steadman; Apostle, Bishop Perry Thomas; Apostle, Frank Soloman
Chpsn. Board of Presbyters, Elder Joseph Frazier
Chpsn. of Board of Bishops, Bishop S. W. Wright
Gen. Sec., Bishop T. E. Woolfolk
Natl. Rec. Sec., Bishop J. W. Parrott, Sr
Natl. Fin. Sec., District Elder Clarence Groover
Natl. Corr. Sec., Elder Fred Rubin
Natl. Treas., Bishop T. Richardson

PERIODICAL

The Contender for the Faith (m), 112 E. 125th St., New York, NY 10035.

†The Church of Revelation, Inc.

Founded 1930 at Long Beach, California, by Rev. Janet Stine Wolford, with Christian love as the basis for membership. Incorporated under the State Laws of California.

GENERAL ORGANIZATION

Board of trustees: annual
Headquarters: P.O. Box 574, Lakewood, CA 90714

OFFICERS

Pres., Rev. Winifred Ruth Mikesell, P. O. Box 574, Lakewood, CA 90714
Vice-Pres., Rev. Moriee Renee Dupree, P. O. Box 574, Lakewood, CA 90714
Sec.-Treas., Donald K. Stine, P. O. Box 574 Lakewood, CA 90714

Church of the Brethren

German pietists-anabaptists founded in 1708 under Alexander Mack, Schwarzenau, Germany, entered the colonies in 1719 and settled at Germantown, Pennsylvania. They have no other creed than the New Testament, hold to principles of nonviolence, temperance, and voluntarism, and emphasize religion in life.

Churches: 1,061 Inclusive Membership: 175,335 Sunday or Sabbath Schools: 1,061 Total Enrollment: 70,156 Ordained Clergy: N.R.

GENERAL ORGANIZATION

General Conference: annual (June 1980)
Headquarters: Church of the Brethren General Offices, 1451 Dundee Ave., Elgin, IL 60120. Tel. (312) 742-5100
Washington Office: 110 Maryland Ave., NE, Box 50, Washington, DC 20002

OFFICERS

Mod. Robert W. Neff
Mod.-Elect, Robert G.Greiner
Treas., Robert Greiner, 1451 Dundee Ave., Elgin, Il 60120

EXECUTIVE STAFF

Gen. Sec., Robert W. Neff
Treas., Robert G. Greiner
Assoc. Gen. Sec. & Exec. Sec. of Parish Ministries Commission, Ralph G. McFadden
Assoc. Gen. Sec. & Exec. Sec. of General Services Commission, Joel K. Thompson
Assoc. Gen. Sec. & Exec. Sec. of World Ministries Commission, Ruby F. Rhoades
Treasurer's Office: Adm. Asst., Joan M. Harrison

GENERAL STAFF

General Secretary's Office: Adm. Asst., Hazel Peters; Office Coord., Esther N. Eichelberger; Dir. of Field Services, J. Bentley Peters
Treasurer's Office: Asst. Treas., Roy L. Hiteshew
General Services Commission: Coord., Office of Personnel Adm.: J. Bentley Peters; Personnel Relations, Hazel Peters; Ministry Consultant, Robert Faus; *Messenger* Ed., Kermon Thomasson; *Agenda/Source* and Books Ed., Fred W. Swartz; Media Education Advocacy, Stewart M. Hoover; Mkt. Dir., Clyde E. Weaver; Stewardship Enlistment; Stewart B. Kauffman, Janine Katonah, Dale Minnich, Donald L. Stern; Prod. Mgr., James Replogle; Dir. of Interpretation, Howard E. Royer
Parish Ministries Commission: Worship and Heritage Resources/Smaller Congregations/Ed., Robert C. Bowman; Outdoor Ministries, Walter D. Bowman; Church Extension and Development/Mission Mutua en las Americas, Merle Crouse; Life Cycle Ministries/Person Awareness, Mary Cline Detrick and Ralph L. Detrick; Health and Welfare/Homes and Hospitals, Jackie Driver; Biblical Studies/Ed. for a Shared Ministry/Ed., Rich Garner; Educational Development/Public and Higher Ed., Shirley Heckman; Educational Resources/Teacher Church Growth, Matthew M. Meyer; Congregations and Communities in Charge Parish Volunteer Service, Thomas Wilson
World Ministries Commission: Asia/Africa Rep., Roger Ingold; Brethren Volunteer Service Dir., Joanne Nesler Davis; Europe-Mid East Rep./Peace and Int'l. Affairs Consultant, H. Lamar Gibble; UN Rep., Shantilal P. Bhagat; Service Ministries Dir., H. McKinley Coffman; Latin American Rep., Merle Crouse; Peace Consultant/On Earth Peace, Charles L. Boyer; SHARE/Community Development Consultant/Foundations Relations, Wilfred F. Nolen; Washington Rep., (Interim) Washington, DC, Ron Hanft
Committee on Interchurch Relations: Exec. Sec., Robert W. Neff
Pension Board: Exec. Sec., Joel K. Thompson; Treas., Robert G. Greiner

PERIODICAL

Messenger (m), Church of the Brethren General Offices, Elgin, IL 60120. Kermon Thommason, Actg. Ed.

†Church of the Living God

(Motto: Christian Workers for Fellowship)

This organization was formed at Wrightsville, Arkansas, in 1889 by the late Chief William Christian. It emphasizes believers' baptism by immersion, the use of water and unleavened bread, and the washing of saints' feet in the celebration of the Lord's Supper, which is required only once—when one unites with the church. The local organizations are known as "temples."

GENERAL ORGANIZATION

National Assembly: annual, second Tuesday in Oct. General Assembly: quadrennial

OFFICERS

Chief Bishop, F. C. Scott, 801 NE 17th St., Oklahoma City, OK 73105
Vice-Chief Bishop, W. E. Crumes, 3547 Washington Ave., Cincinnati, OH 45229
Overseer, A. L. Ponder, 5609 N. Terry St., Oklahoma City, OK 73111
Gen. Treas., Elder Harvey R. Jones, 2928 Newton Ave., San Diego, CA 92113

Church of the Lutheran Brethren of America

Organized in Milwaukee, Wisconsin, in 1900. It adheres to the Lutheran confessions and accepts into membership those who profess a personal faith in Jesus Christ. It practices congregational autonomy and conducts its services in a nonliturgical pattern. The synod has an advisory rather than ruling function on the congregational level, but in the cooperative efforts of all congregations (Education, American and World Missions, Ministries to the Aged, and Publications) it exercises a ruling functon.

Churches: 95 Inclusive Membership: 9,192 Sunday or Sabbath Schools: 94 Total Enrollment: 8,586 Ordained Clergy: 154

GENERAL ORGANIZATION

Convention: annual (June)
Headquarters: Fergus Falls, MN 56537. Tel. (218) 736-5666

OFFICERS

Pres., Rev. E. H. Strom, Box 655, Fergus Falls, MN 56537
1st Vice-Pres., Rev. Omar Gjerness, Lutheran Brethren Schools, Fergus Falls, MN, 56537
2nd Vice-Pres., Rev. Burton Bundy, 1908 26th Ave., S., Fargo, ND 58102
Sec., Rev. George Aase, 1 Tonneson Dr., Succasunna, NJ 07876

Treas., Rev. Robert Wallin, Box 655, Fergus Falls, MN 56537
Pres., Lutheran Brethren Schools, Rev. C. Lloyd Bjornlie, Lutheran Brethren Schools, Fergus Falls, MN 56537
Exec. Sec. World Missions, Rev. Robert Overgaard, Box 655, Fergus Falls MN 56537
Dir. of Home Missons, Rev. Harland Helland, Box 655, Fergus Falls, MN 56537
Dir. of Development, Rev. Theodore Thompson, Box 655, Fergus Falls, MN 56537

PERIODICAL

Faith and Fellowship (m), 704 Vernon Ave., W. Fergus Falls, MN 56537

Church of the Lutheran Confession

This conservative Lutheran body was organized in January, 1961 by clergy and laity who withdrew from synods affiliated with the Synodical Conference of North America.

Members uncompromisingly believe in the Holy Scriptures as the verbally inspired Word of God and subscribe without reservation to all historic Confessions of the Lutheran Church as a clear and correct exposition of Scriptural doctrine.

Churches: 72 Inclusive Membership: 9,316 Sunday or Sabbath Schools: 57 Total Enrollment: 1,540 Ordained Clergy: 75

GENERAL ORGANIZATION

Biennial Synodical Convention (Next meeting, 1980)
Headquarters: Markesan, WI 53946. Tel. (414) 398-2778

OFFICERS

Pres., Rev. Egbert Albrecht, Markesan, WI 53946
Vice Pres., Rev. Robert Reim 8361 Solana Dr., Thornton, CO 80229
Mod., Rev. George Barthels, 710 4th Ave., SW, Sleepy Eye, MN 56085
Sec., Rev. Paul Nolting, 2415 Hemlock, No. 515 Ketchikan, AK 99901
Treas., Lowell Moen, 3455 Jill Ave., Eau Claire, WI 54701
Archivist-Historian, John Lau
Statistician, Harvey Callies

PERIODICALS

The Lutheran Spokesman (m), 1534 West Ave., Red Wing, MN 55066, David Lau, Ed.
Ministry by Mail (w), 2415 Hemlock, No. 515 Ketchikan, AK 99901; Business Address: 313 Bel Air Dr., W. Columbia, SC 29169. Paul E. Nolting, Ed.
C.L.C. Directory (a), 994 Emerald Hill Rd., Redwood City, CA 94061. Rollin Rein, Ed.
Journal of Theology (5 times a year), Immannel Lutheran College, Eau Claire, WI 54701. C. M. Gullerud, Ed.

Church of the Nazarene

One of the larger holiness bodies organized in Pilot Point, Texas, in October, 1908. It is in general accord with the early doctrines of Methodism and emphasizes entire sanctification as a second definite work of grace.

Churches: 4,719 Inclusive Membership: 462,724 Sunday or Sabbath Schools: 4,615 Total Enrollment: 896,989 Ordained Clergy: 7,590

GENERAL ORGANIZATION

General Assembly: quadrennial (Next meeting, Kansas City, MO, June 1980)
International Headquarters: 6401 The Paseo, Kansas City, MO 64131. Tel. (816) 333-7000

OFFICERS

Gen. Supts.: V. H. Lewis, George Coulter, Eugene L. Stowe, Orville Jenkins, Charles Stickland and William Greathouse
Gen. Sec., B. Edgar Johnson
Gen. Treas., Norman O. Miller

OTHER ORGANIZATIONS

General Board: Sec., B. Edgar Johnson; Treas., Norman O. Miller
General Church Department and Agencies: Communications, Exec. Dir., Paul Skiles; Education and the Ministry, Exec. Dir., Mark R. Moore; Evangelism, Exec. Dir., Donald J. Gibson; Home Missions, Exec. Dir., Raymond Hurn; Pensions and Benevolence, Exec. Dir., Dean Wessels; Publication, Exec. Dir., M. A. (Bud) Lunn; NWMS, Exec. Dir., Wanda Knox; Division of Life Income Gifts, Exec. Consultant, Robert Crew; Book Committee, Ed., Fred Parker; Stewardship, Exec. Dir., Leon Doane; World Mission, Exec. Dir., Jerald Johnson; Christian Life, Exec. Coord., Kenneth Rice; Children's Ministries, Exec. Dir., Miriam Hall; Youth Ministries, Exec. Dir., Gary Henecke; Christian Service Training, Dir., Earl C. Wolf.

PERIODICALS

Herald of Holiness (w), W. E. McCumber, Ed.
World Missions (m), Jerald Johnson, Ed.
Preacher's Magazine (m) Neil Wiseman, Ed.
Bread (m), Debbie Salter, Ed.
All published by the Nazarene Publishing House, Box 527, Kansas City, MO 64141

Churches of Christ

This body is made up of a large group of churches, formerly reported with the Disciples of Christ, but since the Religious Census of 1906 reported separately. They are strictly congregational and have no organization larger than the local congregation.

Churches: 17,550 Inclusive Membership: 3,000,000 Sunday or Sabbath Schools: 16,000 Total Enrollment: 1,860,000 Ordained Clergy: 16,200

NO GENERAL ORGANIZATION

PERIODICALS

Gospel Advocate (w), 1006 Elm Hill Road, Nashville, TN 37210. J. Roy Vaughan, Ed.
Firm Foundation (w), 3110 Guadalupe St., Austin, TX 78705. Reuel Lemmons, Ed.
Christian Leader (bi-w), 4507 W. Wilson Ave. Chicago, IL 60630. Elza Huffard, Ed.
20th Century Christian, 1121 W. 79th St., Los Angeles, CA 90044. M. Norvel Young, Ed.
The Christian Chronicle, 110 21st Ave. S. Nashville, TN 37215. Haskell Cheshire, Ed.
Gospel Herald (m), Beamsville, Ontario, Canada, Roy D. Merritt, Ed.
North American Christian (m), 60 West St., Keene, NH 03431. James Robert Jarrell, Ed.
Christian Bible Teacher (m), Box 1060, Abilene, TX 79604. Bill Patterson, Ed.
Voice of Freedom (m), Box 150, Nashville, TN 37202. P. D. Wilmeth, Ed.
Mission (m), Box 2822, Abilene, TX 79604. Roy B. Ward, Ed.

Truth (m), Rt. 2, Box 177, Marion, IN 46952
Spiritual Sword, 1511 Getwell Rd., Memphis, TN 38111, Thomas B. Warren, Ed.

Churches of Christ in Christian Union

Organized in 1909 at Washington Court House, Ohio, as the Churches of Christ in Christian Union. This body believes in the new birth and the baptism of the Holy Spirit for believers. It is Wesleyan with an evangelistic and missionary emphasis.

Reformed Methodist Church merged in September, 1952, with Churches of Christ in Christian Union.

Churches: 262 Inclusive Membership: 10,300 Sunday or Sabbath Schools: 262 Total Enrollment: 20,900 Ordained Clergy: 536

GENERAL ORGANIZATION

General Council: biennial (Next meeting 1980)
District Councils: annual
General Headquarters: 459 E. Ohio St. (Mailing address: Box 30), Circleville, OH 43113

OFFICERS

Gen. Supt., Rev. Robert Kline, Box 30, Circleville, OH 43113
Asst. Gen. Supt., Rev. Grover Blankenship, Rt. 1, Box 198, Waverly, Oh 45690
Gen. Sec., Rev. Paul Dorsey, P.O. Box 188, Alma, GA 31510
Gen. Treas., Bevery R. Salley, Box 30, Circleville, OH 43113
Gen. Board of Trustees: Chm., Rev. Robert Kline, Box 30, Circleville, OH 43113; Vice-Chpsn., Rev. Grover Blankenship; Sec., Rev. Robert Barth, 4205 Cedar St., New Boston, OH 45662
District Superintendents (all District Superintendents are also members of the Gen. Bd. of Trustees); Mid-West District, Rev. Joseph Johnson, P.O. Box 92, London, OH 43140; Mid-East District, Rev. Robert Trimble, 76 Fifth Ave., S.W., Pataskala, OH 43062. South Central District, Rev. G. L. Blankenship, Rt. 1, Box 163A, Bainbridge, OH 45612; Southern District, Rev. L. R. Fitts, 8328 W. Pocahontas St., Tampa, FL 33615, Northeastern Dist., Rev. Elmer Hurles, Jr., Rt. 2 Port Crane, NY 13833

PERIODICALS

Advocate (m), P. Lewis Brevard, Ed.
Missionary Tidings (m), Martha Hollabaugh Ed.

Churches of God, General Conference

This body emerged out of a revival movement among the Germans in Pennsylvania in 1825, under the leadership of John Winebrenner, a German Reformed minister. The Bible is the only rule of faith and practice.

GENERAL ORGANIZATION

General Conference: meets triennially
Legal Headquarters: United Church Center, Rm. 200, 900 So. Arlington Ave., Harrisburg, PA 17109. Tel. (717) 652-0255
Administrative Offices: General Conference Administrator, Dr. Richard Wilkin, 2200 Jennifer Lane, Findlay, OH 45840. Tel. (419) 424-1961
Assoc. to the General Conference Administrator, Rev. Darrell Prichard, Rev. Stephen Dunn, Rev. Richard Dosh, Rev. David Draper, Rev. L. J. Miller, 2200 Jennifer Lane, Findlay, OH 45840. Tel. (419) 424-1961

OFFICERS

Pres., Pastor Lloyd Harlan, Rt. 4 Box 495, Franklin, PA 16323
Vice-Pres., Pastor Gordon Jenkins, 1835 W. Laurel St., Freeport, IL 62526
Journalizing Sec., Rev. Harry G. Cadamore, 1934 Candlewick Dr., Findlay, OH 45840
Treas., Mr. Larry Witherup, 1379 Pittsburgh Rd., Franklin, PA 16323. Tel. (814) 432-5694

COMMISSIONS

Evangelism: Chpsn., Pastor Terry O. Frederick, 2735 Canby St., Harrisburg, PA 17103. Sec., Pastor Gordon Jenkins, 1835 W. Laurel St., Freeport, IL 61032
Education: Chpsn., Dr. K. E. Blodosser, 900 S. Arlington Ave., 200, Harrisburg, PA 17109; Sec., Pastor Robert Bistline, 100 College St. Findlay, OH 45840
Stewardship and Finance: Chpsn., Pastor Larry G. White, 936 W. Main St., Mt. Pleasant, PA 15666; Dr. Herbert O. Now, 1316 N. Cory St., Findlay, OH 45840
Lay Activities: Chpsn., Pastor Daune Beck, Rt. 8, Box 400, Frederick, MD 21701; Sec., Mrs. Kathy Bistline, 2530 Log Cabin Rd., York, PA 17404
Publication: Chpsn., Pastor A. G. Dunn, 2211 Market St., Harrisburg, PA 17103; Sec., Pastor Randall L. Bistline, 2350 Log Cabin Rd., York, PA 17404
National Missions: Chpsn., Mr. Clayton L. Peck, Rt. 1, Yates Center, KS 66783; Sec., Rev. Donald Cohick P. O. Box 234, Valley View, PA 17983
World Missions: Chpsn., Pastor W. S. Darrah, 508 E. Walnut St., Nappanee, IN 46550; Sec., Pastor Lloyd Harlan, Rt. 4, Box 945, Franklin, PA 16323

PERIODICAL

The Church Advocate (m), P. O. Box 926, Findlay, Oh 45840, Rev. David Draper, Ed.

Community Churches, National Council of

This body is a fellowship of locally autonomous, ecumenically minded, congregationally governed, non-creedal Protestant Churches, all located within the continental United States. The Council came into being in 1950 as the union of two former councils of community churches, one formed of black churches known as the Biennial Council of Community Churches, and the other of white churches which had the same name as the present body.

Churches: 200 Inclusive Membership: 190,000 Sunday or Sabbath Schools: N.R. Total Enrollment: N.R. Ordained Clergy: 210

GENERAL ORGANIZATION

Summer Conference: Annual
National Office: 89 East Wilson Bridge Rd., Worthington, OH 43085. Tel. (614) 888-4501

OFFICERS

Pres., Dr. R. C. Thomas
Vice-Pres., Mr. J. Bradford (Barbara) Holt & Mrs. M. C. (Dorothy) Bascoda
Sec., Mrs. James (Mabel E.) Rogers
Treas., Edward H. Baldwin

OTHER ORGANIZATIONS

(All may be contacted through the Central Office)

Commission on Ecumenical Relations, Chpsn., Robert H. Taylor
Commission on Program, Chpsn., Robert M. Puckett
Commission on Information Services & Public Relations, Chpsn., Barbara Holt
Commission on Membership Development, Chpsn., Gerald A. Stevens
Women's Christian Fellowship, Pres., Mrs. Kathleen Holmes
Samaritans (Men's Fellowship), Pres., Sylvester Smith.
Young Adult Fellowship, Pres., Stephen Leonard
Youth Fellowship, Ms. C. Grimes

PERIODICAL

The Christian Community (m), 89 East Wilson Bridge Rd., Worthington, OH 43085. Herbert F. Freitag, Ed.

Congregational Christian Churches, National Association of

Organized 1955 in Detroit, Michigan by delegates from Congregational Christian Churches committed to continuing the Congregational way of faith and order in church life. It has no doctrinal requirements. Participation by member churches is voluntary.

Churches: 382 Inclusive Membership: 95,000 Sunday or Sabbath Schools: N.R. Total Enrollment: N. R. Ordained Clergy: 554

GENERAL ORGANIZATION

Annual Meeting: (1979, Pomona College, Pomona, CA)

OFFICERS

Mod., Dr. Norman S. Ream, Wauwatosa, WI; Exec. Secs., Dr. Erwin A. Britton; Dr. A. Ray Appelquist; Dr. George W. Brown, Jr., P.O. Box 1620, Oak Creek, WI 53154. Tel. (414) 764-1620

PERIODICAL

The Congregationalist (m), Nancy Manser, Ed.

Congregational Holiness Church

A body which separated from the Pentecostal Holiness Church in 1921; carries on mission work in Mexico, Honduras, Costa Rica, Cuba, Brazil, Spain, and Guatemala.

GENERAL ORGANIZATION

General Conference, meets every two years. General Committee, meets as called. Represents ten state conferences.
General Headquarters: 3888 Fayetteville Hwy., Griffin, GA 30223. Tel. (404) 228-4833

EXECUTIVE BOARD

Gen. Supt., Bishop James H. Martin
1st Asst. Gen. Supt., Rev. Hugh B. Skelton
Sec. Asst. Gen. Supt., Rev. Euel Gilstrap
Gen. Sec., Rev. Wayne Hicks
Gen. Treas., Rev. Dennis Phillips
Supt. of Home Mission & Evangelism, Rev. William L. Lewis
Supt. of Foreign Missions, Rev. L. M. Reese
Supt. of Youth, Mr. Franklin Creswell

PERIODICAL

The Gospel Messenger (m), 3888 Fayetteville Hwy., Griffin, GA 30223, James H. Martin, Ed.

Conservative Baptist Association of America

Organized May 17, 1947, at Atlantic City, New Jersey. The Old and New Testaments are regarded as the divinely inspired Word of God and are therefore infallible and of supreme authority. Each local church is independent and autonomous, and free from ecclesiastical or political authority.

GENERAL ORGANIZATION

Meets annually
Headquarters: Geneva Rd., Box 66, Wheaton, IL 60187. Tel. (312) 653-5350

OFFICERS

Pres., Rev. Robert C. Becker, 1 Washington St., Bloomfield, NJ 07003
Sec., Rev. Murray Hicks, 5532 Wooddale Ave., S., Edina, MN 55424
Treas., Dr. Kenneth Stephens, 2500 N. Scottdale Rd., Scottdale, AZ 05257
Eastern Vice-Pres., Rev. Glenn Blossom, P.O. Box 156, Dresher, PA 19025
Central Vice-Pres., Rev. Douglas B. Brown, 28301 Middlebelt Rd., Farmington Hills, MI 48018
Northwestern Vice-Pres., Rev. Roy Kooshian, 2004 Siskiyou Blvd., Ashland, OR 97520
Southwestern Vice-Pres., Rev. Thomas Geshay, 736 W. Islay St., Santa Barbara, CA 93101
Gen. Dir., Dr. Russell A. Shive, Box 66, Wheaton, IL 60187. Tel. (312) 653-5350

OTHER ORGANIZATIONS

Conservative Baptist Foreign Mission Society: Box 5, Wheaton, IL 60187, Gen. Dir., Dr. Warren W. Webster
Conservative Baptist Home Mission Society: Box 828, Wheaton, IL 60187, Gen. Dir., Dr. Rufus Jones

PERIODICAL

Conservative Baptist, P.O. Box 999, Wheaton, IL 60187

Conservative Congregational Christian Conference

The Conference was founded in Chicago, Illinois, in 1948 by a group of Congregational Christian Churches and ministers in order to maintain the historic biblical doctrines and the autonomous polity of the Congregational way. Present membership includes churches from varied denominational backgrounds.

Churches: 130 Inclusive Membership: 22,750 Sunday or Sabbath Schools: 124 Total Enrollment: 12,333 Ordained Clergy: 364

GENERAL ORGANIZATION

General Conference: annual.
Headquarters: 25W626 St. Charles Rd., Wheaton, IL 60187, Tel. (312) 682-3110

OFFICERS

Pres., Rev. George S. Buhl, 207 Main St., Kingston, MA 02364
1st Vice-Pres., Rev. Bruce R. Brown, 1831 El Camino Real, Encinitas, CA 92024

2nd Vice-Pres., Rev. Lynn Scovil, 318 Church Ave., Oshkosh, WI 54901
Conf. Sec., Rev. Samuel T. Hemberger, 235 N. Mill Rd., #316-B, Addison, IL 60101
Treas., William Nygren, 89 Morningside, St. Paul, MN 55119
Recording Sec., Rev. Clarence Schultz, 1916 Lackawanna, Superior, WI 54880
Editor, Rev. Gary Pollitt, 4941 N. Knowle Ave., Portland, OR 97217
Historian, Mr. Glenn Dawson, 141 Anita Dr., Pasadena, CA 91105

Coptic Orthodox Church

This body is part of the ancient Coptic Orthodox Church of Egypt which is currently headed by His Holiness Pope Shenouda III. In the United States many parishes have been organized consisting of Egyptian immigrants to the United States. Copts exist outside of Egypt in Ethiopia, Europe, Asia, Australia, Canada, and the United States. In all, the world Coptic community is estimated at 8 million, the vast majority being located in Egypt, however.

CORRESPONDENT

Archpriest Fr. Gabriel Abdelsayed, 427 West Side Ave., Jersey City, NJ 07304

Cumberland Presbyterian Church

An outgrowth of the revival of religion in 1800, the Cumberland Presbytery was organized February 4, 1810, in Dickson County, Tennessee, by three Presbyterian ministers. Revs. Finis Ewing, Samuel King, and Samuel McAdow, who rejected the doctrine of predestination as taught in the Westminster Confession of Faith. The first synod was constituted in 1813. The General Assembly was constituted at Princeton, KY in 1829. A union with the Presbyterian Church, U.S.A., in 1906 was only partially successful and the Cumberland Presbyterian Church continued as a distinct communion.

Churches: 850 Inclusive Membership: 93,268 Sunday or Sabbath Schools: 850 Total Enrollment: 49,924 Ordained Clergy: 706

GENERAL ORGANIZATION

General Assembly: (Next meeting June 16-20, 1980, Evansville, TN)

OFFICERS

Mod., James E. Gilbert, P.O. Drawer G, Denton, TX 76201
Stated Clk., T. V. Warnick, Box 4149, Memphis, TN 38104

INSTITUTIONS

Cumberland Presbyterian Center, 1978 Union Ave., Memphis, TN 38104. Box 40149 (Headquarters for program boards, Frontier Press, and resource center.)

BOARDS

Board of Christian Education: Exec. Sec., Rev. Harold Davis, Box 4149, Memphis TN 38104
Board of Missions: Exec. Sec., Rev. Joe R. Matlock, Box 4149, Memphis, TN 38104
Board of Finance: Exec. Sec., Mr. Eugene Warren, Box 4149, Memphis, TN 38104

PERIODICALS

The Cumberland Presbyterian (bi-w), Box 4149, Memphis, TN 38104, C. Ray Dobbins, Ed.
The Missionary Messenger (m), Box 4149, Memphis, TN 38104, Rev. Dudley Condron, Ed.
Church School Literature (q). Bd. of Christian Ed., Box 4149, Memphis, TN 38104

Duck River (and Kindred) Associations of Baptists

A group of Baptist associations found in Tennessee, Alabama, Georgia, Kentucky, and Mississippi.

GENERAL ORGANIZATION

Meets yearly, in October

OFFICERS

Duck River Association: Mod., Elder A. B. Ray, 500 Ragan St. Tullahoma, TN 37388; Clk., Elder Marvin Davenport, Auburntown, TN
General Association: Mod., Elder Calvin Jenkins, 607 State Line Rd., Rossville, GA 30741; Clk., Elder James F. Patton, Morrison, TN 37357

Elim Fellowship

The Elim Fellowship, a Pentecostal Body, established in 1947, is an outgrowth of the Elim Ministerial Fellowship, which was formed in 1933.

It is an association of churches, ministers and missionaries seeking to serve the whole Body of Christ. It is of Pentecostal conviction and charismatic orientation providing credentials and counsel and encouraging fellowship among local churches. Elim Fellowship sponsors leadership seminars at home and abroad and serves as a transdenominational agency sending missionaries and other personnel to work with national movements.

GENERAL ORGANIZATION

Annual Representative Assemblies; Board of Administration meets biannually and council of Elders meets bimonthly.

OFFICERS

Gen. Chpsn., Carlton Spencer, Elim Fellowship, Lima, NY 14485. Tel. (716) 582-1230
Gen. Vice-Chpsn., George Veach, 1303 Main Mt., Avocoa, PA 18641
Gen. Sec., Bernard Evans, 7240 Park St., Lima, NY 14485
Gen. Treas., Ronald Taylor, 407 Kettering Dr., Columbia, SC 29210

The Episcopal Church

This body entered the colonies with the earliest settlers (Jamestown, Virginia, 1607), as the Church of England. It became autonomous as the Protestant Episcopal Church in the U.S.A. and adopted that name in 1789. It is an integral part of the Anglican Communion. In 1967 the General Convention adopted "The Episcopal Church" as an alternate name for the Church.

EPISCOPAL CHURCH

Churches: 7,009 Inclusive Membership: 2,815,359 Sunday or Sabbath Schools: N. R. Total Enrollment: 574,693 Ordained Clergy: 12,310

GENERAL ORGANIZATIONS

General Convention: Triennial (Next meeting, 1982)
Headquarters: 815 Second Ave., New York, NY 10017. Tel. (212) 867-8400

OFFICERS OF THE GENERAL CONVENTION

Presiding-Bishop, Rt. Rev. John M. Allin. Sec. Ho. of Bishops, Rt. Rev. Scott Field Bailey, Box 6885, San Antonio, TX 78209
Pres. Ho. of Deputies, Dr. Charles R. Lawrence, 34 Dogwood La., Pomona, NY 10970
Exec. Sec. Gen. Conv., Rev. James R. Gundrum
Treas.: Gen. Conv., Kenneth W. Miller

THE EXECUTIVE COUNCIL

Pres., and Chpsn, Rt. Rev. John M. Allin
Vice Chpsn, Dr. Charles R. Lawrence
Treas., Matthew Costigan
Sec., Rev. Canon James R. Gundrum

"The Domestic and Foreign Missionary Society of PECUSA"

Pres., Presiding Bishop; Vice Pres., Rt. Rev. Milton L. Wood; Treas., Matthew Costigan; Sec., Exec. Council, Rev. Canon James R. Gundrum; Board of Directors, Exec. Council

EPISCOPAL CHURCH CENTER

Episcopal Church Center, 815 Second Ave., New York, NY 10017. Tel. (212) 867-8400

Office of the Presiding Bishop:

Presiding Bishop, Rt. Rev. John M. Allin; Asst. to the Presiding Bishop, Rev. Canon Richard J. Anderson; Suffragan Bishop for Chaplaincies to Military, Prisons, and Hospitals, Rt. Rev. Charles L. Burgreen; Asst. to Bishop Burgreen, Rev. James L. Jones; Suffragan Bishop for Europe and the Diaspora, Rt. Rev. John M. Krumm; Treas, Matthew Costigan; Sec., Rev. Canon James R. Gundrum; Exec. for Admin., Rt. Rev. Milton L. Wood; Admin. Asst. to the Presiding Bishop, Mrs. Nancy Marvel

EPISCOPAL CHURCH CENTER STAFF

Education for Mission and Ministry:

Exec. for Education and Ministry, Rt. Rev. Richard B. Martin; Adm. Asst. to Bishop Martin, Mrs. Ruby H. Miller; Field Officer for the Development of Ministry, Rt. Rev. Elliot L. Sorge; Exec. Dir., Clergy Deployment Office, Rev. Roddey Reid, Jr.; Assoc. Dir., Clergy Deployment William A. Thompson; Rel. Edu. Coordinator, Rev. David W. Perry; Assoc. Coord., Rel. Edu., Rev. Frederick J. Howard; Youth and College Ministries Coord., Ms. Elizabeth Crawford; Youth and College Ministries Coord., Rev. James. J. McNamee; Lay Ministries Staff Officer, D. Barry Menuez; Coord. for Women's Ministries, Dr. Anne Harrison; Evangelism and Renewal Officer, Rev. A. Wayne Schwab; Exec. Dir., Bd. for Theol. Edu., Dr. Fredrica H. Thompsett; Dir. Committee on Pastoral Development, Rt. Rev. David E. Richards; Suffragan Bishop for Chaplaincies to Military, Prisons, and Hospitals, Rt. Rev. Charles L. Burgreen

National Mission in Church and Society:

Exec. for National Mission in Church and Society, Mrs. Richard R. Emery; Staff Officer for Housing and Training, Howard Quander; Staff Officer for Coalition for Human Needs Commission, Rev. Earl A. Neil; Staff Officer for Hunger Program, Rev. Charles A. Cesaretti; Staff Officer for Social and Specialized Ministries, Woodrow S. Carter, Sr.; Staff Officer for Black Ministries, Rev. Franklin D. Turner; Staff Officer for Indian Ministries, Steve Charleston; Staff Officer for Hispanic Ministries, Rev. Herbert Arrunategui; Staff Officer for Asiamerica Ministries, Rev. Winston W. Ching; Staff Officer for Public Issues, ———; Staff Officer for National Mission Development, Rev. Richard E. Gary; Assoc. Ecumenical Officer for Washington Affairs, Rev. William L. Weiler

World Mission in Church and Society:

Exec. for World Mission in Church and Society, Rev. Samuel Van Culin, Jr.; Exec. Asst., Mrs. Jeannie A. Willis; Mission Information Officer, Rev. Onell A. Soto; Assoc. Ecumenical Officer, Rev. William A. Norgren; Staff Officer, Overseas personnel and Scholarships, Rev. David B. Birney, IV; Dir., Presiding Bishop's Fund for World Relief, Rev. Samir J. Habiby; Asst. Dir., Presiding Bishop's Fund for World Relief, Marion E. Morey; Immigration and Refugee Administrator, Mrs. Isis E. Brown; United Thank Offering Coord., Judith M. Gillespie; Volunteers for Mission, Rev. David B. Birney, IV; Suffragan Bishop for Europe and the Diaspora, Rt. Rev. John M. Krumm; Suffragan Bishop for the Episcopal Church in Micronesia, Rt. Rev. Charles L. Burgreen

Stewardship/Development:

Exec. for Stewardship/Development and Venture in Mission, Rev. Dr. Thomas H. Carson, Jr.; Stewardship Officer, Rev. Henry J. Free, Jr.; Admin. Asst. Mrs. Laura E. Wright

Communication:

Exec. For Communication, John C. Goodbody; Assoc. Communication Officer, Mrs. Robert P. Andersen; Press Officer, Walter Boyd; Asst. Press Officer, Rev. William D. Dearnaley; Broadcast Representative, Sonia J. Francis; Editorial Coord., Frank L. Tedeschi

Finance:

Treas. Matthew Costigan; Asst. Treas. Louis H. Gill; Controller, Robert E. Brown; Asst. Controller, Paul D. Urso; Internal Auditor, Thomas C. Kunik; Statistical Officer, Rev. John A. Schultz; Clerical Supervisor, Mrs. Barbara Wilson; Data Processing Supervisor, Mrs. Barbara Price

Administration:

Exec. for Admin., Rt. Rev. Milton L. Wood; Service Manager, Terence Adair; Personnel Officer, Barbara Quinn; Insurance and Benefits Admin., Lloyd I. Jones

General Convention Executive Office:

Exec. Officer, Rev. Canon James R. Gundrum; Sec. and Registrar, Rev. Canon James R. Gundrum; Treas. Kenneth W. Miller; Admin. Asst. and Asst. Sec.-Treas., Rev. John A. Schultz

OFFICIAL AGENCIES

Church Pension Fund and Affiliates: Pres., Robert A. Robinson, 800 Second Ave., New York, NY 10017
Episcopal Church Building Fund: Exec., Rev. Sherrill Scales, Jr., 815 Second Ave., New York, NY 10017, Tel. (212) 697-6066
The Episcopal Church Foundation: Exec., Frederick L. Redpath, 815 Second Ave., New York, NY 10017. Tel. (212) 698-2858
The Episcopalian: Ed., Henry L. McCorkle, 1930 Chestnut St., Philadelphia, PA 19103
Forward Movement Publication: Dir.-Ed., Rev. Charles H. Long, Jr., 412 Sycamore St., Cincinnati, OH 45202. Tel. (513) 721-6659
Historical Society of the Episcopal Church: Archivist, V. Nelle Bellamy; Ed., John F. Woolverton, P.O. Box 2247, Austin, TX 78768. Tel. (212) 557-0500
Seabury Press, Inc.: Pres., Werner Mark Linz, 815 Second Ave., New York, NY 10017. Tel. (212) 557-0500

PUBLICATIONS

The Episcopalian (m), 1930 Chestnut St., Philadelphia, PA 19103, Henry L. McCorkle, Ed.
Forward Movement Publications: 412 Sycamore St., Cincinnati, OH 45202, Ed., Rev. Charles H. Long
The Living Church (w), 407 E. Michigan St., Milwaukee, WI 53202, Rev. H. Boone Porter, Jr. Ed.
Historical Magazine (q), Box 2247, Austin, TX 78705, Rev. J. F. Woolverton, Ed.
The Churchman (m), 1074 23rd Ave., N., St. Petersburg, FL 33704, Edna Ruth Johnson
Anglican Theol. Review (q), 600 Haven St., Evanston, IL 60201, Rev. W. Taylor Stevenson, Seabury-Western Theological Seminary, 2122 Sheridan Rd., Evanston, IL 60201
Pan-Anglican (occ.), 1335 Asylum Ave., Hartford, CT 06105.
Seabury Press, Inc., Pres., Werner Mark Linz, 815 Second Ave., New York, NY 10017
Cathedral Age, Mt. St. Albans, Washington, DC, Nancy Montgomery, Ed.
The Episcopal Church Annual, 78 Danbury Rd., Wilton, CT 06897, Margaret Sheriff, Ed.
Episcopal Clerical Directory, Church Pension Fund, 800 Second Ave., New York, NY 10017
St. Luke's Journal of Theology, The School of Theology, University of South, Sewanee, TN 37375

ACTIVE BISHOPS IN THE U.S.A.

(Note: CO, Coadjutor; S, Suffragan)
(Address: Right Reverend)
Headquarters Staff: Presiding Bishop, John M. Allin; Exec. Vice-Pres., Rt. Rev. Milton L. Wood; Exec. for Mission and Ministry, Rt. Rev. Richard B. Martin: Field Officer, Council for the Development of Ministry, Rt. Rev. Elliott L. Sorge; Suffragan Bishop for Chaplaincies to Military, Prisons and Hospitals, Rt. Rev. Charles L. Burgreen, 815 Second Ave., New York, NY 10017
Alabama, Furman C. Stough, 521 N. 20th St., Birmingham 35203
Alaska, David R. Cochran, Box 441, Fairbanks 99707
Albany, Rt. Rev. Wilbur E. Hogg 62 S. Swan St., Albany, NY 12210.
Arizona, Joseph T. Heistand, 110 W. Roosevelt St., Phoenix 85003
Arkansas, Christoph Keller, 300 W. 17th St., P.O. Box 6120, Little Rock 72206
Atlanta, Bennett J. Sims, C. Judson Child Jr., (S), 2744 Peachtree Rd., N.W., Atlanta, GA 30305.
Bethlehem, Lloyd E. Gressle, 826 Delaware Ave., Bethlehem, PA 18015
California, C. Kilmer Myers, William E. Swing (CO), 1055 Taylor St., San Francisco 94108
Central Florida, William H. Folwell, 324 N. Interlachen Ave., Box 790, Winter Park, 32789
Central Gulf Coast, George M. Murray, 3809 Old Shell Rd., P.O. Box 8395, Mobile, AL 36608
Central N.Y. Ned Cole, Jr., 310 Montgomery St., Syracuse 13203
Central Pennsylvania, Dean T. Stevenson, 221 N. Front St., Harrisburg 17101, P.O. Box W, Harrisburg 17108
Chicago, James W. Montgomery, Quintin E. Primo, Jr. (S), 65 E. Huron St., Chicago, IL 60611
Colorado, William C. Frey, P.O. Box M, Capitol Hill Sta., Denver 80218
Connecticut, Morgan Porteus, Arthur E. Walmsley (CO), 1335 Asylum Ave., Hartford 06105.
Dallas, A. Donald Davies; Robert E. Terwilliger (S), 1630 Garrett St., Dallas, TX 75206
Delaware, William Hawley Clark, 2020 Tatnall St., Wilmington 19802
East Carolina, Hunley A. Elebash, Brice S. Sanders (CO), 305 S. 3rd St., Wilmington, NC 28401
Eastern Oregon, William B. Spofford, Jr., 1336 West Glacier, Redmond, OR
Easton, Moultrie Moore, P.O. Box 1027, Easton, MD 21601
Eau Claire, Stanley H. Atkins, 510 S. Farwell St., Eau Claire, WI 54701
Erie, Donald J. Davis, 145 W. 6th St., Erie, PA 16501
Florida, Frank S. Cerveny, 325 Market St., Jacksonville 32202
Fond du Lac, Wm. H. Brady, P.O. Box 149, Fond du Lac, WI 54935
Georgia, G. Paul Reeves, 611 East Bay St., Savannah 31401
Hawaii, Edmond L. Browning, Queen Emma Square, Honolulu 96813
Idaho, Hanford L. King, Box 936, Boise 83701
Indianapolis, Edward W. Jones, 1100 W. 42nd St., Indianapolis 46208
Iowa, Walter C. Righter, 225 37th St., Des Moines 50312
Kansas, Edward C. Turner, Bethany Place, Topeka 66612
Kentucky, David B. Reed, 421 S. 2nd St., Louisville 40202
Lexington, Addison Hosea, 530 Sayre Ave., Lexington, KY 40508
Long Island, Robert Campbell Witcher, 36 Cathedral Ave., Garden City, NY 11530
Los Angeles, Robert C. Rusack, 1220 W. 4th St., Los Angeles, CA 90017
Louisiana, James Barrow Brown, P.O. Box 15719, New Orleans 70175
Maine, Frederick B. Wolf, 143 State St., Portland 04101
Maryland, David Leighton, Sr., 105 W. Monument St., Baltimore 21230; William J. Cox (S), 106 W. Church St., Frederick 21701
Massachusetts, John B. Coburn, 1 Joy St., Boston 02108; Morris F. Arnold (S), 1 Joy St., Boston 02108
Michigan, H. Coleman McGehee, Jr., H. Irving Mayson (S), 4800 Woodward Ave., Detroit 48201
Milwaukee, Charles T. Gaskell, 804 E. Juneau Ave., Milwaukee, WI 53202
Minnesota, Robert M. Anderson, 309 Clifton Ave., Minneapolis 55403
Mississippi, Duncan M. Gray, Jr., P.O. Box 1636, Jackson 39205
Missouri, William Augustus Jones, Jr., 1210 Locust St., St. Louis 63103
Montana, Jackson E. Gilliam, 303 Horsky Block, Helena 59601

Nebraska, James Daniel Warner, 200 N. 62nd St., Omaha 68132

Nevada, Wesley Frensdorff, 2930 W. 7th St., Reno 89503

New Hampshire, Philip A. Smith, 63 Green St., Concord 03301

New Jersey, Albert W. Van Duzer, G. P. Mellick Belshaw (S), 808 W. State St., Trenton 08618

New York, Paul Moore, Jr., J. Stuart Wetmore (S), Walter D. Dennis (S), 1047 Amsterdam Ave., New York 10025

Newark, John Shelby Spong, 24 Rector St., Newark, NJ 07102

North Carolina, Thomas A. Fraser, Jr.; 201 St. Alban's, P.O. Box 17025, Raleigh 27609

North Dakota, Harold A. Hopkins Jr., 809 8th Ave. S., Fargo 58102

Northern California, John L. Thompson, III, 1322 27th St., P.O. Box 161268, Sacramento 95816

Northern Indiana, William C. R. Sheridan, 117 No. Lafayette Blvd., South Bend 46601

Northern Michigan, William Arthur Dimmick, 131 E. Ridge St., Marquette 49855

Northwest Texas, Willis R. Henton, Texas Commerce Bank Bldg., Ste. 506, 1314 Ave. K, P.O. Box 1067, Lubbock 79408

Ohio, John H. Burt, 2230 Euclid Ave., Cleveland, 44115

Oklahoma, Gerald N. McAllister P. O. Box 1098; Frederick W. Putnam, Jr. (S)

Olympia, Robert H. Cochrane, 1551 Tenth Ave., East, Seattle, WA 98102

Oregon, Matthew P. Bigliardi, Hal R. Gross (S), 11800 S. W. Military La., Portland 97219, P.O. Box 467, Portland, OR 97034

Panama, Lemuel B. Shirley (MB), Box R, Balboa, Panama.

Pennsylvania, Lyman C. Ogilby, 1700 Market St., Ste. 1600, Philadelphia 19103

Pittsburgh, Robert B. Appleyard, 325 Oliver Ave., Pittsburgh, PA 15222

Puerto Rico, Francisco Reus-Froylán (MB), P.O. Box C, Saint Just 00750

Quincy, Donald J. Parsons, 3601 N. North St., Peoria, IL 61604

Rhode Island, George Hunt, 275 N. Main St., Providence 02903

Rio Grande, Richard M. Trelease, Jr., 120 Vassar S.E., Ste. 1-B, P.O. Box 4130 Albuquerque, NM 87106

Rochester, Robert R. Spears, Jr., 935 East Ave., Rochester, NY 14607

San Diego, Robert M. Wolterstorff, St. Paul's Church, 2728 6th Ave., San Diego, CA 92103

San Joaquin, Victor M. Rivera, 4159 East Dakota, Fresno, CA 93726

South Carolina, Gray Temple, 1020 King St., Drawer 2127, Charleston 29403

South Dakota, Walter H. Jones, 200 W. 18th St., P.O. Box 517, Sioux Falls 57101

Southeast Florida, Calvin O. Schofield, Jr., 525 NE 15 St., Miami 33132.

Southern Ohio, William G. Black, 412 Sycamore St., Cincinnati 45202

Southern Virginia, Claude Charles Vaché, 600 Talbot Hill Rd., Norfolk 23505

Southwest Florida, Emerson Paul Hayes, Box 20899, St. Petersburg 33742

Southwestern Virginia, A Heath Light, P.O. Box 2068, Roanoke 24009

Spokane, Leigh Allen Wallace, Jr., 245 E. 13th Ave., Spokane 99202

Springfield, Albert W. Hillestad, 821 S. 2nd St., Springfield, IL 62704

Tennessee, William E. Sanders, Box 3807, Knoxville 37917; William F. Gates, Jr. (S), 692 Poplar Ave., Memphis 38105

Texas, J. Milton Richardson, Roger H. Cilley (S), 520 San Jacinto St., Houston 77002

Upper South Carolina, William A. Beckham, P.O. Box 1789, Columbia 29202

Utah, E. Otis Charles, 231 E. First St., South, Salt Lake City 84111

Vermont, Robert S. Kerr, Rock Point, Burlington 05401

Virgin Islands, Edward M. Turner (MB), P.O. Box 1589, St. Thomas, U.S. Virgin Islands 00801

Virginia, Robert B. Hall 110 W. Franklin St., Richmond 23220

Washington, John T. Walker, Mt. St. Alban, Washington, DC 20016

West Missouri, Arthur Vogel, 415 W. 13th St., P.O. Box 23216, Kansas City 64141

West Texas, Scott Field Bailey, P.O. Box 6885, San Antonio 78209

West Virginia, Robert P. Atkinson 1608 Virginia St. E., Charleston, 25311

Western Kansas, William Davidson, 142 S. 8th St., P.O. Box 1383, Salina 67401

Western Massachusetts, Alexander D. Stewart, 37 Chestnut St., Springfield 01103

Western Michigan, Charles E. Bennison, 2600 Vincent Ave., Kalamazoo 49001

Western New York, Harold B. Robinson, 1114 Delaware Ave., Buffalo 14209

Western North Carolina, William G. Weinhauer, P.O. Box 368, Black Mountain 28711

Wyoming, Bob Gordon Jones, 104 S. 4th St., Box 1007, Laramie 82070

American Churches in Europe—Jurisdiction, John M. Krumm, The American Cathedral, 23 Avenue Georges V, 75008, Paris, France

Navajo Area Mission, Frederick W. Putnam, P.O. Box 720, Farmington, NM 47401

The Estonian Evangelical Lutheran Church

The Estonian Evangelical Lutheran Church (EELC) was founded in 1917 in Estonia and reorganized in Sweden in 1944. The teachings of the EELC are based on the Old and New Testaments, explained through the Apostolic, Nicean and Athanasian confessions, the unaltered Confession of Augsburg and other teachings found in the Book of Concord.

Churches: 25 Inclusive Membership: 8,548 Sunday or Sabbath Schools: N.R. Total Enrollment: N.R. Ordained Clergy: 28

GENERAL ORGANIZATION

Executive Board headed by the Archbishop, Consisterium, Auditing Committee and District Conference.

Headquarters: Wallingatan 32, Box 45074, 10430 Stockholm 45, Sweden.

OFFICERS

Bishop in North America, Rev. Karl Raudsepp, Box 291, Jordan Station, Ontario LOR 1SO. Tel. (416) 562-7438.

Assts. to the Bishop: Dr. Arthur Voobus, 230 So. Euclid Ave., Oak Park, IL 60302. Tel. (312) 386-6274; Dean Oscar Puhm, 84 Dinnick Crescent, Toronto, Ontario M4N 1L8. Tel. (416) 483-4103

PERIODICAL

Eesti Kirik (m), Mandelblomsgatan 15, S-722 25 Vasteras, Sweden. Richard Koolmeister, Ed.

Ethical Culture Movement

A national federation of Ethical Humanist Societies—religious and educational fellowships based on ethics, believing in the worth, dignity, and fine potentialities of the individual, encouraging freedom of thought, committed to the democratic ideal and method, issuing in social action.

Churches: 21 Inclusive Membership: 5,000 Sunday or Sabbath Schools: 19 Total Enrollment: 539 Ordained Clergy: 27

AMERICAN ETHICAL UNION

Assembly: annual (April)
Headquarters: 2 West 64th St., New York, NY 10023. Tel. (212) 873-6500

OFFICERS

Pres., Rose R. Elbert
Vice-Pres., Mark Huber
Treas., Richard Lynn
Sec., Annabelle Glasser
Exec. Dir., Jean S. Kotkin

ORGANIZATIONS

National Ethical Youth Organization (NEYO), Dirs., Donna Kerner, Jon Kerner
National Leaders Council, Chpsn., Don Montagna
National Women's Conference, Pres., Lottie Bernard
Encampment for Citizenship, Exec. Dir., Robert Lubetsky
A.E.U. Ecology Center, Mgr., Robert Kirschner
A.E.U. Race Commission, Chpsn., Robert M. Stein
International Humanist & Ethical Union, Representative, Sidney H. Scheuer
Washington Office for Social Concern, Dir., Raymond Nathan
Rel. Ed. Dir., Emily Thorn

The Evangelical Church of North America

This body was formed in Portland, Oregon in June, 1968. It consists of congregations which declined to enter The United Methodist Church, which resulted from a merger of the Evangelical United Brethren and The Methodist Church. The Evangelical Church of North America incorporated congregations from across the nation including those of the former Holiness Methodist Church. The church is Arminian-Wesleyan in doctrinal orientation.

Churches: 138 Inclusive Membership: 12,210 Sunday or Sabbath Schools: 138 Total Enrollment: 15,398 Ordained Clergy: 251

GENERAL ORGANIZATION

Council of Superintendents which has the power to integrate program and to recommend policy. Such recommendations require the approval of the annual conferences.

OFFICERS

Gen. Supt., Dr. V.A. Ballantyne, 8719 John Dr., Indianapolis, IN 46234. Tel. (317) 297-4379
Chpsn., Council of Superintendents, Dr. George K. Millen, 18121 S. E. River Rd., Portland, OR 97222. Tel. (503) 659-5622

PERIODICAL

The Evangelical Advocate (m), 4200 S.E. Jennings Ave., Portland, OR 97222, Rev. John F. Sills, Ed.

Evangelical Congregational Church

This denomination had its beginning in the movement known as the Evangelical Association, organized by Jacob Albright in the early nineteenth century. In 1891 a division occurred in the Evangelical Association, which resulted in the organization of the United Evangelical Church in 1894. An attempt to heal this division was made in 1922, but a portion of the United Evangelical Church was not satisfied with the plan of merger and remained apart, taking the above name in 1928. This denomination is Arminian in doctrine, evangelistic in spirit, and Methodistic in church government, with congregational ownership of local church property.

Churches: 161 Inclusive Membership: 28,459 Sunday or Sabbath Schools: 160 Total Enrollment: 23,999 Ordained Clergy: 186

GENERAL ORGANIZATION

General Conference: quadrennial. (Next meeting, Sept. 1982)
Headquarters: Church Center, 100 W. Park Ave., Myerstown, PA 17067
Presiding Bishop, Rev. J. E. Moyer, Myerstown, PA 17067

OFFICERS

1st Vice-Chpsn., Rev. H. H. Scanlin, 1409 N. 18th St., Allentown, PA 18104
2nd Vice-Chpsn., Rev. J. A. Smith 27 N. 11th St., Akron, PA 17501
Sec., Rev. A. E. Anderson, 1935 Thronapple St., Akron, OH 44301
Asst. Sec's.: Rev. R. T. Baily, Palmyra, PA and Rev. D. M. Ray, Winnebago, IL 61088
Stat. Sec., Rev. C. C. Reeder, Myerstown, PA 17067
Treas., Howard E. Suhr, Myerstown, PA 17067
Sec., of Missions: Rev. R. A. Cattermole, 100 W. Park Ave., Myerstown, PA 17067
Supt., E. C. Church Retirement Village, Rev. Franklin H. Schock, Myerstown, PA 17067

OTHER ORGANIZATIONS

Administrative Council: Chpsn., Bishop J. E. Moyer; Vice-Chpsn., Rev. D. P. Heil; Sec., Rev. D. R. Wolfe, Treas., Mr. H. Suhr
Board of Church Extension: Pres., Dr. J. D. Yoder, Meyerstown, PA; Sec., Rev. C. C. Reeder, Myerstown, PA
Board of Missions: Pres., Dr. H. H. Scanlin; Sec., R. T. Bailey
Board of Publication: Pres., Rev. R. T. Bailey, Palmyra, PA; Sec., Rev. R. T. Haupt, Bethlehem, PA
Board of Christian Education: Pres., D. G. Roof; Sec., Mrs. Mary Stringer, Girard, OH
Board of Pensions: Pres., Rev. D. P. Heil, Allentown, PA; Sec., Dr. J. D. Yoder, Myerstown, PA

PERIODICALS

The United Evangelical (m), The New Illustrator (q); Venture Series, S.S. lessons (q); Rev. R. B. Kuntz, Ed. Pub., Church Center Press, Myerstown, PA

The Evangelical Covenant Church of America

This church has its roots in historical Christianity as it emerged in the Protestant Reformation in the biblical instruction of the Lutheran State Church of Sweden, and in the spiritual awakenings of the nineteenth century. The denomination was organized on February 20, 1885, in Chicago. Prior to 1957 it was named the Evangelical Mission Covenant Church of America.

Churches: 520 Inclusive Membership: 74,678 Sunday or Sabbath Schools: 509 Total Enrollment: 64,577 Ordained Clergy: 751

EVANGELICAL FREE CHURCH OF AMERICA

GENERAL ORGANIZATION

General Conference: annual (June 10-13, 1980, North Park College & Theological Seminary, Chicago, IL
Headquarters: 5101 N. Francisco Ave., Chicago, IL 60625

OFFICERS

Pres., Dr. Milton B. Engebretson, Chicago, IL
Vice-Pres., Rev. Norbert E. Johnson, Omaha, NE
Sec., Rev. Clifford W. Bjorklund, Chicago, IL
Treas., Dr. Gordon A. Bengtson, Dassel, MN

ADMINISTRATIVE BOARDS

Board of Christian Education: Chpsn., Mrs. Myrtle A. Erickson; Sec., Mrs. Kathleen Pearson; Exec. Sec., Christian Education, Rev. David S. Noreen
Board of Evangelism: Chpsn., Rev. Albert C. Magnuson; Sec., Mrs. Marilyn Peterson; Exec. Sec., Rev. Randolph J. Klassen
Board of Home Mission: Chpsn., Rev. Ernest L. Hansen; Sec., Rev. David L. Elowson; Exec. Sec., Home Mission, Dr. Robert C. Larson
Board of the Ministry: Chpsn., Rev. Vernon A. Anderson; Sec., Rev. Paul E. Sparrman; Exec. Sec. of the Ministry, Rev. Earl M. VanDerVeer.
Board of Pensions: Chpsn. Donald E. Waklquist; Sec. & Dir. of Pensions, Rev. Earl M. VanDerVeer
Board of Publication: Chpsn., ———; Sec., Rev. John S. Benson; Exec. Sec. of Publications, Rev. James R. Hawkinson
Board of Women's Work: Chpsn, Mrs. Betty Carlson; Sec., Mrs. Bette Vetvick; Exec. Dir., Erma G. Chinander
Board of World Mission: Chpsn., Betty J. Nelson; Sec., Dr. Robert P. Stromberg, Exec. Sec., World Mission, Rev. Raymond Dahlberg
Board of Benevolence: Chpsn., Dr. Paul W. Brandel; Sec., Norman W. Nelson; Pres, of Covenant Benevolent Institutions, Nils G. Axelson, 5145 N. California Ave., Chicago, IL 60625
Board of Directors of North Park College and Theological Seminary: Chpsn., Rev. Arthur A. R. Nelson; Sec., Ivan M. Johnson; Pres., ———, 5125 N. Spaulding Ave., Chicago, IL 60625

PERIODICALS

Covenant Companion (s-m), Chicago, IL Rev. James R. Hawkinson, Ed.
Covenant Quarterly (q), Chicago, IL, Dr. F. Burton Nelson, Ed.
Covenant Home Altar (q), Chicago, IL, Rev. James R. Hawkinson, Ed.

The Evangelical Free Church of America

Organized in Boone, Iowa, in the 1880s, as the Swedish Evangelical Free Mission; name later changed to above. The Evangelical Free Church Association merged with this group in June, 1950. The merged body is known as the Evangelical Free Church of America.

GENERAL ORGANIZATION

Conference: annual
Headquarters: 1515 E. 66 St., Minneapolis, MN 55423. Tel. (612) 866-3343

OFFICERS

Pres., Dr. Thomas A. McDill, 1515 E. 66th St., Minneapolis, MN 55423
Pres. Emeritus, Dr. Arnold T. Olson, 6126 Park Ave., Minneapolis, MN 55417
Mod., E. James Rodine, 2709 Gerald Ave., North, St. Paul, MN 55109
Vice-Mod., Rev. Clarence R. Balmer, 4204—75th Des Moines, IA 50322
Gen. Sec., Roland O. Sollie, 4201-13th Ave., S. Minneapolis, MN 55407
Vice-Sec., Rev. James R. Leonard, 201 Charles St., Muscatine, IA 52761
Treas., James A. Hagman, 1895 Hampshire Lane, N., Minneapolis, MN 55427
Fin. Sec., Carlyle D. Jacobson, 5700 Johnson Dr., Minneapolis, MN 55436
Sec. of Overseas Missions, Dr. Lester Westlund, 1515 E. 66th St., Minneapolis, MN 55423
Sec. of Church Ministries, Rev. R. Dean Smith, 1515 E. 66th St., Minneapolis, MN 55423
Sec. of Communication, Dr. Edwin L. Groenhoff, 1515 E. 66th St., Minneapolis, MN 55423

PERIODICAL

Evangelical Beacon (bi-m), 1515 E. 66 St., Minneapolis, MN 55423 George Keck, Ed.

Evangelical Friends Alliance

Formed in 1965 as an organization representing one corporate step of denominational unity, brought about as a result of several movements of spiritual renewal within the Society of Friends. These movements are: (1) the general evangelical renewal within Christianity, (2) the New scholarly recognition of the evangelical nature of seventeenth century Quakerism, and (3) the Association of Evangelical Friends.

The EFA is conservative in theology and makes use of local pastors. Sunday morning worship includes singing, Scripture reading, a period of open worship—usually—and a sermon by the pastor.

YEARLY MEETINGS

Rocky Mountain YM, Arthur James Ellis, 3343 E. 114th Dr., Thornton, CO 80233
Kansas YM, David Smitherman, 2018 Maple, Wichita, KS 67213
Northwest YM, Richard H. Beebe, Box 190, Newberg, OR 97132
Evangelical Friends Church, Eastern Region, Galen Weingart, 2462 Easton St., NE, North Canton, OH 44721

Evangelical Lutheran Church in America (Eielsen Synod)

A small Lutheran body, the first Norwegian synod in the U.S., taking its name from its organizer, Elling Eielsen, in 1846.

GENERAL ORGANIZATION

Synod: annual

OFFICERS

Pres., Rev. Thore Larson, Jackson, MN 56143
Vice-Pres., Alvin Anderson, 4503 Tilly Mill Rd., Doraville, GA 30360
Treas., Truman Larson, Rt. 1, Jackson, MN 56143
Sec., Janette Larson, Rt. 1, Winston, MN 56101

Evangelical Lutheran Churches, Association of

Members of the Association of Evangelical Lutheran Churches acknowledge and confess without reservation the Scriptures of the Old and New Testament as the written Word of God and the only rule and norm of faith and practice; and all the Symbolical Books of the Evangelical Lutheran Church as a true and unadulturated statement and exposition of the Word of God, to wit: the three Ecumenical Creeds (the Apostolic Creed, the Nicene

Creed, the Athanasian Creed), the Unaltered Augsburg Confession, The Apology of the Augsburg Confession, the Smalcald Articles, the Treatise on the Power and Primacy of the Pope, Luther's Large and Small Catechisms, and the Formula of Concord.

The AELC is a church body whose members, both congregations and individuals, have joined together to be in mission and ministry.

The congregations that have formed the Association of Evangelical Lutheran Churches are primarily and in vast majority former affiliates of the Lutheran Church-Missouri Synod. Some are new congregations; some are previously independent.

During 1976 five regional associations of congregations formed. These five regional synods held their initial conventions in November, 1976. The constituting convention of the AELC took place on December 3-4, 1976 in Chicago.

Churches: 250 Inclusive Membership: 106,684 Sunday or Sabbath Schools: N.R. Total Enrollment: N.R. Ordained Clergy: 545

GENERAL ORGANIZATION

Convocation meets biennially. Next meeting, 1980
Headquarters: 12015 Manchester Rd. Ste. 80LL, St. Louis, MO 63131. Tel. (314) 821-3889

OFFICERS

Pres., Dr. William Kohn, 2707 N. 67th St., Milwaukee, WI 53210
Vice-Pres., Dr. Will Herzfeld, 959 12th St., Oakland, CA 94607
Exec. Sec., Elwyn Ewald
Sec., Ms. Charlotte Light, 6084 W. Cabanne Pl., St. Louis, MO 63112
Other Officers: Ms. Chris Grumm, San Francisco, CA; Ms. Virginia Broderius, Golden, CO; Rev. Joel Benbow, Cahokia, IL; Dr. Walter Schur, Oxford, MA; Dr. C. Thomas Spitz, Manhasset, NY; Mrs. Melba Bangert, St. Louis, MO; Rev. John Frey, Prairie Village, KS; Mr. Don Jones, Oklahoma City, OK, Dr. Paul Krause, Minneapolis, MN; Mrs. Thelma Mills, New Orleans, LA, and the five presidents of synods.

SYNODS

East Coast Synod, Lutheran Center, 360 Park Ave., S., New York, NY 10010. Tel. (212) 532-6350. Bishop Rudolph P. F. Ressmeyer; Sec. pro tem, Charles Hughes
English Synod, Box 19307, Detroit, MI 48219. Tel. (313) 522-8440. Pres., Harold L. Hecht; Sec., Craig Settlage
Great Rivers Synod, Box 72, Belleville, IL 62222. Tel. (618) 233-1825. Pres., Herman L. Neunaber; Sec., Kay Mollenhoff
Pacific Synod, 888 Turk St., San Francisco, CA 94102. Tel. (714) 963-2982. Pres./Bishop, Walter Grumm, Exec. Sec., James De Lange
Southwest Synod, 24th and Adams, Great Bend, KS 67530. Tel. (316) 793-7894. Pres., Robert Studtmann; Sec., Norma Heinicke

PERIODICAL

Foreword (m)

Evangelical Lutheran Synod

The Evangelical Lutheran Synod had its beginning among the Norwegian settlers who brought with them their Lutheran heritage and established it in this country. It was organized in 1853. It was reorganized in 1917 by those who desired to adhere to these principles not only in word, but also in deed.

To carry out the above-mentioned objectives, the Synod owns and operates Bethany Lutheran College in Mankato, Minnesota. It also owns and operates Bethany Lutheran Theological Seminary for the training of pastors. The seminary is also at Mankato, MN

Churches: 108 Inclusive Membership: 19,705 Sunday or Sabbath Schools: 100 Total Enrollment: 3,918 Ordained Clergy: 92

GENERAL ORGANIZATION

Synod: annual (June)

OFFICERS

Pres., Rev. W. W. Petersen, 1209 Marsh St., Mankato, MN 56001
Sec., Rev. Alf Merseth, 106 13th St. S., Northwood, IA 50459
Treas., Mr. LeRoy W. Meyer, 1038 S. Lewis Ave., Lombard, IL 60148

OTHER ORGANIZATIONS

Lutheran Synod Book Co.: Office, Bethany Lutheran College, Mankato, MN 56001

PERIODICAL

Lutheran Sentinel, (bi-m), Lake Mills, IA 50450. Rev. N. Tjernagel, Ed., 626 Landing Rd., N., Rochester, NY 14625
Lutheran Synod Quarterly, (q), J. B. Madson, Ed., Bethany Lutheran College, 734 Marsh St., Mankato, MN 56001

Evangelical Mennonite Brethren Conference

Formerly known as the Defenseless Mennonite Brethren in Christ of North America, this body emanates from the Russian immigration of Mennonites into the United States in 1873-74.

GENERAL ORGANIZATION

Conference: annual (June or July)
Headquarters: 5800 S. 14th St., Omaha, NB 68107 (Tel. (402) 731-4800

OFFICERS

Executive Committee

Pres., Rev. Jerry Franz, Henderson, NE 68371
Vice-Pres., Rev. Allan Tschiegg, 1175 S.E. Howe St., Dallas, OR 97338
Rec. Sec., Rev. Eldin Classen, Box 354
Adm. Sec., Willaim Regehr, 5800 So. 14th, Omaha, NE 68107
Commission on Churches, Chpsn., Rev. Loyal Schmidt
Commission on Missions, Chpsn. Rev. Allan Wiebe, RR 1, Wymark, Saskatoon SON 2YO
Commission of Trustees, Chpsn., Mr. C. H. Penner, 4517 Wilson Rd., Yarrow, British Columbia VOX 2AO
Commission on Education & Publication, Chpsn., Rev. Frank Funk, Box 100, Dalmeny, Saskatoon SOK 1EO

PERIODICAL

Gospel Tidings, 5800 S. 14th St., Omaha, NB 68107. William Regehr, Ed.

Evangelical Mennonite Church, Inc.

An independent conference of Mennonites which separated in 1865 from the Amish Mennonite Church over the question of conversion.

Churches: 21 Inclusive Membership: 3,634 Sunday or Sabbath Schools: 21 Total Enrollment: 4,788 Ordained Clergy: 37

GENERAL ORGANIZATION

Conference: annual (August)
Headquarters: 1420 Kerrway Ct., Fort Wayne, IN 46805

OFFICERS

Pres., Rev. Andrew Rupp, 1420 Kerrway Ct., Ft. Wayne, IN 46805

Chpsn., Rev. Donald W. Roth, 6535 Maplecrest Rd., Ft. Wayne, IN 46815

Vice-Chpsn., Dr. Gordon Zimmerman, 821 West Leggett, Wauseon, OH 43567

Sec. R. David Boyer, 5334 Bluffside, Ft. Wayne, IN 46815

Treas., Ronald J. Habegger, 5214 Pleasant Run, Ft. Wayne IN 46815

PERIODICALS

Build (q), Grabill, IN 46741. Andrew M. Rupp, Ed.

Headquarters Communique (m), 1420 Kerrway Ct., Ft. Wayne, IN 46805. Andrew M. Rupp, Ed.

Evangelical Methodist Church

Organized 1946 at Memphis, Tennessee, largely as a movement of people who opposed modern liberalism and wished for a return to the historic Wesleyan position.

GENERAL ORGANIZATION

General Conference, District Conference, and Annual Church Conference

Headquarters: 3000 West Kellogg Drive, Wichita, KS 67213. Tel. (316) 943-3278

OFFICERS

Gen. Supt., John F. Kunkle, Wichita, KS 67213

Gen. Conf. Sec.-Treas., Rev. Ronald D. Driggers, Wichita, KS 67213

PERIODICAL

The Voice of Evangelical Methodism (m), 3000 West Kellogg Dr., Wichita, KS 67213, Rev. Warren L. Banks, Acting Ed.

The Fire Baptized Holiness Church (Wesleyan)

This church came into being about 1890 as the result of definite preaching on the doctrine of holiness in some Methodist churches in southeastern Kansas. It became known as The Southeast Kansas Fire Baptized Holiness Association, which name in 1945 was changed to The Fire Baptized Holiness Church. It is entirely Wesleyan in doctrine, episcopal in church organization, and intensive in evangelistic zeal.

GENERAL ORGANIZATION

Headquarters: 600 College Ave., Independence, KS 67301. Tel. (316) 331-3049

OFFICERS

Gen. Supt., Clarence W. Smith

Gen. Sec., Wayne Knipmeyer, 4819 W. 3rd, Wichita, KS 67212

Gen. Treas., Victor White, Rt. 3, Independence, KS 67301

PERIODICALS

The Flaming Sword (m), 10th St. & Country Club Rd., Independence, KS 67301

John Three Sixteen (w), 10th St. & Country Club Rd., Independence, KS 67301

Free Christian Zion Church of Christ

Organized 1905, at Redemption, Arkansas, by a company of Negro ministers associated with various denominations, with polity in general accord with that of Methodist bodies.

GENERAL ORGANIZATION

General Assembly: annual (November)

Headquarters: 1315 Hutchinson St., Nashville, AR 71852

Chief Pastor, Willie Benson, Jr.

Free Lutheran Congregations, The Association of

The Association of Free Lutheran Congregations was organized in 1962. It lays emphasis on: 1) the authority and inerrancy of the Word of God—the Bible, 2) the authority and freedom of the local congregation. The congregation is the right form of the Kingdom of God on earth and has no authority over it but the Word and Spirit of God, 3) the spiritual union of believers in Christ and the cooperation and fellowship of these believers transcending synodical, racial, and national lines, 4) an evangelistic ministry calling upon all to come to a personal relationship with Jesus Christ, 5) a wholesome Lutheran pietism with the believers being the salt and light in the community.

Churches: 132 Inclusive Membership: 14,738 Sunday or Sabbath Schools: 119 Total Enrollment: 5,402. Ordained Clergy: 91

GENERAL ORGANIZATION

Conference: annual (June)

Headquarters: 3110 E. Medicine Lake Blvd., Minneapolis, MN 55441; Tel. (612) 545-5631

OFFICERS

Pres., Rev. Richard Shipstead, 3110 E. Medicine Lake Blvd, Minneapolis, MN 55441

Vice Pres., David Molstre, St. 4, 29H, Dickinson, ND 58601

Sec., Rev. Einar Unseth, 1308 N. 2nd St., Bismarck, ND 58501

PERIODICAL

The Lutheran Ambassador (bi-w), 3110 East Medicine Lake Blvd., Minneapolis, MN 55441. Rev. Raymond Huglen, Ed.

Free Methodist Church of North America

This body grew out of a movement in the Genesee Conference of the Methodist Episcopal Church about 1850 toward a move original Methodism. It was organized in 1860.

Churches: 1,148 Inclusive Membership: 73,294 Sunday or Sabbath Schools: 1,118 Total Enrollment: 119,385 Ordained Clergy: 1,805

GENERAL ORGANIZATION

General Conference (next meeting, 1979)

Headquarters: 901 College Ave., Winona Lake, IN 46590. Tel. (219) 267-7656

Free Methodist Publishing House: 999 College Ave., Winona Lake, IN 46590. Tel. (219) 267-7161

OFFICERS

Bishops Donald N. Bastian, W. Dale Cryderman, Paul N. Ellis, Elmer E. Parsons, Clyde E. Van Valin

Gen. Conf. Sec., C. T. Denbo

Gen. Miss. Sec., C. D. Kirkpatrick

Gen. Dir. of Christian Education, Robert Crandall

Gen. Dir. of Evangelism and Church Growth, Forest C. Bush

Gen. Sec. of Higher Education and the Ministry, Lawrence R. Schoenhals

Gen. Church Treas., Mr. Jack Crandell

Publisher, Donald E. Chilcote

Communications, Donald E. Riggs

Gen. Dir. of Planned Giving, Stanley B. Thompson

Gen. Dir. of Special Ministries, Jack H. Mottweiler

PERIODICALS

Light and Life (bi-w), G. Roger Schoenhals, Ed.

Missionary Tidings (m), Marian W. Groesbeck, Ed.

Youth in Action (m), Esther Angel, Ed.

All the officers listed above should be contacted at the headquarters address

Free Will Baptists

This evangelical group of Arminian Baptists was organized by Paul Palmer in 1727 at Chowan, North Carolina. Another movement (teaching the same doctrines of free grace, free salvation, and free will) was organized June 30, 1780, in New Durham, New Hampshire, but there was no connection with the southern organization except for a fraternal relationship.

The northern line expanded more rapidly and extended into the West and Southwest. This body merged with the Northern Baptist Convention October 5, 1911, but a remnant of churches reorganized into the Cooperative General Association of Free Will Baptists December 28, 1916, at Pattonsburg, Missouri.

Churches in the southern line were organized into various conferences from the beginning and they finally united into one General Conference in 1921.

Representatives of the Cooperative General Association and the General Conference joined together November 5, 1935 to form the National Association of Free Will Baptists.

Churches: 2,436 Inclusive Membership: 216,831 Sunday or Sabbath Schools: 2,436 Total Enrollment: 187,778 Ordained Clergy: 4,367

GENERAL ORGANIZATION

National Association meets annually (July)

National Offices: 1134 Murfreesboro Rd., Nashville, TN 37217. Tel. (615) 361-1010

Mailing Address: P.O. Box 1088, Nashville, TN 37202

OFFICERS

Exec. Sec., Rev. Rufus Coffey, P.O. Box 1088, Nashville, TN 37202. Tel. (615) 361-1010

Mod., Rev. Bobby Jackson, 1412 E. 14th Greenville, NC 27834

DENOMINATIONAL AGENCIES

Free Will Baptist National Offices, P.O. Box 1088, Nashville, TN 37202

Board of Foreign Missions: Dir., Rev. Rolla Smith

Board of Home Missions: Dir., Rev. Roy Thomas

Board of Retirement and Insurance: Dir., Rev. Herman Hersey

Sunday School and Church Training Dept.: Dir., Dr. Roger Reeds

Woman's Auxiliary Convention: Exec. Sec., Mrs. Paul Purcell

Master's Men Dept.:, Dir., Mr. Loyd Olsan

PERIODICALS

Contact (m), 1134 Murfreesboro Rd., Nashville, TN 37217, Jack Williams, Ed.

Free Will Baptist Gem (m), P. O. Box 991., Lebanon, MO 65536, Rev. Clarence Burton, Ed.

Bible College Bulletin (m), 3606 West End Ave., Nashville, TN 37205, Bert Tippett, Ed.

Heartbeat, Foreign Missions Office, P. O. Box 1088, Nashville, TN 37202, Don Robirds, Ed.

Friends General Conference

An association of Yearly Meetings organized in 1900 to further the concerns for the advancement of Quakerism and the religious education of Friends.

GENERAL ORGANIZATION

General Conference: annual (June)

Headquarters: 1520-B Race St., Philadelphia, PA 19102. Tel. (215) 567-1965

OFFICERS

Clk., Dorothea C. Morse

Treas., Boyd M. Trescott

Exec. Dir., Dwight L. Wilson

PERIODICAL

FGC Quarterly (q), 1520-B Race St., Philadelphia, PA 19102, Carolyn N. Terrell, Ed.

YEARLY MEETINGS

(Note: * denotes Meetings which are also affiliated with Friends United Meeting)

Philadelphia YM Barbara Sprogell Jacobson, 1515 Cherry St. Philadelphia, PA 19102

Lake Erie YM, Ralph Liske, Samuel Prellwitz, 572 Briar Cliff Rd., Pittsburgh, PA 15221

*New England YM, Sylvia Perry, 40 Pleasant St., Dover, MA 02030

*New York YM, Henry Wheeler, Bulls Head Rd., Clinton Corner, NY 12514

*Baltimore YM Virginia R. Sutton 10707 Rain Dream Hill, Columbia, MD 21044

*Canadian YM, Vivien Abbott, 60 Lowther Ave., Toronto, Ontario M5 1C7

Illinois YM, Margaret B. Dupree, 4816 Francisco Ave., Downers Grove, IL 69515

Ohio Valley YM, Merritt S. Webster, 225 Connolly St., West Lafayette, IN 47906

South Central YM, Elmer Carter, 247 E. Rosewood, San Antonio, TX 78212

*Southeastern YM Marguerite Rece, 3021 Fox Springs Rd., Augusta, GA 30909

Northern YM, Joann Elder, 1112 Grant St., Madison, WI 53711

Piedmont FF, George White, 924 Greenwood Dr., Greensboro, NC 27410

Southern Appalachian YM & Assoc., George Oldham, 17 Foxfire Lane, Hendersonville, NC 29739

Friends United Meeting

The Friends United Meeting became the new name in 1965 for that worldwide fellowship of Friends formerly known as the Five Years Meeting of Friends. The latter body was founded in 1902 as a loose federation to coordinate and facilitate a united Quaker witness in missions, peace education, Christian education, and the publication of a monthly magazine, Quaker Life.

Since then additional programs in evangelism, stewardship, social concerns, and leadership have been added. Other Yearly Meetings within and beyond the United States have joined, making a total of fifteen member Yearly Meetings representing about half the Friends in the world.

Churches: 522 Inclusive Membership: 62,080 Sunday or Sabbath Schools: 369 Total Enrollment: 27,041 Ordained Clergy: 617

GENERAL ORGANIZATION

Friends United Meeting: triennial (next meeting, 1981)

OFFICERS

Presiding Clk., Walter Schutt, 101 Quaker Hill Dr., Richmond, IN 47374

Treas., Keith Kendall, 101 Quaker Hill Dr., Richmond, IN 47374

Adm. Sec., Kara Cole, 101 Quaker Hill Dr., Richmond, IN 47374

Field Sec., John W. Kirk

DEPARTMENTS

(All located at 101 Quaker Hill Dr., Richmond, IN 47374)

Wider Ministries Commission, Assoc. Gen. Sec., Harold V. Smuck

Meeting Ministries Commission, Assoc. Gen. Sec., Wayne C. Allman

General Services Commission, Exec. Asst. for Finance, Virginia Esch
Quaker Hill Bookstore (Friends United Press), Mgr. and Ed., Earl J. Prignitz

PERIODICALS

Quaker Life, 101 Quaker Hill Dr., Richmond, IN 47374, John W. Kirk, Ed.
Friends Missionary Advocate, Catherine McCracken, Rt. 4, Tudor Addition, Columbus, IN 47201

YEARLY MEETINGS

(Note: * denotes Meetings which are also affiliated with the Friends General Conference)
Nebraska YM, Kay Mesner, Central City, NB 68826
California YM, Sheldon Jackson, P. O. Box 1607, Whittier, CA 90609
*New England YM, Caleb A. Smith, 374 Hawthorn St., New Bedford, MA 02740
*New York YM, Katherine A. Nicklin, 15 Rutherford Pl., New York, NY 10003
*Baltimore YM, Virginia R. Sutton, 17100 Quaker La., Sandy Spring, MD 20860
Iowa YM, Levi Willits, Box 552, Oskaloosa, IA 52577
Western YM, Daniel W. Carter, P.O. Box 235, Plainfield, IN 46168
North Carolina YM Clifford Winslow, P.O. Box 8328, Greensboro, NC 27410
Indiana YM, Russell Goff, 1403 Briar Rd., Muncie, IN 47304
Wilmington YM, James W. Ellis, Jr., Box 1194, Wilmington College, Wilmington, OH 45177
Cuba YM, Sr. Maulio Ajo, Apartado 183, Banes, Oriente, Cuba
*Canadian YM, Vivien Abbott, 20 Hounslaw Ave., Willowdale, Ontario M2N 2A8
Jamaica YM, Frank Davis, 11 Caledonia Ave., Kingston 5, Jamaica, W.I.
*Southeastern YM, Marguerite Rece, 3021 Fox Springs Rd., Augusta, GA 30909
East Africa YM, Hezekiah W. Ngoya, P.O. Box 71, Webuye, Kenya, E.A.

Full Gospel Assemblies International

This Pentecostal body was founded in 1947 by the Rev. Herman Ponge. Charles E. Strauser succeeded as head in 1951. The FGAI teaches a two-stage theory of conversion and baptism of the Holy Spirit.

Churches: 105 Inclusive Membership: 2,800 Sunday or Sabbath Schools: 35 Total Enrollment: 938 Ordained Clergy: 488

GENERAL ORGANIZATION

Headquarters: 75 West 5th Ave., Coatesville, PA 19320. Tel. (215) 857-2357

OFFICERS

Pres.: Dr. Charles E. Strauser
Board of Directors: Rev. Richard McCauley, P. O. Gen. Del., Coatesville, PA 19320; James Wiggins, 55 Beach St., Coatesville, PA 19320; Rev. Simeon Strauser, Box 26, Sadsburyville, PA 19369; Betty Stewart, 14 Lloyd Ave., Downingtown, PA 19335; Dr. Annamae Strauser, 75 West 5th Ave., Coatesville, PA 19320; Dr. C. E. Strauser, 75 West 5th Ave., Coatesville, PA 19320, Rev. Samuel T. Strauser

PERIODICAL

The Charisma Courier, P. O. Box 429, Coatesville, PA 19320. C. E. Strauser, Ed.

Fundamental Methodist Church, Inc.

This group traces its origin through the Methodist Protestant Church. It withdrew from The Methodist Church and organized on August 27, 1942.

GENERAL ORGANIZATION

Conference: Annual (at Conference Grounds, Lawrence Country, Ash Grove, MO)
Headquarters: 1034 N. Broadway, Springfield, MO 65802

OFFICERS

Gen. Supt., Rev. Fred Cunningham, 224 W. Anderson, Aurora, MO 65605. Tel. (417) 678-3692
District Supt., Rev. Roy Keith, Rt. 2, Box 398, Ash Grove, MO 65604. Tel. (417) 672-3807
Asst. Supt., Rev. George Kelly, 912 Cambridge, Springfield, MO 65730. Tel. (417) 887-0272
Sec.-Treas., Mr. Everett Etheridge, 2652 Horning, Springfield, MO 65802
Missionary Exec., Rev. Robert Blodget, Box 1131, Brownsville, TX 78520
Education and Chaplain Exec., Dr. Wayne W. Mouritzen, Box 611, Hobe Sound, FL 33455

PERIODICAL

The Evangelical Methodist (m), Street, MD 21154. Dr. Donald McKnight, Ed.

General Association of Regular Baptist Churches

Founded in May, 1932, in Chicago, Illinois, by a group of churches which had withdrawn from the Northern Baptist Convention (now the American Baptist Churches in the U.S.A.) because of doctrinal differences. Its Confession of Faith, which it requires all churches to subscribe to, is essentially the old, historic New Hampshire Confession of Faith with a premillennial ending applied to the last article.

Churches: 1,544 Inclusive Membership: 240,000 Sunday or Sabbath Schools: N. R. Total Enrollment: N.R. Ordained Clergy: N.R.

GENERAL ORGANIZATION

Meets annually
Headquarters: 1300 N. Meacham Rd., Schaumburg, IL 60195. (312) 843-1600

OFFICERS

Chpsn., Dr. John G. Balyo
Vice-Chpsn., Dr. David Nettleton
Treas., Dr. Merle R. Hull
Sec., Dr. Ralph G. Colas
National Representative, Dr. Paul Tassell, 1300 N. Meacham Rd., Schaumburg, IL 60195

PERIODICAL

Baptist Bulletin (m), 1300 N. Meacham Rd., Schaumburg, IL 60195 Dr. Merle R. Hull, Ed.

General Baptists (General Association of)

An Arminian group of Baptists first organized by John Smyth and Thomas Helwys in England, 1607. Transplanted to the colonies in 1714. Died out along the Seaboard, but revived in the Midwest in 1823 by Rev. Benoni Stinson.

GENERAL ORGANIZATION

General Association: annual

OFFICERS

Mod., Rev. Royce Schanda, 113 South Tenth, Poplar Bluff, MO 63901
Clerk, Rev. Edwin Runyon, 801 Kendall, Poplar Bluff, MO 63901
Exec. Sec., Rev. Glen O. Spence, Box 537, Poplar Bluff, MO 63901

OTHER ORGANIZATIONS

General Board: Sec., Rev. Edwin Runyon, 801 Kendall, Poplar Bluff, MO 63901
Foreign Mission Board: Exec. Dir., Rev. Charles Carr, Box 537, Poplar Bluff, MO 63901
Board of Christian Education and Publications: Exec. Dir., Rev. Riley Mathias, Box 790, Poplar Bluff, MO 63901
Home Mission Board Exec. Dir., Rev. Leland Duncan, Box 537, Poplar Bluff, MO 63901
Ministers' Aid Board: Sec., Mr. Charles Weir, 7300 Oakdale Dr., Newburgh, IN 47630
Women's Mission Board: Exec. Dir., Mrs. Brenda Kennedy, Box 537, Poplar Bluff, MO 63901
Stewardship Dir., Rev. Ron D. Black, Box 537, Poplar Bluff, MO 63901
Nursing Home Adm., Ms. Wanda Britt, Highway 62 W., Campbell, MO 63933
College Board: Pres., Rev. Jim Marray, Oakland City College, Oakland City, IN 47660
Publishing House, General Baptist Press, Box 790, Poplar Bluff, MO 63901. Rev. Riley Mathias

PERIODICALS

General Baptist Messenger (w), Box 790, Poplar Bluff, MO 63901, Rev. Wayne Foust, Ed.
Capsule, Rev. Charles Carr, Ed.

General Church of the New Jerusalem

The General Church of the New Jerusalem is the result of a reorganization in 1897 of the General Church of The Advent of the Lord. It stresses the full acceptance of the doctrines contained in the theological writings of Emanuel Swedenborg.

GENERAL ORGANIZATION

General Assembly (International), meets every three or four years
Headquarters: Bryn Athyn, PA 19009. Tel. (215) 947-4660

OFFICERS

Presiding Bishop, Rt. Rev. L. B. King
Actg. Sec., Rev. Lorentz R. Soneson
Treas., L. E. Gyllenhaal

PERIODICAL

New Church Life (m), Bryn Athyn, PA 19009 Rev. Ormond deC. Odhner, Act 9., Ed.

General Conference of Mennonite Brethren Churches

An immigration of Mennonite Brethren from Russia in the year 1874. (In 1960, the Krimmer Mennonite Brethren Conference merged with this body.)

Churches: 120 Inclusive Membership 16,042 Sunday or Sabbath Schools: 120 Total Enrollment: 11,894 Ordained Clergy: 135

GENERAL ORGANIZATION

General Convention: triennial (next meeting, August 3-6, 1979)

OFFICERS

Chpsn., Henry H. Dick, 1362 L St., Reedley, CA 93654
Vice-Chpsn., Herb Brandt, 10200 No. 5 Rd., Richmond, British Columbia V7A 4E5
Sec., Nick Rempel, Box 126, Buhler, KS 67522

PERIODICAL

Christian Leader (bi-w), Hillsboro, KS 67063, Wally Kroeker, Ed.
Mennonite Brethren Herald, Winnipeg, Manitoba Canada, Harold Jantz, Ed.

General Conference of the Evangelical Baptist Church, Inc.

This denomination is an Arminian, Wesleyan, premillennial group whose form of government is congregational.

It was organized in 1935, and was formerly known as the Church of the Full Gospel, Inc.

GENERAL ORGANIZATION

General Conference: annual (Third Week in October)
Headquarters: Kevetter Bldg., 2400 E. Ash St., Goldsboro,
NC 27530. Tel. (919) 735-0831

OFFICERS

Pres., Dr. Wm. Howard Carter, Kevetter Bldg., 2400 E. Ash St., Goldsboro, NC 27530
1st Vice-Pres., Rev. Leonard I. Drew, P.O. Box 10396, Goldsboro, NC 27532
2nd Vice-Pres., Rev. T. T. Floyd, R-8, Res. 1008 Oswego Rd., Sumter, SC 29150
3rd Vice-Pres., Dr. L. S. Miller, 1200 Park Dr., Elizabeth City, NC 27909
Sec., Mrs. Harold K. Thomas, 204 S. Lee Dr., Goldsboro, NC 27530
Treas., Mrs. Jessie Byrd Carter, 711 E. Pou St., Goldsboro, NC 27530
Admin. Sec., Ms. Clyde Dawson, Kevetter Bldg., 2400 E. Ash St., Goldsboro, NC 27530
Dir. of Evangelism, Rev. B. L. Proctor, Rt. 3, Box 442, Nashville, NC 27856
Dir. of Youth Work, Rev. Ralph Jarrell, P.O. Box 1261, Burgaw, NC 28425
Dir. of Women's Auxiliaries, Mrs. Pamela Quinn, Rt. 1, Box 208, Beulaville, NC 28518
Dir. of Christian Ed., Dr. H. E. Jones, 3744 Sunset Ave., Rocky Mount, NC 27801

PERIODICAL

The Evangelical Baptist, Kevetter Bldg., 2400 E. Ash St., Goldsboro, NC 27530. Dr. William Howard Carter, Ed.

General Convention The Swedenborgian Church

Followers of Emanuel Swedenborg, Swedish scientist, philosopher, and theologian (1688-1772). They organized their first church society in the U.S. in 1792 in Baltimore. Their church is officially called The Church of the New Jerusalem, but they are usually referred to as Swedenborgians.

GENERAL SIX PRINCIPLE BAPTISTS

GENERAL ORGANIZATION

General Convention: annual (June)

OFFICERS

Pres., Rev. Eric J. Zacharias, Pretty Prairie, KS 67570
Vice-Pres., Frederick G. Perry, Jr., 133 Nagog Woods, Acton, MA 01718
Sec., Mrs. Wilfred Rice, 48 Sargent St., Newton, MA 02158
Treas., Capt. August A. Ebel, 7311 Arrowwood Rd., Bethesda, MD 20034
Exec. Dir., Roger Dean Paulson, 48 Sargent St., Newton, MA 02158

PERIODICAL

The Messenger (m), Box 2642 Sta. B. Kitchener, Ontario, Canada N2H 6N2, Rev. Paul Zacharias, Ed.

†General Six Principle Baptists

A Baptist Group, organized in Rhode Island in 1653, drawing its name from Heb. 6:1-2.

GENERAL ORGANIZATION

Conferences in Rhode Island and Pennsylvania: annually, in September

OFFICERS

Rhode Island Conference: Pres., Rev. Henry R. Bell, Hill Farm Rd., Coventry, RI 02816
Clk., Pauline C. Josefson, 146 Brunswick Dr., Warwick, RI 02886
Pennsylvania Association: Pres., Elder Daniel E. Carpenetti, Nicholson, PA 18446
Clk., Mrs. Eleanor Warner, Rt. 1, Tunkhannock, PA 18657

The Gospel Mission Corps

A nonsectarian, united, evangelistic church and home missionary society incorporated in 1962 in New Jersey. The ordinances of believer's baptism and holy communion are observed. Emphasis is placed on the doctrines and experience of full salvation and practical Christian living. Gospel Mission Christians desire to be biblical in both their faith and their work.

GENERAL ORGANIZATION

Annual Meetings: Spring Encampment, Fall Conference
Headquarters: Box 175, Highstown, NJ 08520. Tel. (609) 448-4387 and 448-4596

OFFICERS

Pres., Pastor Paul J. Rowley; Supt., Pastor Robert S. Turton III, Highstown, NJ 08520
Vice-Pres., Pastor Edward Miller, Philadelphia, PA 08901
Sec., Gloria M. Rowley, Grace B. Turton
Treas., Sandra B. Turton and Grace B. Turton

PERIODICALS

The Gospel Missionary (bi-m)
Loyalty to the Gospel (q), P.O. Box 175, Highstown, NJ 08520

Grace Brethren Churches, Fellowship of

A division occurred in the Church of the Brethren in 1882 on the question of the legislative authority of the annual meeting. It resulted in the establishment of this body under a legal charter requiring congregational government.

Churches: 262 Inclusive Membership: 39,605 Sunday or Sabbath Schools: 262 Total Enrollment: 32,776 Ordained Clergy: 529

OFFICERS

Mod., Rev. Jesse B. Deloe, 706 Robson Rd., Winona Lake, IN 46590
Vice-Mod., Rev. Knute Larson, c/o Grace Brethren Church, 1144 W. Main, Ashland, OH 44805
Sec., Clyde K. Landrum, P. O. Box 219, Clayhole, KY 41317
Asst. Sec., Rev. Gary M. Cole, Camelot Mobile Village, 446 S. Nova Rd., Lot 15, Ormond Beach, FL 32074
Treas., Mr. Larry Chamberlain, c/o Brethren Home Missions Council, P.O. Box 587, Winona Lake, IN 46590
Statistician, Rev. A. Rollin Sandy, 900 Robson Rd., Winona Lake, IN 46590

OTHER BOARDS

Foreign Missionary Society: Exec. Dir., Rev. John Zielasko; Treas., Homer A. Kent, Sr., Grace Village, Apt. 113, Winona Lake, IN 46590
Home Missions Council: Pres., Richard P. De Armey, 1818 Staffordshire Rd., Columbus, OH 43229; Treas., Harry Shipley, 60 W. Oak St., West Alexandria, OH 45381; Exec. Sec., Dr. Lester E. Pifer, 505 School St., Winona Lake, IN 46590
Women's Missionary Council: Pres., Mrs. Miriam Pacheco, 413 Kings Hwy., Winona Lake, IN 46590; Fin. Sec.-Treas., Miss Joyce Ashman, 602 Chestnut Ave., Winona Lake, IN 46590
Brethren Missionary Herald Company: Pres., Rev. Ralph J. Colburn, 3490 LaJara, Long Beach, CA 90805; Treas., Dr. E. William Male, RR 3, Warsaw, IN 46580
SMM: Dir., Girls Ministry, Ms. Judy Kaye Ashman, P.O. Box 365, Winona Lake, IN 46590

PERIODICAL

Brethren Missionary Herald, P.O. Box 544, Winona Lake, IN 46590 Ed., Rev. Charles Turner

Grace Gospel Fellowship

This Fellowship, whose churches are always strictly autonomous in polity, had its origin in 1944. The Fellowship believes in the deity and saviorship of Christ and subscribes to the inerrant authority of Scripture. Its method of biblical interpretation is dispensational with emphasis on the distinctive revelation to, and the ministry of, the Apostle Paul.

Churches: 48 Inclusive Membership: 3,500 Sunday or Sabbath Schools: N.R. Total Enrollment: N.R. Ordained Clergy: 138

GENERAL ORGANIZATION

National Cabinet which recommends policies and programs to the annual convention for approval. After approval it presents them to the constituent churches for voluntary united action.

OFFICERS

Pres., Charles E. O'Connor, 1011 Aldon St., SW, Grand Rapids, MI 49509. Tel. (616) 531-0046

OTHER ORGANIZATIONS

Bethesda Mission, Inc., 3745 26th Ave., S., Minneapolis, MN 55406. Exec. Dir., Harry Rosbottom

Grace Bible College, 1011 Aldon St., S.W., Grand Rapids, MI 49509. Pres., Dr. John Dean
Grace Mission, Inc., 2125 Martindale Ave., SW, Grand Rapids, MI 49509. Exec. Dir., Daniel Bultema
Missionary Literature Distributors, 7514 Humbert Rd., Godfrey, IL 62305. Dir., Mr. Rollie Phipps
Prison Mission Association, P.O. Box 3397, Riverside, CA 92509. Gen. Dir., Mr. Joe Mason

PERIODICAL

Truth (bi-m), 1011 Aldon, S.W., Grand Rapids, MI 49509

Greek Orthodox Archdiocese of North and South America

The Greek Orthodox Archdiocese of North and South America is under the jurisdiction of the Ecumenical Patriarchate of Constantinople, in Istanbul. It was chartered in 1922 by the State of New York and has parishes in the United States, Canada, Central and South America. The first Greek Orthodox Church was founded in New Orleans, Louisiana, in 1864.

GENERAL ORGANIZATION

Headquarters: 8-10 E. 79th St., New York, NY 10021. Tel. (212) 628-2500

OFFICERS

Archdiocesan Council:
Pres., His Eminence Archbishop Iakovos
Vice-Pres., Charles Maliotes (Cambridge, MA)
Sec., Mr. Peter Kourides (New York, NY)
Treas., Mr. Sotiros Cachules (Valley Stream, NY)

BISHOPS

His Eminence Archbishop Iakovos, Primate of the Greek Orthodox Church in North and South America and President of the Synod of Bishops
His Grace Bishop Silas of New York, 8 E. 79th St., New York, NY 10021
His Grace Bishop John of Charlotte, 528 E. Blvd., Charlotte, NC 28203
His Grace Bishop Anthimos of Boston, 1124 W. Roxbury Pkwy., Brookine, MA 02146
His Grace Bishop Iakovos of Chicago, Forty Burton Pl., Chicago, IL 60610
His Grace Bishop Sotirios of Toronto, 27 Teddington Park, Ave., Toronto M4N 2C4
His Grace Bishop Timothy of Detroit, 19405 Renfrew, Detroit, MI 48221
His Grace Bishop Anthony of San Francisco, 372 Santa Clara Ave., San Francisco, CA 94127
His Grace Bishop Maximos of Pittsburgh, 5201 Ellsworth Ave., Pittsburgh, PA 15232
His Grace Bishop Gennadios of Buenos Aires, Ave. Figueroa Alcorta 3187, Buenos Aires, Argentina
His Grace Bishop Philotheos of Meloa, Auxiliary and Assistant to Archbishop Iakovos
The Diocese of Denver is administered by an Archdiocesan Vicar, The Very Rev. Kallistos Samaras, 10225 East Gill Pl., Denver, CO 80231

ARCHDIOCESAN DEPARTMENTS

(All located at 8-10 E. 79th St., New York, NY 10021)
Camping; Campus Commission; Chaplaincy; Education: Parochial, Jr. High Schools, Greek Culture and Language afternoon schools; Department of Religious Education: Church Schools, Adult Religious Classes, Religious Education materials published, 50 Goddard Ave., Brookline, MA 01246; Real Estate and Special Accounts; Economic Development: Financial, Stewardship; Foreign Missions; Interchurch Relations; Laity; Registry: Marriage, Baptismal Records and Statistics; Public Affairs: Press, Radio, Television; Publications; Social, Health and Welfare Center; Youth Ministry: Scouting, Jr. GOYA, Young Adult League; Church and Society

ORGANIZATIONS

(All located at 8-10 E. 79th St., New York, NY 10021)
Philoptohos Society—Women's Auxiliary
LOGOS, League of Greek Orthodox Stewards
ARCHONS of Ecumenical Patriarchate
Holy Cross Orthodox Press (Publishing Co.) 50 Goddard Ave., Brookline, MA 02146

PERIODICAL

The Orthodox Observer (bi-w), 8-10 E. 79th St., New York, NY 10021

The Holiness Church of God, Inc.

Established at Madison, North Carolina, in 1920; incorporated in 1928 at Winston-Salem, North Carolina

GENERAL ORGANIZATION

General Assembly: annual
Headquarters: Winston-Salem, NC

OFFICERS

Pres., Bishop B. McKinney, 602 E. Elm St., Graham, NC 27253
Vice-Bishop, O. M. Gray, 2509 Druid Hill Dr., Winston-Salem, NC 27105
Gen. Sec., Mrs. L. M. McNair, 1838 Gola Dr., Fayetteville, NC 28301
Asst. Sec., Laura Earnestine Ford, 234 Melody Ln., Winston-Salem, NC 27105
Overseer, Northern Area of N.E. Dist., Elder James Radcliff, 21 Jackson St., Mount Vernon, NY 10553
Overseer, Southern Area of N.E. Dist. Elder Ray Alston, R. 1, Box 190, Graham, NC 27253
Overseer, So. Dist., Bishop B. McKinney, 602 E. Elm St., Graham, NC 27253
Overseer, Va. & W. Va., Area of N.W. Dist., Elder Arnie Joyce, Thorpe, WV 24888
Overseer, North Carolina Area of N.W. Dist., Bishop O. M. Gray, 2509 Druid Hill Dr., Winston-Salem, NC 27105

Holy Orthodox Church in America (Eastern Catholic and Apostolic)

This body was instituted in 1934 for the presentation in the English language of the Eastern Liturgies and primitive Christianity. Its orders were derived through the Syro-Russian line.

GENERAL ORGANIZATION

Holy Synod: semi-annual
Headquarters: See House, 321 W. 101st St., New York, NY 10025. Tel. (212) 864-3729

Holy Ukrainian Autocephalic Orthodox Church in Exile

Organized in a parish in New York in 1951. The laymen and clergy who organized it came from among the

Ukrainians who settled in the Western Hemisphere after World War II. In 1954 two bishops, immigrants from Europe, met with clergy and laymen and formally organized the religious body.

GENERAL ORGANIZATION

Headquarters: Holy Trinity Cathedral Church, 185 S. 5th St., Brooklyn, NY 11211

Administrator: Rt. Rev. Serhij K. Pastukhiv, 103 Evergreen St., W. Babylon, NY 11704

†House of God, Which is the Church of the Living God, the Pillar and Ground of the Truth, Inc.

Organized 1919

GENERAL ORGANIZATION

Meets annually, in October

OFFICERS

Bishop A. H. White, 6107 Cobbs Creek Pkwy., Philadelphia, PA 19143

Gen. Sec., Sister Mildred Johnson, 41 N. 50th St., Philadelphia, PA 19139

PERIODICAL

Spirit of Truth Magazine (m), 3943 Fairmont Ave., Philadelphia, PA 19104. Bishop A. H. White, Ed.

Hungarian Reformed Church in America

A Hungarian Reformed Church was organized in New York in 1904 in connection with the Reformed Church of Hungary. In 1922 the Church in Hungary transferred most of her congregations in the U.S. to the Reformed Church in the U.S. Some, however, preferred to continue as an autonomous, self-supporting American denomination, and these formed the Free Magyar Reformed Church in America. This group changed its name in 1958 to Hungarian Reformed Church in America.

Churches: 29 Inclusive Membership 10,500 Sunday or Sabbath Schools: 21 Total Enrollment: 633 Ordained Clergy: 39

OFFICERS

Bishop, Rt. Rev. Dezso Abraham, 18700 Midway A., Allen Park, MI 48101

Chief Lay-Curator, John Nemish, 22 Matthew St., Carteret, NJ 07008. Tel. (201) 541-6378

Gen. Sec., The Very Rev. Stephen Kovacs, 180 Home Ave., Trenton, NJ 08611

Dean, New York Classis, The Very Rev. Gabor Csordas, 229 E. 82nd St., New York, NY 10028

Dean, Western Classis, The Very Rev. Tibor Dömötör, 1657 Centerview Dr., Akron, OH 44321

Dean, Eastern Classis, The Very Rev. Dr. Andrew Harsanyi, 175 Pershing Ave., Carteret, NJ 07008

Legal Adviser, Alex B. Eger Jr., 214 Smith St., Perth Amboy, NJ 08861

PERIODICAL

Magyar Egyhaz (Magyar Church) (m), 1657 Centerview Dr., Akron, OH 44321. The Very Rev. Tibor Dömötör, Ed.

Hutterian Brethren

Small groups of Hutterites deriving their names from an early martyr, Jacob Huter (1536). They have all things in common and share income and expenses. There are 77 colonies in the U.S., 27 of which are in Montana, 41 in South Dakota, 3 in North Dakota, 2 in Minnesota and 4 in Washington. The total membership in these 77 colonies numbered 7,800 in June 1977

CORRESPONDENT

Joseph J. Waldner, P.O. Box 628, Havre, MT 59501

Independent Assemblies of God, International

A body formerly known as Scandinavian Assemblies in the U.S., Canada, and other lands.

GENERAL ORGANIZATION

Convention: annual

Headquarters: 3840 5th Ave., San Diego, CA 92103. Tel. (714) 295-1028

OFFICERS

Sec., International: Rev. A. W. Rasmussen, Rev. T. A. Lanes, Assoc., 3840 5th Ave., San Diego, CA 92103

Sec., Eastern Canada: Rev. Harry Nunn, Sr., 15 Beecher St., St. Catherines, Ontario, Canada

REGIONAL SECRETARIES

Rev. Gil Belec, P.O. Box 2286, New Castle, PA 16101

Rev. Edward Bender, 720 Lake St., White Plains, NY 10604

Rev. Bobby Burnette, P.O. Box 3332, Cocoa, FL 32922

Rev. John Gamble, 4511 Bray Rd., Tampa, FL 33614

Rev. Les Gilpin, Rt. 4, Box 246, Madison Heights, VA 24572

Rev. C. L. Gruver, 3202 Humbert Rd., Alton, IL 62002

Rev. Robert Laughlin, 2714 Glen Oaks Dr., Wichita, KS 67216

Rev. Clyde McCullough, 4900 Hern Dr., St. Louis, MO 63134

Rev. Raymond Mosely, P.O. Box 122, Billings, MT 59103

Rev. Stanford Raleigh, 1533 E. Creston Ave., Des Moines, IA 50317

Rev. William Smith 2131 Southern Ave., Kalamazoo, MI 49001

Rev. Joseph Terlizzi, 2029 W. Harding, Stockton, CA 95203

Rev. Paul Tucker, 1830 E. First St., Duluth, MN 55812

Rev. Delbert Wells, 1100 No. 32nd St., Springfield, IL 62702

Independent Fundamental Churches of America

Organized 1930, at Cicero, Illinois, by representatives of various independent churches.

Churches: 614 Inclusive Membership: 87,582 Sunday or Sabbath Schools: N.R. Total Enrollment: 125,563 Ordained Clergy: 1,252

GENERAL ORGANIZATION

Headquarters: 1860 Mannheim Rd., Box 250 Westchester, IL 60153

EXECUTIVE OFFICERS

Pres., Rev. Robert L. Gray, 2105 Sunnyside, Westchester, IL 60153

National Exec. Dir., Rev. Bryan J. Jones, 1860 Mannheim Rd., Westchester, IL 60153. Tel. (312) 562-0234

PERIODICAL

The Voice (m), 912 Newcastle, Westchester, IL 60153. Rev. Harold Freeman, Ed.

International Church of the Foursquare Gospel

An evangelistic missionary body organized by Aimee Semple McPherson in 1927. The parent church is Angelus Temple in Los Angeles, organized in 1923, with mission stations and meeting places in 30 foreign countries.

GENERAL ORGANIZATION

International Foursquare Convention: annual
Headquarters: Angelus Temple, 1100 Glendale Blvd., Los Angeles, CA 90026. Tel. (213) 484-1100

OFFICERS

Pres., Dr. Rolf K. McPherson
Vice-Pres., Dr. Howard P. Courtney
Gen. Supervisor, Dr. Merrill E. Nicholls
Sec. and Dir. of Missions International, Dr. Leland E. Edwards
Board of Directors: Dr. Rolf K. McPherson, Dr. Howard P. Courtney, Dr. M. E. Nicholls, Dr. Leland Edwards, Dr. N. M. Van Cleave, Rev. Lorna De McPherson, George Corsello, Dick Schmidt
District Supervisors:
Eastern, Dr. Howard Clark
Great Lakes, Rev. Lynn Charter
Midwest, Glen Metzler
Northwest, Rev. Roy H. Hicks
South Central, Rev. Sidney Westbrook
Southeast, Rev. Glenn Burris
Southern California, Dr. Paul E. Jones
Southwest, Rev. John Holland
Western, Rev. Fred Wymore
Western Canada, Rev. Victor Gardner
Missionary Cabinet: Composed of Board of Directors, District Supervisors, Dr. Charles Duarte, Rev. John Bowers, Rev. Jerry Cook, Eugene Kurtz, and Rev. Phillip Hyde

OTHER ORGANIZATIONS

International Department of Youth and Christian Education: ———
United Foursquare Women: Pres., Katie Loggins
Council of Foursquare Men: Pres., Gary Cooper

PERIODICALS

(All published at 1100 Glendale Blvd., Los Angeles. CA 90026
Foursquare World Advance (m) Margaret Gomez, Ed.
United Foursquare Women's Magazine, Katie Loggins

The International Pentecostal Church of Christ

This body is the result of a consolidation, made at London, Ohio on August 10, 1976 of the International Pentecostal Assemblies and the Pentecostal Church of Christ.

The International Pentecostal Assemblies, one of the merged bodies, was the successor of the Association of Pentecostal Assemblies and the International Pentecostal Missionary Union. The other body involved in the merger, the Pentecostal Church of Christ, was founded by John Stroup of Flatwoods, Kentucky, May 10, 1917 and was incorporated at Portsmouth, Ohio in 1927.

GENERAL ORGANIZATION

Headquarters: State Route #42 & Roberts Mill Rd., Mailing Address: P. O. Box 263, London, OH 43140. Tel. (614) 852-2421

OFFICERS

Gen. Overseer, Rev. Chester I. Miller, P. O. Box 263, London, OH 43140. Tel. (614) 842-2421
Asst. Gen. Overseer, Tom G. Grinder, P. O. Box 324, London OH 43140. Tel. (614) 852-0348
Gen. Sec., Rev. William Houck, Jr., 885 Berne St., S.E., Atlanta, GA 30316. Tel. (404) 622-2253
Gen. Treas., Rev. Lindsey T. Hayes, 1451 Hilbish Ave., Akron, OH 44312. Tel. (216) 724-1821
Dir. of Global Missions, Dr. James B. Keiller, P. O. Box 18145, Atlanta, GA 30316. Tel. (404) 627-2681

PERIODICAL

The Bridegroom's Messenger, P. O. Box 18145, Atlanta, GA 30316

Israelite House of David

Established at Benton Harbor, Michigan, by Benjamin Purnell, in 1903.

No statistics available

GENERAL ORGANIZATION

Headquarters: P.O. Box 1067, Benton Harbor, MI 49022. Tel. (616) 926-6695

OFFICERS

Pillar, Mabel Blackburn
Chpsn. of Bd., Lloyd H. Dalager
Pillar & Sec., H. Thomas Dewhirst

Jehovah's Witnesses

It is the belief of Jehovah's Witnesses that they adhere to the oldest religion on earth, the worship of Almighty God revealed in his Bible as Jehovah.

They use the Watch Tower Bible and Tract Society of Pennsylvania, Watchtower Bible and Tract Society of New York, Inc., International Bible Students Association, and other corporations in their earthwide preaching activity, and preach to all regardless of denomination.

All of Jehovah's Witnesses preach the good news and have no human leader. Their Yearbook shows them active during 1978 in 205 countries of the world, where there are approximately 2,182,341 individuals preaching and teaching the people of all nations that God's word is true and that their only hope is in the Kingdom of Jehovah under Christ Jesus which has been established to rule over earth and which will replace all governments of man.

Churches: 7,526 Inclusive Membership: 519,218 Sunday or Sabbath Schools: N.R. Total Enrollment: N.R. Ordained Clergy: None

GENERAL ORGANIZATION

Headquarters: 124 Columbia Heights, Brooklyn, NY 11201. Tel. (212) 625-1240

OFFICER

Pres. Frederick W. Franz

PERIODICALS

The Watchtower and Awake! 124 Columbia Heights, Brooklyn, NY 11201

Jewish Congregations

Jews arrived in the colonies before 1650. The first congregation is recorded in 1654, in New York City, the Shearith Israel (Remnant of Israel).

CONGREGATIONAL AND RABBINICAL ORGANIZATIONS

*Union of American Hebrew Congregations (Reform): 838 Fifth Ave., New York, NY 10021; Pres., Rabbi Alexander M. Schindler

*United Synagogue of America (Conservative): 155 Fifth Ave., NY 10010; Pres., Simon Schwartz; Exec. Vice Pres., Rabbi Benjamin Z. Kreitman

*Union of Orthodox Jewish Congregations of America: 116 E. 27th St., New York, NY 10016, Pres., Julius Berman; Exec. Vice Pres., Rabbi Pinchas Stolper

*Central Conference of American Rabbis (Reform): 790 Madison Ave., New York, NY 10021; Pres., Rabbi Jerome R. Malino; Exec. Vice-Pres., Rabbi Joseph B. Glaser

Rabbinical Alliance of America (Orthodox): 156 Fifth Ave., New York, NY 10011; Pres., Rabbi David B. Hollander

*The Rabbinical Assembly, (Conservative): 3080 Broadway, New York, NY 10027; Pres., Saul I. Teplitz; Exec. Vice-Pres., Rabbi Wolfe Kelman

*Rabbinical Council of America, Inc., (Orthodox): 1250 Broadway, New York, NY 10003; Pres., Bernard Rosenweig; Exec. Vice-Pres., Rabbi Israel Klavan

Union of Orthodox Rabbis of the United States and Canada: 235 E. Broadway, New York, NY 10002; Pres., Rabbi Moshe Feinstein; Chpsn., Rabbi Symcha Elberg

*Synagogue Council of America: 432 Park Ave. S., New York, NY 10016; Pres., Rabbi Arthur J. Lelyveld; Exec. Vice-Pres., Rabbi Bernard Mandelbaum. Meets annually

*Synagogue Council of America is the coordinating body of the organizations starred above.

EDUCATIONAL AND SOCIAL SERVICE ORGANIZATIONS

American Association for Jewish Education: 114 5th Ave., New York, NY 10011, Pres., Arthur Brody; Exec. Vice-Pres., Isaac Toubin

American Council for Judaism, The: 309 Fifth Ave., New York, NY 10016, Pres., Clarence L. Coleman, Jr.; Sec., Alan V. Stone

American Jewish Committee: 165 E. 56th St., New York, NY 10022, Pres., Richard Maass; Exec. Vice-Pres., Bertram H. Gold

American Jewish Congress: 15 E. 84th St., New York, NY 10028, Pres., Arthur Hertzberg; Exec. Dir., Naomi Levine

American Jewish Historical Society: 2 Thornton Rd., Waltham, MA 02154, Pres., David R. Pokross; Dir., Bernard Wax

American Jewish Joint Distribution Committee, 60 E. 42nd St., New York, NY 10017. Pres., Donald M. Robinson; Exec. Vice-Chpsn., Ralph I. Goldman

Anti-Defamation League of B'nai B'rith: 315 Lexington Ave., New York, NY 10016, Natl. Chpsn., Burton M. Joseph; Natl. Dir., Benjamin R. Epstein

B'nai B'rith Hillel Foundations; Inc.: 1640 Rhode Island Ave. NW, Washington, DC 20036, Chpsn., B'nai B'rith Hillel Com., Seymour Martin Lipset; Intl. Dir., Norman E. Frimer

Conference of Presidents of Major American Jewish Organizations, 515 Park Ave., New York, NY 10022. Chpsn., Alexander M. Schindler; Exec. Dir., Yehuda Hellman

Council of Jewish Federations and Welfare Funds, 575 Lexington Ave., New York, NY 10022. Pres., Jerold C. Hoffberger; Exec. Vice-Pres., Philip Bernstein

Hadassah-Women's Zionist Organization of America, 50 W. 58th St., New York, NY 10019, Pres., Bernice S. Tannenbaum; Exec. Dir., Aline Kaplan

HIAS, Inc.: 200 Park Ave., S., New York, NY 10003, Pres., Carl Glick; Exec. Vice-Pres., Gaynor I. Jacobson

Jewish Publication Society of America: 117 S. 17th St., Philadelphia, PA 19103, Pres., Edward B. Shils; Vice Pres., Bernard I. Levinson

JWB (National Jewish Welfare Board) 15 E 26th St., New York, NY 10010. Pres., Robert L. Adler; Exec. Vice-Pres., Arthur Rotman

Jewish War Veterans of the United States of America, Inc.: 1712 New Hampshire Ave. N.W., Washington, DC 20009, Natl. Comdr., Herman H. Moses; Natl. Exec. Dir., Irwin R. Ziff

National Council for Jewish Education: 114 5th Ave., New York, NY 10011, Pres., Leivy Smolar; Exec. Sec., Jack M. Horden

National Federation of Jewish Men's Clubs of the United Synagogue of America: 475 Riverside Dr., Ste. 244, New York, NY 10027, Pres., Morton R. Lang; Sec. David L. Blumenfeld

National Federation of Temple Brotherhoods: 838 Fifth Ave., New York, NY 10021, Pres., Robert E. Katz; Exec. Dir., Av Bandarin

National Federation of Temple Sisterhoods; 838 Fifth Ave., New York, NY 10021, Pres., Lillian Maltzer; Exec. Dir., Eleanor R. Schwartz

National Jewish Community Relations Advisory Council, 55 W. 42nd St., New York, NY 10036. Chpsn., Theodore R. Mann; Exec. Vice-Chpsn. Albert D. Chernin

United Jewish Appeal: 1290 Ave. of Americas, New York, NY 10019, Gen. Chpsn., Leonard R. Strelitz, Exec. Vice-Chpsn., Irving Bernstein

Women's Branch of the Union of Orthodox Jewish Congregations of America: 84 Fifth Ave., New York, NY 10011, Pres., Mrs. Samuel A. Turk; Exec. Vice-Pres., Mrs. Mordecai A. Stern

Women's League for Conservative Judaism of United Synagogue of America: 48 E. 74th St., New York, NY 10021, Pres., Mrs. Ruth Perry

Zionist Organization of America: 4 E. 34th St., New York, NY 10016, Pres., Joseph P. Sternstein; Natl. Exec. Dir., Leon J. Ilutovich

PERIODICALS

ORTHODOX

Jewish Life (q), 116 E. 27th St., New York, NY 10016, Yakov Jacobs, Ed.

Tradition (q), 1250 Broadway, Ste. 802, New York, NY 10001, W. S. Wurzburger, Ed.

CONSERVATIVE

United Synagogue Review (q), 3080 Broadway, New York, NY 10027. Alvin Kass, Ed.

The Torch (q), 3080 Broadway, New York, NY 10027, Rabbi Joel Geffen, Ed.

Conservative Judaism (q), 3080 Broadway, New York, NY 10027 Myron M. Fenster, Ed.

The Reconstructionist (m), 432 Park Ave. S., New York, NY 10016, Rabbi Ira Eisenstein, Ed.

REFORM

CCAR Journal (q), 790 Madison Ave., New York 10021, Bernard Martin, Ed.

Reform Judaism (formerly Dimensions in American Judaism) (m), 838 5th Ave., New York, NY 10021, Aron Hirt-Manheimer, Ed.

Jewish Education (q), National Council for Jewish Education, 114 5th Ave., New York, NY 10011, Alvin I. Schiff, Ed.

The Pedagogic Reporter (3/yr.) American Assn. for Jewish Education, 114 5th Ave., New York, NY 10011, Mordecai H. Lewittes, Ed.

The Synagogue School (q), United Synagogue Comm. on Jewish Education, 155 Fifth Ave., New York, NY 10021, Dr. Morton Siegel, Ed.

American Jewish Historical Quarterly (q), American Jewish Historical Society, 2 Thornton Rd., Waltham, MA 02154, Nathan M. Kaganoff, Ed.

Note: For details concerning many aspects of Jewish life and organization in the United States and throughout the world, consult American Jewish Yearbook, 1979 prepared by the American Jewish Committee, Morris Fine and Milton Himmelfarb, Eds.

†Kodesh Church of Immanuel

Founded 1929 by Rev. Frank Russell Killingsworth, from among a group withdrawing from the African Methodist Episcopal Zion Church, and others.

GENERAL ORGANIZATION

General Assembly or Quadrennial Assembly, Also Annual Assembly

OFFICERS

Supervising Elders: Rev. Fred Almond, 1336 N. Hobart St., Philadelphia, PA 19131; Rev. Alphonso Benjamin, 5040 Brown St., Philadelphia, PA 19139; Rev. Ellsworth Holmes, 6537 Deary St., Pittsburgh, PA 15206

OTHER ORGANIZATIONS

Church Extension Board: Chmn., Mrs. Thelma P. Homes, Pittsburgh, PA

Home and Foreign Missions Board: Chmn., Mrs. Florence E. Woodruff

Young People's Societies: Gen. Pres., Mrs. Catherine B. Harris, Philadelphia, PA

Sunday Schools: Gen. Supt., Mr. Joseph Rollins, Pittsburgh, PA.

The Latvian Evangelical Lutheran Church in America

This body was organized into a denomination on April 10, 1976, after having existed as the Federation of Latvian Evangelical Lutheran Churches in America since 1957. This church is a regional constituent part of the Lutheran Church of Latvia in Exile, a member of the Lutheran World Federation and the World Council of Churches.

The Latvian Evangelical Lutheran Church in America works to foster religious life, traditions and customs in its congregations in harmony with the Holy Scriptures, the Apostles', Nicean and Athanasian Creeds, the unaltered Augsburg Confession, Martin Luther's Small and Large Catechisms and other documents of the Book of Concord.

The LELCA is ordered by its Synod (General Assembly), executive board, auditing committee, and district conferences.

Churches: 56 Inclusive Membership: 12,308 Sunday or Sabbath Schools: 24 Total Enrollment: 629 Ordained Clergy: 70

CORRESPONDENT

Pres., Rev. Arturs Voitkus, 3438 Rosedale Ave., Montreal, Quebec H4B 2G6. Tel. (514) 489-3224

The Liberal Catholic Church—Province of the United States of America

Founded February 13, 1916 by the Rt. Rev. James Ingall Wedgwood. The Province of the USA was established under its first Regionary Bishop, Irving S. Cooper of Ojai, CA in 1919; Bishop Cooper died in 1935 and the Rev. Charles Hampton became the Church's second Regionary Bishop (1935–1945).

GENERAL ORGANIZATION

Board of Trustees, meets July 1, annually. Triennial Assembly

OFFICERS

Pres. and Regionary Bishop, The Rt. Rev. Gerrit Munnik, Krotona 62, Ojai, CA 93023. Tel. (805) 646-5936

Vice-Pres., Very Rev. Alfred Strauss, 10525 Downey Ave., Downey, CA 90241

Sec., The Rev. Lawrence Williams, P.O. Box 1051, Ojai, CA 93023

Treas., The Rt. Rev. Victor A. Neuman, 8435 Bloomington Ave., Minneapolis, MN 55420

PERIODICAL

Ubique, 732 Adams, Kiel, WI 53042, Rev. Kenneth F. Drewek, Ed.

Lutheran Church in America

This body was organized June 28, 1962, by consolidation of the American Evangelical Lutheran Church, 1874; the Augustana Evangelical Lutheran Church, 1860; the Finnish Evangelical Lutheran Church, 1890; and the United Lutheran Church in America, 1918. The new body began to function formally on January 1, 1963. It includes congregations and ministers organized in 33 synods in both Canada and the U. S. A.

Churches: 5,778 Inclusive Membership: 2,942,002, Sunday or Sabbath Schools: 5,640 Total Enrollment: 639,306 Ordained Clergy: 7,822

GENERAL ORGANIZATION

Convention: biennial. Next meeting, 1980

Headquarters: 231 Madison Ave., New York, NY 10016. Tel. (212) 481-9600

OFFICERS

Pres., Rev. James R. Crumley, Jr.

Sec., Rev. Reuben T. Swanson

Treas., L. Milton Woods

OTHER ORGANIZATIONS

Division for Mission in North America: 231 Madison Ave., New York, NY 10016, Exec. Dir., Rev. Kenneth C. Senft

Division for Parish Services: 2900 Queen La., Philadelphia, PA 19129, Exec. Dir., Rev. W. Kent Gilbert

Division for Professional Leadership: 2900 Queen La., Philadelphia, PA 19129, Exec. Dir., Rev. Lloyd E. Sheneman

Division for World Mission and Ecumenism: 231 Madison Ave., New York, NY 10016, Exec. Dir., Rev. David L. Vikner

Office for Administration and Finance: 231 Madison Ave., New York, NY 10016, Exec. Dir., Ralph P. Brighton
Office for Communications: 231 Madison Ave., New York, NY 10016, Exec. Dir., William P. Cedfeldt
Office for Research and Planning: 231 Madison Ave., New York, NY 10016, Exec. Dir., Rev. Albert L. Haversat, Jr.
Board of Pensions: 608 Second Ave., S., Ste. 280, Minneapolis, MN 55402, Adm., L. Edwin Wang
Board of Publication: 2900 Queen La., Philadelphia, PA 19129, Gen. Mgr., Rev. Robert W. Endruschat
Lutheran Church Women: 2900 Queen La., Philadelphia, PA 12129, Exec. Dir., Kathryn E. Kopf

PERIODICAL

The Lutheran (bi-w), 2900 Queen La., Philadelphia, PA 19129, Rev. Edgar R. Trexler, Ed.

SYNODICAL PRESIDENTS

Caribbean, Rev. Henry E. Dierk, P.O. Box 10225, St. Thomas, VI 00801
Central Canada, Rev. Gottlieb W. Luetkehoelter, 2281 Portage Ave., Rm. 211, Winnipeg, Man. R3J 0M1
Central Pa., Rev. Howard J. McCarney, 900 S. Arlington Ave., Room 208, Harrisburg, PA 17109
Central States, Rev. Roger J. Gieschen, 440 General Square Center, 9800 Metcalf, Overland Park, KS 66212
Eastern Canada, Rev. William D. Huras, Commerce House, 3rd fl., 50 Queen St., N., Kitchener, Ont., N2H 6P4
Florida, Rev. Royall A. Yount, Synod Office Bldg. 3838 W. Cypress St., Tampa, FL 33607
Illinois, Rev. Paul E. Erickson, 18 S. Michigan Ave., Rm 800, Chicago, IL 60603
Ind.-Ky., Rev. Ralph A. Kempshi, 3733 N. Meridian St., Indianapolis, IN 46208
Iowa, Rev. Paul M. Werger, Lutheran Church Center, 3125 Cottage Grove Ave., Des Moines, IA 50311
Maryland, Rev. Paul M. Orso, 7604 York Rd., Baltimore, MD 21204
Metropolitan N.Y., Rev. James A. Graefe, 360 Park Ave., S., New York, NY 10010
Mich., Rev. Howard A. Christensen, 19711 Greenfield Rd., Detroit, MI 48235
Minn., Rev. Herbert W. Chilstrom, 122 W. Franklin Ave., Rm. 600, Minneapolis, MN 55404
Nebr., Rev. Dennis A. Anderson, Ste. 204, 124 S. 24th St., Omaha, NB 68102
New England, Rev. Eugene A. Brodeen, 5 Wexford St., Needham Hights, MA 02194
N.J., Rev. Herluf M. Jensen, 1930 State Hwy. 33, Trenton, NJ 08690
N.C., Rev. Ernest L. Misenheimer, Jr., Klumac Rd., (P.O. Box 2049), Salisbury, NC 28144
Northeastern Pa., Rev. Wilson E. Touhsaent, 13 E. Main St., Wescosville, PA 18106
Ohio, Rev. Kenneth H. Sauer, 1233 Dublin Rd., Columbus, OH 43215
Pacific N.W., Rev. A. O. Fjellman, 5519 Phinney Ave., N., Seattle, WA 98103
Pacific S.W., Rev. Stanley E. Olson, 1340 S. Bonnie Brae St., Los Angeles, CA 90006
Red River Valley, Rev. Carl W. Larson, 1022-8th St. S., Ste. 6, Box 758, Moorhead, MN 56560
Rocky Mountain, Rev. Franklin C. Heglund, 240 Josephine St., P.O. Box 6820, Denver, CO 80206
Slovak Zion, Rev. Paul Brndjar, 194 Grove St. Montclair, NJ 07042
S.C. Rev. Herman W. Cauble, 1003 Richland St. (P.O. Box 43), Columbia, SC 29202
Southeastern, Rev. Gerald S. Troutman, 1644 Tully Circle, NE, Ste. 124, Atlanta, GA 30329
Southeastern Pa., Rev. William A. Janson Jr., 2900 Queen La., Philadelphia, PA 19129
Texas-La., Rev. Philip L. Wahlberg, 408 W. 45th St., (P.O. Box 4367), Austin, TX 78765
Upper N. Y., Rev. Edward Kersten Perry, 3049 E. Genesee St., Syracuse, NY 13224
Va., Rev. Virgil A. Moyer, Jr., 317 Washington Ave., S.W., Roanoke, VA 24016
Western Canada, Rev. Donald W. Sjoberg, 9901 107th St., Edmonton Alberta T5K 1G4
Western Pa.-W. Va., Rev. Kenneth R. May, 9625 Perry Hwy., Pittsburgh, PA 15237
Wis.-Upper Mich., Rev. Robert S. Wilch, 1933 W. Wisconsin Ave., Milwaukee, WI 53233

The Lutheran Church—Missouri Synod

The LC-MS was organized in 1847 and is the country's second largest Lutheran church and is at work in over thirty other countries. It holds to an unwavering confessionalism coupled with a strong outreach in ministry and has been a leader in mass media proclamation.

Churches: 5,669 Inclusive Membership: 2,631,374 Sunday or Sabbath Schools: 5,428 Total Enrollment: 638,074 Ordained Clergy: 7,161

GENERAL ORGANIZATION

General Convention: biennial, next meeting, 1981
Headquarters: 500 N. Broadway, St. Louis, MO 63102. Tel. (314) 231-6969

OFFICERS

Pres., Dr. Jacob A. O. Preus
Sec., Dr. Herbert A. Mueller
Treas., Dr. Norman Sell
Adm. Officer of Bd. of Dir., John P. Schuelke
Dir. of Personnel: Mr. William J. Barge
Board of Directors: Pres., Sec., and Treas. of the Synod, and the following: Mr. David H. Goertz, 33 Old Coach Rd, St. Catharines, Ontario, L2N 2P6; Mr. Robert W. Hirsch, 2110 Mulberry, Yankton, SD 57078; Rev. Henry Koepchen, Box 326 Conscience Bay Rd., Setauket, NY 11733; Rev. Ervin R. Lemke, 3225 N. 85th St., Milwaukee, WI 53222; Mr. William E. Ludwig, 594 4th Ave., WN, Kalispell, MT 59901; Mr. Gus Melde, 4511 Cherokee Trail, Dallas, TX 75209; Mr. George H. Mohr, 2531 N. 67th St. Wauwatosa, WI 53213; Mr. Harold Olsen, 712 S. Second St., Springfield, IL 62704; Mr. Lester W. Schultz, 3725 Delahaut St., Green Bay, WI 54301; Mr. Edward S. Scott, 3400 S. Reed, Lakewood, CO 80227

BOARDS AND COMMISSIONS

(All at 500 N. Broadway, St. Louis, MO 63102, unless different address is given)
Board for Public Relations: Exec. Sec., Mr. Victor Bryant
Board for Missions: Executive Sec., Dr. Edward A. Wescott
Board for Higher Education: Exec. Sec., Dr. A.M. Ahlschwede
Board of Parish Education: Offices at 3558 S. Jefferson Ave., St. Louis, MO 63118. Exec. Sec., Dr. Victor Constein
Board of Social Ministry and World Relief: Exec. Sec., Dr. Leslie Weber
Board of Stewardship: Exec. Sec., Rev. Marcus Zill.
Board of Managers, The Concordia Plans Manager, Earl Haake
Armed Forces Commission: Exec. Sec., Rev. Milton S. Ernstmeyer
Church Extension Board: Exec. Sec., Dr. Fred E. Lietz

AUXILIARY ORGANIZATIONS

Concordia Publishing House: 3558 S. Jefferson Ave., St. Louis, MO 63118. Pres., Dr. Ralph Reinke
Concordia Historical Institute: Concordia Seminary, 801 De Mun Ave., St. Louis, MO 63105. Dir., Dr. August R. Suelflow
Lutheran Laymen's League: 2185 Hampton Ave., St. Louis, MO 63110. Exec. Dir., John A. Daniels
Lutheran Women's Missionary League: 3558 S. Jefferson Ave., St. Louis, MO 63118 Pres., Mrs. Walter (Helen) Gienapp

PERIODICALS

The Lutheran Witness (m), 3558 S. Jefferson, Ave., St. Louis, MO 63118. Dr. Geoge Wittmer, Interim Exec. Ed., Roland Lovstad, Asst. Ed.
Reporter (w), 3558 S. Jefferson Ave., St. Louis, MO 63118. Dr. George Wittmer, Interim Exec. Ed., Roland Lovstad, Asst. Ed.

Mennonite Church

The largest group of the Mennonites who began arriving in the U. S. as early as 1683, settling in Germantown, Pennsylvania. They derive their name from Menno Simons, their outstanding leader, b. 1496.

Churches: 1,081 Inclusive Membership: 97,142 Sunday or Sabbath Schools: 753 Total Enrollment: 93,685 Ordained Clergy: 2,393

GENERAL ORGANIZATION

General Assembly: biennial. Next meeting, 1981
General Office: 528 E. Madison St., Lombard, IL 60148. Tel. (312) 620-7802

OFFICERS

Mod., Glendon Blosser, R. 5, Box 314, Harrisonburg, VA 22801

OTHER ORGANIZATIONS

General Board: Gen. Sec., Ivan Kauffmann, 528 E. Madison St., Lombard, IL 60148. Tel. (312) 620-7802
Council on Faith, Life, and Strategy: Chpsn., Virgil Vogt, 726 Monroe, Evanston, IL. Tel. (312) 869-4599
Board of Congregational Ministries: Exec. Sec., Gordon D. Zook, Box 1245, Elkhart, IN 46515, Tel. (219) 294-7536
Board of Education: Exec. Sec., Albert Meyer, Box 1142, Elkhart, IN 46515. Tel. (219) 294-7531
Board of Missions: Exec. Sec., H. Ernest Bennett, Box 370, Elkhart, IN 46515. Tel. (219) 294-7523
Mutual Aid Board: Pres., Dwight L. Stoltzfus, 1110 North Main, Goshen, IN 46526 Tel. (219) 533-9511
Mennonite Publication Board: Publisher, Ben Cutrell, 616 Walnut Ave., Scottdale, PA 15683. Tel. (412)

887-8500PERIODICALS

Gospel Herald (w), Scottdale, PA 15683 Daniel Hertzler, Ed.
Christian Living (m), Scottdale, PA 15683. J. Lorne Peachey, Ed.
Builder (m), Scottdale, PA 15683. Levi Miller, Ed.
Rejoice! (q) Scottdale, PA. Marjorie Waybill Assoc. Ed.
Mennonite Yearbook (annual), Scottdale, PA 15683. James E. Horsch, Ed.
Mennonite Quarterly Review (q), Goshen, IN 46526 John S. Oyer Ed.
With (m), Scottdale, PA 15683. Richard A. Kauffman, Ed.
Purpose (w), Scottdale, PA 15683. David E. Hostetler, Ed.
On the Line (w), Scottdale PA 15683. Helen Alderfer, Ed.
Sent (bi-m.), Elkhart, IN 46515. Willard E. Roth, Ed.
Sharing (2/yr.) Goshen, IN 46526. Maggie Glick, Ed.
Story Friends (w), Scottdale, PA 15683. Marjorie Waybill, Ed.
Information: James E. Horsch, Ed., Mennonite Yearbook, Scottdale, PA 15683

Mennonite Church, The General Conference

One of the oldest Mennonite conferences in the United States. The present denominational organization dates from 1860 (in Iowa).

GENERAL ORGANIZATION

General Conference: triennial. Next meeting, 1980
Central Office: 722 Main, Newton, KS 67114. Tel. (316) 283-5100

OFFICERS

Pres., Elmer Neufeld, Bluffton College, Bluffton, OH 45817
Vice-Pres., Donovan Smucker, 57 McDougall Rd., Waterloo, Ontario, Canada N2L 2W4
Sec., La Vernae J. Dick 588 SW Maple St., Dallas, OR 97338
Gen. Sec., Heinz D. Janzen, 722 Main St., Newton, KS 67114

OTHER ORGANIZATIONS

(All at central office)
Commission on Home Ministries: Exec. Stanley Bohn
Commission on Overseas Mission: Exec. Sec., Howard Habegger
Women in Mission: Coordinator, Joan Wiebe
Commission on Education: Exec. Sec., John Gaeddert
Division of Administration: Exec. Sec., Ted Stuckey

PERIODICALS

The Mennonite (w), 600 Shaftesbury Blvd., Winnipeg, Manitoba R3P 0M4 Canada, Bernie Wiebe, Ed.
Builder (m), 722 Main St., Newton, KS 67114
Window to Mission (q), 722 Main St., Newton, KS 67114, Jeannie Zehr, Ed.
Der Bote (w) 600 Shaftesbury Blvd., Winnipeg, Manitoba, Canada R3P 0M4, Gerhard Ens, Ed.

The Metropolitan Church Association, Inc.

Organized as the result of a revival movement in Chicago in 1894, as the Metropolitan Holiness Church, and in 1899 chartered as the Metropolitan Church Association. It has Wesleyan theology.

GENERAL ORGANIZATION

General Assembly: annual
International Headquarters: 323 Broad St., Lake Geneva, WI 53147

OFFICERS

Pres., Rev. Murdo MacKay
Vice-Pres. Rev. W. T. Pettengell
Sec., Mr. Elbert L. Ison
Treas., Gertrude L. Puckhaber

PERIODICAL

The Burning Bush (bi-m), Lake Geneva, WI, Rev. W. T. Pettengell, Ed. (Publishing House, The Metropolitan Church Association, Lake Geneva, WI 53147)

Metropolitan Community Churches, Universal Fellowship of

Founded October 6, 1968 by the Rev. Troy D. Perry in Los Angeles, California with a particular but not exclusive outreach to the gay community. Since that time, the Fellowship has grown to include congregations throughout the world.

The group is trinitarian and accepts the Bible as the divinely inspired Word of God. The Fellowship has two sacraments, baptism and holy communion, as well as a number of traditionally recognized rites such as ordination.

"This Fellowship acknowledges the Holy Scriptures interpreted by the Holy Spirit in conscience and faith, as its guide in faith, discipline, and government. The government of this Fellowship is vested in its Elders, Ministers, and church delegates, who exert the right of control in all of its affairs, subject to the provisions of its Articles of Incorporation and By-Laws."

Churches: 118 Inclusive Membership: 25,520 Sunday or Sabbath Schools: N.R. Total Enrollment: N.R. Ordained Clergy: 157

GENERAL ORGANIZATION

General Conference. 10th General Conference (biennial) Houston, TX, August 1981
Headquarters: 5300 Santa Monica Blvd., #304, Los Angeles, CA 90029. Tel: (213) 464-5100

OFFICERS

(All at headquarters unless otherwise noted)
Mod., Rev. Elder Troy D. Perry
Vice-Mod., Rev. Elder Freda Smith, P.O. Box 5282, Sacramento, CA 95817
Treas., Rev. Elder John H. Hose, P.O. Box 8356, Atlanta, GA 30306
Clk., Rev. Elder Nancy L. Wilson
Rev. Elder Charlie Arehart, POB 9536, Denver, CO 80209
Rev. Elder Jeri Ann Harvey, 1050 S. Hill St., Los Angeles, CA 90015
Rev. Elder Jean A. Whie, Exec. Sec. of World Church Extension, 79 Glennie Rd., W. Norwood, London SE27 OLX, England

PERIODICALS

(Published at 5300 Santa Monica, Blvd., Los Angeles, CA 90029)
In Unity (bi-m), Ms. Jean Gralley
Gay Christian (q), Rev. F. Jay Deacon

The Missionary Church

The Missionary Church was formed in 1969 through a merger of the United Missionary Church (organized in 1883) and the Missionary Church Association (founded in 1898). It is evangelical and conservative with a strong emphasis on missionary work at home and abroad.

There are three levels of church government with local, district, and general conferences. There are nine church districts in the United States and two in Canada. The general conference meets every two years. The denomination operates two colleges in the U. S. and two colleges in Canada.

GENERAL ORGANIZATION

International Headquarters: 3901 S. Wayne Ave., Ft. Wayne, IN 46807. Tel. (219) 744-1291
Publishing Headquarters: Bethel Publishing Co., 1819 S. Main St., Elkhart, IN 46514. Tel. (219) 293-8585

OFFICERS

Pres., Dr. Kenneth E. Geiger
Vice-Pres., Dr. Gordon Bacon
Sec., Rev. Robert Magary
Asst. Sec., Dr. Timothy Warner
Treas., Edwin W. Crewson
Dir., Overseas Missions, Rev. Eugene Ponchot
Dir., Home Ministries, Rev. Wm. Hesse
Dir., Services, Mr. Paul Beck
Dir., Youth, David Mann
Dir., Children, Mrs. Paul Grabill
Missionary Men International: Pres., Robert Wisler
Women's Missionary Societies: Pres., Mrs. Wayne Brenneman
Board of Publications: Dir., Jerry R. Freed, 1819 S. Main St., Elkhart, IN 46514

PERIODICAL

Emphasis (s-m), 336 Dumfries Ave., Kitchener, Ontario N2H 2G1. Dr. Everek Storms, Ed.

Moravian Church in America (Unitas Fratrum)

In 1735 Moravian missionaries of the preReformation faith of John Hus came to Georgia, in 1740 to Pennsylvania, and in 1753 to North Carolina. They established the Moravian Church, which is broadly evangelical, liturgical, with an episcopacy as a spiritual office and in form of government "conferential."

GENERAL ORGANIZATION

Two Provincial Synods (Northern and Southern)

NORTHERN PROVINCE

Headquarters: 69 W. Church St., P.O. Box 1245, Bethlehem, PA 18018. Tel. (215) 867-7566

Churches: 95 Inclusive Membership: 32,519 Sunday or Sabbath Schools: 93 Total Enrollment: 7,624 Ordained Clergy: 148

OFFICERS

Provincial Elders' Conference:
Pres., Dr. John S. Groenfeldt
Vice-Pres. and Sec., (Eastern District), Rev. Gordon L. Sommers
Vice-Pres. (Western District), Dr. Warren A. Sautebin, Madison, WI
Treas., John F. Ziegler, 69 W. Church St., P.O. Box 1245, Bethlehem, PA 18018

PERIODICAL

The North American Moravian (m), 5 W. Market St., Bethlehem, PA 18018

SOUTHERN PROVINCE

Headquarters: 459 S. Church St., Winston-Salem, NC 27108. Tel. (919) 725-5811

Churches: 52 Inclusive Membership: 21,002 Sunday or Sabbath Schools: 52 Total Enrollment: 9,121 Ordained Clergy: 72

OFFICERS

Provincial Elders' Conference:
Pres., Dr. Richard F. Amos
Vice-Pres., The Rev. Henry E. May
Sec., C. T. Leinbach, Jr.
Treas., Ronald R. Hendrix, 500 S. Church St., Winston-Salem, NC 27101 (Mailing Address: Drawer O. Salem Station, Winston-Salem, NC 27108)

PERIODICAL

The North American Moravian, 5 W. Market St., Bethlehem, PA 18018, Rev. Bernard E. Michel, Ed.

Muslims

Islam now claims over two million adherents in the U.S. Some of them are immigrants who represent almost every part of the world, or children of such immigrants. Others are Americans who converted to Islam or children of such converts. Most of the latter are black Americans who have been fascinated by the simple egalitarian teachings of the Islamic religion which gives them identity and a clear purpose of life. These are apart from those who come to America temporarily, such as Muslim diplomats, students, and those who work in international institutions such as the World Bank, the International Monetary Fund, and the United Nations.

Muslims are found in nearly every American town, and are engaged in all professions, including teaching, medicine, accounting, engineering, and business. Their number increases in large industrial and commercial cities in the East and Midwest, but there are also large numbers of Muslims in some areas on the West Coast such as Los Angeles and San Francisco.

Many Islamic organizations exist in the U.S. under such titles as Islamic Society, Islamic Center, or Muslim Mosque. The aim is to provide a group in a locality with a place of worship and of meeting for other purposes. These societies and organizations are not regarded as religious sects or divisions. Their multiplication arises from the needs of each group in a given area, long distances separating the groups, and the absence in Islam of organized hierarchy, a factor which gives liberty to ambitious personalities to start their own group. All the groups hold the same beliefs, aspire to practice the same rituals: namely, prayers, fasting, almsgiving, and pilgrimage to Mecca. The only difference that may exist between black organizations and other Muslim institutions is that the former may mix civil rights aspirations with Islamic objectives and may, therefore, follow a rigid discipline for their members.

The main Islamic organizations are the Islamic centers which are found in all 300 large cities. Their objectives are cultural, religious, and educational; and each one has a mosque or a prayer hall.

Prominent among these is:

The Islamic Center of Washington, 2551 Massachusetts Ave., NW, Washington, DC 20008, Tel. (202) 332-3451. Dir., Dr. Muhammad Abdul-Raul. Publication: The Bulletin (q).

REGIONAL AND NATIONAL GROUPS

Apart from the Islamic Centers, a number of regional and national groups were started with the objective of helping local groups coordinate their work, and promote closer unity among them. These include:

The Federation of Islamic Associations in the United States and Canada, 300 E. 44th St., 2nd Fl., New York, NY 10017, Tel. (201) 986-6824. Pres., Mr. Dawud Assad. Publication: *The Muslim Star,* 17514 Woodward Ave., Detroit, MI 48203.

The Muslim Students Association of the U.S. and Canada, P. O. Box 38, Plainfield, Indianapolis, IN 46168, Tel. (317) 839-8157. Publications: *The Islamic Horizons* (m); Al-Itti*had* (q).

Council of Muslim Communities of Canada, P. O. Box 400, Sta. D, Toronto, Ontario M6P 3J9, Sec. Gen., Mr. Qasim Mahmound. Publication: *Islam Canada,* P.O. Box 771, Sta. B, Willowdale, Ontario M2K 2R1, Tel. (416) 270-9215.

The World Community of Islam in the West, 7351 South Stoney Island, Chicago, IL 60649, Leader, Mr. Wallace D. Muhammad. Publication: *Bilalian News,* 7801 South College Groves, Chicago, IL 60619, Tel. (312) 651-7600.

The Council of Islamic Organizations of America, 676 St. Marks Ave., Brooklyn, NY 11216. Pres., Hajj Amir Hassan.

Council of Imams in North America, 1214 Cambridge Crescent, Sarnia, Ontario N7S 3W4, Mr. Abudl-Monem Khattab; Sabil al-Rashad (The Path of Righteousness)

National Baptist Convention of America

This is the "unincorporated" body of National Baptists which was organized in 1880 following a dispute over control of the publishing board in which another Convention was organized. Membership of the churches is largely black.

GENERAL ORGANIZATION

Convention: annual (September)

OFFICERS

Pres., Dr. James C. Sams, 954 Kings Rd., Jacksonville, FL 32204

Corr. Sec., Albert E. Chew, 2823 N. Houston, Fort Worth, TX 76106

Treas., Dr. John Francis, 3715 Dryades New Orleans, LA 70115

Hist., Rev. Marvin C. Griffin, 1010 E. Tenth St., Austin, TX 79102

OTHER ORGANIZATIONS

Baptist Training Union: Chpsn., Rev. Alexander Bernard, 3069 Orchard St., Indianapolis, IN 46218

Benevolent Board: Chpsn., Rev. W. M. Bowie, 3401 Southmore Blvd., Houston TX 77004

Educational Board: Chpsn., Rev. J. B. Adams, 609 S.W. 9th St., Belle Glade, FL 33430

Evangelical Board: Chpsn., Dr. E. H. Branch, 4919 Rosedale Circle, Houston, TX 77004

Foreign Mission Board: Exec. Sec., Rev. Robert H. Wilson, National Baptist Convention of America, P.O. Box 1680, Dallas, TX 75221

Home Mission Board: Chpsn., Dr. Luke K. Mingo, 3993 S. King Dr., Chicago, IL 60653

Junior Mission Auxiliary: Pres., Ms. Susan Turner

Mission Number Two Auxiliary, Pres., Ms. Hattie L. E. Williams, 1166 Rapides St., Alexandria, LA 71301

National Baptist Brotherhood: Pres., Dr. Ira L. Clark, 3615 Rosedale St., Houston, TX 77004

National Baptist Youth Convention: Pres., Quaford Coleman, 4269 S. Figueroa St., Los Angeles, CA 90037

National Ushers Auxiliary: Pres., Sr. Katie Allen, 1806 Chestnut Ave., Austin, TX 78702

Nurses Corps: Exec. Sec., Sr. Ernestine Sims, 5007 N. Roman, New Orleans, LA 70117

Senior Woman's Auxiliary: Pres., Mrs. Fannie C. Thompson, 516 E. Waverly St., Tuscon, AZ 85705

†National Baptist Convention, U.S.A., Inc.

The older and parent convention of black Baptists. This body is to be distinguished from the National Baptist Convention of America, usually referred to as the "unincorporated" body.

GENERAL ORGANIZATION

Convention: annual

OFFICERS

Pres., Rev. J. H. Jackson, 405 E. 31st St., Chicago, IL 60616
Vice-Pres.-at-large, Rev. E. D. Billoups, 904 N. 33rd St., Baton Rouge, LA 70802
Vice-Pres.: Rev. C. H. Hampton, 605 S. 32nd St., San Diego, CA 92113; Rev. David Matthews, P.O. Box 627, Indianola, MS; Rev. A. E. Campbell, 2500 Carnes Ave., Memphis, TN 38114; Rev. Sandy F. Ray, 574 Madison St., Brooklyn, NY 11221
Sec., Rev. T. J. Jemison, 915 Spain St., Baton Rouge, LA 70802
Treas., ———
Stat., Dr. B. Joseph Johnson, Sr., 1211 Hunter St., NW, Atlanta, GA 30314
Hist., Rev. E. T. Caviness, 10515 Tacoma Ave., Cleveland, OH 44108

OFFICERS OF BOARDS

Foreign Mission Board: 701 S. 19th St. Philadelphia, PA 19146. Sec., Rev. William J. Harvey, III
Home Mission Board: Exec. Sec.,———
Sunday School Publishing Board; 330 Charlotte Ave., Nashville, TN 37201. Exec. Dir., Mrs. C. N. Adkins
B.T.U. Board: 412 4th Ave., Nashville, TN 37219. Sec., ———
Education Board: 903 Looney St., Memphis, TN 38107. Chpsn., Rev.W. H. Brewster
Evangelism Board: 7201 Claremont St., Albuquerque, NM 87110. Sec., Rev. W. C. Trotter
Laymen's Movement: Pres., Walter Cade, 537 N. 82nd St., Kansas City, KS 66112
Woman's Auxiliary Convention: 584 Arden Pk., Detroit, MI 48202. Pres., Mrs. Mary O. Ross
Congress of Christian Education: 3620 Oak St., Kansas City, KS 66104. Pres., Dr. E. A. Freeman

PERIODICAL

National Baptist Voice (s-m), 902 N. Good St., Dallas, TX 75204. Rev. C. A. Clark, Ed.

†National Primitive Baptist Convention, Inc.

A group of Baptists having associations, state conventions, and a National Convention (organized in 1907).

GENERAL ORGANIZATION

Headquarters: P.O. Box 2355, Tallahassee, FL

CHIEF OFFICERS

National Convention: Pres., Elder F. L. Livingston, 1334 Carson St., Dallas, TX 75216; Rec. Sec., Elder T. W. Samuels, 6433 Hidden Forest Dr., Charlotte, NC 28206; Sec. Bd. of Dirs., Elder M. G. Miles, 1525 S. Bronough St., Tallahassee, FL 32301
National Church School Training Union: Pres., Elder David Tolbert, 818 Irvine Ave., Florence, AL; Sec., Mrs. Icylene B. Horne, 2222 Metropolitan St., Dallas TX 75215
National Ushers Congress: Pres., Willie Campbell, 1321 E. Scott St., Pensacola, FL 32503; Sec., Mrs. R. H. Howard, 3305 25th Ave., Tampa, FL 33605
Publication Board: Chpsn., Elder T. M. Batts, 19713 Holiday La., Warrenville Heights, OH; Sec., Elder J. L. Fitzgerald, 2703 Aspen Dr., Nashville, TN
Women's Congress: Pres., Mrs. E. C. Raye, 2112 Russell St., Charlotte, NC 28208; Sec., Mrs. W. M. Miles, 1525 S. Bronough St., Tallahassee, FL 32301
National Laymen's Council: Pres., Dea. J. L. Warren, 4209 Curtis St., Tampa, FL; Sec., Bro. J. L. Byrd, 4829 Fairmount Ave., Elyria, OH 44035
Young People's Congress, Pres., Br. Harold Batts, 2805 Penland Rd., Huntsville, AL 35810. Sec., Sr. Cecelia Meeks, 3227 Burbank Dr., Charlotte, NC 28216

The National Spiritual Alliance of the U.S.A.

This body, founded in 1913, believes in supernormal, personal, and impersonal manifestations and in intercommunication between denizens of different worlds.

GENERAL ORGANIZATION

Convention: annual (July)
Headquarters: Lake Pleasant, MA

OFFICERS

Pres., Rev. George Caesar, 28 Orne St., West Haven, CT 06516
Sec., Mrs. Wilma M. Doucette, 14 Edgewood St. Stafford Springs, CT 06076

National Spiritualist Association of Churches

This organization is made up of believers that Spiritualism is a science, philosophy, and religion based upon the demonstrated facts of communication between this world and the next.

Churches: 164 Inclusive Membership 5,168 Sunday or Sabbath Schools N.R. Total Enrollment: N.R. Ordained Clergy:144

GENERAL ORGANIZATION

Convention: annual (October)
Pres., Joseph H. Merrill, 13 Cleveland Ave., Lily Dale, NY 14752
Vice-Pres., Ernst A. Schoenfeld 3501 W. Shakespeare Ave., Chicago, IL 60647
Sec., Rev. Alice M. Hull, P.O. Box 128, Cassadaga, FL 37206
Treas., Rev. Edwin Ford, 1521 W. Edgemont, Phoenix, AZ 85007

OTHER ORGANIZATIONS

Bureau of Education: Morris Pratt Institute, 11811 Watertown Plank Rd., Milwaukee, WI 53226
Bureau of Public Relations: The Stow Memorial Foundation, Cassadaga, FL 32706, Sec.-Treas., Evelyn Muse
Spiritualist Benevolent Society, Inc.: Cassadaga, FL 32706

PERIODICAL

The National Spiritualist (m), P.O. Box 40172, Indianapolis, IN Wm. F. Melick, Ed.

Netherlands Reformed Congregations

Formed from among immigrations from Holland; a secession from the State Church there. The present body dates from 1907. The doctrines are the Belgic Confession, the Heidelborg Catechism, and the Canons of Dort.

Churches: 14 Inclusive Membership: 4,904 Sunday or Sabbath Schools: N.R. Total Enrollment: N.R. Ordained Clergy: 4

GENERAL ORGANIZATION

Synod meets every two years (next meeting, 1980)

OFFICERS

Pres. of Synod: Rev. A. M. Den Boer, Main St., P.O. Box 42, E. Norwich, Ontario N0J 1P0 Dr., N.E., Grand Rapids, MI 49503. Tel. (616) 456-6323

PERIODICAL

The Banner of Truth (m)

New Apostolic Church of North America

This body is a variant of the Catholic Apostolic Church, which movement began in England in 1830. The New Apostolic Church distinguished itself from the parent body in 1863 by recognizing a succession of Apostles.

Churches: 362 Inclusive Membership: 26,384 Sunday or Sabbath Schools: 362 Total Enrollment: 9,502 Ordained Clergy: 579

GENERAL ORGANIZATION

Headquarters: 3753 N. Troy St., Chicago, IL 60618

OFFICERS

Pres., Rev. Michael Kraus, 267 Lincoln Rd., Waterloo, Ontario, Canada
First Vice-Pres., Rev. John W. Fendt, 36 Colony La., Manhasset, NY 11030
Second Vice-Pres., Rev. Erwin Wagner, 330 Arlene Pl., Waterloo, Ontario, Canada
Sec., Rev. William K. Schmeerbauch, 312 Ladue Woods Court, St. Louis, MO 63141
Treas. and Asst. Sec., A. Walter Eckhardt, 6380 N. Indian Rd., Chicago, IL 60646

PERIODICALS

(All published at 3753 N. Troy St., Chicago, IL 60618)
Word of Life (s-m)
Youth Guide (m)
New Apostolic Review (s-m)
The Good Shepherd (m)
Our Family (m)

North American Baptist Conference

These churches emanated from German Baptist immigrants of more than a century ago. Some are still bilingual in their ministry. Although scattered on the North American continent, they are bound together by a common heritage, a strong spiritual unity, a Bible-centered faith, and a deep interest in missions.

Churches: 253 Inclusive Membership: 42,499 Sunday or Sabbath Schools: 249 Total Enrollment: 28,270 Ordained Clergy: 353

GENERAL ORGANIZATION

Triennial Conference: Next meeting, 1982
Headquarters: 1 S. 210 Summit Ave., Oakbrook Terrace, IL 60181. Tel. (312) 495-2000

OFFICERS

Mod., Dr. Peter Fehr
Vice-Mod., Rev. Donald Miller
Exec. Sec., Dr. John Binder
Sec. of Stewardship and Com., Rev. Connie Salios
Treas., Mr. Milton Hildebrandt

OTHER ORGANIZATIONS

General Missionary Society: Gen. Sec., Rev. Fred Folberts
Church Ministries Dept.: Gen. Dir., Rev. Bruce Rich
Church Extension Dept.: Gen. Sec., Rev. John Ziegler
Stewardship & Communications Dept.: Sec., Rev. Connie Salios

PERIODICAL

The Baptist Herald (m), Dr. Reinhold Kerstan, Ed. published by the North American Baptist Conference, 1 S. 210 Summit Ave., Oakbrook Terrace, IL 60181

North American Old Roman Catholic Church

A body with the doctrine of the Old Catholics in right and succession of Catholic orders. Knott Missal used for Masses. Traditional Mass and Seven Sacraments are used. Baltimore Catechism used for all instruction classes. Pontificale used for all Order Rights. Not under Papal jurisdiction.

Churches: 121 Inclusive Membership: 67,314 Sunday or Sabbath Schools: 41 Total Enrollment: 8,504 Ordained Clergy: 123

OFFICERS

Presiding Archbishop of the Americas and Canada. Most Rev. John E. Schweikert, 4200 N. Kedvale Ave., Chicago, IL 60641

North American Old Roman Catholic Church (Archdiocese of New York)

This body is identical with the Roman Catholic Church in worship, faith, etc., but differs from it in discipline. It was received into union with the Eastern Orthodox Church by the Archbishop of Beirut on August 5, 1911, and by the Orthodox Patriarch of Alexandria on February 26, 1912

Churches: 6 Inclusive Membership: 2,500 Sunday or Sabbath Schools: 3 Total Enrollment: 79 Ordained Clergy: 10

GENERAL ORGANIZATION

Synod: biennial; next meeting, May 1981.
Chancery Address: Box 1647, G.P.O., Brooklyn, NY 11202. Tel. (212) 855-0600

OFFICERS

Primate Metropolitan, The Most Rev. Archbishop James H. Rogers, 238 Wyona St., Brooklyn, NY 11207
Vicar Gen.-Treas., The Most Rev. George T. Koerner
Chancellor, Rev. Albert J. Berube

COMMITTEES

Committee on the Liturgy: Chmn., Most Rev. Joseph Mahurter
Seminary Committee: Chmn., Most Rev. George T. Koerner
Canon Law Committee: Chmn., Most Rev. Joseph M. Nevilloyd
Committee on Church Unity, Chmn., Rev. Albert J. Berube

PERIODICAL

The Augustinian (occ), Box 1647, G.P.O., Brooklyn, NY 11202

Old German Baptist Brethren

A group which separated from the Church of the Brethren (formerly German Baptist Brethren) in 1881 as a protest against a liberalizing tendency.

Churches: 50 Inclusive Membership: 4,898 Sunday or Sabbath Schools: N.R. Total Enrollment: N.R. Ordained Clergy: 221

GENERAL ORGANIZATION

Conference, annual

OFFICERS

Foreman, Elder Clement Skiles, Rt. 1, Box 140, Bringhurst, IN 46913
Reading Clk., Elder Herman Shuman, Rt. 4, Box 301, Pendleton, IN 46064
Writing Clk., Elder Lester Fisher, 4664 N. St., Rt. 48, Covington, OH 45318

PERIODICAL

The Vindicator, Covington, OH, Donald Boyd, Ed.

Old Order Amish Church

The congregations of this Old Order Amish group have no annual conference. They worship in private homes. They adhere to the older forms of worship and attire. This body has bishops, ministers, and deacons.

Churches: 513 Inclusive Membership: 33,000 Sunday or Sabbath Schools: N.R. Total Enrollment: N.R. Ordained Clergy: 2,007

NO GENERAL ORGANIZATION

INFORMATION

Der Neue Amerikanische Calendar, c/o Raber's Book Store, Baltic, OH 43804

†Old Order (Wisler) Mennonite Church

This body arose from a separation of Mennonites dated 1870, under Jacob Wisler, in opposition to what were thought to be innovations.

At present, this group is located in the Eastern United States and Canada. There are approximately 8400 members and 60 congregations, with 19 bishops, 76 ministers, and 48 deacons.

Each state, or district, has its own organization or government and holds a yearly conference.

NO GENERAL ORGANIZATION
INFORMATION

Henry W. Riehl, Rt. 1, Columbiana, OH 44408. Tel. (216) 482-4832

Open Bible Standard Churches, Inc.

An evangelical, full gospel denomination emphasizing evangelism, missions, and the message of the Open Bible. Originally composed of two separate groups, namely Bible Standard Churches and Open Bible Evangelistic Association, a merger took place July 26, 1935, and the name Open Bible Standard Churches, Inc., was adopted.

GENERAL ORGANIZATION

General Conference: annual (June)
Headquarters: 2020 Bell Ave., Des Moines, IA 50315. Tel. (515) 288-6761.

Churches; 280 Inclusive Membership: 60,000 Sunday or Sabbath Schools: N.R. Total Enrollment: N.R. Ordained Clergy: 781

OFFICERS

Gen. Supt., Ray E. Smith, Des Moines, IA Asst. Gen. Supt., Milton J. Stewart, Eugene, OR
Sec.-Treas., O. Ralph Isbill, Des Moines, IA
Dir. of World Missions, Paul V. Canfield, Des Moines, IA
National Christian Education & Youth Dir., Edward Anderson, Des Moines, IA

PERIODICALS

Address for periodicals: 2020 Bell Ave., Des Moines, IA 50315
Message of the Open Bible (m), Ray E. Smith, Managing Ed.
The New Overcomer (q), Edward Anderson Ed.
World Vision (m), Paul V. Canfield, Ed.

The (Original) Church of God, Inc.

This body was organized in 1886 as the first church in the U.S.A., to take the name "The Church of God." In 1917 a difference of opinion led this particular group to include the word (Original) in its name. It is a holiness body and believes in the whole Bible, rightly divided, using the New Testament as its rule and government.

GENERAL ORGANIZATION

General Convention: annual (October) at Chattanooga, TN
Headquarters: P.O. Box 3086, Chattanooga, TN 37404

OFFICERS

Gen. Supt., Dr. Lacy Cagle
Asst. Gen. Supt., Dr. O. E. Lambeth
Bus. Mgr., Rev. W. D. Sawyer,
Asst. Bus. Mgr., Dr. Paul Hopkins
Sec.-Treas., Mary H. Furguson
Supt. Y.P.C.U.W., Rev. Johnny Albertson
Camp. Mgr., Roy Wm. Kyzer; Dir., Ronald Reeves

PERIODICALS

The Messenger (m), 2214 E. 17th St., Chattanooga TN 37404, Rev. W. D. Sawyer, Ed.
Youth Messenger (m), Billy Perkins, Ed.

The Orthodox Church in America

The Russian Orthodox Greek Catholic Church of America entered Alaska in 1792 before its purchase by the U.S.A. in 1867. Its canonical status of independence (autocephaly) was granted by its Mother Church, the Russian Orthodox Church, on April 10, 1970, and it is now known as The Orthodox Church in America.

Churches: 440 Inclusive Membership: 1,000,000 Sunday or Sabbath Schools: N.R. Total Enrollment: N.R. Ordained Clergy; 531

GENERAL ORGANIZATION

All-American Council (biennial, next meeting, October, 1980)
Primate: The Most Blessed Theodosius, Metropolitan of All America and Canada; Sec. to the Metropolitan; Serge Troubetzkoy, P.O. Box 675, Syosset, NY 11791
Chancellor: V. Rev. Daniel Hubiak

SYNOD

The Rt. Rev. Boris, Bishop of Chicago, 8200 S. Country Line Rd., Hinsdale, IL 60521
The Most Rev. Sylvester, Archbishop of Montreal, 1175 Champlain St., Montreal, Canada H2L 2R7
The Most Rev. Valerian, Archbishop of Detroit, 2522 Grey Tower Rd., Jackson, MI 49201
The Most Rev. Kiprian, Archbishop of Philadelphia, St. Tikhon Monastery, South Canaan, PA 18459
The Rt. Rev. Kyrill, Bishop of Pittsburgh, P.O. Box R, Wexford, PA 15090
The Rt. Rev. Dmitri, Bishop of Dallas, 4112 Throckmorton, Dallas, TX 75219
The Rt. Rev. Gregory, Bishop of Sitka, St. Michael's Cathedral, Box 697, Sitka, AK 99835
The Rt. Rev. Jose, Bishop of Mexico, Apartado' No. 1877, Mexico 1, D.F. Mexico
The Rt. Rev. Herman, Bishop of Wilkes-Barre, St. Tikhon's Monastery, South Canaan, PA 18459

The Orthodox Presbyterian Church

On June 11, 1936, certain ministers, elders, and lay members of the Presbyterian Church in the U.S.A. withdrew under the leadership of the conservative scholar, the late Rev. J. Gresham Machen.

Churches: 136 Inclusive Membership: 15,806 Sunday or Sabbath Schools: N.R. Total Enrollment: N.R. Ordained Clergy: 238

GENERAL ORGANIZATION

General Assembly: annual Headquarters: 7401 Old York Rd., Philadelphia, PA 19126. Tel. (215) 224-1883

OFFICERS

Mod., Geoge E. Haney, 7401 Old York Rd., Philadelphia, PA 19126
Stated Clk., Richard A. Barker, 7401 Old York Rd., Philadelphia, PA 19126

Pentecostal Assemblies of the World, Inc.

An interracial Pentecostal holiness of the Apostolic Faith, believing in repentance, baptism in Jesus' Name, and being filled with the Holy Ghost, with the evidence of speaking in tongues. This organization, originating in the early part of the century in the Middle West has now spread throughout the country.

GENERAL ORGANIZATION

Convention: annual (August)
Headquarters; 3040 N. Illinois St., Indianapolis, IN 46208

OFFICERS

Presiding Bishop, Francis L. Smith, 783 New Castle Dr., Akron, OH 44313; Asst. Presiding Bishop, Lawrence E. Brisbin, 3841 Wedgewood Dr., Grand Rapids, MI; 49509; Paul A. Bowers, 1021 Egan Hills, Cincinnati, OH 45229; Arthur Brazier, 500 E. 33rd St., Chicago, IL 60616; David Braziel, 10 Pineridge Dr., Rt. 2, Silver Creek, GA; David Braziel, 112 Wilson Ave., Rome, GA 30161; George Brooks, 75 Brooklynlawn Circle, Westville, CT 06515; Ramsey Butler, 4627 Clay St., Washington, DC 20019; William Crossely, 79 McArthur Dr., Williamsville, NY 14221; Morris E. Golder, 7474 Holliday W. Dr., Indianapolis, IN 46260; John S. Holly, 7337 Eberhart St., Chicago, IL 60619; James A. Johnson, 12643 Conway Downs Dr., St. Louis, MO 63141; Brooker T. Jones, P.O. Box 1479, Princeton, WV 24740; C. R. Lee, 533 Oak St., Mansfield, OH 44707; Robert McMurray, 1639 Wellington Rd., Los Angeles, CA 90019; Benjamin T. Moore, 8048 Hollybrook Ct., Indianapolis, IN 46250; Ross P. Paddock, 818 Dwillare Dr., Kalamazoo, MI 49001; Philip L. Scott, 7133 Blue Spruce Dr., St. Louis, MO 63110; William L. Smith, 2460 Gramercy Pk., Los Angeles, CA 90019; A. J. Street 3906 N. 32nd St., Pine Bluff, AR 70601; Thomas Streitferdt. P.O. Box 386 Port Jefferson, L.I., NY 11777; Freeman M. Thomas, 436 Fielding Dr., Penn Hills Pk., VA 15235; James E. Tyson, 6431 N. Sunset La., Indianapolis, IN 64260; Charles Watkins, 1147 Brandon Rd., Cleveland, OH 44112; Thomas Weeks, 147 Ruthven, Grove Hill. MA 02121
Gen. Sec., Dist., Elder Raymond E. Lloyd, 1435 Villa Rd., Springfield OH 45503; Treas, Elder Samuel A. Layne, 1240 N. Euclid, St. Louis, MO 63113

PERIODICAL

Christian Outlook (m) P.O. Box 386, Port Jefferson, L.I., NY 11777 Bishop Thomas Streitferdt, Ed.

Pentecostal Church of God

Organized in 1919 at Chicago, Illinois, the first convention was held in October, 1953.

Churches: 1,189 Inclusive Membership: 110,670 Sunday or Sabbath Schools: 1,179 Total Enrollment: 135,000 Ordained Clergy: 2,168

GENERAL ORGANIZATION

Headquarters: Messenger Plaza, 211 Main St., Joplin, MO 64801

PENTECOSTAL FIRE-BAPTIZED HOLINESS CHURCH

OFFICERS

Gen. Supt., Rev. Roy M. Chappell
Gen. Sec.-Treas., Rev. Ray J. Smith

†Pentecostal Fire-Baptized Holiness Church.

Organized in 1918, consolidated with Pentecostal Free Will Baptists in 1919. Maintains rigid discipline over members.

GENERAL ORGANIZATION

General Convention every two years. (Next meeting, 1979)
Headquarters: Taccoa, GA 30577

OFFICERS

Gen. Mod., Wallace B. Pittman, Jr., P.O. Box 261, LaGrange, GA 30240
Gen. Sec., Foreign Mission Board Rev. William H. Preskitt, Jr., Apt. J-106, Area III, University Village, Athens, GA 30602
Gen. Treas. H. J. Barrett, Rte. 4, Commerce GA 30529

PERIODICAL

Faith and Truth (m) Rt. 4, Commerce, GA 30529. Rev. D. E. Beauchamp, Ed.

The Pentecostal Free Will Baptist Church, Inc.

Organized 1855, as the Cape Fear Conference of Free Will Baptists. Reorganized in 1959 and renamed the Pentecostal Free Will Baptist Church, Inc. The doctrines include regeneration, sanctification, the Pentecostal baptism of the Holy Ghost, the Second Coming of Christ, and divine healing.

Churches: 128 Inclusive Membership: 12,272 Sunday or Sabbath Schools: 128 Ordained Clergy: 195

GENERAL ORGANIZATION

General Meeting: Meets annually beginning Wednesday and Thursday following 2nd Sunday in August.
General Headquarters: P.O. Box 1081, Dunn, NC 28334. Tel. (919) 892-4161
Heritage Bible College, P.O. Box 1221, Dunn, NC 28334. Tel. (919) 892-4161

OFFICERS

Gen. Supt., Rev. Herbert Carter
Asst. Gen. Supt., Dr. Ned D. Sauls
Gen. Sec., Rev. Don Sauls
Gen. Treas., Rev. W. L. Ellis
World Witness Dir., Rev. W. L. Ellis
Christian Education Dir., Rev. Don Sauls
Ministerial Dir., Herbert Carter
Ladies' Auxiliary Dir., Mrs. Shirley Hardison
Brotherhood Dir., Don Worley
Ministerial Council Dir., Herbert F. Carter
Heritage Bible College: Pres., Dr. Ned Sauls

Pentecostal Holiness Church, International

This body grew out of the holiness movement in the South and Middle West from 1895 to 1900. It is premillennial in belief, emphasizes Christian perfection as taught by John Wesley, and believes in the Pentecostal baptism with the Holy Spirit, accompanied by glossolalia.

GENERAL ORGANIZATION

General Conference: quadrennial (Next meeting, 1981)
Headquarters: P.O. Box 12609, Oklahoma City, OK 73157 Tel. (405) 787-7110

OFFICERS

Gen. Supt., Bishop J. Floyd Williams
Asst. Gen. Supts.: Rev. Leon Stewart, Vice Chpsn., Dr. Vinson Synan; Rev. Bernard Undersood
Gen. Sec./Treas., Rev. A. D. Beacham

OTHER ORGANIZATIONS

The Publishing House (Advocate Press), Franklin Springs, GA 30639. Charles Bradshaw, Gen. Administrator
Lifeliners (Youth): Gen. Dir., Rev. Jim Eby, P.O. Box 12526, Oklahoma City, OK 73112
General Sunday School Dept.: Pres., Rev. Wiley T. Clark
General Woman's Auxiliary: Pres., Mrs. Agnes Robinson

PERIODICALS

Publications Editorial Office:
P.O. Box 12609, Oklahoma City, OK 73157
The Pentecostal Holiness Advocate (bi-w), Dr. Frank Tunstall, Ed.
Reach (m), Mrs. Alfreda Flowers, Ed.
Helping Hand (m), Mrs. Alfreda Flowers, Ed.
Tips, Mrs. Shirley G. Spencer, Ed.
Sunday School Literature, Rev. A. M. Long, Ed.
Witness (bi-m), Rev. Leon Stewart, Ed.
Worldorama (q), Rev. Ronald Moore, Ed.

Pillar of Fire

This is a holiness, Methodistic group, organized by Mrs. Alma White in 1901 under the name Pentecostal Union. The name was changed in 1917, as above.

GENERAL ORGANIZATION

Headquarters: Zarephath, NJ 08890
Western Headquarters: 1302 Sherman St., Denver, CO 80203

OFFICERS

Pres., Bishop Arlene W. Lawrence, Vice-Pres., and Gen. Supt., Bishop E. Jerry Lawrence; Sec., Mildred E. Portune; Treas., Bishop A. R. Stewart; Trustees, Bishop Arthur K. White, Rev. Harry Ross, Rev. Bertha White, Rev. Lois Stewart

PERIODICALS

Pillar of Fire (bi-m), Zarephath, NJ 08890
Pillar of Fire Junior (w), Zarephath, NJ 08890
Pillar of Fire Bay Chronicle (m), 24 Beulah St., San Francisco, CA 94117
Arthur K. White, Editor of all periodicals listed above; Arlene White, Asst. Ed.

Plymouth Brethren (Also known as Christian Brethren)

An orthodox and evangelical movement which began in the British Isles in the 1820's and is now worldwide. The name "Plymouth Brethren" was given by others because the group in Plymouth, England, was a large congregation. Congregations in the U.S. and Canada are usually simply called "assemblies." Plymouth Brethren are known as Christian Brethren in Quebec.

The congregations observe the Lord's Supper as a

separate meeting each Sunday and do not view their full-time ministers as being a separate clerical order, but rather consider every believer a "priest." Much ministry is given by qualified men of spiritual gift, secularly employed.

In the 1840's the movement divided. The "exclusive branch," which is now smaller, stresses the interdependency of congregations. It has subdivided and has had reunions. There are now six groups in the U.S. with around 250 congregations.

By contrast, the "Open" branch stresses congregational independence, each assembly being guided by local elders. The "Open" branch has a large foreign missions effort and is cooperative with other evangelicals. The "Open" branch statistics are given below.

Churches: 800 Inclusive Membership: 74,000 Sunday or Sabbath Schools: N.R. Total Enrollment: N.R. Ordained Clergy: 380

NO GENERAL ORGANIZATION

Correspondent: Letters of Interest Associates, P. O. Box 294, 218 West Willow, Wheaton, IL 60187. Tel. (312) 653-6550.

OTHER ORGANIZATIONS

Christian Missions in Many Lands, Box 13, Spring Lake, NJ 07762
Stewards Foundation, Box 294, Wheaton, IL 60187
Letters of Interest Associates, Box 294, Wheaton, IL 60187
Literature Crusades, Prospect Heights, IL 60070

PUBLISHERS

Interest Magazine (m), Box 294, Wheaton, IL 60187, James A. Stahr, Ed.
Loiseaux Brothers, Inc., 1238 Corlies, Neptune, NJ 17753
Walterick Publishers, Box 2216, Kansas City, KS 66110
Christian Missions Press, Waynesboro, GA 30830
The Uplook (m), Box 2041, Grand Rapids, MI 49501, Peter Pell, Ed.

Polish National Catholic Church of America

After a long period of dissatisfaction with Roman Catholic administration and ideology and, in addition, through the strong desire for religious freedom, this body was organized in 1897.

GENERAL ORGANIZATION

General Synod: every four years. (Next General Synod, October 1982)
Headquarters: 529 East Locust St., Scranton, PA 18505. Tel. (717) 356-9131

OFFICERS

Prime Bishop, Most Rev. Thaddeus F. Zielinski, 115 Lake Scranton Rd., Scranton, PA 18505
Bishop of the Central Diocese, Rt. Rev. Anthony M. Rysz, 529 E. Locust St., Scranton, PA 18505
Bishop of the Eastern Diocese, Rt. Rev. Walter A. Slowakiewicz, 635 Union St., Manchester, NH 03104
Bishop of the Buffalo-Pittsburgh Diocese, ——— 182 Sobieski St., Buffalo, NY 14212
Bishop of Western Diocese, Rt. Rev. Francis Rowinski, 2019 W. Charleston St., Chicago, IL 60647
Bishop of the Canadian Diocese, Rt. Rev. Joseph I. Nieminski, 186 Cowan Ave., Toronto, Ontario M6K 2N6

Presbyterian Church in America

With a strong commitment to missionary work both at home and abroad and to continuing historic Presbyterianism in the nation, this body was formally organized in December 1973 in Birmingham, Alabama. Most of its original members were formerly affiliated with the Presbyterian Church in the United States. Unlike PCUS, the PCA has no sectional boundaries and now has members in many parts of the country. After using the name National Presbyterian Church in its first year, the body adopted the name Presbyterian Church in America at its second general assembly. The PCA believes the Bible is the inerrant Word of God and the only infallible and sufficient rule of faith and practice. All officers are required to subscribe, without reservation, to the Reformed faith as set forth in the Westminster Confession and Catechisms.

Churches: 440 Inclusive Membership: 82,095 Sunday or Sabbath Schools: 440 Total Enrollment: 40,595 Ordained Clergy: 584

GENERAL ORGANIZATION

General assembly: meets annually (1980 meeting: Savannah, Georgia, June 16-20)

OFFICERS

Mod., William F. Joseph
Stated Clk., Rev. Morton H. Smith, P. O. Box 312, Brevard, NC 28712. Tel. (704) 883-8203

PERMANENT COMMITTEES

Adm., Dan Moore, P. O. Box 6287, Columbus, A 31907
Christian Education and Publications, Rev. Charles Dunahoo, P.O. Box 39, Decatur, GA 30031
Mission to the United States, Rev. J. Philip Clark, P.O. Box 1703, Decatur, GA 30031
Mission to the World, Rev. Paul McKaughan, P.O. Box 1744, Decatur, GA 30031

PERIODICAL

The PCA Messenger (m), P.O. Box 39, Decatur, GA 30031, Arthur H. Matthews, Ed.

Presbyterian Church in the United States

The Presbyterian Church in the United States (PCUS) is a branch of the major American Presbyterian tradition which broke apart during the Civil War. It was organized as a separate denomination at the General Assembly at Augusta, Georgia, in 1861 and was constituted as the Presbyterian Church in the United States in 1865.

The PCUS is the dominant branch of American Presbyterianism in the South and Southeast. The Church is confined to an area bounded by Maryland and the Virginias, the Ohio River, Missouri, Kansas, Oklahoma and Texas.

The Constitution of the Church consists of the Westminster Confession of Faith, the Westminster Larger and Shorter Catechisms, and the Book of Church Order, all of which were originally adopted by the General Assembly at Philadelphia in 1789. These have since undergone separate modification without major change to the system or corpus of the documents.

The PCUS maintains a consistent ecumenical outlook, has been deeply involved in overseas mission commitments, and has been a major influence in Southern Protestantism.

Close relationships with the United Presbyterian Church in the United States of America are maintained, with major negotiations looking toward reunion of these two presbyterian bodies currently under way. Eleven of the 60 presbyteries of the Presbyterian Church in the United States are union presbyteries with the United

Presbyterian Church in the United States of America, and union churches are numerous in areas where both denominations are present.

Denominational offices are located at 341 Ponce de Leon Ave., NE, Atlanta, GA 30308. There are seven synods and 59 presbyteries, each with separate regional offices.

Churches: 4,007 Inclusive Membership: 862,416 Sunday or Sabbath Schools 4,000 Total Enrollment: 405,926 Ordained Clergy: 5,254

GENERAL ORGANIZATION

The General Assembly: Meets annually. Next meeting: Myrtle Beach, SC, May 30-June 6, 1980

OFFICERS

Mod., Albert C. Winn
Stated Clk., James E. Andrews
Assoc. Stated Clk., Flynn V. Long, Jr.

OFFICE OF THE GENERAL ASSEMBLY

341 Ponce de Leon Ave., NE, Atlanta, GA 30308. Tel. (404) 873-1531
Office of the Stated Clk., James E. Andrews
Office of Review and Evaluation, Richard G. Hutcheson, James E. Womack, Jr., Beverly Myres
Council on Theology and Culture, B. Harrison Taylor
Committee on Women's Concerns, Carole Goodspeed
Council on Church and Race, Otis Turner

GENERAL ASSEMBLY MISSION BOARD

Administrative Unit: Adm. Dir., Patricia McClurg; Budget and Planning, John Coffin; Interpretation and Advocacy, William Crawford; Personnel, Linda Thomas

Division of National Mission: Dir., Robert Miller; Youth Ministry, William Forbes; Leader Development, Byron Jackson; Editor, Children's Materials, Frances Johns; Church Officer and Educational Leader Development and Shared Approaches, Mary Jean McFadyen; Editor, Adult Material, Marvin Simmers; Curriculum Resources and Interpretation, Henrietta Wilkinson; Minority Church Development, Elias Hardge; Evangelism and Membership Growth, Bing Kong Han; Congregational and Church Development, James Vande Berg; Women's Work, Lois Stover, Lillian Weaver; Joint Office of Worship, Harold M. Daniels

Division of International Mission: Dir., G. Thompson Brown; Missionary Support and Itineration, Ann Broom; Missionary Resources and Communication, James Magruder; Overseas Program Coord., William Rice, Africa/Europe/Middle East, John Pritchard; Asia/Pacific, Insik Kim; Latin America/Caribbean, Edla Gabriel Oliveira; Missionary Personnel Services and Enlistment, Miriam Dunson; Pastoral Care of Missionaries, Harry Phillips; International Leadership Development, Elizabeth Dunlap; Missionary Communicators: Alastair J. Scougal, Africa/Europe/Middle East; Alma Grubbs, Asia/South Pacific; Chess Campbell, Latin America/Caribbean

Division of Court Partnership Services: Dir., A. Milton Riviere; Professional Develop., Mary V. Atkinson, Donald K. Campbell, Diane Tennis; Stewardship and Funding, Robert Richardson, Bruce Berry, Byron Knight; Management of Court Systems, Robert Rea; Regional Communicators: Dorothy Barnard, Mid-America; J. Calvin Chesnutt, Southeast; Robert Grigsby, Mid-South; Andrea Ahlers, Florida; James M. McChesney, Jr., North Carolina; Mabel T. Franz, Red River; William E. Pauley, Virginias

Division of Corporate and Social Mission: Dir., George B. Telford, Jr.; Ecumenical Coordination, David W. A. Taylor, Lewis H. Lancaster, Jr.; Washington Communicator, George Chauncey; Minority Affairs, Winston Lawson; Corporate Witness in Public Affairs, Belle Miller McMaster, Gaspar Langella; ———, Education Through Mission; Higher Education, J. Rodney Fulcher, Clyde Robinson; World Service/World Hunger, James A. Cogswell, Colleen Shannon-Thornberry

Division of Central Support Services: Dir. (Treas.), J. Richard Hacke; Communications Group: Mgr., Bill Huie; Electronic Media, Carole Etzler; Presbyterian News Services, Marj Carpenter, Editor, Presbyterian Survey, Bill Lamkin; Electronic Media, Fran Terranella; Fiscal Group: Mgr., (Controller and Assist. Treas.), Paul J. Case; Accounting, Marta Machado; Accounting and Missionary Support, William P. Partenheimer; Operations Group: Mgr., Samuel N. Hezlep; Property Management Group: Mgr., Charles Harris; Publishing Group: Mgr., Ross Cockrell; Dir., John Knox Press, Richard A. Ray; Assist. John Knox Press Editor, Donald Hardy; Design Services, Robert Stratton; Data Processing Dept.: William R. Washburn

OTHER OFFICES AND AGENCIES OF THE GENERAL ASSEMBLY

Board of Annuities and Relief: Exec. Sec., Charles C. Cowsert
The Historical Foundation of the Presbyterian and Reformed Churches, Inc.: Dir., Jerrold L. Brooks

SYNOD EXECUTIVES

Florida, R. P. Douglas, 1221 Lee Rd., Ste. 214, Orlando, FL 32810. Tel. (305) 295-1243
Mid-America, C. Edward Brubaker, 6400 Glenwood, Ste. 111, Overland Park, KS 66202. Tel. (913) 384-3020
Mid-South, J. Harold Jackson, Acting Exec. for Admin., Ste. 416 1701 21st Ave., S., Nashville, TN 37212. Tel. (615) 383-2830
North Carolina, Vernol R. Jansen, Jr., P.O. Box 10785, Raleigh, NC 27605. Tel. (919) 834-4379
Red River, William J. Fogleman, 920 Stemmons Freeway, Denton, TX 76201. Tel. (817) 382-9656
Southeast, James A. Nisbet, 509 Executive Pk., Augusta, GA 30907. Tel. (404) 738-0201
Virginias, H. Davis Yeuell, 4841 Williamson Rd., Roanoke, VA 24012. Tel. (703) 563-0393

Primitive Advent Christian Church

A development from the Advent Christian Church; all churches are located in West Virginia

Churches: 10 Inclusive Membership: 550 Sunday or Sabbath Schools: 9 Total Enrollment: 568 Ordained Clergy: 10

OFFICERS

Pres., Elza Moss, Sissonville, WV 25185. Tel. (304) 984-3528
Vice-Pres., Donald Young, 1640 Clay Ave., South Charleston, WV
Sec. and Treas., Hugh W. Good, 395 Frame Rd., Elkview, WV 25071

Primitive Baptists

A large group of Baptists, mainly through the South, who are opposed to all centralization and to modern missionary societies. This body believes, preaches Salvation by Grace alone.

GENERAL ORGANIZATION

Headquarters: Cayce Publ. Co., S. Second St., Thornton, AR 71766. Tel. (501) 352-3694

OFFICERS

Elder W. H. Cayce, S. Second St., Thornton, AR 71766. Tel. (501) 352-3694

PERIODICALS

Primitive Baptist (m), Thornton, AR W. H. Cayce, Ed.
For the Poor (m), Thornton, Ar 71766. W. H. Cayce, Ed.
Baptist Witness, Box 17037, Cincinnati, OH 45217. L. Bradley, Jr., Ed.

Primitive Methodist Church, U.S.A.

This body was established at Mow Cop in England as an offshoot of the Wesleyan Connection. It was brought to America by immigrants in 1829, and organized into a General Conference in 1889. The Annual and General Conferences were merged to form The Conference in 1975.

Churches: 88 Inclusive Membership: 10,222 Sunday or Sabbath Schools: 82 Total Enrollment: 6,639 Ordained clergy: 91

GENERAL ORGANIZATION

The Conference, annual (Next Meeting, May 1980)

OFFICERS

Pres., Rev. G. Kenneth Tyson, 408 E. Market St., Scranton, PA 18509
Sec., Rev. K. Gene Carroll, 55 Cherry St., Plymouth, PA 18651
Treas., Mr. Raymond C. Baldwin, 11012 Langton Arms Ct., Oakton, VA 22124

PERIODICAL

The Primitive Methodist Journal (m), 5227 Holmes St., Pittsburgh, PA 15201. Rev. Russell Masartis, Ed.

Progressive National Baptist Convention, Inc.

A body which held its organizational meeting at Cincinnati, November, 1961, and subsequent regional sessions, followed by the first annual session in Philadelphia in 1962

GENERAL ORGANIZATION

Convention: annual

OFFICERS

Pres., Rev. William A. Jones, Jr., Bethany Baptist Church, 460 Sumner Ave., Brooklyn, NY 11216
Gen. Sec., Dr. S. S. Hodges, 601 50th St., N.E., Washington, DC 20019. Tel. (202) 396-0558
Dir., Publicity, Mrs. Merdean Fielding, 47 Pricewoods La., St. Louis, MO 63132

OTHER ORGANIZATIONS

Dept. of Christian Education: Sec., Rev. C. B. Lucas, 3815 W. Broadway, Louisville, KY 40211
Women's Auxiliary: Pres., Ms. Peggy A. Garnett, 313 Oak St., Elmwood Pl., Cincinnati, OH 45216
Home Mission Bd., Exec. Dir., Dr. Joseph O. Bass, 601 50th St., N.E., Washington, DC 20019.
Baptist Foreign Mission Bureau: Exec. Sec., ———
Congress of Christian Education: Pres., Rev. Howard W. Creecy, Mt. Moriah Bapt. Ch., 200 Ashby St., S.W., Atlanta, GA 30314

PERIODICAL

Baptist Progress (q), Mt. Carmel Baptist Church, 712-14 Quincy St., Brooklyn, NY 11221. Rev. V. Simpson Turner, Ed.

The Protestant Conference (Lutheran), Inc.

Organized in 1927 in Wisconsin as a result of differences with the Evangelical Lutheran Joint Synod of Wisconsin and Other States.

GENERAL ORGANIZATION

Conference: meets 3 times annually

OFFICERS

Rec. Sec., Pastor Gerald Hinz, Shiocton, WI 54170
Fin. Sec.-Treas., Michael Meler, 1023 Colan Blvd., Rice Lake, WI 54868

PERIODICAL

Faith-Life (bi-m), P.O. Box 2141, LaCrosse, WI 54601. Pastor Marcus Albrecht, Rt. 1, Mindoro, WI 54644, Ed.

Protestant Reformed Churches in America

Organized in 1926 in Grand Rapids, Michigan. The doctrinal tenets are those of Calvinism, the Belgic Confession, the Heidelberg Catechism, and the Canons of Dordrecht.

Churches: 21 Inclusive Membership: 4,040 Sunday or Sabbath Schools: 16 Total Enrollment: 669 Ordained Clergy: 25

GENERAL ORGANIZATION

General Synod: meets annually (June)
Headquarters: 16515 South Park Ave., South Holland, IL 60473. Tel. (312) 333-1314

OFFICER

Stat. Clk., Rev. M. Joostens, 2016 Tekonsha, S.E., Grand Rapids, MI 49506

Reformed Baptists

This group is a contemporary movement which began in the mid 1950s. However, its "newness" is deceiving for the movement's theology reflects a return to the London Confession (1689) and Philadelphia Confession (1742). Reformed Baptists stress the teachings of the Calvinistic Reformation regarding salvation. But they also emphasize that a church should consist only of those who have publicly confessed personal faith in Christ by immersion in water.

Although individual churches are independent, they are interdependent in terms of supporting missionaries, literature work, and discussion of doctrine and discipline.

Churches: 250 Inclusive Membership: 5,000 Sunday or Sabbath Schools: N.R. Total Enrollment: N.R. Ordained Clergy: 350

NO GENERAL ORGANIZATION

Correspondent: Pastor Jon Zens, 171 Luna Dr., Nashville, TN 37211. Tel. (615) 832-4860

PERIODICALS

Baptist Reformation Review (q), Box 40161, Nashville, TN 37204. Tel. (615) 269-9600. Jon Zens, Ed.
Reformation Today (bi-m), 2817 Dashwood St., Lakewood, CA 90712. Erroll Hulse, Ed
Sword and Trowel (m), P. O. Box 1659, Plano, TX 75074 McKinney, Ed.

Reformed Church in America

The Reformed Church in America was established in 1628 by the earliest settlers of New York. It is the oldest Protestant denomination with a continuous ministry in North America. Until 1867 it was known as the Reformed Protestant Dutch Church.

Churches: 898 Inclusive Membership: 348,080 Sunday or Sabbath Schools: 898 Total Enrollment: 108,540 Ordained Clergy: 1,418

GENERAL ORGANIZATION

General Synod: annual (Next meeting, June 16-20, 1980. Schenectady, New York)
National Office: 475 Riverside Dr., New York, NY 10027. Tel. (212) 870-2841

OFFICERS AND STAFF OF GENERAL SYNOD

Pres., Edwin G. Mulder, 620 W. 24 St., Holland, MI 49423
Gen. Sec., Rev. Arie R. Brouwer

OTHER ORGANIZATIONS

Board of Direction: Pres., Harry E. De Bruyn, 6721 Wyandot Dr., Palos Heights, IL 60463
General Program Council: Chpsn., Thomas J. Harris, 1445 Main St., Sommerville, NJ 08876; Exec. Sec. for Program, John R. Walchenbach
Office of Human Resources: Coord., Alvin J. Poppen; Beth E. Marcus, Adult Voluntary Services
Office of Operations and Finance: Sec., Marvin D. Hoff; Treas., Donald Moss
Office of Promotion and Communications: Lois M. Joice, Dir.
Eastern Metropolitan Regional Center: 475 Riverside Dr., NY 10027, Arthur O. Van Eck, Sec. for Regional Services; John E. Buteyn, Sec. for World Ministries, Roland Ackerman, Sec. for Development
Northeastern Regional Center, 1790 Grand Blvd., Schenectady, NY 12309: Herman E. Luben, Sec. for Regional Services and Evangelism; Ms. Patricia L. Stere., Sec. for Christian Nurture and Young Adult Ministry
Midwestern Regional Center, 18525 Torrence Ave., Lansing, IL 60438: Gordon Timmerman, Sec. for Regional Services; Joseph B. Muyskens, Sec. for Social Ministries, Box 247, Grandville, Mi 49418; Glenn Bruggers, Sec. for Asian and African Ministries; Harry Pofahl, Sec. for Development
Western Regional Center: Delbert Vander Haar, Sec. for Regional Services, Orange City IA 51041; Harold M. Hakken, Sec. for Devel., 421 N. Brookhurst, Ste. 218, Anaheim, CA 92801; Donald Jansma, Sec. for Evangelism and Renewal, c/o Central College, Box 62, Pella, IA 50219
Reformed Church Women: Beth E. Marcus, Exec. Dir., 475 Riverside Dr., New York, NY 10027
The Black Council: M. William Howard, Jr., Exec. Dir., 475 Riverside Dr., New York NY 10027
The Hispanic Council: Ray Rivera, National Sec., 475 Riverside Dr., New York, NY 10027
The American Indian Council: Kenneth Mallory, Chpsn., Winnebago, NB 68071
Board of Pensions: Pres., Exec. Sec., Arie R. Brouwer, 475 Riverside Dr., New York, NY 10027

PERIODICAL

The Church Herald (bi-m), 1324 Lake Dr., SE, Grand Rapids, MI 49506, John C. Stapert, Ed.

Reformed Church in the United States

The Eureka Classis, organized in 1910 in South Dakota, continued as the Reformed Church in the United States, when that body merged into the Evangelical and Reformed Church in 1934. The doctrines are Calvinistic as set forth in the Heidelberg Catechism.

GENERAL ORGANIZATION

Classis: annual

OFFICERS

Pres., Rev. Vernon Pollema, 3930 Mason Dr., Lincoln, NB 68521. Tel., (402) 477-7289
Vice-Pres., Rev. Paul Treick, 927 E. Graceway Dr., Napoleon, OH 43545
Clerk, Rev. Steven Work, Rte. 3, Garner, IA 50438
Treas., Donald Greiman, Route 3, Garner, IA 50438

PERIODICAL

The Reformed Herald (m), 317 So. Garfield, Pierre, SD 57501. N. Jones, Ed.

Reformed Episcopal Church

In 1873, Bishop Cummins withdrew from the Protestant Episcopal Church in protest against certain sacramentalist and ritualistic tendencies and, with other clergymen and laymen, organized the church as above.

GENERAL ORGANIZATION

General Council: triennial (Next meeting, 1978) Sec., Gen. Council, Rev. D. Ellsworth Raudenbush, 560 Fountain St., Havre de Grace, MD 21078. Tel. (301) 939-3210

OFFICERS

Pres. and Presid. Bishop, Rev. Theophilos J. Herter, 26 Strath Haven Dr., Broomall, PA 19008
Vice-Pres., G. Arnold Pfaffenbach, 209 N. Union Ave., Havre de Grace, MD 21078
Sec., Rev. D. Ellsworth Raudenbush, 560 Fountain St., Havre de Grace, MD 21078
Treas., David B. Boon, 4106 Hain Dr., Lafayette Hill, PA 19444

OTHER ORGANIZATIONS

Board of Foreign Missions: Pres., Rev. Samuel M. Forster, 901 Church Rd., Oreland, PA 19075; Treas.,

Maurice C. Mower, 3021 Cedar Bridge Ave., Northfield, NJ 08225
Board of National Church Extension: Pres., Rev. D. Ellsworth Raudenbush, 560 Fountain St., Havre de Grace, MD 21078; Sec., Rev. Frank C. Roppelt; Treas., Robert T. Laur, 574 Edmondson Ave., Catonsville, MD 21228
Trustees Sustentation Fund: Pres.———; Treas., Harry Moock, 7625 A William Way, Elkins Park, PA 19117
Publication Society: Pres., Rev. Harold Mulvaney, Hartford Rd., Moorestown, NJ 08057
The Reapers: Pres., Ms. Mary Longenecker; Treas., Mrs. James Browne, Upper Black Eddy, PA 18972

BISHOPS

Joseph E. Kearney, Summerville, SC 29483
Howard D. Higgins, Four Brooks, Pipersville; R.D., PA 18947
William H. S. Jerdan, Summerville, SC 29483.
Sanco K. Rembert, 121 Moultrie St., Charleston, SC 29403
Theophilus J. Herter, 26 Strath Haven Dr.; Broomall, PA 19008
Franklin H. Seller, 1629 W. 99th St., Chicago, IL 60643
Leonard W. Riches, 1162 Beverly Rd., Jenkintown, PA 19046

PERIODICAL

Episcopal Recorder (m), 25 S. 43rd St., Philadelphia, PA 19104. Bishop Howard D. Higgins, Ed.

Reformed Mennonite Church

This group was reorganized in 1812 under John Herr because they did not know of any other organization that fully carried out New Testament teachings. They believe there can be only one true church, consisting of regenerated persons who are united in love and doctrine.

OFFICER

Bishop Earl Basinger, 1036 Lincoln Heights Ave., Ephrata, PA 17522

Reformed Methodist Union Episcopal Church

Organized in 1885 at Georgetown, S.C. among persons withdrawing from the African Methodist Episcopal Church; the doctrines were generally those of the Methodist Episcopal Church.

GENERAL ORGANIZATION

General Conference: annual Headquarters: Charleston, SC 29407

OFFICERS

Rt. Rev. Leroy Gethers, 1136 Brody Ave., Charleston, SC 29407. Tel. (803) 766-3539
Sec., Rev. Eugene Davis, Jr., 1219 Carnegie Ave., Charleston, SC 29407. Tel. (803) 556-1372
Sec. of Education, Fred E. German
Treas., Rufus German
Sec. of Books Concerns, Earnest McKeever
Sec. of Pension Fund, Rev. Joseph Powell
Sec. of Church Extension, Joseph Gadsden
Sec. of Church Contingent, Sammie Mitchell
Sec. of Sunday Union, Benjamin H. Bolds.
Sec. of Mission, Rev. John Moore

Reformed Presbyterian Church, Evangelical Synod

This church was formed on April 6, 1965 by a union of the Reformed Presbyterian Church in North America, General Synod, and the Evangelical Presbyterian Church. It is Biblical in its theology, subscribes to the Westminster Confession of Faith and Catechisms as its doctrinal standards, subordinate to Holy Scripture.

GENERAL ORGANIZATION

General Synod: annual

OFFICERS

Mod., Dr. P. Robert Palmer, 12330 Conway Rd., St. Louis, MO 63141
Stated Clk., Dr. Paul R. Gilchrist, 107 Hardy Rd., Lookout Mountain, TN 37350

Reformed Presbyterian Church of North America

Also known as the Church of the Covenanters. Origin dates back to the Reformation days of Scotland when the Covenanters signed their "Covenants" in resistance to the king and the Roman Church in the enforcement of state church practices. The Church in America has signed two "Covenants" in particular, those of 1871 and 1954.

GENERAL ORGANIZATION

Synod: annual

OFFICERS

Mod., J. Renwick Wright, 3000 Graham Blvd., Pittsburgh, PA 15235
Clk., Rev. Paul M. Martin, 1031 E. Glenrosa, Phoenix, AZ 85014. Tel. (602) 266-1454
Asst. Clk., Rev. Stanley Copeland, 3920 S. Kennedy, Bloomington, IN 47401
Stated Clk., Louis D. Hutmire, 7418 Penn Ave., Pittsburgh, PA 15208. Tel. (412) 731-1177

PERIODICALS

The Covenanter Witness (bi-w), 800 Wood St., Pittsburgh, PA 15221. Philip R. Beard, Ed.
Blue Banner Faith and Life (q), 3408 7th Ave., Beaver Falls, PA 15010. Dr. J. G. Vos, Ed.

†Reformed Zion Union Apostolic Church

Organized in 1869, at Boydton, Va., by Elder James R. Howell of New York, a minister of the A.M.E. Zion Church; with doctrines of the Methodist Episcopal Church.

GENERAL ORGANIZATION

Annual Conferences (in August After the Third Sunday) General Conference: quadrennial (Next meeting, 1978)

RELIGIOUS SOCIETY OF FRIENDS

OFFICER

Sec., Deacon, James C. Feggins, 416 South Hill Ave., South Hill, VA 23970

Religious Society of Friends (Conservative)

These Friends mark their present identity from separations occurring by regions at different times from 1845 to 1904. They hold to a minimum of organization structure. Unprogrammed Meetings for Worship, which are basically silent, demonstrate the belief that all individuals may commune directly with God and may share equally in vocal ministry.

They continue to stress the importance of the Living Christ and the experience of the Holy Spirit working with Power in the lives of individuals who obey him.

YEARLY MEETINGS

North Carolina, YM, David H. Brown, 1208 Pinewood Dr., Greensboro, NC 27410

Iowa YM, Olive Wilson, Primghar, IA 51245

Ohio YM, William L. Cope, 44550 S.R. 517, R. 2, Columbiana, OH 44408

Religious Society of Friends (Unaffiliated Meetings)

Elements of the early Friends movement are to be found in this small but significant category of meetings and groups which are marked by spontaneity, fluidity, variety, and experimentation. These groups are not formally associated in traditional ways with the larger organizations within the Society. Some of these unaffiliated groups have begun within the past twenty-five years.

UNAFFILIATED YEARLY MEETINGS

Bolivian Natl. Church of Evangelical Friends, Casilla 544, La Paz, Bolivia

Central Alaska Friends Conf., P.O. Box 252, Fairbanks, AK 99707

Southern Appalachian YM, c/o Oldham, 17 Foxfire Lane, Hendersonville, NC 28739

Mexico, General Meeting, Casa De Los Amigos, Ignacio Mariscal 132, Mexico 1, D.F., Mexico

Alaska YM, P.O. Box 687, Kotzebue, AK 99752

Pacific YM, Lowell Tozer, 4919 Cresita Dr., San Diego 92115

Central YM of the Friends Church, 302 S. Black St., Alexandria, IN 46001

Missouri Valley Conference YM, Marilyn Miriani, Penn Valley Meeting, 4405 Gillham Rd., Kansas City, MO 64110

Central America YM of Evangelical Friends Churches, Apartado 8, Chiquimula, Quatemala, Central America

North Pacific YM, Jackie Van Dyke, Clk., Steering Committee, 3300 N.W. VanBuren Ave., Corvallis, OR 97330

Intermountain YM, Francis McAllister, Clk., Box 922, Flaggstaff, AZ 86002

Reorganized Church of Jesus Christ of Latter Day Saints

Founded April 6, 1830, by Joseph Smith, Jr., and reorganized under the leadership of the founder's son, Joseph Smith III, in 1860. The Church, with headquarters in Independence, MO is established in 35 countries in addition to the United States and Canada. A biennial world conference is held in Independence, Missouri. The current president is Wallace B. Smith, great-grandson of the original founder.

Churches: 1,048 Inclusive Membership: 185,636 Sunday or Sabbath Schools: N.R. Total Enrollment: N.R. Ordained Clergy: 16,039

GENERAL ORGANIZATION

Conference: (World Conference: Biennial in April of even numbered years)

Headquarters: The Auditorium, P.O. Box 1059, Independence, MO 64051. Tel. (816) 833-1000

OFFICERS

First Presidency: Wallace B. Smith, Duane E. Couey, Counselor; Howard S. Sheehy, Jr., Counselor

Pres. of Council of 12 Apostles: Clifford A. Cole

Presiding Bishopric, Francis E. Hansen, Presiding Bishop; Gene M. Hummel, Counselor; Ray E. McClaran, Counselor

Presiding Bishop: Francis E. Hansen, Gene M. Hummel, Ray E. McClaren

Church Sec., Roy Stearns

Div. of Public Affairs: Maurice L Draper, Dir.

PERIODICALS

Saints Herald (bi-m), Independence, MO. Wallace B. Smith, Duane E. Couey, Howard S. Sheehy, Jr., and Paul Wellington, Eds.

Commission (published (3/yr.) by Pastoral Services Commission), Fred Bozarth, Ed.

Armed Forces Newsletter (bi-m), Pershing Tousley, Ed.

Restoration Witness (missionary, m), Independence MO, Norman Rouff, Ed.

The Roman Catholic Church

The largest single body of Christians in the U.S., the Roman Catholic Church, is under the spiritual leadership of His Holiness the Pope. Its establishment in America dates back to the priests who accompanied Columbus on his second voyage to the New World. A settlement, later discontinued, was made at St. Augustine, Florida. The continuous history of this Church in the Colonies began at St. Mary's in Maryland, in 1634.

Churches: 25,542 Inclusive Membership: 49,602,035 Sunday or Sabbath Schools: 10,513 Total Enrollment: 8,527,153 Ordained Clergy: 58,856

(The following information has been furnished by the editor of The Official Catholic Directory, published by P. J. Kenedy & Sons, P.O. Box 729, New York, NY 10022. Reference to this complete volume will provide more adequate information.)

INTERNATIONAL ORGANIZATION

His Holiness the Pope, Bishop of Rome, Vicar of Jesus Christ, Supreme Pontiff of the Catholic Church.

POPE JOHN PAUL II, Karol Wojtyla (born May 18, 1920; installed October 22, 1978)

APOSTOLIC DELEGATE IN THE UNITED STATES

Most Rev. Jean Jadot, 3339 Massachusetts Ave., N.W., Washington, DC 20008. Tel. (202) 333-7121

U.S. ORGANIZATION

National Conference of Catholic Bishops, 1312 Massachusetts Ave., NW, Washington, DC 20005. Tel. (202) 659-6600

The National Conference of Catholic Bishops (NCCB) is a canonical entity operating in accordance with the

Vatican II Decree, **Christus Dominus.** Its purpose is to foster the Church's mission to mankind by providing the Bishops of this country with an opportunity to exchange views and insights of prudence and experience and to exercise in a joint manner their pastoral office.

OFFICERS

Pres., Archbishop John Raphael Quinn
Vice-Pres., Archbishop John R. Roach
Sec., Bishop Thomas C. Kelly, O.P.
Treas., Archbishop John J. Maguire

GENERAL SECRETARIAT

Gen. Sec., Bishop Thomas C. Kelly, O.P.
Assoc. Gen. Secs., Rev. Daniel F. Hoye; Msgr. Thomas J. Leonard

COMMITTEES

Ecumenical and Interreligious Affairs (Ecumenism):
Chpsn., Bishop Bernard F. Law
Secretariat: Exec. Dir., Rev. John Hotchkin
Asst. Exec. Dir., Rev. Peter Sheehan
Liturgy:
Chpsn., Archbishop John R. Quinn of San Francisco
Secretariat: Dir., Rev. Thomas Krosnicki; Asst., Rev. John Gurrieri
Priestly Formation:
Chpsn., Bishop John A. Marshall
Secretariat: Dir., Rev. Daniel Pakenham
Permanent Diaconate:
Chpsn., Bishop Ernest L. Unterhoefler
Secretariat: Dir., Msgr. Ernest Fiedler
Priestly Life and Ministry:
Chpsn., Bishop Raymond J. Gallagher
Secretariat: Dir., Msgr. Colin MacDonald
Pro-Life Activities: Rev. Edward M. Bryce
Secretariat for Latin America, Ms. Frances Neason

United States Catholic Conference, 1312 Massachusetts Ave. NW, Washington, DC 20005, Tel. (202) 659-6600

The United States Catholic Conference (USCC) is a civil entity of the American Catholic Bishops assisting them in their service to the Church in this country by uniting the people of God where voluntary, collective action on a broad diocesan level is needed. The USCC provides an organization structure and the resources needed to insure coordination, cooperation, and assistance in the public, educational, and social concerns of the Church at the national, regional, state, interdiocesan and, as appropriate, diocesan levels.

OFFICERS

Pres., Archbishop John R. Quinn
Vice-Pres., Archbishop John R. Roach
Treas., Archbishop John J. Maguire

GENERAL SECRETARIAT

Gen. Sec., Bishop THomas C. Kelly, O.P.
Assoc. Gen. Sec., Msgr. Thomas J. Leonard
Assoc. Gen. Sec., Rev. Daniel F. Hoye
Sec. for Planning, John J. O'Neill
Sec. for Research, Msgr. George Higgins
Sec. for Public Affairs, Russell Shaw

STAFF OFFICES

Finance & Administration, Dir., Francis Doyle
Accounting, Robert Bailey
Personnel & General Services, Samuel DiMisa
Publications, Angela Ricciardelli
General Counsel, George Reed
Actg. Government Liaison, Dir., James Robinson

RELATED STAFF OFFICES

Secretariat for Spanish-Speaking. Sec. Paul Sedillo
Migration & Refugee Services, Dir., John McCarthy

COMMITTEES AND DEPARTMENTS

Communication: Chpsn., Bishop Joseph R. Crowley; Sec., Richard Hirsch; Film & Broadcasting, Rev. Patrick Sullivan; Creative Services, Francis Frost; National Catholic News Services Richard Daw
Education: Chpsn., Bishop William E. McManus; Sec., Msgr. Wilfred H. Paradis; Assoc. Sec. Sr. Ruth McDonell; Young Adult Ministry, Rev. Patrick O'Neill; Family Life, Rev. Donald Conroy; Federal Assistance Programs, Richard Duffy; Youth Activities, Marisa Guerin; Adult Ed., Thomas Tewey; Religious Ed., Rev. David E. Beebe; Coord. of Research & Program Development, Rev. Eugene Hemrick; Coord., NCD Implementation, Sr. Mariella Frye
Social Development and World Peace: Chpsn., Bishop Joseph A. McNicholas; Sec., Msgr. Francis Lally; Domestic Social Development, Francis Butler, Health Affairs, Charlotte M. Mahoney; Rural Issues, David Byers; International Justice and Peace, Rev. J. Bryan Hehir; African Section, Rev. Rollins Lambert; Europe & East Asia, Edward Doherty; Latin American Section, Thomas Quigley; Strategic & Political Section, Rev. Joseph Nangle; Economic Section, Henry Brodie

RELATED ORGANIZATIONS

Campaign for Human Development, Dir., Rev. Marvin Mottet
Catholic Relief Services, Exec. Dir., Bishop Edwin B. Broderick

U.S.CATHOLIC BISHOPS' ADVISORY COUNCIL

Chpsn., Joseph Monte

CORPORATE ENTITIES AFFILIATED WITH USCC

National Council of Catholic Laity, Pres., Mrs. John Eckstein, 1415 Wm. White Blvd., Iowa City, IA 52240
National Council of Catholic Women, Pres., Mrs. Arthur Horsell: Exec. Dir., Ms. Mary Helen Madden, 1330 Massachusetts Ave., NW, Washington, DC 20005
National Council of Catholic Men, Pres., William Sandweg, 4712 Randolph Dr., Annandale, VA 22003

ASSOCIATIONS

Canon Law Society of America, Exec. Coord., Rev. Donald Heintschel, 1933 Spielbush Ave., Toledo OH 43624
Conference of Major Religious Superiors of Men, Exec. Sec., Bro. Thomas More Page: 1330 Massachusetts Ave., NW, Washington, DC 20005
Leadership Conference of Women Religious, Sec., Sr. Lora Ann Quinonez, 1330 Massachusetts Ave., NW, Washington, DC 20005
National Catholic Educational Association, Pres., Rev. John F. Myers, One Dupont Circle, NW, Washington, DC 20036

ROMAN CATHOLIC CHURCH

National Conference of Catholic Charities, Exec. Dir., Msgr. Lawrence Corcoran, 1347 Connecticut Ave., NW, Washington, DC 20006

National Office for Black Catholics, Exec. Dir., Brother Cyprian Rowe, 734 15th St., NW, Washington, DC 20005

Word of God Institute, Exec. Dir., Rev. John Burke, 487 Michigan Ave., NE, Washington, DC 20017

ARCHDIOCESES AND DIOCESES

There follows an alphabetical listing of Archdioceses and Dioceses of The Roman Catholic Church. Each Archdiocese or Diocese contains the following information in sequence: Name of incumbent Bishop; name of Auxiliary Bishop with right to succession, if any; name of the Apostolic Administrator for vacant Sees; name of Episcopal Vicars, if any, and their territorial jurisdiction; name and address of Ecumenical officers, if any; address and telephone number of the Chancery office. Archdioceses are designated in the text.

Cardinals are addressed as "His Eminence" and Archbishops and Bishops as "Most Reverend."

Albany, Bishop Howard J. Hubbard, Ecumenical Officer, Mr. William A. Toomey, 40 N. Main, Ave., Albany, NY 12203. Tel. (518) 438-6681. Chancery Office, 465 State St., Albany, NY 12206. Tel. (518) 462-5476

Alexandria-Shreveport, Bishop Lawrence P. Graves, Office, 2315 Texas Ave., P.O. Box 5665, Alexandria, LA 71301. Tel. (318) 445-2401

Allentown, Bishop Joseph McShea, Ecumenical Officer, Rev. Edward B. Connolly, 1200 S. Cedar Crest Blvd., Allentown, PA 18105. Tel. (215) 821-2121. Chancery Office, 202 N 17th St., Allentown, PA 18104. Tel. (215) 437-0755

Altoona-Johnstown, Bishop James J. Hogan. Ecumenical Officer, Rev. Msgr. Philip P. Saylor, 309 Lotz Ave., Lakemont, Altoona, PA 16602. Chancery Office, Box 126, Logan Blvd., Hollidaysburg, PA 16648. Tel. (814) 695-5579.

Amarillo, Bishop Lawrence M. De Falco. Ecumenical Officer, Rev. Ronald F. Krisman, 4011 54th St., Lubbock, TX 79413. Tel. (806) 792-6168. Chancery Office, 1800 N. Spring St., P.O. Box 5644, Amarillo, TX 79107. Tel. (806) 383-2243

Archdiocese of Anchorage, Archbishop Francis T. Hurley. Chancery Office, P.O. Box 2239, Anchorage, AK 99510. Tel. (907) 277-1628

Arlington, Bishop Thomas J. Welsh Ecumenical Officer, Rev. John A. O'Connell, 5312 10th St., N. Arlington, VA 22205. Tel. (703) 528-6276. Chancery, Ste. 704, 200 Glebe Rd., Arlington, VA 22203. Tel. (703) 841-2500

Archdiocese of Atlanta, Archbishop Thomas A. Donnellan. 30305. Chancery Office, 756 W. Peachtree St., N.W., Atlanta, GA 30308. Tel. (404) 881-6708

Austin, Bishop Vincent M. Harris. Chancery Office, N. Congress and 16th, P.O. Box 13327 Capital Sta. Austin, TX 78711. Tel. (512) 476-4888

Baker, Bishop Thomas J. Connolly, Ecumenical Officer, Very Rev. Joseph B. Hayes, 815 High St., Klamath, OR 97601. Tel. (503) 884-4566. Chancery Office, Baker and First Sts., P.O. Box 826, Baker, OR 97814. Tel. (503) 523-2373

Archdiocese of Baltimore, Archbishop William D. Borders, Chancery Office, 320 Cathedral St., Baltimore, MD 21201. Tel. (301) 547-5446. Ecumenical Officer, Rev. Brian M. Rafferty, 320 Cathedral St., Baltimore, MD 21201. Tel. (301) 461-9111

Baton Rouge, Bishop Joseph V. Sullivan. Ecumenical Officer, Rev. Michael Maroney, P. O. Box 2028, Baton Rouge, LA 70821. Tel. (504) 387-0561. Chancery Office, P.O. Box 2028, Baton Rouge, LA 70821. Tel. (504) 387-0561

Beaumont, Bishop Bernard J. Ganter, Ecumenical Officer, ———. Chancery Office, P.O. Box 3948, Beaumont, TX 77704, Tel. (713) 838-0451

Belleville, Bishop William M. Cosgrove, Ecumenical Officer, ———. Tel (618) 327-3232. Chancery Office, 5312 W. Main St., Box 896, Belleville, IL 62223. Tel. (618) 233-1100

Biloxi, Bishop Joseph Howse, Ecumenical Officer, Rev. John Izral, 512 College St., Wiggins, MS 39577. Tel. (601) 928-2592. Chancery Office, P.O. Box 1198, Biloxi, MS 39533

Birmingham, Bishop Joseph G. Vath. Ecumenical Officer, Rev. Peter Sheehan, P.O. Box 2086, Birmingham, AL 35201. Chancery Office, P.O. Box 2086, Birmingham, AL 35201. Tel. (205) 833-0171

Bismarck, Bishop Hilary B. Hacker, Chancery Office, 420 Raymond St., Box 1575, Bismarck, ND 58501. Tel. (701) 223-1347

Boise, Bishop Sylvester W. Treinen. Ecumenical Officer, Rev. Roger LaChance, 2020 12th Ave., Lewiston, ID 83501. Chancery Office, Box 769, 420 Idaho St., Boise, ID 83701. Tel. (208) 342-1311

Archdiocese of Boston, Archbishop Humberto Cardinal S. Medeiros; Ecumenical Officer, Rev. Msgr. Edward G. Murray. Tel. (617) 899-5500. Chancery Office, 2121 Commonwealth Ave., Brighton, MA 02135. Tel. (617) 254-0100

Bridgeport, Bishop Walter W. Curtis, Ecumenical Officer, Rev. Thomas J. Driscoll, 84 Long Lots Rd., Westport, CT 06880. Tel. (203) 227-7245. Chancery Office, 238 Jewett Ave., Bridgeport CT 06606. Tel. (203) 372-4301

Brooklyn, Bishop Francis J. Mugavero. Ecumenical Officer: Rev. Ignatius A. Catanello, 157-04 82nd St., Howard Beach, NY 11414. Tel. (212) 738-1616. Chancery Office, 75 Greene Ave., Brooklyn, NY 11238 Tel. (212) 638-5500

Brownsville, Bishop John J. Fitzpatrick, Ecumenical Officer: Rev. John J. Singer, P.O. Box 451, Rio Hondo, TX 78583. Tel. (512) 748-2327. Chancery Office, P.O. Box 2279, Brownsville, TX 78520. Tel. (512) 542-2501

Buffalo, Bishop Edward D. Head, Ecumenical Officer: Rev. Robert S. Sweeny, Chancery Office, 35 Lincoln Parkway, Buffalo, NY 14222. Tel. (716) 883-1372

Burlington, Bishop John A. Marshall. Ecumenical Officer: Rev. Raymond J. Doherty, S.S.E., St. Michael's College, Winooski, VT 05404 Tel. (802) 655-2000. Chancery Office, 351 North Ave., Burlington, VT 05401. Tel. (802) 658-6110

Camden, Bishop George H. Guilfoyle, Ecumenical Officer, Rev. Msgr. James J. Gaffney, 3107 Alabama Rd., Camden, NJ 08104. Tel. (609) 962-8642. Chancery Office, 1845 Haddon Ave., Camden, NJ 08101. Tel. (609) 541-2100

Charleston, Bishop Ernest L. Unterkoefler. Ecumenical Officer, Rev. Msgr. Charles J. Baum, 338 W. Washington St., Greenville, SC 29601. Tel. (803) 271-8422. Chancery Office, 119 Broad St., Charleston, SC 29401. Tel. (803) 723-3488

Charlotte, Bishop Michael S. Begley, Chancery Office P.O. Box 3776 Charlotte, NC 28203. Tel. (704) 377-6871

Cheyenne, Bishop Joseph H. Hart. Ecumenical Officer Msgr. John Corrigan, 1009 9th St., Wheatland, WY 82201. Tel. (307) 322-2070. Chancery Office, Box 426, Cheyenne, WY 82001. Tel. (307) 638-9394

Archdiocese of Chicago, John Cardinal Cody. Ecumenical Officer: Rev. William Lion, 201 E. Ohio, Chicago, IL 60611. Chancery Office, 155 E. Superior Ave., Chicago, IL 60611. Tel. (312) 751-8200

Archdiocese of Cincinnati, Archbishop Joseph L. Bernadin. Ecumenical Officer, Rev. Ralph J. Lawrence, 5440 Moeller Ave., Cincinnati, OH 45212. Chancery Office, 29 E. 8th St., Cincinnati, OH 45202. Tel. (513) 721-1532.

Cleveland, Bishop James A. Hickey. Ecumenical Officer, Rev. John L. Fiala, 1031 Superior Ave., Cleveland, OH 44114. Tel. (216) 696-6525. Tel. (216) 526-1686. Chancery Office, 350 Chancery Bldg., Cathedral Square, 1027 Superior Ave., Cleveland, OH 44114. Tel. (216) 696-6525

Columbus, Bishop Edward J. Herrmann. Ecumenical Officer, Most Rev. George A. Fulcher, 212 E. Broad St., Columbus, OH 43215. Chancery Office, 198 E. Broad St., Columbus, OH 43215. Tel. (614) 224-2251

Corpus Christi, Bishop Thomas J. Drury. Ecumencial Officer, Rev. James Tamayo, Chancery Office, 620 Lipan St., Corpus Christi, TX 78401. Tel. (512) 882-6191

Covington, Bishop Richard H. Ackerman, C.S. Sp., Ecumenical Officer, Rev. Msgr. Edward T. Hickey, 1680 Dixie Hwy., Fort Wright, Covington, KY 41011. Chancery Office, 1140 Madison Ave., P.O. Box 192, Covington, KY 41012. Tel. (606) 291-4240

Crookston, Bishop Victor Balke. Ecumenical Officer, ——— Chancery Office, 1200 Memorial Dr., P.O. Box 610, Crookston, MN 56716. Tel. (218) 281-4533.

Dallas, Bishop Thomas Tschoepe, Ecumenical Officer, Rev. Robert C. Rehkemper. Chancery Office, 3915 Lemmon Ave., P.O. Box 19507, Dallas, TX 75219. Tel. (214) 528-2240

Davenport, Bishop Gerald Francis O'Keefe, Ecumenical Officer, Rev. John F. Hynes, 615 Marquette St., Davenport, IA 52802. Tel. (319) 322-3473. Chancery Office, 2706 Gaines St., Davenport, IA 52804. Tel. (319) 324-1911

Archdiocese of Denver. Archbishop James V. Casey. Chancery Office, 200 Josephine St., Denver, CO 80206. Tel. (303) 388-4411 Tel. (303) 388-4411

Des Moines, Bishop Maurice J. Dingman. Ecumenical Officer, Rev. Frank S. Palmer, Chancery Office, 2910 Grand Ave., P.O. Box 1816, Des Moines, IA 50306. Tel. (515) 243-7653.

Archdiocese of Detroit, John Cardinal Dearden. Chancery Office, 1234 Washington Blvd., Detroit, MI 48226. Tel. (313) 237-5800

Dodge City, Bishop Eugene Gerber. Ecumenical Officer, Rev. John Lavrih, 706 E. Sixth St., Kinsley, KS 67547. Chancery Office, 910 Central Ave., P.O. Box 849, Dodge City, KS 67801.Tel. (316) 227-3131

Archdiocese of Dubuque, Archbishop James J. Byrne. Chancery Office, 1229 Mt. Loretta Ave., Dubuque, IA 52001. Tel. (319) 556-2580

Duluth, Bishop Paul F. Anderson, Chancery Office, 215 W. Fourth St., Duluth, MN 55806. Tel. (218) 727-6861

El Paso, Bishop Patrick F. Flores, Chancery Office, 1200 N. Mesa St., El Paso, TX 79902. Tel. (915) 533-5549

Erie, Bishop Alfred M. Watson. Chancery Office, 205 W. Ninth St., Erie, PA 16501. Tel. (814) 454-4563

Evansville, Bishop Francis R. Shea. Ecumenical Officer, Rev. Camillus Ellspermann, O.S.B., East 10th St., Ferdinand, IN. Tel. (812) 367-1411. Chancery Office, 4200 N. Kentucky Ave., Evansville, IN 47711. Tel. (812) 424-5536

Fairbanks, Bishop Robert Louis Whelan. Ecumenical Officer, Rev. F. E. Mueller, S.J., 1316 Peger Rd., Fairbanks, AK 99701. Tel. (907) 456-6753. Chancery Office, 1316 Peger Rd., Fairbanks, AK 99701. Tel. (907) 456-6753

Fall River, Bishop Daniel A. Cronin. Ecumenical Officer, Rev. Edward J. Burns, Box 2577, Fall River, MA 02722. Tel. (617) 673-2122. Chancery Office, 47 Underwood St., Box 2577, Fall River, MA 02722. Tel. (617) 675-1311.

Fargo, Bishop Justin A. Driscoll. Ecumenical Officer, Rev. Gerald A. McCarthy. Chancery Office, 1310 Broadway, Fargo, ND 58107. Tel. (701) 235-6429

Fort Wayne-South Bend, Bishop William E. McManus. Ecumenical Officer, Rev. Daniel E. Peil, 3402 S. Locust Rd., South Bend, IN 46614. Tel. (219) 282-2317. Chancery Office, 1103 S. Calhoun St., P.O. Box 390. Fort Wayne, IN 46614. Tel. (219) 422-4611

Fort Worth, Bishop John J. Cassata. Ecumenical Officer, Rev. Leon Flusche, 331 N.E. Cindy La., Burleson, TX 76028. Tel. (817) 295-5621. Chancery Office, 1206 Throckmorton St. Fort Worth, TX 76102. Tel. (817) 335-2697

Fresno, Bishop Hugh A. Donohoe. Chancery Office, P.O. Box 1668, 1550 N. Fresno St., Fresno, CA 93717. Tel. (209) 237-5125

Gallup, Bishop Jerome J. Hastrich. Ecumenical Officer, Very Rev. James Dunphy, 300 W. 2nd St., Winslow, AR 86047. Tel. (602) 289-2350. Chancery Office, 711 Puerco Dr., P.O. Box 1338, Gallup, NM 87301. Tel. (505) 863-5083

Galveston-Houston, Bishop John L. Morkovsky. Ecumenical Officer: Very Rev. Edward J. Lyons, 2131 Lauder Rd., Houston, TX 77088. Tel. (713) 449-2820. Chancery Office, 1700 San Jacinto St., Houston, TX 77002. Tel. (713) 659-5461

Gary, Bishop Andrew Gregory Grutka. Chancery Office, P.O. Box 474, 975 W. 6th Ave., Gary, IN 46401. Tel. (219) 886-3141

Gaylord, Bishop Edmund C. Szoka. Chancery Office M-32 West, P.O. Box 700, Gaylord, MI 49735. Tel. (517) 732-5147

Grand Island, Bishop Lawrence J. McNamara. Chancery Office, 311 W. 17th St., P.O. Box 996, Grand Island, NB 68801. Tel. (308) 382-6565

Grand Rapids, Bishop Joseph M. Breitenbeck. Ecumenical Officer, Lorraine Watson, 317 High St., Ionia, MI 48846. Chancery Office, 265 Sheldon Ave., S.E., Grand Rapids, MI 49502. Tel. (312) 459-4509

Great Falls, Bishop Thomas J. Murphy. Ecumenical Officer, Rev. Robert Fox, 725 3rd Ave., N., Great Falls, MT 59403. Chancery Office, 725 Third Ave., N., P.O. Box 1399, Great Falls, MT 59403. Tel. (406) 453-9389

Green Bay, Bishop Aloysius J. Wycislo. Ecumenical Officer, Rev. Msgr. James Feely, 333 Hilltop Dr., Green Bay WI 54301. Tel. (414) 336-7768. Chancery Office, Box 66, Green Bay, WI 54305. Tel. (414) 435-4406

Greensburg, Bishop William G. Connare. Ecumenical Officer, Mrs. Johanna Cambruzzi. Chancery Office, 723 E. Pittsburgh St., Greensburg, PA 15601. Tel. (412) 837-0901

Harrisburg, Bishop Joseph T. Daley. Ecumenical Officer, Rev. Lawrence J. McNeil, 26 N. 3rd St., McSherrytown, PA 17344. Tel. (717) 637-1191. Chancery Office, 4800 Union Deposit Rd., Harrisburg, PA 17105. Tel. (717) 652-3920

Archdiocese of Hartford, Archbishop John F. Whealon. Ecumenical Officer, Rev. John P. Hannon, 129 Edwards St., New Haven, CT 06511. Chancery Office, 134 Farmington Ave., Hartford, CT 06105. Tel. (203) 527-4201

Helena, Bishop Elden F. Curtiss. Ecumenical Officer, Rev. James H. Provost. Chancery Office, 612 Harrison Ave., P.O. Box 1729, Helena, MT 59601. Tel. (406) 442-5820

Honolulu, Bishop John J. Scanlan, Ecumenical Officer, Rev. Msgr. Daniel Dever, P.O. Box 699, Kaneohe, HI 96744. Chancery Office, 1184 Bishop St., Honolulu, HI 96813. Tel. (808) 533-1791

Houma-Thibodaux, La. Bishop Warren L. Boudreaux. Ecumenical Officer, Rev. Gerald Prinz, P.O. Box 1066 Houma, LA 70361. Tel. (504) 876-2047. Chancery Office, 1220 Aycock St., Houma, LA 70360. Tel. (504) 868-7720

Archdiocese of Indianapolis, Archbishop George J. Biskup. Ecumenical Officer, Rev. Kenneth Murphy. Chancery Office, 1350 N. Pennsylvania St., P.O. Box 1776 Indianapolis, IN 46202. Tel. (317) 635-2579

ROMAN CATHOLIC CHURCH

Jackson, Bishop Joseph B. Brunini. Chancery Office, 237 E. Amite St., P.O. Box 2248, Jackson, MI 39205. Tel. (601) 948-6551

Jefferson City, Bishop Michael F. McAuliffe, Ecumenical Officer, Rev. Joseph Starmann, P.O. Box 417, Jefferson City, MO 65101. Tel. (314) 635-9127. Chancery Office, 605 Clark Ave., P.O. Box 417, Jefferson City, MO 65101. Tel. (314) 635-9127

Joliet, Joseph L. Imesch. Chancery Office, 425 Summit St., Joliet, IL 60435. Tel. (815) 722-6606

Juneau, Archbishop Francis T. Hurley, Adm. Ecumenical Officer, Rev. James Ryan, S.J., Box 495, Sitka, AK 99835. Tel. (907) 983-2271 Chancery Office, 416 5th St. Juneau, AK 99801. Tel. (907) 586-2227

Kalamazoo, Bishop Paul V. Donovan, Chancery Office, 215 N. Westnedge, Kalamazoo, MI 49006. Tel. (616) 349-8714

Archdiocese of Kansas City in Kansas, Archbishop Ignatius J. Strecker, Chancery Office, 2220 Central Ave., P.O. Box 2328, Kansas City, KS 66110. Tel. (913) 621-4131

Kansas City-St. Joseph, Bishop John J. Sullivan. Ecumenical Officer, ———, Chancery Office, P.O. Box 1037, Kansas City, MO 64141. Tel. (816) 756-1850

La Crosse, Bishop Frederick W. Freking. Chancery Office, 3710 East Ave., P.O. Box 69, La Crosse, WI 54601. Tel. (608) 788-7700

Lafayette in Indiana, Bishop Raymond J. Gallagher. Chancery Office, 610 Lingle Ave., Lafayette, IN 47902. Tel. (317) 742-0275

Lafayette, Bishop Gerard L. Frey. Ecumenical Officer, Rev. Msgr. Robert C. Landry, P.O. Box 186, Maurice, LA 70555. Tel. (318) 893-4099. Chancery Office, Diocesan Office Bldg., P.O. Drawer 3387, Lafayette, LA 70502. Tel. (318) 232-5150

Lansing, Bishop Kenneth J. Povish. Ecumenical Officer Rev. Lawrence P. Delaney, Chancery Office, 300 W. Ottawa, Lansing, MI 48933. Tel. (517) 372-8540

Lincoln, Bishop Glennon P. Flavin, Ecumenical Officer, Rev. Msgr. Raymond B. Hain, 301 W. 7th St., Hastings, NB 68901. Tel. (402) 463-1336. Chancery Office, 3400 Sheridan Blvd., P.O. Box 80328, Lincoln, NB 68501. Tel. (402) 488-0921

Little Rock, Bishop Andrew J. McDonald. Ecumenical Officer: Rev. James R. Savary. Chancery Office 2415 N. Tyler St., Little Rock, AR 72210. Tel. (501) 664-0340

Archdiocese of Los Angeles, Archbishop Timothy Cardinal Manning. Ecumenical Officer, Rev. Royal M. Vadakin, 4112 W. Washington Blvd., Los Angeles, CA 90018. Tel. (213) 734-6066. Chancery Office, 1531 W. Ninth St., Los Angeles, CA 90015. Tel. (213) 388-8101

Archdiocese of Louisville, Archbishop Thomas J. McDonough. Ecumenical Officer, Rev. Stanley A. Schmidt, 1020 E. Burnett St., Lousiville KY 40217. Tel. (502) 636-3706. Chancery Office. 212 E. College St., Louisville, KY 40203. Tel. (502) 585-3291

Madison, Bishop Cletus F. O'Donnell. Chancery Office, 15 E. Wilson St., Madison, WI 53701. Tel. (608) 256-2677

Manchester, Bishop Odore J. Gendron, Ecumenical Officer, Rev. Robert G. Boisvert. Chancery Office, 153 Ash St., Manchester, NH 03104. Tel. (603) 669-3100

Marquette, Bishop Mark F. Schmitt. Ecumenical Officer, Rev. Peter A. Minelli. Chancery Office, 444 S. Fourth St., P.O. Box 550, Marquette, MI 49855. Tel. (906) 225-1141

Memphis Bishop Carroll T. Dozier. Ecumenical Officer, Rev. Thomas Kirk, 3825 Neely Rd., Memphis, TN 38109. Tel. (901) 396-9996. Chancery Office, 1325 Jefferson Ave., Memphis, TN 38104. Tel. (901) 725-6761

Archdiocese of Miami, Archbishop Edward A. McCarthy, Ecumenical Officer, Rev. John D. McGrath. Chancery Office, 6301 Biscayne Blvd., Miami, FL 33138. Tel. (305) 757-6241

Archdiocese of Milwaukee, Archbishop Rembert G. Weakland, O.S.B. Ecumenical Officer, Sr. Maureen Hopkins, S.D.S. Chancery Office, 345 N. 95th St., Milwaukee, WI. 53266 Tel. (414) 476-2101

Mobile, Bishop John L. May. Ecumenical Officer, Rev. Msgr. Joseph Lyons, P.O. Box 1031, Andalusia, LA 36420. Tel. (205) 222-4808. Chancery Office, 400 Government St., P.O. Box 1966, Mobile, AL 36601. Tel. (205) 433-2241

Monterey, Bishop Harry Anselm Clinch. Ecumenical Officer, Rev. James Van Lanen. Chancery Office, 580 Fremont Blvd., Monterey, CA 93940. Tel. (408) 373-4345

Nashville, Bishop James D. Niedergeses. Ecumenical Officer, Rev. Robert J. Hofstetter. Chancery Office, 2400 21st Ave., S., Nashville, TN 37212. Tel. (615) 383-6393

Archdiocese of Newark, Archbishop Peter L. Gerety. Ecumenical Officer, Rev. Msgr. John H. Koenig, 971 Suburban Rd., Union, NJ 07083. Tel. (201) 687-3327. Chancery Office, 31 Mulberry St., Newark, NJ 07102. Tel. (201) 483-8500

Archdiocese of New Orleans, Archbishop Philip M. Hannan. Ecumenical Officer, Mt. Rev. Stanley J. Ott. Chancery Office, 7887 Walmsley Ave., New Orleans, LA 70125. Tel. (504) 861-9521

Melkite Apostolic Exarchate of Newton, Bishop Joseph Tawil. Chancery Office, 19 Dartmouth St., P.O. Box 83, West Newton, MA 02165. Tel. (617) 969-8957

New Ulm, Bishop Raymond A. Lucker. Ecumenical Officer, Rev. John P. Murphy, 509 So. Lincoln St., Redwood Falls, MN 56283. Tel. (507) 637-2278. Chancery Office, 140 Chancery Drive, New Ulm, MN 56073. Tel. (507) 359-2966

Archdiocese of New York, Terence Cardinal Cooke Ecumenical Officer: Rev. Msgr. James F. Rigney, 1011 First Ave., New York, NY 10022. Chancery Office, 1011 First Ave., New York, NY 10022. Tel. (212) 371-6100

Norwich, Bishop Daniel P. Reilly, Ecumenical Officer, Rev. Theodore J. Klein. Chancery Office, 201 Broadway, P.O. Box 587, Norwich, CT 06360. Tel. (203) 887-9294

Oakland, Bishop John S. Cummins. Ecumenical Officer, Rev. Anthony Harcar, 6266 Camden St., Oakland, CA 94605. Tel. (415) 638-1447. Chancery Office, 2900 Lakeshore Ave., Oakland, CA 94610. Tel. (415) 893-4711

Ogdensburg, Bishop Stanislaus J. Brzana. Ecumenical Officer, Rev. Msgr. Robert A. Farmer, St. Patrick's Church, Rouses Point, NY 12979. Tel. (315) 297-7361. Chancery Office, 622 Washington St., Ogdensburg, NY 13669. Tel. (315) 393-2920

Archdiocese of Oklahoma City, Archbishop Charles A. Salatka, Ecumenical Officer, Rev. Larry Gatlin, Box 32286, Oklahoma City, OK 73132. Tel. (405) 721-8366. Chancery Office, 4720 N. Classen, Oklahoma City, OK 73118. Tel. (405) 528-7807

Archdiocese of Omaha, Archbishop Daniel E. Sheehan. Ecumenical Officer, Rev. Robert Preisinger, 3020 Curtis Ave., Omaha, NB. Tel. (402) 455-5200. Chancery Office, 100 N. 62nd St., Omaha, NB 68132. Tel. (402) 558-3100

Orange, Bishop William R. Johnson. Chancery Office, 440 S. Batavia St., Orange, CA 92668. Ecumenical Officer, Rev. Lawrence Baird. Tel. (714) 973-2973.

Orlando, Bishop Thomas J. Grady. Ecumenical Officer, Joseph Calderone, 408 E. Lyman Ave., Winter Park, FL 32789. Chancery Office, 421 E. Robinson, P.O. Box 1800, Orlando, FL 32802. Tel. (305) 425-3556

Owensboro, Bishop Henry J. Soennecker. Ecumenical Officer, Very Rev. Anthony G. Higdon. RR 10, Box 110, Paducah, KY 42001. Tel. (502) 554-3810. Chancery

Office, c/o Chancellor's Residence, 4003 Frederica St., P.O. Box 364, Owensboro, KY 42301. Tel. (502) 683-1545

Parma Eparchy, Bishop Emil Mihalik. Chancery Office, 1900 Carlton Rd., Parma, OH 44134. Tel. (216) 741-8773

Passaic (Greek Rite), Bishop Michael J. Dudick. Ecumenical Officer, Rev. John J. Rebouich. Passaic, NJ 07055. Tel. (201) 777-2553. Chancery Office, 101 Market St., Passaic, NJ 07055. Tel. (201) 778-9595

Paterson, Bishop Frank J. Rodimer Chancery Office, 777 Valley Rd., Clifton NJ 07013. Tel. (201) 777-8818.

Pensacola-Tallahassee, Bishop Rene H. Gracida Ecumenical Officer, Rev. Richard Altenbaugh, P.O. Drawer 17329, Pensacola, Fl 32522. Tel. (904) 763-1821. Chancery Office, 11 N. "B" St., Pensacola, FL 32501. Tel. (904) 432-1515

Peoria, Bishop Edward W. O'Rourke. Ecumenical Officer, Mrs. Ralph Meismer, 323 N. Niles St., Metamora, IL 61548. Chancery Office, 607 NE Madison Ave., Peoria, IL 61655. Tel. (309) 673-6318

Archdiocese of Philadelphia, John Cardinal Krol. Chancery Office, 222 N. 17th St. Philadelphia, PA 19103. Tel. (215) 587-3550

Ukrainian Rite--Philadelphia ———. Chancery Office, 815 N. Franklin St., Philadelphia, PA 19123. Tel. (215) 627-0143

Phoenix, Bishop James S. Rausch. Ecumenical Officer, Rev. Msgr. Robert J. Donohoe. Chancery Office, 400 E. Monroe St., Phoenix, AZ 85004. Tel. (602) 257-0030

Pittsburgh, Bishop Vincent M. Leonard. Ecumenical Officer, Rev. William J. Erkens, 111 Blvd. of Allies, Pittsburgh, PA 15222. Chancery Office, 111 Blvd. of Allies, Pittsburgh, PA 15222. Tel. (412) 465-3000

Metropolitan Archdiocese of Pittsburgh (Byzantine) Archbishop Stephen J. Kocisko. Chancery Office, 54 Riverview Ave., Pittsburgh, PA 15214. Tel. (412) 322-7300.

Portland, Bishop Edward C. O'Leary. Ecumenical Officer, Rev. Paul E. Cote, 110 Silver St., Waterville, ME 04901. Tel. (207) 872-6662. Chancery Office, 510 Ocean Ave., Portland, ME 04103. Tel. (207) 773-6471

Archdiocese of Portland in Oregon, Archbishop Cornelius M. Power. Chancery Office, 2838 E. Burnside St., Portland, OR 97207. Tel. (503) 234-5334

Providence, Bishop Louis E. Gelineau. Ecumenical Officer, Rev. Lionel A. Blain, 69 Quincy Ave., Pawtucket, RI 02860. Tel. (401) 722-9054. Chancery Office, Cathedral Square, Providence, RI 02903. Tel. (401) 278-4500

Pueblo, Bishop Charles A. Buswell. Ecumenical Officer, Rev. William T. Gleeson, 650 Elm St., Las Animas, CO 81054. Tel. (303) 456-0357. Chancery Office, 1426 Grand Ave., Pueblo, CO 81003. Tel. (303) 544-9861

Raleigh, Bishop F. Joseph Gossman. Chancery Office, 300 Cardinal Gibbons Dr., Raleigh, NC 27606. Tel. (919) 821-0350

Rapid City, Bishop Harold J. Dimmerling. Ecumenical Officer, Rev. Ignatius Potts, O.S.B., Newell, SD 57760. Tel. (605) 456-2221. Chancery Office, 606 Cathedral Dr., P.O. Box 678, Rapid City, SD 57709. Tel. (605) 343-3541

Reno-Las Vegas, Bishop Norman F. McFarland. Chancery Office, 515 Court St., Reno, NV 89509. Tel. (702) 329-9274

Richmond, Bishop Walter F. Sullivan. Ecumenical Officer, Rev. James R. von Meysenbug, 4400 Beulah Rd., Richmond, VA 23234. Tel. (804) 275-7962. Chancery Office, 807 Cathedral Pl., Richmond, VA 23220. Tel. (703) 649-9353

Rochester, Bishop Joseph L. Hogan. Ecumenical Officer, Rev. Henry Atwell, 108 Prospect St., Avon, NY 14414. Tel. (716) 226-2100, R.S.M. Chancery Office, 1150 Buffalo Rd., Rochester, NY 14624. Tel. (716) 328-3210

Rockford, Bishop Arthur J. O'Neill. Chancery Office, 1245 N. Court St., Rockford, IL 61101 Tel. (815) 962-3709

Rockville Centre, Bishop John R. McGann. Ecumenical Officer, Rev. Daniel Hamilton, 2000 Jackson Ave., Seaford, NY 11783. Tel. (516) 785-1266. Chancery Office, 50 N. Park Ave. Rockville Centre, NY 11570. Tel. (516) 678-5800

Sacramento, Bishop Alden J. Bell. Ecumenical Officer, Rev. Msgr. Richard C. Dwyer, 10497 Coloma Rd., Rancho Cordova, CA 95670. Tel. (916) 362-1385. Chancery Office, 1119 K St., P.O. Box 1706, Sacramento, CA 95808. Tel. (916) 443-1996

Saginaw, Bishop Francis F. Reh. Chancery Office, 5800 Weiss St., Saginaw, MI 48603. Tel. (517) 799-7910

St. Augustine, Bishop Paul F. Tanner. Chancery Office, Ste. 1648, Gulf Life Tower, Jacksonville, FL 32207. Tel. (904) 396-2509

St. Cloud, Bishop George H. Speltz. Ecumenical Officer, Rev. William Yos, 396 First Ave., St. Cloud, MN 56301. Tel. (612) 251-3260. Chancery Office, P.O. Box 1248, St. Cloud, MN 56301. Tel. (612) 251-2340

Archdiocese of St. Louis, John Cardinal Carberry. Ecumenical Officer, Rev. Msgr. Joseph W. Baker, 4445 Lindell Blvd., St. Louis, MO 63108. Chancery Office, 4445 Lindell Blvd., St. Louis, MO 63108. Tel. (314) 533-1887

St. Maron-Detroit, Bishop Francis M. Zayek, Chancery Office, 205 82nd St., P.O. Box 333, Ft. Hamilton Sta., Brooklyn, NY 11209. Tel. (212) 680-6270

St. Nicholas in Chicago for the Ukrainians, Bishop Jaroslav Gabro. Chancery Office, 2245 W. Rice St., Chicago, IL 60622. Tel. (312) 276-5080

Archdiocese of St. Paul and Minneapolis, Archbishop John R. Roach. Ecumenical Officer, Rev. Patrick J. Ryan, 2633 Harvester Ave., Maplewood, MN 55119. Tel. (612) 738-2646. Chancery Office, 226 Summit Ave., St. Paul, MN 55102. Tel. (612) 291-4400.

St. Petersburg, Bishop W. Thomas Larkin. Ecumenical Officer, Rev. Harold Bumpus, P.O. Box 2407, St. Leo, FL 32574. Tel. (904) 588-8288. Chancery Office, 6363 9th Ave. N., P.O. Box 13109. St. Petersburg, FL 33733. Tel. (813) 344-1611

Salina, Bishop Cyril J. Vogel. Chancery Office, 421 Country Club Rd., P.O. Box 999, Salina, KS 67401. Tel. (913) 827-8746

Salt Lake City, Bishop Joseph Lennox Federal. Ecumenical Officer, Rev. Victor G. Bonnell, 333 E. South Temple, Salt Lake City, UT 84111. Chancery Office, 333 E. South Temple, Salt Lake City, UT 84111. Tel. (801) 328-8641

San Angelo, Bishop Stephen A. Leven. Chancery Office, 116 S. Oakes (Mailing Address Box 1829) San Angelo, TX 76901. Tel. (915) 653-2466

Archdiocese of San Antonio, Archbishop Francis J. Furey. Ecumenical Officer, Rev. Robert P. Kownacki, 758 W. Ramsey, San Antonio, TX 78216. Chancery Office, 9123 Lorene Lane, P.O. Box 32648, San Antonio, TX 78284. Tel. (512) 344-2331

San Bernardino, Bishop Phillip F. Straling, Chancery Office, 1450 North D St., San Bernadino, CA 92405 Tel. (714) 889-8351

San Diego, Bishop Leo T. Maher. Ecumenical Officer, Rev. Msgr. John R. Portman, 672 B. Ave., Coronado, CA 92118. Tel. (714) 435-4858. Chancery Office, Alcala Park, San Diego, CA 92110. Tel. (714) 298-7711

Archdiocese of San Francisco, Archbishop John R. Quinn. Ecumenical Officer, Rev. John M. Ring, P.O. Box 409, Mill Valley, CA 94941. Tel. (415) 388-4190. Chancery Office, 445 Church St., San Francisco, CA 94114. Tel. (415) 863-5112

Archdiocese of Santa Fe, Archbishop Robert F. Sanchez. Chancery Office, 202 Morningside Dr., S.E., Albuquerque, NM 87108. Tel. (505) 268-4572

Santa Rosa, Bishop Mark J. Hurley. Chancery Office, 398 10th St., P.O. Box 1297, Santa Rosa, CA 95402. Tel. (707) 545-7610

Savannah, Bishop Raymond W. Lessard. Ecumenical Officer, Rev. John A. Kenneally, 4937 Bloomfield Rd., Macon, GA 31201. Tel. (912) 788-2837. Chancery Office, 225 Abercorn St., P.O. Box 8789, Savannah, GA 31412. Tel. (912) 232-6475

Scranton, Bishop J. Carroll McCormick, Ecumenical Officer, Rev. Constantine V. Siconolfi, 300 Wyoming Ave., Scranton, PA 18503. Chancery Office, 300 Wyoming Ave., Scranton, PA 18503. Tel. (717) 346-8910

Archdiocese of Seattle, Archbishop Raymond G. Hunthausen. Ecumenical Officer, Rev. Roger O'Brien, 907 Terry Ave., Seattle, WA 98104. Tel. (206) 723-4750. Chancery Office, 907 Terry Ave., Seattle, WA 98104. Tel. (206) 622-8880

Sioux City, Bishop Frank H. Greteman. Ecumenical Officer, Rev. Msgr. Frank J. Brady, 1212 Morningside Ave., Sioux City, IA 51106. Tel. (712) 276-4821. Chancery Office, 1821 Jackson St., P.O. Box 1530, Sioux City, IA 51102. Tel. (712) 255-7933

Sioux Falls, Bishop Paul V. Dudley. Ecumenical Officer, Rev. Msgr. Louis J. Delahoyde, 423 N. Duluth Ave., Sioux Falls, SD 57104. Chancery Office, 423 N. Duluth Ave., Sioux Falls, SD 57104. Tel. (605) 334-9861

Spokane, Bishop Lawrence H. Welsh. Chancery Office, 1023 W. Riverside Ave., Spokane, WA 99201. Tel. (509) 456-7100

Springfield-Cape Girardeau, Bishop Bernard Law. Chancery Office, 200 McDaniel, Springfield, MO 65806. Tel. (417) 866-0841

Springfield in Illinois, Bishop Joseph A. McNicholas. Ecumenical Officer, Rev. Msgr. Lawrence Wiskirchen. Chancery Office, 524 E. Lawrence Ave., Springfield, IL 62705. Tel. (217) 522-7781

Springfield, Bishop Joseph F. Maguire. Chancery Office, 76 Elliot St., P.O. Box 1730, Springfield, MA 01101. Tel. (413) 732-3175

Byzantine Ukainian Rite—Stamford, Bishop Basil H. Losten. Chancery Office, 161 Glenbrook Rd., Stamford, CT 06902. Tel. (203) 324-7698

Steubenville, Bishop Albert H. Ottenwell. Ecumenical Officer, Rev. Charles J. Sargus, 852 Main St., Wintersville, OH 43952. Tel. (614) 264-0868. Chancery Office, 422 Washington St., P.O. Box 969, Steubenville, OH 43952. Tel. (614) 282-3631

Stockton, Bishop Merlin J. Guilfoyle. Ecumenical Officer, Robert J. Silva, 4101 Manchester Ave., Stockton, CA 95204. Tel. (209) 951-0881. Chancery Office, 1105 N. Lincoln St., Stockton, CA 95203, P.O. Box 4237, Stockton, CA 95204. Tel. (209) 466-0636

Superior, Bishop George A. Hammes. Ecumenical Officer, Rev. George Gleason, Box 30, Woodruff, WI 54568. Tel. (715) 356-6284. Chancery Office, 1201 Hughitt Ave., Superior, WI 54880. Tel. (715) 392-2937

Syracuse, Bishop Frank J. Harrison, Ecumenical Officer: Rev. Msgr. Daniel B. O'Brien, 4112 E. Genessee St., Dewitt, NY 13214. Tel. (315) 446-0473. Chancery Office, 240 E. Onondaga St., Syracuse, NY 13202. Tel. (315) 422-7203

Toledo, Bishop John A. Donovan. Ecumenical Officer, Rev. Robert Holden, 333 Brookside Dr., Swanton, OH 43558. Tel. (419) 826-2791, Chancery Office, 2544 Parkwood Ave., Toledo, OH 43610. Tel. (419) 255-1670

Trenton, Bishop George W. Ahr. Ecumenical Officer, Rev. Joseph C. Shenrock, 716 Bellevue Ave., Trenton, NJ 08618. Tel. (609) 396-9231. Chancery Office, 701 Lawrenceville Rd., Trenton, NJ 08648. Tel. (609) 882-7125

Tucson, Bishop Francis J. Green. Chancery Office, 192 S. Stone Ave., Box 31, Tucson, AZ 85702. Tel. (602) 792-3410

Tulsa, Bishop Eusebius J. Beltran. Ecumenical Officer, Rev. Bernard C. Jewitt, 2720 S. 129th East Ave., Tulsa, OK 74106. Tel. (918) 437-0168. Chancery Office, 824 S. Boulder St., P.O. Box 2009, Tulsa, OK 74101. Tel. (918) 587-3115

Archdiocese of Washington, Archbishop William Cardinal Baum. Ecumenical Officer, Rev. Gabriel F. Duffy, 4902 Berwyn Rd., College Park, MD 20740. Tel. (301) 474-3920. Chancery Office, 1721 Rhode Island Ave. NW, Washington, DC 20036. Tel. (202) 783-1465

Wheeling-Charleston, Bishop Joseph H. Hodges. Ecumenical Officer: Rev. John H. McDonnell, P.O. Box 230, Wheeling, WV 26003. Tel. (304) 233-0880. Chancery Office, 1300 Byron St., Wheeling, WV 26003. Tel. (304) 233-0880

Wichita, Bishop David M. Maloney. Ecumenical Officer, Rev. Msgr. Charles F. Walsh. 307 E. Central Ave., Wichita, KS 67202. Tel. (316) 263-6574. Chancery Office, 424 N. Broadway, Wichita, KS 67202. Tel. (316) 263-6262

Wilmington, Bishop Thomas J. Mardaga. Ecumenical Officer, Rev. Leonard J. Kempski, 1925 Delaware Ave., Wilmington, DE 19806. Tel. (302) 654-3131. Chancery Office, P.O. Box 2030, 1925 Delaware Ave., Ste 1A, Wilmington, DE 19899. Tel. (302) 656-2578

Winona, Bishop Loras J. Watters. Chancery Office, 55 W. Sanborn, P.O. Box 588, Winona, MN 55987. Tel. (507) 454-4643

Worcester, Bishop Bernard J. Flanagan. Ecumenical Officer, Sister Therese Dion, S.S.A., 49 Elm St., Worcester, MA 01609. Chancery Office, 49 Elm St., Worcester, MA 01609. Tel. (617) 791-7171

Yakima, Bishop William S. Skylstad. Chancery Office, 222 Washington Mutual Bldg., P.O. Box 505, Yakima, WA 98907. Tel. (509) 248-6857

Youngstown, Bishop James W. Malone. Ecumenical Officer, Rev. Joseph Witmer, 26 W. Rayen Ave., Youngstown, OH 44503. Tel. (216) 452-9539. Chancery Office, 144 W. Wood St., Youngstown, OH 44503. Tel. (216) 744-8451

The Romanian Orthodox Church in America

The Romanian Orthodox Church in America is an autonomous Archdiocese chartered under the name of the "Romanian Orthodox Missionary Archdiocese in America."

It was founded as a Diocese in 1929 and approved by the Holy Synod of the Romanian Orthodox Church in Romania in 1934. By a decision of the Holy Synod of the Romanian Orthodox Church of July 12, 1950, it was granted the status of ecclesiastical autonomy in America, continuing to hold only dogmatical and canonical ties with the Holy Synod and the Romanian Orthodox Patriarchate of Romania.

In 1951, a group of approximately 40 parishes with their clergy from USA and Canada separated from this church and eventually joined in 1960 the Russian Orthodox Greek Catholic Metropolia now called the Orthodox Church in America which reordained for these parishes a bishop with the title "Bishop of Detroit and Michigan."

The Holy Synod of the Romanian Orthodox Church, in its session of June 11, 1973, elevated the Bishop of Romanian Orthodox Missionary Episcopate in America to the rank of Archbishop. Consequently the Annual Congress of the Romanian Orthodox Church in America, held on July 21, 1973, at Edmonton-Boian, Alberta, decided to change the title of the Diocese from "Episcopate" to that of "Archdiocese." This decision was approved by the Holy Synod of the Romanian Orthodox

Church of Romania in its session of December 12, 1974, renewing at the same time the status as an Autonomous Archdiocese with the right to elect in addition to the Archbishop an Auxiliary Bishop for the Archdiocese.

GENERAL ORGANIZATION

Headquarters: 19959 Riopelle, Detroit, MI 48203. Tel. (313) 893-7191

Annual Congress in July, and biannual Archdiocesan Council

OFFICERS

Archbishop, His Eminence The Most Rev. Archbishop Victorin (Ursache), 19959 Riopelle, Detroit, MI 48203. Tel. (313) 893-7191

Vicar, Very Rev. Archim. Dr. Vasille Vasilachi, 19959 Riopelle St., Detroit, MI 48203. Tel. (313) 366-1998

Vicar, Very Rev. Archpriest John Bugariu, 17601 Wentworth Ave., Lansing, IL 60438. Tel. (312) 474-7392

Dir., Inter-Church Relations, V. Rev. Archim, B.V. Anania, 19965 Riopelle St., Detroit, MI 48203. Tel. (313) 366-1998

Sec., Rev. Fr. Gerome L. Hewville, 19959 Riopelle St., Detroit, MI 48203. Tel. (313) 893-7191

PERIODICALS

Credinta—The Faith (m), 19959 Riopelle. Detroit, MI 48203. Very Rev. Archim, Dr. Vasile Vasilachi, Ed.

Calendarul Credinta (yearbook), 19959 Riopelle, Detroit, MI 48203. Very Rev. Archim. Dr. Vasile Vasilachi, Ed.

The Romanian Orthodox Episcopate of America

This body of Eastern Orthodox Christians of Romanian descent was organized in 1929 as an autonomous Diocese under the jurisdiction of the Romanian Patriarchate. In 1951 it severed all relations with the Orthodox Church of Romania. The Diocese is under the canonical jurisdiction of the autocephalous Orthodox Church in America, but enjoys full administrative autonomy and is headed by its own bishop.

Churches: 34 Inclusive Membership: 40,000 Sunday or Sabbath Schools: 34 Total Enrollment: 1,600 Ordained Clergy: 55

GENERAL ORGANIZATION

Church Congress: annual (July)

Headquarters: 2522 Grey Tower Road, Jackson, MI 49201. Tel. (517) 522-4800

OFFICERS

The Bishop: His Eminence Archbishop Valerian; (D. Trifa)

The Council of the Episcopate: Pres., His Eminence Archbishop Valerian; Sec., Rev. Fr. Laurence Lazar, 3355 Ridgewood Rd., Akron, OH 44313; Treas., Mr. Peter Metes, 1580 Tottenham, Birmingham, MI 48009

OTHER ORGANIZATIONS

The American Romanian Orthodox Youth (AROY): Pres. Miss Stefanie Yova, 1308 Herberich, Akron, OH 44301. Sec., Miss Doina Magda, 1387 Grayton, Grosse Pointe Park, MI 48230. Spiritual Advisor, Rev. Fr. Laurence C. Lazar, 3355 Ridgewood Rd., Arkon OH 44313

Association of Romanian Orthodox Ladies' Auxiliaries (ARFORA): Pres. Mrs. Anne Groza, 1336 N. Plainview Dr., Copley, OH 44321

Orthodox Brotherhood: Chpsn., Mrs. Virginia Martin, 3315 W. 157 St., Cleveland, OH 44111

PERIODICAL

SOLIA, Romanian News (m), 11341 Woodward Ave., Detroit, MI 48202

Russian Orthodox Church in the U.S.A., Patriarchal Parishes of the

This group of parishes is under the direct jurisdiction of the Patriarch of Moscow and All Russia, His Holiness Pimen, in the person of a Vicar Bishop, His Grace Ireney, Bishop of Serpukhov.

GENERAL ORGANIZATION

Headquarters: St. Nicholas Patriarchal Cathedral, 15 E. 97th St., New York, NY 10029. Tel. (212) 289-1915

Vicar Bishop: His Grace Ireney, Bishop of Serpukhov

PERIODICALS

One Church (bi-m), P.O. Box 1863, East Lansing, MI 48823. Rt. Rev. Photius F. M. Donahue, Ed.

Journal of the Moscow Patriachate (In English (m), subscription list, St. Nicholas Cathedral, New York, NY 10029

The Russian Orthodox Church Outside Russia

(Formerly The Russian Orthodox Church Abroad)

Organized in 1920 to unite in one body of dioceses the missions and parishes of the Russian Orthodox Church outside of Russia. The Governing body was set up in Constantinople sponsored by the Ecumenical Patriarchate. In November 1950, it came to the United States. The Russian Orthodox Church Outside Russia lays emphasis on being true to the old traditions of the Russian Church, but it does not compromise with official church leaders in Moscow, "since that would amount to being under the influence and direction of a godless State."

GENERAL ORGANIZATION

Headquarters: 75 E. 93rd St., New York, NY 10028. Tel. (212) 534-1601

(Summer residence): Hermitage of Our Lady of Kursk, Mahopac, NY 10541, and 744 El Camino Real, Burlingame, CA 94010

Council of Bishops, Synod (elected by the Council): Pres., His Eminence, the Most Rev. Metropolitan Philaret

Other Members: Rt. Rev. Bishop Gregory, Sec.; Most Rev. Seraphim, Archbishop of Chicago and Detroit; Most Rev. Vitaly, Archbishop of Montreal and Canada; Anthony, Archbishop of Western America and San Francisco

Director of Public and Foreign Relations Dept., Rt. Rev. Bishop Gregory, 75 E. 93rd St., New York, NY 10028

PERIODICAL

Orthodox Life, Holy Trinity Monastery, Jourdanville, NY 13361

Pravoslavnaya Rus (2-mo), in Russian Holy Trinity Monastery, Jordanville, NY

The Orthodox Word (m), in English, St. Herman of Alaska Brotherhood, Platina, CA 96076

The Salvation Army

The Salvation Army, founded in 1865 by William Booth (1829-1912) in London, England, and introduced into America in 1880, is an international religious and charitable movement organized and operated on a paramilitary pattern, and is a branch of the Christian church. To carry out its purposes, The Salvation Army has established a widely diversified program of religious and social welfare services which are designed to meet the needs of children, youth, and adults in all age groups.

Churches: 1,117 Inclusive Membership: 414,035 Sunday or Sabbath Schools: 1,067 Total Enrollment: 107,549 Ordained Clergy: 5,104

SALVATION ARMY

GENERAL ORGANIZATION

National Headquarters:120-130 W. 14th St., New York, NY 10011. Tel. (212) 620-4900

OFFICERS

Natl. Commander, Commissioner Ernest W. Holz
Natl. Chief Sec., Col. G. Ernest Murray

TERRITORIAL ORGANIZATIONS

Eastern Territory, 120-130 W. 14th St., New York, NY 10011; Territorial Commander, Commissioner W. R. H Goodier; Chief Sec., Col. Albert Scott

Central Territory, 860 N. Dearborn St., Chicago, IL 60610; Territorial Commander, Commissioner John D. Needham; Chief Sec., Col. Andrew S. Miller

Western Territory, 30840 Hawthorne Blvd., Rancho Palos Verdes, CA 90274. Territorial Commander, Commissioner Richard E. Holz; Chief Sec., Col. Will Pratt

Southern Territory, 1424 Northeast Expressway, Atlanta, GA 30329. Territorial Commander, Commissioner Arthur Pitcher; Chief Sec., Col. John W. Paton

PERIODICALS

War Cry (w), The Young Soldier (m), SAY (m), The Musician (m), National Publications Dept., 120 W. 14th St., New York, NY 10011. Lt. Col. Ralph I. Miller, Ed.-in-Chief

The Schwenkfelder Church

Descendants of a German migration from Silesia into Pennsylvania in 1734, followers of a Reformation leader, Caspar Schwenckfeld Von Ossig.

GENERAL ORGANIZATION

General Conference: semi-annual
Headquarters: Pennsburg, PA 18073

OFFICERS

Mod., Andrew A. Anders, 958 Anders Rd., Lansdale, PA 19446

Sec., Miss Florence Schultz, P.O. Box 221, Palm, PA 18070

Treas., Ellis W. Kriebel, 523 Meetinghouse Rd., Harleysville, PA 19438

PERIODICAL

The Schwenkfeldian (q), Pennsburg, PA 18073. Jack R. Rothenberger, Ed.

†Second Cumberland Presbyterian Church in U.S.

In 1869 the black churches of the Cumberland Presbyterian Church were set apart by the General Assembly with their own ecclesiastical organization.

GENERAL ORGANIZATION

General Assembly: annual 2nd Thurs. in June

OFFICERS

Mod.: Rev. Dr. Henry Bradford, Jr., 228 Church St., Huntsville, AL 35801

Stated Clk.: Rev. Robert Earl Thomas, 2404 N. Grand Ave., Tyler, TX 75701

SYNODS

Alabama, Stated Clk., Arthur Hinton, 511 10th Ave., N.W., Aliceville 35442

Kentucky, Stated Clk., Leroy Hunt, 1317 Monroe St., Paducah, Ky 42001

Tennessee, Stated Clk., Mrs. S. E. Wilson, 206 Ferry Ave., Loudon 37774

Texas, Stated Clk., ———

PERIODICAL

The Cumberland Flag, 545 Vanderhorst Dr., Nashville, TN 37209. Mrs. Helen B. Nichols, Ed.

Separate Baptists in Christ

A group of Baptists found in Indiana, Ohio, Kentucky, Tennessee, Illinois and North Carolina, dating back to an association formed in 1758 in North Carolina.

GENERAL ORGANIZATION

General Association

OFFICERS

Mod., Rev. Roger Popplewell, Rt. 5, Russell Springs, KY 42642

Asst. Mod., Rev. David Freeman, R.R. 3, Spencer, IN 47460

Clk., Bro. Floyd Wilson, 59 Greensprings Rd., Indianapolis, IN 46224

Serbian Eastern Orthodox Church for the U.S.A. and Canada

GENERAL ORGANIZATION

National Assembly
Chancery: St. Sava Monastery, P.O. Box 519, Libertyville, IL 60048. Tel. (312) 362-2440

OFFICERS

Diocese of the Midwest, Rt. Rev. Bishop Firmilian, St. Sava Monastery, P.O. Box 519 Libertyville, IL 60048. Tel. (312) 362-2440

Western Diocese, Rt. Rev. Bishop Gregory, 2511 W. Garvey Ave., Alhambra, CA 91803

Diocese for the Eastern States of America and Canada, Bishop Christophor, Way Hollow Rd., Edgeworth, Sewickley, PA 15143

OTHER ORGANIZATIONS

Brotherhood of Serbian Orthodox Clergy in the U.S.A. and Canada, Pres., V. Rev. George Lazich, Gary, IN
Serbian Orthodox Teacher's and Youth Association
Circle of Serbian Sisters

Seventh-day Adventists

This Protestant body developed out of a interdenominational movement that appeared in different countries of Christendom in the early decades of the nineteenth century, stressing the imminence of the Second Advent of Christ. However, Seventh-day Adventists were not formally organized until 1863. Taking the Bible as their sole rule of faith and practice, they are fundamentally evangelical, holding to the full inspiration of the Scriptures and the deity of Christ. Their two cardinal points of faith are: (1) belief in the personal, imminent, premillennial return of Christ, and (2) observance of the seventh day as the Sabbath.

Churches: 3,591 Inclusive Membership: 535,705 Sunday or Sabbath Schools: 3,673 Total Enrollment: 477,208 Ordained Clergy: 4,016

GENERAL ORGANIZATION

General Conference: quinquennial (next meeting, 1980)
Headquarters: 6840 Eastern Ave. NW, Washington, DC 20012. Tel. (202) 723-0800

OFFICERS

Pres., Neal C. Wilson
Sec., Clyde O. Franz
Treas., K. H. Emmerson

DEPARTMENTS

Communication Dept.: Dir., J. E. Chase
Education Dept.: Dir., W. J. Brown
Health Dept.: Dir., S. L. DeShay
Lay Activities Dept.: Dir., G. E. Knowles
Ministerial Association: Sec., N. R. Dower
Public Affairs Dept. and Religious Liberty: Dir. W. Melvin Adams
Publishing Dept.: Dir., Bruce M. Wickwire

Sabbath School Dept.: Dir., H. F. Rampton
Stewardship and Development Dir., P. G. Smith
Temperance Dept.: Dir., E. H. J. Steed
Youth Dept.: Dir., John H. Hancock

NORTH AMERICAN ORGANIZATIONS

The North American Division of Seventh-day Adventists, 6840 Eastern Ave. NW, Washington, DC 20012, Vice-Pres., Charles E. Bradford; Secretary, J. W. Bothe; Treasurers, M. E. Kemmerer and W. L. Murrill. This Division includes the United States and Canada and is divided into 61 Conferences which are grouped together into 10 organized Union Conferences. The various Conferences work under the general direction of these Union Conferences. The Canadian Union Conference is listed under the Canadian Section of this **Yearbook.** Following is a list of the 9 Union Conferences in which the Seventh-day Adventist Churches are organized in the United States.

Atlantic Union Conference, P.O. Box 458, South Lancaster, MA 01561. Pres., Earl W. Amundson; Sec., Aaron N. Brodgen; Treas., L. W. Crooker, (Territory: Connecticut, Maine, Massachusetts, New Hampshire, New York, Rhode Island, Vermont, and the Bermuda Islands)
Central Union Conference, P.O. Box 6127, Lincoln, NB 68506. Pres., E. S. Reile; Sec., W. S. Lee; Treas., Harry L. Haas, (Territory: Colorado, Kansas, Missouri, Nebraska, Wyoming, and San Juan County in New Mexico)
Columbia Union Conference, 7710 Carroll Ave., Takoma Park, MD 20012. Pres., W. O. Coe; Sec., W. A Thompson; Treas., D. J. Russell, (Territory: Delaware, Maryland, New Jersey, Ohio, Pennsylvania, Virginia, West Virginia, and District of Columbia)
Lake Union Conference, P.O. Box C, Berrien Springs, MI 49103, Pres., L. L. Bock; Sec., R. H. Carter; Treas., George Crumley, (Territory: Illinois, Indiana, Michigan, and Wisconsin)
North Pacific Union Conference, P.O. Box 16677, Portland, OR 97216. Pres., M. C. Torkelsen; Sec., R. C. Remboldt; Treas., D. P. Huey, (Territory: Alaska, Idaho, Montana, Oregon, and Washington)
Northern Union Conference, P.O. Box 27067, Minneapolis, MN 55427. Pres., E. L. Marley; Sec.-Treas., Lee Allen, (Territory: Iowa, Minnesota, North Dakota, and South Dakota)
Pacific Union Conference, P. O. Box 5005, Westlake Village, CA 91359 Pres., W. D. Blehm; Sec., Major C. White; Treas., S. D. Bietz, (Territory; Arizona, California, Hawaii, Nevada, and Utah)
Southern Union Conference, P.O. Box 849, Decatur, GA 30031. Pres., H. H. Schmidt; Sec., H. F. Roll; Treas., J. H. Whitehead, (Territory: Alabama, Florida, Georgia, Kentucky, Mississippi, North Carolina, South Carolina, and Tennessee)
Southwestern Union Conference, P.O. Box 606, Keene, TX 76059. Pres., B. E. Leach; Sec., W. R. May; Treas., V. L. Roberts, (Territory: Arkansas, Louisiana, New Mexico [excepting San Juan Country], Oklahoma, and Texas)

PERIODICALS

The Adventist Layman (m), 6840 Eastern Ave N.W., Washington, DC 20012. G. E. Knowles, Ed.
The Adventist Review (w), 6856 Eastern Ave. NW, Washington, DC 20012. K. H. Wood, Ed.
Christian Record, (m), 4444 South 52nd St., Lincoln NB 68506.
Guide (w), 6856 Eastern Ave. NW, Washington, DC 20012. Lowell Litten, Ed.
Insight, (w), 6856 Eastern Ave., NW, Washington, DC 20012. Donald John, Ed.
Israelite, 6840 Eastern Ave., NW, Washington, DC 20012. R. L. Odom, Ed.
Journal of Adventist Education (five issues yearly), 6856 Eastern Ave. NW, Washington, DC 20012. G. J. Millet, Ed.
Liberty (bi-m), 6856 Eastern Ave. NW, Washington, DC 20012. R. R. Hegstad, Ed.
Life and Health (m), 6856 Eastern Ave. NW, Washington, DC 20012. Joyce McClintock, Ed.
Listen (m), Pacific Press Publishing Association, Mountain View, CA 94040. F. A. Soper, Ed.
Message Magazine (8/yr), 1900 Elm Hill Pike, Nashville, TN 37210. L. B. Reynolds, Ed.
Ministry, The (m), 6840 Eastern Ave. N.W., Washington, DC 20012. J. R. Spangler, Ed.
Our Little Friend (w), Pacific Press Publishing Association, Mountain View, CA 94040. L. P. Schutter, Ed.
Primary Treasure (w), Pacific Press Publishing Association, Mountain View, CA 94040. L. P. Schutter, Ed.
Sabbath School Lesson Quarterlies, Pacific Press Publishing Association, Mountain View, CA 94040
Signs of the Times (m), Pacific Press Publishing Association, Mountain View, CA 94040. Lawrence Maxwell, Ed.
Smoke Signals, (m), 6840 Eastern Ave. NW, Washington DC 20012. F. A. Soper, Ed.
These Times (m), 1900 Elm Hill Pike, Nashville, TN 37210 K. J. Holland, Ed.
Worker: Journal of Sabbath School Action, (m), 6856 Eastern Ave., Washington, DC 20012. H. F. Rampton, Ed.
Youth Ministry Accent (q), 6840 Eastern Ave., NW, Washington, DC 20012. James Joiner, Ed.

Seventh Day Baptist General Conference

A group of Baptists organized in Rhode Island in 1671; they are distinguished from other groups by their observance of Saturday as the Sabbath.

Churches: 60 Inclusive Membership: 5,181 Sunday or Sabbath Schools: 53 Total Enrollment: 1,790 Ordained Clergy: 76

GENERAL ORGANIZATION

General Conference: annual
Headquarters: Seventh Day Baptist Bldg., 510 Watchung Ave., Box 868, Plainfield, NJ 07061. Tel. (201) 561-8700

OFFICERS

Pres., Rev. Duane L. Davis, 755 S. Homer St., Seattle, WA 98108
Rec. Sec., Mrs. Mae Bottoms, Box 64 Almond, NY 14804
Exec. Sec., Dr. K. Duane Hurley, 510 Watchung Ave., Box 868, Plainfield, NJ 07061
Treas., Richard W. Burdick, 3705 Tracy, N.E., Albuquerque, NM 87111
Treas., Denom, Budget, Gordon L. Sanford, R. 1, Little Genesee, NY 14754

OTHER ORGANIZATIONS

Seventh Day Baptist Missionary Society: Exec. Vice-Pres., Rev. Leon R. Lawton, 401 Washington Trust Bldg., Westerly, RI 02891
Seventh Day Baptist Board of Christian Education: Exec. Sec., Mrs. Mary Clare, 15 S. Main St., Alfred, NY 14802
Women's Society of the General Conference: Pres., Mrs. Ada Davis, 500 Manhattan Dr., Boulder, CO 80303, Corr. Sec., Ms. Patricia Williams, 13012 King Circle, Broomfield, CO 80020

American Sabbath Tract Society Seventh Day Baptist Publishing House: Publishing Dir., John D. Bevis, 510 Watchung Ave., Box 868, Plainfield, NJ 07061

Seventh Day Baptist Historical Society: Librarian, Thomas Merchant, 510 Watchung Ave., Box 868, Plainfield, NJ 07061

Seventh Day Baptist Center on Ministry: Dean, Rev. Herbert E. Saunders, 510 Watchung Ave., Box 868, Plainfield, NJ 07061

PERIODICAL

Sabbath Recorder (m) Seventh Day Baptist Bldg., 510 Watchung Ave., Box 868, Plainfield, NJ 07061. John D. Bevis, Ed.

Social Brethren

Organized 1867 among members of various bodies; confession of faith has nine articles; evangelical.

GENERAL ORGANIZATION

General Assembly: biennial

OFFICERS

Mod., of General Assembly, Rev. John Bailey, R.R. #1, Box 122 Simpson, IL 62985

Mod. (Union Association), Rev. John D. Tucker, P.O. Box 125, Harrisburg, IL 62946

Mod. (Illinois Association), Rev. Bill Jones, R.R. #3, Eldorado, IL 62930

Mod. (Midwestern Association), Rev. Edward Darnell, 1705 Chapel Pike, Marion, IN 46952

Southern Baptist Convention

In 1845 Southern Baptists withdrew from the General Missionary Convention over the question of slavery and other matters and formed the Southern Baptist Convention.

The men who formed the Southern Baptist Convention were moved by a spirit of conquest; they founded a society of co-operating believers who organized, to quote from the preamble to the constitution of the Convention, "a plan for eliciting, combining and directing the energies of the whole denomination in one sacred effort, for the propagation of the Gospel."

The glory of the Southern Baptist Convention is that the design of its organization was to preach the gospel in its entirety to the entire world, motivated by the belief that He who has saved us to the uttermost has called for the conquest of the uttermost.

The Southern Baptist Convention does its work through twenty boards, institutions and commissions known as agencies. These did not come into existence all at the same time, and they were not established until there was need for them. All of them reflect the life and work of the churches. They are rooted deeply in the experiences of the church members and their leaders, as they seek to fulfill their obligations to the commandments of Jesus Christ.

In addition, the Southern Baptist Convention has an Executive Committee organized for the first time in 1917, seventy-two years after the 1845 meeting. It first had only limited duties and was mostly concerned with the details of the annual convention. It was reorganized in 1925 and made the central business committee of the Convention.

Churches: 35,357 Inclusive Membership: 13,191,394 Sunday or Sabbath Schools: 34,450 Total Enrollment: 7,331,954 Ordained Clergy: 56,000

GENERAL ORGANIZATION

Convention: annual

OFFICERS

Pres., Adrian P. Rogers, Box 4837, Crosstown Sta., Memphis, TN 38104; Rec. Sec., Martin B. Bradley, 127 9th Ave., N., Nashville, TN 37234, Executive Committee: Offices, 460 James Robertson Pkwy., Nashville, TN 37219. Tel. (615) 244-2355; Exec. Sec., Harold C. Bennett; Dir. of Program Planning, Albert McClellan; Dir. of Fin. Planning, Tim Hedquist; Dir. of Public Relations, W. C. Fields

GENERAL BOARDS AND COMMISSIONS

Foreign Mission Board: 3806 Monument Ave., Richmond, VA 23220. Tel. (804) 353-0151. Exec. Sec., James Cauthern; Exec. Sec., R. Keith Parks

Home Mission Board: 1350 Spring St., NW, Atlanta, Ga 30309. Tel. (404) 873-4041. Exec. Sec.-Treas., William G. Tanner.

Annuity Board: 511 N. Akard, Dallas, TX 75201. Tel. (214) 747-9611. Pres., Darold H. Morgan; Exec. Vice Pres., Pat McDaniel

Sunday School Board: 127 Ninth Ave., N., Nashville, TN 37234. Tel. (615) 251-2000. Pres., Grady C. Cathen; Exec. Vice-Pres., James W. Clark.

Brotherhood Commission: 1548 Poplar Ave., Memphis, TN 38104. Tel. (901) 272-2461. Exec. Dir.-Treas., James H. Smith

Southern Baptist Commission on the American Baptist Theological Seminary: Room 318, 460 James Robertson Pkwy., Nashville, TN 37219. Tel. (615) 244-2362. Exec. Sec., Arthur H. Walker; Pres., of the Seminary, Charles E. Boddie

Christian Life Commission: 460 James Robertson Pkwy., Nashville, TN 37219. Tel. (615) 244-2495. Exec. Sec., Foy Valentine

Education Commission; 460 James Robertson Pkwy., Nashville, TN 37219. Tel. (615) 244-2362. Exec. Sec., Arthur H. Walker

Historical Commission: 127 Ninth Ave., N., Nashville, TN 37234. Tel. (615) 251-2660. Exec. Dir., Lynn E. May, Jr.; Asst. Exec. Dir., A. Ronald Tonks

The Radio and TV Commission: 6350 West Freeway, Ft. Worth, TX 76150. Tel. (817) 737-4011. Harold C. Martin, Exec. Vice Pres.

Stewardship Commission: 460 James Robertson Pkwy., Nashville, TN 37219. Tel (615) 244-2303. Exec. Dir., A. R. Fagan; Assoc. Exec. Dir., Michael L. Speer

STATE CONVENTIONS

Alabama, George E. Bagley, 4001 E. South Blvd., Montgomery 36106. Tel. (205) 288-2460

Alaska, Allen Meeks, Box 80, Anchorage 99501. Tel. (907) 344-9627

Arizona, Jack Johnson, 316 W. McDowell Rd., Phoenix 85003. Tel. (602) 264-9421

Arkansas, Charles H. Ashcraft, Baptist Bldg., Little Rock 72201. Tel. (501) 376-4791

California, Robert D. Hughes, 678 E. Shaw Ave., Fresno 93726. Tel. (Tel. (209) 229-9533

Colorado, Glen Braswell, P.O. Box 22005, Denver 80222. (Tel.) (303) 771-2480

District of Columbia, James Langley, 1628 16th St. NW, Washington 20009. Tel. (202) 265-1526

Florida, Interim Exec., Woodrow Fuller, 1230 Hendricks Ave., Jacksonville 32207. Tel. (904) 396-2351

Georgia, Searcy S. Garrison, 2030 Flowers Rd., S., Atlanta, GA 30341. Tel. (404) 455-0404

Hawaii, Edmond Walker, 2042 Vancouver Dr., Honolulu 96822. Tel. (808) 946-9581

Illinois, James H. Smith, Baptist Bldg., P.O. Box 3486 Springfield, 62708. Tel. (217) 786-2626

Indiana, E. H. Moore, 900 N. High School Rd., Indianapolis 46224. Tel. (317) 241-9317

Kansas-Nebraska, R. Rex Lindsay, 5410 W. Seventh St., Topeka 66606. Tel. (913) 273-4880
Kentucky, Franklin Owen, P.O. Box 43433, Middletown 40243. Tel. (502) 245-4101
Louisiana, Robt. L. Lee, Box 311, Alexandria 71301. Tel. (318) 443-3611
Maryland, Roy D. Gresham, 1313 York Rd., Lutherville 21093. Tel. (301) 321-7900
Michigan, Robert Wilson, 15635 W. 12 Mile Rd., Southfield 48076. Tel. (313) 557-4200
Mississippi, Earl Kelley, P.O. Box 530, Jackson 39205. Tel. (601) 354-3704
Missouri, Rheubin L. South, 400 E. High, Jefferson City 65101. Tel. (314) 635-7931
New Mexico, Chester O'Brien, P.O. Box 485, Albuquerque 87103. Tel. (505) 247-0586
New York, Jack P. Lowndes, 500 S. Salina St., Syracuse 13202. Tel. (315) 475-6173
North Carolina, Cecil Ray, 301 Hillsboro Rd., Raleigh 27611. Tel. (919) 833-1605
Northern Plains, Roy Owens, P.O. Box 1278 Rapid City, SD 57709. Tel. (605) 343-5572
Northwest Baptist Convention, Dan C. Stringer, 1033 N.E. 6th Ave., Portland, OR 97232. Tel. (503) 238-4545
Ohio, Tal Bonham, 1680 E. Broad St., Columbus 43203. Tel. (614) 258-8491
Oklahoma, Joe L. Ingram, 1141 N. Robinson, Oklahoma City 73103. (405) 236-4341
Pennsylvania-South Jersey, Ellis M. Bush, 900 S. Arlington Ave., Harrisburg 17109. Tel. (717) 652-5856
South Carolina, A. Harold Cole, 907 Richland St., Columbia 29201. Tel. (803) 765-0030
Tennessee, Tom Madden, P.O. Box 647, Brentwood, 37027. Tel. (615) 373-2255
Texas, James Landes, 703 North Ervay, Dallas 75201. Tel. (214) 741-1991
Utah-Idaho, Darwin E. Welsh, Sec., P.O. Box 2545, Salt Lake City 84101. Tel. (801) 322-3565
Virginia, Richard M. Stephenson, Va. Baptist Bldg., P. O. Box 8568, Richmond 23226. Tel. (804) 282-9751
West Virginia, Thomas E. Halsell, Sr., 801 Sixth Ave., St. Albans 25177. Tel. (304) 727-2974

PERIODICALS

Accent, 600 N. 20th, Birmingham, AL 35203 Oneta Gentry, Ed.
Alabama Baptist (w), 3310 Independence Dr., Birmingham, AL 35209. Tel. (205) 870-4720. Hudson Baggett, Ed.
Alaska Baptist Messenger, Box 80, Anchorage, AK 99507. Troy Prince, Ed. Tel. (907) 344-9627.
Ambassador Life, 1548 Poplar Ave., Memphis, TN 38104
Arkansas Baptist Newsmagazine (w), 525 W. Capitol Ave., Little Rock, AR 72203. Tel. (501) 376-4791. J. Everett Sneed, Ed.
Aware, 600 N. 20th, Birmingham, AL 35203. Mrs. Jesse A. Tucker, Ed.
Baptist and Reflector (w), P.O. Box 647, Brentwood, TN 37027. Alvin Shackleford, Ed. Tel. (615) 373-2255
Baptist Beacon (w), 400 W. Camelback Rd., Phoenix, AZ 85013. C. L. Pair, Ed. Tel. (602) 264-9421
Baptist Courier (w), 100 Manly St., Greenville, SC 29602. John Roberts, Ed. Tel. (803) 232-8736
Baptist Digest (w), 5410 W. 7th, Topeka, KS 66606. John Hopkins, Ed. Tel. (913) 273-4880
Baptist Message (w), Box 311, Alexandria, LA 71301. Lynn Clayton, Ed. Tel. (318) 442-7728
Baptist Messenger (w), 1141, N. Robinson, Oklahoma City, OK 73103. Jack L. Gritz, Ed. Tel. (405) 236-4341
Baptist New Mexican (w), Box 485, Albuquerque, NM 87103. C. Eugene Whitlow, Ed. Tel. (505) 247-0586
Baptist Program, SBC, 460 James Robertson Pkwy., Nashville, TN 37219. Albert McClellan, Ed. Tel. (615) 244-2355
Baptist Record (w), P.O. Box 530, Jackson, MS 39205. Don McGregor, Ed. Tel. (601) 354-3704
Baptist Standard (w), P.O. Box 226330, Dallas, TX 75266. Tel. (214) 630-4571. Presnall Wood, Ed.
Biblical Recorder (w), P.O. Box 26568, Raleigh, N. C. 27611. Marse Grant, Ed. Tel. (919) 832-4019
California Southern Baptist (w), P.O. Box 5168, Fresno, CA 93755. Elmer Gray, Ed. Tel. (209) 229-9533
Capital Baptist, 1628 16th St. NW, Washington, DC 20009. James Langley, Ed. Tel. (202) 265-1526
Christian Index (w), 2930 Flowers Rd., S., Atlanta, GA 30341. Jack U. Harwell, Ed. Tel. (404) 455-0404
Commission, The, 3806 Monument Ave., Richmond, VA 23230. Floyd North, Ed.
Contempo, 600 N. 20th, Birmingham, AL 35203. Laurella Owens, Ed.
Discovery, 600 N. 20th, Birmingham, AL 35203. Mrs. Jesse A. Tucker, Ed.
Florida Baptist Witness (w), 1230 Hendricks Ave., Jacksonville, TL 32207. Edgar Cooper, Ed. Tel. (904) 396-2351
Hawaii Baptist, 2042 Vancouver Dr., Honolulu 96822. Edmond Walker, Ed. Tel. (808) 946-9581
Home Missions, 1350 Spring St. NW, Atlanta, GA 30303. Walker L. Knight, Ed.
Illinois Baptist (w), P.O. Box 3486, Springfield, 62708. Robert J. Hastings, Ed. Tel. (217) 529-6721
Indiana Baptist (m), P.O. Box 24038, Indianapolis, IN 46224. Gene Medaris, Ed. Tel. (317) 241-9317
Maryland Baptist (w), 1313 York Rd., Lutherville, MD 21093. Larry High, Assoc, Ed. Tel. (301) 321-7905
Michigan Baptist Advocate, 15635 W. Twelve Mile Rd., Southfield MI 48076. Robert Wilson, Ed. Tel. (313) 557-4200
New York Baptist, 500 S Salina St., Syracuse, NY 13202, Jack P. Lowndes, Ed. Tel. (315) 475-6173
Northern Plains News, P. O. Box 1278, Rapid City, SD 57709. Roy W. Owen, Ed. Tel. (605) 343-5572
Northwest Baptist Witness, 1033 N. 6th Ave., Portland, OR 97232, Dan Stringer, Ed. Tel. (503) 238-4545
Ohio Baptist Messenger (m), 1680 E. Broad, Columbus, OH 43203. Theo Sommerkamp Ed. Tel. (614) 253-8527
Penn.-Jersey Baptist, 900 S. Arlington Ave., Harrisburg, PA 17109. Ellis M. Bush, Ed. Tel. (717) 564-7550
Quarterly Review (q), 127 Ninth Ave. N., Nashville, TN 37203. Reggie McDonough, Ed.
Religious Herald (w), P.O. Box 8377, Richmond, VA 23226. Julian Pentecost, Ed. Tel. (804) 288-1973
Review and Expositor (q), 2825 Lexington Rd., Louisville, KY 40206
Rocky Mountain Baptist, P.O. Box 22005, Denver, CO 80222. James Young, Ed. Tel. (303) 771-2480
Royal Service, 600 N. 20th St., Birmingham, AL 35203. Rosanne Osborn, Ed.
Southwestern News, P.O. Box 22000, Seminary Hill, Fort Worth, TX 76122. John Seelig, Ed.
Start, 600 N. 20th, Birmingham, AL 35203. Mrs. Helen M. Allan, Ed.
Utah-Idaho Southern Baptist Witness, P.O. Box 2545, Salt Lake City, UT 84110. Darwin E. Welsh, Ed. Tel. (801) 322-3565
Western Recorder (w), Box 43401, Middletown, KY 40243. C. R. Daley, Ed. Tel. (502) 245-4101
West Virginia Southern Baptist, 801 Sixth Ave., St. Albans, WV 25177. Jackson C. Walls, Ed. Tel. (304) 727-2974
Word and Way (w), Mo. 400 E. High, Jefferson City, MO 65101. Bob Terry, Ed. Tel. (314) 635-7931

Southern Methodist Church

Organized in 1939, this body is composed of congregations desirous of continuing in true Methodism and preserving the fundamental doctrines and beliefs of the Methodist Episcopal Church, South that declined to be a party to the merger of the Methodist Episcopal Church, The Methodist Episcopal Church, South, and the Methodist Protestant Church into The Methodist Church.

GENERAL ORGANIZATION

General Conference: quadrennial (next meeting, May 1982)

Annual Conferences: (1) South Carolina Conference (Virginia, North Carolina, South Carolina); (2) Alabama, Florida, Georgia Conference; (3) Mid-South Conference (Mississippi, Tennessee); (4) South-Western Conference (Arkansas, Louisiana, Texas)

OFFICERS

Pres., Rev. Julian B. Gamble, P.O. Box 132, Orangeburg, SC 29115. Tel. (803) 536-1378

Vice-Presidents:

South Carolina Conf., Rev. E. Legrand Adams, 408 W. Pine St., Florence, SC 29501

Alabama, Florida, Georgia Conf., Rev. H. Emmett Hutto 2622 Garden Lakes Blvd., Rome, GA 30161

Mid-South Conf., Rev. David S. Moore, 4139 Parkchester Ave., Memphis, TN 38118

South-western Conf., Rev. Wallace R. Terry, Jr., 6011 Fairfield Ave., Shreveport,LA 71106

Treas., Gen. Conference, Mr. George K. Nelson, 2424 Marling Dr., Columbia, SC 29204

PERIODICAL

The Southern Methodist (m), P.O. Drawer A, Orangeburg, SC 29115

Syrian Orthodox Church of Antioch (Archdiocese of the U.S.A. and Canada)

An archdiocese in North America of the Syrian Orthodox Church of Antioch. Composed of several archdioceses, numerous churches, schools and seminaries, the Syrian Orthodox Church, numbering faithful in the Middle East, India, the Americas, Europe and Australia, traces its origin to the earliest Patriarchate established in Antioch by St. Peter the Apostle and is under the supreme ecclesiastical jurisdiction of the Syrian Orthodox Patriarch of Antioch and All the East.

The first Syrian Orthodox faithful came to North America during the late 1800's, and by 1907 the first Syrian Orthodox priest arrived to tend to the community's spiritual needs. In 1949, His Eminence Archbishop Mar Athanasius Y. Samuel came to America and was soon appointed Patriarchal Vicar. The Archdiocese of the Syrian Orthodox Church in the U.S. and Canada was formally created in 1957.

There are 13 official archdiocesan parishes in the United States located in California, Illinois, Massachusetts, Michigan, New Jersey, New York, Pennsylvania, Rhode Island and Texas. In Canada, there are 3 official parishes one in the Province of Ontario and two in the Province of Quebec.

Churches: 13 Inclusive Membership: 30,000 Sunday or Sabbath Schools: N.R. Total Enrollment: 335 Ordained Clergy: 18

ORGANIZATION

Archdiocese of the U.S. and Canada, 293 Hamilton Pl., Hackensack, NJ 07601

Archdiocesan Advisory Council: Appointed regularly by the Primate

Archdiocesan Convention: Annual

OFFICERS

Primate: Archbishop MarAthanasius Y. Samuel, 293 Hamilton Pl., Hackensack, NJ 07601

Advisory Council Chpsn., Mr. Charles Koorey, 45 Broadview Ave., Maplewood, NJ 07040

Archdiocesan Gen. Sec., Rev. Father John Meno, 45 Fairmount Ave., Hackensack, NJ 07601

Archdiocesan Treas., Dr. Fehmi Aydin, 4 Jockey Ln., New City, NY 10956

†Triumph the Church and Kingdom of God in Christ (International)

This church was given through the wisdom and knowledge of God himself to the Late Apostle Elias Dempsey Smith, on October 20, 1897, at 12:00 noon in Issaquena, County, Mississippi, while he was pastor of a Methodist church.

The Triumph Church, as this body is more commonly known, was founded in 1902, its doors opened in 1904, and confirmed in Birmingham, Alabama, with 225 members in 1915. It was incorporated in Washington, DC, 1918 and currently operates in 31 states and overseas. The General Church is divided into 18 districts including the Africa District and the South American District.

Triumphant doctrine and philosophy is based on the following concepts and principles: Life, Truth and Knowledge; God in man, and being expressed through man; Manifested Wisdom; Complete and Full Understanding; Constant New Revelations. Its concepts and methods of teaching "the second coming of Christ" are based on these and all other attributes of goodness.

Triumphians put strong emphasis on the fact that God is the God of the living, and not the God of the dead.

GENERAL ORGANIZATION

Quarterly and Annual Conferences, International Religious Congress: quadrennial

National Headquarters, 213 Farrington Ave., Atlanta, GA 30318. Tel. (404) 413-0315

International Headquarters, 7122 Campania Ave., Pittsburgh, PA 15206

OFFICERS

Archbishop, The Rt. Rev. D. H. Harris, 7122 Campania Ave., Pittsburgh, PA 15206

Exec. Sec. to the Archbishop, Rev. Clinton J. LeVert, 255 Raeburn St., Pontiac, MI 48053

Nat. Gen. Rec. Sec., Bishop A. L. Williams, Rt. 4, Box 385, Bessemer, AL 35020

Ukrainian Orthodox Church in the U.S.A.

Formally organized in U.S.A. in 1919. Archbishop John Theodorovich arrived from Ukraine in 1924.

GENERAL ORGANIZATION

The Sobor, which elects a Council of Bishops, meets every three years. Next meeting of the Sobor, 1980

Headquarters: South Bound Brook, NJ 08880

OFFICERS

Metropolitan: Most Rev. Mstyslav S. Skrypnyk, South Bound Brook, NJ 08880; Archbishop Mark Hundiak, 641 Roosevelt Ave., Carteret, NJ 07008; Bishop Constantine Buggan, 2238 W. Cortex St., Chicago, IL 60622

Consistory: Pres., Protopresbyter Artem Selepyna; Vice Pres., Protopresbyter Stephen Bilak, Sec., Mrs. Larissa

Palyvoda; Treas., Protopresbyter Theodore Forosty; Member, T. Burka

PERIODICAL

Ukrainian Orthodox Word, South Bound Brook, NJ 08880

Ukrainian Orthodox Church in America (Ecumenical Patriarchate)

This body was organized in America in 1928, when the first convention was held. In 1932 Dr. Joseph Zuk was consecrated as first Bishop. His successor was the Most Rev. Bishop Bohdan, Primate, who was consecrated by the order of the Ecumenical Patriarchate of Constantinople on Februrary 28, 1937, in New York City. The present primate is the Most Rev. Bishop Andrei Kuschak.

GENERAL ORGANIZATION

Sobor meets on call.
Headquarters: St. Andrew's Ukrainian Orthodox Diocese, 90-34 139th St., Jamaica, N.Y. 11435. Tel. (212) 297-2407

OFFICERS

Primate: Most Rev. Bishop Andrei Kuschak
Chancellor: Very Rev. H. Wroblewsky
Dean: Boris Zabrodsky

PERIODICAL

Ukrainian Orthodox Herald (q), Fr. Ivan Tkaczuk, Ed.

Unitarian Universalist Association

The Unitarian Universalist Association is the consolidated body of the former American Unitarian Association and the Universalist Church of America. The Unitarian movement arose in Congregationalism in the 18th century, producing the American Unitarian Association in 1825. In 1865 a national conference was organized. The philosophy of Universalism originated with the doctrine of universal salvation in the first century, and was brought to America in the 18th century. Universalists were first formally organized in 1793. In May, 1961, the Unitarian and Universalist bodies were consolidated to become the Unitarian Universalist Association. The movement is noncreedal.

Churches: 936 Inclusive Membership: 136,207 Sunday or Sabbath Schools: N.R. Total Enrollment: 37,783 Ordained Clergy: 898

GENERAL ORGANIZATION

General Assembly: annual
Headquarters: 25 Beacon St., Boston, MA 02108. Tel. (617) 742-2100. District offices, 23 in number

OFFICERS

Pres., Dr. O. Eugene Pickett
Exec. Vice-Pres., Rev. Robert Senghas
Mod., Sandra Mitchell Caron
Sec., Lori Pederson
Treas., Arthur J. Root
Ministerial & Congregational Services, ———
Communications and Development, Doris Pullen
Beacon Press, Mary Ann Lash
Minister, Church of the Larger Fellowship: Rev. George N. Marshall

OTHER ORGANIZATIONS

(Address unless otherwise noted, 25 Beacon St., Boston, MA 02108)
Unitarian Universalist Ministers' Association: Pres., Rev. Virgil Murdock
Unitarian Universalist Women's Federation: Exec. Dir., Nancy Prichard
Liberal Religious Youth: Contact: Nada Velimirovic
Unitarian Universalist Service Committee, Inc.: 78 Beacon St., Boston, MA 02108. Exec. Dir., Richard Scobie
Unitarian Universalist Historical Society, Pres., Dr. Spencer Lavan

PERIODICALS

UU World (twice monthly), William Gagnon, Ed., 25 Beacon St., Boston, MA 02108
Wayside Community Pulpit, Kerry O'Donnell, Ed., 25 Beacon St., Boston, MA 02108

United Brethren in Christ

The Church of the United Brethren in Christ had its beginning with Philip William Otterbein and Martin Boehm, who were leaders in the revivalistic movement in Pennsylvania and Maryland during the late 1760s and which continued into the early 1800s.

On September 25, 1800, they and others associated with them, formed a society under the name of United Brethren in Christ. Subsequent conferences adopted a Confession of Faith in 1815 and a constitution in 1841. The Church of the United Brethren in Christ adheres to the original constitution as amended in 1957, 1961 and 1977.

GENERAL ORGANIZATION

General Conference, quadrennial (next meeting, 1981)
Headquarters: 302 Lake St., P.O. Box 650, Huntington, IN 46750. Tel. (219) 356-2312

OFFICERS

Bishops: Chpsn., C. Ray Miller, Duane A. Reahm, Raymond Waldfogel, Wilbur L. Sites, Jr.
Adm. Asst.-Gen. Treas., David G. Jackson
Exec. Dir., Dept. of Education, E. DeWitt Baker
Exec. Dir., Dept. of Church Ministries, Howard Anderson
Exec. Dir., Dept. of Stewardship, E. Carlson Becker

PERIODICAL

The United Brethren (m), Huntington, IN 46750, Stanley Peters, Ed.

United Christian Church

A group which separated in 1862-70 from the United Brethren in Christ; organized at Campbelltown, PA 1878.

GENERAL ORGANIZATION

General Conference: annual (1st Saturday in May)

OFFICERS

Mod., Elder Henry C. Heagy, Lebanon, R.D. 4, Lebanon County, PA 17042. Tel. (717) 867-2611
Presiding Elder, Elder Henry C. Heagy, Lebanon, R.D. 4. Lebanon County, PA 17042

OTHER ORGANIZATION

Mission Board: Pres., Elder Henry C. Heagy; Sec., Elder Landis E. Tice; Treas., Elder John P. Ludwig

United Church of Christ

A union in 1957 of the Evangelical and Reformed Church and the General Council of the Congregational Christian Churches. The union was completed in July 1961, when the Constitution was adopted in Philadelphia.

Churches: 6,491 Inclusive Membership: 1,769,104 Sunday or Sabbath Schools: N.R. Total Enrollment: 508,764 Ordained Clergy: 9,704

GENERAL ORGANIZATION

Synod: biennial

Headquarters: 105 Madison Ave., New York, NY 10016. Tel. (212) 683-5656

OFFICERS

Pres., Rev. Avery Post
Sec., Rev. Joseph H. Evans
Dir. of Finance & Treas., Charles H. Lockyear
Exec. Assoc. to the Pres., Rev. Norman W. Jackson
Asst. to Pres.: Rev. Robert Phillip Noble, Jr., Rev. Carol Joyce Burn
Chpsn. Exec. Council, Rev. John M. Bracke
V-Chpsn., Mrs. Jean M. Edwards
Mod., Rev. Nathanael M. Guptill
Asst. Mod., The Hon. William Counsins, Jr.
Asst. Mod., Ms. Virginia Held

ORGANIZATIONS

United Church Board for World Ministries: Offices, 475 Riverside Dr., New York, NY 10027. Tel. (212) 870-2637; 14 Beacon St., Boston, MA 02108; Box 179, 115 N. Jefferson St., Louis, MO 63166; Executive Office and General Program: Exec. Vice Pres., Rev. David M. Stowe; Overseas Personnel Sec., Rev. Elinor G. Galusha; Sec. for World Hunger Action, Rev. E. Neill Richards; World Issues & Regional Sec. for Europe, Sec., Rev. Howard Schomer; Asst. to the Exec. Vice Pres., Mr. Dalton Smith

Division of World Mission: Gen. Sec., and Regional Sec., Southern Asia, Rev. Telfer H. Mook; Regional Sec., Near East, Miss Margaret R. Blemker; Regional Sec., Pacific, Rev. Paul R. Gregory; Regional Sec., Africa, Rev. L. Marcus; Assoc. Regional Sec., Africa, Rev. Richard E. Stenhouse; Regional Sec., Latin America/Carribbean, Rev. Jeffrey H. Utter

Division of World Service: Gen. Sec., Rev. Alfred C. Bartholomew; Consultant on Development Education and the United Nations, Ms. Hazel T. Johns; Program Sec., Rev. Gustav H. Kuether.

Treasury: Treas. Rev. Myles H. Walburn; Assoc. Treas., Mr. John F. Fairfield; Asst. Treas. and Dir. of Planned Giving, Rev. Leonard G. Clough; Dir. of Purchasing & Transportation, Ms. Marcella Z. Begovic; Dir. of Accounting and Finance, Mr. Adolf W. Simonides.

United Church Board for Homeland Ministries: Offices 132 W. 31st St., New York, NY 10001; Tel. (212) 239-8700. Exec. V-Pres., Rev. Howard E. Spragg; Treas., Richard H. Dubie; Asst. Treas., Edward C. Fitzgerald; Osborne D. Nichols; Sec. for Admin., Nils E. Forstner; Exec. Assoc. for Planning and Sec. for Div. of Publication, Rev. Paul H. Sherry; Sec. for Mission Coordination, Rev. Theodore H. Erickson; Sec. for Division of Higher Education and the American Missionary Association; Rev. Wesley A. Hotchkiss; Sec. for Division of Health and Welfare, Mrs. Helen B. Webber; Interim Sec. for Div. of Evangelism, Church Extention, and Education, Rev. Carl A. Bade; Sec. for Office of Church Building, Mr. John R. Potts.

A.D., United Church Edition (Published jointly with the United Presbyterian Church): Editorial and Circulation Offices, 475 Riverside Dr., New York, NY 10027; Publisher, Roy A. Lord; Editor, Rev. J. Martin Bailey Assoc. Eds., Thomas O. Bentz, Sarah Cunningham, James A. Gittings, Mayo Y. Smith, James E. Solheim.

Commission for Racial Justice: 105 Madison Ave., New York, NY 10016, 1029 Vermont Ave., NW, Ste. 208, Washington, DC 20005; 5 West Hargett, St., Ste. 809, Raleigh, NC 27601. (All addresses in New York unless otherwise noted.) Exec. Dir., Rev. Charles E. Cobb; Assoc. Dir., Ms. Marilyn Adams Moore; Consultant, Consumer Protection, Mr. James Brennan; Office Manager, Ms. Alice Douglas; Dir. of Research, Information, Education; Ed. of Commission News, Criminal Justice, Issues, CRJ Reporter, Mr. Travis Francis; Dir., Child Abuse Program, Ms. Gina Toppins; Dir., Washington, DC Field Office, Rev. Benjamin Chavis; Staff Assistant, Criminal Justice & Penal Reform, Mr. William Jones; Dir., Special Higher Education, Ms. Toni Killings; Community Organizer, Ms. Kristine Curtis; Dir., N.C.-Virginia Field Office, Rev. Leon White; Staff Assists; Ms. Edna McLaren-Bartley (NY); Ms. Armanta Eaton (NC).

Council for American Indian Ministry: 122 W. Franklin Ave., Rm. 300, Minneapolis, MN 55404. Exec. Dir., Rev. Mitchell Whiterabbit; Exec. Sec., Ms. Donna Richardson.

Office for Church in Society: 105 Madison Ave., New York, NY 10016; 110 Maryland Ave., N.E., Washington, DC 20002; 2525 E. Newton Ave., Milwaukee, WI 53211. Exec. Dir., Rev. S. Garry Oniki (NY); Assoc. for Information and Publication, Rev. James E. Lintner (NY); Assoc. for Constituency Devel., Rev. Yvonne V. Delk (NY); Dir., Washington Office, Rev. Paul L. Kittlaus (DC); Legislative Counsel and Assoc. for Policy Advocacy, Rev. Barry W. Lynn (DC); Assoc. for Policy Advocacy, Ms. Gretchen C. Eick (DC); Assoc for Constituency Devel., Rev. David C. Rohlfing (WI)

Office for Church Life and Leadership: 105 Madison Ave., New York, NY 10016; 870 Market St., San Francisco, CA 94102; 122 W. Franklin Ave., Rm. 323, Minneapolis, MN 55404; P.O. Box 179, St. Louis, MO 63166; 750 Chatham Rd. Winston-Salem, NC 27101; 41 Crosswell Rd., Columbus, OH 43214; P.O. Box 369 Framingham, MA 01701; P.O. Box 29883, Atlanta GA 30359; Exec. Dir., Rev. Ruben A. Sheares, II (NY); Exec. Assoc., Rev. Thomas R. Tupper (MO); Ms. Marilyn M. Brietling (MO); Rev. Anthony Carpenter, (NY); Rev. Richard B. Griffis (NY); Rev. William A. Hulteen, Jr. (OH); Rev. Kenneth K. Iha (CA); Rev. Roger D. Knight (MN); Rev. Ralph C. Quellhorst (NY); Rev. Joyce B. Myers (GA); Ms. Dorothy L. Robinson (NC); Rev. Robert D. Witham (MA)

Office of Communication: 105 Madison Ave., New York, NY 10016. Dir., Rev. Everett C. Parker, Deputy Dir., Dr. Ralph M. Jennings; Assoc. Dirs., Rev. Eugene A. Schneider, Mr. William C. Winslow; Staff Writer, Mr. Frederick Blake; Field Rep., Ms. Janice Engsberg; Gen. Exec., Fr. Donald Matthews; Gen. Mgr., Ms. Doris Smith.

17/76 Achievement Fund: 105 Madison Ave., New York, NY 10016. Treas., Charles H. Lockyear.

Stewardship Council: 105 Madison Ave., New York, NY 10016 and 1505 Race St., Philadelphia, PA 19102. (All addresses at New York City unless otherwise stated.) Exec. Dir., Rev. George W. Otto; Gen. Sec. for Adm., Rev. William M. Thompson (Phila.); Gen. Sec. for Program Development, Rev. Theodore S. Horvath; Admin. Sec., Ms. Sherry Marshall; Bus. Mgr., Mrs. Joan M. Hasher (Phila.); Sec. for OCWM Information, and Editor of Sunday Bulletin Service, Rev. Charles W. Cooper, Jr.; Sec. for Promotion, Rev. Milton E.

Gockley, Jr.; Editorial Sec., John M. Haverstick; Sec. for Special A-V Resources, and Editor of Desk Calendar & Plan Book, Rev. Earl D. Miller; Sec. for Program Info. and Speakers Bureau, Ms. Jean Schwertfager (Phila.); Sec. for Stewardship Ed., Rev. George Siudy, Jr. (Phila.); Coordinator of Special Projects, Rev. William E. Wimer. Conference-based Staff: Conn., R.I., Vt., Rev. Ray L. Harwick, 125 Sherman St. Hartford CT 06105; Mass., N.H., Maine, Rev. George Condon, Box 2246, Salem End & Badger Rds., Framingham, MA 01701; Southern and Middle Atlantic Regions, Rev. C. David Langerhans (Phila.); Ohio, Rev. Paul E. Baumer, 41 Croswell Rd. Columbus OH 43214; Ill., Rev. Donald G. Stoner, 302 South Grant St., Hinsdale IL 60521; Neb., No. Dak., So. Dak. and Kans.-Okla., Rev. Earle R. Potts, 2055 E St. Lincoln, NE 68510; South Central and Southeast, Rev. Edwin Mehlhaff, 4054 Coltwood Dr., Spring, TX 77373.

Historical Council: 105 Madison Ave., New York, NY 10016. Office of Archivist, George H. Bricker, Philip Schaff Library, Lancaster Theological Seminary, 555 W. James St., Lancaster, PA 17603

Pension Board: 132 W. 31st S., New York, NY 10001. Exec. Vice Pres., Dr. John D. Ordway; Sec., Rev. Don A. Bundy; Adm. Sec., Maria Lucia; Sec. for Benefits, Mr. James P. Devane; Ministerial Asst., Sec., Rev. William T. Green, Supervisor, Actuarial Dept., Mr. Robert Peirsa; Treas., Mr. Richard H. Dubie.

United Church Foundation, Inc.: 132 W. 31st St., New York, NY 10001. Financial Vice Pres. and Treas., Richard H. Dubie.

CONFERENCES

Western Region:

California, Northern, Rev. Mineo Katagirl, 677 Flood Bldg., 870 Market St., San Francisco, CA 94102

California, Southern, Rev. Fred P. Register, 466 E. Walnut St., Pasadena 91101

Hawaii, Rev. Teruo Kawata, 2103 Nuuanu Ave., Honolulu 96817

Montana/Northern Wyoming, Rev. George P. Barber, 1511 Poly Dr., Billings 59102

Central Pacific, ———, 0245 SW Bancroft St., Portland 97201

Rocky Mountain, Rev. W. Harper Welch, Acting, 222 Clayton St., Denver, CO 80206

Southwest, Rev. Edward H. Hastings, 10 E. Roanoke, Phoenix, AZ 85004

Washington-North Idaho, Rev. W. James Halfaker, 720 14th Ave. E., Seattle, WA 98102

West Central Region:

Iowa, Rev. Scott S. Libbey, 600 42nd St., Des Moines 50312

Kansas-Oklahoma, Rev. A. Gayle Engle, 216 E. 2nd, Rm. 401, Wichita, KS 67202

Minnesota, Rev. Francis X. Pirazzini, 122 W. Franklin Ave., Minneapolis 55404

Missouri, Rev. Rueben P. Koehler, 1720 Chouteau Ave., St. Louis 63103

Nebraska, Rev. David J. Jamieson, 2055 "E" St., Lincoln 68510

North Dakota, Rev. Lester L. Soberg, 202½ Third St. N., Bismarck 58501

South Dakota, Rev. Jack A. Batten, Ste. B, 801 E. 41st St., Sioux Falls, SD 57105

Great Lakes Region:

Illinois, Rev. W. Sterling Cary, 302 S. Grant St., Hinsdale 60521

Illinois South, Rev. William Koshewa, 1312 Broadway, Highland 62249

Indiana-Kentucky, Rev. Harry W. Bredeweg, 1100 W. 42nd St., Indianapolis, IN 46208

Michigan, Rev. John Rogers, P.O. Box 1006, East Lansing 48823

Ohio, Rev. William K. Laurie, 41 Croswell Rd., Columbus 43214

Wisconsin, Rev. Ralph P. Ley, 2719 Marshall Ct. Madison 53705

Southern Region:

Florida, Rev. Charles L. Burns Jr., 222 E. Welbourne Ave., Winter Park, FL 32789

South Central, Rev. James Tomasek, Jr., 2704 Rio Grande #8, Austin TX 78705

Southeast, Rev. William J. Andes, P.O. Box 29883, Atlanta, GA 30359

Southern, Rev. James H. Lightbourne, Jr., 328 W. Davis St., P.O. Box 2410, Burlington, NC 27215

Middle Atlantic Region:

Central Atlantic, Rev. Curtis Clare, 620 Pershing Dr., Silver Spring, MD 20910

New York, Rev. James R. Smucker, The Church Center, Rm. 260, 3049 E. Genesee St., Syracuse, NY 13224

Penn Central, Rev. Horace S. Sills, The United Church Center, Rm. 126, 900 South Arlington Ave., Harrisburg, PA 17109

Penn Northeast, Rev. William T. Longsdorf, 431 Delaware Ave., P.O. Box 177, Palmerton, PA 18071

Pennsylvania Southeast, Rev. John C. Shetler, 620 Main St., Box G, Collegeville, PA 19426

Penn West, Rev. Paul L. Westcoat, Jr., 320 South Maple Ave., Greensburg, PA 15601

Puerto Rico, Rev. Osvaldo Malave, Box 20519, Rio Peidras, PR 00925

New England Region:

Connecticut, Rev. Nathanael M. Guptill, 125 Sherman St., Hartford, CT 06105

Maine, Rev. Otto E. Sommer, 53 Baxter Blvd., Portland 04101

Massachusetts, Rev. Alfred Williams, P. O. Box 2246, Salem and Badger Rds., Farmingham, MA 01701

New Hampshire, Rev. Benjamin R. Andrews, Jr., Rev. Edward D. Brueggemann, Rev. Robert D. Fiske, Rev. Stephen V. Weaver, 85 N. State St., Concord 03301

Rhode Island, Rev. Robert L. Bergfalk 2 Stimson Ave., Providence 02906

Vermont, Rev. Charles G. Chamberlain, 285 Maple St., Burlington, VT 05401

Nongeographic:

Calvin Synod, Rev. Desmond D. Parragh, 8260 W. Foster Ter., Norridge, IL 60659

†The United Free Will Baptist Church

A body which set up its organization in 1870

GENERAL ORGANIZATION

General Conference: every 3 years

Headquarters: Kinston College, 1000 University St., Kinston, NC 28501

OFFICERS

Vice-Mod., Rev. O. L. Williams, 1052 N. Missouri Ave., Lakeland, FL 33801

Chpsn. Exec. Board, Rev. W. F. Cox 1106 Holt St., Durham, NC 27701

Gen. Fin. Sec., Rev. W. L. Jones, 606 Bancraff Ave., Greenville, NC 27834

Gen. Rec. Sec., Rev. J. H. O'Neal, 203 De Soto St., Daytona Beach, FL 32014

Gen. Pres., Women's Home Mission Dept., Mrs. J. M. Reaves, Ayden, NC 28513

Mgr. Lit. Dept., Rev. J. C. Smith, 209 Freemon St., Raleigh, NC 27601

PERIODICAL

The Free Will Baptist Advocate (s-m), Kinston, NC 28501. E. L. Brown, New Bern, NC, Ed.

United Holy Church of America, Inc.

Organized in 1886 at Method, North Carolina. Ordinances of baptism by immersion, the Lord's supper, and Feet Washing are observed. We accept the premillennial teaching of the Second Coming of Christ. Divine healing, but not to the exclusion of medicine, justification by faith, sanctification as a second work of grace, and spirit baptism.

GENERAL ORGANIZATION

Convocation: quadrennial (next meeting, May, 1980)
Headquarters: 159 W. Coulter St., Philadelphia, PA 19144. Tel. (215) 849-1233
General Convocation, annually in May 1978—Bermuda District; 1979—Central Western District

OFFICERS

Gen. Pres., Bishop W. N. Strobhar, 268 Orange Rd., Montclair, NJ 07042
1st Vice-Pres., Bishop Joseph T. Bowens, 825 Fairoak Ave., Chillum, MD 20783
2nd Vice-Pres., Bishop Thomas E. Talley, 2710 Magnolia St., Portsmouth, VA 23704
Gen. Rec. Sec., Sadie Walker, 5425 Cedar Ave., Philadelphia, PA 19143
Gen. Fin. Sec., Rev. Mr. Iris Fischer, 28 Cooper St., Brooklyn, NY
Gen. Asst. Rec. Sec., Rev. A. Thomas Godfrey, Chicago, IL
Gen. Asst. Fin. Sec., Rev. Mrs. Clarice L. Chambers, Harrisburg, PA.
Gen. Treas., Rev. Edward M. Burnett, Randleman, NC
Pres., Missionary Dept., Rev. Savannah W. Edwards
Gen. Supt., Bible Church School, David Williams, Philadelphia, PA
Pres., Youth Dept., Rev. Elroy Lewis, E. 10 Village Green, Chapel Hill, NC 27514
Gen. Education Dept., Rev. Roosevelt Alston, Henderson, NC

PERIODICAL

The Holiness Union (m), Open Door Press, Box 5393, St. Louis, MO 63115

The United Methodist Church

The United Methodist Church was formed April 23, 1968 in Dallas, Texas, by the union of The Methodist Church and The Evangelical United Brethren Church. The two churches shared a common historical and spiritual heritage. The Methodist Church resulted in 1939 from the unification of three branches of Methodism—the Methodist Episcopal Church; the Methodist Episcopal Church, South; and the Methodist Protestant Church. The Methodist movement began in 18th-century England under the preaching of John Wesley, but the so-called Christmas Conference of 1784 in Baltimore is regarded as the date on which the organized Methodist Church was founded as an ecclesiastical organization. It was there that Francis Asbury was elected the first bishop in this country. The Evangelical United Brethren Church was formed in 1946 with the merger of the Evangelical Church and the Church of the United Brethren in Christ, both of which had their beginnings in Pennsylvania in the evangelistic movement of the 18th and early 19th centuries. Philip William Otterbein and Jacob Albright were early leaders of this movement among the German-speaking settlers of the Middle Colonies.

Churches: 38,682 Inclusive Membership: 9,731,779 Sunday or Sabbath Schools: 36,485 Total Enrollment: 4,410,471 Ordained Clergy: 35,939

GENERAL ORGANIZATION

General Conference: quadrennial (next meeting will be held April, 1984 in Baltimore, MD)

OFFICERS

Sec. of Gen. Conference, John B. Holt, Perkins School of Theology, Southern Methodist University, Dallas, TX 75222
Council of Bishops: Pres., Bishop Ralph T. Alton, 1100 W 42nd St., Indianapolis, IN 46208; Pres-designate, Bishop Roy C. Nichols, 223 Fourth Ave., Pittsburgh, PA 15222; Sec., Bishop James K. Mathews, 100 Maryland Ave., NE, Washington, DC 20002. Tel. (202) 547-2991

BISHOPS IN U.S.A.

L. Scott Allen, P.O. Box 12005, Charlotte, NC 28205
Ralph T. Alton, 1100 W. 42nd St., Indianapolis, IN 46208
Edsel A. Ammons, 155 W. Congress, Ste. #200, Detroit, MI 48226
A. James Armstrong, Berkshire Plaza, 405 NW 8th Ave., Aberdeen, SD 57401
James M. Ault, Valley Forge Corporate Center, P.O. Box 820, Valley Forge, PA 19482
Robert M. Blackburn, Methodist Bldg., 1307 Glenwood Ave., P.O. Box 10955, Raleigh, NC 27605
Monk Bryan, 2641 N. 49th St., Lincoln, NE 68504
William R. Cannon, 159 Forrest Ave., NE Suite 208, Atlanta, GA 30308
Alsie H. Carleton, 1201 First National Bank Bldg. E., Albuquerque, NM 87108
Edward G. Carroll, 581 Boylston St., Rm. 84, Boston, MA 02116
Wilbur W. Y. Choy, 800 Olympic National Bldg., 920 Second Ave., Seattle, WA 98104
Wayne K. Clymer, 122 W. Franklin St., Minneapolis, MN 55404
Finis A. Crutchfield, 5215 S. Main St., Houston, TX 77002
Jesse R. DeWitt, 325 Emerald Terrace, Sun Prairie, WI 53590
Ernest T. Dixon, 4201 W. 15th St., Topeka, KS 66604
H. Ellis Finger, Jr. 1111 Northshore Dr., Ste. 235, Knoxville, TN 37919
Charles F. Golden, 5250 Santa Monica Blvd., Los Angeles, CA 90029
Robert E. Goodrich, Jr., City Bank Bldg., Ste. 420, 4625 Lindell Blvd., St. Louis, MO 63108
W. Kenneth Goodson, 108-110 Methodist Bldg., P.O. Box 11367, 4016 W. Broad St., Richmond, VA 23230
Kenneth W. Hicks, 723 Center St., Little Rock, AR 72201
Leroy C. Hodapp, 501 E. Capitol Ave., Springfield, IL 62701
Earl G. Hunt, Jr., The Cavalier Bldg., Rm. 415, 95 White Bridge Rd., Nashville, TN 37205
Dwight E. Loder, 471 E. Broad St., Columbus, OH 43215

J. Chess Lovern, P.O. Box 28509 (The Methodist Bldg., 535 Bandera Rd.), San Antonio, TX 78228
James K. Mathews, 100 Maryland Ave., NE, Washington, DC 20002
Joel D. McDavid, P.O. Box 1747, Lakeland, FL 33802
Paul W. Milhouse, 2420 N. Blackwelder, Oklahoma City, OK 73106
Roy C. Nichols, Benedum-Trees Bldg., 223 Fourth Ave., Pittsburgh, PA 15222
Frank L. Robertson, 1115 S. Fourth St., Louisville, KY 40203
Carl J. Sanders, 6 Office Park Cir., Suite 301, Birmingham, AL 35223
J. Kenneth Shamblin, 1915 American Bank, Bldg., 200 Carondelet St., New Orleans, LA 70130
Mack B. Stokes, P.O. Box 931 (Meth. Bldg., 321 E. Mississippi St.), Jackson, MS 39205
W. McFerrin Stowe, P.O. Box 8127 (3300 Mockingbird Ln), Dallas, TX 75205
R. Marvin Stuart, P.O. Box 467 (330 Ellis St.), San Francisco, CA 94101
James S. Thomas, 1226 Market Ave., N., Canton, OH 44714
Jack M. Tuell, United Methodist Center, 1505 SW 18th Ave., Portland, OR 97201
Edward L. Tullis, 1420 Lady St., Columbia, SC 29201
W. Ralph Ward, United Methodist Center, 210 Boston Post Rd., Rye, NY 10580
John B. Warman, 900 S. Arlington Ave., Rm. 214, Harrisburg, PA 17109
Paul A. Washburn, 77 W. Washington St., Suite 1806, Chicago, IL 60602
Lance Webb, 1019 Chestnut St., Des Moines IA 50309
D. Frederick Wertz, 900 Washington St., E., Charleston, WV 25301
Melvin E. Wheatley, Jr., 2200 S. University Blvd., Denver, CO 80210
C. Dale White, Opinion Research Corporation Bldg., N. Harrison St., Princeton, NJ 08540
Joseph H. Yeakel, 3049 E. Genesee St., Syracuse, NY 13224

OTHER ORGANIZATIONS

Judicial Council: Pres., Tom Matheny; Vice-Pres., Truman W. Potter; Sec., Hoover Rupert, 212 S. Park St., Kalamazoo, MI 49006

General Council on Finance and Administration: 1200 Davis St., Evanston, IL 60201. Tel. (312) 869-3345. Pres., Bishop H. Ellis Finger, Jr.; Vice-Pres., Bishop Paul W. Milhouse; Rec. Sec., Mrs. Ross E. Hanna; Gen. Sec.and Treas., Ewing T. Wayland; Administrative Assoc.: Asst. Gen. Sec., DeWayne S. Woodring; Section on Episcopal Affairs: Asst. Gen Sec., Marie Kitazumi; Section on Legal Services, Property, Trustee Matters, Investments: Asst. Gen. Sec., Craig R. Hoskins; Section on Systems and Procedures: Asst. Gen. Sec., Vernon Sidler

Division of Financial Services: Assoc. Gen. Sec., Beverley C. Berry; Controller, Gary K. Bowen; Section on Accounting and Reporting: Asst. Gen. Treas., Frances L. Braker; Section on Central Payroll and Special Services: Asst. Gen. Sec., Marjorie R. Philbrick. Service Centers: (Dayton) Asst. Gen. Treas., Marian R. Nixon; (Nashville) Comptroller, W. C. Hawkins; (Washington) Asst. Gen. Treas., Harold W. Stephens; (Evanston) Asst. Gen. Treas., Frances L. Braker; (New York) Asst. Gen. Treas., Stephen F. Brimigion

Division of Administrative Services: Assoc. Gen. Sec., John F. Norwood; Section on Insurance, Wills and Annuities: Asst. Gen. Sec., K. Joan Cole; Section on Church Business Administration: Assoc. Gen. Sec., John F. Norwood; Section on Records and Statistics: Assoc. Gen. Sec., John L. Schreiber; Dirs.: Dept. of Records, Cynthia Haralson; Dept. of Statistics, Daniel A. Nielsen

General Council on Ministries: 601 W. Riverview Ave., Dayton, OH 45406 Tel. (513) 222-6761. Pres., John T. King; Vice-Pres., Richard W. Cain; Rec. Sec., Mariam E. Isaacs; Treas., Alice F. Lee; Gen. Sec., Norman E. Dewire; Assoc. Gen. Secs., Edith H. Goodwin, Ezra Earl Jones, C. Leonard Miller, Alan K. Waltz. Spec. Asst. to Gen. Sec., Gerald L. Clapsaddle

Advance Committee: 475 Riverside Dr., New York, NY 10027. Tel. (212) 678-6131. Dir., ———

Joint Committee on Communications/United Methodist Communications: 601 W. Riverview Ave., Dayton, OH 45406. Tel. (513) 222-7068. Pres., Charles Cappleman; Vice-Pres., Mrs. Barbara Blackstone; Rec. Sec., Noah C. Long; Treas., Ewing T. Wayland; Gen. Sec., Curtis A. Chambers; Asst. Gen. Sec., Edwin H. Maynard; Dir. of Public Relations, Lyndell D. Smith; Dir. of Finance, Peggy Welshans

Division of Program and Benevolence Interpretation: 1200 Davis St., Evanston, IL 60201. Tel. (312) 869-3770. Assoc. Gen. Sec., Readus J. Watkins; Asst. Gen. Sec., Donald Collier; Ed., *The Interpreter,* Darrell R. Shamblin; Assoc. Eds., Ralph E. Baker, Leonard M. Perryman; Mng. Ed., Jane G. Cavey; Ed., *El Interprete,* Fines Flores, Editorial Dir.; Promotional Materials, Donald B. Moyer; Art Dir., ———; Consultants (Field Service): Ervin Dailey (Atlanta, GA); W. Cannon Kinnard (St. Louis); Gene W. Carter (Walnut Creek, CA); Paula C. Watson (Rye, NY)

Division of Production and Distribution: 1525 McGavock St., Nashville, TN 37203. Tel. (615) 327-0911. Assoc. Gen. Sec., Peggy West; Dept. of AV Media: Dir., Edgar A. Gossard; Producers, Kay Henderson, J. Fred Rowles, Jeffrey C. Weber (NY). Dept. of Technical Services: Dir., Anton J. Pilversack. Dept. of AV Distribution: Dir., Wilford V. Bane, Jr. Supervisors: Special Projects, Donald E. Hughes; Sound Recording, Vilmars M. Zile. Dir. INFOSERV, Sam S. Barefield.

Division of Public Media: 475 Riverside Dr., New York, NY 10027. Tel. (212) 663-8900. Assoc. Gen. Sec., Nelson Price: Asst. Gen. Sec. and Dir. of News and Special Services, Martha Man; Information Services Officer, Sue Couch (Nashville); News Dirs., Robert Lear (Evanston); Thomas S. McAnally (Nashville); Frances S. Smith (New York); Winston H. Taylor (Washington). Coordinator, Special Services, Louise V. Gray. Program Services: Producers, (New York) Ben T. Logan, Bruce C. Mosher; (Nashville) William R. Richards; Assoc. Producers Kathleen H. Dale, William Hall, Stanley Nelson. Marketing Coordinator, Lee Parkison.

Office of Communication Education: 1525 McGavock St., Nashville, TN 37203. Tel. (615) 327-0911. Asst. Gen. Sec., Gene W. Carter (307 Fenway Dr., Walnut Creek, CA 94958). Consultants: Thomas Nankervis; Diane Bowden

Board of Church and Society: 100 Maryland Ave., NE, Washington, DC. 20002. Tel. (202) 488-5600. Pres. Bishop Joseph H. Yeakel; Vice-Pres., Mrs. Barbara Lavery, Richard Truitt, Mrs. J. LaVon Wilson, Christine Modisher, Barbara Wilcox; Rec. Sec., Josephine Bigler; Treas., Mrs. Martha Styron; Gen. Sec., George H. Outen. Office of Constituency Services: Assoc. Gen. Sec. Carolyn W. McIntyre; Ed. of Resources and *engage/social action,* Lee Ranck; U.N. Seminars on National and International Affairs: Designers, Rosamond Steere, Beverly Jackson, Irene Adame, Trish Ahern. Business and Finance: Asst.

Gen. Sec., Harold Stephens; Chpsn., Trustees, John Stumbo

Dir., Service Dept., Samuel P. Griffin

Division of General Welfare: Assoc. Gen. Sec. and Dir., Dept. of Social Welfare and Social Health, Grover C. Bagby; Dirs.; Dept. of Drug and Alcohol Concerns, Dolores F. Wright; Dept. of Law, Justice and Community Relations, John P. Adams

Division of Human Relations: Assoc. Gen. Sec. and Dir. Dept. of Intergroup Relations, Thomas M. Fassett, Dirs., Dept. of Economic Life, Luther E. Tyson; Dept. of Church-Government Relations, J. Elliott Corbett

Division of World Peace: Assoc. Gen. Sec. and Dir., Dept. of U.S. Foreign and Military Policy, Herman Will, Jr.: Dir., Dept. of Population, Mrs. Thomas N. Blockwick. United Methodist Office for the U.N. 777 U.N. Plaza, New York, NY 10017. Tel. (212) 682-3633. Assoc. Dir., Robert McClean

Board of Discipleship: P. O. Box 840 (1908 Grand Ave. and 1001 19th Ave. S.), Nashville, TN 37202. Tel. (615) 327-2700. Pres. Bishop W. Kenneth Goodson; Vice-Pres., Bishop Edward L. Tullis, Bishop Joel D. McDavid, Mike Hernandez; Sec., Mrs. Charles N. Gilreath; Treas., Isaac W. Brown; Gen Sec. Melvin G. Talbert.

Division of Education: Assoc. Gen. Sec., Howard M. Ham. Section on Church School Development: Asst. Gen Sec., Warren J. Hartman; Dirs., Roy H. Ryan, Richard Cookson, Afrie Joye. Section on Church School Teaching and Learning: Asst. Gen. Sec., ———; Dirs. Mary Calhoun, Clifford Kolb, Robert Cagle, William Pearce, Wayne Lindecker. Section on Experimental Developments in Church School and Christian Education: Asst. Gen. Sec., George E. Koehler; Dept. of Hunger and Value Formation; Neil M. Alexander, Thomas J. Van Loon. Section on Ethnic Local Church: Asst. Gen. Sec., Fletcher J. Bryant; Dir., Dorothy Turner

Division of Evangelism, Worship and Stewardship: Assoc. Gen. Sec., Roberto Escamilla. Section on Evangelism: Asst. Gen. Sec., George G. Hunter III; Dirs., Vance D. Archer, Harold Bales, H. Eddie Fox, James D. Bass, Robert A. Ochsenrider, William Ellington, Edward E. Bufford. Ronald K. Crandall, Josefat Curti, L. Ray Sells. Section on Stewardship: Asst. Gen. Sec., Thomas Rieke; Dirs., Albert V. Hooke, William Miller, J. LaVon Kincaid. Section on Worship: Asst. Gen. Sec., Hoyt L. Hickman; Dirs., Richard Eslinger, Elsie Shoemaker; Section on *The Upper Room:* Ed., Maxie Dunnam; Assoc. Ed. and Dir. Chaplain Services; Richard W. Ricker, Assoc. Ed., and Dean of Upper Room Chapel, W. Maurice King, Dirs., Kenneth Diehl, Janice T. Grana, Danny E. Morris; Ed., *Alive Now,* Mary Ruth Coffman

Division of Lay Life and Work: Assoc. Gen. Sec., David W. Self. Section on United Methodist Men: Asst. Gen. Sec., John Lundy; Dirs., James H. Snead, Jr. Allen L. Brown; Section on Leadership Development and Training: Asst. Gen. Sec., Sidney R. Nichols; Dirs., Charles P. Jaeger, Ronald T. Lynch, Alvin T. Mayberry, Felix Morales, Inis L. Wyrick; Section on Age Level and Family Ministries: Asst. Gen. Sec., Richard S. Smith; Dirs., Donald C. Cottrill, William E. Wolfe, Richard F. Monroe, Lina H. McCord, C. Leon Smith

Curriculum Resources Committee: Ed., Church School Publications, Ewart G. Watts; Assoc. Ed., Harold L. Fair; Curriculum Planning, M. Franklin Dotts; Interpretive Services, Howard E. Walker, David L. Hazelwood, Gloria Simmons; Eds., H. Myron Braun, Ruth McDowell; Audiovisual Services, Lucelia B. Reed; Business Services, Mildred H. Bateman. Exec. Eds., Younger Children's Publications, Leo N. Kisrow; Older Children, Pat Floyd; Youth Richard H. Rice; Adult, Horace R. Weaver. Assoc. Eds., Annella Creech, Donn C. Downall, John P. Gilbert.

Administrative Services: Communications and Data Gathering, James E. Alexander; Gen. Business, Jean Suiter; Personnel, Carl D. Case; Discipleship Resources, Chester Custer, Mary Pugh.

Board of Global Ministries: 475 Riverside Dr., New York, NY 10027. Tel. (212) 678-6161. Pres., Bishop D. Frederick Wertz; Vice-Pres., Bishop Wayne K. Clymer, Bishop Jesse R. Dewitt, Mrs. C. Jarrett Gray, Bishop Roy C. Nichols, Mrs. Donald T. Strong, Bishop Jack M. Tuell, H. Claude Young Jr.; Gen. Sec., Tracey K. Jones Jr.; Assoc. Gen Secs., Betsy K. Ewing, J. Harry Haines, Theressa Hoover, Robert W. Huston, Lois C. Miller, John A. Murdock, Randolph Nugent, Betty Thompson; Ombudsman, Harry B. Gibson Jr.; Personnel Dir., Raymond Jones; Rec. Sec., Jane S.L. Brice; Gen. Treas., Stephen F. Brimigion; Assoc. and Div. Treas., Enid Belle, Florence Little, Joyce Sohl, Florence Walter; Gen. Comptroller, Frank A.W. Morrison; Office of Missionary Personnel, Ex. Sec., Avery C. Manchester; Secs., Lois Dauway, Anne Unander; Crusade Scholarship, Ex. Sec., Constance Hawkins

Ecumenical and Interreligious Concerns Division: Pres., Bishop Jack M. Tuell; Vice-Pres., Mrs. Jean Dowell; Rec. Sec., Mrs. Donald Alguire; Assoc. Gen. Sec., Robert W. Huston; Asst.Gen. Sec., Jeanne Audrey Powers; Exec. Secs., Janice L. Frederick, Robert L. Turnipseed

Education and Cultivation Division: Pres., H. Claude Young Jr.; Vice-Pres., Mrs. Robert Pratt, Jr.; Rec. Sec., Perry Saito; Assoc. Gen. Sec., Betty Thompson; Asst. Gen. Sec. for Administration, Marian T. Martin Section of Cultivation: Asst. Gen. Sec., ———; Exec. Secs.Section of Mission Development: Asst. Gen. Sec., William T. Carter; Exec. Secs., Howard Brinton, Roy Katayama, James V. Lyles; Assoc. Sec. for Cultivation, Lionel P. A. Muthiah; Exec. Sec. for Field Interpretation, Beverly Judge; Coords., Mission Education, ———; Dirs. of Current/Deferred Gifts, Doris Gidney, Warren Loesch; Mission Leaders, Donald E. Struchen; Consultative Services, Elinor Kajiwara

Section of Mission Resources: Asst. Gen. Sec., Beverly J. Chain; Dirs., Service Center, Mary Jane Shahan; Promotion/Utilization, B. Elizabeth Marchant; Audiovisual Resources, Gilbert Galloway; Literature, Roger Sadler; Editors: Literature, Nancy Carter Goodley; *New World Outlook,* Arthur J. Moore Jr.; *response,* Carol Marie Herb; Assoc. Editors: Nancy Sartin, Charles E. Brewster, Ellen Clark, Betty Gray; Dir. of Interpretive Services, George M. Daniels; Senior Staff Writer, Constance Myer; Communicator, Charles Lerrigo; Spanish-speaking Communicator, Ana Martinez

Health and Welfare Ministries Division: 1200 Davis St., Evanston, IL 60201. Tel. (312) 869-9600. Pres., Mrs. Donald T. Strong; Vice-Pres., Richard Church; Rec. Sec., Priscilla Pierce; Treas., Florence Walter; Assoc. Gen. Sec., John A. Murdock (New York); Asst. Gen. Sec. for Administration and Planning and Exec. Dir. of Certification Council, Cathie Lyons; Asst. Gen. Sec., Services to the Aging, Lynn A. Bergman; Serivces to Children and Youth, Bertha Swindall; Exec. Sec., Overseas Medical Work, Duvon C. Corbitt Jr., M.D. (New York); Office of Minority Services and National Assn. of Health and

Welfare Ministries, Charles P. Kellogg; Liaison to National Division and Annual Conferences, June Shimokawa; Services to Aging, ———; Office of Ministries with Persons with Handicapping Conditions, ———; Health Care Consultant, Louis Blair

National Division: Pres., Jesse R. DeWitt, Vice-Pres., F. Herbert Skeete; Mrs. Wm. H. Yaggy; Rec. Sec., Robert L. Johnson; Treas., Enid Belle; Assoc. Gen. Sec., Randolph Nugent; Asst. Gen. Sec. for Admn., Betty Henderson; Asst. Gen. Sec., Agency Concerns, Lula Garrett; Congregational Development, James Davis; Mission Leadership, John Jordan; Parish Ministries, Negail Riley; Dirs.,: Planning, Robert J. Harman; Research, Sarla Lall; Exec. Secs., Coalition for Human Development, Betty J. Letzig; Community Development, Lucy Gist; University and Young Adult Ministries, ———; Youth Serving Ministries, ———; Goodwill Industries, Joseph E. Pouliot; Architecture, Douglas R. Hoffman; New Church Development, ———; United Methodist Development Fund, George Williams; Finance and Field Service, C. Clifford Sargent; Deaconess/Home Missionary Service, Christine Brewer; Community Developers, Louis Hodge; Church and Community Ministries ———; Voluntary Services, Sheila Collins; Ethnic and Language Ministries, Joel Martinez; Town and Country Ministries, Gladys Campbell; Urban Ministries, Kinmoth Jefferson

United Methodist Committee on Relief: Pres., Bishop Wayne K. Clymer; Vice-Pres., Mrs. Edgar Lashford; Rec. Sec., Bonnie Totten; Assoc. Gen. Sec., J. Harry Haines; Asst. Gen. Sec. for Administration, Doreen F. Tilghman; Exec. Sec., Hunger Coord., Franklin P. Smith; Secs., Program, Gerald Schmidt; Refugee Concerns, Lilia V. Fernandez; Specialized Ministries, Paul Morton

Women's Division: Pres., Mrs. C. Jarrett Gray Sr.; Vice-Pres., Mrs. Charles H. Neuman; Mrs. Charles Dorsett, Mrs. Wayne A. Bellamy, Mrs. John W. Gordon; Rec. Sec., Mrs. William Barnes; Assoc. Gen. Sec., Theressa Hoover, Asst. Gen. Sec, Barbara E. Campbell; Exec. Sec., Ellen Kirby; Staff Rec. Sec., Helen L. Abshire. Staff in Regions: Marion L. Baker, Evanston, IL.; Bernice Dvorak, Syracuse, N.Y.: Lois E. Kohler, Nashville, Tenn.; Gene Maxwell, Denver, Colo.; Maryruth Nickels, Atlanta, Ga.; Mary F. Ryan, Dallas, Tex.; Mae F. Spencer, Washington; Helen Swett, Dayton, Ohio; Murden Woods, San Francisco, CA. Section of Christian Social Relations; Asst. Gen. Sec., Peggy Billings; Exec. Secs., UN/International Affairs, Mia Adjali; Development Education, Annette Hutchins-Felder; Secs., Community Action, Ruth Gilbert; Legislative Affairs, Joyce Hamlin; Racial Justice, Consuelo Urquiza. Section of Finance: Treas., Joyce D. Sohl; Comptroller, Mrs. Betty J. Edwards, Asst. Treas., Rosalind M. Lesher; Secys., Financial Interpretation, Peggy Halsey; Property Management, Mary Harvey; Section on Mission and Membership Development: Asst. Gen. Sec., Elaine Gasser; Exec. Secs., Program Development, Mary Lou Van Buren; Schools/Leadership Development, Josephine Harris; Secs., Schools and Mission Education, Ann Eaton; Organizational Development, Marjorie Crossman; Membership Concerns, Bernadette J. Sanders

World Division: Pres., Bishop Roy Nichols; Vice-Pres., Dollie Crist; Harry Vanderpood; Rec. Sec. and Dir. of Admininistrative Services, Patricia Ewald; Treas., Florence Little. Assoc. Gen. Sec., Lois C. Miller; Asst. Gen. Secs., Program Administration, Charles H. Germany; Research and Planning, L. M. McCoy. Africa Team, Asst. Gen. Sec., Isaac Bivens; Exec. Secs., Omar L. Hartzler, Patricia Rothrock; Asia/Pacific Team, Asst. Gen. Sec., Barbara Chase; Exec. Secs., Edwin O. Fisher, Jr., Patricia Patterson, Henry A. Lacy, Jiro Mizuno, Latin America/Caribbean, Asst. Gen. Sec., Nora Q. Boots; Exec. Secs., Joyce Hill, Joseph A. Perez. Exec. Secs., Personnel Development/Communications, Doris Hess; University/Youth and Urban/Rural, Ruth Harris; Church Development and Renewal, Albert J. D. Aymer; Ministry of Women, Rose Catchings; Medical, Duvon C. Corbitt Jr., M.D.; Treasury Staff: Assoc. Treas., James Brentlinger; Comptroller, Nabil Abou-Daoud; Systems Analyst, Hans L. Aurbakken; Internal Auditor, Leora Landmesser.

Board of Higher Education and Ministry: P.O. Box 871 (1001 Nineteenth Ave. S.), Nashville, TN 37202. Tel. (615) 327-2700. Pres. Bishop Ralph T. Alton; Vice-Pres., Bishop James M. Ault, Claus H. Rohlfs, Gordon Bender, Ms. Rena M. Yocom; Sec., Roy I. Sano; Treas., Edwin E. Smith, Jr.; Gen. Sec., F. Thomas Trotter; Assoc. Gen. Sec. for Administration, John D. Humphrey. Assoc. Gen. Sec. for Interpretation; Judith L. Weidman. Assoc. Gen. Sec. for Program, Douglas Fitch; Office of Loans and Scholarships: Asst. Gen. Sec., Esther E. Edwards

Office of Career Planning and Personnel Services: Asst. Gen. Sec., Ruben Salcido

Division of Chaplains and Related Ministries: 1501 Wilson Blvd., 8th Floor Arlington, VA 22209. Tel. (703) 522-1050. Chpsn., Claus H. Rohlfs, Vice-Chpsn., C. Dendy Garrett; Sec., Mark Wethington; Assoc. Gen. Sec., Orris Kelly; Dirs., M. Douglas Blair, James P. Rickards

Division of Diaconal Ministry: Chpsn., Ms. Rena Yocom; Vice-Chpsn., Mrs. Burl Wyckoff; Sec., Roger L. Loyd; Assoc. Gen. Sec., Rosalie Bentzinger; Dir., R. Harold Hipps, Juaquin Garcia

Division of Higher Education: Chpsn. Ralph M. Tanner: Vice-Chpsn., Gordon R. Bender; Sec., Ms. Mareyjoyce Green; Assoc. Gen. Sec., James Barrett; Asst. Gen. Sec. for Campus Ministry, Joe L. Gipson; Office of the Black College Fund: Dir., Lina McCord, Ken Yamada. National Methodist Foundation for Christian Higher Education: Pres., Jack C. Phillips, Consultant, Ralph Tanner

Division of the Ordained Ministry: Chpsn., Bishop James M. Ault; Vice-Chpsn., Ms. Janice R. Huie; Sec., Lee B. Shaeffer; Assoc. Gen. Sec., Donald H. Treese; Dirs., Robert Kohler, Richard Yeager, Hector Grant

General Board of Pensions: 1200 Davis St., Evanston, IL. 60201. Tel. (312) 869-4550. Pres., Bishop Alsie H. Carleton; Vice-Pres., Roger B. Roberts; Rec. Sec., Mrs. Betty L. Nusbaum; Gen. Sec., Gerald K. Hornung. Assoc. Gen. Secs., Gerald A. Beam, Dale M. Knapp, James F. Parker; Treas., Donald R. McKee; Asst. Treas., Wilbert A. Blum, G. Warren Dare; Actuary, Frank L. Markel; Asst. Actuary, Susan Wilson; Gen. Counsel, James M. Walton-Myers; Adm. Asst. & Dir. Adm. Dept., Joyce E. Gilman; Office Service Mgr., Bryce W. Wilmot; Asst. Gen. Secs., Raul B. Algria, Wayne L. BonDurant, Cheryl Haack, Allen M. Mayes, H. Howard Miller, David L. Mohr, Eugene J. Moore, Vernon A. Sladek, Connie J. Takamine, Ray E. Whatley; Dir. Data Proc. Dept., Ruth K. Pankiw; Sr. Systems Analyst, Gale W. Brenner, Kenneth L. Helfers, Christopher A. Postlewaite, Bruce E. Slown

Board of Publication: Chpsn, John B. Russell, 1200 Ross Bldg., Richmond, VA 23219; Vice-Chpsn, Mrs. William F. Dunlap, 129 Forest View Dr., Wintersville, OH; Sec., J. Kenneth Forbes, 1100 W. 42nd St., Indianapolis, IN 46208

The United Methodist Publishing House: Pres. & Publisher, John E. Procter; Treas. & Chief Financial Officer,

John H. Laird; Senior Vice-Pres., Manufacturing Division, Donald A. Theuer; Senior Vice-Pres., Retail Sales (Cokesbury) Division, Thomas E. Carpenter; Senior Vice-Pres., Publishing Division, Thomas K. Potter, Jr.; Book Ed./Dir. of General Publishing, Ronald P. Patterson; Manager, Abingdon Press, Charles O. McNish; Manager, Graded Press, Gary H. Vincent; Vice-Pres., Public Relations Division; Roger L. Burgess; Vice-Pres., Personnel Services Division, James C. Peters, Sr.

Commissions on Archives and History: P.O. Box 488 Lake Junaluska, NC 28745. Tel. (704) 456-9433. Pres. Bishop John B. Warman; Vice-Pres., Carroll Hart; Rec. Sec., Donald K. Gorrell; Exec. Sec., John H. Ness, Jr.; Asst. Exec. Sec., Mrs. Louise Queen, Archivist, William C. Beal, Jr.

Commission on Religion and Race: 100 Maryland Ave., N.E., Washington, DC 20002. Tel. (202) 547-4270. Pres., Bishop A. James Armstrong; Vice-Pres., Bishop Charles F. Golden; Rec. Sec., Don Hayashi; Exec. Sec., Woodie W. White; Assoc. Exec. Secs., Albert H. Hammond, Jr., Dalila Kruger, Kenneth S. Deere, Samuel P. Wong, Evelyn Fitzgerald

Commission on the Status and Role of Women: 1200 Davis St., Evanston, IL 60201. Tel. (312) 869-7330. Pres., Carolyn Oehler; Rec. Sec., H. Sharon Howell; Secretariat, Nancy G. Self, Kiyoko Fujiu, Trudie K. Preciphs

Fellowship of United Methodist in Worship, Music and Other Arts: P.O. Box 840, Nashville, TN 37202. Tel. (615) 327-2700; Pres., Janet Lee, Clawson, Mich.

PERIODICALS

Circuit Rider (w), 516 N. Charles St., Rm. 208, Baltimore, MD 21201. Charles Biedka, Ed.

Arkansas Methodist (w), P.O. Box 3547, Little Rock, AR 72203. Jerry Canada, Ed.

California-Nevada United Methodist (w), 1530 Altemont Ave., San Jose, CA 95125. Mrs. Gerri Hodson, Ed.

Central Illinois United Methodist Reporter, P.O. Box 2050, Bloomington, Il, Bettie W. Story

Central New York United Methodist Reporter (w), 210 Hill St., Chittenango, NY 13037. Cuthbert Rowe, Ed.

Christian Home, The (m), 201 Eighth Ave., S., Nashville, TN 37202. David I. Bradley, Ed.

Church School, The (m), 201 Eighth Ave., S., Nashville, TN 37202. Ruth McDowell, Ed.

Circuit Rider (m), 201 Eighth Ave., So., Nashville, TN 37202. J. Richard Peck, Ed.

Circuit West (w), 5250 Santa Monica Blvd., Los Angeles, CA 90029. Peg Parker, Ed.

Communicator, The (bi-m), 405 NW Eighth Ave., Berkshire Plaza, Aberdeen, SD 57401. Russell Dilley, Ed.

Communicator, The (w), 139 N. State St., Dover, DE 19901. Richard D. Bailey, Ed.

Contact (m), 2420 N. Blackwelder, Oklahoma City, OK 73106. Frances L. Williams, Ed.

Crossfire (m), 710 Loch Lommond, Hutchinson, KS 67501, Mrs. Majorie Matthaei, Ed.

Dimensions (m), 325 Emerald Terrace, Sun Prairie, WI 53590. Muriel F. Anderson, Ed.

East Ohio Today (m), 1300 S. Main St., Ste. 100, N. Canton, OH 44720. Thelma Monbarren, Ed.

Eastern Pennsylvania United Methodist Reporter (w), P.O. Box 820, Valley Foge, PA 19482 John McEllhenney, Ed.

El Interprete (q), 1200 Davis St., Evanston, IL 60201. Finees Flores, Ed.

engage/social action (m), 100 Maryland Ave., NE, Washington, DC 20002. Lee Ranck, Ed.

Florida United Methodist, The P.O. Box 3767, Lakeland, FL 33802. Barbara Wilcox, Ed.

Hawkeye United Methodist (m), 1019 Chestnut St., Des Moines, IA 50309. Robert L. Sands, Ed.

Holston United Methodist, The P.O. Box 1178, Johnson City, TN 37601. Don Sluder, Ed.

Hoosier United Methodist (m), 1100 W. 42 St., Indianapolis, IN 46208. Newman Cryer, Ed.

Indian Mission Advocate (m), P.O. Box 60427, Oklahoma City, OK 73106. David Adair, Ed.

Interchange (w), P.O. Box 4187, Topeka, KS 66604. Karen Sexton, Ed.

Interpreter, The (m), 601 W. Riverview Ave., Dayton, OH 45406. Darrell R. Shamblin, Ed.

Kentucky United Methodist (w), P.O. Box 5107, Lexington, KY 40555. Cheryl Hendrix, Ed.

Link, The (m), 900 S. Arlington Ave., Harrisburg, PA 17109. Martin W. A. Trostie. Ed.

Louisiana United Methodist (w), P.O. Box 4325, Shreveport, LA 71104. Ray Branton, Ed.

Maine United Methodist, The (bi-m), Box 277, Winthrop, ME 04364, Ralph Miller, Ed.

Mature Years (m), 201 Eighth Ave., S., Nashville, TN 37202. Mrs. Daisy D. Warren, Ed.

Methodist Christian Advocate (w), 1100 Campus Cir., Birmingham, AL 35204. Herschel T. Hammer, Ed.

Methodist History (q), Box 488, Lake Junaluska, NC 28745. John H. Ness, Jr., Ed.

Michigan Christian Advocate (w), 316 Springbrook Ave., Adrian, MI 49221. Keith Pohl, Ed.

Minnesota United Methodist Reporter (w), 122 W. Franklin Ave., Minneapolis, MN 55404. Beverly Boche, Ed.

Mississippi Methodist Advocate (w), Box 1093, Jackson, MS 39205. George Roy Lawrence, Ed.

Missouri United Methodist (m), 101 N. Bemiston Ave., St. Louis, MO 63105. James Steele, Ed.

Nebraska United Methodist Messenger (m), 2641 N. 49 St., Lincoln, NE 68504. A. Elwood Fleming, Ed.

New Mexico United Methodist (w), 209 San Pedro, NE, Albuquerque, NM 87108. B. C. Goodwin, Ed.

New World Outlook (m), 475 Riverside Dr., New York, NY 10027. Arthur J. Moore, Jr., Ed.

Newscope (w), 201 Eighth Ave., S., Nashville, TN 37202, Richard Peck, Ed.

North Carolina Christian Advocate (w), Box 508, Greensboro, NC 27402. Charles A. Simonton, Sr., Ed.

Northwest United Methodist (m), 810 Olympic National Bldg., Seattle, WA 98104, Carol Mariano, Ed.

Ohio West News (m), 471 E. Broad St., Columbus, OH 43215. John F. Young, Ed.

Peninsula United Methodist Communicator (w), 139 N. State St., Dover, De 19901. Richard D. Bailey, Ed.

Religion in Life (q), 201 Eighth Ave., S., Nashville, TN 37202. Ronald P. Patterson, Ed.

response (m), 475 Riverside Dr., Room 1323, New York, NY 10027. Carol M. Herb, Ed.

Rio Grande Methodist (w) (Spanish), P.O. Box 28090, San Antonio, TX 78284. Dan Rodriguez, Ed.

Rocky Mountain United Methodist (w), 2200 S. University Blvd., Denver, CO 80210. ———, Ed.

South Carolina United Methodist Advocate (w), 1420 Lady St., (Box 11589, Capitol Sta.) Columbia, SC 29211. Maryneal Jones, Ed.

Spark, The (m), Box 66-559 Center St., West Oneonta, NY 13861. Linda Jump, Ed.

Tennessee United Methodist Reporter (w), 1907 Acklen Ave., Nashville, TN 37212. Donald K. Small, Ed.

Texas Methodist, The (w), Box 1076, Dallas, TX 75221. Spurgeon M. Dunnam III, Ed.

United Methodist, The (m), 77 W. Washington St., Rm. 1806, Chicago, IL 60602. James Moore, Ed.

United Methodist (m), 1505 SW 18th Ave., Portland, OR 97209. Asa Mundell, Ed.

United Methodist Relay (m), 460 Pulis Ave., Franklin Lakes, NJ 07417. Howard Eemaly, Ed.

Upper Room (bi-m), 1908 Grand Ave., Nashville, TN 37203. Maxie Dunnam, Ed.
Virginia Advocate (w), 4016 W. Broad St., Richmond, VA 23230. W. Hewlett Stith, Jr., Ed.
Wesleyan Christian Advocate (w), 159 Forest Ave., NE, Atlanta, GA 30303. William M. Holt, Ed.
Western New York Conference Communicator (m), 8499 Main St., Buffalo, NY 14211. David Fessenden, Ed.
Western Pennsylvania United Methodist (w), 223 4th Ave., Pittsburgh, PA 15222. ———, Ed.
West Virginia United Methodist (w), P.O. Box 2313 Charleston, WV 25328. John Henry Shadburn, Ed.
World Parish (m), Box 518, Lake Junaluska, NC 28745. Joseph R. Hale, Ed.
Yellowstone United Methodist (w), 3622 4th Ave., Great Falls, MT 59405. Doris Bjork, Ed.
Zion's Herald (m), 581 Boylston St., Boston, MA 02116. T. C. Whitehouse, Ed.

United Pentecostal Church International

Pentecostal Church, Inc., and Pentecostal Assemblies of Jesus Christ merged September 25, 1945 at St. Louis, Missouri.

Churches: 2,830 Inclusive Membership: 450,000 Sunday or Sabbath Schools: N.R. Total Enrollment: N.R. Ordained Clergy: 5,881

GENERAL ORGANIZATION

Conference: annual
Headquarters: 8855 Dunn Rd., Hazelwood, MO 63042. Tel. (314) 837-7300

OFFICERS

Gen. Supt., Nathaniel A. Urshan, 8855 Dunn Rd., Hazelwood, MO 63042
Asst. Gen. Supts., James Kilgore, Box 15175, Houston, TX 77020; C. M. Becton, 8207 Sawyer Brown Rd., Nashville, TN 37221
Gen. Sec., Robert L. McFarland, 8855 Dunn Rd., Hazelwood, MO 63042
Dir. of For. Miss., Harry Scism, 8855 Dunn Rd., Hazelwood, MO 63042
Gen. Dir. of Home Miss., Jack E. Yonts, 8855 Dunn Rd., Hazelwood, MO 63042
Editor-in-Chief, Calvin Rigdon, 8855 Dunn Rd., Hazelwood, MO 63042
Gen. Sunday School Dir., James Boatman, 8855 Dunn Rd., Hazelwood, MO 63042

OTHER ORGANIZATIONS

The Pentecostal Publishing House, Hazelwood David Schroeder, Mgr.
Pentecostal Conquerors (Young People's Division); Pres., Dan L. Rigdon, Hazelwood
Ladies Auxiliary: Pres., Vera Kinzie, 4840 Elm Pl., Toledo, OH 43608
Harvestime Radio Broadcast: Dir., Ray Agnew, Hazelwood
Stewardship Dept.: Dir. David Wheeler, 1470 Hugo Ln., San Jose, CA 95118
Education Division: Supt. Arless Glass, 4502 Aztec, Pasadena, TX 77504

PERIODICAL

The Pentecostal Herald, Hazelwood. Calvin Rigdon Clanton, Ed.
The Global Witness, J. S. Leaman, Ed.
The Outreach, D. E. Gwaltney, Ed.
The Ephphatha, Jerry Harper, Ed.
Homelife, C. P. Williams, Ed.
Conqueror, Stephen Judd, Ed.

The United Presbyterian Church in the United States of America

The United Presbyterian Church in the United States of America as formed in May 1958 through a merger of the United Presbyterian Church of North America and the Presbyterian Church in the United States of America. The uniting General Assembly was held in Pittsburgh, Pennsylvania from May 28 to June 3, 1958. Of the two uniting bodies the Presbyterian Church in the United States of America dated from the first Presbytery organized in Philadelphia in 1706. The first General Assembly was held in Philadelphia in 1789.

The United Presbyterian Church of North America was formed in 1858, when the Associate Reformed Presbyterian Church and the Associate Presbyterian Church united.

Churches: 8,567 Inclusive Membership: 2,520,367 Sunday or Sabbath Schools: 8,657 Total Enrollment: 886,100 Ordained Clergy: 13,871

THE GENERAL ASSEMBLY

Meets annually: next meeting May 27-June 4, 1980, Detroit, MI

OFFICERS

Mod. (1979-80) Rev. Howard L. Rice
Vice-Mod., Rev. Robert R. Woods
Stated Clerk, William P. Thompson
Assoc. Stated Clerks, Otto K. Finkbeiner, Rev. Robert F. Stevenson, Rev. Robert T. Newbold, Jr.
Treas., Otto K. Finkbeiner

THE OFFICE OF THE GENERAL ASSEMBLY

475 Riverside Dr., Rm. 1201, New York, NY 10027 Dept. of Operations, Otto K. Finkbeiner, Mgr.: Department of History, William B. Miller, Mgr. 425 Lombard St., Philadelphia, PA 19147
Presbyterian Council for Chaplains and Military Personnel (joint with the Associate Reformed Presbyterian Church, the Cumberland Presbyterian Church, the Presbyterian Church in the United States, and the Second Cumberland Presbyterian Church), Chprsn., Mark R. Thompson; Dir., Rev. S. David Chambers, Assoc. Dir., Rev. Ike C. Barnett, Jr., 4125 Nebraska Ave. NW, Washington, DC 20016

THE UNITED PRESBYTERIAN CHURCH IN THE U.S.A., A CORPORATION (UNITED PRESBYTERIAN FOUNDATION)

Chpsn. of the Board, David A. Cort, Pres., Horace B. B. Robinson; Dir., Rev. Charles C. Griffin; 475 Riverside Dr., New York, NY 10027. Assoc. Dir. for Finance, Earl Kelz; Assoc. Dir. for Development, Rev. Donn G. Jann; Asst. Dir., Rev. Marvin C. Wilbur; Asst. Dir., James B. Potter; Controller, Catherine M. Sinclair; Regional Representatives: Southern California—Paul M. Kroesen, 1501 Wilshire Blvd., Los Angeles, CA 90017; Pennsylvania, New York—Rev. Richard W.

Firth, 203 Oakbourne Rd., West Chester, PA 19380; Florida—Rev. Howard Lee, 2600 N. Flagler Dr., West Palm Beach, FL 33407, Michigan, Ohio—Charles H. McCracken, 4805 Oak Glen Dr., Toledo, OH 43613; Northern California, Oregon, Southern Idaho, Nevada—Richard B. Cole, 802 Clearfield Dr., Millbrae, CA 94030; Wisconsin, Minnesota, Iowa, the Dakotas, Western Nebraska—Illinois and Indiana—Robert B. Turner, 1100 W. 42nd St., Indianapolis, IN 46208; Rev. Roscoe M. Wolvington, 5608 53rd Ave., Kenosha, WI 53142; New Jersey, New England, Metropolitan New York City—Alfred V. Danielson, 22 Round Hill Rd., Scarsdale, NY 10583

THE GENERAL ASSEMBLY MISSION COUNCIL

Chpsn., Rev. William P. Lytle; Exec. Dir., Rev. G. Daniel Little, 475 Riverside Dr., New York, NY 10027
Deputy Exec. Dir., Rev. Margaret J. Thomas
Assoc. Exec. Dir. Mission Policy Coordination, Rev. Kyoji Buma
Dir. of Budgeting, Edna McCarthy
Assoc. Exec. for Coordination with Judicatories, Rev. David B. Lowry
Assoc. Exec. for Social Witness Policy, Rev. Dean H. Lewis
Dir., Adv. Council on Discipleship and Worship, Rev. James G. Kirk

THE PROGRAM AGENCY

Pres., Rev. Victor E. Makari; Gen. Dir., Rev. J. Oscar McCloud, 475 Riverside Dr., New York, NY 10027
Assoc. Gen. Dir. for Program Coord., Rev. Donald Black
Assoc. Gen. Dir. for Interchurch Relations, Rev. W. H. Vernon Smith.
Dir. of Budget Admn., Ms. Hope M. Bezold
Dir. for Judicatory and Personnel Relations, Max E. Browning
Executive Asst. to the Gen. Dir., Mrs. Roberta L. London
Exec. Asst. to the Assoc. Gen. Dir. for Program Coord., Ms. Blanche Allen
Rec. Sec. of the Program Agency, Admin. Cabinet Sec., Ms. Constance E. Lobody

Area Liaisons
Coordinator and Liaison with S. Asia and Europe, Rev. Frederick R. Wilson
Liaison with Africa, Paul A. Hopkins
Liaison with E. Asia, Rev. L. Newton Thurber
Liaison with Middle East & Assoc. for Internationalization of Mission, Rev. Syngman Rhee
Liaison with Latin America and the Carribean, Rev. Benjamin F. Gutierrez

Studies and Planning Services
Coord., Program Dir., Rev. Frederick C. Maier; Assoc. for Planning and Theological Studies, Rev. Edward M. Huenemann; Assoc. for Review & Evaluation, Rev. David L. Zuverink
United Pres. Reps. Overseas: Europe (Joint with UCC/BWM), Dr. Robert C. Lodwick; Korea, Rev. Stanton R. Wilson; Pakistan, Mr. Robert F. Tebbe; Syria, Lebanon and Iran, Rev. Benjamin M. Weir
Stony Point Center: Dir., Rev. James E. Palm
Jarvie Commonweal Service: Dir., Ellsworth G. Stanton III; Assoc. Dir., Mrs. Alice W. Stutz; Soc. Caseworkers: Ms. Jule M. Creed; Ms. Adele Malhotra; Mrs. Margaret B. Russin; Ms. Florence M. Wolin; Admn. Coord., Ms. Josephine H. Breedlove
Ministries with the Laity: Coord., Ms. Lois E. Montgomery; Men's Program: Prog. Dir., Archibald F. Pieper; Women's Program: Prog. Dir., Ms. Lois E. Montgomery; Assoc. for United Presbyterian Women & Admin. Secy. of Natl. Exec. Com., Ms. Ruth W. Zimmerman; Assoc. for Council on Women and the Church, Ms. Elizabeth H. Verdesi; Assoc. for Women's Giving; Ms. Marilyn Clark; Assoc. for Relations with Women on Six Continents, Rev. Aurelia T. Fule; Assoc. for Communications, Resource & Leader Dev., Ms. M. Virginia Stieb-Hales. *Concern* Magazine: Ed., Ms. Jane Jarrad, Assoc. Ed., Ms. Ann Yeargin. Women's Area Staff; Eastern Area; Ms. Gladys Strachan, Ms. Linda L. Pierce; E. Central Area: Ms. Glendora Paul: W. Central Area: Ms. Barbara Tilton; Western Area: Ms. Alice V. McGuire, Ms. Joan Richardson. Youth Relations HallProgram: Prog. Dir., Rev. Ray T. Woods; Assoc. for Youth Resources, Rev. Bernie C. Dunphy-Linnartz
Ministries of Health, Education & Social Justice: Coord., Rev. Donald J. Wilson; Assoc., Coord., ———; Corporate Social Justice: Assoc., for Economic Justice, Rev. Philip R. Newell, Jr.; Assoc, for Justice System Issues, Rev. Kathy Young; Assoc. for Peace and Internatl. Affairs, Rev. Robert F. Smylie; Washington Office, Dir., Ms. Mary Jane Patterson; Assoc. Dir., Robert Barrie; Racial Justice and Mission Devl: Assoc. for Asian Mission Devl., Rev. J. Philip Park; Assoc. for Black Mission Devl., Rev. Clarence L. Cave; Assoc. for Hispanic Mission Devl., Rev. Cecilio Arrastia; Assoc. Coord., Rev. Charles W. Watt; Health, Welfare and Community Devl.: Assoc. for Community Devl., S. Douglas Brian; Assoc. for Health Ministries, Rev. Ronald W. McNeur; Assoc. for Social Welfare-Program Relations, Ms. Roxanna Coop; Assoc. for Social Welfare-Institutional Relations, Rodney T. Martin; Development Assistance: World Relief, Emergency and Resettlement Services and Jinishian Memorial Program, Rev. William K. DeVal; Asst. for Refugee and Resettlement Service, Ms. Shirley G. Nichols; Hunger Program, Dir., Mrs. Ann N. Beardslee; Assoc, Dir., Rev. Joseph D. Keesecker; Natl. Committee on Self Devl., Exec. Dir., Rev. St. Paul Epps; Assoc. Exec. Dir., Ms. Christina R. Bellamy; Presbyterian Economic Devl. Corp. (PEDCO), Exec. Dir., Milton Page; Assoc. Exec. Dir., David Liston; Assoc. Coord., Earl K. Larson, Jr.; Education and Leadership Devl.: Assoc. for Ministries in Higher Education, Rev. A. Myrvin DeLapp; Assoc. for Educational Services, Rev. Yenwith K. Whitney; Assoc. for Leadership Devl., Mrs. Esther C. Stine; Asst. for leadership Devl., ———; Assoc. for Regional Services, UMHE (NW), Rev. William E. Hallman.
Ministries with Congregations: Coord., Rev. Robert H. Kempes; Asst. Coord., Ms. Sarah E. Roberts; Church Education Services: Program Dir., ———; Dir., of Educational Resources, Rev. John C. Purdy; Educational Media Consultant, Rev. W. Benjamin Lane; Educational Resources Section: Assoc. for Adult Resources, Social Education, Rev. Dieter H. Hessel; Assoc. for Adult Resource Devl., Rev. Frank T. Hainer; Assoc. for Children's Resources and Program, Ms. Mary Ducker; Assoc. for Early Childhood Education, Ms. Donna J. Blackstock; Assoc. for Youth Education Ms. Barbara A. Withers; Leadership/Support Section: Assoc. for Adult Planning and Program, Rev. Haydn O. White; Assoc. for Adult Leader Education and Program, Rev. Lindell L. Sawyers; Assoc. for Communication and Support, Rev. Jack M. MacLeod; Assoc. for Educational Planning and Support, Rev. Edna May Mosley; Assoc. for Teacher Education, Rev. David B. McDowell; Congregational Devl., Program Dir. and Admin. Sec. of The Mission Developments Grants Committee, Rev. Harold H. Byers; Discipleship and Worship Program: Program Dir., (Joint with the General Assembly Mission Council) and Exec. Dir. of the Advisory Council on Discipleship and Worship, Rev. James G. Kirk; Dir., Joint Office of Worship, PCUS/UPCUSA, Rev. Harold M. Daniels, Louisville Theological Seminary, 1044 Alta

Vista Rd., Louisville, KY 40205. Evangelism Program: Program Dir., Rev. Grady N. Allison; Assoc. for Developing Resources and Services, Rev. Jeffrey C. Wood; Assoc. for Implementing Strategy, Rev. Morton S. Taylor; Assoc. for Implementing Strategy, Rev. Morton S. Taylor; Office of Capital Resources: Program Dir., Rev. S. Charles Shangler; Assoc. for Program Services, Ms. Diana A. Stephen, Ghost Ranch Conference Center, Abiquiu, New Mexico 87510, Dir., Rev. James W. Hall.

Ministries through People in Mission: Program Dir., Rev. William H Miller; Asst. to Coord., Ms. Martha E. Havens; Prog. Dir., People in Mission, Rev. William H. Miller; Program Dir., Patterns of Ecumenical Sharing, Ms. Margaret Flory; Assoc. for Fraternal Worker Concerns; Ms. Hazel J. McGeary; Program Specialist for Medical and Retirement Concerns, Ms. Marjorye A. Keyser; Volunteer in Mission Section: Program Dir. for Volunteers in Mission, Rev. J. Wilbur Patterson; Assoc. for Volunteers in Mission/Overseas, Rev. John B. Linder; Assoc. for Volunteers in Mission/USA, Rev. Jean Anne Swope; Program Specialist for Mobile Health Fairs, Ms. Martha E. Havens.

Publications: Coord. and Program Dir., Robert D. McIntyre; Asst. to Coord., Ms. Jane W. Tyas; Business Mgr., Mr. Philip A. McLaughlin; Religious Book Ed., Rev. Paul L. Meacham; Assoc. Ed., Religious Books, Rev. Edward K. Trefz; Children's Book Ed., Ms. Barbara S. Bates; Prod. Mgr., Michal Bergamo; Asst. Production Mgr., Joseph M. Grosso; Art Dir., Ed. Resource materials, Mrs. Dorothy E. Jones; Art Dir., Books, Ms Dorothy A. Smith; Art. Dir., Books, Mr. Gene Harris, Supervisor, Copy-Editing and Proofreading Books, Ms. Marian S. Noecker; Supervisor, Copy-Editing & Proofreading Ed. Materials, Ms. Louise W. Hunt; Dir. of Advertising, John F. Ahrens; Asst. to Dir. of Advertising, Walter I. Roberts; Public Relations Dir., Mrs. Jacquelene A. Sabat; Dir. of Curriculum Services, Rev. Arthur A. Wahmann; Supervisor, Curriculum Order & *These Days* Curriculum Sections, Ms. Catherine Di Ienno; Sales Mgr., The Westminster Press, Rev. Robert S. House; Special Sales Rep., Cornelius V. R. Bogert, III; Sales Rep., Mrs. Elizabeth House; Sales Rep., Mrs. Elizabeth L. Morris; Sales Rep., Robert G. Wilson; Supervisor, Sales Dept., Order Section, Ms. Louise M. Wagner

THE VOCATION AGENCY

Chpsn., Rev William C. Howell; Gen. Dir., Rev. Donald P. Smith, 475 Riverside Dr., New York, NY 10027. Exec. Asst., Gen. Dir., Ruth Reifel; Coord. of Personnel Planning, and Administration and Compensation Coord. for Gen. Assembly Agencies, Rev. Donald L. Leonard; Mgr., Headquarters Personnel Office, Helen E. Irvine

Personnel Development: Assoc. Gen. Dir., Rev. James L. Mechem; Mgr. of Financial Aid for Studies, Susan Ellison; Coord. of Professional Development, Rev. James F. Reese; Coord. of Counseling Resources, Rev. Jerome J. Leksa; Rev. Carlos Santin, Assoc. for Racial/Ethnic Enlistment

Personnel Services: Assoc. Gen. Dir., Rev. Edgar Ward; Mgr., Information Services for Personnel, Margaret C. Pols; Assoc. Mgr., Evelyn Hwang; Coord. of Ministerial Relations, Rev. Alan G. Gripe; Coord. of Employment Opportunities, Rev. Ann Conrad; Prog. Assoc. for Women in Ministry, Penelope Morgan Colman; Coord. of Professional Recruitment, Dorothy Gist; Assoc. for Minority Placement, JoRene Willis

Compensation and Benefits; Board of Pensions; Assoc. Gen. Dir. and President, Board of Pensions, Arthur W. Brown; Mgr., Finance and Treas., Board of Pensions, William Irwin Arbuckle II, Mgr., Pensions and Benefits, Harold A. Clark; Mgr., Assistance Program and Sec., Board of Pensions, Rev. Robert Moreland Adm., Home Program, ———

THE COUNCIL ON ADMINISTRATIVE SERVICES

Chpsn., Mrs. M. Frances Dyer; Vice-Chpsn., Rev. Andrew M. Sebben; Dir., Rev. James L. Hogue; Assoc. Dirs., Rev. Robert Kerr, Jr., Rev. Howard A. Bryant, Sr.; Asst. Dir., Rev. Richard Pacini; Lesly L. Jones, Exec. Asst.

THE COUNCIL OF THEOLOGICAL SEMINARIES

Chpsn., Dr. James I. McCord; Vice-Chpsn., Dr. Frank T. Wilson; Dir., Dr. John H. Galbreath, Rm. 1060, New York, NY 10027

THE SUPPORT AGENCY

Chpsn., J. Morgan Cox; Gen. Dir., Rev. Robert J. Rodisch; 475 Riverside Dr., New York, NY 10027; Asst. for Adm., Rosa C. Nesbitt; Assoc. for Personnel Relations, Margaret Ferns; Assoc. for Special Services, Granville C. Smith

Communications Division: Man. Dir., Rev. Frank H. Heinze; Exec. Asst., Rebecca A. Gatho; Dept. of Information: Dir., Vic Jameson; Assoc. Dir., Ann Anderson; Assoc. Dir., Robert J. Thomson; Asst. in Information, Jill Schaeffer; Department of Multi-Media Production: Dir., Joseph M. Elkins; Assoc. Dir., Audio-Visual Services, Carlos Alvarez; Assoc. Dir., Projects, Philip R. Steer; Electonic Engineer, James Harris; Department of Interpretation; Dir., Nancy A. Battye; Exec. Asst., Doris Watterson; Assoc. Dir., David M. Eddy; Assoc. Dir., Ray Yeager

Financial Services Division: Man. Dir., Delmar R. Byler; Exec. Asst., Jean C. Jones; Controller's Department: Mgr. Edgar B.B. Matthews; Assoc. Mgr., Robert J. Collins; Acctg. Specialist, Gerard van Amstel; Accounting Depart.: Mgr. Arthur R. Clark; Assoc. Mgr., Kurt A. Zimmermann; Assoc. Man. Disbursements, Gladys E. Sumersille; Supervisor, Payroll Office, Helen W. Durr; Supervisor, Gen. Acctg., Barbara Berryman; Supervisor, Accts. Receivable, Delores Grier; Treasury Department: Mgr., (also for Foreign Acctg.), ———; Assoc. Mgr. Insurance Management, Dorothy P. Romaine; Assoc. Mgr., Mission Treasury Service, Chester Kusterveck; Coord. Spec. Receipts, Eileene Johnson; Middle East Treasurer, Judson W. Allen; Asst. Foreign Accounts, Ester A. Amago; Assist. for Missionary Accounts, L. Vernelle Blair; Legal Services Depart.: Mgr., Kenneth W. Linsley; Attorney, Linda Norton; Property Management Department: Mgr., Charles L. Marshall, Jr., Asst. Mgr., Emeterio L. Rueda

Management Service Division: Man. Dir., ———; Information Systems Department (includes Computer Services): Mgr., Bruce Smith; Business Systems Department: Mgr., Robert T. Mehrhoff; Assoc. Mgr. for Purchasing, Rev. Harvey Smith; Assoc. Mgr., Ruth Kelley; Business Service Department: Mgr. Leon A. Payne; Assoc. Mgr., Eva Marshall; Assoc. Mgr., Paul Rochester; Facilities and Office Support Department (includes Presbyterian Distribution Service Order Processing): Mgr., Charles Frisby; Assoc. Mgr., Brenda Y. Reid

Mission Funding Division: Man. Dir., William S. Rowling; Exec. Asst., Gertrude V. Affinito; Department of Mission Promotion: Dir., ———; Assoc. Dir., Special Offerings, Barbara Gerak; Assoc. Dir., Congregational Relationships in Mission, ———; Department of Stewardship Training: Dir., Rev. Mark H. Landfried; Department of Fund Raising: Dir., Donald E. MacFalls; Coord. Church Building Campaign Service, Rev. Donald R. Kellian; Field Representatives, Church Building Campaign Service, Rev. J. Wallace Carlson; Rev. Donald R. Killian; Rev. Franklin R. Lane; Rev.

Donald S. Myer; Rev. Clifford A. Post; Department of Major Mission: Dir., James D. Nesbitt

Research Division: Man. Dir., Dr. Mary C. Mattis; Dir., Gay H. Tennis; Research Analysts; Rev. Arthur L. Benjamin; Rev. Robert C. Tomlinson; Research Asst., Marjorie R. Cunningham

A.D. Publications Incorporated

Publisher, Roy A. Lord; Ed., Rev. J. Martin Bailey; Assoc. Eds., Rev. Thomas Orrin Bentz; Sarah Cunningham; James A. Gittings; Rev. Mayo Y. Smith; James E. Solheim; Gen. Mgr., Arthur M. Lupfer; Natl. Circ. Fulfillment Mgr., George Olthoff; Advertising Sales Dir., Arthur W. Van Dyke

PERIODICALS

Journal of Presbyterian History (q), 425 Lombard St., Philadelphia, PA 19147. Rev. James H. Smylie, Ed.

Monday Morning (bi-w), 475 Riverside Dr., New York, NY 10027. Rev. Frank H. Heinze, Ed.

Concern Magazine/Newsfold Magazine (q), Newsfold (8/yr.), United Presbyterian Women, Pub., Jane Jarrard, Ed., Rm. 454, 475 Riverside Dr., New York, NY 10027

A.D. (10/yr.) (Jointly with the United Church of Christ), Pres., Margot Sherman Peet; Publisher, Roy A. Lord; Ed., Rev. J. Martin Bailey, 475 Riverside Dr., New York, NY 10027

Church and Society Magazine (bi-m), 475 Riverside Dr., New York, NY 10027. Earl K. Larson, Belle Miller McMaster, Ed.

These Days (bi-m), (jointly with the Cumberland Presbyterian Church, the Presbyterian Church in Canada, the Presbyterian Church in the United States, The United Church of Canada, The United Presbyterian Church in the U.S.A. and the United Church of Christ), Ed., Larry M. Correu, Editorial Office, 341 Ponce de Leon Ave., NE, Atlanta, GA 30308

SYNOD EXECUTIVES

Alaska-Northwest, Rev. Casper Glenn, 720 Senaca St., Seattle, WA 98101

Covenant, Rev. George P. Morgan, 6172 Bush Blvd., Ste. 3000, Columbus, OH 43229

Lakes & Prairies, Rev. Robert T. Cuthill, Interim, 8012 Cedar Ave., S., Bloomington, MN 55420

Lincoln Trails, Rev. Carl R. Smith, 1100 W. 42nd St., Indianapolis, IN 46208

Mid-America, Rev. Edward C. Brubaker, 6400 Glenwood, Ste. 111, Overland Park, KS 66104

Northeast, Rev. Eugene Turner, 3049 Genesee St., Syracuse, NY 13224

Pacific, Rev. Richard E. Moore, 1 Hallidie Plaza, Ste. 405, San Francisco, CA 94102

Piedmont, Rev. Hugh Bean Evans, Interim, Quadrangle, 153 West Block, Cross Keys, Baltimore, MD 21210

Puerto Rico, Rev. Samuel Velez, Medical Center Plaza, Rm. 216, Rd. #2, Mayaguez, PR 00708

Rocky Mts., Rev. John Sensenig, 1737 Vine St., Denver, CO 80206

South, Rev. Clinton M. Marsh, Acting Head of Staff, Rm. 217-C, 1001 Virginia Ave., Atlanta, GA 30354

Southern Calif., Rev. Frederick J. Beebe; Exec. Ste. 1501, Wilshire Blvd., Los Angeles, CA 90017

Southwest, Rev. Richard K. Smith, 10 E. Roanoke Ave., Phoenix, AZ 85004

Sun, Rev. Raymond V. Kearns, Jr. (Interim), Box 901, Denton, TX 76201

Trinity, Rev. William G. Rusch, 3040 Market St., Camp Hill, PA 17011

United Zion Church

A branch of the Brethren in Christ, which settled in Lancaster County, Pennsylvania, and was organized under the leadership of Matthias Brinser, in 1855.

Churches: 13 Inclusive Membership: 952 Sunday or Sabbath Schools: 13 Total Enrollment: 1,294 Ordained Clergy: 24

GENERAL ORGANIZATION

Conference: annual

OFFICERS

Bishops: Alvin H. Eberly, Rt. 2, Denver, PA 17517. Brinser Heistand, Rt. 3, Elizabethtown, PA 17022; Amos Weidman, R.D. 2, Manhiem, PA 17545

Gen. Conf. Sec.: Eugene Dreider, RC#2, Manhiem, PA 17545

Unity of the Brethren

Czech and Moravian immigrants in Texas (beginning about 1855) established congregations which grew into an Evangelical Union in 1903, and with the accession of other Brethren in Texas, into the Evangelical Unity of the Czech-Moravian Brethren in North America. In 1959, it shortened the name to the original name used in 1457, the Unity of the Brethren (Unitas Fratrum, or Jednota Bratrska).

GENERAL ORGANIZATION

Synod: Every two years.

OFFICERS

Pres., Rev. John Baletka, 3829 Sandstone, San Angelo, TX 76901

1st Vice Pres., Rev. Milton Maly, 2205 Carnation, Temple, TX 76501

Sec., Mrs. Dean Hodon, Austin, TX

Fin. Sec., Mr. Larry Zabeik, Temple, TX

Treas., Jerry Vitek, 822 Estate Dr., Belton, TX 76513

ORGANIZATIONS

Sunday School Union: Chmn., Mr. Stanley Mrnustik, 205 N. Shaw, Caldwell, TX 77836; Sec., Mrs. Joe Kocian, 107 S. Barbara, Waco, TX 76705; Chpsn., Board of Christian Education: Rev. Lawrence Junek, 6731 Kury Lane, Houston, TX 77088

Christian Sisters Society: Pres., Mrs. Joe Kocian, 107 S. Barbara, Waco, TX 76705; Sec., Mrs. Earl Hinson, 5823 Kuldell, Houston, TX 77036

Brethren Youth Fellowship: Ray Griggs, 1901 S. 45th St., Temple, TX 76501

PERIODICAL

Brethren Journal (m), 5905 Carleen Dr., Austin, TX 78731, Rev. Jesse E. Skrivanek, Ed.

Vedanta Society of New York

Followers of the Vedas, the scriptures of the Indo-Aryans, doctrines expounded by Swami Vivekananda at the Parliament of Religions, Chicago, 1893. There are altogether 12 such Centers in the U.S.A. All are under the control of the Ramakrishna Mission, organized by Swami Vivekananda in India.

Churches: 12 Inclusive Membership: 1,000 Sunday or Sabbath Schools: N.R. Total Enrollment: N.R. Ordained Clergy: 1

GENERAL ORGANIZATION

Headquarters: 34 W. 71st St., New York, NY 10023. Tel. (212) 877-9197

LEADER

Swami Tathagatananda

Volunteers of America

A religious social welfare organization, founded in 1896 by Ballington and Maud Booth; it provides spiritual and material aid for those in need, through approximately 892 churches and service units in the continental U.S.

Churches: 607 Inclusive Membership: 36,634 Sunday or Sabbath Schools: 102 Total Enrollment: 8,590 Ordained Clergy: 704

GENERAL ORGANIZATION

National Headquarters: 340 West 85th St., New York, NY 10024. Tel. (212) 873-2600

NATIONAL OFFICERS

Commander-in-Chief, Gen. John F. McMahon
National Field Sec., Lt. Col. Belle Leach
National Fin. Sec., Lt. Col. Don Schwartz
National Religious Activities Sec., Col. Elizabeth J. Hartman
National Sec. for the Aging, Major M. Clelland Bone
National Correctional Services Sec., Maj. J. Clint Cheveallier
National Social Welfare Sec., Lt. Col. Belle Leach
National Youth Services Sec., Maj. James R. Simmons
National Rehabilitation Services Sec., Maj. David W. Bordenkircher
Eastern Region Headquarters: 18 Exchange St., Binghamton, NY 13901; Regional Dir., Col. Clifford S. Hartman
Midwest Region Headquarters: 6550 York Ave., S., Minneapolis, MN 55435; Regional Dir., Col. Robert E. Nolte
Southern Region Headquarters: Ste. 515, 433 Metairie Rd., New Orleans, LA 70005; Regional Dir., Col. Ray C. Tremont
Western Region Headquarters: 1501 Wilshire Blvd., Los Angeles, CA Regional Dir., Col. Paul H. Nolte
Metropolitan Division Headquarters: 340 W. 85th St., New York, NY 10024. Exec. Dir., Gen. J. F. McMahon; Operations Dir., Lt. Col. Don Schwartz

PERIODICAL

The Volunteer (m), published at National Headquarters

The Wesleyan Church

The Wesleyan Church originated through the uniting of the Pilgrim Holiness Church (1897) and The Wesleyan Methodist Church of America (1843) at a merging conference held on June 26, 1968. The Wesleyan Church emphasizes scriptural truth concerning the new birth, the entire sanctification of believers, the personal return of Christ, and worldwide holiness evangelism.

Churches: 1,714 Inclusive Membership: 99,016 Sunday or Sabbath Schools: 1,714 Total Enrollment: 201,238 Ordained Clergy: 2,367

GENERAL ORGANIZATION

General Conference: quadrennial (next session, 1980) Headquarters: P.O. Box 2000. Marion, IN 46952. Tel. (317) 674-3301

OFFICERS

Gen. Supts.: Dr. J. D. Abbott, Dr. R. W. McIntyre, Dr. Virgil A. Mitchell, Dr. Melvin H. Snyder
Gen. Sec., Rev. D. Wayne Brown
Gen. Treas., Rev. Charles E. Lewis
Gen. Ed., Dr. George E. Failing
Gen. Publisher, Mr. Richard J. Halt
Gen. Sec. Extension and Evangelism, Rev. Joe C. Sawyer
Gen. Sec. World Missions, Dr. Robert N. Lytle
Gen. Sec., Local Church Edu., Dr. O. D. Emery
Gen. Sec. Youth, Rev. David Keith
Gen. Sec. Educational Institutions, Dr. Leo Cox

PERIODICALS

The Wesleyan Advocate, Dr. George E. Failing, Ed.
Wind, Rev. David Keith, Ed.
Wesleyan World, Rev. Paul Swauger, Ed.

Wesleyan Holiness Association of Churches

This body was founded Aug. 4, 1959 near Muncie, Indiana by a group of ministers and laymen who were drawn together for the purpose of spreading and conserving sweet, radical, scriptural holiness. These men came from various church bodies. This group is Wesleyan in doctrine and standards.

GENERAL ORGANIZATION

General Conference meets every two years.
Headquarters: 726 W. 13th St., Tempe, AZ 85281. Tel. (602) 967-2734

OFFICERS

Gen. Supt., Rev. Matthew M. Harden, 7107 N. 43rd Ave., Phoenix, AZ 85021. Tel. (602) 937-2400
Asst. Gen. Supt., Rev. William H. Owen, 37626 Miller Rd., Lisbon, OH 44432. Tel. (216) 424-7968
Gen. Sec.-Treas., Rev. Duane H. Watkins, 726 W. 13th St., Tempe, AZ 85281. Tel. (602) 967-2734

PERIODICAL

Eleventh Hour Messenger (m), Rev. Matthew M. Harden, Ed.

Wisconsin Evangelical Lutheran Synod

Organized in 1850 at Milwaukee, Wisconsin by three pastors sent to America by a German mission society. The name Wisconsin Evangelical Lutheran Synod still reflects its origins, although it has lost its local character and presently has congregations in 46 states and 4 Canadian provinces.

In 1872 the Wisconsin Synod became a charter member of the Synodical Conference, a conservative federation which included the Lutheran Church—Missouri Synod as a church member. In 1963, the Wisconsin Synod withdrew from the Conference because of a dispute with the Missouri Synod over fellowship.

The Wisconsin Synod federated with the Michigan and Minnesota Synods in 1892 in order to more effectively carry on education and mission enterprises. A merger of these three Synods followed in 1917 to give the Wisconsin Evangelical Lutheran Synod its present form.

Although at its organization in 1850 the Synod turned away from conservative Lutheran theology, today it is ranked as one of the most conservative Lutheran bodies in the U.S. The Synod confesses that the Bible is the verbally inspired, infalliable Word of God and subscribes without reservation to the confessional writings of the Lutheran Church. Its interchurch relations are determined by a firm commitment to the principle that unity of doctrine and practice are the prerequisites of pulpit and altar fellowship and ecclesial cooperation. Consequently it does not hold membership in ecumenical organizations.

ADVENTIST BODIES

Churches: 1,116 Inclusive Membership: 402,972 Sunday or Sabbath Schools: 1,045 Total Enrollment: 47,862 Ordained Clergy: 1,247

GENERAL ORGANIZATION

Synod: biennial (Next meeting, 1979)

OFFICERS

Pres., Rev. Carl H. Mischke, 3512 W. North Ave., Milwaukee, WI 53208
1st Vice-Pres., Rev. George W. Boldt, 8637 Fernald, Ave., Morton Grove, IL 60053
2nd Vice-Pres., Rev. Gerald E. Free, 1922 S. 50th Ave., Omaha, NB 68106
Sec., Prof. Heinrich J. Vogel, 11757 N. Seminary Dr. 65W., Mequon, WI 53092

OTHER ORGANIZATIONS

Board of Trustees:
3512 W. North Ave. Milwaukee, WI 53208. Exec. Sec. Rev. Elton H. Huebner; Treas. and Comptroller: Norris Koopmann; Fiscal Exec., Paul A. Unke; Real Estate Mgr., Warren Hanson;
Commission on Higher Education:
Exec. Sec., Rev. Robert J. Voss, 3512 W. North Ave., Milwaukee, WI 53208
Board for Parish Education: Office, 3614 West North Ave., Milwaukee, WI 53208
Exec. Sec., Donald H. Zimmerman
Gen. Board for Home Missions:
Exec. Sec., Rev. Norman W. Berg, 3512 W. North Ave., Milwaukee, WI 53208
Gen. Board for World Missions:
Exec. Sec., Rev. Theodore A. Sauer, 3512 W. North Ave., Milwaukee, WI 53208
Stewardship Board: Deferred Giving Counselor, A. W. Schaefer; Exec. Sec., Rev. James P. Schaefer, 3512 W. North Ave., Milwaukee, WI 53208
Special Ministries Board:
Exec. Sec., Alfons Woldt, 3512 W. North Ave., Milwaukee, WI 53208
Public Relations Committee:
Dir. of Publ. Inf., Rev. James P. Schaefer, 3512 W. North Ave., Milwaukee, WI 53208

PERIODICALS

Wisconsin Lutheran Quarterly (q), 11831 N. Seminary Dr., 65 W. Mequon, WI 53092. Prof. Edward C. Frederich, Mng. Ed.
Northwestern Lutheran (bi-w), 3624 W. North Ave., Milwaukee, WI 53208. Rev. Harold E. Wicke, Ed.
Junior Northwestern (m), Editorial Committee: 3512 W. North Ave., Milwaukee, WI 53208
Yearbook, 3624 W. North Ave., Milwaukee, WI 53208. Rev. Mentor E. Kujath, Ed.
The Lutheran Educator, 3614 W. North Ave., Milwaukee, WI 53208. Donald H. Zimmerman, Ed.

RELIGIOUS BODIES IN THE UNITED STATES ARRANGED BY FAMILIES

The following list of religious bodies appearing in the Directory Section of this **Yearbook** shows the "families," or related clusters into which American religious bodies can be grouped. For example, there are many communions that can be grouped under the heading "Baptist" for historical and theological reasons. It is not to be assumed, however, that all denominations under one family heading are similar in belief or practice. Often, any similarity is purely coincidental. The family clusters tend to represent historical factors more often than theological or practical ones. The family categories provided one of the major pitfalls of church statistics because of the tendency to combine the statistics by "families" for analytical and comparative purposes. Such combined totals are almost meaningless, although often used as variables for sociological analysis. **Religious bodies not grouped under family headings appear alphabetically and are not indented in the following list.**

ADVENTIST BODIES

Advent Christian Church
Church of God General Conference (Oregon, Ill.)
Primitive Advent Christian Church
Seventh-day Adventists

The African Orthodox Church
Amana Church Society
American Evangelical Christian Churches
American Rescue Workers
Apostolic Christian Church (Nazarean)
Apostolic Christian Churches of America
The Anglican Orthodox Church
Baha'i Faith

BAPTIST BODIES

American Baptist Association
American Baptist Churches in the U.S.A.
Baptist General Conference
Baptist Missionary Association of America
Bethel Ministerial Association, Inc.
Conservative Baptist Association of America
Duck River (and Kindred) Associations of Baptists
Free Will Baptists
General Association of Regular Baptist Churches
General Baptists, General Association of
General Conference of the Evangelical Baptist Church, Inc.
General Six-Principle Baptists
National Baptist Convention of America
National Baptist Convention, U.S.A., Inc.
National Primitive Baptist Convention, Inc.
North American Baptist General Conference
Primitive Baptists
Progressive National Baptist Convention, Inc.
Reformed Baptists
Separate Baptists in Christ
Seventh Day Baptist General Conference
Southern Baptist Convention
The United Free Will Baptist Church

Berean Fundamental Church

BRETHREN (German Baptists)

Brethren Church (Ashland, Ohio)
Church of the Brethren
Grace Brethren Churches, Fellowship of
Old German Baptist Brethren

BRETHREN, RIVER

Brethren in Christ Church
United Zion Church

Buddhist Churches of America,
Christadelphians
The Christian and Missionary Alliance
Christian Catholic Church
Christian Church (Disciples of Christ)
Christian Churches and Churches of Christ
The Christian Congregation
Christian National Church U.S.A.
Christian Union
Church of Christ (Holiness), U.S.A.
Church of Christ, Scientist
Church of Daniel's Band
The Church of Illumination
The Church of Revelation
Church of the Nazarene
Churches of Christ
Churches of Christ in Christian Union.

CHURCHES OF GOD

Church of God (Anderson, Ind.)
Church of God by Faith
The Church of God (Seventh Day)
The Church of God (Seventh Day), Denver, Colo.,
Church of God (Which He Purchased With His Own Blood)
Churches of God, General Conference

CHURCHES OF THE LIVING GOD

Church of the Living God
House of God, Which is the Church of the Living God, the Pillar and Ground of the Truth, Inc.

CHURCHES OF THE NEW JERUSALEM

General Church of the New Jerusalem
General Convention, The Swedenborgian Church

Community Churches, National Council of
Congregational Christian Churches, National Association of
Conservative Congregational Christian Conference

EASTERN CHURCHES

Albanian Orthodox Archdiocese in America
Albanian Orthodox Diocese of America
The American Carpatho-Russian Orthodox Greek Catholic Church
The Antiochian Orthodox Christian Archdiocese of N.A.
Armenian Apostolic Church of America
Armenian Church of America, Diocese of the (including Diocese of California)
Bulgarian Eastern Orthodox Church
Coptic Orthodox Church
Greek Orthodox Archdiocese of North and South America
Holy Orthodox Church in America
Holy Ukrainian Autocephalic Orthodox Church in Exile
The Orthodox Church in America
Romanian Orthodox Church in America
The Romanian Orthodox Episcopate of America
Russian Orthodox Church in the U.S.A., Patriarchal Parishes of the
The Russian Orthodox Church Outside Russia
Serbian Eastern Orthodox Church for the U.S.A. and Canada
Syrian Orthodox Church of Antioch (Archdiocese of the U.S.A. and Canada)
Ukrainian Orthodox Church in the U.S.A.
Ukrainian Orthodox Church in America (Ecumenical Patriarchate)

The Episcopal Church
Ethical Culture Movement
Evangelical Church of North America
Evangelical Congregational Church
The Evangelical Covenant Church of America
The Evangelical Free Church of America
The Fire-Baptized Holiness Church (Wesleyan)
Free Christian Zion Church of Christ

FRIENDS

Evangelical Friends Alliance
Friends General Conference
Friends United Meeting
Religious Society of Friends (Conservative)
Religious Society of Friends (Unaffiliated Meetings)

The Gospel Mission Corps
Grace Gospel Fellowship
The Holiness Church of God, Inc.
Independent Fundamental Churches of America
Israelite House of David
Jehovah's Witnesses
Jewish Congregations
Kodesh Church of Immanuel

LATTER DAY SAINTS

Church of Christ
The Church of Jesus Christ (Bickertonites)
The Church of Jesus Christ of Latter-day Saints
Reorganized Church of Jesus Christ of Latter Day Saints

The Liberal Catholic Church-Province of the United States of America

LUTHERANS

The American Lutheran Church
Apostolic Lutheran Church of America
Church of the Lutheran Brethren of America
Church of the Lutheran Confession
Estonian Evangelical Lutheran Church
Evangelical Lutheran Church in America (Eielsen Synod)
Evangelical Lutheran Churches, Association of
Evangelical Lutheran Synod
Free Lutheran Congregations, The Association of
Latvian Evangelical Lutheran Church in America
Lutheran Church in America
The Lutheran Church—Missouri Synod
The Protestant Conference (Lutheran)
Wisconsin Evangelical Lutheran Synod

MENNONITE BODIES

Beachy Amish Mennonite Churches
Church of God in Christ (Mennonite)
Evangelical Mennonite Brethren Conference
Evangelical Mennonite Church
General Conference of Mennonite Brethren Churches
Hutterian Brethren
Mennonite Church
Mennonite Church, The General Conference
Old Order Amish Church
Old Order (Wisler) Mennonite Church
Reformed Mennonite Church

METHODIST BODIES

African Methodist Episcopal Church
African Methodist Episcopal Zion Church
Bible Protestant Church
Christian Methodist Episcopal Church
Evangelical Methodist Church
Free Methodist Church of North America
Fundamental Methodist Church, Inc.
Primitive Methodist Church, U.S.A.
Reformed Methodist Union Episcopal Church
Reformed Zion Union Apostolic Church
Southern Methodist Church
The United Methodist Church

The Metropolitan Church Association
Metropolitan Community Churches, Universal Fellowship of
The Missionary Church

MORAVIAN BODIES

Moravian Church in America (Unitas Fratrum)
Unity of the Brethren

Muslims
New Apostolic Church of North America
North American Old Roman Catholic Church (Archdiocese of New York)

OLD CATHOLIC CHURCHES

The American Catholic Church, Archdiocese of New York
The American Catholic Church (Syro-Antiochian)
Christ Catholic Church (Diocese of Boston)
North American Old Roman Catholic Church

PENTECOSTAL BODIES

Holiness-Pentecostal Denominations*

The Apostolic Faith
The Church of God
Church of God (Cleveland, Tenn.)
The Church of God in Christ
Church of God in Christ, International
The Church of God of Prophecy
The Church of God of the Mountain Assembly
Congregational Holiness Church
Full Gospel Church
International Pentecostal Church of Christ
The (Original) Church of God
Pentecostal Fire-Baptized Holiness Church
Pentecostal Free-Will Baptist Church, Inc.
Pentecostal Holiness Church, Inc.
United Holy Church of America

*Baptistic-Pentecostal Denominations**

Assemblies of God
The Bible Church of Christ, Inc.
Christian Church of North America, General Council
Elim Fellowship
Full Gospel Asemblies, International
Independent Assemblies of God, International
International Church of the Foursquare Gospel
Open Bible Standard Churches
Pentecostal Church of God

*Unitarian (Oneness)-Pentecostal Denominations**

Apostolic Overcoming Holy Church of God
Bible Way Church of Our Lord Jesus Christ, World Wide, Inc.
Church of Our Lord Jesus Christ of the Apostolic Faith
Pentecostal Assemblies of the World
United Pentecostal Church, International

(*The above typology for Pentecostal Bodies was supplied by Dr. H. Vinson Synan, Emmanuel College, Franklin Springs, Georgia, to whom the editor is grateful. According to Dr. Synan, "Holiness-Pentecostal" bodies are those that teach the three stages theory of Christian experience [i.e., conversion, sanctification, baptism of the Holy Spirit]. "Baptistic-Pentecostal" denominations are those that teach a two-stage theory [i.e., conversion and baptism of the Holy Spirit]. "Unitarian-Pentecostal" bodies deny the traditional concept of the Trinity and teach that Jesus Christ alone is God.)

Pillar of Fire
Plymouth Brethren
Polish National Catholic Church of America

PRESBYTERIAN BODIES

Associate Reformed Presbyterian Church (General Synod)
Cumberland Presbyterian Church
The Orthodox Presbyterian Church
Presbyterian Church in America
Presbyterian Church in the U.S.
Reformed Presbyterian Church, Evangelical Synod
Reformed Presbyterian Church of North America
Second Cumberland Presbyterian Church in U.S.
The United Presbyterian Church in the U.S.A.

REFORMED BODIES

Christian Reformed Church in North America
Hungarian Reformed Church in America
Netherlands Reformed Congregations
Protestant Reformed Churches in America
Reformed Church in America
Reformed Church in the U.S.

Reformed Episcopal Church
The Roman Catholic Church
The Salvation Army
The Schwenkfelder Church
Social Brethren

SPIRITUALIST BODIES

The National Spiritual Alliance of the U.S.A.
National Spiritualist Association of Churches

Triumph the Church and Kingdom of God in Christ
Unitarian Universalist Association

UNITED BRETHREN BODIES

United Brethren in Christ
United Christian Church

United Church of Christ
Vedanta Society of New York
Volunteers of America
The Wesleyan Church
Wesleyan Holiness Association of Churches

4. RELIGIOUS BODIES IN CANADA

A large number of Canadian religious bodies were organized by immigrants from Europe and elsewhere and a smaller number of them sprang up originally on Canadian soil. In the case of Canada, moreover, many denominations overlapping the U.S.-Canadian border have headquarters in the United States.

In the past year, a concerted effort has been made to develop completeness in this directory and much improvement over the previous listing has been made. The editor of the **Yearbook of American and Canadian Churches** would be grateful for information on any major Canadian religious body not now included.

What follows is, first, an alphabetical directory of religious bodies in Canada that have supplied information for this edition of the **Yearbook.** The second section is an alphabetical list, with addresses and other information, of bodies known to exist in Canada that have not yet supplied directory information. This second section is entitled "Other Religious Bodies in Canada."

Those denominations that have not checked and returned their directory for this edition carry the symbol (†) in front of the title.

A listing of Canadian religious bodies classified by family groups (e.g., Baptists) appears at the end of this directory.

Complete statistics for Canadian denominations will be found in the table "Canadian Current and Non-Current Statistics" in Section III of this **Yearbook.** Statistics appearing in the denominational directories which follow are Current only; that is, those gathered in 1979 and 1978:

The Anglican Church of Canada

Anglicanism came to Canada with the early explorers such as Martin Frobisher and Henry Hudson. Continuous services began in Newfoundland about 1700 and in Nova Scotia in 1710. The first Bishop, Charles Inglis, was appointed to Nova Scotia in 1787. The numerical strength of Anglicanism was increased by the coming of American Loyalists and by massive immigration both after the Napoleonic wars and in the later 19th and early 20th centuries.

The Anglican Church of Canada has enjoyed self-government for over a century and is an autonomous member of the worldwide Anglican Communion. The General Synod, which normally meets biennially, consists of the Archbishops, Bishops, and elected clerical and lay representatives of the 30 dioceses and one Episcopal district. Each of the Ecclesiastical Provinces—Canada, Ontario, Rupert's Land, and British Columbia—is organized under a Metropolitan and has its own Provincial Synod and Executive Council. Each diocese has its own Diocesan Synod meeting usually annually.

Churches: 3,030 Inclusive Membership: 961,952 Sunday or Sabbath Schools: 2,049 Total Enrollment: 107,505 Ordained Clergy: 2,832

GENERAL SYNOD OFFICERS

Primate of the Anglican Church of Canada, Most Rev. E. W. Scott, 600 Jarvis St., Toronto, Ontario M4Y 2J6

Prolocutor, Chancellor J. H. C. Harradence, 685-20th St., W., Prince Albert, Saskatchewan S6V 4H4

Gen. Sec., Ven. H. St. C. Hilchey, 600 Jarvis St., Toronto, Ontario M4Y 2J6

Gen. Treas. and Treas. of all Departments, John R. Ligertwood, 600 Jarvis St., Toronto, Ontario M4Y 2J6

DEPARTMENTS AND DIVISIONS

Offices: Church House, 600 Jarvis St., Toronto, Ontario M4Y 2J6. Tel. (416) 924-9192

Exec. Dir. of Program, L. C. Raymond.

Missionary Society of the Anglican Church of Canada. Exec. Sec., T. M. Anthony

Division of National and World Program: Dir., T. M. Anthony

Division of Planning: Dir., W. E. Lowe

Division of Pensions: Dir., G. E. Hobson

Department of Administration and Finance: Dir., J. R. Ligertwood

Anglican Book Centre: Dir., M. J. Lloyd

METROPOLITANS (ARCHBISHOPS)

(Address: The Most Reverend)

Ecclesiastical Province of:

Canada: Robert Seaborn, 19 King's Bridge Rd., St. John's, Newfoundland A1C 3K4

Rupert's Land: F. H. W. Crabb, Box 279, Peace River, Alberta T0H 2X0. Tel. (403) 624-2767.

British Columbia: T. David Somerville, #101-325 Howe St., Vancouver, British Columbia V6C 1Z7

Ontario: J. A. Watton, Box 830, Schumacher, Ontario P0N 1G0

DIOCESAN ARCHBISHOPS AND BISHOPS

(Address: The Most Reverend; The Right Reverend)

Algoma: F. F. Nock, Box 1168, Sault Ste. Marie, Ontario P6A 5N7. Tel. (705) 256-5061

Arctic: J. R. Sperry, 1055 Avenue Rd., Toronto, Ontario M5N 2C8. Tel. (416) 481-2263

Athabasca: F. H. W. Crabb (Archbishop), Box 279, Peace River, Alberta T0H 2X0. Tel. (403) 624-2767

Brandon: J. F. S. Conlin, 341-13th St., Brandon, Manitoba R7A 4P8. Tel. (204) 727-7550

British Columbia: F. R. Gartrell, 912 Vancouver St., Victoria, British Columbia V8V 3V7. Tel. (604) 386-7781

Caledonia: D. W. Hambidge, #208-4th Ave., Prince Rupert, British Columbia V8J 1P3. Tel. (604) 624-6044

Calgary: M. L. Goodman, 3015 Glencoe Rd. S. W., Calgary, Alberta T2S 2L9. Tel. (403) 243-3673

Cariboo: J. S. P. Snowden, 360 Nicola St., Kamloops, British Columbia. Tel. (604) 372-3912

Edmonton: J. A. W. Langstone, 10033-84th. Edmonton, Alberta T6E 2S6. Tel. (403) 439-7344

Fredericton: H. L. Nutter, 791 Brunswick St. Fredericton, New Brunswick E3B 1H8. Tel. (506) 455-8667

Huron: T. D. B. Ragg, 4-220 Dundas St., London, Ontario N6A 1H3, Tel. (519) 434-6893

Keewatin: H. J. P. Allan, Box 118, Kenora, Ontario P9N 3X1. Tel. (807) 468-7011

Kootenay: R. E. F. Berry, Box 549, Kelowna, British Columbia V1Y 7P2 Tel. (604) 762-3306

Montreal: R. Hollis, 1444 Union Ave., Montreal, Quebec H3A 2B8. Tel. (514) 845-6211

Moosonee: J. A. Watton (Archbishop), Box 841, Schumacher, Ontario P0N 1G0. Tel. (705) 264-9759

Eastern Newfoundland and Labrador: R. L. Seaborn, (Archbishop), 19 King's Bridge Rd., St. John's, Newfoundland A1C 3K4. Tel. (709) 726-6697

Central Newfoundland: Mark Genge, 34 Fraser Rd., Gander, Newfoundland A1V 1K7 Tel. (709) 256-2372
Western Newfoundland, Stuart S. Payne, 311, Millbrook Hall, Corner Brook Newfoundland. Tel. (709) 639-8712
New Westminster: T. D. Somerville (Archbishop), #101-325 Howe St., Vancouver, British Columbia V6C 1Z7. Tel. (604) 684-6306
Niagara: J. C. Bothwell, 67 Victoria Ave. S., Hamilton, Ontario. L8N 2S8. Tel. (416) 527-1117
Nova Scotia: G. F. Arnold, 5732 College St., Halifax, Nova Scotia B3H 1X4. Tel. (902) 423-8301
Ontario: H. G. Hill, 90 Johnson St., Kingston, Ontario. K7L 1X7. Tel. (613) 544-4774
Ottawa: W. J. Robinson, 71 Bronson Ave., Ottawa, Ontario K1R 6G6. Tel. (613) 232-7124
Quebec: A. Goodings, 36 rue Desjardins, Quebec, Quebec G1R 4L5. Tel. (418) 692-3858
Qu'Appelle: M. G. Peers, 1501 College Ave., Regina, Saskatchewan S4P 1B8. Tel. (306) 527-8606
Rupert's Land: Barry Valentine, 935 Nesbitt Bay, Winnipeg, Manitoba R3T 1W6. Tel. (204) 453-6248
Saskatchewan: H. V. R., Short, Box 1088, Prince Albert, Saskatchewan S6V 5S6. Tel. (306) 763-2455
Saskatoon: D. A. Ford, Box 1965, Saskatoon, Saskatchewan S7K 3S5. Tel. (306) 244-5651
Toronto: L. S. Garnsworthy, 135 Adelaide St., E., Toronto, Ontario M5C 1L8. Tel. (416) 363-6021
Yukon: J. T. Frame, Box 4247, Whitehorse, Yukon. Tel. (403) 667-7746

The Antiochian Orthodox Christian Archdiocese of North America

There are approximately 25,000 members of the Antiochian Orthodox community living in Canada. They are under the jurisdiction of the Patriarch of Antioch and All the East, with headquarters in Damascus, Syria. There are churches in Ottawa, Toronto, Montreal, Alberta, Windsor and new missions in Prince Edward Island and other cities.

GENERAL ORGANIZATION

Metropolitan Archbishop, Philip (Saliba), 358 Mountain Rd., Englewood, NJ 07631
In Canada: V. Rev. Anthony Gabriel, St. George's Orthodox Church, 555-575 Jean Talon St., E., Montreal, Quebec H2R 1T8

Apostolic Christian Church (Nazarean)

This church was formed in Canada as a result of immigration from various European countries. The body began as a movement originated by the Rev. S. H. Froehlich, a Swiss pastor, whose followers are still found in Switzerland and Central Europe.

GENERAL ORGANIZATION

Headquarters: Apostolic Christian Church Foundation, P.O. Box 151, Tremont, IL 61568

OFFICER

Gen. Sec. Walter H. Meyer, P.O. Box 151, Tremont, IL 61568. Tel. (309) 925-3551

PERIODICAL

Newsletter (q)

The Apostolic Church in Canada

Founded in Wales in 1904 and brought over to Canada thereafter.

GENERAL ORGANIZATION

The Apostolic Church Council, twice yearly.

OFFICERS

Pres., Rev. D. S. Morris, 388 Gerald St., La Salle, Quebec.
Natl. Sec., Rev. S. Hammond, 43 Marlbank Rd., Agincourt, Ontario M1T 1Y6

Apostolic Church of Pentecost of Canada Inc.

This body was founded in 1921 at Winnipeg, Manitoba, by Pastor Frank Small. Doctrines include belief in eternal salvation by the grace of God, baptism of the Holy Spirit with the evidence of speaking in tongues, water baptism by emersion in the name of the Lord Jesus Christ.

Churches: 120 Inclusive Membership: N.R. Sunday or Sabbath Schools: N.R. Total Enrollment: N.R. Ordained Clergy: 209

GENERAL ORGANIZATION

Annual Ministers Conference: Next meeting June 3-5, 1980, Surrey, British Columbia
Headquarters: 3026 Taylor St. E., Saskatoon, Saskatchewan S7H 4J2. Tel. (306) 374-1944

OFFICERS

Moderator, D. W. Breen, 3026 Taylor St., E., Saskatoon, Saskatchewan S7H 4J2
Clerk, B. W. Conrad, 3026 Taylor St. E., Saskatoon, Saskatchewan S7H 4J2
Missionary Council Chpsn., E. G. Bradley, 10324—107 Ave., Edmonton, Alberta T5H 0V8

PERIODICAL

End Times' Messenger (11/yr.), 4—3026 Taylor St. E., Saskatoon, Saskatchewan S7H 4J2. I. W. Ellis, Ed.

The Armenian Church of North America, Diocese of Canada

The Canadian branch of the Ancient Church of Armenia founded in A.D. 301 by St. Gregory the Illuminator. It was established in Canada at St. Catherines, Ontario, in 1930. The diocesan organization is under the jurisdiction of the Holy See of Etchmiadzin, Armenia, U.S.S.R. The Diocese of Canada is normally under the jurisdiction of a suffragan bishop within the Diocese of the Armenian Church of North America.

Churches: 4 Inclusive Membership: 23,500 Sunday or Sabbath Schools: 4 Total Enrollment: 500 Ordained Clergy: 5

GENERAL ORGANIZATION

Diocesan Offices: Holy Trinity Armenian Church, 14 Woodland Ave. W, Toronto, Ontario M4V 1G7

OFFICERS

Vicar Of Canada: Very Rev. Vazken Keshishian, Pastor of Holy Trinity Church

ARMENIAN EVANGELICAL CHURCH

Very Rev. Kagham Zakarian, Pastor of St. Gregory the Illuminator Armenian Apostolic Church, 49 Carlton St., St. Catherine, Ontario L2R 1P7

Vicar of Quebec: Very Rev. Baret Yeretzian, Pastor of Montreal and Ottawa St. Gregory the Illuminator Armenian Cathedral 615 Stuart Ave., Montreal, Quebec H2V 3H2

PERIODICALS

Nor Serout (m) in Armenian and English, 14 Woodlawn Ave., Toronto, Ontario M4V 1G7.

Pourastan (m) in Armenian, 615 Stuart Ave., Montreal, Quebec H2V 3H2

Armenian Evangelical Church

Founded in 1960 by immigrant Armenian evangelical families from the Middle East. This body is conservative doctrinally, with an evangelical, biblical emphasis. The polity of churches within the group differ with congregationalism being dominant, but there are Presbyterian Armenian Evangelical churches as well. Most of the local churches have joined main-line denominations. All of the Armenian Evangelical (Congregational or Presbyterian) local churches in the U.S. and Canada have joined with the Armenian Evangelical Union of North America.

GENERAL ORGANIZATION

Armenian Evangelical Union of North America. Meets every two years. Next meeting, San Francisco, CA, June, 1980.

OFFICERS

Moderator, Mr. George Philibassian, c/o Armenian Presbyterian Church, 140 Forrest Ave., Paramus, NJ 07652

Minister, Rev. A. K. Jizmejian, 28 Glenforest Rd., Toronto, Ontario M4N 1Z8

PERIODICAL

Canada Armenian Press (q), 28 Glenforest Rd., Toronto, Ontario M4N 1Z8. Rev. A. Jizmejian, Ed.

Associated Gospel Churches

Founded in 1922 by Dr. Peter Philpott and H. E. Irwin, K. C., in Hamilton and Toronto, Ontario. Letters of Patent obtained from the Canadian Government in 1925. This body stresses historical, conservative theology.

GENERAL ORGANIZATION

Annual Conference. A 22-member Executive Committee acts in the interim.

Headquarters: 280 Plains Rd. W., Burlington, Ontario L7T 1G4

OFFICERS

Pres., Rev. G. M. Crosby, 713 Leeder Ct., Newmarket, Ontario L3Y 5A8. Tel. (416) 895-7460

Vice-Pres., Rev. S. R. Sadlier, 3057 Driftwood Dr., Burlington, Ontario L7M 1X8.Tel. (416) 335-4631.

Exec. Sec., Rev. J. L. Hockney, 280 Plains Rd. W., Burlington, Ontario L7T 1G4. Tel. (416) 522-2398

PERIODICAL

Advance (bi-m), Box 3023, Sta. C, Hamilton, Ontario L8H 7K6. Rev. D. C. Ralph, Ed.

The Association of Regular Baptist Churches (Canada)

Organized in 1957 by a group of churches for the purpose of mutual cooperation in missionary activities. The Association believes the Bible to be God's word, stands for historic Baptist principles, and opposes modern ecumenism.

Headquarters: 337 Jarvis St., Toronto, Ontario, M5B 2C7. Tel. (416) 925-3261

OFFICERS

Pres., Rev. G. B. Hicks, Box 162, Brownsburg, Quebec J0V 1A0

Sec., Rev. Ronald E. Matthews, 337 Jarvis St., Toronto, Ontario M5B 2C7

PERIODICAL

The Gospel Witness, 130 Gerrard St. E., Toronto, Ontario M5A 3T4. Rev. W. P. Bauman, Man. Ed.

Bahá'i Faith

(National Spiritual Assembly of Bahá'ís in Canada).

Bahá'ís are followers of Bahá'úllah (1817-1892) whose religion upholds the basic principles of progressive revelation, religious unity, and a new world order.

The Bahá'i administrative order consists of institutions which function at the local, national, and international level. The international administrative institutions are located in Haifa; Israel, surrounding the burial places of the Founders.

In Canada, the Bahá'i Faith is administered by the National Spiritual Assembly. This body was incorporated by Act of Parliament in 1949. There are approximately 1500 Bahá'i centers in Canada, one-fifth of them electing local Spiritual Assemblies.

GENERAL ORGANIZATION

National Spiritual Assembly Headquarters: 7200 Leslie St., Thornhill, Ontario L3T 2A1. Sec., Mr. J. D. Martin

Baptist Federation of Canada

The Baptist Federation of Canada has four federated member bodies: (1) Baptist Convention of Ontario and Quebec, (2) Baptist Union of Western Canada, (3) the United Baptist Convention of the Atlantic Provinces, (4) Union d'Eglises Baptistes Françaises au Canada (French Baptist Union). Its main purpose is to act as a coordinating agency for the four groups.

Churches: 1,117 Inclusive Membership: 128,391 Sunday or Sabbath Schools: 896 Total Enrollment: 56,305 Ordained Clergy: 1,032

GENERAL ORGANIZATION

Office: 91 Queen St., Box 1298, Brantford, Ontario N3T 5T6. Tel. (519) 752-9114

OFFICERS

Pres., Dr. J. K. Zeman, Acadia Divinity College, Wolfville, Nova Scotia B0P 1X0

Vice-Presidents, Dr. Bruce Neal, Walmer Road Baptist Church, 188 Lowther Ave. at Walmer, Toronto, Ontario M5R 1E8; Mrs. Shirley Bentall, Site 13, Box 14, R.R. #4, Calgary, Alberta T2M 4L4; Rev. Maurice Boillat, c/o French Baptist Union, 3674 Ontario St., East, Montreal, Quebec H1W 1R9

Gen. Sec.-Treas., Dr. R. F. Bullen, Box 1298, Brantford, Ontario N3T 5T6
Gen. Sec., Canadian Baptist Overseas Mission Board, 217 St. George St., Toronto, Ontario M5R 2M2. Rev. R. Berry

1. *Baptist Convention of Ontario and Quebec*
Office: 217 St. George St., Toronto, Ontario M5R 2M2. Tel. (416) 922-5163

Churches: 378 Inclusive Membership: 47,600 Sunday or Sabbath Schools: 350 Total Enrollment: 23,000 Ordained Clergy: 478

NOTE: *The above statistics are a subtotal for the Baptist Federation of Canada whose total statistics are reported initially.*

OFFICERS

Pres., Rev. Albert E. Coe, Rexdale, Ontario
1st Vice-Pres., Mr. W. Laurence Evans, Uxbridge, Ontario
2nd Vice-Pres., Rev. James Taylor, Tilsonburg, Ontario
Gen. Sec., Dr. Ronald F. Watts, 217 St. George St. Toronto, Ontario M5R 2M2
Treas., Mr. Peter Kaups, Toronto, Ontario

DEPARTMENTS

Dept. of Canadian Missions: Chpsn., Mr. James Humphrey, Brockville, Ontario Sec., Rev. A. R. Goldie, Toronto, Ontario
Dept. of Christian Education: Chpsn., Mr. Don Lancaster, Ottawa, Ontario, Sec., Rev. William F. Steeper, Toronto, Ontario
Dept. of Communications: Chpsn., Rev. David U. Houghland, Norwich, Ontario, Sec., Rev. Phil Karpetz, Toronto, Ontario
Dept. of Ministry: Chpsn., Mr. Ian McClung, Queensville, Ontario, Sec., ———

PERIODICAL

The Canadian Baptist, 217 St. George St., Toronto, Ontario M5R 2M2. Rev. Dr. William H. Jones, Islington, Ontario, Ed.

2. *Baptist Union of Western Canada*
Office: Baptist Centre, 4404-16 St., S.W., Calgary, Alberta T2T 4H4

Churches: 153 Inclusive Membership: 19,020 Sunday or Sabbath Schools: 120 Total Enrollment: 11,702 Ordained Clergy: 181
Note: *The above statistics are a subtotal for the Baptist Federation of Canada whose total statistics are reported initially.*

OFFICERS

Pres., Rev. J. W. Dick
Exec. Minister, Dr. Harry A. Renfree
Area Minister, Alberta, Rev. R. M. Steeves, 7516-131A Ave., Edmonton, Alberta T5C 1Z8
Area Minister, British Columbia, Rev. Philip Collins, 8411 Rosebank Cres., Richmond, British Columbia V7A 2K8
Area Minister, Manitoba, Rev. J. Farr, 61 Columbus Cres., Winnipeg, Manitoba R3K 0C5
Area Minister, Saskatchewan, Rev. B. Medgett, No. 4306, 79 Cambridge Ave., Regina, Saskatchewan S4N 5N4

3. *United Baptist Convention of the Atlantic Provinces*
Office: 112 Princess St., Saint John, New Brunswick E2L 1K4, P.O. Box 7053, Sta. A, Saint John, New Brunswick E2L 4S5

Churches: 571 Inclusive Membership: 61,130 Sunday or Sabbath Schools: 426 Total Enrollment: 21,603 Ordained Clergy: 359

Note: *The above statistics are a subtotal for the Baptist Federation of Canada whose total statistics are reported initially.*

OFFICERS

Pres., Rev. Frank E. Locke, 36 Fairview Dr., Truro, Nova Scotia B2N 1S3.
Exec. Min., Rev. Dr. Keith R. Hobson, P.O. Box 7053, Sta. A., Saint John, New Brunswick E2L 4S5
Administrator-Treas., Rev. W. E. O'Grady, P. O. 7053, Sta. A., Saint John, New Brunswick E2L 4S5
Dir. of Evangelism, Rev. Roy D. Campbell, Box 7053, Sta. A., Saint John, New Brunswick E2L 4S5
Dir. of Christian Training, Mrs. Mary Raymond, Box 7053, Sta. A., Saint John, New Brunswick E2L 4S5

PERIODICAL

The Atlantic Baptist, Box 756, Kentville, Nova Scotia B4N 3X9. Rev. George E. Simpson, Ed.

4. *Union of French Baptist Churches in Canada* (Union d'Eglises Baptistes Françaises au Canada)

Headquarters: 3674 rue Ontario est, Montreal, Quebec H1W 1R9. Tel. (514) 526-6643. Gen. Sec., ———

Churches: 15 Inclusive Membership: 641 Sunday or Sabbath Schools: N.R. Total Enrollment: N.R. Ordained Clergy: 14
Note: *The above statistics are a subtotal for the Baptist Federation of Canada whose total statistics are* reported *initially.*

Baptist General Conference

Founded in Canada by missionaries from the United States. Originally a Swedish body, but no longer an ethnic body. The BGC includes people of many nationalities and is conservative and evangelical in doctrine and practice.

Churches: 69 Inclusive Membership: 5,279 Sunday or Sabbath Schools: 69 Total Enrollment 7,345 Ordained Clergy: 87

The Baptist General Conference has three conferences in Canada, all separately incorporated as follows:

1. *The Central Canada Baptist Conference* (Manitoba, Saskatchewan, and part of Ontario)
2. *Baptist General Conference of Alberta*
3. *Columbia Conference* (partly in British Columbia and the remainder in the Northwest U.S.)

1. *The Central Canada Baptist Conference*
The Annual Conference in May
Headquarters: 10 Westmount Bay, W., Winnipeg, Manitoba R2J 1Y8. Tel. (214) 256-6217

OFFICERS

Mod., Rev. Dr. Grant C. Richison 261 Colony St., Winnipeg, Manitoba R3C 1W4
Exec. Sec., Roy A. Campbell, 10 Westmount, Bay, W., Winnipeg, Manitoba R2J 1Y8

PERIODICAL

The Christian Link (m), 50 Gauvin Rd., Winnipeg, Manitoba R2H 1Y3. Walter Lint, Ed.

2. *Baptist General Conference of Alberta*
Annual Conference in June

Headquarters: 5011-122A St., Edmonton, Alberta T6H 3S8. Tel. (403) 435-4974

OFFICERS

Mod., Mr. Wayne Wicks, Box 3126, Sherwood Park, Alberta T8A 2A6
Exec. Sec., Abe Funk, 5011-122A St., Edmonton, Alberta. T6H 3S8

PERIODICAL

The ALbERTa, 5011-122A St., Edmonton, Alberta T6H 3S8 Rev. Abe Funk, Ed.

3. *Columbia Baptist Conference*
Annual Conference in May.
Headquarters: 925 N. 130th St., Seattle, WA 98133 or 7650 Jasper Crescent, Vancouver, British Columbia V5P 3S5

OFFICERS

Mod., Robert Freeman, 29322 11th Place S., Federal Way, WA 98002
Exec. Sec., John H. Bergeson, 925 N. 130th St., Seattle, WA 98133, or 7650 Jasper Crescent, Vancouver, British Columbia V5P 3S5

PERIODICAL

The Conference Call, 925 N. 130th St., Seattle, WA 98133. Rev. John Bergeson, Ed.

Bible Holiness Movement

A missionary and evangelistic movement organized at Vancouver, British Columbia in 1949. It emphasizes the original Methodist faith of salvation and Scriptural holiness with principles of exacting discipleship, nonconformity, and nonresistance. Overseas indigenous missionary centers have been developed.

Churches: 26 Inclusive Membership: 372 Sunday or Sabbath Schools: N.R. Total Enrollment: N.R. Ordained Clergy: 16

International Headquarters: Box 223 Postal Stn. A, Vancouver, British Columbia V6C 2M3. Tel. (604) 683-1833

DIRECTORS

Evangelist Wesley H. Wakefield, Pres. (International Leader)
Evangelist M. J. Wakefield
Evangelist Napoleon Sneed, 155 Windemere, Calgary, Alberta T3C 3K9
Evangelist C. C. Jamandre, Artacho, Sison, Pangasinan, Philippines
Pastor Daniel Stinnett, 1425 Mountain View W. Phoenix, AZ 85021
Mr. G. Egbosimba (pro tempore), Aba, Nigeria
Pastor A. Sanon, Port-au-Prince, Haiti
Evangelist A. Theo Seongbae, Sr. Monrovia, Liberia

PERIODICAL

Truth on Fire (bi-m), Box 223 Postal Stn. A., Vancouver, British Columbia V6C 2M3. Rev. Wesley H. Wakefield, Ed.

Brethren in Christ Church, Canadian Conference

The Brethren in Christ, formerly known as Tunkers in Canada, arose out of a religious awakening in Lancaster County, Pa., late in the eighteenth century. Representatives of the new denomination reached Ontario in 1788 and established the church in the southern part of the present province. Presently the conference has congregations in Ontario, Alberta, and Saskatchewan. In doctrine the body is evangelical, Arminian, holiness, and premillennial.

Headquarters: 301 N. Elm St., Nappanee, IN 46550. Tel. (219) 773-3164. Canadian Headquarters (Bishop's office): Stevensville, Ontario L0S 1S0. Tel. (416) 382-3144

OFFICERS

Mod., Bishop Harvey Sider, Stevensville, Ontario L0S 1S0. Tel. (416) 382-3144
Sec., Leonard J. Chester, 509 Bellview, Ridgeway, Ontario L0S 1N0

PERIODICAL

Evangelical Visitor (bi-w), Nappance, IN 46550. Rev. John E. Zercher, Ed.

British Methodist Episcopal Church

The British Methodist Episcopal Church was organized in 1856 in Toronto, Ontario and incorporated in 1913. It has congregations across the Province of Ontario.

Churches: 13 Inclusive Membership: 2,000 Sunday or Sabbath Schools: N.R. Total Enrollment: N.R. Ordained Clergy:9

GENERAL ORGANIZATION

Annual Conference: Last week in June
Headquarters: 460 Shaw St., Toronto Ontario M6G 2L3. Tel. (416) 534-3831.

OFFICERS

Bishop, A. S. Markham
Gen. Sec., Rev. M. A. Aylestock
Annual Sec., Rev. F. H. Boyce
Treas., Rev. Ronald Blackwood

PERIODICAL

The Apostle (q), Mrs. Jean Markham, Ed.

Buddhist Churches of Canada

Founded at Vancouver, British Columbia in 1904. The first minister was the Rev. Senju Sasaki. This body is the Mahayana division of Buddhism, and its sectarian belief is the Pure Land School based on the Three Canonical Scriptures with emphasis on pure faith.

GENERAL ORGANIZATION

Churches: 15 Inclusive Membership: 2,600 Sunday or Sabbath Schools: 10 Total Enrollment: 330 Ordained Clergy: 10

GENERAL ORGANIZATION

National Conference: Annual.
Headquarters: 918 Bathurst St., Toronto, Ontario M5R 3G5. Tel. (416) 534-4302. Bishop Seimoku Kosaka

OFFICERS

Chpsn., Harry H. Yonekura
Vice Chpsn., ———
Sec., Mr. Roy Sato
Treas., ———
Dirs., Richard Tanaka; Harry Yonekura; Mrs. Terrie Komori; Fukashi Nakatsumi; Bishop Seimoku Kosaka; Dr. Ted Izukawa, Mr. Kunio Suyama

PERIODICAL

Canadian Buddist (m).

The Canadian Baptist Conference

This conference was founded in 1959 at Kamloops, British Columbia by pastors of existing churches. It is associated with the Northwest Baptist Convention of the Southern Baptist Convention with offices at 1033 N.E. 6th Ave., Portland, OR 97232

Headquarters: Contact Cecil Sims, 5300 Rundle Horn Dr., N.E., #505, Calgary, Alberta T1Y 3V5. Tel. (403) 385-5250

OFFICER

Pres., Rev. Jack Conner, Scarborough Baptist Fellowship, Box 1174, Prince Albert, Saskatchewan S6V 5S7. Tel. (306) 764-0720

PERIODICAL

Northwest Baptist Witness (bi-m), 1033 N.E. 6th Ave., Portland, OR 97232. ———.

Canadian Jewish Congress

The Canadian Jewish Congress was founded in 1919 and reorganized in 1934. It is the national representative body of Canadian Jewry having as its functions the protection of the status, rights, and welfare of Canadian Jews; the promotion of understanding and goodwill among ethnic and religious groups, and the combatting of anti-semitism; the improvement, through the establishment of cooperative relationships with other Jewish agencies, of social, economic, and cultural conditions, and the rehabilitation of Jewish refugees and immigrants; the establishment of central community organizations to provide for the social, philanthropic, educational, and cultural needs of Jews.

GENERAL ORGANIZATION

Headquarters: 1590 Ave. Docteur Penfield, Quebec H3G 1C5. Tel. (514) 931-7531

OFFICERS

Natl. Pres., Rabbi W. Gunther Plaut
Exec. Vice-Pres., Alan Rose
Chpsn., National Religious Dept., Moe Seidman; Dir., Rabbi Robert Sternberg

PERIODICALS

Bulletin du Cercle Juif (m), 1590 McGregor Ave., Montreal, Quebec H3G 1C5. Charles Dadoun, Ed.
Congress Bulletin (m), 1590 McGregor Ave., Montreal, Quebec H3G 1C5
Viewpoints Magazine, 1590 Ave. Docteur Penfield Montreal, Quebec, H3G 1C5 Borys Wajsman, Ed.

The Canadian Yearly Meeting of the Religious Society of Friends

Founded in Canada as an offshoot of the Quaker movement in colonial America. Genesee Yearly Meeting, founded 1834, Canada Yearly Meeting (Orthodox), founded in 1867, and Canada Yearly Meeting, founded in 1881, united in 1955 to form the Canadian Yearly Meeting. The Canadian Yearly Meeting is affiliated with the Friends United Meeting and the Friends General Conference.

Churches: 27 Inclusive Membership: 1,075 Sunday or Sabbath Schools: N.R. Total Enrollment: N.R. Ordained Clergy: None.

GENERAL ORGANIZATION

Meeting: annual
Headquarters: 60 Lowther Ave., Toronto, Ontario M5R 1C7. Tel. (416) 922-2632

CLERK

Vivien Abbott, 60 Lowther Ave., Toronto, Ontario M5R 1C7

PERIODICAL

The Canadian Friend, Dorothy Chapman, Ed.

The Christian and Missionary Alliance in Canada

The ministry of the Alliance first began in Canada in 1897 at Peterborough, Ontario. Meetings were held in Ottawa, Toronto, Peterborough, Montreal, and other Canadian cities. The founder, Rev. A. B. Simpson, D.D., was born in Prince Edward Island, educated in Toronto, and served in the Presbyterian ministry, having as his first church, Knox, in Hamilton, Ontario.

The Alliance in Canada is part of the worldwide fellowship of The Christian and Missionary Alliance. It has been chartered by the Federal Government as a corporation for the Canadian affairs of the Society.

Churches: 224 Inclusive Membership: 32,900 Sunday or Sabbath Schools: 213 Total Enrollment: 33,483 Ordained Clergy: 251

BOARD OF DIRECTORS

Pres., Rev. Melvin Sylvester, Box 1030, Waterdown, Ontario L0R 2H0
Vice-Pres., Rev. Roy McIntyre, 1230 A-17th Ave., S.W., Calgary, Alberta T2T 0B8
Sec., Rev. R. J. Gould, 3585 Hillsdale St., Regina, Saskatchewan S4S 3Y4
Treas., M.D. Feather, Box 4048, Regina, Saskatchewan S4P 3R9

Christian Church (Disciples of Christ) in Canada

Disciples have been in Canada since 1810 but were organized nationally in 1922 when the All-Canada Committee was formed. It seeks to serve the Canadian context as part of the whole Christian Church (Disciples of Christ) in the United States and Canada.

Churches: 39 Inclusive Membership: 4,753 Sunday or Sabbath Schools: 39 Total Enrollment: 824 Ordained Clergy: 49

Headquarters: 39 Arkell Rd., Rt. 2, Guelph, Ontario N1H 6H8. Tel. (519) 823-5190

OFFICERS

Moderator, Kenneth MacDougall, RR 1, Waverley, Nova Scotia B0N 2S0
Vice Moderator, Dr. Russell Legge, 259 Lourdes St., Waterloo, Ontario N2L 1P2
Rec. Sec., Rev. F. Thomas Rutherford, 36 Park Ave., St. Thomas, Ontario N5R 4W1
Exec. Min., Rev. Robert K. Leland, 39 Arkell Rd., Rt. 2, Guelph, Ontario N1H 6H8

PERIODICAL

Canadian Disciple (8/yr.), 39 Arkell Rd., Rt. 2, Guelph, Ontario N1H 6H8. Mrs. J. W. Hutcheson, Ed.

Christian Churches and Churches of Christ in Canada

This fellowship, dedicated to the "restoration of the New Testament Church in doctrine, ordinances and life," has been operating in Canada since 1820. There is no general organization. Each church within the fellowship is completely independent. For detailed information see: Directory *of the Ministry,* Christian Churches and Churches of Christ, 1525 Cherry Rd., Springfield, IL 62704, U.S.A.

Churches: 69 Inclusive Membership; 4,871 Sunday or Sabbath Schools: N.R. Total Enrollment: N.R. Ordained Clergy: 110

The Christian Congregation, Inc.

This church was incorporated March 10, 1887 in Indiana. Organizers were a group of independent clergymen who desired a free pulpit in an established denomination. Doctrines are centered around the New Commandment, John 13:34-35. There are no authoritative, sectarian dogmas. Individual search for truth is encouraged. The common denominator is pacifism and opposition to warfare. Churches in Canada are supervised from U.S. Headquarters.

Churches: 26 Inclusive Membership: 2,650 Sunday or Sabbath Schools: 26 Total Enrollment: 1,751 Ordained Clergy: 26

GENERAL ORGANIZATION

Board of Trustees meets annually March 15.
Headquarters: 804 W. Hemlock St., La Follette, TN 37766

OFFICERS

Gen. Supt., Rev. Ora Wilbert Eads, 804 W. Hemlock St., La Follette, TN 37766

Christian Reformed Church in North America

The Christian Reformed Church in North America represents the historic faith of Protestantism and is creedally united in the Belgic Confession (1561), the Heidelberg Catechism (1563), and the Canons of Dort (1618-19). The denomination was founded in the U.S. in 1857. Canadian congregations have been formed since 1908.

Churches: 191 Inclusive Membership: 77,709 Sunday or Sabbath Schools: N.R. Total Enrollment: N.R. Ordained Clergy: 192

GENERAL ORGANIZATION

Headquarters: 2850 Kalamazoo Ave., S.E., Grand Rapids, MI 49560. Tel. (616) 241-1691.
Council of Christian Reformed Churches in Canada: Exec. Sec., Arie G. Van Eek, Box 82D, S.S.I., Waterdown, Ontario L0R 2H0 Tel. (416) 689-5266

Church of God (Anderson, Ind.)

This body is one of the largest of the groups which have taken the name "Church of God." Its headquarters are at Anderson, Indiana. It originated about 1880 and emphasizes Christian unity.

Churches: 46 Inclusive Membership 2,529 Sunday or Sabbath Schools: 44 Total Enrollment: 3,408 Ordained clergy: 44

GENERAL ORGANIZATION

Ontario Assembly: Chpsn., E. Sonnenburg, 1510 Queenston St., Cambridge, Ontario N3H 3L9
Western Canada Assembly: Interim Exec. Sec., Delmar D. Holbrook, 5509 48th Ave., Camrose, Alberta T4V 0J8

PERIODICALS

Ontario Messenger (m), 85 Emmett Ave., #1109, Toronto, Ontario M6M 5A2. Paul Kilburn, Ed.
The Gospel Contact (m), 4703 56th St., Camrose, Alberta T4V 2C4. Richard N. Yamabe, Ed.

Church of God (Cleveland, Tenn.)

This body began in the U.S. in 1886 as the outgrowth of the holiness revival under the name Christian Union, and in 1902 it was reorganized as the Holiness Church. In 1907, the church adopted the name Church of God. Its doctrine is fundamental and Pentecostal, it maintains a centralized form of government and an evangelistic and missionary program.

The first church in Canada was established in 1919 in Scotland Farm, Manitoba. Paul H. Walker became the first overseer of Canada in 1931.

Churches: 55 Inclusive Membership: 2,067 Sunday or Sabbath Schools: 57 Total Enrollment: 3,038 Ordained Clergy: 108

GENERAL ORGANIZATION

General Assembly: biennial (Next Meeting, 1980.)
General Offices: Keith St. at 25th, N.W., Cleveland, TN 37311. Tel. (615) 472-3361
Exec. Office in Canada: Rev. Mark Summers, P.O. Box 2036, Bramalea, Ontario L6T 3S3. Tel. (416) 459-6588; Western Canada: Rev. John S. Bridal, 1630 Albert St., Ste. 7, Regina; Saskatchewan S4P 2S6. Tel. (306) 527-5373

PERIODICAL

Church of God Beacon (m), P.O. Box 2036, Bramalea, Ontario L6T 3S3

The Church of God of Prophecy in Canada

The first Church of God of Prophecy congregation was organized in Swan River, Manitoba in 1937. There are now established churches in British Columbia, Manitoba, Alberta, Saskatchewan, Ontario, and Quebec.

Churches: 26 Inclusive Membership: 1,215 Sunday or Sabbath Schools: 28 Total Enrollment: 1,962 Ordained Clergy: 29

GENERAL ORGANIZATION

National headquarters for the Church of God of Prophecy in Canada is located at 3269 Academy Dr., Windsor, Ontario N9E 2H7. Tel. (519) 969-6768.

General Meetings: annually held in the various Provinces in June and July

OFFICERS

Natl. Overseer, Bishop Elmer E. Van Deventer
First Line East, RR#2 Brampton, Ontario L6V 1A1 Tel. (416) 843-2379

BOARD OF DIRECTORS

Pres., Bishop E. E. Van Deventer
Sec., Bishop A. R. Morrison
Member, Bishop H. L. Martin
Member, Bishop Adrian Varlack
Member, Bishop M. A. Tomlinson

PERIODICALS

Canadian Trumpeter (m), Elmer E. Van Deventer, Ed.
English Coed., John Doroshuk
French Coed., A. Sylvester Smith

The Church of Jesus Christ of Latter-day Saints in Canada

This body has no central headquarters in Canada, only stake and mission offices. One of the Church's General Authorities, Elder Rex D. Pinegar of the First Quorum of the Seventy, residing in Salt Lake City, is Executive administrator with special responsibilities for overseeing the Church's activities in Canada. All General Authorities may be reached at 47 East South Temple St., Salt Lake City, UT 84150. [See U. S. Directory, "Religious Bodies in the United States" in this edition for further details.]

In Canada, there are 23 stakes, 6 missions, 15 districts, 184 branches and 150 wards. Those holding the Priesthood in Canada total 25,000 men and boys. There are no career clergy, only lay clergy.

A listing of "Mission and Stake (Diocese) Officers of Church of Jesus Christ of Latter-day Saints in Canada" may be obtained from Public Communications Department, 50 E. North Temple St., Salt Lake City, UT 84150.

Churches: 269 Inclusive Membership: 74,900 Sunday or Sabbath Schools: 270 Total Enrollment: 70,100 Ordained Clergy: 927

Church of the Foursquare Gospel of Western Canada

The Western Canada District was formed in 1964 with the Rev. Roy Hicks as supervisor. Prior to 1964 it had been a part of the Northwest District of the International Chruch of the Foursquare Gospel with headquarters in Portland, Oregon.

A society, Church of the Foursquare Gospel of Western Canada was formed in 1977.

Churches: 27 Inclusive Membership: 2,025 Sunday or Sabbath Schools: 23 Total Enrollment: 1,794 Ordained Clergy: 75

GENERAL ORGANIZATION

International Convention, Annual.
Headquarters: 7875 Welsley Dr., V5E 3X4

OFFICER

District Supervisor, Victor F. Gardner, 7875 Welsley Dr., V5E 3X4

PERIODICAL

The Canadian Challenge (2/Yr.)

Church of the Lutheran Brethren

Founded in December 1900, organized in convention at Milwaukee, Wis. Lutheran in doctrine.

Churches: 11 Inclusive Membership: 1,430 Sunday or Sabbath Schools: 10 Total Enrollment: 522 Ordained Clergy: 9

GENERAL ORGANIZATION

Convention: annual in June
Headquarters: 1007 Westside Dr., Box 655, Fergus Falls, MN 56537. Tel. (218) 736-5666

Church of the Nazarene

The first Church of the Nazarene in Canada was organized in November, 1902, by Dr. H. F. Reynolds. It was in Oxford, Nova Scotia. The Church of the Nazarene is Wesleyan Arminian in theology, representative in church government, and warmly evangelistic.

Churches: 138 Inclusive Membership: 8,537 Sunday or Sabbath Schools: 136 Total Enrollment: 18,860 Ordained Clergy: 193

GENERAL ORGANIZATION

Executive Board: meets annually in January.

OFFICERS

Pres., Rev. Alexander Ardrey, 2236 Capitol Hill Cres., Calgary, Alberta T2M 4B9
Vice-Pres., Rev. Neil E. Hightower, 1301 Lee Blvd., Winnipeg, Manitoba R3T 2P7
Sec., Rev. Daniel Derksen, 5443 Meadedale Dr., Burnaby, British Columbia V5B 2E6
Treas., Robert Rimington, P. O. Box 3456, Sta. B, Calgary, Alberta T2M 4M1

Conference of Mennonites in Canada

The Conference of Mennonites in Canada began in 1902 as an organized fellowship of Mennonite immigrants from Russia clustered in southern Manitoba and around Rosthern, Saskatchewan. The first annual sessions were held in July, 1903. Its members hold to traditional Christian beliefs, believer's baptism, and congregational polity. They emphasize practical Christianity: opposition to war, service to others, and personal ethics. Further immigration from Russia in the 1920s and 1940s increased the group which is now located in all provinces from Ontario to British Columbia. This conference is affiliated with the General Conference Mennonite Church whose offices are at Newton, Kansas.

Churches: 133 Inclusive Membership: 25,818 Sunday or Sabbath Schools: 133 Total Enrollment: 18,122 Ordained Clergy: 447

GENERAL ORGANIZATION

Conference of Mennonites in Canada meets annually in July.
Headquarters: 600 Shaftesbury Blvd., Winnipeg, Manitoba R3P 0M4. Tel. (204) 888-6781

OFFICERS

Chpsn., David P. Neufeld, 2630 Langdon St., Clearbrook, British Columbia V2T 3L2
Vice Chpsn., Jake Fransen, Smithville, Ontario L0R 2A0
Sec., Helen Rempel, 75 Garnet Bay, Winnipeg, Manitoba R3T 0L4
Gen. Sec., Henry J. Gerbrandt, 600 Shaftesbury Blvd., Winnipeg, Manitoba R3P 0M4

The Coptic Church in Canada

The Coptic Church in Canada was begun in Canada in 1964 and was registered in the Province of Ontario in 1965. The Coptic Church has spread since then to a number of locations in Canada.

The governing body of each local church is an elected Board of Deacons. The Diocesan Council is the national governing body and meets at least once a year.

OFFICER

Prelate, Fr. M. A. Marcos, St. Mark's Coptic Orthodox Church, 41 Glendinning Ave., Agincourt, Ontario M1S 3B2. Tel. (416) 494-4449, (416) 298-3355

The Estonian Evangelical Lutheran Church

The Estonian Evangelical Lutheran Church (EELC) was founded in 1917 in Estonia and reorganized in Sweden in 1944. The teachings of the EELC are based on the Old and New Testaments, explained through the Apostolic, Nicean and Athanasian confessions, the unaltered Confession of Augsburg and other teachings found in the Book of Concord.

GENERAL ORGANIZATION

Executive Board headed by the Archbishop, Consisterium, Auditing Committee and District Conference.
Headquarters: Wallingatan 32, Box 45074, 10430 Stockholm 45, Sweden.

OFFICERS

Bishop in North America, Rev. Karl Raudsepp, Box 291 Jordan Station, Ontario L0R 1S0. Tel. (416) 562-7438.
Assts. to the Bishop: Dr. Arthur Vööbus, 230 So. Euclid Ave., Oak Park, IL 60302. Tel. (312) 386-6274; Dean Oscar Puhm, 84 Dinnick Crescent, Toronto, Ontario M4N 1L8. Tel. (416) 483-4103.

PERIODICAL

Eesti Kirik (m), Mandelblomsgatan 15, S-722 25 Västeras, Sweden. Richard Koolmeister, Ed.

Evangelical Baptist Churches in Canada, The Fellowship of

Formed in 1953 by the merging of the Union of Regular Baptist Churches of Ontario and Quebec with the Fellowship of Independent Baptist Churches of Canada.

Headquarters: 74 Sheppard Ave. W., Willowdale, Ontario M2N 1M3. Tel. (416) 223-8696

OFFICERS

Pres. Mr. J. Edwin Warkentin
Gen. Sec.-Treas., Rev. R. W. Lawson

PERIODICALS

Evangelical Baptist, 74 Sheppard Ave. W., Willowdale, Ontario, Dr. R. W. Lawson, Ed.
Intercom, Rev. R. W. Lawson, Ed.

The Evangelical Church in Canada

Founded early in the 19th century by Jacob Albright and William Otterbein in Pennsylvania as the Evangelical Church, this body became known later as the Evangelical United Brethren Church, which in the U.S. became a part of The United Methodist Church in 1968. This Canadian body is Methodist in organization and Arminian, Wesleyan, and Methodist in doctrine. It was incorporated in 1928 by Dominion Charter as The Northwest Canada Conference Evangelical Church. In 1970, this Canadian Conference was granted autonomy and became a separate denomination.

GENERAL ORGANIZATION

Council of Administration: Meets 2 to 4 times each year. Annual Conference. Quadrennial Conference, next meeting, June, 1982

Headquarters: Evangelical Church Office Bldg., 2805 13th Ave., S.E., Medicine Hat, Alberta T1A 3R1

OFFICERS

Conference Supt., Rev. L. V. Myers, 386—14th St., N.E., Medicine Hat, Alberta T1A 5V8
Conference Chpsn., Rev. A. W. Riegel, 2802 17th Ave. SE, Medicine Hat, Alberta T1A 3V7
Conference Sec., Rev. A. Hein, 4335 2nd St. NW, Calgary, Alberta T2K 0Z2

PERIODICAL

Northwest Canada Echoes (m), 2801—13th Ave., S.E., Medicine Hat, Alberta T1A 3R1. Rev. A. W. Riegel, Ed.

The Evangelical Covenant Church of Canada

A Canadian denomination organized in Canada at Winnipeg in 1904 which is affiliated with the Evangelical Covenant Church of America and with the International Federation of Free Evangelical Churches, which includes churches in eleven European countries.

This body believes in the one triune God as confessed in the Apostles' Creed, that salvation is received through faith in Christ as Saviour, that the Bible is the authoritative guide in all matters of faith and practice. Christian Baptism and the Lord's Supper are accepted as divinely ordained sacraments of the church. As descendants of the 19th century pietistic awakening, the group believes in the need of a personal experience of commitment to Christ, the development of a virtuous life, and the urgency of spreading the gospel to the "ends of the world."

Most of the members of this group came from Northern Europe originally, primarily from Scandinavia.

Churches: 24 Inclusive Membership: 1,127 Sunday or Sabbath Schools: 22 Total Enrollment: 1,803 Ordained Clergy: 22

GENERAL ORGANIZATION

Headquarters: 8501 82nd Ave., Edmonton, Alberta T6C 0Y7. Tel. (403) 466-0462
Mailing Address: 8024 Ranchero Dr., N.W., Calgary, Alberta T3G 1C3
Conference: annual.

OFFICERS

Supt. Rev. Keith C. Fullerton, 8024 Ranchero Dr., N.W., Calgary, Alberta T3G 1C3
Chpsn., Rev. Tom Wilkinson, Rt. 1, Nelson, British Columbia V1L 5P4
Sec., Rev. A. L. Fullerton, Box 424, Norquay, Saskatchewan S0A 2V0
Treas., Paul Benson, 3843 Varsity Dr., N.W., Calgary, Alberta T3A 0Z3

PERIODICAL

The Covenant Messenger (m), 165 Silvermead Cres., N.W., Calgary, Alberta T3B 3W3. Rev. Wesley Morris, Ed.

Evangelical Free Church of Canada

The Canadian branch of the Evangelical Free Church of America which was officially organized as a suitable celebration of the 50th anniversary of our Free Church work in Canada. On March 29th, 1967, the Evangelical Free Church of Canada was voted into being as a vehicle to better facilitate the forward thrust of our Free Church work in Canada as well as our witness around the world.

GENERAL ORGANIZATION

Board of Trustees.
Headquarters: 732—55th Ave., S.W., Calgary, Alberta

T2V 0G3. Mailing Address: Postal Sta. F., Box 8593, Calgary, Alberta T2J 2V6

OFFICERS

Pres., Rev. Ken Lawrence, 15845—96th Ave., Surrey, British Columbia V3R 5W5
Vice Pres., Rev. Vern Beck, Box 655, Bow Island, Alberta T0K 0G0
Sec., Rev. Dan Nicholson, Box 8, Bow Island, Alberta T0K 0G0
Treas., Walter Ehrenholz, 4343—216th St., RR 1, Langley, British Columbia V3A 4P4
Fin. Sec., Mr. Gordon Fryer, 11153-84 B Ave., Delta, British Columbia V4C 7E4

The Evangelical Lutheran Church of Canada

This body was formerly the Canada District of The American Lutheran Church. On January 1, 1967, it became autonomous. The Confessional Statements are identical with those of The American Lutheran Church.

Churches: 317 Inclusive Membership: 82,065 Sunday or Sabbath Schools: 237 Total Enrollment: 16,294 Ordained Clergy: 284

GENERAL ORGANIZATION

Biennial Convention: 1980
Headquarters: 247-1st Ave. N., Saskatoon, Saskatchewan S7K 4H5. Tel. (306) 653-0133

OFFICERS

Pres., Dr. S. T. Jacobson, 247-1st Ave. N., Saskatoon, Saskatchewan S7K 4H5.
Vice-Pres., Dr. Roger W. Nostbakken 114 Seminary Crescent, Saskatoon, Saskatchewan S7N 0X3
Sec., Rev. Irvin H. Holm, 10624 Capilano St., Edmonton, Alberta T6A 3R9

PERIODICAL

The Shepherd (m), 247-1st Ave. N., Saskatoon, Saskatchewan S7K 4H5. Rev. Oscar Sommerfeld, Ed.

Evangelical Mennonite Conference

This body was founded in Southern Russia in 1812. One of the founders was Klaas Reimer.

Churches: 45 Inclusive Membership: 4,680 Sunday or Sabbath Schools: N.R. Total Enrollment: N.R. Ordained Clergy: 180

GENERAL ORGANIZATION

Annual Meeting
Headquarters: Box 1268, 440 Main St., Steinbach, Manitoba R0A 2A0. Tel. (204) 326-6401

OFFICERS

Conf. Mod., Henry Kornelsen, R.R. 1, Box 18, Steinbach, Manitoba R0A 2A0
Bd. of Missions, Exec. Sec., Henry Klassen, Box 1268, Steinbach, Manitoba R0A 2A0
Bd. of Education and Publication, Exec. Sec., Dave K. Schellenberg, Box 1268, Steinbach, Manitoba R0A 2A0

PERIODICALS

The Messenger (bi-w), Box 1268, Steinbach, Manitoba R0A 2A0. Dave K. Schellenberg, Ed.
Familienfreund (bi-w), Box 1268, Steinbach, Manitoba R0A 2A0. A. R. Reimer, Ed.

Evangelical Mennonite Mission Conference

Founded in 1936 as the Rudnerwelder Mennonite Church in Southern Manitoba and organized as the Evangelical Mennonite Mission Conference in 1959. It was incorporated in 1962.

Churches: 17 Inclusive Membership: 1,924 Sunday or Sabbath Schools: 17 Total Enrollment: 1,730 Ordained Clergy: 20

GENERAL ORGANIZATION

Annual Conference meeting in July
Headquarters: Box 126, Winnipeg, Manitoba R3C 2G1. Tel. (204) 775-2774

OFFICERS

Pres., Rev. B. W. Sawatsky, 125 Sterling Ave., Winnipeg, Manitoba R2M 2R8
Vice Pres., Rev. David H. Dyck, Bagot, Manitoba R0H 0E0
Sec., Neil Neufeld, 30 Poplarwood Ave., Winnipeg, Manitoba R2M 1K6 Tel. (204) 253-0359

OTHER ORGANIZATIONS

Missions Dir., Rev. Hildebrand, Box 2128, Winkler, Manitoba R0G 2X0
Radio Dir., Rev. John D. Friesen, 1712 Avenue E North, Saskatoon, Saskatchewan S7L 1V4
Radio Office, The Gospel Message, Box 1622, Saskatoon, Saskatchewan S7K 3R8

PERIODICAL

The Recorder (m), Box 1420, Steinbach, Manitoba. Ben Hoeppner, Ed.

Free Methodist Church in Canada

Organized in 1880 by General Superintendent Benjamin T. Roberts. Methodist in doctrine.

Churches: 125 Inclusive Membership: 5,951 Sunday or Sabbath Schools: 125 Total Enrollment: 11,088 Ordained Clergy: 191

GENERAL ORGANIZATION

Canadian Jurisdictional Conference, or Exec. Bd.: meets annually in early August.
Headquarters: 833-D Upper James St., Hamilton, Ontario L9C 3A3. Tel. (416) 385-1145

OFFICERS

Pres., Bishop Donald N. Bastian, 3 Harrowby Ct., Islington, Ontario M9B 3H3. Tel. (416) 233-6580
Sec., Rev. Claude A. Horton, 833-D Upper James, Hamilton, Ontario L9C 3A3
Treas., Mr. Leslie A. Freeman, 40 Harrisford St., Harris Towers Ste. 901, Hamilton, Ontario L8N 6N1

PERIODICAL

Canadian Free Methodist Herald (m), 4397 Dorchester Rd., Niagara Falls, Ontario L2E 6N5. Alan R. Harley, Ed.

General Church of the New Jerusalem

The Church of the New Jerusalem is founded on the Writings of Emanuel Swedenborg (1688-1772). These were first brought to Ontario in 1835 by Christian Enslin.

GENERAL ORGANIZATION

Canadian National Assembly, Kitchener, Ontario, 1978
Annual Meeting General Church of the New Jerusalem in Canada each fall in Toronto or Kitchener.
Headquarters: 40 Chapel Hill Dr., R.R. 2, Kitchener, Ontario N2G 3W5. Tel. (519) 742-9789.

OFFICERS

Pres., Rt. Rev. L. B. King Bryn Athyn, PA 19009
Exec. Vice-Pres., Rev. Geoffrey S. Childs, 2 Lorraine Gardens, Islington, Ontario M9B 4Z4
Sec., Reinhold J. Kauk, 442 Biehn Dr., Kitchener, Ontario N2G 3W5
Treas., Douglas Raymond, 6 Bannockburn Rd., Kitchener, Ontario N2G 3W5

PERIODICAL

New Church Life (m), Bryn Athyn, PA 19009, Rev. Morley D. Rich, Ed.

The Gospel Missionary Association

Initially organized in 1951 under the chairmanship of Rev. W. J. Laing of the Bethel Baptist Church and a group of clergymen of independent missions and churches; then incorporated by the Province of Alberta in 1956.

The doctrines of this body are: fundamental, premillennial, pre-tribulation rapture, evangelical, and congregational in church government.

Annual Meeting: fourth Wednesday in June

OFFICERS

Pres., Rev. Irvin Krause, 7120 Hunterdale Rd. N.W., Calgary, Alberta T2K 4S1
Sec.-Treas., Rev. A. D. Cornell, Postal Bag 3900, Postal Sta. B, Calgary, Alberta T2M 4N2. Tel. (403) 277-5084

PERIODICAL

Impact

Greek Orthodox Diocese of Toronto

Greek Orthodox Christians in Canada under the jurisdiction of the Ecumenical Patriarchate of Constantinople (Istanbul).

GENERAL ORGANIZATION

Headquarters: 27 Teddington Park Ave, Toronto, Ontario M4N 2C4. Tel. (416) 481-4643

OFFICERS

Primate, The Most Rev. Iakovos. (See U.S. listing.)
The Rt. Rev. Bishop Sotirios of Toronto, 27 Teddington Park Ave., Toronto, Ontario M4N 2C4

†Independent Assemblies of God—Canada

This fellowship of churches has been operating in Canada for over twenty-five years. It is a branch of the Pentecostal Church in Sweden. Each church within the fellowship is completely independent.

GENERAL ORGANIZATION

General Convention, annual
Headquarters: 60 Facer St., St. Catharines, Ontario L2M 5J1. Tel. (416) 685-5392

OFFICER

Sec.-Treas., Rev. Harry Nunn, Sr., 15 Beecher St., St. Catharines, Ontario L2R 5S4. Tel. (416) 685-5392

PERIODICAL

The Mantle (m), 3840 5th Ave., San Diego, CA 92103. Rev. A. W. Rassmussen, Ed.

Independent Holiness Church

The former Holiness Movement of Canada merged with the Free Methodist Church in 1958. Some churches remained independent of this merger and they formed the Independent Holiness Church in 1960, in Kingston, Ontario. The doctrines are Methodist and Wesleyan.

General Conference: every three years, next meeting, 1980

OFFICERS

Pres., Rev. R. E. Votary, Sydenham, Ontario K0H 2T0. Tel. (613) 376-3114
Vice-Pres., Rev. L. A. Copeland, Nipawin, Saskatchewan
Gen. Sec., Mr. Dwayne Reaney, Manotick, Ontario K0A 2N0.

PERIODICAL

Gospel Tidings (m)

The Italian Pentecostal Church of Canada

This body had its beginnings in Hamilton, Ontario, in 1912 when a few people of an Italian Presbyterian Church banded themselves together for prayer and received a Pentecostal experience of the Baptism in the Holy Spirit. Since 1912, there has been a close association with the teachings and practices of the Pentecostal Assemblies of Canada.

From Hamilton the work spread to Toronto, which became a center for all of Southern Ontario. The Church then spread to Montreal, where it also flourished.

In 1959, the Church was incorporated under its present name, in the Province of Quebec, Canada, and authorized by charter and Letters' Patent.

The early leaders of this body were the Rev. Luigi Ippolito and the Rev. Ferdinand Zaffuto. The churches have carried on active missionary work in Italy and among many thousands of immigrants recently arrived in Canada.

GENERAL ORGANIZATION

General Conference, annual, Oct.
Headquarters: 6724 Fabre St., Montreal, Quebec H2G 2Z6. Tel. (514) 721-5614

OFFICERS

Gen. Supt. Rev. Daniel Ippolito, 384 Sunnyside Ave., Toronto, Ontario M6R 2S1. Tel. (416) 766-6692

Gen. Sec., Rev. David Distaulo, P.O. Box 1, Station St. Michel, Montreal, Quebec H2A 3L8 Tel. (514) 729-2644
Gen. Treas., Rev. Rinaldo Remoli, 61 Hatton Dr., Ancaster, Ontario. L9G 2H5. Tel. (416) 648-1219
Overseers, Rev. Alberico DeVito, 7685 Tremblay St., Boussard, Quebec J4W 2W2; Joseph Manafo, 22 Sparrow Ave., Toronto, Ontario M6A 1L4

PERIODICAL

Voce Evangelica (Evangel Voice) (q) Joseph Manafo, Daniel Ippolito, Eds.

Jehovah's Witnesses

For details on Jehovah's Witnesses see the directory in this edition "Religious Bodies in the United States."

There are 1,035 congregations and 61,836 Witnesses actively teaching the Bible in Canada

GENERAL ORGANIZATION

Headquarters: 124 Columbia Heights, Brooklyn, NY 11201. Tel. (212) 625-1240
Canadian Branch Office: 150 Bridgeland Ave., Toronto, Ontario M6A 1Z5

The Latvian Evangelical Lutheran Church in America

This body was organized into a denomination on April 10, 1976, after having existed as the Federation of Latvian Evangelical Lutheran Churches since 1957. This church is a regional constituent part of the Lutheran Church of Latvia in Exile, a member of the Lutheran World Federation and the World Council of Churches.

The Latvian Evangelical Lutheran Church in America works to foster religious life, tradition and customs in its congregations in harmony with the Holy Scriptures, the Apostles', Nicaean, and Athanasian Creeds, the unaltered Augsburg Confession, Martin Luther's Small and Large Catechisms and other documents of the Book of Concord.

The LELCA is ordered by its Synod, executive board, auditing committee, and district conferences.

Churches: 11 Inclusive Membership: 4,275 Sunday or Sabbath Schools: 2 Total Enrollment 72 Ordained Clergy: 17

GENERAL ORGANIZATION

Synod: Meets every three years. Next meeting, 1978
Headquarters: 3438 Rosedale Ave., Montreal, Quebec H4B 2G6. Tel. (514) 489-3224

OFFICERS

Pres., Rev. Arturs Voitkus, 3438 Rosedale Ave., Montreal, Quebec H4B 2G6. Tel. (514) 489-3224
Vice-Pres., Rev. Roberts Abolins, 9405 17th Ave., N.E., Seattle, WA 98115. Tel. (206) 523-0238; Dr. Janis Robins, 11 Ludlow Ave., St. Paul, MN 55108, Tel. (612)646-1980
Sec., Dr. Ernests Reinbergs, 32 Hales Cres., Guelph, Ontario N1G 1P6
Treas., Mr. Alfreds Trautmanis, 103 Rose St., Freeport, NY 11520. Tel. (516) 623-2646

PERIODICAL

Cela Biedrs (10/yr.), Rev. J. V. Strautnieks, Ed., 425 Elm St., Glenview, IL 60025. Tel. (312) 729-1768

Lutheran Church—Canada

Founded April 23, 1959, at Edmonton, Alberta, by the Canadian congregations of the Lutheran Church—Missouri Synod.

Churches: 354 Inclusive Membership: 92,939 Sunday or Sabbath Schools: 273 Total Enrollment: 18,977 Ordained Clergy: 275

GENERAL ORGANIZATION

Biennial Convention. Next meeting, 1979
Headquarters: Tel. (604) 433-4744

OFFICERS

Pres., Rev. Elroy Treit, 3022 E. 49th Ave., Vancouver, British Columbia V5S 1K9
Vice-Pres., Rev. A. Stanfel, 15 Eastwood Dr., Kitchener, Ontario N2A 2A1
Sec., Rev. E. Lehman, #205, 10645 Jasper Ave., Edmonton, Alberta T5J 1Z8
Treas., Mr. Bill Buller, 1225 Pelissier St., Windsor, Ontario N8Y 1M2
Dirs., Rev. Ph. Fry, 1927 Grant Dr., Regina, Saskatchewan S4S 4V6; Mr. Arno Ginther, R.R. 1, Ft. Saskatchewan, Alberta T0B 1P0

Lutheran Church in America—Canada Section

The Lutheran Church in America's three synods in Canada jointly constitute its Canada Section. Where there is a common Canadian concern, it establishes inter-Lutheran, ecumenical and governmental relationships, and engages in social action programs and projects.

Churches: 325 Inclusive Membership: 121,693 Sunday or Sabbath Schools: 302 Total Enrollment: 19,888 Ordained Clergy: 344

OFFICERS

Pres., Rev. G. W. Luetkehoelter, 211—2281 Portage Ave., Winnipeg, Manitoba R3J 0M1 Tel. (204) 889-3760
Sec., Rev. V. Cronmiller, 825 King St., W., Kitchener, Ontario N2G 1E3 Tel. (509) 743-6309
Treas., Walter A. Schultz, 365 Hargrave St., Rm. 500, Winnipeg, Manitoba R3B 2K3. Tel. (204) 942-0096
Exec. Sec., Dr. John M. Zimmerman, 600 Jarvis St., Rm. 206, Toronto, Ontario M4Y 2J6. Tel. (416) 961-8917.

SYNOD PRESIDENTS

Central Canada Synod, Rev. Gottlieb W. Luetkehoelter, 211-2281 Portage Ave., Winnipeg, Manitoba R3J 0M1.
Eastern Canada Synod, Rev. William D. Huras, 509-251 King St. W., Kitchener, Ontario N2G 1B5. Tel. (519) 743-1461.
Western Canada Synod, Rev. Donald Sjoberg, 9901-107 St., Edmonton, Alberta T5K 1G4. Tel. (403) 424-4677

Mennonite Brethren Churches of North America, Canadian Conference of

Incorporated, November 22, 1945

Churches: 131 Inclusive Membership: 20,900 Sunday or Sabbath Schools: 131 Total Enrollment: 18,926 Ordained Clergy: 152

GENERAL ORGANIZATION

Annual Conference: next meeting July, 1978
Headquarters: 9002 Ashwell Rd., Chilliwack, British Columbia V2P 6W4 Tel. (604) 792-1708

OFFICERS

Mod., Rev. P. R. Toews, 145 Henderson Hwy., Winnipeg, Manitoba R2L 1L4
Asst. Mod., David Redekop, 101 Lamont Blvd., Winnipeg, Manitoba R3P 0E7
Sec., Mr. C. J. Rempel, 20 Idlewood Dr., Kitchener, Ontario N2A 1J1

PERIODICAL

Mennonite Brethren Herald (bi-w), 159 Hendenson Hwy., Winnipeg, Manitoba R2L 1L4. Harold Jantz, Ed.

Mennonite Church (Canada)

This body had its origins in Europe in 1525 as an outgrowth of the Anabaptist movement. It was organized in North America in 1898. Canada has been considered Region 1 of the North American Mennonite Church since 1971.

Churches: 113 Inclusive Membership: 9,819 Sunday or Sabbath Schools: 75 Total Enrollment: 9,947 Ordained Clergy: 226

GENERAL ORGANIZATION

Mennonite Church (Canada) consists mainly of three conferences which form Region I of the Mennonite Church with general offices in Lombard, IL. (See listing in the section "Religious Bodies in the U.S." of this edition.) The General Assembly of the Mennonite Church meets biennially. Next meeting is 1979.

OFFICERS

Chpsn., James Mullet, Box 1120, Watrous, Saskatchewan S0K 4T0
Vice-Chpsn. Gerald Schwartzentruber, RR 1, Wellesley, Ontario N0B 2T0
Treas., Amsey Martin, Box 323, Milverton, Ontario N0K 1M0
Exec. Sec., ———

PERIODICAL

Mennonite Reporter (bi-w), Waterloo, Ontario. David Kroeker, Ed.

The Missionary Church of Canada

This body, organized in 1883, was formerly known as the Mennonite Brethren in Christ and changed its name to the United Missionary Church in 1947. In 1969, it merged with the Missionary Church Association and is now called The Missionary Church. It is an Anabaptist body.

GENERAL ORGANIZATION

District Conferences meet annually.

OFFICERS

Canada East District: Dist. Supt., Rev. Grant Sloss, 130 Fergus Ave., Kitchener, Ontario N2A 2H2; Sec., Rev. H. R. Priddle, 120 Rutherford Dr., Kitchener, Ontario N2A 1R1
Canada West District: Dist. Supt., Rev. Norman Reimer 2610 First Ave., N.W., Calgary, Alberta T2N 0C4; Sec., Rev. Willard Swalm, 10 Fremont Close, Red Deer, Alberta T4N 4Y6

Moravian Church in America, Northern Province, Canadian District of the

Note: The work in Canada is under the general oversight and rules of the Moravian Church, Northern Province, general offices for which are located at 69 W. Church St., Bethlehem, PA 18018

Churches: 9 Inclusive Membership: 1,684 Sunday or Sabbath Schools: 8 Total Enrollment: 594 Ordained Clergy: 10

OFFICER

Pres., Rev. John H. Weinlick, 15106 76th Ave., Edmonton, Alberta. Tel. (403) 487-0211

Muslims

There are many thousands of Muslims in Canada, primarily in the larger cities. The Muslim community in Canada is gathered together by Islamic societies and Muslim Mosques. These societies and other organizations are not regarded as religious sects or divisions. Their multiplication arises from the needs of each group in a given area, long distances between groups, and the absence in Islam of organized hierarchy. All the groups hold the same beliefs, aspire to practice the same rituals; namely, prayers, fasting, almsgiving, and pilgrimage to Mecca.

REGIONAL AND NATIONAL GROUPS

A number of regional and national groups exist which were started with the objective of helping local groups, coordinating their work, and promoting closer unity among them.

These include:

The Federation of Islamic Associations in the United States and Canada, 99 Woodview Dr., Old Bridge, NJ 08857 Tel. (201) 679-8617. Pres., Mr. Dawud Assad. Publication: *The Muslim Star,* 17514 Woodward Ave., Detroit, MI 48203
The Muslim Students Association of the United States and Canada, P. O. Box 38, Plainfield, Indianapolis, IN 46168. Tel. (317) 839-8157. Publications: *The Islamic Horizons* (m); *Al-Ittihad* (q)
Council of Muslim Communities of Canada, 100 Gloucester, Ste. 600, Ottawa, K2P 0A4, Tel. (613) 238-6657. Sec. Gen., Mr. Qasim Mahmoud. Publication: *Islam Canada,* P. O. Box 771, Sta. B. Willowdale, Ontario M2K 2R1. Tel. (416) 444-8697

North American Baptist Conference

These churches emanated from German Baptist immigrants of more than a century ago. A limited number are still bilingual in their ministry. Although scattered on the North American continent, they are bound together by a common heritage, a strong spiritual unity, a Bible-centered faith, and a deep interest in missions.

Churches: 102 Inclusive Membership: 14,742 Sunday or Sabbath Schools: 102 Total Enrollment: 9,018 Ordained Clergy: 144

Note: The details of general organization, officers, and periodicals of this body will be found in the North

American Baptist conference directory in the United States directory. The office at 1 S. 210 Summit Ave., Oakbrook Terrace, IL 60181, serves the Canadian churches.

The Old Catholic Church of Canada

Founded in 1948 in Hamilton, Ontario. The first bishop was the Rt. Rev. Georges Davis. The Old Catholic Church of Canada accepts all the doctrines of the Eastern Orthodox Churches and, therefore, not Papal Infallibility or the Immaculate Conception. The ritual is Western (Latin Rite) and is in the vernacular. Celibacy is optional. The Old Catholic Church of Canada is affiliated with the North American Old Roman Catholic Church, whose Presiding Bishop is Most Rev. John E. Schweikert of Chicago (see U.S. directory).

GENERAL ORGANIZATION

Headquarters: 216 Tragina Ave., N., Hamilton, Ontario L8H 5E1 Tel. (416) 544-9198

OFFICERS

Bishop, Rt. Rev. Robert Ritchie, 216 Tragina Ave., N., Hamilton, Ontario L8H 5E1

Sec., Mrs. Mary R. Darlington, 32 Wexford St., N. Hamilton, Ontario

Treas., Allan Hall, 4 Beaucourt Rd., Hamilton, Ontario L8S 2P9

Old Order Amish Church

This is the most conservative branch of the Mennonite Church and direct descendants of Swiss Brethren (Anabaptists) who emerged from the Reformation in Switzerland in 1525. The Amish, followers of Bishop Jacob Ammann, became a distinct group in 1693. They began migrating to America about 1720 where 95 percent of them still reside. They first migrated to Ontario in 1824 directly from Bavaria, Germany and also from Pennsylvania and Alsace-Lorraine.

In 1979, there were 14 congregations in Ontario, each being autonomous. No membership figures are kept by this group but membership has been estimated at 700. Being congregational in structure, there is no central headquarters. Each congregation is served by a bishop, two ministers, and a deacon, all of whom are chosen by lot for life.

CORRESPONDENT

Mr. David Luthy, Pathway Publishers, Rte. 4, Aylmer, Ontario, N5H 2R3

PERIODICALS

Blackboard Bulletin; The Budget; The Diary; Die Botschaft; Family Life; Herold der Wahrhiet; Young Companion

The Pentecostal Assemblies of Canada

Incorporated under the laws of the Dominion of Canada in 1919.

Churches: 868 Inclusive Membership: 200,000 Sunday or Sabbath Schools: 579 Total Enrollment: 131,344 Ordained Clergy: 997

OFFICERS

Gen. Supt., Rev. Robert W. Taitinger

Gen. Sec., Rev. Charles Yates

Gen. Treas., Rev. A. Graydon Richards

Exec. Dir. Overseas Missions, Rev. C. W. Lynn

Exec. Dir. Christian Education and Youth Departments, Rev. S. D. Feltmate

Exec. Dir. Home Missions and Bible Colleges, Rev. R. M. Argue

Dir. Women's Missionary Council, Mrs. Elma Scratch

Man. Full Gospel Publishing House, Mr. Victor T. Smalridge

Man. Testimony Press, Harry Anderson

DISTRICT SUPERINTENDENTS

British Columbia, Rev. J. M. House, 339 E. Carisbrooke Rd., North Vancouver, British Columbia V7N 1N4

Alberta, Rev. I. A. Roset, 11617-106 Ave., Edmonton, Alberta, T5H 0S1

Saskatchewan, Rev. J. C. Tyler, 1219 Idylwyld Ave., Saskatoon, Saskatchewan S7L 1A1

Manitoba, Rev. W. G. Reinheimer, 3081 Ness Ave., Winnipeg, Manitoba R2Y 2G3

Western Ontario, Rev. H. J. Cantelon, 3419 Mainway, Burlington, Ontario L7M 1A9

Eastern Ontario and Quebec, Rev. Gordon R. Upton, Box 1600, Belleville, Ontario K8N 5J3

Maritime Provinces, Rev. A. Donald Moore, Box 1184, Truro, Nova Scotia B2N 5H1

CONFERENCES

German Conference, Rev. Gustav Kurtz, 5 Manitou Dr., Kitchener, Ontario N2D 2J6

French Conference, Rev. André Gagnon, 1705 Henri-Bourassa E., Montreal, Quebec H2C 1J5

Slavic Conferences: Eastern District, Rev. Walter Senko, R.R. 1, Wilsonville, Ontario N0E 1Z0; Western District, Rev. Peter Kerychuk, 7104—39th Ave., Edmonton, Alberta T6K 0R5

Finnish Conference, Rev. A. Wirkkala, Box 27 Naselle, WA 98638

PERIODICAL

The Pentecostal Testimony, 10 Overlea Blvd., Toronto, Ontario M4H 1A5. Miss Joy Hansell, Ed.

Pentecostal Assemblies of Newfoundland

This body began in 1910 and held its first assembly at the Bethesda Pentecostal Mission at St. John's. It was incorporated in 1925 as the Bethesda Pentecostal Assemblies and changed its name in 1930 to the Pentecostal Assemblies of Newfoundland.

Churches: 152 Inclusive Membership: 30,000 Sunday or Sabbath Schools: 152 Total Enrollment: 16,500 Ordained Clergy: 165

GENERAL ORGANIZATION

Headquarters: 57 Thorburn Rd., St. John's, Newfoundland A1B 3M2. Tel. (709) 753-6314

General Conference: Bi-Annual, Next meeting, June, 1980

OFFICERS

Pres. and Gen. Supt., A. Stanley Bursey, 10 Cornwall Hgts., St. John's Newfoundland A1E 3G7

Asst. Gen. Supt. and Treas., Roy D. King, 10 Symonds Ave., St. John's, Newfoundland A1E 3A2

Gen. Sec., A. E. Batstone, 39 Weymouth St., St. John's, Newfoundland A1B 2B7

Youth and S.S. Dir., R. H. Dewling, 26 Wicklow St., St. John's, Newfoundland A1B 3H2

PENTECOSTAL HOLINESS CHURCH OF CANADA

PERIODICAL

Good Tidings (bi-m), 57 Thorburn Rd., St. John's Newfoundland A1B 3M2, A. Stanley Bursey, Ed.

Pentecostal Holiness Church of Canada

The first General Conference convened in May, 1971 in Toronto. Prior to this, the Canadian churches were under the leadership of the Pentecostal Holiness Church in the U.S.A.

GENERAL ORGANIZATION

General Conference every four years. Next meeting, 1982
Headquarters: 139 Winding Way, Kitchener, Ontario Tel. (519) 745-3941

OFFICERS

Gen. Supt., G. H. Nunn, 139 Winding Way, Kitchener, Ontario N2N 1N3
Asst. Supt., F. P. Thomson, 22 York Mills Rd., Willowdale, Ontario; G. A. McDonald, 3414 Douglas Rd., Burnaby, British Columbia; Rev. E. A. Gagnon, Summerville, Hants County, Nova Scotia B2N 4M4
Sec.-Treas., W. B. Gamble, 127 Huntford Close, N.E., Calgary T2K 3Y7

PERIODICAL

Impact (bi-m), P. O. Box 584, Calidonia, Ontario N0A 1A0. Rev. Jack Chamberlin, Ed.

Plymouth Brethren

(Also known as Christian Brethren)

An orthodox and evangelical movement which began in the British Isles in the 1820's and is now worldwide. The name "Plymouth Brethren" was given by others because the group in Plymouth, England was a large congregation. Congregations in Canada and the U.S. are usually called "assemblies." Plymouth Brethren are known as Christian Brethren in Quebec.

The congregations observe the Lord's Supper as a separate meeting each Sunday and do not view their full-time ministers as being a separate clerical order, but rather consider every believer a "priest." Much ministry is given by qualified men of spiritual gift, secularly employed.

In the 1840's the movement divided. The "exclusive" branch, which is now smaller, stresses the interdependence of congregations. It has subdivided and has had reunions. There are now five groups in Canada with around 50 congregations in all.

By contrast, the "Open" branch stresses the independence of congregations, each assembly being guided by local elders. The "Open" branch has a large foreign missions effort and is cooperative with other evangelicals. Statistics below are for the "Open" branch."

GENERAL ORGANIZATION

Christian Brethren Church of Quebec, Box 420, Lennoxville, Quebec J1M 1Z6. Arnold J. M. Reynolds, Sec.

OTHER ORGANIZATIONS

Missionary Service Committee, 1562A Danforth, Toronto, Ontario M4J 1N4
Stewards Foundation (0), Box 181, Don Mills, Ontario M3C 2S2.
Letters of Interest (0), Box 181, Don Mills, Ontario M3C 2S2

PUBLISHERS

Interest Magazine (m), Box 294, Wheaton, IL 60187, James A. Stahr, Ed.
Publications Chretiennes, 230 Lupien, Cap de la Madeleine, Quebec G8T 6W4
Everyday Publications, 230 Glebemount, Ave., Toronto, Ontario M4C 3T4
Focus, Box 353, Etobicoke, Ontario M9C 4V3, W. Ross Rainey, Ed.

†Polish National Catholic Church of Canada

This Diocese was created at the XII General Synod of the Polish National Catholic Church of America in October, 1967. Formerly, the Canadian parishes were a part of the Western Diocese and Buffalo-Pittsburgh Diocese of the Polish National Catholic Church in America.

GENERAL ORGANIZATION

Headquarters: St. John's Cathedral, 186 Cowan Ave., Toronto, Ontario M6K 2N6

OFFICER

The Rt. Rev. Joseph Nieminski, Bishop of the Canadian Diocese, 186 Cowan Ave., Toronto, Ontario M6K 2N6. Tel. (416) 532-8249

The Presbyterian Church in Canada

The nonconcurring portion of the Presbyterian Church in Canada that did not become a part of The United Church of Canada in 1925.

Offices: 50 Wynford Dr., Don Mills, Ontario M3C 1J7. Tel. (416) 441-1111

OFFICERS

Mod., Dr. K. G. McMillan
Clerks of Assembly: Dr. L. H. Fowler, Principal Clerk, Emeritus; Rev. D. C. MacDonald, Principal Clerk; Rev. E. H. Bean; Rev. D. B. Lowry
Treas., Russell Merifield, Q.C.
Compt., Mr. Norman Creen

NATIONAL BOARDS

Board of World Mission: Sec., Rev. George Malcolm; Sec. for Research, Planning and Finance, Rev. C. R. Talbot; Sec. for Mission Education, Rev. H. Glen Davis; Sec. for Field Operations—Canada Mission Fields, Dr. A. F. MacSween; Sec. for Field Operations—Mission Personnel & Overseas Scholarships, Miss M. E. Whale; Sec. for Field Operations—Canada Special Ministries, Miss G. G. Kelly; Sec. for Field Operations—Overseas Program, Rev. E. F. Roberts; Consultant in Church & University, Rev. A. G. MacDougall; Sec. of Church Extension, Rev. J. C. Elder
Board of Congregational Life: Gen. Sec., Rev. W. L. Young; Assoc. Sec's., Resources Dev., Rev. David Murphy, Rev. John Duncan; Leadership Dev., Miss H. Tetley, Rev. (Miss) M. MacNaughton, Mr. Hamish Livingston, Support Services, Rev. B. P. Loper

Communication Services: Consultant, Mr. Donald Stephens
Board of Ministry: Sec. Rev. J. C. Cooper
Presbyterian Church Building Corporation: Dir., Dr. R. G. Mac Millan
Women's Missionary Society (WD): Pres., Miss Isabella T. Hunter, Toronto, Ontario
Women's Missionary Society (ED): Pres., Mrs. A. J. Murchison, Charlottetown, Prince Edward Island

PERIODICAL

The Presbyterian Record (m), Rev. James Ross Dickey, Ed.

Primitive Baptist Conference of New Brunswick

Started in 1874-75 by Rev. George Orser at Carlisle, New Brunswick. He broke away from the Baptists of his day over a number of concerns. The body is evangelical and Arminian. There are about 15 active churches. Recently it has opened up discussions for fellowship with the Freewill Baptist Assn. in the U.S.

GENERAL ORGANIZATION

Annual Conference meets in early July at Hartland, New Brunswick

OFFICER

Conference Chpsn., Rev. Fred Hanson, Box 355, Hartland, New Brunswick

PERIODICAL

The Gospel Standard, Box 355, Hartland, New Brunswick E0J 1N0. Rev. Philip Giberson, Bath, New Brunswick, E0J 1E0, Ed.

Reformed Church in America

The Canadian branch of the Reformed Church in America consists of 28 Churches organized under the Council of the Reformed Church in Canada and within the Classes of Ontario (19 churches), Cascades (7 churches), Lake Erie (1 church) and Montgomery (1 church). The Reformed Church in America was established in 1628 by the earliest Dutch settlers in America as the Reformed Protestant Dutch Church. It is evangelical in theology and Presbyterian in government.

Churches: 19 Inclusive Membership: 5,541 Sunday or Sabbath Schools: 19 Total Enrollment: 1,252 Ordained clergy: 23

GENERAL ORGANIZATION

Gen. Sec., Rev. Arie R. Brouwer, 475 Riverside Dr., New York, NY 10027
Council of the Reformed Church in Canada; Pres., Mr. Peter Greene,
Sec., Siebrand Wilts, 201 Paradise Rd. N., Hamilton, Ontario L8S 3T3

PERIODICAL

Pioneer Christian Monthly (m), 201 Paradise Rd. N., Hamilton, Ontario L8S 3T3 Tel. (416) 427-0998

Reformed Doukhobors, Christian Community and Brotherhood of (Formerly known as Sons of Freedom Doukhobors)

Doukhobors were founded in the late 17th century in Russia. Their doctrine is the "Living Book," which is based on traditional songs and chants and on contents of the Bible. The Living Book is memorized by each generation.

Churches: 1 Inclusive Membership: 3,075 Sunday or Sabbath Schools: 1 Total Enrollment: 308 Ordained Clergy: 1

GENERAL ORGANIZATION

Headquarters: Site 8, Comp. 50, R.R. 1, Crescent Valley, British Columbia V0G 1H0

OFFICERS

Pastor, Stephan S. Sorokin (assisted by a 30-member Executive Committee)

The Reformed Episcopal Church

OFFICERS

Bishop, Rev. W. W. Lyle, 211 Osborne Ave., New Westminster, British Columbia V3L 1Y7
Vice Pres., Laurence Jackson, 600 Foul Bay Rd., Victoria, British Columbia V8S 4H3
Sec., W. J. Calhoun, 626 Cumberland St., New Westminster, British Columbia V3L 3G8. Tel. (604) 521-2475
Treas., George Fetherstonhaugh, 6437 Cottonwood La., R. R. 7, Langley, British Columbia V3A 4B0

Reformed Presbyterian Church Evangelical Synod

This body was founded as a presbytery in Canada in 1832 and reconstituted in 1950. The RPC believes the Bible to be the Word of God and therefore requires that all officers be men who accept the written Scriptures as the Word of God, inerrant and infallible. Doctrines of the church are derived from the Bible, the catholic creeds, and the Westminster Confession of Faith. Congregations are located in eight cities from Vancouver to Sydney.

Note: This body is related to the Reformed Presbyterian Church, Evangelical Synod with headquarters in the United States located at the Office of the Stated Clerk, 107 Hardy Rd., Lookout Mountain, TN 37350.

CORRESPONDENT

Rev. William D. McColley, 3116 49th St., SW, Calgary, Alberta T3E 3Y3.

Reinland Mennonite Church

This group was founded in 1958 when ten ministers and approximately 600 members separated from the Sommerfelder Mennonite Church. In 1968, four ministers and about 200 members migrated to Bolivia.

Churches: 7 Inclusive Membership: 780 Sunday or Sabbath Schools: 5 Total Enrollment: 216 Ordained Clergy: 13

CORRESPONDENT

Bishop Peter A. Rempel, R. R. 1, Box 434, Winkler, Manitoba R0G 2X0. Tel. (204) 325-4596.

Reorganized Church of Jesus Christ of Latter Day Saints

Founded April 6, 1830, by Joseph Smith, Jr., and reorganized under the leadership of the founder's son, Joseph Smith III, in 1860. The Church is established in 35 countries in addition to the United States and Canada. A biennial world conference is held in Independence, Mo. The current president is Wallace B. Smith, greatgrandson of the original founder.

Churches: 86 Inclusive Membership: 10,152 Sunday or Sabbath Schools: N.R. Total Enrollment: N.R. Ordained Clergy: 988

Headquarters: World Headquarters, The Auditorium, Independence, Mo.; Canadian Office, 390 Speedvale Ave., E., Guelph, Ontario N1E 1N5

CHURCH OFFICERS IN CANADA

Region Pres., D. Franklin Silverthorn, 390 Speedvale Ave., E., Guelph, Ontario N1E 1N5
Region Bishop, Kenneth G. Fisher, 390 Speedvale Ave., E. Guelph, Ontario N1E 1N5
District Presidents:
Alberta, G. Ivan Miller, 2206 14th Ave., S. Lethbridge, Alberta T1K 0V5
British Columbia, James W. Hodgson, 10615-142 A St., Surrey, British Columbia V3T 5A1
Chatham, Ontario, Allen M. Badder, R. R. No. 1, Thamesville, Ontario N0P 2K0
London, Ontario, Stephen A. Koehler, 303 Commissioner Rd. W., London, Ontario N6K 1Y4
Niagara Falls, Ontario, Victor H. Byrnes, 26 Holborn St., Brantford, Ontario N3R 2B8
Northern Ontario, Clair F. Shepherdson, Box 525, New Liskeard, Ontario P0J 1P0
Ottawa, Ontario, Wilbert L. Canniff, 1 Cedarcrest Dr., Ottawa, Ontario K2E 5P7
Owen Sound, Ontario, Alma J. V. Leeder, P.O. Box 192, Wiarton, Ontario N0H 2T0
Saskatchewan, Frank W. Ward, 411 Preston Ave., Saskatoon, Saskatchewan S7H 2V1
Toronto, Ontario, Bryce Taylor, 260 Seneca Hill Dr., Apt. 605, Willowdale, Ontario M2J 4S6

The Roman Catholic Church in Canada

The largest single body of Christians in Canada, the Roman Catholic Church is under the spiritual leadership of His Holiness the Pope. Catholicism in Canada dates back to 1534, when the first Mass was celebrated on the Gaspé Peninsula, on July 7, by a priest accompanying Jacques Cartier. There seems little doubt that Catholicism had been implanted earlier by fishermen and sailors from Europe. Priests came to Acadia as early as 1604. Traces of a regular colony go back to 1608 when Champlain settled in Quebec. The Recollets (1615), followed by the Jesuits (1625) and the Sulpicians (1657), began the missions among the Indians. The first official Roman document relative to the Canadian missions dates from March 20, 1618. Bishop Francois de Montmorency-Laval, the first Bishop, arrived in Quebec in 1659. The Church developed in the East but not until 1818 did systematic missionary work begin in Western Canada.

INTERNATIONAL ORGANIZATION

His Holiness the Pope, Bishop of Rome, Vicar of Jesus Christ, Supreme Pontiff of the Catholic Church.
POPE JOHN PAUL II, Karol Wojtyla (born May 18, 1920; installed October 22, 1978)
APOSTOLIC PRO NUNCIO TO CANADA Archbishop Angelo Palmas, 724 Manor Ave., Ottawa, Ontario K1M 0E3. Tel. (613) 746-4914

Churches: 5,880 Inclusive Membership: 10,082,341 Sunday or Sabbath Schools: N.R. Total Enrollment: N.R. Ordained Clergy: 13,374

CANADIAN ORGANIZATION

Canadian Conference of Catholic Bishops (Conferénce des évêques catholiques du Canada) 90 Parent Ave. Ottawa, Ontario, K1N 7B1. Tel. (613) 236-9461. (All offices below are at this address and telephone number unless otherwise stated.)

The Canadian Conference of Catholic Bishops is an Association of Cardinals, Archbishops, and Bishops of Canada established to assure the progress of the Church and the Coordination of Catholic activities in Canada.

OFFICERS

General Secretariat of the Episcopacy
Secrétaire général (French Sector) ———
General Secretary (English Sector) Rev. Dennis J. Murphy
Assistant General Secretary (English Sector), ———
Secrétaire général adjoint (French Sector), ———

EXECUTIVE COMMITTEE

Pres., S. E. Mgr. Gilles Ouellet
Vice Pres., Archbishop Joseph MacNeil
General Treasurer: Mgr. Adolphe Proulx

EPISCOPAL TEAM

1. Department of Theology, Liturgy, and Canon Law (Theology, Liturgy, Canon Law), Most Rev. Adam Exner
2. Department for Christian Education (Christian Education), Most Rev. A. L. Penney
3. Department of Internal Relations (Laity, Clergy-Seminaries/Vocations, Religious, Inter-Rite), S. E. Mgr. Henri Legaré
4. Department for Mission (Missions, Ecumenism, Non-Believers, S. E. Mgr. Gérard Dionne
5. Department for Social Life (Social Affairs-Action/Welfare, Family), Most Rev. John M. Sherlock
6. Department for Social Communications and Extraordinary Affairs (Social Communications, Migration and Tourism), Mgr. Robert Lebel

OFFICES

Secteur Francais
Office des Missions, Dir., Abbé H. Laurin
Office des Communications Sociales, Dir., Abbé Lucien Labelle, 4635 de Lorimier, Montreal, Québec. H2H 2B4 Tel. (514) 526-9165
Office National de liturgie, coordonnateur: M. Jean-Bernard Allard, p.s.s., 1225 est, boul. St. Joseph, Montréal, Québec H2J 1L7. Tel. (514) 277-2133
Office pour le Dialogue avec les Non-Croyants, Dir., Père Paul Morisset, 2930 Lacombe, Montréal, Québec H3T 1L4. Tel. (514) 735-1565
Office National d'Ocumenisme, Père Irenée Beaubien,

2065 ouest rue Sherbrooke, Montréal, Québec H3H 1G6. Tel. (514) 937-9176
Services des Relacions Publiques, Dir., M. Jacques Binet
Service des Editions, Dir., Mlle Claire Dubé.

English Sector

National Liturgical Office, Dir., Rev. David Walsh; Rev. P. Bryne
National Office of Religious Education, Director, Rev. Peter A. Sanders
Office for Missions, Dir., Abbé H. Laurin
Public Information Office, Dir., Miss Bonnie Brennan
Social Affairs, Dir., Mr. Tony Clarke

REGIONAL EPISCOPAL ASSEMBLIES

Atlantic Episcopal Assembly, Pres., Most Rev. F. J. Spence; Sec., Msgr. Augustin-E. Burke. Secretariat: 53 Park St., C.P. 278, Yarmouth, Nova Scotia B5A 4B2. Tel. (902) 742-7163

Assemblée des Évêques du Quebec, Prés., Monsieur le Cardinal Maurice Roy; Secrétaire, M. l'abbé Raynald Brillant, Secrétariat: 1225, boulevard Saint Joseph est, Montréal, Québec H2J 1L7. Tél. (514) 272-1179

Ontario Conference of Catholic Bishops, Pres., Most Rev. Alexander Carter; Sec., Rev. Angus J. MacDougall, S.J. Secretariat: 67 Bond St., Ste. 304, Toronto, Ontario M5B 1X5. Tel. (416) 368-5298

Western Catholic Conference, Pres., Msgr. Henri Légaré, O.M.I., Sec., Most. Rev. Adam Exner, O.M.I. Secretariat: P. O. Box 388, McLennan, Alberta T0H 2L0. Tel. (403) 324-3002

MILITARY VICARIATE (VICARIAT MILITAIRE)

Vicaire aux Forces canadiennes (Military Vicar), M. le Cardinal Maurice Roy, 2 rue Port Dauphin, C.P. 459, Québec, Québec G1R 4R6. Tél. (418) 692-3935

ARCHDIOCESES AND DIOCESES

The Roman Catholic Church in Canada has 17 Archdioceses, 46 Dioceses, 4 Ukrainian Eparchies and 1 Abbacy. Each of these ecclesiastical jurisdictions appears alphabetically in the following list and contains this information in sequence: Name of incumbent bishop, address of Chancery office (Evêché) or other headquarters, and telephone number.

Cardinals are addressed as "His Eminence" (in French as "Son Eminence") and Archbishops and Bishops as "Most Reverend" (in French as "Son Excellence").

Alexandria-Cornwall, Mgr. Eugène P. LaRocque. Evêché, C. P. 1388 Cornwall, Ontario K6H 5V4. Tel. (613) 933-1138

Amos, Mgr. Gérard Drainville, Evêché, 450, Principale Nord, Amos, Québec J9T 2M1. Tel. (819) 732-6515

Antigonish, Bishop William E. Power. Chancery Office, P.O. Box 1330, Antigonish, Nova Scotia B2G 2L7. Tel. (902) 863-4818

Bathurst, Mgr. Edgar Godin, Evèché, 645, avenue Murray, C.P. 460, Bathurst, New Brunswick E2A 3Z4. Tel. (506) 546-3484

Calgary, Bishop Paul J. O'Byrne. Chancery, P.O. Box 4130 Sta. "C" Calgary, Alberta. T2T 5M9. Tel. (403) 263-3371

Charlottetown, Bishop F. J. Spence, Chancery Office, P.O. Box 907, Charlottetown, Prince Edward Island C1A 7L9. Tel. (902) 892-1357

Chicoutimi, Mgr. Jean-Guy Couture. Evêché: 602 est, rue Racine, C.P. 278, Chicoutimi, Québec G7H 5C3. Tel. (418) 543-0783

Churchill-Baie D'Hudson. Mgr. Omer Robidoux. Evêché, C.P. 10, Churchill, Manitoba, R0B 0E0. Tel. (204) 675-2252

Archdiocese of Edmonton, Archbishop Joseph N. MacNeil. Archdiocesan Office. 10044-113th St. Edmonton, Alberta T5K 1N8 Tel. (403) 488-0118

Eparchy of Edmonton, Bishop Neil N. Savaryn. Bishop's Residence, 6240 Ada Blvd., Edmonton, Alberta T5W 4P1. Tel. (403) 479-0381

Edmundston, Mgr. Fernand Lacroix, Evêché, Centre diocésain, Edmundston, New Brunswick E3V 3K1. Tel. (506) 735-5578

Gaspé, Mgr. Bertrand Blanchet. Evêché, C. P. 440 Gaspé, Québec G0C 1R0. Tel. (418) 368-2274

Grand Falls, Bishop A. L. Penney. Bishop's Residence, 8A Church Rd., Grand Falls, Newfoundland, A2A 2M4. Tel. (709) 489-2778

Gravelbourg, Mgr. Noel Delaquis, Evêché C.P. 690, Gravelbourg, Saskatchewan S0H 1X0. Tel. (306) 648-2235

Archidiocèse de Grouard-McLennan, Mgr. Henri Légaré, Chancellerie, C.P. 388 McLennan, Alberta T0H 2L0, Tel. (403) 324-3002

Archdiocese of Halifax, Archbishop James M. Hayes. Archbishop's Residence, 6541 Coburg Rd., P.O. Box 1527, Halifax, Nova Scotia B3J 2Y3. Tel. (902) 429-9388

Hamilton, Bishop Paul F. Reding, Chancery Office, 700 King St. W., Hamilton, Ontario L8P 1C7. Tel. (416) 528-7988

Hauterive, Mgr. Roger Ebacher, Evêché, 639 Rue de Bretagne, C.P. 10, Hauterive, Québec G5C 2S8. Tel. (418) 589-5744

Hearst, Mgr. Roger A. Despatie, Evêché, C.P. 1330, Hearst, Ontario P0L 1N0. Tel. (705) 362-4903

Hull, Mgr. Adolphe Proulx, Evêché, 119, rue Carillon, Hull, Québec J8X 2P8. Tel. (819) 771-8391

Joliette, Mgr. René Audet, Evêché, 2, rue St-Charles Borromée, Nord. C.P. 470, Joliette, Québec J6E 6H6. Tel. (514) 753-7596

Kamloops, Bishop Adam Exner. Bishop's Residence, 635A Tranquille Rd., Kamloops, British Columbia V2B 3H5. Tel. (604) 376-2749

Archidiocèse de, Keewatin-LePas, Mgr. Paul Dumouchel. Résidence, 108, 1st St., W., C.P. 270, Le Pas, Manitoba R9A 1K4. Tel. (204) 623-3529

Archdiocese of Kingston, Archbishop J. L. Wilhelm. Archbishop's Residence, 279 Johnson St., Kingston, Ontario K7L 4X8. Tel. (613) 546-5521

Labrador-Schefferville, Mgr. Peter Sutton. O.M.I., Evêché, 303 A.P. Low, C.P. 700 Schefferville, Québec G0G 2T0 Tel. (418) 585-2470

London, Bishop John M. Sherlock. Chancery Office, 1070 Waterloo St., London Ontario N6A 3Y2, Tel. (519) 433-0658

Mackenzie-Fort Smith (T.No.O.), Mgr. Paul Piché. Résidence, B. P. 25, Fort Smith, T.N.O. X0E 0P0. Tel. 872-2537

Archidiocèse de Moncton, Mgr. Donat Chiasson. Archevêché, C.P. 248, Moncton, New Brunswick E1C 8K9. Tel. (506) 389-9531

Mont-Laurier, Mgr. Jean Gratton. Evêché, 435, rue de la Madone, C.P. 1290, Mont Laurier, Québec J9L 1S1. Tel. (819) 623-5530

Archidiocèse, de Montréal, Mgr. Paul Grégoire. Archevêché, 2000 ouest, rue Sherbrooke, Montréal, Québec H3H 1G4. Tel. (514) 931-7311

Moosonee, Mgr. Jules LeGuerrier, Résidence, C.P. 40, Moosonee, Ontario P0L 1Y0. Tel. (705) 336-2908

Abbatia Nullius of Muenster, Abbott Ordinary Jerome Weber, OSB. Abbot's Residence, St. Peter's Abbey, Muenster, Saskatchewan S0K 2Y0. Tel. (306) 682-3373

Nelson, Bishop W. Emmett Doyle. Bishop's Residence, 813 Ward St., Nelson. British Columbia V1L 1T4. Tel. (604) 352-6921

Eparchy of New Westminster, Bishop Jerome J. Chimy. Bishop's Residence, 502 5th Ave., New Westminster, British Columbia V3L 1S2. Tel. (604) 521-8015

Nicolet, Mgr. J. Albertus Martin. Evêché, C.P. 820, Nicolet, Québec J0G 1E0. Tel. (819) 293-4234

Archidiocèse D'Ottawa, Mgr. Joseph-Auréle Plourde.

Archevêché, 256, King Edward, Ottawa, Ontario K1N 7M1 Tel. (613) 237-4540

Pembroke, Bishop J. R. Windle. Bishop's Residence, 188 Renfrew St., P.O. Box 7, Pembroke, Ontario K8A 6X1. Tel. (613) 732-7933

Peterborough, Bishop James L. Doyle. Bishop's Residence, 350 Hunter St. W., Peterborough, Ontario K9J 6Y8. Tel. (705) 745-5123

Prince-Albert, Mgr. Laurent Morin. Evêché, 1415-ouest, 4e Ave., Prince-Albert, Saskatchewan S6V 5H1. Tel. (306) 763-2778.

Prince-George, Bishop Fergus J. O'Grady. Bishop's Residence, College Rd., Prince George, British Columbia V2N 2K6. Tel. (604) 964-4755

Archidiocèse de Québec, Son Eminence le Cardinal Maurice Roy. Archevêché, 2, rue Port Dauphin, C.P. 459, Québec, Québec G1R 4R6. Tel. (418) 692-3935

Archdiocese of Regina, Archbishop Charles A. Halpin, Chancery Office, 3225 13th Ave., Regina, Saskatchewan S4T 1P5. Tel. (306) 523-1651

Archidiocèse de Rimouski, Mgr. Gilles Quellet. Archevêché, 34 ouest, rue de l'evêché, C.P. 730, Rimouski, Québec. G5L 7C7. Tel. (418) 723-3320

Rouyn-Noranda, Mgr. Jean-Guy Hamelin, Evêché, 515, rue Cuddihy, C.P. 1060, Rouyn, Québec J9X 4C5. Tel. (819) 764-4660

Ste-Anne de la, Pocatière, Mgr. Charles-Henri Lévesque. Evêché, C.P. 430 La Pocatière, Québec G0R 1Z0. Tel. (418) 856-1811

Archidiocèse de Saint-Boniface, Mgr. Antoine Hacault. Archevêché, 151, ave de la Cathédrale, St-Boniface Manitoba R2H 0H6. Tel. (204) 247-9851

St. Catharines, Bishop Thomas B. Fulton. Bishop's Residence, 122 Riverdale Ave., St. Catharines, Ontario L2R 4C2. Tel. (416) 684-0154

St. George's, Bishop Richard McGrath. Bishop's Residence, 16 Hammond Dr., Corner Brook, Newfoundland A2H 2W2. Tel. (709) 639-9411

Saint Hyacinthe, Mgr. Louis-de-Gonzaque Langevin. Evêché 1900, Girouard, C. P. 190, Saint-Hyacinthe, Québec J2S 7B4. Tel. (514) 773-8581

Saint-Jean-de-Québec, Mgr. Bernard Hubert. Evêché, 740 boul. Ste-Foy, C.P. 40, Longueuil, Québec J4K 4X8. Tel. (514) 679-1100

Saint-Jérôme, Mgr. Charles Valois, Evêché, 355, rue St-Georges, C.P. 580, Saint-Jérôme, Québec J7Z 5V3. Tel. (514) 432-9741

Saint John, Bishop Arthur Joseph Gilbert, Bishop's Residence, 91 Waterloo St., Saint John, New Brunswick E2L 3P9. Tel. (506) 693-6583

Archdiocese of St. John's, Archbishop Alphonsus Penney, Archbishop's Residence, P.O. Box 37, Basilica Residence, St. John's, Newfoundland A1C 5H5. Tel. (709) 726-3660

Saint-Paul, Mgr. Raymond Roy, Evêché, 4410 51e Ave., C.P. 339, St-Paul, Alberta T0A 3A0. Tel. (403) 645-3277

Saskatoon, Bishop James P. Mahoney. Bishop's Residence, 1036 College St., Saskatoon. Saskatchewan S7N 0W1. Tel. (306) 652-8379

Eparchy of Saskatoon, Bishop Andrew Roborecki. Bishop's Residence, 866 Saskatchewan. Crescent East, Saskatoon, Saskatchewan S7N 0L4. Tel. (306) 653-0138

Sault Ste. Marie, Bishop Alexander Carter Bishop's Residence, 480 McIntyre St., W., P.O. Box 510, North Bay, Ontario, P1B 8J1 Tel. (705) 476-1300

Archidiocèse de Sherbrooke, Mgr. Jean-Marie Fortier, Archevêché, 130, rue de la Cathedrale, C.P. 430, Sherbrooke, Québec J1H 5K1. Tel. (819) 569-6070

Thunder Bay, Bishop John A. O'Mara. Bishop's Residence, P.O. Box 113, Thunder Bay, Ontario PC7 4V5. Tel. (807) 622-4645

Timmins, Mgr. Jacques Landriault. Evêché, 65, avenue Jubilee est, Timmins, Ontario P4N 5W4. Tel. (705) 267-6224

Archdiocese of Toronto, Archbishop G. Emmett Carter, Chancery Office, 55 Gould St., Toronto, Ontario M5B 1G1. Tel. (416) 362-6571

Eparchy of Toronto, Bishop Isidore Borecky. Bishop's Residence, 61 Glen Edyth Dr., Toronto, Ontario M4V 2V8. Tel. (416) 924-2381

Trois-Rivièrés, Mgr. Laurent Noël. Evêché, 362, rue Bonaventure, C.P. 879, Trois-Rivièrès, Québec G9A 5J9. Tel. (819) 374-9847

Valleyfield, Mgr. Robert Lebel. Evêché, 31 rue Fabrique, C.P. 338, Valleyfield, Québec J6T 4G9. Tel. (514) 373-8122

Archdiocese of Vancouver, Archbishop James F. Carney, Chancery Office, 150 Robson St., Vancouver, British Columbia, V6B 2A7. Tel. (604) 683-0281

Victoria, Bishop Remi J. De Roo. Bishop's Residence, 740 View St., Victoria, British-Columbia V8W 1J8. Tel. (604) 384-4951

Whitehorse (Yukon), Bishop Hubert P. O'Connor, O.M.I. Bishop's Residence, 5119 5th Ave., Whitehorse, Yukon Y1A 1L5. Tel. (403) 667-2052

Archdiocese of Winnipeg, Archbishop George Bernard Cardinal Flahiff. Chancery Office 50 Stafford Street, Winnipeg, Manitoba R3M 2V7. Tel. (204) 474-2361

Archeparchy of Winnipeg, Archbishop Maxim Hermaniuk. Archbishop's Residence, 235 Scotia St., Winnipeg, Manitoba R2V 1V7. Tel. (204) 339-7457

Yarmouth, Mgr. Augustin Emile Burke. Evêché, 53, rue Park, Yarmouth, Nova Scotia B5A 4B2. Tel. (902) 742-7163

Romanian Orthodox Church in America (Canadian Parishes)

The first Romanian Orthodox immigrants in Canada called for Orthodox priests from their native country of Romania. Between 1902-1914, they organized the first Romanian parish communities and built Orthodox churches in different cities and farming regions of western Canada (Alberta, Saskatchewan, Manitoba) as well as in the eastern part (Ontario and Quebec).

In 1929, the Romanian Orthodox parishes from Canada joined with those of the U.S. in a Congress held in Detroit, Mich., and asked the Holy Synod of the Romanian Orthodox Church of Romania to establish a Romanian Orthodox Missionary Episcopate in America (which was the legal title of this body). The first Bishop, Policarp (Morushca), was elected and consecrated by the Holy Synod of the Romanian Orthodox Church and came to the U.S. in 1935. He established his headquarters in Detroit with jurisdiction over all the Romanian Orthodox parishes in the U.S. and Canada.

In 1950, the Romanian Orthodox Church in America (i.e. the Romanian Orthodox Missionary Episcopate in America) was granted administrative autonomy by the Holy Synod of the Romanian Orthodox Church of Romania, and only doctrinal and canonical ties remain with this latter body.

The Holy Synod of the Romanian Orthodox Church of Romania, in its session of Dec. 12, 1974, recognized and approved the Decision taken by the Annual Congress of the Romanian Church in America, held on July 21, 1973, at Edmonton-Boian, Alberta, relating to the elevation of the Episcopate to the rank of "Archdiocese" with the official title **The Romanian Orthodox Missionary Archdiocese in America,** renewing at the same time its status of Ecclesiastical Autonomy.

GENERAL ORGANIZATION

Archbishop assisted by his Vicar and the Canadian Diocesan Council. Annual Congress for both U.S. and Canada.

Canadian Office: St. Demetrios Romanian Orthodox Church, 103 Furby St., Winnipeg, Manitoba R3C 2A4. Tel. (204) 775-3701

OFFICERS

Archbishop: Most Rev. Archbishop Victorin, 19959 Riopelle St., Detroit, MI 48203. Tel. (313) 893-7191

Vicar, V. Rev. Archim, Dr. Vasile Vasilachi 19959 Riopelle St., Detroit, MI 48203

Cultural Councilor, V. Rev. Archpriest George Nan, 1480 Cadillac St., Windsor, Ontario N8Y 2V1

Administrative Councilor, V. Rev. Fr. Mircea Panciuk, 11020-165th Ave., Edmonton, Alberta T5X 1X9

Sec., V. Rev. Fr. Gheorghe Chisea, 6340 boul. St. Michel, Montréal, Québec

PERIODICALS

Credinta—The Faith (m), and Calendarul Credinta (Yearbook with the Church Directory of the Archdiocese) (a). 19959 Riopelle St., Detroit, MI 48203. V. Rev. Archim., Dr. Vasile Vasilachi, Ed.

The Romanian Orthodox Episcopate of America (Jackson, Michigan)

Some of the Canadian churches of Romanian origin are under the canonical jurisdiction of the Romanian Orthodox Episcopate of America, of the Orthodox Church in America.

The Episcopate, chartered in 1929, is headed by the Most Reverend Archbishop Valerian (D. Trifa).

Churches: 13 Inclusive Membership: 8,000 Sunday or Sabbath Schools: 10 Total Enrollment: 535 Ordained Clergy: 9

GENERAL ORGANIZATION

Church Congress, held annually in July

OFFICERS

Vicar to the Bishop: The Very Rev. Archim. Martinian Ivanovici, 421 Victoria Ave., Regina, Saskatchewan S4N 0P7. Tel. (306) 523-3501

PERIODICAL

Solia, Romanian News (m), 11341 Woodward Ave., Detroit, MI 48202

Russian Orthodox Church in Canada, Patriarchal Parishes of the

Diocese of Canada of the former Exarchate of North and South America of the Russian Orthodox Church. Originally founded in 1897 by the Russian Orthodox Archdiocese in North America.

Churches: 24 Inclusive Membership: 4,000 Sunday or Sabbath Schools: 3. Total Enrollment: 56. Ordained Clergy: 7

GENERAL ORGANIZATION

General Conference: Meets annually at call from Bishop, St. Barbara's Russian Orthodox Cathedral, 10105—96th St., Edmonton, Alberta T5H 2G3.

OFFICERS

Administrator: His Excellency the Most Rev. Iriney (Seradny), Bishop of Serpukhov, #19, 10630-83rd Ave., Edmonton, Alberta T6E 2E2. Tel. (403) 433-8623

The Salvation Army in Canada

An evangelistic organization with a military government, first set up by General William Booth (1829-1912) in England in 1865. Converts from England started Salvation Army work in London, Ontario, in 1882. In 1884, Canada became a separate command which also has included Bermuda since 1933. An act to incorporate the Governing Council of The Salvation Army in Canada received royal assent on May 19, 1909.

Headquarters for Canada and Bermuda: 20 Albert St., Toronto, Ontario; P. O. Box 4021 Postal Sta. A, Toronto, Ontario M5W 2B1 Tel. (416) 598-2071

OFFICERS

Territorial Commander, Commissioner John D. Waldron
Territorial Pres., Women's Organizations, Mrs. Commissioner, John D. Waldron
Chief Sec., Col Kenneth Rawlins
Field Sec., Col. Edward Read
Fin. Sec., Lt. Col. Norman Sampson
Personnel Sec., Lt. Col. J. Sloan
Pub. Relations Sec., Lt. Col. George Oystryk
Information Services Sec., Major Kenneth Evenden

PERIODICAL

War Cry, Maj. Dudley Coles, Ed.

Serbian Orthodox Church in America and Canada, Diocese of Eastern America and Canada

The Serbian Orthodox Church is an organic part of the Eastern Orthodox Church. As a local church it received its autocephaly from Constantinople in 1219 A.D. The Patriarchal seat of the church today is in Belgrade, Yugoslavia. In 1921, a Serbian Orthodox Diocese in the United States of America and Canada was organized. In 1963, it was reorganized into three dioceses: The Diocese of Eastern America and Canada; The Midwest Diocese; and the Western Diocese. The Serbian Orthodox Church is in absolute doctrinal unity with all other local Orthodox Churches.

Churches: 8 Inclusive Membership: 10,036 Sunday or Sabbath Schools: 6 Total Enrollment: 315 Ordained Clergy:10

GENERAL ORGANIZATION

Headquarters: Serbian Orthodox Diocese of Eastern America and Canada, Way Hollow Rd., Edgeworth, PA 15143, Tel. (412) 741-5686; Canadian Deanery, 333 Glengarry Ave., Apt. 108, Windsor, Ontario N9A 1P6. Tel. (519) 258-0951.

OFFICERS

Rt. Rev. Christopher, Bishop of Eastern America and Canada, Way Hollow Rd., Edgeworth, PA 15143. Tel. (412) 741-5686.

Dean of Canadian Deanery. V. Rev. Mirko Visnjich, 333 Glengarry Ave., Apt. 108, Windsor, Ontario N9A 1P6. Tel. (519) 258-0951.

PERIODICAL

The Path of Orthodoxy, P. O. Box 36, Leetsdale, PA 15056. Tel. (412) 741-8660. Mrs. Victoria Trbuhovich, Eng. Ed.; V. Rev. Uros Ocokoljic, Serbian Ed.

Seventh-day Adventist Church in Canada

The Seventh-day Adventist Church in Canada is the legal title of the Canadian Union Conference of the Seventh-day Adventist Church with world headquarters in Washington, D.C. The Seventh-day Adventist Church in Canada was organized in 1901 and reorganized in 1932.

Churches: 252 Inclusive Membership: 29,258 Sunday or Sabbath Schools: 293 Total Enrollment: 23,851 Ordained Clergy: 218

GENERAL ORGANIZATION

Headquarters: 1148 King St., E., Oshawa, Ontario L1H 1H8. Tel. (416) 723-3401

OFFICERS

Pres., L. L. Reile
Treas., R. W. Wilmot
Sec., A. N. How

DEPARTMENTS

A.S.I.: L. L. Reile
Education: M. S. Graham
Lay Activities, Sabbath School: L. A. Shipowick
Communication Dept., L.R. Krenzler
Medical: Dr. R. Matiko
Ministerial: L. G. Lowe
Public Affairs: D. L. Michael
Temperance and Y.P.M.V.: Bill Edsell
Publishing: Walter Ruba
Stewardship: D. E. Crane
Revivalist: J. W. Lehman
Trust Services: ———
Consultant to Health Care Institutions: A. G. Rodgers

PERIODICAL

Canadian Adventist Messenger, (s-m), Maracle Press, Oshawa, Ontario, A. N. How, Ed.

Sikhs

Sikhism was born in the northwestern part of the Indo-Pakistan sub-continent in Punjab province about five hundred years ago. Guru Nanak, founder of the religion, was born in 1469. He was followed by nine successor Gurus. The Guruship was then bestowed on the Sikh Holy Book, popularly known as the Guru Granth. The Granth contains writings of the Sikh Gurus and some Hindu and Muslim saints and was compiled by the fifth Guru, Arjan Dev. For the Sikhs, the Granth is the only object of worship. It contains, mostly, hymns of praise of God, the Formless One.

Sikhs started migrating from India more than a half century ago. A number of them settled on the West coast of North America, in British Columbia and California. More recently, a sizeable group has settled in the Eastern part of the Continent as well, particularly in Ontario, New York and Michigan. Sikhs are found in all major cities of the U.S. and Canada.

When Sikhs settle, they soon establish a Gurdwara, or Sikh temple, for worship and social gathering. Gurdwaras are found, among other places, in Toronto, Vancouver, Victoria, and Yuba City, California. At other places, they meet for worship in schools and community centers.

The First Sikh Conference was held on March 24-25, 1979 in Toronto. This is the first step in establishing a federation of all the Sikh Associations in Canada, and, if possible, in USA as well.

There are approximately 120-150,000 Sikhs in North America.

CORRESPONDENT

The Sikh Social and Educational Society, 70 Cairnside Crescent, Willowdale, Ontario M2J 3M8

Ukrainian Greek Orthodox Church of Canada

Toward the end of the 19th century the Ukrainian people began leaving their homeland, and many immigrated to Canada, which has been their homeland for over 75 years. At Saskatoon, in 1918, the Ukrainian pioneers organized this Church. The Ukrainian Greek-Orthodox Church of Canada has grown rapidly in the past 50 years so that today it is the largest Ukrainian Orthodox Church beyond the borders of the Ukraine.

GENERAL ORGANIZATION

General Organization: Sobor (General Council) meets every five years, Presidium meets monthly, Full Consistory, semi-annually
Headquarters: Consistory of the Ukrainian Greek-Orthodox Church of Canada, 9 St. John's Ave., Winnipeg, Manitoba R2W 1G8. Tel. (204) 586-3093

OFFICERS

Presidium, Chpsn., V. Rev. D. Luchak, 9 St. John's Ave., Winnipeg, Manitoba R2W 1G8

PERIODICALS

Visnyk (s-m), 9 St. John's Ave., Winnipeg, Manitoba, R2W 1G8. Rev. T. Minenko, Ed.
The Herald (English Supplement) (bi-w), 9 St. John's Ave., Winnipeg Manitoba R2W 1G8. Rev. T. Minenko, Ed.

Union of Spiritual Communities of Christ (Orthodox Doukhobors in Canada)

Groups of Canadians of Russian origin living in the western provinces of Canada whose beginnings in Russia are unknown. The name "Doukhobors," or "Spirit Wrestlers," was given in derision by the Russian Orthodox clergy in Russia as far back as 1785. Victims of decades of persecution in Russia, about 7,500 Doukhobors finally arrived in Canada in 1899.

The whole teaching of the Doukhobors is penetrated with the Gospel spirit of love; worshiping God in the spirit they affirm that the outward Church and all that is performed in it and concerns it has no importance for them; the Church is where two or three are gathered together, united in the name of Christ. Their teaching is founded on tradition, which is called among them the "Book of Life," because it lives in their memory and hearts. In this book are recorded sacred songs or chants, partly composed independently, partly formed out of the contents of the Bible, and these are committed to memory by each succeeding generation. Doukhobors observe complete pacifism and non-violence.

The Doukhobors were reorganized in 1938 by their leader, Peter P. Verigin, shortly before his death, into the Union of Spiritual Communities of Christ, commonly called Orthodox Doukhobors. It is headed by a democratically elected Executive Committee which executes the will and protects the interests of the people.

In the present day at least 90 percent of the Doukhobors are law-abiding, pay taxes, and definitely, "do not burn or bomb or parade in the nude" as they say a fanatical offshoot called the "Sons of Freedom" does.

GENERAL ORGANIZATION

General Meeting: Annual in February
Headquarters: USCC Central Office, Box 760, Grand Forks, British Columbia V0H 1H0. Tel. (604) 442-8252

OFFICERS

Honorary Chpsn. of the Exec. Comm., John J. Verigin, Box 760, Grand Forks, British Columbia V0H 1H0

Chpsn., William E. Kootnekoff
Adm., S. W. Babakaiff

PERIODICAL

Iskra (bi-w) in Russian with part of Youth Section in English, Box 760, Grand Forks, British Columbia, V0H 1H0. Peter J. Soloveoff, Ed.

Unitarian Universalist Association

The headquarters of the Unitarian Universalist Association is located at 25 Beacon St., Boston, MA 02108. Tel. (617) 742-2100. Three of the twenty-three districts of the UUA are located partly or wholly in Canada, as are 43 of the 991 congregations. There is a Canadian Unitarian Council—Conseil Unitaire Canadien which handles matters of particular concern to Canadian churches and fellowships. Its office is located at 175 St. Clair Ave. W. Toronto, Ontario M4V 1P7

Churches: 43 Inclusive Membership: 4,858 Sunday or Sabbath Schools: N.R. Total Enrollment: N.R. Ordained Clergy: 30

DISTRICTS AND OFFICERS

Pacific Northwest, Rod Stewart, 675-21st. St., West Vancouver, British Columbia V7V 4A7. Tel. (604) 926-1621
St. Lawrence, Rev. Raymond Nasemann, 1150 Meadowbrook Dr., Syracuse, NY 13224. Tel. (315) 853-5459
Western Canada, Herman Boerma, 1710 Prince of Wales Ave., Saskatoon, Saskatchewan S7K 3E5. Tel. (306) 242-1362

United Brethren in Christ, Ontario Conference

Founded in 1767 in Lancaster County, PA, missionaries came to Canada about 1850. The first class was held in Kitchener in 1855, and the first building was erected in Port Elgin in 1867.

The Church of the United Brethren in Christ had its beginning with Philip William Otterbein and Martin Boehm who were leaders in the revivalistic movement in Pennsylvania and Maryland during the late 1760s.

GENERAL ORGANIZATION

Ontario conference, Annual. Next meeting: June 6-8, 1980; Quadrennial conference: Next meeting, June 1981
Headquarters: Rev. Martin Magnus, Conference Supt., 1360 Orchard Ave., Fort Erie, Ontario L2A 3E6. Tel. (416) 871-0430

OFFICERS

Conf. Supt., Rev. Martin Magnus, 1360 Orchard Ave., Fort Erie, Ontario L2A 3E6
Treas., Mr. Don Nash, 1 Ponoca Rd., Toronto, Ontario M9W 3Y4

PERIODICAL

The United Brethren (m), 302 Lake St., P.O. Box 650, Huntington, IN 46750. Rev. Stanley Peters, Ed.

The United Church of Canada

The United Church of Canada was formed in 1925 through the union of the Methodist Church, the Congregational Union of Canada and the Councils of Local Union Churches, and 70 per cent of the Presbyterian Chruch in Canada. On January 1, 1968, the Canada Conference of the Evangelical United Brethren became part of The United Church of Canada. The United Church is a full member of the World Methodist Council, the World Alliance of Reformed Churches (Presbyterian and Congregational) and the Canadian and World Council of Churches.

Churches: 4,271 Inclusive Membership: 2,087,313 Sunday or Sabbath Schools: 3,543 Total Enrollment: 225,388 Ordained Clergy: 3,688

Headquarters: The United Church House, 85 St. Clair Ave. E., Toronto, Ontario M4T 1M8, Tel. (416) 925-5931
General Council, meeting every two years. Next meeting, 1979

GENERAL COUNCIL

Mod., Rt. Rev. George M. Tuttle
Sec., Rev. Donald G. Ray
Deputy Sec., (Regionalism and Personnel), Rev. Albion R. Wright; (Theology and Faith), Rev. Peter G. White
Personnel Officer, Mr. James A. H. MacFadzean
Research Officer, Rev. David R. Stone
Archivist-Historian, Rev. C. Glenn Lucas, 73 Queen's Park Cr., E., Toronto, Ontario M5S 2C4. Tel. (416) 978-3832

DIVISIONS

Communication: Sec., Rev. F. G. Brisbin; Regional Relations, Education for Mission and Stewardship: Rev. R. C. Plant; Rev. Keith Woollard; News Services, Ms. Alayne Scanlon; Audio-Visuals Consultant, Mrs. Margaret Nix
CANEC Publishing and Supply House: 47 Coldwater Rd., Don Mills, Ontario M3B 1Y9, Tel. (416) 449-7440, Gen. Mgr., Mr. Alun Hughes
Media Services: 315 Queen St. E., Toronto, Ontario M5A 1S7, Tel. (416) 366-9221, Dir. Rev. G. Earl Leard; Still Pictures, Alice Foster; Television and Films, Rev. R. D. McCalmont; Radio, Miss Nancy Edwards; Cassettes, Mrs. Betty Richardson; Photographer, Mr. Wolf Kutnahorsky; Operations Manager, Mr. Dennis Stanbrook

Finance: Sec., Mr. D. N. Borgal
Dept. of the Treasury: Treas., Mr. W. R. Davis
Dept. of Pensions: Sec., Rev. D. Weatherburn
Dept. of Stewardship Services: Sec., Rev. M. Jewitt Parr

Ministry, Personnel and Education: Sec., Rev. Howard M. Mills
Continuing Education and Career Development, Lay Supply Training, ———

Personnel Services and Campus Ministries, Rev. Robert K. Shorten
Student Services, Field Education and Women's Concerns, Miss Mary Sanderson
Grants, Admissions, Rev. Peter Collins

Mission in Canada: Sec., Rev. Howard L. Brox
Christian Development, Miss Jessie MacLeod
Church in Society, Rev. W. Clarke MacDonald
Administration and Financial Policy, Mr. John D. L. Robertson; Curriculum Resources, Rev. Gordon J. Freer; Evangelism, Rev. Gordon Turner, Ministry with Adults, Laity, Mr. Alan Staig and Marion Logan; Marriage and Family Life, Rev. Robin Smith; Persons of Special Need, David Hallman; Social Issues, Rev. Robert Lindsey; Youth, Mardi Tindal and Rev. John Sloan; Senior Adults, Elaine Kaye; Resource, Rev. Fritz Schmidt; French-English Relations, Rev. Guy Deschamps; Human Rights-Immigration, Elizabeth Loweth
Superintendent, Hospitals and Medical Work: Dr. W. Donald Watt, 6762 Cypress St., Vancouver, British Columbia V6P 5L8. Tel. (604) 266-5426

World Outreach: Sec., Rev. Garth W. Legge
Africa, Rev. James A. Kirkwood; Caribbean and Latin America, Rev. Garth Legge; Asia, Rev. E. Frank Carey; Inter-Faith Dialogue, Rev. James F. Seunarine; Personnel, Ms. Janet MacPherson
World Development, Service, Relief, Miss Glenna Graham; Admin., Rev. Fred M. Bayliss

CONFERENCE EXECUTIVE SECRETARIES

Alberta: Rev. P. A. Cline, 6724-99 St., Edmonton, Alberta T6E 5B8, Tel. (403) 432-0287
Bay of Quinte: ———, 218 Barrie St., Kingston, Ontario K7L 3K3, Tel. (613) 549-2503
British Columbia: Rev. A. M. Anderson, 1955 W. 4th Ave., Vancouver, British Columbia V6B 1M7, Tel. (604) 682-7556
Hamilton: ———, P. O. Box 100, Carlisle, Ontario L0R 1H0 (416) 659-3343
London: Rev. L. T. C. Harbour, 363 Windermere Rd., London, Ontario N6G 2K3, Tel. (519) 672-1930
Manitoba: Rev. W. J. Hickerson, 120 Maryland St., Winnipeg, Manitoba R3G 1L1, Tel. (204) 786-8911
Manitou: Rev. F. A. Sorensen, 198 Hughes Rd., North Bay, Ontario P1A 3E8, Tel. (705) 474-3350
Maritime: Rev. J. H. Tye, Box 1560, Sackville, New Brunswick E0A 3C0, Tel. (506) 536-1334
Montreal and Ottawa: ———, Ste. 204B, 352 Dorval Ave., Dorval, Quebec H9S 3H8, Tel. (514) 613-8594
Newfoundland: Rev. W. J. Baker, Box 248, St. John's, Newfoundland, A1C 5J2, Tel. (709) 576-4011
Saskatchewan: Rev. R. S. Harper, 1805 Rae St., Regina, Saskatchewan S4T 2E3, Tel. (306) 525-9155
Toronto: Rev. L. H. Walsh, Rm. 321, 85 St. Claire Ave. E., Toronto Ontario M4T 1M8, Tel. (416) 967-1880

PERIODICAL

United Church Observer, Toronto, Ontario, Hugh McCullum, Ed.

†United Pentecostal Church in Canada

This body, which is affiliated with the United Pentecostal Church, International with headquarters in Hazelwood, Missouri, accepts the Bible standard of full salvation, which is repentance, baptism by immersion in the Name of the Lord Jesus Christ for the remission of sins, and the baptism of the Holy Ghost with the initial signs of speaking in tongues as the Spirit gives utterance. Other tenets of faith include the Oneness of God in Christ, holiness, divine healing and the second coming of Jesus Christ.

Churches: 124 Inclusive Membership: 20,000 Sunday or Sabbath Schools: N.R. Total Enrollment: N.R. Ordained Clergy: 250

ORGANIZATION

Atlantic District, District Supt., Rev. J. D. Mean, Box 286, Dartmouth, Nova Scotia B2Y 3Y3
Ontario District, District Supt., Rev. William V. Cooling, Box 2128, Preston, Ontario K0K 2T0. Tel. (613) 476-4219
Minnesota-Manitoba District, District Presbyter, Rev. I. Wurch, 128 Whyte Ave., Dryden, Ontario P8N 1Z7
Canadian Plains District, District Supt., Rev. R. Sirstad, 1730-46th Ave., SW, Calgary, Alberta T2T 2R5
British Columbia District, District Supt., Rev. R. V. Reynolds, Midway, British Columbia V0H 1M0

The Wesleyan Church

The Canadian portion of The Wesleyan Church which consists of the Atlantic and Central Canada districts. The Central Canada District of the former Wesleyan Methodist Church of America was organized at Winchester, Ontario, in 1889 and the Atlantic District was founded in 1888 as the Alliance of the Reformed Baptist Church which merged with the Wesleyan Methodist Church in July, 1966.

The Wesleyan Methodist Church and the Pilgrim Holiness Church merged in June, 1968, to become The Wesleyan Church. The doctrine is evangelical and Arminian and stresses holiness beliefs. For more details, consult the U.S. listing under The Wesleyan Church.

Churches: 76 Inclusive Membership: 4,750 Sunday or Sabbath Schools: 76 Total Enrollment: 13,925 Ordained Clergy: 110

GENERAL ORGANIZATION

Central Canada District Conference: meets third week in July.
Atlantic District Conference: meets first week in July.
Headquarters: Colonial Rd., Box 108, Rt. 3, Belleville, Ontario K8N 4Z3
Office: 41 Summit Ave., Box 20, Sussex, New Brunswick E0E 1P0. Tel. (506) 433-1007

OFFICERS

District Supt. (Central Canada District), Dr. J. S. A. Spearman, Colonial Rd., Box 108, Rt. 3, Belleville, Ontario K8N 4Z3
District Supt. (Atlantic District), Rev. H. R. Ingersoll, P.O. Box 20, Sussex, New Brunswick E0E 1P0

PERIODICALS

Wesleyan Advocate (s-m), George E. Failing, Ed.
Central Canada District News (bi-m), Dr. J. S. A. Spearman, Colonial Rd., Rt. 3, Box 108, Belleville, Ontario K8N 4Z3, Ed.
Atlantic Wesleyan (m), Box 20, Sussex, New Brunswick E0E 1P0. Rev. H. R. Ingersoll, Ed.

Wisconsin Evangelical Lutheran Synod

The W.E.L.S. was founded in Milwaukee, WI, in 1850. The Synod believes in a verbally inspired, inerrant Bible and embraces without reservation the Lutheran Confessions as found in the Book of Concord.

Churches: 7 Inclusive Membership: 938 Sunday or Sabbath Schools: 7 Total Enrollment: 161 Ordained Clergy: 6

GENERAL ORGANIZATION

No separate Canadian organization. National Convention meets biennially. Next meeting in Watertown, WI, in 1979.

For additional details, consult Wisconsin Evangelical Lutheran Synod listing in Directory 3, "Religious Bodies in the U.S."

OTHER RELIGIOUS BODIES IN CANADA

Although a sizable majority of Canadian religious bodies, having most of the Canadian church membership, is accounted for by denominations providing directory materials in the section immediately preceding, a number of important groups have not yet provided directory information.

For the sake of completeness, an alphabetical listing of these religious bodies not yet supplying directory information appears below.

The editor of the **Yearbook of American and Canadian Churches** would be grateful for any information concerning significant omissions from this listing of Religious Bodies in Canada as well as for any other information concerning this section.

African Methodist Episcopal Church in Canada, 765 Lawrence Ave. W., Toronto, Ontario M6A 1B7. Rev. L. O. Jenkins

Bergthaler (Mennonite) Congregations, John Neudorf, LaCrete, Alberta T0H 2H0.

Canadian Reformed Churches, Box 152, Smithville, Ontario L0R 2A0

Chortitz (Mennonite) Congregations, Ben Hoeppner, Box 1420, Steinbach, Manitoba R0A 2A0. (2,007 members)

Christadelphians in Canada, P.O. Box 221, Weston, Ontario M9N 3M7

Christian Science in Canada, Mr. J. Donald Fulton, 696 Yonge St., Ste. 403. Toronto, Ontario M4Y 2A7. Tel. (416) 922-7473

Evangelical Mennonite Brethren Conference, c/o William Regehr, 5800 S. 14th St., Omaha, NE 68107

Hutterian Brethren, Joseph J. Waldner, P. O. Box 628, Havre, MT 59501. (15,920 members)

New Apostolic Church of North America in Canada, c/o Rev. Michael Kraus, President, 267 Lincoln Rd., Waterloo, Ontario N2J 2P6

Old Colony Mennonite Church in Canada, Alberta, Deacon Herman Geisbrecht, La Crete, Alberta T0H 2H0, (650 members); British Columbia, Deacon Jacob Giesbrecht, Ft. St. John, British Columbia V0C P20, (320 members); Manitoba, Deacon Abram Driedger, Box 601, Winkler, Manitoba R0G 2X0, (915 members); Ontario, Bishop Henry Reimer, R. R. 3, Wheatley, Ontario N0P 2P0, (260 members); Saskatchewan, Deacon Klass Dyck, R. R. 4, Saskatoon, Saskatchewan, (1,087 members).

Orthodox Church in America (Canada Section), c/o The Most Rev. Sylvester, Archbishop of Montreal and Canada, 1175 Champlain St., Montreal, Quebec H2L 2R7

Reformed Presbyterian Church of North America, Louis D. Hutmire, 7418 Penn Ave., Pittsburg, PA 15208

Sommerfelder (Mennonite) Congregations, Andrew Knelson, La Crete, Alberta T0H 2H0. (4,000 members)

Standard Church of America (Canadian Section), 243 Perth St., Brockville, Ontario K6V 5E7

United Brethren Churches, c/o Rev. Evan Sider, 29 Priscilla Ave., Toronto, Ontario M6S 3W1. Tel. (416) 766-8902

RELIGIOUS BODIES IN CANADA ARRANGED BY FAMILIES

The following list of religious bodies appearing in Directory 4, "Religious Bodies in Canada," including "Other Religious Bodies in Canada," shows the "families" or related clusters into which Canadian religious bodies can be grouped. For example, there are many bodies that can be grouped under the heading "Baptist" for historical and theological reasons. It is not to be assumed, however, that all denominations under one family heading are necessarily similar in belief or practice. Often any similarity is purely coincidental since ethnicity, theological divergence, and even political and personality factors have shaped the directions denominational groups have taken.

Family categories provide one of the major pitfalls of church statistics because of the tendency to combine statistics by "families" for analytical and comparative purposes. Such combined totals are almost meaningless, although often used as variables for sociological analysis.

The editor would be grateful for any additions or corrections in the family table below. **Religious bodies not grouped under family headings appear alphabetically and are not indented in the following list.**

The Anglican Church of Canada
Apostolic Christian Church (Nazarean)
Armenian Evangelical Church
Associated Gospel Churches
Baha'i Faith

BAPTIST BODIES

- *The Association of Regular Baptist Churches (Canada)*
- *Baptist Federation of Canada*
    - Baptist Convention of Ontario and Quebec
    - Baptist Union of Western Canada
    - Union of French Baptist Churches in Canada
    - United Baptist Convention of the Atlantic Provinces
- *Baptist General Conference*
    - The Central Canada Baptist Conference
    - Baptist General Conference of Alberta
    - Columbia Conference
- *Canadian Baptist Conference*
- Evangelical Baptist Churches in Canada, The Fellowship of
- North American Baptist Conference
- Primitive Baptist Conference of New Brunswick

Bible Holiness Movement
Brethren in Christ Church, Canadian Conference
Buddhist Churches of Canada
Canadian Jewish Congress
The Canadian Yearly Meeting of the Religious Society of Friends
Christadelphians in Canada

The Christian and Missionary Alliance in Canada
Christian Church (Disciples of Christ) in Canada
Christian Churches and Churches of Christ in Canada
The Christian Congregation, Inc.
Christian Science in Canada
Church of God, (Anderson, Ind.)
Church of the Nazarene

DOUKHOBORS

Reformed Doukhobors, Christian Community and Brotherhood of
Union of Spiritual Communities of Christ (Orthodox Doukhobors in Canada)

EASTERN CHURCHES

The Antiochian Orthodox Christian Archdiocese of North America
The Armenian Church of North America, Diocese of Canada
The Coptic Church in Canada
Greek Orthodox Diocese of Toronto
Orthodox Church in America (Canada Section)
Romanian Orthodox Church in America (Canadian Parishes)
The Romanian Orthodox Episcopate of America (Jackson, Michigan)
Russian Orthodox Church in Canada, Patriarchal Parishes of the
Serbian Eastern Orthodox Church in America and Canada, Diocese of Eastern America and Canada
Ukrainian Greek Orthodox Church of Canada

The Evangelical Covenant Church of Canada
Evangelical Free Church of Canada
General Church of the New Jerusalem
Gospel Missionary Association in Canada
Independent Holiness Church
Jehovah's Witnesses

LATTER DAY SAINTS

The Church of Jesus Christ of Latter-day Saints
Reorganized Church of Jesus Christ of Latter Day Saints

LUTHERANS

Church of the Lutheran Brethren
The Estonian Evangelical Lutheran Church
The Evangelical Lutheran Church of Canada
The Latvian Evangelical Lutheran Church in America
Lutheran Church—Canada
Lutheran Church in America—Canada Section
Wisconsin Evangelical Lutheran Synod

MENNONITE BODIES

Bergthaler Congregations
Chortitz Congregations
Conference of Mennonites in Canada
Evangelical Mennonite Brethren Conference
Evangelical Mennonite Conference
Evangelical Mennonite Mission Conference
Hutterian Brethren
Mennonite Brethren Churches of North America, Canadian Conference of
Mennonite Church (Canada)
Old Colony Mennonite Church in Canada
Old Order Amish Church
Rhineland Mennonite Church
Sommerfelder Congregations

METHODIST BODIES

African Methodist Episcopal Church in Canada
British Methodist Episcopal Church
The Evangelical Church in Canada
Free Methodist Church in Canada

The Missionary Church of Canada
Moravian Church in America, Northern Province
Muslims
New Apostolic Church of North America in Canada
The Old Catholic Church of Canada

PENTECOSTAL BODIES

The Apostolic Church in Canada
Apostolic Church of Pentecost of Canada
Church of God (Cleveland, Tenn.)
The Church of God of Prophecy in Canada
Church of the Foursquare Gospel of Western Canada
Independent Assemblies of God—Canada
The Italian Pentecostal Church of Canada
The Pentecostal Assemblies of Canada
Pentecostal Assemblies of Newfoundland
Pentecostal Holiness Church of Canada
United Pentecostal Church in Canada

Plymouth Brethren (a.k.a. Christian Brethren)
Polish National Catholic Church of Canada

PRESBYTERIAN BODIES

The Presbyterian Church in Canada
Reformed Presbyterian Church, Evangelical Synod
Reformed Presbyterian Church of North America

REFORMED BODIES

Canadian Reformed Churches
Christian Reformed Church in North America
Reformed Church in America

The Reformed Episcopal Church
The Roman Catholic Church in Canada
The Salvation Army in Canada
Seventh-day Adventist Church in Canada
Sikhs
Standard Church of America (Canadian Section)
Unitarian Universalist Association
United Brethren Churches
United Brethren in Christ, Ontario Conference
United Church of Canada
The Wesleyan Church

5. INTERNATIONAL AGENCIES: CONFESSIONAL, INTERDENOMINATIONAL, COOPERATIVE

A listing of major confessional, interdenominational, and cooperative international agencies follows. The editor of the **Yearbook of American and Canadian Churches** would be grateful for details on major groups omitted from this listing.

WORLD COUNCIL OF CHURCHES

The World Council of Churches is a fellowship of more than 295 churches of the Protestant, Anglican, Orthodox, and Old Catholic traditions banded together for study, witness, service, and the advancement of unity. It includes in its membership churches in more than 90 countries with various forms of government, and its life reflects the immense richness and variety of Christian faith and practice.

The World Council of Churches came into being after many years of preparation on August 23, 1948, when its First Assembly was held in Amsterdam, Holland.

The basis for World Council membership is: "The World Council of Churches is a fellowship of Churches which confess the Lord Jesus Christ as God and Saviour according to the Scriptures and therefore seek to fulfill together their common calling to the glory of the one God, Father, Son, and Holy Spirit."

Membership is open to churches which express their agreement with this basis and satisfy such criteria as the Assembly or Central Committee may prescribe.

The fundamental reorganization of the World Council was approved at the meeting of the Central Committee in Addis Ababa, Ethiopia, in January, 1971. The changes were effective immediately, although the restructuring process was not completed until 1975.

Headquarters: 150 route de Ferney, 1211 Geneva, 20, Switzerland
Office in the U.S.: 475 Riverside Dr., Rm. 1062, New York, NY 10027

HONORARY PRESIDENT

Rev. Dr. Willem A. Visser 't Hooft, Switzerland

PRESIDENTS

Ms. Annie Jiagge, Ghana.
Rev. J. Miguez-Bonino, Argentina.
His Holiness Ilia, Georgia, USSR.
Gen. T. B. Simatupang, Indonesia.
Archbishop O. Sundby, Sweden.
Dr. Cynthia Wedel, United States.

CENTRAL COMMITTEE

Chpsn., Most Rev. E. W. Scott, Canada.
Vice-chpsns., His Holiness Karekin II, Lebanon; Ms. Jean Skuse, Australia.

GENERAL SECRETARIAT

Gen. Sec., Rev. Dr. Philip A. Potter.
Deputy Gen. Secs., Dr. Konrad Raiser, Dr. Todor Sabev; Asst. Gen. Sec. for Finance and Administration, Mr. Wesley Kenworthy.
Coordination for Budget Development, Mr. Patrick Coidan; Consultant, Mrs. Midge Meinertz.
Librarian, Rev. Dr. Ans J. van der Bent.
Reference Librarian and Cataloguer, Mr. Pierre Beffa.
Personnel Dir., Trevor Davies; Assoc Dir., Ms. Malena Wiehe
Ecumenical Institute: Dr. Karl Hertz, Dir.; Asst. Dir., Rev. Alain Blancy
  Assoc. Dir., Mr. Van den Burg
Communication:
  Exec. Sec., J. Victor Koilpillai, Jan H. Kok, Publications; Mrs. Tomoko Evdokimoff, Translation: Rev. J. J. Bauswein, French-German Press Officer; Robin Gurney, English Language News Editor; John Taylor, Ms. Ishbel Mac Lellan Radio/TV; Rev. John Bluck, Ed., One World.

PROGRAM UNIT 1—FAITH AND WITNESS

Staff Moderator: Dr. Todor Sabev

Commission on Faith and Order:
  Dir., ———.
  Rev. Stephen Cranford, Exec. Sec.;
  Assoc. Dir., Rev. Dr. C. S. Song; Exec. Sec., Rev. Stephen Cranford.
  Study Sec.: Rev. Constance Parvey (Community of Men and Women in the Church)
Commission on World Mission and Evangelism:
  Dir., Dr. Emilio Castro.
  Dep. Dir., Mrs. Ruth Sovik.
  Secs.: Dr. George E. Todd; Prof. Ion Bria; Dr. John Kurewa, Ms. Gwen Cashmore, Pontas Nasution, Rev. Samuel Kobia.
  Consultant-Melbourne Conference: Jacques Matthey.

INTERNATIONAL AGENCIES

Department on Church and Society:
Exec. Sec., Dr. Paul R. Abrecht.
Dialogue with Men of Living Faiths and Ideologies:
Dr. Stanley J. Samartha, Dir.
Asst. Secs., Dr. John B. Taylor, Rev. Alan Brockway
Program on Theological Education
Rev. Aharon Sapsezian, Dir.; Dr. Ross Kinsler, Dr. Samuel Amirtham, Asst. Dirs.

PROGRAM UNIT II—JUSTICE AND SERVICE
Staff Moderator: Dr. Konrad Raiser

Commission on Inter-Church Aid, Refugee and World Service:
Dir., Mr. Jean Fischer; Dep. Dir., Archpriest Georgios Tsetsis
Sec. for Finance and Fund Raising, Mr. Willem Schot
Area Secs.: Africa: Mr. Maxime Rafransoa; Consultant, Mr. Huibert van Beek; Asia: Rev. William Tung; Latin America: Rev. Gerson Meyer; Middle East: Ghassan Rbeiz; Europe ———
Refugee Service: Ms. Ruud van Hoogevest; Ms. Mercedes Saitzew, Mr. Carl Neilsen.
Health and Related Concerns: Ms. Lois Meyhoffer.
Material Aid: Mr. Helmut Reuschle; Emergency Officer: Mr. Robin Morison-Turnbull
Ecumenical Sharing of Resources: Rev. William Perkins
Ecumenical Church Loan Fund: Dir.: Mr. Archibald Turnbull; Assoc. Dir., Mr. Reginald Stober
Commission of the Churches on International Affairs: Dir.: Dr. Leopoldo Niilus; Secs.: Mr. Ninan Koshy, Mr. Victor Hsu; Human Rights, Rev. Erich Weingartner; Exec. Sec., New York Office, Rev. Dwain Epps; Human Rights Resources Officer for Latin America: Rev. Charles Harper
Commission on the Churches' Participation in Development: Dir.: Dr. Julio de Santa Ana; Sec. Ecumenical Development Fund: Mr. Wolfgang Schmidt; Sec. for Technical Services: Mr. Pascal de Pury; Exec. Sec. for Development Education: Dr. Reinhild Traitler; Exec. Sec. for People's Participation: Dr. Koson Srisang; Study Sec.: Prof. Nikolai Zabolotsky
Ecumenical Program to Combat Racism: Dir. Dr. Baldwin Sjollema; Prog. Sec., Rev. José Chipenda; Research Officer, Mr. Prexy Nesbitt.
Program Unit on Justice and Service: Sec. for Migration: Rev. Alan Matheson
Christian Medical Commission: Dir.: Ms. Ruth Nita Barrow; Assoc. Dirs.: Dr. Stuart Kingma, Dr. Eric Ram.

PROGRAM UNIT III—EDUCATION AND RENEWAL
Acting Moderator: Dr. Philip Potter

Sub-Unit on Women in Church and Society:
Dir., ———
Sub-Unit on Renewal & Congregational Life:
Dir., ———
Sub-Unit on Education:
Dr. Ulrich Becker, Dr. Paulo Freire, Special Consultant; Hans-Reudi Weber, Portfolio on Biblical Studies; ———
Family Ministries: Exec. Sec., Dr. ma Mpolo Masamba; Church Sponsored/Related Edu. Inst., Exec. Sec., Ms. Atsede Kahssay; Scholarships Dir., ———
Sub-Unit on Youth: Peter Moss, Coordinator, Assoc. Coord., Agnes Chepkwony

FINANCE AND CENTRAL SERVICES

Asst. Gen. Sec. for Finance and Administration, Wesley Kenworthy
WCC/Roman Catholic Commission on Society, Development and Peace (SODEPAX):
Gen. Sec.: Fr. John Lucal; Asst. Sec.: Theo Tschuy.

PERIODICALS

The Ecumenical Review (q), Dr. Philip Potter.
The Ecumenical Press Service (w), Mr. Robin E. Gurney, Ed., English edition.
International Review of Mission (q), Dr. Emilio Castro.
One World, Rev. John Bluck, Ed.

THE UNITED STATES CONFERENCE FOR THE WORLD COUNCIL OF CHURCHES

The United States Conference for the World Council of Churches, Inc. is a corporation composed of representatives named by member churches in the United States to the Assembly of the World Council of Churches. There are currently 28 member churches in the U.S. Conference.

The purposes as stated in the Certificate of Incorporation are:

"to aid the World Council of Churches and its Central Committee in implementing their policy in the United States of America; to interpret the program of the World Council of Churches to the churches in the United States of America;

to represent the American member churches of the World Council of Churches and to secure budgetary support for them; and to perform any and every function and service directly related and appropriate to the foregoing."

The New York office of the World Council of Churches is maintained jointly by the U.S. Conference and the World Council of Churches. As such, it is the executive arm of both for carrying out of the above purposes.

The Ecumenical Courier is a quarterly publication of the U.S. Conference. It is sent regularly to all who become "Friends of the World Council of Churches."

Headquarters: 475 Riverside Dr., New York, NY 10027.
Tel. (212) 870-2528
Meets annually.

OFFICERS

Chpsn., Dr. Robert J. Marshall
Vice-Chpsn., Ms. Barbara Thompson
Sec., Dr. John S. Groenfeldt
Treas., Ms. Ann W. Hilliard
Asst. Treas., Jean E. Schmidt

STAFF

Exec. Dir., Dr. Keith Bridston
Information Officer, Bruno Kroker

PERIODICAL

The Ecumenical Courier (4 issues a year), 475 Riverside Dr., New York, NY 10027.

Constituent Bodies of the World Council of Churches and Associate Member Churches

MEMBER CHURCHES

Argentina
Iglesia Evangêlica del Río de la Plata
(Evangelical Church of the River Plata)
Iglesia Evangêlica Metodista Argentina
(Evangelical Methodist Church of Argentina)

Australasia
Methodist Church of Australasia
The United Church in Papua, New Guinea and the Solomon Islands

Australia
Churches of Christ in Australia
The Church of England in Australia
The Congregational Union of Australia
The Presbyterian Church of Australia
The Uniting Church in Australia

Austria
Alt-katholische Kirche Österreichs
(Old Catholic Church of Austria)
Evangelische Kirche A.B. in Österreich
(Evangelical Church of the Augsburg Confession)

Bangladesh
Baptist Church of Bangladesh

Belgium
Eglise Protestante de Belgique
(Protestant Church of Belgium)
Eglise Réformée de Belgique
(Reformed Church of Belgium)

Brazil
Igreja Episcopal do Brasil
(Episcopal Church of Brazil)
Igreja Evangélica de Confissão Lutherana no Brasil

(Evangelical Church of Lutheran Confession in Brazil)
Ireja Evangélica Pentecostal "O Brasil para Cristo"
(The Evangelical Pentecostal Church "Brazil for Christ")
Igreja Metodista do Brasil
(Methodist Church of Brazil)
Ireja Reformada Latino Americana
(The Latin American Reformed Church)

Bulgaria
Eglise Orthodox Bulgare
(Bulgarian Orthodox Church)

Burma
Burma Baptist Convention
Church of the Province of Burma

Cameroon
Eglise évangélique du Cameroun
(Evangelical Church of Cameroon)
Eglise presbytérienne Camérounaise
(Presbyterian Church of Cameroon)
Presbyterian Church in Cameroon
Union des Eglises baptistes du Cameroun
(Union of Baptist Churches of Cameroon)

Canada
The Angelican Church of Canada
Canadian Yearly Meeting of the Society of Friends
Christian Church (Disciples of Christ)
The Evangelical Lutheran Church of Canada
The Presbyterian Church in Canada
The United Church of Canada

Central Africa
Church of the Province of Central Africa

Chile
Iglesia Evangélica Luterana en Chile
(Evangelical Lutheran Church in Chile)
Iglesia Pentecostal de Chile
(Pentecostal Church of Chile)
Misión Iglesia Pentecostal
(Pentecostal Mission Church)

China
China Baptist Council
Chung-Hua Chi-Tu Chiao-Hui
(Church of Christ in China)
Chung Hua Sheng Kung Hui
(Angelican Church in China)
Hua Pei Kung Li Jui
(Congregational Church in North China)

Congo (People's Republic of the)
Eglise Evangélique du Congo
(Evangelical Church of the Congo)

Cook Islands
Cook Islands Christian Church

Cyprus
Church of Cyprus

Czechoslovakia
Ceskobratrská církev evangelická
(Evangelical Church of Czech Brethren)
Ceskoslovenská církev husitská
(Czechoslovak Hussite Church)
Pravoslavná církev v CSSR
(Orthodox Church of Czechoslovakia)
Ref. krest. církev na Slovensku
(Reformed Christian Church in slovakia)
Slezská címrkev evangelická a.v.

(Silesian Evangelical Church of the Augsburg Confession)
Slovenská evanjelická církev a.v. v CSSR
(Slovak Evangelical Church of the Augsb. Conf. in the CSSR)

People's Republic of Benin (Dahomey)
Eglise Protestante Methodiste au Dahomey-Togo
(The Protestant Methodist Church in Dahomey and Togo)

Denmark
Det danske Baptistsamfund
(The Baptist Union of Denmark)
Den evangelisk-lutherske Folkekirke i Danmark
(The Church of Denmark)

East Africa
Presbyterian Church of East Africa

Egypt
Coptic Orthodox Church
Evangelical Church—The Synod of the Nile
Greek Orthodox Patriarchate of Alexandria

Ethiopia
Ethiopia Orthodox Church
Evangelical Church Mekane Yesus (Ethiopia)

Fiji
Methodist Church in Fiji

Finland
Suomen Evankelis-Luterilainen Kirkko
(Evangelical-Lutheran Church of Finland)

France
Eglise de la Confession d'Augsbourg d'Alsace et de Lorraine
(Evangelical Church of the Augsburg Confession of Alsace and Lorraine)
Eglise Evangélique Luthérienne de France
(Evangelical Lutheran Church of France)
Eglise Réformée d'Alsace et de Lorraine
(Reformed Church of Alsace and Lorraine)
Eglise Réformée de France
(Reformed Church of France)

Gabonese Republic
Eglise Evangélique du Gabon
(Evangelical Church of Gabon)

German Churches
Federal Republic of Germany
Katholisches Bistum der Alt-Katholiken in Deutschland
(Catholic Diocese of the Old Catholics in Germany)
Evangelische Brüder-Unität
(Moravian Church)
Evangelische Kirche in Deutschland
(Evangelical Church in Germany)
Evangelische Landeskirche in Baden
Evangelisch-Lutherische Kirche in Bayern*
Evangelische Kirche in Berlin-Brandenburg
Evangelische-Lutherische Landeskirche in Braunschweig*

*This Church is directly a member of the World Council of Churches in accordance with the resolution of the General Synod of the United Evangelical Lutheran Church of Germany, dated 27 January, 1949, which recommended that the member churches of the United Evangelical Lutheran Church should make the following declaration to the Council of the Evangelical Church in Germany concerning their relation to the World Council of Churches:

Bremische Evangelische Kirche
Evangelisch-Lutherische Landeskirche Eutin*
Evangelisch-Lutherische Kirche im Hamburgischen Staate*
Evangelisch-Lutherische Landeskirche Hannovers*
Evangelische Kirche in Hessen und Nassau
Evangelische Kirche von Kurhessen-Waldeck
Lippische Landeskirche
Evangelisch-Lutherische Kirche in Lübeck*
Evangelisch-reformierte Kirche in Nordwestdeutschland

Evangelisch-Lutherische Kirche in Oldenburg
Vereinigte Protestantisch-Evangelisch-Christliche Kirche der Pfalz
Evangelische Kirche im Rheinland
Evangelisch-Lutherische Landeskirche Schaumburg-Lippe*
Evangelisch-Lutherische Landeskirche Schleswig-Holsteins*
Evangelische Kirche von Westfalen
Evangelische Landeskirche in Württemberg
Vereinigung der Deutschen Mennonitengemeinden
(Mennonite Church)

"The Evangelical Church in Germany has made it clear through its constitution that it is a federation (Bund) of confessionally determined churches. Moreover, the conditions of membership of the World Council of Churches have been determined at the Assembly at Amsterdam. Therefore, this Evangelical Lutheran Church declares concerning its membership in the World Council of Churches:
i) It is represented in the World Council as a church of the Evangelical Lutheran confession.
ii) Representatives which it send to the World Council are to be identified as Evangelical Lutherans.
iii) Within the limits of the competence of the Evangelical Church in Germany it is represented in the World Council through the intermediary of the Council of the Evangelical Church in Germany."

German Democratic Republic
Bund der Evangelischen Kirchen in der Deutschen Demokratischen Republik
(Federation of the Evangelical Churches in the GDR)
Evangelische Landeskirche Anhalts†
Evangelische Kirche in Berlin-Brandenburg†
Evangelische Kirche des Görlitzer Kirchengebietes†
Evangelische Landeskirche Greifswald†
Evangelisch-Lutherische Landeskirche Mecklenburgs†
Evangelische Kirche der Kirchenprovinz Sachsen†
Evangelische-Lutherische Landeskirche Sachsens†
Evangelisch-Lutherische Kirche in Thüringen†
Evangelische Brüder-Unität (Distrikt Herrnhut)
(Moravian Church)
Gemeindeverband der Alt-Katholischen Kirche in der Deutschen Demokratischen Republik
(Federation of the Old Catholic Church in the GDR)

Ghana
Evangelical Presbyterian Church
The Methodist Church, Ghana
Presbyterian Church of Ghana

Greece
Ekklesia tes Ellados
(Church of Greece)
Hellenike Evangelike Ekklesia
(Greek Evangelical Church)

Hong Kong
The Church of Christ in China, The Hong Kong Council

Hungary
Magyarországi Baptista Egyház
(Baptist Church in Hungary)
Magyarországi Evangélikus Egyház
(Lutheran Church in Hungary)
Magyarországi Reformatus Egyház
(Reformed Church in Hungary)

Iceland
Evangelical Lutheran Church of Iceland

India
Church of North India
Church of South India
Federation of Evangelical Lutheran Churches in India
Mar Thoma Syrian Church of Malabar
The Orthodox Syrian Church, Catholicate of the East
The Samavesam of Telugu Baptist Churches

Indonesia
Banua Niha Keriso Protestan Nias
(The Church of Nias)

†United in a fellowship of Christian witness and service in the Federation of Evangelical Churches in the GDR, these churches are represented in the Council through agencies of the Federation of Evangelical Churches in the GDR.

Christian Protestant Church in Indonesia
Evangelical Christian Church in Halmahera
Gereja Batak Karo Protestan
(Karo Batak Protestant Church)
Gereja-Gereja Kristen Java
(Christian Churches of Java)
Gereja Kalimantan Evangelis
(Kalimantan Evangelical Church)
Gereja Kristen Indonesia
(Indonesian Christian Church)
Gereja Kristen Injili di Irian Jaya
(Evangelical Christian Church in West Irian)
Gereja Kristen Jawi Wetan
(Christian Church of East Java)
Gereja Kristen Pasundan
(Pasundan Christian Church)
Gereja Kristen Sulawesi Tengah
(Christian Church in Mid-Sulawesi)
Gereja Masehi Injili Minahasa
(Christian Evangelical Church in Minahasa)
Gereja Masehi Injili Sangihe Talaud (GMIST)
(Evangelical Church of Sangir Talaud)
Gereja Masehi Injili di Timor
(Protestant Evangelical Church in Timor)
Gereja Protestan di Indonesia)
(Protestant Church in Indonesia)
Gereja Protestan Maluku
(Protestant Church of the Moluccas)
Gereja Kristen Protestan Simalungun
(Simalungun Protestant Christian Church)
Gereja Toraja
(Toraja Church)
Huria Kristen Batak Protestan
(Protestant Christian Batak Church)
Huria Kristen Indonesia (H.K.I.)
(The Indonesian Christian Church)

Iran
Apostolic Catholic Assyrian Church of the East
Synod of the Evangelical Church of Iran

Italy
Chiesa Evangelica Metodista d'Italia
(Evangelical Methodist Church of Italy)
Chiesa Evangelica Valdese
(Waldensian Church)

Jamaica
The Moravian Church in Jamaica
The United Church of Jamaica and Grand Cayman

Japan
Japanese Orthodox Church
Nippon Kirisuto Kyodan
(The United Church of Christ in Japan)
Nippen Sei Ko Kai
(Angelican-Episcopal Church in Japan)

Jerusalem
Episcopal Church in Jerusalem and the Middle East
Greek Orthodox Patriarchate of Jerusalem

Kenya
African Christian Church and Schools
African Israel Church, Ninevah
Church of the Province of Kenya
The Methodist Church in Kenya

Korea
The Korean Methodist Church
The Presbyterian Church in the Republic of Korea
The Presbyterian Church in Korea

Lebanon
Armenian Apostolic Church
Union of the Armenian Evangelical Churches in the Near East

Lesotho
Lesotho Evangelical Church

Liberia
Lutheran Church in Liberia

Madagascar
Eglise de Jésus Christ à Madagascar
(Church of Jesus Christ in Madagascar)
Eglise Luthérienne Malgache
(Malagasy Lutheran Church)

Malaysia
The Methodist Church in Malaysia

Mauritius
Church of the Province of the Indian Ocean

Mexico
Iglesia Metodista de México
(Methodist Church of Mexico)

Netherlands
Algemene Doopsgezinde Sociëteit
(General Mennonite Society)
Evangelisch Lutherse Kerk
(Evangelical Lutheran Church)
De Gereformeerde Kerken in Nederland
(The Reformed Churches in the Netherlands)
Nederlandse Hervormde Kerk
(Netherlands Reformed Church)
Oud-Katholieke Kerk van Nederland
(Old Catholic Church of the Netherlands)
Remonstrantse Broederschap
(Remonstrant Brotherhood)

New Caledonia
Eglise Evangélique en Nouvelle Calédonie et aux Iles Loyauté
(Evangelical Church in New Caledonia and the Loyalty Isles)

New Hebrides
Presbyterian Church of the New Hebrides

New Zealand
Associated Churches of Christ in New Zealand
The Baptist Union of New Zealand
Church of the Province of New Zealand
The Methodist Church of New Zealand
The Presbyterian Church of New Zealand

Nigeria
Church of the Lord (Aladura)
Methodist Church, Nigeria
Nigerian Baptist Convention
The Presbyterian Church of Nigeria

Norway
Den Norske Kirke
(Church of Norway)

Pakistan
The Church of Pakistan
United Presbyterian Church of Pakistan

Philippines
Iglesia Filipina Independiente
(Philippine Independent Church)
United Church of Christ in the Philippines
Iglesia Evangelica Metodista en las Islas Filipinas
(The Evangelical Methodist Church in the Philippines)

Poland
Autocephalous Orthodox Church in Poland

Kosciola Ewangelicko-Augsburskiego w PRL
(Evangelical Church of the Augsburg Confession in Poland)
Kosciola Polskokatolickjego w PRL
(Polish Catholic Church in Poland)
Staro-Katolickiego Kosciola Mariatowitow w PRL
(Old Catholic Mariavite Church in Poland)

Romania
Biserica Evangelica Dupa Confesiunea Dela Augsburg
(Evangelical Church of the Augsburg Confession)
Biserica Ortodoxa Romane
(Romanian Orthodox Church)
Biserica Reofrmata Din Romania
(Reformed Church of Romania)
Evangelical Synodal Presbyterial Church of the Augsburg Confession in the Socialist Republic of Romania

Samoa
The Congregational Christian Church in Samoa

Sierra Leone
The Methodist Church, Sierra Leone

South Africa
The Bantu Presbyterian Church of South Africa
Church of the Province of South Africa
Evangelical Lutheran Church in Southern Africa
The Methodist Church of South Africa
Moravian Church in South Africa
The Presbyterian Church of Southern Africa
The United Congregational Church of Southern Africa

Spain
Iglesia Evangélica Española

Sri Lanka
The Angelican Church in Sri Lanka
Methodist Church, Sri Lanka

Sudan
Episcopal Church of the Sudan

Surinam
Moravian Church

Sweden
Svenska Kyrkan
(Church of Sweden)
Svenska Missionsförbundet
(The Mission Covenant Church of Sweden)

Switzerland
Christkatholische Kirche der Schweiz
(Old Catholic Church of Switzerland)
Schweizerischer Evangelischer Kirchenbund
(Swiss Protestant Church Federation)

Syria
The National Evangelical Synod of Syria and Lebanon
Patriarcat Grec-Orthodoxe d'Antioche et de tout l'Orient
(Greek Orthodox Patriarchate of Antioch and All the East)
Syrian Orthodox Patriarchate of Antioch and All the East

Tahiti
Eglise évangélique de Polynésie Francaise
(Evangelical Church of French Polynesia)

Taiwan
Tai-Oan Ki-Tok Tiu Lo Kau-Hoe
(The Presbyterian Church in Taiwan, Republic of China)

Tanzania
Church of the Province of Tanzania
Evangelical Lutheran Church in Tanzania

INTERNATIONAL AGENCIES

Thailand
The Church of Christ in Thailand

Togo
Eglise évangélique de Polynésie francaise
(Evangelical Church of Togo)

Tonga
Methodist Church of Tonga

Trinidad
The Presbyterian Church in Trinidad and Grenada

Turkey
Ecumenical Patriarchate of Constantinople

Uganda
The Church of Uganda, Rwanda and Burundi

Union of Soviet Socialist Republics
Eglise apostolique arménienne
(Armenian Apostolic Church)
Eesti Evangeeliumi Luteri usu Kirik
(Estonian Evangelical Lutheran Church)
Georgia Orthodox Church
Latvijas Evangeliska-Luteriska Baznica
(Evangelical Lutheran Church of Latvia)
Russian Orthodox Church
The Union of Evangelical Christian Baptists of USSR

United Kingdom and the Republic of Ireland
The Baptist Union of Great Britain and Ireland
Churches of Christ in Great Britain and Ireland
The Church of England
The Church of Ireland
The Church of Scotland
The Church in Wales
The Congregational Union of Scotland
Episcopal Church in Scotland
The Methodist Church
The Methodist Church in Ireland
The Moravian Union
The Presbyterian Church in Ireland
The Presbyterian Church of Wales
The Salvation Army
Union of Welsh Independents
United Free Church of Scotland
The United Reformed Church of England and Wales

United States of America
African Methodist Episcopal Church
African Methodist Episcopal Zion Church
American Baptist Churches in the U.S.A.
American Lutheran Church
The Antiochian Orthodox Christian Archdiocese
Christian Church (Disciples of Christ)
Christian Methodist Episcopal Church
Church of the Brethren
The Episcopal Church
Hungarian Reformed Church in America
International Evangelical Church
Lutheran Church in America
Moravian Church in America (Northern Province)
Moravian Church in America (Southern Province)
National Baptist Convention of America
National Baptist Convention, U.S.A., Inc.
National Council of Community Churches
The Orthodox Church in America
Polish National Catholic Church of America
Presbyterian Church in the United States
Progressive National Baptist Convention
Reformed Church in America
Religious Society of Friends

Friends General Conference
Friends United Meeting
The Romanian Orthodox Episcopate of America
United Church of Christ
The United Methodist Church
The United Presbyterian Church in the United States of America

West Africa
The Church of the Province of West Africa

West Indies
The Church in the Province of the West Indies
The Methodist Church in the Caribbean and the Americas
Moravian Church, Eastern West Indies Province

Yugoslavia
Reformatska Crke u SFRJ
(The Reformed Church in Yugoslavia)
Serbian Orthodox Church
Slovenska ev.-kr. a.v. cirkev v. Juhuslavii
(Slovak Evangelical Church of the Augsburg Confession in Yugoslavia)

Zaïre (Republic of)
Eglise du Christ au Zaïre (Communauté des Disciples)
(Church of Christ in Zaïre—Community of Disciples)
Eglise du Christ au Zaïre (Communauté du Christ Lumière)
(Church of Christ in Zaïre—Community of Christ the Light)
Eglise du Christ au Zaïre (Communauté Mennonite au Zaïre)
(Church of Christ in Zaïre—Mennonite Community in Zaïre)
Eglise du Christ sur la Terre par le Prophète Simon Kimbangu
(Church of Christ on Earth by the Prophet Simon Kimbangu)
Eglise évangélique du Zaïre
(Evangelical Church of Zaïre)
Eglise Presbytérienne au Zaïre)
(Presbytérian Church in Zaïre)

Zambia
United Church of Zambia

ASSOCIATE MEMBER CHURCHES

Algeria
Eglise Protestante d'Algérie
(Protestant Church of Algeria)

Argentina
Junta de los Discípulos de Cristo
(Disciples of Christ)
Iglesia Evangélica Luterana Unida
(United Evangelical Lutheran Church)

Bangladesh
Church of Bangladesh

Bolivia
Iglesia Evangélica Metodista en Bolivia
(Evangelical Methodist Church in Bolivia)

Cameroon
Eglise Protestante Africaine
(African Protestant Church)

Chile
Iglesia Metodista de Chile
(The Methodist Church of Chile)

Costa Rica
Iglesia Evangélica Metodista
(Evangelical Methodist Church)

Cuba
Iglesia Metodista en Cuba

(Methodist Church in Cuba)
Iglesia Presbiteriana-Reformada en Cuba
(Presbyterian-Reformed Church in Cuba)

India
Bengal-Orissa-Bihar Baptist Convention

Indonesia
Protestant Christian Church in Bali
Punguan Kristen Batak

Italy
Union of Christian Evangelical Baptists of Italy

Japan
The Korean Christian Church in Japan

Kenya
African Church of the Holy Spirit

Liberia
Presbytery of Liberia

Malaysia
Protestant Church in Sabah

Netherlands Antilles
Protestantse Kerk van de Nederlandse Antillen
(Protestant Church of the Netherlands Antilles)

Peru
Iglesia Metodista del Peru
(The Methodist Church of Peru)

Portugal
Igreja Evangélica Presbiteriana de Portugal
(Evangelical Presbyterian Church of Portugal)
Igreja Lusitana Catolica Apostolica Evangélica
(Lusitanian Catholic-Apostolic Evangelical Church)

Samoa
Methodist Church of Samoa

Singapore
Methodist Church in Singapore

Spain
Iglesia Española Reformada Episcopal
(Spanish Reformed Episcopal Church)

Sudan
The Presbyterian Church in the Sudan

Uruguay
Iglesia Evangélica Metodista en el Uruguay
(The Evangelical Methodist Church in Uruguay)

West Africa
Iglesia Evangélica de Guinea Ecuatorial
(Evangelical Church of Equatorial Guinea)

Zaïre
Eglise du Christ au Zaïre (Communauté Episcopale Baptiste en Afrique (C.E.B.A.)
(Church of Christ in Zaïre)

Anglican Consultative Council

The Anglican Consultative Council is the central council for the worldwide Anglican Communion. Its creation was proposed by the Lambeth Conference of Bishops of the Anglican Communion in 1968, and came into being by the end of 1969 with the consent of all the Provinces (or member Churches). Council meetings are held in different parts of the world. Its first meeting was held in Limuru, Kenya, in 1971; the second in Dublin, Ireland, in July, 1973; the third in Trinidad, April, 1976 and the fourth meeting was in Canada in May, 1979.

The membership includes bishops, priests, and lay people. Each Province (or member Church) is represented by up to three members and meetings are held every second or third year; the Standing Committee meets every year.

True to the Anglican Communion's style of working, the Council has no legislative powers. It fills a liaison role, consulting and recommending, and at times representing the Anglican Communion. Among its functions are "to share information about developments in one or more provinces with the other parts of the Communion and to serve as needed as an instrument of common action"; "to develop as far as possible agreed Anglican policies in the world mission of the Church and to encourage national and regional Churches to engage together in developing and implementing such policies by sharing their resources of manpower, money, and experience to the best advantage of all"; "to encourage and guide Anglican participation in the Ecumenical Movement and the ecumenical organizations."

OFFICERS

Pres., The Archbishop of Canterbury, Most Rev. Robert Runcie, Lambeth Palace, London, SE1 7JU., England.
Chpsn., Mr. J. G. Denton, P.O. Box Q190, Queen Victoria Buildings, Sydney, N.S.W. 2000, Australia
Sec. Gen., Rt. Rev. J. W. A. Howe, 14 Great Peter St., London SW1P 3NQ, England.

Baptist World Alliance

The Baptist World Alliance is a voluntary association of Baptist conventions and unions which was formed at the first world gathering of Baptists in Exeter Hall, London, England, July 11-18, 1905. There have been thirteen meetings of the Alliance's Baptist World Congress, the most recent of which was held in Stockholm, Sweden in 1975.

One hundred and fifteen Baptist bodies around the world participate in the Alliance, and these bodies represent approximately 29.6 million baptized, communicant members. Each body retains its autonomy.

BWA functions as: 1) An agency of communications between Baptists through publications, dissemination of news, film, radio, personal visits, and correspondence; 2) A forum for study and fraternal discussion of doctrines, practice and ways of witness to the world; 3) A channel of cooperation in extending help to each other and those in need; 4) A vigilant force for safeguarding religious liberty and other God-given rights; 5) a sponsor of regional and worldwide gatherings for the furtherance of the gospel; 6) an agency for promotion consultation and cooperation among Baptists; 7) an agency for promotion of evangelism and education; and 8) a sponsor of program for lay development.

Headquarters: 1628 16th St. NW, Washington, DC 20009. Tel. (202) 265-5027. Congress convenes every five years. Next meeting: Toronto, Canada, July 8-13, 1980.

OFFICERS

Pres., Dr. Duke K. McCall So. Bapt. Theol. Sem., Louisville, KY 40206
Gen. Sec., Dr. Gerhard Claas, 1628 16th St. NW, Washington, DC 20009
Associate Secs., Dr. Cyril E. Bryant, Dr. C. Ronald Goulding, Rev. Charles F. Wills, 1628 16th St. NW, Washington, DC 20009; Dr. Gerhard Class, Postfach 610 340, 2000 Hamburg 61, West Germany; Alan C. Prior, P. O. Box 163, Beecroft, NSW 2119, Australia
Assistant Sec., Betty Lee Smith, 1628 16th St., NW, Washington, DC 20009
Treas., Fred B. Rhodes, Washington, DC.

Heads of Eastern Orthodox Churches

The term "Eastern Orthodox Churches" relates to three main groups: 1) The Orthodox, composed of sixteen bodies listed below, which recognize each other and are recognized by the Ecumenical Patriarch of Constantinople, who is considered the keeper of the "canons" of Orthodoxy. 2) The Ancient Oriental Orthodox, commonly referred to as Monophysite (e.g., Copts; Ethiopian, Armenian, Syrian Orthodox, Syrian Malabar (India); and the Nestorians, known as the Assyrian Church of the East). 3) Churches which have authentic Orthodox roots and adhere to Orthodox doctrine, but which are historically estranged.

Ecumenical Patriarchate: His All-Holiness Demetrios I, Archbishop of Constantinople, and Ecumenical Patriarch, Fener, Istanbul, Turkey.
Patriarchate of Alexandria: Nicolaos V, Patriarch of Alexandria and All Egypt, Greek Orthodox Patriarchate, Alexandria, Egypt.
Patriarchate of Antioch: His Holiness Ignatius IV (Hazim), Patriarch of Antioch, Damascus, Syria.
Patriarchate of Jerusalem: His Holiness Benediktos, Patriarch of Jerusalem, Jerusalem, Israel.
Patriarchate of Russia: His Holiness Pimen, Patriarch of Moscow and All Russia, 5 Tchisty Pereulok, Moscow 34, U.S.S.R.
Patriarchate of Serbia: His Holiness German, Patriarch of the Serbian and Macedonian Orthodox Church, Belgrade, Yugoslavia.
Patriarchate of Romania: His Holiness Justin, Patriarch of Romania, Bucharest, Romania.
Patriarchate of Bulgaria: His Holiness Maxime, Patriarch of Bulgaria, Sofia, Bulgaria.
Church of Greece: His Beatitude Seraphim, Archbishop of Athens and Primate of All Greece, Athens, Greece.
Church of Cyprus: Most Rev. Archbishop Chrysostomos, Archbishop of Cyprus, Nicosia, Cyprus
Church of Sinai: The Archbishop-Abbot Damian, Mt. Sinai, Arabia.
Church of Georgia: His Beatitude Elia II, Catholicos Patriarch of All Georgia, Urbni, Georgian Republic, U.S.S.R.
Church of Albania: ———.
Church of Finland: Most Rev. Archbishop Paavali, Archbishop of Karelia and All Finland, Kupio, Finland.
Church of Poland: His Beatitude Vasili, Metropolitan of Warsaw and All Poland, Swiercxewskiego 52 Warsaw, Poland.
Church of Czechoslovakia: His Beatitude Dorotej, Metropolitan of Prague and All Czechoslovakia, V. Jame 6, Prague, Czechoslovakia.

Friends World Committee for Consultation Section of the Americas

The Friends World Committee for Consultation (FWCC) was formed in 1937. There has been an American Section as well as a European Section from the early days and an African Section was organized in 1971. In 1974 the name Section of the Americas was adopted by that part of the FWCC with constituency in North, Central and South America and in the Caribbean area. The purposes of the Section of the Americas can be summarized as follows:

1) To encourage and strengthen the spiritual life within the Society of Friends through such measures as the promotion of intervisitation, study, conferences, and a wide sharing of experience on the deepest spiritual level.

2) To help Friends to gain a better understanding of the worldwide character of the Society of Friends and its vocation in the world today.

3) To promote consultation amongst Friends of all cultures, countries, and languages. The Committee seeks to bring the different groups of Friends into intimate touch with one another on the basis of their common Quaker heritage, with a view to sharing experience and coming to some measure of agreement in regard to their attitude to modern world problems.

4) To promote understanding between Friends of all countries and members of other branches of the Christian Church and members of other religious faiths, and to interpret the specific Quaker message to those who seek for further religious experience.

5) To keep under review the Quaker contribution in world affairs and to facilitate both the examination and presentation of Quaker thinking and concern.

Headquarters: 1506 Race St., Philadelphia, PA 19102. Tel. (215) 563-0757.
Sec. Herbert M. Hadley.
Midwest Office: P. O. Box 235, Plainfield, IN 46168. Tel. (317) 839-6317.
Assoc.. Sec., Robert J. Rumsey.

Hierarchy of the Roman Catholic Church

The Hierarchy of the Roman Catholic Church consists of His Holiness, the Pope, Supreme Pastor of the Roman Catholic Church and the various bishops from around the world joined with the Pope in one apostolic body to care for the Church. Cardinals, now always bishops, number about one hundred and fifty. They serve as the chief counselors to the Pope.

The Supreme Pastor is further assisted by the Roman Curia, which consists of the Secretariat of State or the Papal Secretariat, and the Council for the Public Affairs of the Church, various Sacred Congregations, Secretariats, Tribunals, and Offices. The bishops, some bearing the title of Patriarch or Archbishop, are united with the Supreme Pastor in the government of the whole Church. The bishops, when assigned to particular sees, are individually responsible for the teaching, sanctification and governance of their particular jurisdictions of the Church.

The Papal territorial possessions are called the State of Vatican City situated within the city of Rome and occupying 108.7 acres. It is the smallest sovereign state in the world. Papal authority is recognized as supreme by virtue of a Concordat reached with the Italian state and ratified June 7, 1929. Included in Vatican City are the Vatican Palace, various museums, art galleries, libraries, apartments, officers, a radio station, post office and St. Peter's Basilica.

HIS HOLINESS THE POPE

John Paul II, Karol Wojtyla, Supreme Pastor of the Roman Catholic Church (born May 18, 1920, installed, October 22, 1978.)

THE ROMAN CURIA

(A few sections of the Roman Curia relevant to ecclesiastical bodies outside the Roman Catholic Church and to other groups and individuals are listed below.)

The Secretariat for Promoting Christian Unity. This Secretariat has responsibility for relations with non–Roman Catholic Christian religious bodies, is concerned with the observance of the principles of ecumenism, promotes bilateral conversations on Christian unity both on national and international levels; institutes colloquies on ecumenical questions and activities with churches and ecclesiastical communities separated from the Holy See; deputes Catholic observers for Christian congresses; invites to Catholic gatherings observers of the separated churches and orders into practice conciliar degrees on ecumenical matters. The Secretariat for Promoting Christian Unity deals with all questions concerning religious relations with Judaism. Cardinal Praeses: Jan Cardinal Willebrands; Vice. Pres., Most Rev. Ramon Torrella Cascante; Sec., Rev. Msgr. Charles Moeller. Office: 1 via dell'Erba, Rome, Italy.

Secretariat for Non-Christians. This Secretariat deals with those who are outside the Christian religion, profess some religion, or have a religious sense. It fosters studies and promotes relations with non-Christians to bring about an increase in mutual respect and seeks ways to establish a dialogue with them. Cardinal Praeses: Sergio Cardinal Pignedoli; Sec., Rev. Msgr. Pietro Rossano. Office: Palazzo S. Calisto, Vatican City.

Secretariat for Non-Believers. This Secretariat studies atheism in order to expore more fully its nature and to establish a dialogue with non-believers who sincerely wish to collaborate. Cardinal Praeses: Franz Cardinal Koenig; Sec., Rev. Vincent Miano, S.D.B.; Undersecretary, Msgr. Bernard Jacqueline. Office: 16 Piazza S. Calisto, Vatican City.

(Note: For a complete description and listing of the Hierarchy of the Roman Catholic Church see: the Official Catholic *Directory, 1978.* New York, P. J. Kenedy & Sons, 1978, pp. 1-7. For a description of the Roman Catholic Church in the United States and in Canada, see under Directory 3, "Religious Bodies in the United States," and Directory 4, "Religious Bodies in Canada," appearing in this **Yearbook**.)

International Association of Women Ministers

This organization was founded in 1919 and was formerly known as the American Association of Women Ministers. Membership is open to women who are licensed or ordained by Evangelical bodies. The IAWM exists to promote equal ecclesiastical rights for women in the church and to encourage young women to enter the ministry. It also aims to develop an enabling fellowship among women ministers to urge women to qualify themselves for increased efficiency in Christian service.

OFFICERS

Pres., Rev. Kathryn Williams, 2909 Lubbock, Ft. Worth, TX 76109
Gen. Sec., Constance Bradshaw, Box 52, Westfield, WI 53964
Rec. Sec., Rev. Pamela Webb, 302 S. Main, Eureka, IL 61530
Treas., Rev. Carol Sue Brown, 143 Locust St., Manchester, KY 40962.

PERIODICAL

The Woman's Pulpit (q), 5227 Castor ST., Philadelphia, PA 19124. Rev. LaVonne Althouse, Ed.

Lambeth Conference of Bishops of the Anglican Communion

The Lambeth Conference consists of all the diocesan bishops (and sometime also the assistant bishops) of the Anglican Communion, and is called together by the personal invitation of the Archbishop of Canterbury.

The first Lambeth Conference was held in 1867 at the request of the bishops in Canada and the United States, and it became a recurring event at approximately ten-year intervals.

The Anglican Communion has no central legislative body, but a practice of consultation and acknowledged interdependence assures its identity as a worldwide family of autonomous Churches and Provinces in communion with the See of Canterbury. The most frequent main instrument of consultation was the Lambeth Conference.

After the Lambeth Conference of 1958, a full-time officer, who became known as the Anglican Executive Officer, was appointed "to collect and disseminate information, keep open lines of communication, and make contact when necessary with responsible authority." The next Lambeth Conference in 1968 proposed the setting up of an Anglican Consultative Council, which, with the consent of all the Provinces (or member Churches), came into being at the end of 1969. The appointment of Secretary General of the Council replaced that of Anglican Executive Officer. The Lambeth Conference of 1978 proposed regular meetings of the Primates of the Anglican Communion.

Pres., The Archbishop of Canterbury, Most Rev. Robert Runcie, Lambeth Palace, London, SE1 7JU., England.

Lutheran World Federation

The Lutheran World Federation is the successor to an earlier organization of Lutheran churches named the Lutheran World Convention and organized in Eisenach, Germany, in 1923. World War II inflicted such tremendous damage upon the spiritual and welfare activities of Lutheran and other churches in western Europe and elsewhere in the world that it was felt necessary to establish a more functional organization. Thus, the Lutheran World Federation was organized on July 1, 1947, at Lund, Sweden, and plunged immediately into programs of emergency relief, interchurch aid, and studies. Currently it functions between assemblies through major departments of Studies, Church Cooperation, and World Service. The 1977 membership consists of 99 member churches from all parts of the world with constituencies exceeding 53 million persons.

The LWF is incorporated under Swiss law and has its headquarters in Geneva. Its constitution stipulates that "the Lutheran World Federation shall be a free association of Lutheran Churches. It shall act as their agent in such matters as they assign to it. It shall not exercise churchly functions on its own authority, nor shall it have power to legislate for the Churches belonging to it or to limit the autonomy of any Member Church.

"In accord with the preceding paragraphs, the Lutheran World Federation shall:

(a) Further a united witness before the world to the Gospel of Jesus Christ as the power of God for salvation.
(b) Cultivate unity of faith and confession among the Lutheran Churches of the world.
(c) Develop fellowship and cooperation in study among Lutherans.
(d) Foster Lutheran interest in, concern for, and participation in ecumenical movements.
(e) Support Lutheran Churches and groups as they endeavor to meet the spiritual needs of other Lutherans and to extend the Gospel.
(f) Provide a channel for Lutheran Churches and groups to help meet physical needs."

Headquarters: 150 Route de Ferney, 1211 Geneva 20, Switzerland
Meets every 5-7 years. Next meeting approximately 1984.

OFFICERS

Pres., Rt. Rev. Josiah Kibira, D.D. Evangelical Lutheran Church in Tanzania, P.O. Box 98, Bukoba, Tanzania
Vice Presidents: Rev. Dr. David W. Preus, American Lutheran Church, Minneapolis, MN; Bishop Johannes Hanselmann, Evangelical Lutheran Church of Bavaria, Munich, Germany; Dr. Andrew Hsiao, Evangelical Lutheran Church of Hong Kong
Treas., Mr. Carl-Gustav Von Ehrenheim, Sweden
Gen. Sec., Rev. Dr. Carl H. Mau, Jr., Geneva, Switzerland.
Gen. Sec., U.S. National Committee, Rev. Dr. Paul A. Wee, 360 Park Ave., S., New York, NY 10010. Tel. (212) 532-6350

PERIODICALS

Lutherische Rundschau (German Ed.), Geneva.
LWF Information (news service in English, German, French)

Mennonite World Conference

The first Conference was held in Basel, Switzerland, in 1925 under the leadership of Christian Neff, elder of the Weierhof, Palatinate, Germany. All of the major Mennonite church bodies around the world participate in the program of the World Conference and these bodies represent approximately 614,000 baptized members. The MWC does not legislate for the member churches; it convenes basically for inspiration and discussion. Each of the participating Mennonite church bodies retains its autonomy. The Mennonite World Conference normally meets every six years.

OFFICERS

Pres., Charles Christano, Jln. K. H. A. Wahid Hasyim 74, Kudus, Jateng, Indonesia.
Exec. Sec., Paul N. Kraybill, 528 East Madison St., Lombard, IL 60148

Pentecostal World Conference

The Pentecostal World Conference was organized in 1947 at Zurich, Switzerland, where Pentecostal leaders met in conference seeking ways to help bring about greater understanding and cooperation among their churches.

Formed and continuing as a nonlegislative body, the conference provides a forum for exchanging ideas, sharing information, and participating in fellowship together.

The main event of the organization is the triennial worldwide convention. Past conventions have been in Zurich, Switzerland; Paris, France; London, England; Stockholm, Sweden; Toronto, Canada; Jerusalem, Israel; Helsinki, Finland; Rio de Janeiro, Brazil; Dallas, Texas; Seoul, Korea; and London, England.

Between conventions the World Conference Advisory Committee supervises the work of the conference and plans the next convention. The 25-member committee is elected at each Pentecostal World Conference convention and has members from around the world.

Conference every three years.

OFFICERS

Chpsn., Dr. Thomas F. Zimmerman, 1445 Boonville Ave., Springfield MO 65802.
Sec., Rev. P. S. Brewster, 64 Forest House; Russell Cotes Rd., Bournemouth, Dorset, England.

PERIODICAL

World Pentecost, (q), Eric Dando, Sans Souci, Forge Lane, Bassaleg, Newport, Gwent NP1 9NG, England.

United Bible Societies

The United Bible Societies is a world fellowship of 64 national Bible Societies and 34 national offices which, through its national, regional, and global organization, coordinates the efforts of Bible Societies and their staff in over 100 countries.

The UBS was founded in 1946 to facilitate consultation and mutual support between its then 16 member Societies, thus helping them to carry out the translation, production and distribution of the Scriptures with ever-increasing effectiveness. In fulfilling this purpose the UBS has evolved over the years, and is now a single partnership of Societies—some old-established, some very recently formed—responsible corporately through national and regional representation in the operation of a World Service Budget (now totaling some $20 million annually), for planning, policy making, financing, and carrying out the worldwide work.

The UBS has functional subcommittees (on translation, production, distribution, fund raising, World Service Budget, etc.) and a team of technical consultants in these same matters, some located at the two World Service Centres (at present in London and New York) but most working in the four Regions of Africa, Americas, Asia-Pacific, and Europe. The UBS organizes training institutes and publishes technical helps for translators; coordinates and advises on the most efficient and economical production of the Scriptures; makes known and stimulates new methods of Scripture distribution, especially by church members, for whom training courses are organized; is currently working on the New Readers Project, a graded series of Scriptures for the millions who study in the worldwide literacy campaigns and have no reading material at the end of their courses; represents Bible Society interests at world and regional interdenominational conferences and committees; and when necessary coordinates arrangements to provide Scriptures in emergency situations.

Headquarters: P.O. Box 755, D-7000 Stuttgart 1, West Germany
Council and Assembly meeting at least once every ten years.

OFFICERS

Pres., The Rev. Dr. Oswald C. J. Hoffmann
Gen. Sec., The Rev. Ulrich Fick.

PERIODICALS

United Bible Societies Bulletin (q); The Bible translator (q); Technical Papers (1 & 3), Practical Papers (2 & 4); World Report (m); Les Cahiers; Prayer Booklet; La Biblia en America Latina.

World Alliance of Reformed Churches (Presbyterian and Congregational)

The World Alliance of Reformed Churches (Presbyterian and Congregational) was formed in 1970 at Nairobi, Kenya, with the union of the former World Alliance of Reformed Churches and the former International Congregational Council. Both organizations were composed of member churches whose origins lie mainly in the Reformation with which the names of Calvin and Zwingli are linked.

Member churches constituent to WARC number 145 in some 80 different countries with a total estimated 60 million people as members.

The constitution provides that *ordinarily* once in five years delegates from member churches will meet in General Council (Assembly). Only this Assembly has the authority to make and administer policies and plans, and to speak as the Alliance. Between Assemblies, the Executive Committee exercises general oversight of the Alliance work; it meets annually.

The Executive Committee consists of the president, three vice-presidents, department heads, and fifteen members, WARC headquarters are in the ecumenical center in Geneva, Switzerland, and its staff members maintain close contact with departments and agencies of the World Council of Churches and with the executives of other world confessional organizations.

Regional needs and growing membership in all parts of the world have produced area organizations within the Alliance. Two areas are fully organized: Europe and North America; an informal consultative group is at work in Latin America. The major object of such area organizations is to provide means of cooperation, fellowship, and study in specific regions of the world.

THE ALLIANCE
OFFICERS

Pres., Rev. Dr. James I. McCord, Princeton Theological Seminary, Princeton, NJ 08540
Vice Presidents: Dr. Chung Hyun Ro, Korea; Rev. Karoly Toth, Hungary; Rev. Samuel Habib, Egypt
Gen. Sec., Rev. Dr. Edmond Perret, 150 route de Ferney, 1211 Geneva 20, Switzerland.
North American Sec., Rev. James E. Andrews, 341 Ponce de Leon Ave. NE, Atlanta, GA 30308
Gen. Treas., Mr. Jean Francois Rochette, 11, Corraterie, 1204 Geneva, Switzerland

THE NORTH AMERICAN AREA
OFFICERS

Chpsn., Dr. Randall T. Ruble (Associate Reformed Presbyterian Church), P.O. Box 172, Due West, SC 29639
Vice Chpsn., Rev. Patricia McClurg (Presbyterian Church in the United States), 341 Ponce de Leon Ave., N.E., Atlanta, GA 30308
North American Sec., Rev. James E. Andrews, 341 Ponce de Leon Ave. NE, Atlanta, GA 30308. (Presbyterian Church in the United States.)
Treas., Rev. Donald C. MacDonald (Presbyterian Church in Canada), Don Mills, Ontario, Canada
Dir. of Information, The Rev. Frank H. Heinze, 475 Riverside Dr., New York, NY 10027 (United Presbyterian Church in the U.S.A.)

World Alliance of Young Men's Christian Associations

The World Alliance of YMCAs was constituted at the First World Conference of Young Men's Christian Associations, held in Paris in 1855. Geneva, Switzerland, was designated as its headquarters, and in the early years the work was largely undertaken by lay and honorary officers, using the professional assistance of the staff of some National Movements. In 1878 a permanent office was acquired and the first General Secretary, with related staff, was appointed.

The World Alliance is basically a confederation, its members being the National YMCAs around the world. At present 66 National YMCA Movements maintain membership in the Alliance, and in addition to these, the World Alliance cooperates with YMCAs in 17 other countries where National Movements have not yet been organized. Thus the World Alliance provides the coordination and service functions for National Movements which National Movements in turn provide for the Member Associations in their several countries.

The basis of the World Alliance, popularly known as the Paris Basis, because it was at the 1855 Conference in Paris that it was formulated, is as follows:

> "The Young Men's Christian Association seek to unite those young men who, regarding Jesus Christ as their God and Saviour according to the Holy Scriptures, desire to be His disciples in their faith and in their life, and to associate their efforts for the extension of His Kingdom amongst young men."
>
> "Any differences of opinion on other subjects, however important in themselves, shall not interfere with the harmonious relations of the Constituent Members and Associates of the World Alliance."

The World Alliance is governed by a World Council of YMCAs, which meets at four-year intervals. An Executive Committee and Committees on Finance, Refugees and Rehabilitation, Development, Leadership, Intermovement Cooperation meet at regular intervals between World Councils and carry the responsibility for the ongoing work. Other Commissions are related to Christian Emphasis, Human Rights, Communication and Constituency.

It helps to coordinate intermovement cooperation, particularly to extend the Movement into new fields and to develop new programs. It represents the World Movements at the United Nations and its agencies. It cooperates with other world Christian bodies, notably the World YWCA, the World Council of Churches and the World Student Christian Federation. Close relationships and cooperation is maintained with the Roman Catholic Church.

Headquarters: 37 Quai Wilson, 1201 Geneva, Switzerland. Tel. (022) 32-31-00

OFFICERS

Pres., Walter Arnold
Sec. Gen., Hector Caselli, 37 Quai Wilson, 1201 Geneva, Switzerland.

World Association for Christian Communication

The World Association for Christian Communication (WACC) is a professional service organization working with churches and other groups in more than 50 countries to use media for the proclamation of the Christian Gospel in its relevance to all of life.

WACC channels more than $2 million yearly to more than 125 communication projects in developing nations as well as providing professional services for management, planning and coordination. Funds come from churches and related agencies, mostly in North America and Europe.

WACC also helps communicators improve skills through training, consultations, research and information exchange.

WACC's 235 corporate members include Protestant, Catholic and Orthodox churches and related groups as well as secular organizations. (WACC also has more than 500 personal members.) Members are divided into regional associations: Africa, Asia, Europe, Latin America-Caribbean, Middle East, Pacific and North America.

Headquarters: 122 King's Rd., London SW3 4TR, England. Tel. (01) 589-1484

OFFICERS

Pres., Dr. Christopher O. Kolade (Nigeria)
Sec., Dr. Curtis A. Chambers (USA)
Treas., Drs. Jan van Dis (Netherlands)
Chpsns., of Regional Associations, Africa, Dr. Christopher O. Kolade (Nigeria); Asia, Mr. Mathew S. Ogawa (Japan); Europe, Rev. Michael de Vries (Switzerland); Latin America-Caribbean, Mr. Pablo LaMoglie (Argentina); Middle East, Mr. Gabriel Habib (Lebanon); Pacific, Rev. Galuefa Aseta (Fiji); North America, Dr. John Mangum (USA)

STAFF

Gen. Sec., Dr. Hans W. Florin (Fed. Rep. of Germany)
Dir., Electronic Media, Mr. Neville D. Jayaweera (Sri Lanka)
Dir. Print Media Development, Dr. Albert D. Manuel (India)
Exec. Sec., Group Media, Rev. Don Roper (USA)
Exec. Sec. for Communication Edu., Mrs. Thelma Awori (Liberia)
Exec. Sec. for Periodicals Development, Dr. Michael Traber (Switzerland)
Information Officer, Editor of *Action,* Rev. Ronald T. Englund (USA)

PERIODICALS

WACC Journal (q), Dr. Michael Traber, Ed.
Action Newsletter (10/yr.), Rev. Ronald T. Englund, Ed.

World Convention of Churches of Christ

The World Convention of Churches of Christ was organized in 1930 in Washington, D.C. It normally meets every five years and is an international confessional grouping including churches and work in 60 countries of the world. It uses the name "Churches of Christ" because it is the name used by many of its churches in various parts of the world.

This organization, according to its constitution, "may in no way interfere with the independence of the churches or assume the administrative functions of existing ongoing organizations among us." It exists "in order, more fully to show the essential oneness of the churches in the Lord Jesus Christ; impart inspiration to the world brotherhood; cultivate the spirit of fellowship; provide unity among the churches; and to cooperate with Christians everywhere toward the unity of the Church upon the basis of the New Testament."

Headquarters: 3603 Lemmon, Dallas, TX 75219
Next Convention: Honolulu, Hawaii, July 15-20, 1980.

OFFICERS

Pres., Rev. Forrest D. Haggard, 7600 W. 75th St., Overland Park, KS 66204
First Vice-Pres., Rev. Richmond I. Nelson, Lawrence Tavern, Jamaica.
Gen. Sec., Dr. Allan W. Lee, Dallas, Texas.

World Council of Synagogues (Conservative)

The World Council of Synagogues (Conservative) was organized in 1957 as an alliance of Conservative synagogues and synagogue organizations throughout the world. Its purpose is to extend fellowship and mutual aid to each other and to foster the growth and development of Conservative Judaism.

OFFICERS

Pres., David Zucker 155 Fifth Ave., New York, NY 10010 Tel. (212) 533-7800.
Act. Pres., Rabbi Mordecai Waxman, Temple Israel of Great Neck, 108 Old Mill Rd., Great Neck, NY 10023, Tel. (516) 372-7800 Exec. Dir., Mrs. Zipporah Liben Cons., Mrs. Muriel Bermar

World Methodist Council

The World Methodist Council is an association of 62 different Methodist, or Methodist-related groups at work in 90 countries of the world. According to its constitution, "it does not seek to legislate for them nor to invade their autonomy. Rather it exists to serve them and to give unity to their witness and enterprise."

Although the name World Methodist Council was adopted in 1951 at Oxford, England, the Council dates from 1881, when the first Ecumenical Methodist Conference met in London, England. As the Ecumenical Methodist Conference, this world organization convened at ensuing ten-year intervals with the exception of the 1941 Conference, which because of World War II was not held until 1947. Since 1951, meetings have been held every five years.

The membership of the Council is composed of autonomous churches or such units of international church organizations as have attained a significant degree of autonomy.

The World Methodist Council seeks: to deepen the fellowship of the Methodist peoples over the barriers of race, nationality, color, and language; to foster Methodist participation in the ecumenical movement and to promote the unity of Methodist witness and service in that movement; to advance unity of theological and moral standards in the Methodist churches of the world; to suggest priorities in Methodist activity; to promote the most effective use of Methodist resources in the Christian mission throughout the world; to encourage evangelism in every land; to promote Christian education and the church's care for youth; to uphold and relieve persecuted or needy Christian minorities; to provide a means of consultation and cooperation between world Methodism and the other world communions of the Christian Church; to study union and reunion proposals which affect Methodist member churches and to offer advice and help as needed; to arrange the exchange of preachers through a committee appointed for that purpose.

OFFICERS

Gen. Sec., Joe Hale, Lake Junaluska, NC 28745; Tel. (704) 456-9432; Geneva Secretary, Frank Northam, 150 Route de Ferney, 1211 Geneva 20, Switzerland; Tel. 33-34-00.

World Evangelical Fellowship

Founded in 1951 in the Netherlands, the World Evangelical Fellowship: 1) organizes and stimulates the development of national evangelical fellowships, 2) serves as a catalyst, an efficient liaison between evangelicals to avoid costly duplication in evangelism, mission, theological research and training, emergency relief, social justice and other biblical concerns, 3) builds bridges between men and women who share the evangelical faith, regardless of denomination or nationality.

Headquarters: P. O. Box 670, Colorado Springs, CO 80901. Tel. (303) 635-1612

OFFICERS

Gen. Sec., Waldron Scott, P. O. Box 670, Colorado Springs, CO 80901. Tel. (303) 635-1612.
Executive Council: Dr. Hudson T. Armerding (USA), Pres.; Mr. Brian Bayston (Australia); Dr. C. Lal Rema (India); Dr. Petros Octavianus (Indonesia); Dr. Claude Noel (Haiti); Mr. Gordon Landreth (Great Britain); Mr. Samuel Odunaike (Nigeria).

WORLD EVANGELICAL FELLOWSHIP MEMBER BODIES

Association of Evangelicals of Angola
Australian Evangelical Alliance
Evangelical Fellowship of Botswana
Evangelical Fellowship of Canada
Association of Evangelical Churches of Central Africa
China Evangelical Fellowship
Evangelical Alliance of Denmark
French Evangelical Alliance
German Evangelical Alliance
Evangelical Alliance of Great Britain
Guyana Evangelical Fellowship
Council of Evangelical Churches of Haiti
Pan-Hellenic Evangelical Alliance
Evangelical Fellowship of India
Indonesia Evangelical Fellowship
Italian Evangelical Fellowship
Evangelical Federation of the Ivory Coast
Jamaica Association of Evangelicals
Evangelical Fellowship of Kenya
Liberia Evangelical Fellowship
Evangelical Association of Malawi
National Evangelical Fellowship, Malaysia
Protestant Evangelicals of Mali
New Zealand Evangelical Alliance
Nigerian Evangelical Fellowship
Evangelical Fellowship of Pakistan
Philippine Council of Evangelical Churches
Evangelical Alliance of Portugal
Evangelical Fellowship of Rhodesia
Evangelical Fraternity of Senegal
Evangelical Fellowship of Sierra Leone
Association of Evangelicals of South Africa
Evangelical Alliance of the South Pacific
Spanish Evangelical Alliance
Evangelical Alliance of Sri Lanka
Swiss Evangelical Alliance
Evangelical Fellowship of Thailand
Trinidad and Tobago Council of Evangelical Churches
National Association of Evangelicals, U.S.A.
Federation of Evangelical Churches and Missions in Upper Volta
Evangelical Fellowship of Vietnam
Evangelical Fellowship of Zambia
Association of Evangelicals in Zwaziland

PERIODICALS

Global Report (bi-m), P. O. Box 760, Colorado Springs, CO 80901.
Evangelical Review of Theology (bi-a), P.O. Box 670, Colorado Springs, CO 80901.

World Student Christian Federation

The World Student Christian Federation was founded in 1895 by a group of Student Christian Movement leaders, John R. Mott prominent among them. WSCF now has movements in more than 90 countries with constituency at all levels of education: high schools, higher education, and the academic community generally. For many years WSCF published the quarterly *Student World*, which has been replaced by regional publications. A new WSCF *Journal* is planned for the coming year. The WSCF North American *Newsletter* is available from the North American Regional Office.

The Federation played a significant role in promoting ecumenism among Christian denominations and therefore in creating the World Council of Churches in 1948.

At the Helsinki, Finland, General Assembly in 1968, a decision was made to regionalize the WSCF. Now, six regional continental offices serve as the coordination points of regional and inter-regional programs for implementing the vocation of Christian community and furthering programs working toward a just world.

At the last General Assembly, in Colombo, Sri Lanka in February, 1977, the WSCF articulated a new project on "Education in the Struggle for Liberation." This is a further development of the WSCF's previous commitments to liberation, and to work within educational institutions. Continued and vigorous commitment to theological reflection and involvement in the church community undergirds the program.

Headquarters: 37 Quai Wilson, 1201 Geneva, Switzerland.
North American Office: 427 Bloor St., W., Toronto, Ontario M5S 1X 7

OFFICERS

Gen. Sec., Dr. Emidio Campi
Chairperson, Mr. Bereket Yebio
North American Secs.: Ms. Debra House and Mr. John Boonstra

World Union for Progressive Judaism

The World Union for Progressive Judaism was established in London, England, in 1926, by representatives of Liberal, Progressive, and Reform congregational associations and individual synagogues from six nations. The movement has grown, and today the World Union stimulates the development of a worldwide movement and its congregations in 25 countries. The membership of these congregations totals approximately 1.1 million Jewish men, women, and children.

The World Union operates a secondary school in Haifa, Israel, a college for training rabbis in London, and a teacher training school for the French-speaking world in Paris. It extends organizational and financial assistance to new congregations in many countries, assigns and employs rabbis wherever Jews are in search of their religious heritage, operates religious and social youth programs in Israel and Europe, publishes prayer books and other texts in many languages, holds biennial conferences for Jewish leaders and scholars from all corners of the world.

Office: 838 5th Ave., New York, NY 10021. Tel. (212) 249-0100.

OFFICERS

Pres., Rabbi Dr. David H. Wice
Exec. Dir., Rabbi Richard G. Hirsch.
Dir., North American Board, Rabbi Ira S. Youdovin.

World Young Women's Christian Association

The World YWCA was founded in 1894 by four of the existing National YWCAs: the Associations of Great Britain, Norway, Sweden, and the United States. During the first years of its history the world movement, reflecting the patterns of its national affiliates, was primarily made up of members of various Protestant denominations. However, as the work spread around the world, Roman Catholic and Orthodox Christians joined the Association and the World YWCA became consciously ecumenical. Today it includes large numbers of women from all confessions and serves many women and girls of many faiths. The latest World YWCA constitution was adopted in 1955 and expressed the functions of the World Association as follows:

> "The World YWCA provides a channel for the sharing of resources and the exchange of experience among its affiliated associations.
>
> It helps its affiliated associations with the development of their leadership and programme.
>
> It surveys new fields and promotes work to meet the needs therein.
>
> It acts in cooperation with world voluntary movements and with intergovernmental organizations in matters of common concern.
>
> It works for international understanding for improved social and economic conditions and for basic human rights for all people.
>
> In times of emergency it undertakes and sponsors international humanitarian, welfare, and relief work, in accordance with Christian principles, irrespective of religious, social, political, national or racial differences."

The YWCA is now at work in 80 countries with programs including a variety of educational activities, vocational training programs for women and girls, hostels, rural projects, and programs of study and action in relation to social and economic issues. A wide network of sharing of financial resources and personnel between Associations and of financial aid from other sources forms the World YWCA program of development aid. The World YWCA also carries on refugee services in cooperation with other ecumenical bodies and with its own member associations.

The World YWCA has a legislative Council which brings together representatives of its national affiliates every four years and an Executive Committee made up of twenty members from all parts of the world which meets annually. An international staff works at the headquarters in Geneva.

Headquarters: 37 Quai Wilson, 1201 Geneva, Switzerland. Tel. (022) 32-31-00.

OFFICERS

Pres., Ms. Nita Barrow
Gen. Sec., Ms. Erica Brodie

World's Christian Endeavor Union

Christian Endeavor is a movement composed of committed followers of Jesus Christ, organized in groups called societies or grades, for the purpose of: leading young people (also children and adults) to accept Jesus Christ as Saviour and Lord; bringing them into the life of the church; sustaining and training them for the service of Christ and his cause; releasing them through all channels of human activity in the service of God and man.

Christian Endeavor societies are generally sponsored by a local church, which determines theology, program, activities, and relationships. In most countries it is a graded program including organizational pattern and materials for various age groups.

The first society was organized February 2, 1881, in Portland, Maine. The idea spread rapidly, and by 1895 Christian Endeavor had become a worldwide movement and the World's Christian Endeavor Union was organized in Boston, Mass. As the movement spread to other lands, many national unions were formed. Presently, Christian Endeavor operates in 78 nations and islands and is used by 93 different Christian groups; there are approximately 2 million members worldwide. The World's Union is composed of two areas for the effective promotion of the work—Area I (the Americas, Caribbean, Pacific Region, and Asia) and Area II (Europe, Africa, India, Pakistan, and the Near East). World conventions are held quadrennially and Area conferences in the intervening years. The union is incorporated and is governed by a Council which meets every four years, a Board of Trustees which meets annually, and an Executive Committee which meets on call. There are no full-time paid employees. Most of the work is carried on by volunteer service.

Headquarters: 1221 E. Broad St., P.O. Box 1110. Columbus, OH 43216. Tel. (614) 253-8541.
Area II Office: "Sunnydene," 23 Leamington Rd., Ryton-on-Dunsmore, Coventry VC8 3FL, England.
Next convention: Portland, Maine, 1981.

OFFICERS

Pres., Rev. Arno Pagel.
Exec. Sec. and Treas., Phyllis I. Rike.
Gen. Sec., Rev. Charles W. Barner.
Area II. Gen. Sec., William J. Sharpe.

6. UNITED STATES REGIONAL AND LOCAL ECUMENICAL AGENCIES

Christians and Christian churches relate to each other through ecumenical agencies in many and varied ways at different regional and local levels. Some agencies have single purpose programs such as ministry to drug addicts, or to persons released from prison, or to senior citizens. Other agencies are broad and inclusive. Some serve an extensive geography, such as Appalachia, whereas others are neighborhood-oriented "cluster parishes." Many agencies bring together church people (ministerial associations, local units of Church Women United, etc.), while others provide for cooperation of congregations, judicatory units, or church agencies. "Council of Churches" is still a standard designation for organization of churches in relation to each other, but new terms have come into use such as "conference of churches," "area church board," "area coalition," "ecumenical ministry," "cooperative ministry," "interchurch agencies" and "association of churches."

If a composite list of all local and regional ecumenical instrumentalities and ministeriums were compiled, it would number into many thousands: however, no such compilation exists at this time. The **Yearbook** listing which follows includes the more standard regional and local ecunenical expressions, including a number that serve on an interstate basis. Interstate agencies are listed first. There are other ecumenical agencies, but accurate information is not available concerning them. More information concerning local ecumenical developments within a state is usually available from the state ecumenical agency.

After the interstate agencies this section lists states, arranged alphabetically, with the state-wide ecumenical agencies listed first; then follow metropolitan, city, or area agencies with paid staff, listed alphabetically by name of agency using significant geographical words in the title.

For councils or agencies with paid staff, the name, address, and telephone number of the agency are given and the names of all professional staff are listed. When the name of the city is omitted from an address, the city is the same as the headquarters of the organization. For councils or agencies with voluntary leadership, consult the state Council of Churches or the Commission on Regional and Local Ecumenism, address below.

Information concerning changes in staff, officers, mailing addresses, and program emphases for those agencies listed here can be secured from the Commission on Regional and Local Ecumenism, National Council of Churches, 475 Riverside Dr., New York, NY 10027, or it may be secured from the executive or the president of the agency.

Listing includes information available through November, 1979, by the Commission on Regional and Local Ecumenism. †Indicates that information is repeated from the previous **Yearbook** listing, since no more recent report was received.

REGIONAL

†Association for Christian Training and Service

1808 W. End Ave., Nashville, TN 37203
Tel. (615) 329-1560
Exec. Dir., Rev. Ted McEachern
Assoc. Dir., Rev. Mance Jackson, P.O. Box 92284, Atlanta, GA 30314. Tel. (404) 525-6827
Adm. Asst., Mrs. Bobbie Roberts
Major Activities: Consultation; Training; Black Training; Research; Evaluation; Ecumenical Cooperation; Mission Development

The Commission on Religion in Appalachia, Inc.

864 Weisgarber Rd., NW, Knoxville, TN 37919
Tel. (615) 584-6133
Coordinator, Rev. John B. McBride
Adm. Asst., Paula Pace
Chpsn., Rev. Donald Steele, P.O. Box 3701, Knoxville, TN 37919
Treas., Rev. Dwayne Yost, Rt. 3, Box 418, Manchester, KY 40962
Appalachian Development Projects Cmte., Coord., Jim Boldenow; Chpsn., Mike Maloney
Social, Economic and Political Issues Task Force, Coord., Ms. Tena Willemsma; Chpsn., Sr. Shawn Scanlan
Resource Mobilization Task Force, Chpsn., Rev. John Price; Coord., Dr. Carl Burke
Parish Development Task Force, Chpsn, Rev. Peter Fulghum

A 13-state regional ecumenical agency composed of 19 communions (national mission boards and judicatories); 10 state councils of churches; The Council of the Southern Mountains, Inc.; Commission on Regional and Local Ecumenism, National Council of Churches; National Catholic Rural Life Conference: Lutheran Council in the USA; and Christian Associates of Southwest Pennsylvania

IMPACT

110Maryland Ave., NE, Washington, DC 20002
Tel. (202) 544-8636
National Director, Rev. Robert Odean

An interfaith legislative information and action network. Design of information flow: education and perspective development; progress and status reports; action alerts with recommendations for immediate response; network organizations with specific response objectives.

National Farm Worker Ministry

1430 W. Olympic Blvd., Los Angeles, CA 90015
Tel. (213) 386-8130
Exec. Dir., Rev. Wayne C. Hartmire

Continuing the National Migrant Ministry. Related to the National Council of the Churches of Christ in the U.S.A.

ALABAMA

No state council at present

ALASKA

Alaska Christian Conference

Box 441, Fairbanks 99707
Pres., John J. Shaffer, Box 907, Nome 99762
Sec.-Treas., Milton Hunt, 740 West Tenth St., Juneau 99801
Major Activities: Legislative & Social Concerns, Resources and Continuing Education, New Ecumenical Ministries, Communication

ARIZONA

North Phoenix Corporate Ministry

555 W. Glendale Ave., Phoenix 85021
Exec. Dir., Rev. Fredrick A. Barnhill

ARKANSAS

Arkansas Council of Churches

715 W. 22nd St., P.O. Box 6011, Little Rock 72216. Tel. (501) 375-1553
Adm.-Coordinator, Mrs. Frances P. Wood
Pres., Rev. Preston H. Russell, 1903 Izard, Little Rock 72206
Sec., Mrs. John Stephans, 811 N.W. 4th St., Bryant 72022
Treas., Mrs. Eugene Wolfe, 1602 Green Mt. Dr., Apt. I-153, Little Rock 72211
Major Activities: Task Forces on Hunger, Aging, Energy & Disasters; Institutional Ministry; Church World Service; Heifer Project; Christian Recreational Ministry; Ecumenical Worship Seminar; Week of Prayer for Christian Unity; Interfaith Executive Roundtable; Theological Studies; Church in Community Seminar; Mt. Sequoyah Ecumenical Mission Conference; T.V. Awareness; Communications; Liaison with State Agencies—Family Planning, Drug Abuse, Rural Health; Governor's Prayer Breakfast; Interfaith Relations; Church Women United

CALIFORNIA

Northern California Ecumenical Council

944 Market St., Rm. 400, San Francisco 94102
Tel. (415) 433-3024
Exec. Dir., Rev. John Pairman Brown
Bookkeeper, Miss Janet Verkuyl
Exec. Dir. of JSAC, Rev. Hector Lopez
Dir., Calif. Food Network, Caryl Weisberg
Sec., Mary Huenink
Pres., Rev. Robert Bulkley
Treas., Beverly Plambeck
Major Activities: Legislation; Hunger; Opposition to Death Penalty; Urban Ministry; Coordination; Native Americans; Farm Worker Ministry; Human Rights; Parks Ministry; Nuclear Energy and Power; Legislation

Office for State Affairs

1300 N. St., Sacramento 95814
Tel. (916) 442-5447
Exec. Dir., Rev. Glen Holman
Calif. Food Policy Advocate, Ms. Anna Hackenbracht
Major Activities: Monitoring State Legislation; Calif. IMPACT Network; Farmers Markets, Preservation of Prime Agricultural Land; Legislative Principles

Southern California Council of Churches

5250 Santa Monica Blvd., Los Angeles 90029
Tel. (213) 665-5771
Exec. Dir., Rev. Priscilla A. Chaplin
Pres., Rev. Leland Wilson
Treas., Dr. Earl Kernahan
Major Activities: Church Women United; Faith and Order Studies; Local Councils; Interreligious Coalition on the Aging; Interfaith Hunger Coalition; Women Committed to Women; Ecumedia; Legislative Issues Studies: Office of State Affairs (Sacramento, California); Church World Service; CROP; Ecology Studies and Action: Ministry to State Parks; Farm Worker's Ministry; Interreligious Council of Southern California; Joint Strategy and Action Coalition (JSAC); Ministers Convocation; Immigration and Refugee Task Force State Advisory Committee for Institutional Religion

†Greater Bakersfield Council of Churches

500 Truxtun Ave., Bakersfield 93301
Tel. (805) 325-8794
Ofc. Sec., Mrs. Phyllis Indermill
Pres., Rev. David C. Campbell, 3017 Hollins 93305
Treas., Dick Bruce, 2624 Cherry 93304
Major Activities: Public Relations; Christian Education; CWS Participation: Easter Work Camps; UNICEF: Hospital Chaplaincy; Christian Missions

Berkeley Area Interfaith Council

2340 Durant Ave., Rm. 206, Berkeley, 94704
Tel. (415) 841-0881
Exec. Dir., William Shive
Office Sec., Geraldine Lambert
Pres., Bettina Gray
Vice Pres., Husayn Neuzil
Sec., Sara Blackstock
Treas., Louise Staltenberg
Major Activities: News/Notes; Weekly Radio program, "Spiritual Resources"; Advocacy for Religious Freedom; Advocacy for Community Service programs; Religious and Social issues Roundtable; Information and Referrals

Pacific and Asian American Center for Theology and Strategies (PACTS)

1798 Scenic Ave. Berkeley 94709
Tel. (415) 848-0173
Interim Dir., Mrs. Kathleen A. Thomas-Sano
Pres., Rev. Lloyd K. Wake
Sec., Rev. Leo K. Constantino
Treas., Rev. Kay Sakaguchi
Major Activities: Collect and Disseminate Resource Materials; Training Conferences; Affirmative Action in Theological Education; Community Action

Council of Churches of Contra Costa County

404 Gregory Lane, Pleasant Hill 94523
Tel. (415) 689-4363
Exec. Director, Mrs. Joyce Bench
Chaplains: Rev. Keith Spooner; Rev. Norman Behrmann; Rev. Virginia Siewert, Rev. J. Richard Flowers; Rev. Nina Alazaqui, Rev. Waldemar B. Petzoldt
Pres., Rev. James Current, St. Mark's United Methodist Church, P.O. Box 436, Moraga 94556
Treas., Mr. Kenneth Bry, 1750 Clayton Way, Concord 94521
Major Activities: Institutional Ministries; Social Education and Action; Christian Education;

†Long Beach Area Council of Churches

1542 E. 7th St., Long Beach 90813
Tel. (213) 436-3350
Exec. Dir., Rev. Don E. Lindblom, 1542 E. 7th St., Long Beach 90813
Dir. of Aging, Rev. Thomas J. Clagett
Dir. of Cmty. Action, Rev. James R. Deemer
Dir. of Refugee Center, Mrs. Mary Arimoto
Pres., Dr. Edward J. Read
Treas., Mr. Willis Bon

Major Activities: Weekday Christian Education; Aging; Hunger; Campus Ministry; Refugee Center; Hispanic Ministries; Community Worship; FISH; Communications; Interfaith Relations

The Los Angeles Council of Churches

760 S. Westmoreland Ave., Los Angeles 90005
Tel. (213) 384-3148
Exec. Dir., Ms. Mildred L. Arnold
Adm. Sec., Mrs. Josie Gant
Coord., Metropolitan Learning Center, Ms. Charlotte Heinen
Coord., Proj. Learn and Job Inf./Resource Bank, Ms. Opal Buchanan
Pres., Rev. J. B. Reese, 2445 W. Washington Blvd. 90018
Treas., Rev. Otis Armistead 320 E. 47th Pl. 90011
Major Activities: United Church Men; Church Women United; Interreligious Council; Resource Lab; Basketball League; Released Time Christian Education; Retired Senior Volunteer Program; Young Adult and Youth Ecumenical Task Group; Chaplaincy Commission; Aging Commission; Community Services; Community Issues

Interfaith Hunger Coalition

5539 W. Pico Blvd. Los Angeles 90019
Tel. (213) 933-5943
Coordinators: Pat Reif, Mike Fonte

†The Social Service Bureau of the East Bay, Inc.

534—22nd St., Oakland 94612
Tel. (415) 832-8542
Exec. Dir., Rev. Roger Boyvey
Asst. Dir., Barbara Ruffner
Senior Action Project Dir., Rev. Leslie L. Sauer
Senior Aide Program Dir., Rev. Nathaniel Linzie, Sr.
Senior Citizen Nutrition Proj., Dir., Fran Bellman
Halfway House & Creative Living Center Dir., Rev. Charles McLain
Pres., George Nobori, 649 Blair Ave., Piedmont 94611
Treas., Mrs. Anne Harper, 5040 Proctor Ave. 94618
Major Activities: Senior Action Project; Senior Aide Program; Nutrition Project for Senior Citizens; Halfway House

†The Ecumenical Council of the Pasadena Area Churches

444 E. Washington Blvd., Pasadena 91104
Tel. (213) 797-2402
Exec. Sec., Rev. Charles B. Milburn
Sec., Mrs. Rev. Robert L. Earhart
Major Activities: Christian Education; Campus Ministry; Housing; Community Worship; Peace Commission; Christian Unity; Youth; Ethnic Ministries; Hunger; Peace; Public Education; Friends in Deed; Placement Service for Older Workers

Pomona Valley Council of Churches

1753 N. Park Ave., Pomona 91768
Tel. (714) 622-3806
Pres. Mrs. Dawn Hall
Exec. Dir., Mrs. Audrey Lightbody
Sec., Dr. Frances Crago
Treas., Mr. Virgil Wilkinson
Major Activities: Leadership Training; Audiovisual Resources; Social Concerns; Low-Income Housing (through Housing Development Corporation); Pastoral Counseling Center; Broadcasting; Ecumenical Events; Church World Service; Catholic-Protestant Dialogue; Information Center; Liaison with Community Agencies

San Fernando Valley Interfaith Council

18210 Sherman Way, Ste. 220 Reseda 91335
Tel. (213) 345-4114
Exec., Mrs. Avanelle Smith
Pres., Rabbi Steven B. Jacobs, Temple Judea, 5429 Lindley Ave., Tarzana 91356
Major Activities: Seniors' Multi-Purpose Centers; Nutrition & Services; Meals to the Homebound; Project Share; "Interfaith Reporter"; Project Share Escort/Outreach; Task Forces on Interreligious Concerns, School Integration, Emergency Needs, Peace and Justice, Gay Rights, Aging

California Church Council

1300 N St., Sacramento 95814
Tel. (916) 442-5447
Administrator, Rev. Glen A. Holman
Food Policy Legislative Advocate, Anna Hackenbracht
Major Activities: Liaison between major Protestant denominations and legislative and governmental programs and offices with major emphasis on food policy

Church Service Bureau

3720 Folsom Blvd., Sacramento 95816
Tel. (916) 456-3815
Exec. Dir., Chaplain Elling E. Ramsey
Pres., Mr. Ephraim Spivek
Major Activities: Youth Chaplaincy; Volunteer Hospital and Jail Chaplaincy; Food Closet Coalition; Blood Reserve Fund; Senior Citizen Program; Contact Teleministry; Mass Media; Credit Union; Interfaith Voice; News Bulletin; Indo-Chinese Rehab. Center

San Diego County Ecumenical Conference

1875 2nd Ave., San Diego 92101
Tel. (714) 232-6385
Exec. Dir., Rev. James W. Mishler
Dirs. of Communication, Rev. Bernard Filmyer
Rev. Christopher Moore
Admin. Asst., Mrs. Mary Lewis
Pres., Rev. Harold M. Heath, Jr.
Treas., Mitchell Prior
Major Activities: Social Services and Issues; Communications: Education & Youth; Ecumenical Relations; Church Women United

San Francisco Council of Churches

944 Market St., 4th Fl., San Francisco 94102
Tel. (415) 433-3024
Exec. Dir., Mrs. Donneter E. Lane
Assoc. Dir., Mr. Jack McKay
Pres., Rev. Roland E. Grumm, 888 Turk St. 94102
Treas., Lindbergh Porter, 433 34th Ave. 94121
Major Activities: Legislation; Community Organization; Leadership Development for Seniors; Interfaith Program on Racial and Social Problems; Night Ministry; Services for Children and Youth

The Council of Churches of Santa Clara County

1229 Naglee Ave., 95129

Tel. (408) 297-2660
Exec. Min., Rev. Dwight L. Kintner
Friendly Visiting Coordinators, Ms. Kathleen McConnell and Mrs. Dona Reddy
Sec., Emergency Aid, Mrs. Ruth Keeley
Job Corps Coord., Mr. Walter Stolar
Correctional Chpln., Rev. Charles Walker
Juvenile Chaplain, Rev. Merritt Metcalf
Telephone Assurance Sec., Mrs. Wayna Tabuchi
Pres., Rev. Dr. William Youngdabl
Treas., Mrs. Wendie Chaddock
Major Activities: Services for Aging; Social Education/Action; Institutional Chaplaincies; Hunger and Emergency Services; Christian Witness and Unity; Migrant Network

Westside Ecumenical Conference

P.O. Box 1402, 1533 4th St., Santa Monica 90406
Tel. (213) 394-1518
Exec. Sec., Mrs. Helen Wallace
Pres., Dr. David Rogne, Westwood Un. Meth. Ch., 10497 Wilshire Blvd., Los Angeles 90024
Major Activities: Convalescent Hospital Visiting; Meals on Wheels; Community Religious Services and Ecumenical Affairs

Ventura County Council of Churches

P.O. Box 661, Camarillo 93010
Exec. Sec., Mark R. van de Erve, 452 Baja Ct. 93010
Pres., Rev. Lester Cleveland, P.O. Box 74, Somis 93066

COLORADO

Colorado Council of Churches

1313 Clarkson St., Denver 80218
Tel. (303) 832-9309
Exec. Dir., Rev. W. Spencer Wren
Dir. Church Community Service, Mr. William Sievers
Dir. Communications, Mrs. Patricia Hutchison
Pres., Rev. Wallace Ford, First Christian Church, Boulder 80303
Treas., Dr. Earl Phillips, Metropolitan State College, 250 W. 14th Ave. 80204
Major Activities: Church Community Service (Ministry to Metro Denver); REACH (Research, Education and Action Coalition on Hunger); Task Force on Energy; Legislation and Social Issues; Ministries (City, Metropolitan and Migrant); Communication and Education

Pikes Peak Association of Churches

1 Stratmoor Dr., Colorado Springs 80906
Tel. (303) 576-7631
Sec., Mrs. Joyce Kuehn
Pres., Rev. Donald E. Bloor
Treas., T. R. Wallace, 4009 Wakely Dr., 80909
Major Activities: Christian Education; Church Directories; Newsletter; Radio and TV Programs; Institutional Chaplaincy; Military Ministry

†Pueblo Interfaith Association of Churches

34735 Jersey Rd., Vineland 81004
Tel. (303) 948-3416
Exec. Sec., Rev. Ross E. Purinton
Pres., Mrs. Courtney Graves, 4044 North Dr. 81008
Treas., George Lowe, 1024 Oxford 81005
Major Activities: Ecumenism

CONNECTICUT

Christian Conference of Connecticut (CHRISCON)

60 Lorraine St., Hartford 06105
Tel. (203) 236-4281
Gen. Sec., Rev. Mark Rohrbaugh
Administrative Asst., Fay Snyder
Dir., Ministry With Special Persons, Sr. Gail Ide
Pres., The Most Rev. John F. Whealon, Archbishop, 134 Farmington Ave., 06105
Treas., Gerald Lamb, CBT, 1 Constitution Plaza 06115
Major Activities: Communications; Education; Institutional Ministries; Social Issues; Commission on Christian Unity; Conn. Bible Society; Council on Alcohol Problems; Ministry With Special Persons; Operation Fuel and Food

Council of Churches of Greater Bridgeport, Inc.

3030 Park Ave., Bridgeport 06604
Tel. (203) 374-9471
Exec. Dir., Rev. Roger W. Floyd
Assoc. Exec. Dir., Rev. Frank S. Denton
Adm. Assist., Miss Barbara E. Bailey
Pres., Rev. Alexander Havadtoy
Sec., Mr. Miller Wachs
Treas., Robert Sammis
Major Activities: Jail Chaplaincy; Hospital Chaplaincy; Leadership training; Nursing Home Ministry; Runaway Youth Project; Jail Inmate Rehabilitation Project; Emergency Food Network

†Association of Religious Communities

248 Main St., Danbury 06810
Exec. Dir., Rev. David E. Simpson

The Capitol Region Conference of Churches

30 High St., Hartford 06103
Tel. (203) 527-2171
Exec. Dir., Rev. Dr. David D. Mellon
Dir. Pastoral Care & Training and Anna M. Fulling Chaplain, Rev. Robert H. Lloyd,
Assoc. Dir., Pastoral Care & Trng. Dept., Rev. Thomas E. Otte
Dir. Social Serv., Ms. Carol Maurer
Dir. Dept. on Aging and B.T.A., Rev. Robert C. Casstevens
Dir. Pastoral Counseling Center, Rev. Robert H. Lloyd
Asst. Dir., Pastoral Counseling Cntr., Rev. Thomas E. Otte
Dir. Voluntary Action Center, M. Deborah Walsh; Coord. of Volunteers, Catha Abrahams
Dir. Retired Senior Volunteer Program, Ms. Carolyn D. Vallieres
Dir., Foster Grandparents Prog., Ms. Lorrie R. Brown
Community Planner/Advocate, Sheila L. Scott
Community Organizer, Ms. Annette Carter
Dir., Senior Employment, 60 Plus, Susan Cummings-Lawrence
Congregate Housing Planner, Jonathan Frankel
Housing Advocate, Richard C. Frost
Hartford Correctional Center Chaplain, Rev. Robert E. Johnson

R.S.V.P. Field Coordinators: Gayle Carta, Hedda Rublin, Joanne West
Broadcast Ministry Consultant, Ivor T. Hugh
Educational Consultant, Dr. Ralph R. Sundquist, Jr.
Pres., Rev. Edward B. Geyer, Jr. 24 Cone St. 06105
Treas., Mr. Joseph P. Hesse, 41 Bradford Dr., Windsor 06095
Major Activities: Social Services; Chaplaincy; Aging; Legislative Action; Cooperative Broadcast Ministry. Retired Senior Volunteer Program; Counseling Center; Foster Grandparent Program; Senior Employment

Center City Churches of Hartford

170 Main St., Hartford 06106
Tel. (203) 728-3201

Exec. Dir., Rev. George H. Welles, Jr.
Adm. Asst., Helen Loughlin
Pres., Rev. Frank R. Hoffman
Sec., Mrs. Barbara Napolitano
Treas., Donald Carlson
Major Activities: Aging; Youth Resources; Friendship Center; Children's City; Children's Theatre; Tutorial Program; Food Pantry; Day Care; Health/Outreach Ministry

Council of Churches and Synagogues

628 Main St., Stamford 06901
Tel. (203) 348-2800
Exec. Dir., Rev. Melvin A. Hoover
Adm. Asst., Mrs. Kathryn B. Harris
Hospital Chaplain, Rev. Claude Peters
Hospital Chaplain Asst., Rev. Leslie Depenbrock
Pres., Rev. William Sexton, 31 Cascade Rd. 06903
Treas., Mr. James Arata, 628 Main St. 06901
Major Activities: Radio Ministry; Prisoner & Parolee Rehabilitation; Counseling, Hospital Chaplaincy; Systems Change; Low Cost Housing; Senior Neighborhood Support Services; Ecumenical Services; Interfaith Dialogues; Co-sponsor of Refugee Resettlement and Domestic Violence Programs

†Waterbury Area Council of Churches

24 Central Ave., Waterbury 06702
Tel. (203) 756-7831
Exec. Coordinator, Mrs. Virginia B. Tillson
Adm. Asst., Mrs. Shirley U. Clark
Pres., Mr. Donald MacKenzie, 52 Green Hill, Middlebury 06762
Treas., Mr. William N. Smith, Nova Scotia Hill Rd. Watertown 06795
Major Activities: Emergency Food Program; Hospital Chaplaincy; Emergency Transportation, Emergency Fuel

DELAWARE

Delmarva Ecumenical Agency

1626 N. Union St., Wilmington 19806, Tel. (302) 655-6151; 803 Miller Dr., Dover 19901, Tel. (302) 678-1124
Exec. Dir., Rev. Donald E. Leiter
Pres., Rev. Raymond Best, 450 Fiddlers Green, Dover 19901
Treas., Mr. Warren Beh, 915 Westover Rd., Wilmington 19807
Dir., Rural Ministries, Ms. Susan Canning, Blue Hen Mall, Dover 19901. Tel. (302) 678-2000
Coord., Resource Center, Ms. Elaine B. Stout, 1626 N. Union St. 19806. Tel. (302) 655-6151
Dir., Pacem in Terris, Mr. Charles Zoller, 1106 N. Adams St., 19806. Tel. (302) 656-2721
Coord., Social Awareness and Action, Rev. James Young, 407 W. 9th St., 19801. Tel. (302) 654-3101
Coord., Hunger Action, Mr. Tom Hunsdorfer, 900 Washington St., Wilmington 19801. Tel. (302) 654-3102
Dir., Problem Gambling Counseling Center, 900 Washington St., Wilmington 19801. Tel. (302) 655-3261
Coord., Pastoral Care Ministries, Chaplain Lynwood Swanson, Wilmington Medical Center, Wilmington 19801. Tel. (302) 428-2780
Major Activities: Facilitates and coordinates the work of churches and public and private agencies in urban, rural and leisure ministries, Education, Worship, Social Concerns and Mass Media

DISTRICT OF COLUMBIA

Interfaith Conference of Metropolitan Washington

1419 V St., N.W. 20009
Tel. (202) 234-6300
Exec. Dir., Rev. Clark Lobenstine
Admin. Asst., Patricia D. Gray
Pres., Rt. Rev. John T. Walker
1st Vice Pres., Rabbi Eugene Lipman
Vice Pres., William Cardinal Baum
Vice Pres., Imam Khalil Abdel Alim
Sec., Rev. Leamon White
Treas., Rev. Richard Taylor
Major Activities: Interfaith Dialogue; Hunger; Aging; Housing; Employment; Criminal Justice; D.C. Full Voting Rights; International Peace and Justice

†The Council of Churches of Greater Washington

1239 Vermont Ave., N.W., Washington 20005
Tel. (202) 638-1077
Exec. Dir., Rev. Ernest R. Gibson
Dir. for Prog., City, Rev. Rodney L. Young
Dir. of Communications, Mrs. Dorothy Monroe
Res. Dir., Hope Valley Camp, Mr. Herbert Amick
Dir. of Public Service Employment, Rev. Robert Williams; Asst. Dir., Rev. Lee Calhoun
Pres., Rev. W. Chris Hobgood
Treas., Rev. Hal. T. Henderson
Major Activities: Development of Group and Community Ministries; Church Development and Redevelopment; Liaison with Public Agencies; Theological Education and Training; Special Projects: Audio-Visual Library; Neighborhood Youth Corps; Hope Valley Camp; Institutional Ministry

FLORIDA

†Florida Council of Churches

122 E. Colonial Dr., Orlando 32801
Admin., Mrs. Ann K. Johnson
Major Activities: Farm Worker/Farmer Issue; Aging; Ecumenism and Communication; Crime/Justice; Postsecondary Education; Florida Growth

†Metropolitan Fellowship of Churches of Southeast Florida

1205 Sunset Dr., Coral Gables 33143
Tel. (305) 665-1120
Actg. Pres., Dr. Carroll L. Shuster, 121 Alhambra Plaza 33134

Major Activities: Representing Protestant Churches of Southeast Florida in a variety of Programs

GEORGIA

†Georgia Interchurch Association

159 Forrest Ave., N.E., Rm. 410, Atlanta 30308
Tel. (404) 659-0935
Coordinator: Rev. Jackson P. Braddy
Pres., Rev. James A. Nisbet, 509 Executive Park, Augusta 30907
Treas., Rev. William J. Andes, Box 29883 30359
Major Activities: Hunger; Criminal Justice and Penal Reform; Legislative Seminar; Marriage and Family Life; Camps and Camping; Ecumenical Clergy Conferences

Christian Council of Metropolitan Atlanta

848 Peachtree St., N.E., Atlanta 30308
Tel. (404) 881-9891
Exec. Dir., Rev. Donald O. Newby
Pres., Dr. Lawrence W. Bottoms
Vice Pres., Mr. Frank O. Broniec
Major Activities: Refugee Services; Emergency Assistance; Hunger Programs; Criminal Justice

HAWAII

Hawaii Council of Churches

200 N. Vineyard Blvd., Room 403, Honolulu 96817
Tel. (808) 521-2666
Exec. Dir., Rev. Stanley E. Kain
Program Asst., Ms. Pat Mumford
Pres., Ms. Relda Loomis
Treas., Rev. Ruth Senter
Major Activities: Education & Training; Legislative Concerns; Ministry to World & Community; Ecumenical Worship

IDAHO

Ecumenical Association of Churches in Idaho

2308 N. Cole Rd., #H, Boise 83704
Tel. (208) 375-8132
Exec., Rev. Sadie Lowrey
Major Activities: Disaster Emergency Relief; Migrant Library; Clergy Training & Lay Education; Church Resource Fair; Legislative Concerns; Prison Ministries; New Church Development; Idaho Hunger Council; Refugee Immigration

The Regional Council for Christian Ministry, Inc.

P.O. Box 2236, Rm. 10 Trinity United Methodist Church, Idaho Falls 83401
Tel. (208) 522-7921
Exec. Sec., Donna Waltman
Major Activities: Kindergarten and Licensed Day Care Programs; Summer Vacation Ministry; Community Observances; Biblical Studies for High School Youth

ILLINOIS

Illinois Conference of Churches

615 S. 5th St., Springfield 62703
Tel. (217) 544-3423
Exec. Sec., Rev. James M. Webb
Dir. Governmental Concerns, Rev. Richard R. Wood
Hunger Associate, Silve Barge
Dir., Peace Ministries, Rev. Thomas D. Kinzie
Dir. Farm Worker Ministry, Ms. Olga Sandman
Field Dir. CROP, Dennis Metger
Dir., Human Services Ministry, ———
Pres., Rev. Dr. R. Paul Sims, 501 E. Capitol Ave., Springfield 62701
Treas., Sr. Helena Henton, 800 S. 5th St., Springfield 62703
Major Activities: Poverty & Race; Migrant & Farm Worker Ministry; Chaplaincy in Institutions; Governmental Concerns and Illinois Impact; Peace Ministries; CROP, Church W. United; Ecumenical Courier; Ministry to Mentally Handicapped; Ministry with Aging; Church-Community Development; Hunger and Welfare Reform

The Church Federation of Greater Chicago

116 S. Michigan Ave., Room 300, Chicago 60603
Tel. (312) 372-2427
Exec. Dir., Mr. Frank T. Mohr, Jr.
Dir. for Communications: Rev. Gary Rowe
Pres., Dr., Donald Benedict
Treas., Mr. George Sisler
Major Activities: Radio & Television; Interfaith Development; Social Welfare; Christian Education; Community Organization

†Council of Hyde Park & Kenwood Churches & Synagogues

1400 E. 53rd St., Chicago 60615
Tel. (312) 324-5300
Hon. Sec., Mr. Claud L. Shaw, 1400 E. 53rd St. 60615
Exec. Sec., Mr. Werner H. Heymann, 1400 E. 53rd St. 60615
Pres., Rev. Gordon A. Humphrey, 4840 S. Dorchester Ave. 60615
Treas., Ms. Gladys Scott, 1164 E. 54th St. 60615

Oak Park-River Forest Community of Churches

324 N. Oak Park Ave., Oak Park 60302
Sec. for the Council, Miss Ruth E. McNutt
Pres., Rev. Preston D. Woods
Major Activities: Community Affairs; Ecumenical Affairs; Youth; Education; Food Pantry; Senior Citizens Worship Services; Laity; Interfaith Thanksgiving Services

River Forest: see Oak Park-River Forest

Churches United of Scott County, Iowa & Rock Island County, Illinois

639 38th St., Rock Island 61201
Tel. (309) 786-6494
Exec. Dir., Thomas N. Kalshoven
Program Coord. in Metropolitan Issues, Sharon M. Lockheart
Pres., Leslie Johnson
Treas., Lauren E. Eldridge
Major Activities: Jail Ministry; Hunger Projects; Minority Enablement; Criminal Justice; Migrant Ministry; Radio-TV; Housing; Aging; Local Church Development

Contact Ministries of Springfield

P. O. Box 1828 Springfield 62705
Tel. (217) 753-3939
Dir., Rev. William Peckham

†Council of Congregations

112 Brady Lane Urbana 61801
Dir., Mr. Greg Albert

INDIANA

Indiana Council of Churches

1100 W. 42nd St. Indianapolis 46208
Tel. (317) 923-3674
Exec. Sec., Rev. Harold Statler
Assoc. Exec. Sec., Rev. Walter F. Horlander
Bookkeeper, Joan Snyder
Dir. of CROP-CWS, Rev. Gerald L. Wilson
Coord. of Migrant Ministry/Literacy Edu., Dr. Henderson S. Davis
Peace/Development Impact-International Affairs, Richard E. Walters
Chaplain, Indiana State Police, Rev. Richard Cooley
Cons., Office of Campus Ministry, Rev. Erwin R. Bode
Development, Office of Campus Ministry ———
Pres., Dr. Otto K. Behrens
Treas., Rev. John McKune
Major Activities: Educational Ministries; Legislation; Migrant Ministries; CROP-CWS; Literacy Education; World Missions Interpretation to the College Campuses; Faith & Order; Evangelism; Institutional Ministries; Campus Ministry; State Police Chaplaincy; Services to Aged; International Affairs

Indiana Interreligious Commission on Human Equality

1100 W. 42nd St., Indianapolis 46208
Tel. (317) 924-4226
Exec. Dir., Rev. Thomas H. Quigley, Jr.
Project Equality Dir., Mr. E. H. Dansby
Pres., Rev. Rabbi Jonathan Stein
Treas., Bishop Ralph Alton
Major Activities: Project Equality; Anti-Racism Training; Racism/Sexism; Inventory; Hispanic Concerns

†Ecumenical Assembly of Bartholomew County Churches

P.O. Box 1421, Columbus 47201
Exec. Dir., Mrs. Lynn Bigley

Clark and Floyd Counties: See Kentuckiana Interfaith Community Kentucky Section

Christian Ministries of Delaware County

300 W. Main St., Muncie 47305
Tel. (317) 288-0601
Exec. Dir., Mary Jane Carpenter
Pres., Dr. Marvin Grooms, 1007 Shellbark Dr., Muncie 47304
Treas., Mr. Joseph Jackson, 1224 Neely Ave., Muncie 47303
Major Activities: Migrant Ministry, Christian Education, Feed-the-Baby Program, Religion and Public Education; Good News Caravan

Evansville Area Council of Churches, Inc.

119 N.W. Sixth St., Evansville 47708
Tel. (812) 425-3524
Adm., Rev. Francis I. Frellick
Weekday Supervisor, Mrs. Walter Foster
Coord. Communications Ministries, Mr. Jerry Graville
Pres., Rev. Clifford Janssen
Sec., Mrs. Patricia Swanson
Fin. Chpsn., Mr. Paul Farmer
Spec. Serv. Coord., Mrs. Charleen Moore
Major Activities: Christian Education; Mass Media Ministries; Community Responsibility & Service; Public Relations; Interpretation; Church Women United; Institutional Ministries; Vietnamese Resettlement; Interchurch Foundation; Hunger Program

The Associated Churches of Fort Wayne & Allen County, Inc.

6430 W. Jefferson Blvd., Fort Wayne 46804
Tel. (219) 432-1521
Exec. Min., Rev. Melvin R. Phillips
Ofc. Sec., Mrs. Virginia M. Adams
Pres., Mr. Marvin Sherman, Mutural Security Life, 3000 Coliseum Blvd., E. 46805
Treas., Mr. Donald Sell, Ft. Wayne Community Schools, 1230 S. Clinton Ave. 46802
Major Activities: Weekday Religious Education; Radio & TV; Community Ministry; Race Relations; Christian Education; Interfaith Commission; Inter-Religious Action Council; Widowed-to-Widowed; Ex-Offenders; Urban Strategy Commission; CROP; UNICEF

Associated Churches of Huntington County

530 Guilford St., Huntington 46750
Tel. (219) 356-6882
Pres., Mr. Stephen Echart, 145 Curray Markle 45770

The Church Federation of Greater Indianapolis, Inc.

1100 W. 42nd St., Indianapolis 46208
Tel. (317) 926-5371
Exec. Dir., Mr. Paul E. McClure
Assoc. Dir., Communications, Rev. Richard E. Davies
Assoc. Dir., Social Service, Rev. Donald Carpenter
Assoc. Dir., Metropolitan Center, Sr. Toni Ressino
Exec. Sec., Mrs. Dolores Harry
Campus Minister, Rev. Daniel Motto
Consultant—Development, Michael Kenney
Consultant—Finance, Cassius Fenton
Consultant—TV-Radio, Rev. Alfred R. Edyvean
Chaplains, Rev. C. T. Boyd, Rev. Harrison C. Neal, Rev. Frank O. Carlson, Rev. Walter Parks, Rev. Wendell Abel; Rev. Wilbert Cunningham
Pres., Margaret S. Robbins
Treas., Mr. Leland Holtman
Major Activities: Congregational Concerns; Communications; Special Ministries; Urban Affairs; Campus Ministries; Metropolitan Center

†Community Inter-Faith Housing, Inc.

2401 N. Central Ave., Indianapolis 46205
Tel. (317) 923-1314
Exec. Dir., Rev. L. Richard Hudson
Dir. of Counseling, Rev. Enos Nelson
Pres., Halbert W. Kunz
Treas., James Miles
Major Activities: Housing Dev.; Housing Management; Tenant Services & Tenant Organization; Housing Counseling; Community Development and Blight Prevention; Home Repair for Senior Citizens

Greater Kokomo Association of Churches

505 W. Mulberry 46901
Tel. (317) 457-3146
Pres., Rev. Daniel C. Kechel
Vice Pres., Mr. William R. Kearney

Sec., Mrs. Juanita Jarratt
Treas., Rev. Glen R. Campton
Major Activities: Mass Media; UNICEF; Migrant Ministry; Week of Prayer for Christian Unity; Health; Nursing Home Volunteers; Welcoming; Preparation for Parenthood & Early Childhood Guidance; Good Friday Services; Youth; Recycling

Marion Area Churches Cooperating in Mission

2302 S. Geneva Ave., Marion 46952
Exec. Dir., Rev. John Bunch

Monroe County United Ministries, Inc.

827 W. 14th St.
Bloomington 47401
Tel. (812) 339-3429
Exec. Dir., Dr. James J. Fisko
Pres., Philip Peak, 2000 E. 2nd 47401
Sec., Timothy Sorrow, 9450 E. Conard Dr. 47401
Treas., Robert Walden, Windermere Woods Dr., 47401
Major Activities: Day Care Preschool; Ecumenical Programs; Emergency and Referral Services; Neighborhood Programs; Summertime Care and Adult Care Programs

Portable Learning Center

240 E. Washington St., Martinsville 46151
Tel. (317) 342-3242
Dir., Rev. Robert H. White, Jr.
Mgr., Mrs. Johnnie White
Major Activities: Church Education; Resource Newsletter; Library Services; Resource Development; Leadership Development; Publication

†Interfaith Community Council, Inc.

702 E. Market St., New Albany 47150
Tel. (812) 948-9248
Exec. Dir., Rev. Dr. George P. Beury
Adm. Asst., Mrs. Marion Nunemacher
Dir., Child Dev. Center, Ms. Joy Smith
Dir., Contact Teleministry, Rev. Dr. Frank Dawkins
Chpsn., Rev. William Benninger, 1307 E. Elm St. 47150
Treas., Mr. Robert Craig, 1607 Hedden Ct. 47150
Major Activities: Contact Kentuckiana Teleministry; Dial-a-Care for Homebound; Food Pantry; Child Development Center; Hospice Volunteers; New Clothing and Toy Drives; Job Training; Convalescent Sitter & Mother's Aides; Emergency Dental Care

United Religious Community of St. Joseph County

319 S. Main St., South Bend 46601
Tel. (219) 282-2397
Exec. Dir., Rev. Bernard R. Palka, S.A.
Adm., Sec., Mrs. John E. Byers
Major Activities: Juvenile Justice, Adult Ex-offenders, Hospital Chaplaincy, Jail Chaplaincy; Family Life; Alcohol Education; Hunger; Boat People

IOWA

Iowa Inter-Church Forum

317 E. 5th St., Des Moines 50309
Tel. (515) 244-2253
Exec. Coord., Rev. Don Manworren
Governmental Concerns Consortium, Legislative Liaison, Virginia Petersen
CIPAR (Peace Consortium) Prog. Dir., Dan Clark
Pres., Rev. Howard B. Goodrich, Jr.
Major Activities: A forum dialogue related to theological faith issues and social concerns; opportunity to develop responses to discern needs and join in common mission; Intercom; Hunger

Churches United, Inc.

222 29th St. Drive, SE, Cedar Rapids 52403
Tel. (319) 366-7163
Exec. Sec., Mrs. Harry R. Mullin
Pres., Rev. Cedric J. Lofdahl, 720 Edgewood Rd. NW, Cedar Rapids 52405
Treas., F. Eugene Bender, MNB Bldg. 52401
Major Activities: Christian Education; Community Food Bank; CROP; Cooperative Low Income Store (O.N.E. Store); Community Information and Referral; Jail Chaplaincy; World Hunger; Community College Campus Ministry; Nursing Home Ministry; Radio and TV Ministry; Ecumenical City-Wide Celebrations

Des Moines Area Religious Council

3829 Grand Ave., Des Moines 50312
Tel. (515) 274-4018
Exec. Dir., Harold A. Varce
Pres., Norman Ullestad
Treas., Jane Alexander
Major Activities: Evangelism, Education; Social Concerns; Mission; Worship; Emergency Food Pantry

Scott County: See Churches United of Scott County, Iowa, etc., in Illinois Section

KANSAS

Consultation of Cooperating Churches in Kansas

4125 Gage Center Dr., Topeka 66604
Tel. (913) 272-9531
Exec. Coord., Dorothy G. Berry
Pres., Rev. H. Paul Osborne
Vice Pres., Ms. Helen Case
Sec., Rev. Don Hammerli
Treas., Rev. Fred Thompson
Major Activities: Legislative Activities; Program Facilitation and Coordination; World Hunger; Lakes Ministry; Retirement Planning; Singles Ministry; Higher Education Concerns; Religion and Rural Life; Education

Cross-Lines Cooperative Council

1620 S. 37th St., Kansas City 66106
Tel. (913) HE 2-5497
Exec. Dir., Rev. Donald C. Bakely
Program Dir., Mr. M. Myron Dice
Pres., Mrs. Helen P. Harper
Treas., Mrs. Jill Buckstead
Major Activities: Community Action Program; Education; Housing; Legislation; Social Service; Team Ministries; Volunteer Services

Interfaith of Topeka, Inc.

234 Kansas Ave., #105, Topeka 66612
Tel. (913) 357-1493
Exec. Dir., ———
Pres., Marianne Wilkinson
Treas., Rev. Lloyd Munger

Inter-Faith Ministries—Wichita

216 E. 2nd St., Wichita 67202
Tel. (316) 264-9303

Exec. Dir., Rev. Donna Meinhard
Adm. Asst., Mrs. Frances Duke
Coord. Jail Ministry, Ralph Allen
Coord. Operation Holiday, Gayle Bishop
Coord. Week Day Church School, Frances Duke
Coord. Indian Social Ministry, Mrs. Irene Heinze
Coord. Give-A-Lift, Mr. Walter Adrian
Coord. Operation Clothesline, Mrs. Pearl Long
Pres., Richard Matassarin
Treas., Halsey Hulburt
Major Activities: Religious Social Action; Urban Education; Jewish-Christian Dialogue; Networking city service agencies and local congregations; Theological and Worship events

KENTUCKY

Kentucky Council of Churches

1500 W. Main St., Lexington 40505
Tel. (606) 255-4402 or 253-3027
Exec. Dir., Rev. John C. Bush
Coord., Kentucky Hunger Task Force, Ms. Anne Joseph
Dir., Kentucky Interchurch Disaster Recovery Program, Fred C. Austin
Pres., Dr. Howard H. Willen, First United Meth. Ch., 1305 S. Main St., Hopkinsville 42240. Tel. (502) 886-0277
Major Activities: Institutional Ministry; Hunger, Church and Government; Media; Disaster Response; Social Concerns Network; Religious Educators Network; Needs & Rights of Children; Family Life; Christian Unity Workshop; Leisure Ministries; Spiritual Renewal; Housing; Health Care Issues

Human/Economic Appalachian Development Corporation (HEAD)

Box 504, Berea 40403
Tel. (606) 986-8423
Dir., Rev. Ben Poage

Federation of Church Social Agencies

850 S. Fourth St. Louisville 40203
Tel (502) 585-4076
Exec. Dir., Rev. John Mitchell
Pres., Rev. Jim Holladay, 400 E. Chestnut 40202
Coord., Hunger Program, Ron Nelson
Treas., Rev. Charles Tachau, P. O. Box 10096, 40210
Major Activities: Referral and Information Service; Emergency Resource Coordinaton: Coordination of Advocacy Efforts

Kentuckiana Interfaith Community

850 S. Fourth, Louisville 40203
Tel. (502) 585-4076
Exec. Dir., Rev. Kenneth D. MacHarg
Pres., Fr. Stan Schmidt
Vice Pres., Rabbi Martin Perley
Sec., Rev. Jim Holladay
Treas., Mr. Ernest Edwards
Major Activities: Refugee Activities; Congregational Blood Donor Program; Speaker's Bureau; Religious Workers Insurance Plan; Radio and TV; Federation of Church Social Agencies; Coalition on Human needs

†Northern Kentucky Interfaith Commission, Inc.

601 Greenup St. Covington 41011
Tel. (606) 581-2237
Admin. Sec., Sr. Martha Walther
Major Activities: Spiritual Social, Cultural Interchurch Programs

†South Louisville Community Ministries

417 W. Ashland Ave., Louisville 40214
Exec. Dir., Sr. Elaine Eckert
Major Activities: Emergency Assistance; Meals on Wheels; Tel-a-Friend; Small Home Repair; Friendly Visitors; Youth Employment Service; Clothing Closet; Counseling; Employment Registry; Health Screening

St. Matthew Area Ministries

5000 Shelbyville Rd., Louisville 40207
Tel. (502) 893-0205
Exec. Dir., A. David Bos

Paducah Cooperative Ministry

1359 South Sixth St. Paducah 42001
Tel. (502) 442-6795
Acting Dir., Mrs. John Listemann
Chpsn., Rev. Herbert J. Simpson
Major Activities: The P.C.M. is a cooperative venture of 24 local churches and five denominational judicatories, serving the community's hungry, elderly, poor, prisoners, alcoholics.

LOUISIANA

Louisiana Interchurch Conference

440 North Foster Dr., Ste. 106, Baton Rouge 70806
Tel. (504) 923-3749
Exec. Sec., Nedra Seay
Pres., Rt. Rev. James B. Brown, P.O. Box 15719, New Orleans 70175
Treas., Mr. Winter Trapolin, 119 Audubon Blvd., New Orleans 70118
Major Activities: Ministries to Aging; Correction Reform; Liaison with State Agencies; Ecumenical Planning; Ecology

Greater New Orleans Federation of Churches

332 Carondelet St., New Orleans 70130
Tel. (504) 524-0246
Exec. Dir., Dr. David E. Mason
Asst. to the Exec. Dir., Mrs. Jan Fitts
Program, Mr. Malcolm Peters
Chaplain Coordinator, Dr. Walton Ehrhandt
Adm. Sec., Mrs. Johanna Slater
Police Chaplain, Dr. Robert Trotter
Religion and the Arts, Ms. Bethany Bultman
Senior Adults, Mrs. Dorothy Boehmer
Fin. Sec., Mrs. Nellie Moulin
Newsletter Editor, Mr. Ken Thompson
Operation Mainstream-Literacy, Mrs. Betsy Latham
Pres., Rev. Woodrow Smith
Treas., Rev. Daniel Long
Major Activities: Radio-TV Programs; Comprehensive Chaplaincy; Central Business District Task Force; Regional Suburban Network; Leadership Training; Senior Citizens; Social Action; Public Information; Religious Census and Survey; Nutritional Programs; Literacy; Disaster Relief; Counseling Coordination; Race Track Ministry; Non-Profit Management; Community Awareness; Evangelism; Religion and the Arts;

Crime Prevention; Comfort Ministry to Widows and other Bereaved Persons

MAINE

Maine Office for Religious Cooperation

143 State St., Portland 04101
Pres., Rt. Rev. Frederick B. Wolf

Maine Council of Churches

17 Chestnut St., Portland 04101
Pres., Rev. William A. Chamberlain

MARYLAND

Maryland Churches United

3107 North Charles St., Baltimore 21218
Tel. (301) 467-6194
Exec. Dir., Rev. N. Ellsworth Bunce
Pres., Rev. Richard L. Clifford
Treas., Michael Cone
Major Activities: Pastoral-Social Care; Communications; Church in Society; Leadership Development; Ecumenical Relations; Faith & Worship; Community Service; Seafarers' Center for Port of Baltimore

Delmarva Ecumenical Agency

(See also under DELAWARE)
Office; Wesley Temple, West Rd., Box 182, Salisbury 21801
Tel. (301) 749-7631
Exec. Dir., Rev. Donald E. Leiter
Dir. Rural Ministries, Ms. Susan Canning
Coord. Hunger Action, Wicomico Co., Mr. Milbourne F. Hull, Sr.
Coord. Hunger Action, Somerset Co., Rev. John Ringgold, P.O. Box 1509, Salisbury 21801. Tel. (301) 742-3514
Coord. Hunger Action, Worcester Co., Ms. Josephine Merrill, R.F. #1, Box 371, Pocomoke City 21851. Tel. (301) 957-0627

MASSACHUSETTS

Massachusetts Council of Churches

14 Beacon St., Boston 02108
Tel (617) 523-2771
Exec. Dir., Rev. Dr. James A. Nash
Assoc. Dir. for Ecumenical Development, ———
Assoc. Dir. for Strategy and Action (SAC), Ms. Diane C. Kessler

Massachusetts Commission on Christian Unity

50 Ridge St., Winchester 01890
Exec. Sec., Rev. Thomas E. MacLeod

Attleboro Area Council of Churches, Inc.

505 N. Main St., Attleboro 02703
Tel. (617) 222-2933
Exec. Sec., Rev. Robert C. Ryder
Admin. Sec., Mrs. Franklyn E. Holbrook
Pres., Mr. Laurence Gower, Clifton St. 02703
Treas., Elmer Forbes, 59 Payson St. 02703
Major Activities: Christian Education; Radio-TV; Men's and Women's Departments; Institutional Ministry; Christian Social Action; Christian Unity

The Cape Cod Council of Churches, Inc.

79 Winter St., Hyannis 02601
Tel. (617) 775-5073
Exec. Dir., Rev. John Scott Everton
Adm. Sec., Mrs. Priscilla T. Crocker
Chaplain, House of Correction & Jail, Rev. David W. Yohn
Chaplain, Cape Cod Hospital, Rev. Charles T. Newberry
Chaplain, Barnstable County Hospital, Rev. Norman C. Jimerson
Pres., Mrs. Carol M. Beaven
Major Activities: Stewardship & Finance; Pastoral Services; Social Concerns; Communications; Christian Education; Youth; Church World Service; Interfaith Relations

†Greater Fall River Council of Churches, Inc.

101 Rock St., Fall River 02720
Tel. (617) 673-4670
Pres., F. M. Hutchinson, 354 Florence St. 02720
Treas., Miss Helene Sunderland, 3555 N. Main St., 02720
Youth Coordinator, Mrs. Patricia Mayall
Major Activities: Youth; Hospital Chaplaincy; TV Church Services; Athletics; Worship

Council of Church of Greater Springfield

152 Sumner Ave. Springfield 01108
Tel. (413) 733-2149
Exec. Dir., Rev. Thomas W. Olcott
Assoc. Dir., Rev. Ronald G. Whitney
Pres., Very Rev. Malcolm Eckel, Dean (Episc.) Christ Church Cathedral, 35 Chestnut St., 01108
Treas., Robert Auchter, Union Fed. Savings, P.O. Box 3930, 01101
Major Activities: Public Relations, Hospital Chaplaincy; Urban Ministry; Counseling; Christian Education; Ecumenical Affairs; Christian Social Relations; Pastoral Service; Peace & World Justice; Ecology-Environment; Health Care; Visitor-Ombudspersons to Nursing Homes; Pre-Retirement Training; Ecumenical Singles Ministry; Ecumenical Task Force on Churches and Retardation; Task Force on Aging; Emergency Fuel Fund; Crisis Counseling; Interfaith Concerns; Relief Collections; Christian Life and Work

Worcester County Ecumenical Council

63 Wachusett St., Worcester 01609
Tel. (617) 757-8385
Exec. Dir., Rev. Henry A. Bearisto
Dir. Public Relations, Mrs. E. Andrew Harvie
Pres., Mr. Gary W. MacConnell
Major Activities: Clusters of Churches; Mass Media;

Family; Economic Justice; Criminal Justice; Youth and Young Adult Ministries; Ecumenical Worship and Dialog; Interfaith Activities; Hospital and Nursing Home Chaplaincies Assistance to Churches

MICHIGAN

Michigan Council of Churches

205 W. Saginaw, P.O. Box 10206, Lansing 48901
Tel. (517) 485-4395
Exec. Dir., Rev. Duane N. Vore
Pres., Dr. Royal J. Synwolt, 155 W. Congress Rd., Detroit 48266
Treas, Henry Larzelere
Chpsn., Goals/Program, Stuart Nisbett
Major Activities: Aging; Ecumenism; Energy; Faith & Order; Family Farm Concerns; Farm Worker Ministry; Interfaith Disaster Response; Interfaith Hunger Action; Juvenile Justice Reform; Legislative Concerns; Taxation & the Church; Welfare Reform

Council of Churches of Ann Arbor

608 East William St., Ann Arbor 48104
Tel. (313) 665-5277
Office Man., Suzanne M. Steiner
Pres., Rev. Terry Smith, 608 E. William St., 48104
Treas., Dan Butler, 439 Riverview 48104
Major Activities: Communication and Coordination of churches and religious agencies; Jail Chaplaincy and Children's Hospital Chaplaincy

Area Council of Churches on Renewed Dedication

72 E. Michigan Mall, Battle Creek 49017
Tel. (616) 963-2280
Adm. Sec., Kay Jaeger
Vice-Pres./Church, Rev. James Moore
Vice-Pres./Community, Ms. Kathy Thornton
Major Activities: Intercity Youth; Elderly and Institutionalized; Ecumenical Community Dialogues; International Relations; Energy Conservation; Christian Education

Berrien County Council of Churches

305 Lake Blvd., St. Joseph 49085
Tel. (616) 983-6535
Exec. Dir., Rev. Arnold R. Bolin
Major Activities: Migrant Day Care Center (summers); Camp Warren; Hospital Chaplaincy and Pastoral Care; Ecumenical Experience and Planning; Information and Referral; Berrien Homes (Low-Income Housing); Continuing Education for Clergy

Christian Communication Council of Metropolitan Detroit Churches

1300 Mutual Building, 28 W. Adams, Detroit 48226
Tel. (313) 962-0340
Exec. Dir., Rev. Edward B. Willingham, Jr.
Program Assoc., Rev. John W. Peoples
Production Associates, Rev. J. Howard Mettee; Sr. Mary Clare Yates
Dir., Meals for Shut-Ins, Mr. Thomas Murphy
Asst. Dir., Meals for Shut-ins, Mr. Clark Churchill
Admin. Sec., Miss Louise Scott
Financial Sec., Mrs. Carrie Finney
Major Activities: Educational Services; Broadcast Services; Multi-Media Services; Print Services; Hospital Chaplaincy; Ecumenical Worship; Interfaith Housing; Meals for Shut-Ins; Summer Feeding Program

Greater Flint Council of Churches

308 W. Third Ave., Flint 48503
Tel. (313) 238-3691
Office Administrator, Miss Elayne A. Pownall
Pres., Rev. F. Robert Davidson
Treas., Mr. Earl Graves, Jr.
Major Activities: Christian Education; Christian Missions; Christian Unity; Church in Society; Filmstrip Library; Hospital and Nursing Home Chaplaincy

Grand Rapids Area Center for Ecumenism

9 Federal Sq. Bldg., Grand Rapids 49503
Tel. (616) 774-2042
Exec. Dir. Rev. Vernon D. Hoffman
Pres., Rev. Donald J. Griffioen
Treas., Bob Mersereau
Major Activities: Ministry to Metropolitan Churches and Community; Administration of Fish Program, Widowed Persons Program; Hunger, Criminal Justice, South Africa, Fine Arts and Christian Education Task Forces; Consultation Services; Radio, TV and Media Programming; Public Relations; Communications.

Jackson County Interfaith Council

425 Oakwood Dr., Box 97, Clarklake 49234
Tel. (517) 529-9721
Exec. Dir., Rev. Loyal H. Wiemer
Treas., Mr. Douglass Bennett, 309 S. Bowen, Jackson 49203
Major Activities: Chaplaincy; Radio & TV; Education; Social Concerns; Worship Services at Rest Homes and Hospitals; Ecumenical Activities

†Lansing Area Council of Churches

205 West Saginaw, Box 10206, Lansing, 48901
Tel. (517) 372-2333
Exec. Dir., Rev. William H. Work
Pres., Mr. John Duff
Treas., Mr. Lamont McAlvey
Major Activities: Week of Prayer; Radio Hours; Chaplaincies; Continuing Education; Human Welfare; Protestant/Catholic and Interfaith Relations; Direct Services; Annual Directory; Newsletter

Muskegon County Cooperating Churches

Jefferson and Hume, Muskegon Heights 49444
Tel. (616) 733-0012
Exec. Dir., Mrs. Marjorie Warner
Major Activities: Emergency Housing Loans; Filmstrip Library; Prison Ministries; Cable TV; Ecumenical Workshops; Friends on Wheels; Foster Grandparent Program

MINNESOTA

†Minnesota Council of Churches

122 W. Franklin Avenue, Minneapolis 55404.
Tel. (612) 870-3604

Exec. Dir., ———
Assoc. Dir., Rev. George K. Tjaden
Business Adm., Rev. Monroe Bell
Consultant, Educ. and Youth, Mr. Gerald C. Fahrenholz
Coord., Jt. Religious Legislative Coalition, Rev. Benno Salewski
Coord., Coalition of Chs. for Migrant Concerns, Sr. Suzanne Menshek
Pres., Rev. Leland Johnson
Treas., Ms. Betty J. Foster, 122 W. Franklin #400, Minneapolis 55404
Major Activities: Continuing Education for Clergy; Church and Community Development; Communications; Indian Work; Administration

Arrowhead Council of Churches

230 E Skyline Pkwy., Duluth 55811
Tel. (218) 727-5020
Exec. Dir., Mrs. A. Dean Headley (Harriet)
Pres., Dr. Michael Rogness
Treas., Dr. E. Paul Sylvester, 2925 Greysolon Rd. 55804
Major Activities: Christian Education; Inter-Church Evangelism; Twin Ports Ministry; Indian Work; Community Concerns; Community Health Center; Leisure Ministry; Joint Religious Legislative Coalition; Campus Ministry; UNICEF; Ecumenical Organ & Choir Festival; Downtown Ecumenical Good Friday Service

Greater Minneapolis Council of Churches

122 W. Franklin Ave., Rm. 218 Minneapolis 55404
Tel. (612) 870-3660
Exec. Dir., Rev. Thomas H. Quigley
Dir. Coordinator of Educational Ministries, Mr. Gerald C. Fahrenholz
Juvenile Court Chaplain; Rev. Henry W. Taxis
Youth Counselor/Street Minister, Rev. Clyston Holman, Jr.
Dir. of Indian Work, ———
Program Asst., Div. of Indian Work, Ms. Ruth J. Fevig
Adm. Asst., CWU, Mrs. June B. Estey
Consultant, Nursing Home Ministries Prog., Rev. Alison D. Crellin
Pres., Rev. Maynard B. Iverson
Treas., Mr. John W. Barber
Major Activities: Chaplaincy Services; Church Women United; Educational Ministries; Faith in Dialogue; Indian Work; Social Ministries

St. Paul Area Council of Churches

1671 Summit Ave., St. Paul 55105
Tel. (612) 646-8805
Exec. Dir., Rev. C. Arthur Scott
Education, Mr. Gerald Fahrenholz
Juvenile Court Chaplain, Rev. John Gilmore
Women's Jail Chaplain and Mt. Airy Community, Rev. Joan Conrad
Kinship, Ms. Ann E. Sieving
Institutional Chaplain, Rev. Fred A. Hueners
Indian Work, Mrs. Sheila White Eagle
Cmty. Chaplain, Rev. Clyston B. Holman, Jr.
Retarded Citizens', Ms. Mary Hinze
Nursing Home Ministry, Rev. Alison D. Crellin
Family Counselor, Rev. Frank Goodlake
Pres., Rev. William G. Kaiser
Treas., Rev. Dewaine Kolbo
Major Activities: Religious Services and Counseling for Prisoners at Detention and Corrections Authority Institutions; Delinquency Prevention Counseling; Kinship Program for Youth; Educational Development; Ecumenical Encounters and Activities; Indian Ministries

MISSISSIPPI

No state ecumenical agency at present.

Delta Ministry

P. O. Box 457, Greenville 38701
Tel. (601) 334-4587
Exec. Dir., Owen H. Brooks
Major Activities: Economic Self-Help Programs: Race Relations

MISSOURI

†Missouri Council of Churches

420 B Madison St., P.O. Box 839, Jefferson City 65102
Tel. (314) 636-3169
Exec. Dir., Rev. Walter B. Price
Assoc. Exec. Dir. & Dir. of Church Planning, Rev. Raymond A. Schondelmeyer
Pres., Elder Lyman Edwards
Vice-Pres., Rev. Rueben P. Koehler; Mrs. Rosamond Oliver
Sec., Mrs. Margaret Sonnenday
Treas., Dr. Warren Chrisman
Program Activities Christian Life and Mission; Criminal Justice; Faith and Order; Full Employment; Commission on Aging; Heifer Project; Ecumenical Prayer Seminar; Disaster Recovery; Higher Education; Legislative Affairs; Ecumenical Ministries; Correlated Agencies: CWU, Coalition on Church Planning, Chaplaincy Commission, and Youth Legislative Forum

†Missouri Delta Ecumenical Ministry

Box 524, Hayti 63851
Tel. (314) 359-1718
Exec. Dir., Emma Walker
Pres., Rev. J. P. Wissman, Caruthersville 63830
Major Activities: Community Economic Development; Social Action; Communications

†Interchurch Council of West Central Missouri

211 S. Washington St., P.O. Box 211, Clinton 64735
Tel. (816) 855-5976
Exec. Dir., Dr. Harvey O. Wilfred
Church and Cmty. Worker and Actg. Director of ICC, Charlotte Burtner
Moderator, Mr. Warren Hargus, Nevada 64772
Treas., Cecil Simpson
Church & Cmty. Worker, Ms. Charlotte Burtner
Dir. Retired Senior Volunteers Prog., Ms. Mary F. Clary
Major Activities: Church Leadership Training; Ecology; Health Issues; Hunger; Lake Ministries; Land Reclamation; Housing; Church Planning; Welfare Reform; Aging

†Metropolitan Inter-Church Agency

4049 Pennsylvania, Ste. 308, Kansas City 64111
Tel. (816) 756-1422

Exec. Dir., Rev. James O. Leffingwell
Emergency Assistance Coordinating Center, Mrs. Virginia Stuhr
Education Task Force, Proj. Dir., Mrs. Ashton Stovall
Pres., Rev. Ray Grant
Treas., Rev. David Downing
Major Activities: Prevention of Teenage Pregnancy; Quality Integrated Education; Emergency Assistance Coordinating Center; Family Planning Training Region

Springfield Area Council of Churches

Box 3686, Glenstone Sta., Springfield 65804
Tel. (417) 862-3586
Exec. Dir., Rev. Dorsey E. Levell
Pres., Mr. Alfred C. Sikes
Major Activities: Poverty Program; Community Treatment Program for Ex-Public Offenders; Volunteers in Corrections; Legislative Affairs; Week-day Religious Education; Ministerial Alliance; Hospital Chaplains' Fellowship; Retired Senior Volunteer Program; Treatment Center for Alcoholics; Vietnamese Refugee Program; Senior Citizen Discount Program; Spiritual Well-Being for Senior Citizens; Ombudsman for Nursing Homes

Interfaith Community Services

200 Cherokee, St. Joseph 64504
Tel. (816) 238-4511
Exec. Dir., Wallace Bloss
Major Activities: Child Development; Neighborhood Family Services; Group Home for Girls; Retired Senior Volunteer Program; Nutrition Program; Mobile Meals; Southside Youth Program; Church and Community; Housing Development; Housing Management

MONTANA

Montana Association of Churches

1511 Poly Dr. Billings 59102
Tel. (406) 252-5138
Exec. Dir., Mr. Cecil E. Gubser
Pres., Rev. David Bielefeld, P. O. Box 646, Livingston 59047
Treas., Mrs. Mary Ann Aaberge, 2204 Sunnyview 59102
Major Activities: Christian Education; Montana Religious Legislative Coalition; Christian Unity; Junior Citizen Camp; Public Information; Ministries Development; Social Ministry

NEBRASKA

Interchurch Ministries of Nebraska

215 Centennial Mall S., Room 303, Lincoln 68508
Tel. (402) 476-3391
Exec. Sec., Rev. Robert W. Jeambey
Admin. Asst., Ms. Sharon K. Kalcik
Pres., Rev. Jim Eikenberry, Carleton 68326
Treas., Rev. Louie Schweppe, 1231 Taylor Ave., Norfolk 68701
Major Activities: Interchurch Planning and Development; Comity; Indian Ministry; Television Ministry; Teacher Training; Audio-Visual Center; Rural Church Strategy; World Hunger; Legislative Information; State Young Adult System; Aging Coalition; Disaster Planning

Lincoln Fellowship of Churches

215 Centennial Mall South, Room 303, Lincoln 68508
Tel. (402) 474-3017
Exec. Sec., Rev. Stephen C. Evans
Pres., Rev. Dr. William Doran, 730 N. 70th St. 68505
Treas., Dr. Otis Young, 20th and D St. 68502
Media Asst.: Mrs. Anita Fussell
Major Activities: Mass Media Ministry; Emergency Food Service; Community Liaison; Research and Planning; Indian Concerns; Police Chaplaincy Corps; Church Directory; Ministerial Fellowship; Center for Christian Growth

†Omaha Metropolitan Association of Churches, Inc.

124 South 24th St., Suite 203, Omaha 68102
Tel. (402) 341-0246
Actg. Exec., Mrs. Orrian I. Craighead, 9517 N. 31st St. 68112
Pres., Mr. Henry R. Roose, 5219 Ida St., 68152
Treas., Mr. Robert A. Falk, Ft. Calhoun 68023

NEVADA

(No current information)

NEW HAMPSHIRE

New Hampshire Council of Churches

24 Warren St., P.O. Box 1107, Concord 03301
Tel. (603) 224-1352
Exec. Sec., Rev. Frank H. Gross
Pres., Rt. Rev. Philip A. Smith, 63 Green St., Concord 03301
Treas., ———
Major Activities: Facilitating cooperative work of member denominations

NEW JERSEY

New Jersey Council of Churches

116 North Oraton Parkway, East Orange 07017
Tel. (201) 675-8600
Gen. Sec., Rev. Paul L. Stagg
Adm. Assoc., Mrs. Alice Schuler
Associate General Secretaries: Commission on Radio & TV, ———
Commissions on Government and Community Life, Rev. Dudley E. Sarafy
Commissions on Research & Church Development and Pastoral and Institutional Ministries, Rev. Jean Paul Richter
Pres., Rev. Arthur S. Jones
Treas., Rev. William Jewett
Major Activities: Consultancy; Advocacy; Service

Bergen County Council of Churches

165 Burton Ave., Hasbrouck Heights 07604
Tel. (201) 288-3784
Ecumenical Minister Emeritus Dr. Stanley I. Stuber

Office Sec., Mrs. A. E. Vander Vliet
Pres., Rev. Warren J. Henseler, First Reformed Church, Burton Ave. at Washington Pl., Hasbrouck Heights 07604
Treas., Mr. George Theuret, 188 Central Ave., Bogota 07603
Major Activities: Family Life Education; Market Place Ministry; Ministries for & with Youth; Services to the Aging; United Campus Ministry; Boy Scouts; Girl Scouts; Evaluation and Planning; Chaplaincy Program at Public Institutions

Council of Churches of Greater Camden

Box 1208, Merchantville 08109
Tel. (609) 665-1919
Exec. Sec., Dr. Samuel A. Jeanes
Pres., Rev. Lawrence L. Dunn
Treas., William G. Mason
Major Activities: Radio & TV; Hospital Chaplaincy; United Services; Good Friday Breakfast; Mayors' Prayer Breakfast; Public Affairs; Mobile Meals

†New Brunswick Area Council of Churches

22A Joyce Kilmer Ave., New Brunswick 08901
Tel. (201) 247-0384
Exec. Sec., Rev. Joseph G. Bodnar
Pres., Rev. Imre Bertalan, 179 Somerset St., 08901
Treas., Mr. V.K. Coffill, Jr., 134 Norris Ave., Metuchen 08840
Major Activities: Chaplaincy; CWS: UNICEF; Ecumenical worship; Transient Aid Program; Flood Relief

Metropolitan Ecumenical Ministry

969 McCarter Highway, Newark 07102
Tel. (201) 623-9259
Exec. Dir., Rev. Arthur C. Thomas
Pres., Rev. Hugh C. Dugan, 190 Rutgers Pl., Nutley 07110
Treas., Dean Dillard Robinson
Major Activities: Urban Crisis; Education; Health; Welfare; Counsel to Churches

Trenton Ecumenical Area Ministry, (TEAM)

1235 Greenwood Ave., Trenton 08609
Tel. (609) 396-9166
Interim Dir., Rev. Art Stanley
Sec., Mrs. Ann Dalton
Pres., Mr. H. Starkey
Treas., Mr. Robert Smith
Major Activities: Urban Ministry; Ecumenical Relations

NEW MEXICO

New Mexico Inter-Church Agency

525 San Pedro NE, Albuquerque 87108
Tel. (505) 255-1509
Exec. Sec., Rev. Harry V. Summers
Coordinator, Refugee Placement, Rev. Glen Mayhew, 827 Pennsylvania Ave., N.E. 87110
Pres., Dr. Robert N. Allen
Treas., Leon A. Wiltse, 2117 Menaul Blvd., N.E. 87107
Major Activities: Home Education Livelihood Program; Chaparral Adoption Services; Day Care Center; Senior Citizen Housing; Police Chaplaincy; Storehouse; Bible in the Schools; Media Ministry; Ecumenical Consultation

NEW YORK

New York State Council of Churches, Inc.

3049 E. Genesee St., Syracuse 13224
Tel. (315) 446-6151
Exec. Dir., Dr. Jon L. Regier
Deputy for Admn., Lucy C. Groening
Assoc. Dir. for Public Policy, Rev. Elenora G. Ivory
Assoc. Dir. for Criminal Justice, Mrs. Nader R. Maroun, Jr.
Pres., Bishop Joseph H. Yeakel
Vice Pres., Rt. Rev. Ned Cole
Treas., Mr. Donald R. Waful, 2005 W. Genesee St., Syracuse 13219
Major Activities: Governmental Relations; Legislation; Chaplancy in State Institutions; Criminal Justice; IMPACT and Community Crisis

†Christians United in Mission, Inc.

40 N. Main Ave., Albany, 12203
Tel. (518) 438-6681
Exec. Dir., Rev. James J. Reid
Eco. Dir., Mrs. Sandra Deitlein
Program Coord., Mrs. May Anne Weinman
Major Activities: To promote cooperation/coordination among member judicatories in the areas of urban ministries, media communications, social action, and criminal justice

Broome County Council of Churches, Inc.

81 Main St., Binghamton 13905
Tel. (607) 724-9130
Exec. Dir., Mr. Kenneth A. Cable
Asst. Exec. Dir., Mrs. Nancy M. Leamon
Hospital Chaplain, Rev. LeRoy Flohr
Jail Chaplain, Rev. Phillip Singer
Campus Minister, Rev. George Hanssen; Rev. C. James Jones
Pres., Rev. Philip H. Mitchell, 30 Main St. 13905
Treas., Mrs. Priscilla Pease
Major Activities: Campus Christian Life; Christian Education; Radio & T.V.; Urban Services; Chaplaincy to Hospital and Jail; Christian Life & Work; Christian Hunger Outreach Warehouse

Buffalo Area Council of Churches

1272 Delaware Ave., Buffalo 14209
Tel. (716) 882-4793
Exec. Dir., Rev. Robert E. Grimm
Dir. Church Supply Agency, Mrs. June Somerville
Admin. Sec., Church Women United, Mrs. Norma Roscover
Chpsn., Literacy Volunteers, Mrs. LaRita Galley
Pres., Mrs. Helen Urban
Treas., Mr. Theodore C. Orr
Major Activities: Radio-TV; Social Services; Hospital Chaplains; Church Women United; Ecumenical Relations; Literacy Volunteers

Buffalo Area Metropolitan Ministries, Inc.

24 Linwood Ave., Buffalo 14209
Tel. (716) 883-7717

Exec. Dir., Rev. Patrick J. Cogan
Pres., Msgr. Robert E. Nesslin
Sec., Marian Beck
Treas., Rev. Joachim K. Wilck
Major Activities: School Desegregation; Housing, Full Employment; Health Care; Criminal Justice; Hunger

Capital Area Council of Churches, Inc.

810 Madison Ave., Albany 12208
Tel. (518) 489-8441
Exec. Dir., Rev. Mrs. Joyce Giles
Adm. Asst., Mrs. Carol Thayer
Pres., Rev. Craig Bartholomew
Treas., Mr. Joseph Lynn, 6 View Ave. 12209
Major Activities: Legislative Concerns; Institutional Ministries; International Affairs Education; Urban Ministry; Community Worship; Faith and Order Discussions; Hospital Chaplaincy; Family Concerns; Inter Faith Cabinet; Martin Luther King Scholarship Fund; Prison Ministry; Half-Way House for Ex-Offenders; Food Pantries

Council of Churches of Chemung County Inc.

330 W. Church St., Elmira 14901
Exec. Dir., Joan Geldmacher, 621 Newton St. 14904
Treas., Mr. D. E. Foote, 123 Sunset Dr., Horseheads 14845
Major Activities: CWS Clothing Collection; UNICEF: Chaplaincy at Chemung County Nursing Facility and Psychiatric Center; Worship Services at Home for Aged; Meals on Wheels; Clergy Seminars; Radio Broadcast; Joint services Easter, Lent

†The Cortland County Council of Churches, Inc.

7 Calvert St., Cortland 13045
Tel. (607) 753-1002
Exec. Dir., Rev. Walter P. Parry
Pres., Rev. Loren House, Box 186, Preble 13141
Treas., Mr. Kenneth Brong, R.D. 4, 13045
Sec., Mr. Wilber Henry
Major Activities: Institutional Ministries: Campus Nursing Home, Retirement Home, Hospital, Jail. Radio; CWS; UNICEF; Alcohol & Drug Program; Local Congregation Support Program; Refugee Resettlement

Dutchess Interfaith Council, Inc.

9 Vassar St., Poughkeepsie 12601
Tel. (914) 471-7333
Exec. Dir., Mrs. Martha S. Miller
Protestant Chaplain, Rev. Dr. Charles E. Byrd
Roman Catholic Chaplain, Rev. A. Francis Burns
Asst. Chaplain, Sr. Eileen McCabe
Dir. Project Gateway, Mr. Charles Milch
Field Worker, Project Gateway, Mr. Ronald Smith
Pres., Sr. Helen Demboski
Treas., Patricia J. Boyd
Major Activities: County Jail Chaplaincy; Inmate counseling & Rehabilitaton (Project Gateway); Radio-TV; CROP Hunger Walk; Interfaith Music Festival; Young Adult Singles Fellowship; Public Worship Events; Indochinese; Migrant Ministry; Interfaith Dialogue; Christian Unity; Refugee Sponsorship

Genesee County Council of Churches

306 E. Main St., Batavia 14020
Tel. (716) 343-9002
Exec. Sec., Ms. Rose Anne Gough
Pres., Mrs. Margaret Watson
Treas., Mr. James Murphy
Major Activities: Ecumenical Service; Radio; Chaplaincy Services; Jail Ministry

Genesee Ecumenical Ministries

17 South Fitzhugh St., Rochester 14614
Tel. (716) 232-6530
Exec. Dir., Rev. Lawrence E. Witmer
Pres., Mrs. Isabel Calkins, 8 Peppermill Dr., Fairport 14450
Treas., Mr. Newton Hall, 61 Barmont Dr., Fairport 14450
Major Activities: Judicial Process Commission; Pastoral Counseling; Church Women United; Jail Ministry; Alternatives to Incarceration; Education Resource Network (Public Schools, Desegregation); Legislative IMPACT Network; Mission Educational & Training Tax Reform; Refugee Resettlement; Hospital Chaplaincies

The Long Island Council of Churches

Eastern Office: 318 Roanoke Ave., Riverhead 11901
Tel. (516) 727-2210
Western Office: 249 Merrick Rd., Rockville Centre 11571
Tel. (516) 536-8707
Exec. Dir., Rev. Jack H. Alford
Pres., Rev. Kenneth Nelson
Treas., Rev. W. H. Perkins
Major Activities: Migrant Ministry; Blood Bank; Radio; Project REAL; Outreach; Emergency Aid and Food; CROP; Counseling; Chaplaincies; Task Force; Human Rights; Advocacy; Coordination; Church World Service; Planning; Bible Distribution; Choir and Worship; Area Projects; Interfaith Cooperation; Protestant Mission Ministries

Council of Churches of the Mohawk Valley Area, Inc.

1644 Genesee St., Utica 13502
Tel. (315) 733-4661
Exec. Dir., Dr. Alan B. Peabody
Adm. Sec., Mrs. Olga Long
Pres., Rev. John W. Morrow
Treas., Mr. Robert Fish
Major Activities: Christian Education; Social Action; Urban Ministry; Ecumenical Relations; Ministry in Higher Education; Church Women United; Radio and TV

The Council of Churches of the City of New York

475 Riverside Dr., Ste. 456, New York 10027
Tel. (212) 749-1214
Exec. Dir., Rev. Robert L. Polk
Program Dir, Rev. Franklin D. Graham
Controller, Mrs. Mary Buckley
Div. Dir. Church Planning & Research, Rev. Leland Gartrell
Div. Dir., Dept. Pastoral Care, Rev. Grant Williams
Div. Dir., Dept. Communications, William Bertenshaw
Chaplain, Protestant Ecumenical Chapel, Kennedy Airport, Rev. Marlin Bowman
Pres., Gordon Brown, 475 Riverside Dr., Ste. 456, 10027
Treas., Mr. Harry F. Reiss, Jr., 475 Riverside Dr., Ste. 456, 10027

Major Activities: Christian Education; Church Planning & Research; Radio & TV; Church Women United; Housing Development Corporation; Youth Services; Specialized Ministries; Pastoral Care; Protestant Chapel, Kennedy International Airport; Public Relations; Task Force Against Racism; Delinquency Prevention

Bronx Division of the Council of Churches of the City of New York

297 E. 206th St., Bronx 10467
Tel. (212) 652-6839
Pres., Rev. Daniel Nickerson
Divisional Dir., Rev. John C. Allan, Jr.
Major Activities: Prayer Breakfasts; Chaplaincy; Youth Services; Unity Celebrations; Christian Educ.

Brooklyn Division of the Council of Churches of the City of New York

66 Court St., Ste. 1107 11201
Tel. (212) 625-5851
Dir., Rev. Charles H. Straut, Jr.
Pres., Rev. Neville N. Simmons-Smith
Treas., Rev. Albert J. Berube
Major Activities: Christian Education; Criminal Justice; Hunger Education & Action; Local Christian Ecumenical Relations; Pastoral Care; Prison Ministry; Community Issues

Manhattan Division of the Council of Churches of the City of New York

475 Riverside Drive, New York 10027
Tel. (212) 749-1214
Prog. Dir., Rev. Bernard Holliday
Pres., Rev. Dr. Frederick B. Williams
Major Activities: Wall Street Ministry; Released Time Education; Family Institute; Drug Abuse Education; Summer Satellite Center Project for Urban Youth; Housing & Criminal Justice; Hunger Project—Summer Food Service for Children; Christian Education; Energy Conservation; Multi-Resource Center

Queens Federation of Churches

86-17 105th St., Richmond Hill 11418
Tel. (212) 847-6764
Exec. Dir., Rev. N. J. L'Heureux, Jr.
Pres., Rev. George H. Ashdown
Treas., Albert M. Dayson
Major Activities: Emergency Food Service; Family Court Counseling Center; Blood Bank; Scouting; Christian Education Workshops; Planning and Strategy; Church Women United; Communications.

Staten Island Division of the Council of Churches of the City of New York

2187 Victory Blvd., Staten Island 10314
Tel. (212) 761-6782
Ofc. Mgr., Mrs. Marjorie R. Bergendale
Pres., Rev. Fred W. Diekman, 292 Kingsley Ave., 10314
Major Activities: Support; Christian Education; Parish Services; Civic Affairs; Community Action

The Niagara Council of Churches

Rainbow Blvd. & 2nd St.
Niagara Falls 14303
Tel. (716) 285-7505
Administrator, Mrs. Ruth Betty Shippee
Pres., Rev. Harold Faba, 350—7th St., Lewiston 14092
Treas., Mr. Donald Ames, 1129 Escarpment Dr., Lewiston 14092
Major Activities: Christian Education; Evangelism and Mission; Services to Tourists; Referral Services; Institutional Ministries; Court Watching; Social Concerns

Rochester: see Genesee Ecumenical Ministries

The Inter-Faith Community of Schenectady

1803 Union St. Schnectady 12309
Tel. (518) 370-2150
Pres., ——
Sec., Mariann D. Barge
Major Activities: Prison Services; Interfaith Dialogue; Hospital Services; Community Concerns

Syracuse Area Interreligious Council

910 Madison St., Syracuse 13210
Tel. (315) 476-2001
Pres., Rabbi Theodore Levy
Exec. Dir., Dorothy F. Rose
Assoc. for Edu. and Community Issues, Ms. Martha Ely
Assoc. for Pastoral Care/Chaplaincies, Rev. Terry Culbertson
Chaplain, Hillbrook Detention Cntr., Rev. Tom Hedges
Chaplain, Onondaga County Correctional Facility, Rev. Gary Bergh
Chaplain, Public Safety Bldg. Jail, Rev. Hyrd Seals
Chaplain, Van Duyn Home & Hospital, Rev. Robert Lucas
Adm. Asst., Ms. Jan Simpson-Clement
Major Activities: Criminal Justice; Health and Life Crisis Issues; Lay and Clergy Education on religious and community issues; Christian/Jewish Relations; Interreligious Task Force on Hunger, Summer Camp for Children; Community Forums

†Tioga County Council of Churches, Inc.

228 Main St., Owego 13827
Tel. (607) 687-2520
Exec. Sec., Miss Pauline Kishpaugh
Pres., Bruce Pierce, R.D. 2, 415 McFall Rd., Apalachin 13732
Treas., Mr. Ray Torrey, R. D. 2, 13827
Major Activities: Adult Work; Children's Work; Leadership Education; Social Concerns; Christian Education; Youth

Troy Area Council of Churches, Inc.

1838 Fifth Ave., Troy 12180
Exec. Dir., Rev. Charles Rice, 27 Westcott Rd., Schnectady 12306
Pres., Rev. Richard Scheu, 15 111th St. 12182
Treas., Mr. Otto E. Kuhl, 170 McChesny Ave., Averill Park 12018
Major Activities: Christian Education; Faith & Order; Evangelism; Communications; Chaplaincy Program

NORTH CAROLINA

North Carolina Council of Churches

Bryan Bldg., Ste. 201A, Raleigh 27605
Tel. (919) 828-6501
Exec. Dir., Rev. S. Collins Kilburn
Pres., Dr. Richard F. Amos, Drawer O, Sal, Sta., Winston-Salem 27108
Treas., Dailey J. Deer, Croasdaile Office Park, Ste. 210 27707
Major Activities: Church Women United; Christian Nurture; Christian Unity; Christian Social Ministries; Legislative Program; Criminal Justice; Labor/Management Issues; ERA; Child Abuse; Migrant Farmworkers

Asheville-Buncombe Community Christian Ministry (ABCCM)

201-203 Broadway, Asheville 28801
Exec. Dir., Rev. Robert A. Wiltshire
Pres., Mrs. Joan Marshall

†Greensboro Urban Ministry

407 N. Eugene St., Greensboro 27401
Tel. (919) 273-6916
Exec. Dir., Rev. Dr. Charles F. Klotzberger

Interchurch Council for Social Service

207 Wilson St., Chapel Hill 27514
Exec. Sec., Mrs. Dorothy Mullen
Pres., Dr. Emily Barrow

†The Robeson County Church and Community Center

Rt. 4, Box 845, Lumberton 28358
Tel. (919) 738-5204
Exec. Dir., Rev. Robert L. Mangum
Chpsn., Mr. Adolph Dial
Treas., Rev. Arnold Walker

†Rowan Cooperative Christian Ministry

117 W. Fisher St., P.O. Box 4026, Salisbury 28144
Exec. Dir., Rev. James R. Cress
Pres., Rev. Floyd Bost

NORTH DAKOTA

North Dakota Conference of Churches

107½ N. Fourth St., Bismarck 58501
Tel. (701) 255-0604
Exec. Dir., Rev. J. Winfred Stoerker
Pres., Rev. Gordon Berntson, Carrington 58412
Treas., Rev. Don Shoemaker, Bismarck 58501
Major Activities: Natural Resources Development; Religious Legislation; Urban-Rural Youth Exchange; Ecumenical Relations; Rural Church

OHIO

Ohio Council of Churches, Inc.

89 E. Wilson Bridge Rd., Columbus 43085
Tel. (614) 885-9590
Exec. Dir., Rev. Carlton N. Weber
Assoc. Dir., Rev. Keene R. Lebold
Legislative Representative, Rev. Robert S. Graetz
Economic Justice, Rev. Jackson E. Pyles
Criminal Justice, Hiram Maddox
Refugee Services, Rev. Robin Tetzloff
Pres., Rev. David S. Sageser
Treas., Mrs. Josephine Marino
Major Activities: Economic Justice; Criminal Justice; Minority Church Empowerment; Ecumenical Development; Public Policy Issues

†Metropolitan Interchurch Ministries

282 W. Bowery St., Akron 44307
Tel. (216) 535-3112
Exec. Officer, ———
Pres., Pat Selwood, 3641 Brookside Dr., Barberton 44203
Sec., Mr. Irven Pettyman, 210 Crescent Dr. 44301
Coordinators Metro Mission, Ms. Fran Koonce, Jerry Egan; Fr. Thomas Dunphy; Sr. Eileen Kazmierowicz
Campus Minister, Rev. Robert Clarke
Coordinator for Program Resources, Mrs. Marie Nolf
Communication, Cosmo Olivieri
Juvenile Court and Youth Counselor, Rev. Byron W. Arledge
Pastoral Counseling Service, Rev. Donald D. Nofziger
Project Together, Joe Schaetzle
Major Activities: Cluster Development; Communications; Church Planning; Resource Center; Metropolitan Mission; Community Relations; FISH; Pastoral Counseling; Juvenile Court Chaplaincy; Campus Ministry; Teen Sexuality Clinic

Alliance Area Council of Churches

470 E. Broadway, Alliance 44601
Tel. (216) 823-2025
Exec. Sec., James L. McBride
Pres., Bernard Taylor
Treas., Joseph Leeson, 879 Wright Ave., 44601
Major Activities: Christian Education; Community Relations & Service; Public Meetings & Evangelism

Canton: see Central Stark County

Council of Christian Communions of Greater Cincinnati

1836 Fairmount Ave., Cincinnati 45214
Tel. (513) 251-4666

Exec. Dir., Dr. Richard P. Jameson
Dir. of Police-Clergy & Good Samaritan Chaplaincies, Bro. Thomas Payne
Dir. of Adult Chaplaincy, Rev. Jack N. Lawson
Chaplain at Juvenile Center, Rev. Maurice Philip
Chaplain at Rollman's Hospital, Rev. William Ross
Coord. of Weekday Released Time Religious Ed., Ms. Terry Keeney
Assoc. Producer, Broadcast Programming, Mr. Chuck Wiggins
Pres., Mrs. Esther S. Zepf, 2879 Marbreit 45209
Treas., Mr. Van J. Wolf, 3561 Glengary Lane 45236
Major Activities: Christian Unity; Broadcasting & Communications; Adult & Juvenile Chaplaincies; Religious Education; Policy-Clergy Counselling Teams; Interfaith Cooperation; Information Service.

Metropolitan Area Religious Coalition of Cincinnati (MARCC)

1418 Enquirer Bldg., 617 Vine St., Cincinnati 45202
Tel. (513) 721-4843
Dir., Rev. Duane Holm
Pres., Mr. Charles H. Tobias, Jr.
Treas., Mr. Arril Bruun
Major Activities: Public Education; Criminal Justice; Health Care; Minority & Women Employment in Government

Greater Cleveland Interchurch Council

2230 Euclid Ave., Cleveland 44115
Tel. (216) 621-5925
Exec. Dir., Dr. Donald G. Jacobs
Dir., Church and Society, Mark Real
Dir., Communications, Ms. Janice Giering
Moderator, Mr. John Bustamonte
Pres., Rev. Dr. Joseph Albrecht
Major Activities: Congregational Development, Church and Society; Communications; Hunger; Project Learn; Criminal Justice Christian Education; Legislation

West Side Ecumenical Ministry

4315 Bridge Ave, Cleveland 44113
Tel. (216) 651-2037
Exec. Dir., Rev. George Nishimoto
Major Activities: Day Care Centers; Elderly Meals Programs; Group Homes; Youth Outreach Ministry; Emergency Food Distribution Ctrs.; Foster Home Placement Network; Church Clusters in Community Development; Shared Ministry; One World Shoppe; Neighborhood Housing; Tutoring; Youth Services

Metropolitan Area Church Board

30 W. Woodruff Ave., Columbus 43210
Tel. (614) 294-3219
Pres., Rev. John T. Frazer
Chpsn., Most Rev. George Fulcher, 212 E. Broad St. 43215
Treas., Rev. T. William Filbern, 1280 Shady Lane 43227
Major Activities: Church Issues; Community Issues; Communications; Area Councils

†Metropolitan Churches United

212 Belmonte Park E., P.O. Box 3, Dayton 45402
Tel. (513) 222-8654
Exec. Dir., Rev. Robert E. Koize
Special Asst., Manfred Orlow
Radio-TV Coord., Mrs. Paul Shank
Pres., Rev. Thomas Dorenbusch, 811 N. Summit St. 45407
Hosp. Notification Service, Mrs. Emma Montgomery
Major Activities: Communications: Service to the Churches and Community; Social Action and Legislation

Churchpeople for Change and Reconciliation

221 W. North St., Lima 45801
Tel. (419) 229-6949
Exec. Dir., Rev. Leonard Stark

Mahoning Valley Association of Churches

631 Wick Ave., Youngstown 44502
Tel. (216) 744-8946
Exec. Dir., Rev. Richard D. Speicher
Hospital Chaplains, William Wolfgang, Rev. Donald Booth, Rev. Wallace Wadland
Social Worker, Miss Elsie Dursi, Mrs. Rita Stubbles
Pres., Rev. Morris W. Lee, 1177 Park Hill 44502
Treas., Mr. Paul Fryman, 42 Venloe Dr., Poland 44514
Major Activities: Support of Campus Ministry; Communications; Christian Education; Ecumenism; Social Action

Pike County Outreach Council

104 S. High St., Waverly 45690
Tel. (614) 947-7151
Dir., Andrew D. Reid

The Council of Churches of Central Stark County

405 2nd St. NW, Canton 44702
Tel. (216) 455-5143
Exec. Dir., Dr. Franklin Trubee
Pres., Mrs. C. R. Looman
Treas., Mr. John Mani, 3021 Rowland NE, 44714
Major Activities: Christian Education; Citywide Activities; United Church Action; Youth; Church School for Retarded Children; Christian Educ.; Special Events; Community Emergency Service; Hospital Chaplaincies

Toledo Area Council of Churches

2130 Madison Ave., Toledo 43624
Tel. (419) 242-7401
Exec. Dir., Rev. Nathan H. VanderWerf
Asst. for Program, Rev. J. A. Clark
Asst. for Administration, Mrs. Barbara Wilson
Asst. for Volunteer Program, Mrs. Jean Morris
Asst. for Communication and Interpretation, Mrs. Marian Sarver
Exec. Dir., Toledo Campus Ministry, Rev. Glenn B. Hosman, Jr.
Exec. Dir., Toledo Metropolitan Mission, Mr. Jerome Ceille
Pres., Rev. Bernard J. Boff
Treas., Mr. Merle Abbott
Major Activities: Metropolitan Mission; Campus Ministry; Social Services; Christian Education; Ecumenical Development; Parish Life; Hunger; Interfaith Relations; Christian Unity; Mental Health; Employment; Institutional Ministries; Development; Communication; Community Organization; Welfare Rights; Housing; Elderly

Tuscarawas County Council for Church and Community

120 First Dr. SE, New Philadelphia 44663
Tel. (216) 343-6012
Exec. Dir., Barbara E. Lauer
Pres., Dr. Judson Roesbush, 420 E. Shafer Ave., Dover, 44622
Treas., Mr. Russell Mullady, 459 E. High Ave. 44663
Major Activities: Welfare; Health; Family Life; Child

Abuse; Housing; Mental Health and Retardation, Employment; Elderly

Youngstown: see Mahoning Valley

OKLAHOMA

†Oklahoma Conference of Churches

Rte. 13, 7501 N.W. Expressway, Oklahoma City 73132
Tel. (405) 722-3100
Exec. Dir., Rev. Max E. Glenn
Pres., Rev. David J. Walker
Treas., Rev. John Thomas
Major Activities: World Hunger and Agricultural Policy; Criminal Justice; State and National Issues; Aging; Faith and Order; Native Americans

AFCCOM (Associates for Christian Cooperative Ministry)

5101 N. May Ave. 73112
Tel. (405) 947-2998
Exec. Dir., Rev. Jim Shields

†Oklahoma Indian Ministries, Inc.

701 N.W. 82 St., Oklahoma City 73102
Tel. (405) 232-3695
Exec. Dir., Rev. Robert Pinezaddleby
Major Activities: Advocate for Indian People; Religious Education in Government Schools

Tulsa Metropolitan Ministry

125 W. Third St., Tulsa 74103
Tel. (918) 582-3147
Exec. Dir., Rev. Bruce Theunissen
Asst. Exec. Dir., Rev. Marvin L. Cooke
Coord. Corrections Ministry Sr. Leona Luecke
Coord. Ecumenical Hunger Program, Bill Major
Dir., Meals on Wheels, Cathy Peppito
Pres., Ronald T. McDaniel
Sec., David M. Breed
Treas., Mary Cherry
Major Activities: Community Needs and Issues; Hunger; Corrections; American Indian Awareness; Black Community; Meals on Wheels; Jewish-Christian Understanding; Disaster Response; Theological Awareness

OREGON

Ecumenical Ministries of Oregon

0245 S. W. Bancroft St., Portland 97201
Tel. (503) 221-1054
Exec. Dir., ———
Assoc. Dir., Rev. Rodney I. Page; Mr. Stephen Schneider
CUE Dir., Mr. Stephen Schneider
Pres., Rev. David E. Baker, 435 NW 21st Corvallis 97330
Treas., Mr. Ron Means, 1730 SW Skyline Blvd. 97221
Major Activities: Christian Education; Communications; Social Action & Legislation; Center for Urban Education; Runaway Youth

PENNSYLVANIA

Pennsylvania Conference on Interchurch Cooperation

P. O. Box 2835, Harrisburg 17105
Tel. (717) 545-4761
Co-Staff: Mr. Howard Fetterhoff, Rev. Albert E. Myers
Co-Chairpersons: Bishop Martin N. Lohmuller, Rev. Howard J. McCarney
Major Activities: Theological Consultation; Social Concerns; Inter-Church Planning; Conferences and Seminars

The Pennsylvania Council of Churches

900 S. Arlington Ave., Harrisburg 17109
Tel. (717) 545-4761
Exec. Dir., Rev. Albert E. Myers
Asst. to the Exec. Dir. for Specialized Min, Rev. Charles C. Frazier
Asst. to the Exec. Dir., for Soc. Min., Rev. Paul D. Gehris
Dir., Office for Refugee Resettlement, Mr. Kim Miller
Pres., Rev. R. Eugene Crow
Treas., Mrs. Zedna Haverstock, 900 S. Arlington Ave. 17109
Major Activities: Institutional Ministry; Migrant Ministry; Social Ministry; Park Ministry; Inter-Church Planning and Dialog; Refugee Resettlement

Allentown; see Lehigh County Conference

Ecumenical Conference of Greater Altoona

1208 Thirteenth St., P. O. Box 305, Altoona 16603
Pres., Mrs. Mary Burgoon
Exec. Dir., Ms. Eileen Becker
Major Activities: Religious Education; Workshops; Ecumenical Activities; TV; Religious Christmas Parade; Campus Ministry

†Christians United in Beaver County

682 Third Street, Rm. 6, Beaver 15009
Tel. (412) 774-1446; 774-0621
Exec. Sec., Mrs. Lysle P. Shaffer
Chaplains, Rev. Delbert Wasser, Str., Rev. David L. Bleiyik
Pres., Mrs. William H. McGraw, Rr. 708, Darlington Rd., Beaver Falls 15010
Treas., Mrs. Alice Melkerson, 836 Sixth St. 15009
Major Activities: Christian Education; Evangelism; Radio; Social Action; Church Women United; United Church Men; Ecumenism

Greater Bethlehem Area Council of Churches

520 E. Broad St., Bethlehem 18018
Tel. (215) 867-8671
Exec. Dir., Rev. William P. Dodd, Jr.
Pres., Dr. R. Wayne Kraft, 645 Biery's Bridge Rd. 18017
Treas., Mr. Roy D. Hagen, 318 Reservoir Rd. Hellertown 18055
Major Activities: Lifeline; Chaplaincy; Ecumedia; Migrants; Church World Service; Institutional Ministry; Interfaith and Brotherhood; Lay Academy

Concerned of Pennsylvania, Inc.

Metcalfe Community House
Rt. 1, Dunbar 15431
Tel. (412) 628-1997
Exec. Dir., Mr. James E. Murphy

Inter-Church Ministries of Northwestern Pennsylvania

235 W. 6th St., P. O. Box 1194, Erie 16512
Tel. (814) 454-2411
Exec. Dir., Rev. C. Edward Geiger
Pres., Gordon Osborn, 1448 W. 44th St. 16509
Treas., Mr. Charles Beckman, 2239 South Shore Dr. 16505
Major Activities: Community Organization and Development; Planning and Resourcing of Ecumenical Clusters of Congregations; Institutional Chaplaincy; Mass Media Communications; Lay and Clergy Continuing Education and Leadership Development; Tutorial Reading Programs for Elementary School Children; Summer Interracial Intercultural Exchange Program for Children

Christian Churches United of the Tri-County Area

900 S. Arlington Ave., Harrisburg 17109
Tel. (717) 652-2771
Exec. Dir., Rev. Charles E. Dorsey
Adm., Sec., Mrs. Eleanor Carnes
Dir. of Development, Rev. Eldridge Brewster
Dir. of Communications, Mrs. Lynn Horchler
Campus Minister, Rev. Karen Layman
Pres., Rev. T. Orestus Wilson, 1001 N. 17th St., Harrisburg 17103
Treas., Mr. James Hoepfer, 1612 Terry Ln. 17112
Major Activities: Institutional Ministries to Aged, Prisons, and Hospitals; Campus Ministry; Communications; Resources for Parish Ministry; Low Income Housing; Prayer and Study; Congregational Sponsorship of Probationers and Parolees; Interreligious Forum

Greater Norwin Council of Churches

408 Main St., Irwin 15642
Tel. (412) 863-0430
Exec. Dir., Rev. J. Richard Coyle
Treas., Charles W. Heidler, 10430 Madison Ave., N. Huntingdon 15642
Pres., Rev. Barry M. Walker, 4th and Maple 15642
Sec., Mrs. Mary Ann Johnstown, R.D. 6, Box 571, Irwin 15642
Major Activities: Spiritual Life; Civic Affairs; Christian Education; Youth; Meals on Wheels; CWU

Lancaster County Council of Churches

447 E. King St., Lancaster 17602
Tel. (717) 291-2261
Exec. Dir., Rev. Richard E. Grant
Hospital Chaplain, Rev. Kenneth A. Burnette
Dir. Christian Social Ministry, Rev. Robert B. Ketcham
Dir. Conestoga Cottage, Mrs. Sheri Hafer
Dir. Horizon House, Mr. Victor P. Slansky
Dir. CONTACT, Mrs. Nancy J. Gieniec
Coordinator, Shared Holiday, Mrs. Alice Heitmueller
Pres., Mrs. Dorothy H. Searles, 837 Olde Hickory Rd. 17601
Treas., James E. Rothernerger, 223 N. Pine St. 17603
Major Activities: Hospital Chaplaincy, Christian Social Ministry; Residential Ministry to Youthful Offenders; Rural Ministry; Prison Ministry; Housing; Parish Resource Center; CONTACT; Widow Support and Divorce Adjustment Groups

Lehigh County Conference of Churches

36 S. Sixth St., Allentown 18101
Tel. (215) 433-6421
Exec. Sec., Mrs. Carol Closson
Ofc. Sec., Pauline Yerk
Pres., Rev. Richard Stough, 32 S. 5th St. 18101
Treas., Mr. James Hottenstein, 152 E. South St. 18103
Major Activities: Chaplaincy Program; Migrant Ministry; Social Concerns and Action

McKeesport Neighborhood Ministry

723 Walnut St., McKeesport, 15132
Tel. (412) 664-9353
Minister-Dir., Rev. James W. Dowell

Monroeville Mall Ministry

Office Complex, Room 231, Monroeville, 15146
Tel. (412) 372-3725
Dir. of Adm. Sr. Grace O'Donnell
Dir. of Interpretation, Mrs. Joan Paul

Northeastern Pennsylvania Congregations in Christian Mission

550 Madison Ave., Scranton 18510
Tel. (717) 347-4730
Ofc. Sec., Mrs. Paul A. Knorr
Pres., Rev. Henry A. Male, Jr.
Treas., Rev. Bruce Gallup
Major Activities: Chaplaincy; Communications; Human Affairs; Special Ministry to Housing Communities; United Churches Book Store; Christian Education for Handicapped and Deaf Children; "Religion in the News" Broadcasts

Metropolitan Christian Council of Philadelphia

1501 Cherry St., Philadelphia 19102
Tel. (215) 563-7854
Exec. Dir., ———
Staff Asst., Mrs. Carol Stone
Adm. Asst., Mrs. Joan G. Shipman
Chairperson: Rev. William L. Johnson, 1701 Arch St. 19103
Pres., Mrs. John W. Forrester, 5306 Master St. 19131
Treas., John A. Clark, 1600, 100 S. Broad St. 19110
Major Activities: Task Forces and Commissions as needed

Christian Associates of Southwest Pennsylvania

239 Fourth Ave., Pittsburgh 15222
Tel. (412) 281-1515
Exec. Dir., Dr. W. Lee Hicks
Assoc. Exec. and Dir. of Planning. Rev. Bruce H. Swenson
Dir. of Communications, Rev. Ronald P. Lengwin
Ecumemo Editor, Mrs. Betty Jane Lehman; Production Asst., Mr. David Wasseman
Adm. Asst., Mrs. Sue Stangl
Pres., Bishop Anthony G. Bosco
Treas., Mr. Robert Reynolds
Major Activities: Communications; Planning; Church and Community; Leadership Development; Theological Dialogue

East End Cooperative Ministry

250 N. Highland Mall, Pittsburgh 15206

Tel. (412) 361-5549
Exec. Dir., Rev. Samuel N. Gibson

North Hills Youth Ministry

1566 Northway Mall, Pittsburgh 15237
Tel. (412) 366-1300
Exec. Minister, John D. Rickloff

†Project 60

P.O. Box 11377, Pittsburgh 15238
Tel. (412) 828-1544
Dir., Mr. Braden L. Walter
Major Activities: Prison Counseling; Advocacy with the Aging

South Hills Interfaith Ministries

300-B South Hills Village, Pittsburgh 15241
Tel. (412) 833-6177
Exec. Dir., Rev. David J. Isch
Exec. Sec., ———
Pres., Marilyn Benson
Treas., Donald Rinald, 281 Old Farm Rd. 15228
Major Activities: Inter-Faith Cooperation; Family Counseling; Lay Training Workshops; Social and Humanitarian Concerns; Family Hospice; Personal Growth

Southwest Interchurch Ministries

50 Stratmore Ave., Pittsburgh 15205
Tel. (412) 921-4000
Pres., Rev. Lawrence Chottiner
Coord., Rev. Margaret Yingling

†University and City Ministries

4401 Fifth Ave., Pittsburgh 15213
Tel. (412) 682-2751
Exec. Min., Rev. Elizabeth M. Scott
Major Activities: Community of Reconciliation; Oakland Children's Center; Urban and Campus Ministries; Hunger Education

†Wilkinsburg Community Ministry; Hunger Education

704 Franklin Ave., Pittsburgh 15221
Tel. (412) 241-8072
Dir., Rev. Park Allis

The Greater Reading Council of Churches

631 Washington St., Reading, 19601
Tel. (215) 375-6108
Exec. Dir., Rev. Earl W. Allen
Pres., Dr. James D. Miller
Rec. Sec., Mrs. C. Walt Hafer
Treas., Mr. Lee M. LeVan
Major Activities: Leadership Educ.; Institutional Ministry; CWU; Scouting; Social Action; Migrant Ministry; CWS; State Park Chaplaincy; Chaplaincy at Hospital; Pastoral Counseling Center

Scranton: see Northeastern Pennsylvania

Christian Associates of the Shenango Valley

240 N. Hermitage Rd., P.O. Box 1081, Sharon 16146
Tel. (412) 347-5021
Sec., Mrs. Arden Morrow
Hospital Chaplain, Rev. Leroy E. Ickes
Treas., Mr. David J. Cole, 2638 Hill Rd., Rt. 1, Sharpsville 16150
Major Activities: Chaplaincy; Christian Education for the Mentally Retarded; School of Religion; Campground Chaplaincy; Hospital Chaplaincy

†Community Ministry Center

416 E. 7th Ave., Tarentum 15084
Tel. (412) 226-0606
Exec. Dir., Rev. Donald B. Power

†Uniontown Area Association of Churches

R.D. 4, 669, Uniontown 15401
Tel. (412) 437-0332
Ofc. Sec., Mrs. Marlene K. Baker
Pres., James L. Ganoe, R.D. 4, Box 250 15401
Treas., Mr. Leroy Fisher, R.D. 1, Box 219, Lemont Furnace 15456
Major Activities: Christian Missions; Spiritual Life; Christian Social Concern;

Pennsylvania Commission for United Ministries in Higher Education

61 Cassatt Ave., Berwyn 19312
Exec., Rev. David Rich

United Churches of Williamsport and Lycoming County

202 E. Third St., Williamsport 17701
Tel. (717) 322-1110
Exec. Dir., Rev. Dr. Alton M. Motter
Ofc. Sec., Mrs. Lois Hunt
Pres., Rev. Melvin L. Whitmire, 60 Ross St. 17701
Treas., Mr. Harold L. Criswell, 343 W. Fourth St. 11701
Dir., Ecumenism, Rev. Dr. Larry A. Coleman
Dir., Evangelism, Rev. Roger Alling, Jr.
Dir., Christian Education, Miss Kathleen Weaver
Dir., Institutional Ministry, Rev. Karl S. Fetterman
Dir., Radio-TV, Rev. James W. Grubb
Dir., Social Concerns, Rev. James T. Dawes
Major Activities: Ecumenism; Educational Ministries; Evangelism; Church Women United; Church World Service; Prison Ministry; Radio-TV; Nursing Homes; Refugee Sponsorships; Ministry to Deaf

Wyoming Valley Council of Churches

35 S. Franklin St., Wilkes-Barre 18701
Tel. (717); 825-8543
Exec. Dir., Miss Anita J. Ambrose
Bookstore Mgrs., Mrs. William Sittner, Mrs. Edward Gavenus
Ofc. Sec., Miss Anne Roberts
Pres., Mr. Harry Hickman
Treas., Mr. James Evans
Major Activities: Hospital and Nursing Home Chaplaincy; Church Women United; High Rise Apartment Ministry; Hospital Referral Service; Emergency Response; Food Bank; Migrant Ministry; Meals on Wheels; Dial-A-Driver; Radio and TV; Leadership Schools; Interfaith Programs

†York County Council of Churches

145 S. Duke St., York 17403
Tel. (717) 854-9504
Exec. Dir., ———
CONTACT-York Teleministry Dir., Mrs. Leuellyn S. Curry
Pres., Mrs. Wallace H. Dunlap
Treas., Mr. Roy E. Livingstone, 1717 Stanton St. 17404
Major Activities: Educational Development; Community Witness; Ecumenical Concerns; Special Ministries; CONTACT Teleministries

PUERTO RICO

Evangelical Council of Puerto Rico (Concilio Evangélico de Puerto Rico)

P.O. Box C, Río Piedras 00928
Tel. (809) 765-5977
Exec. Sec., Mr. Félix M. Cintrón-Cruz
Pres., Rev. Samuel J. Vélez
Treas., Mrs. Emma Roura
Major Activities: Christian Social Action; Ecology; Chaplaincy; Evangelism; Ecumenism; Higher Education; Public Relations; Radio-TV; Parochial Schools; Head Start Program

RHODE ISLAND

Rhode Island State Council of Churches

2 Stimson Ave., Providence 02906
Tel. (401) 861-1700
Exec. Minister, Rev. Dr. Paul G. Gillespie
Div. of Ministry in Higher Education: Chaplain at U.R.I. & Campus Ministry Coordinator, Rev. Edmund W. Fetter
Chaplain, R.I. Junior College, Warwick, Rev. David O'Brien
Chaplain R.I. Junior College, Blackstone Valley, Rev. Jeffrey N. Leath
Chaplain, R.I. College, Rev. Glendon Heath
Chaplain, Johnson & Wales, Rev. Janet P. Aquavella
Dir., Center for Church & University Consultation, Rev. Richard Bausman
Communications:
Rev. Robert Hargreaves; Rev. Earnest E. Ryden; Rev. Dr. Lawrence van Heerden
Urban Ministry Division: Dir., Rev. Dr. Paul G. Gillespie
Pres., Rev. Birger J. C. Johnson, 15 Hayer, St. 02908
Treas., Mr. Robert A. Mitchell, 175 Barney St., Rumford 02916
Major Activities: Urban Ministries; Radio-TV; Chaplaincy; Social Action; Legislative Liaison; Faith & Order; CWS; Leadership Development; Ministries in Higher Education

†Rhode Island Interfaith Health Care Ministries

Rm. 112, Aldrich Bldg., Rhode Island Hospital, Providence 02902
Tel. (401) 277-8356
Dir. of Pastoral Care, Rev. Duane Parker
Major Activities: Clinical-Pastoral Education for Clergy and Laity

SOUTH CAROLINA

Christian Action Council

Lutheran Theol. Southern Sem.
4201 N. Main St., P.O. Box 3663, Columbia 29230
Tel. (803) 786-7115
Exec. Minister, Rev. Howard G. McClain
Pres., Rev. John Gillison
Major Activities: Citizenship; Community Services; Continuing Education; Interchurch Affairs; Publications

Community Care, Inc.

1611 Devonshire Dr., Columbia 29204
Tel. (803) 256-4925
Rev. Marvin Lare

Greenville Urban Ministry

P.O. Box 3105
Greenville 29602
Rev. Harlan Wilson, Jr.

†Greater Spartanburg Ministries

659 N. Church St., Spartanburg 29303
Tel. (803) 585-9371
Exec. Dir., Rev. Roy E. Russell

SOUTH DAKOTA

†Association of Christian Churches

200 W. 18th St., Sioux Falls 57104
Tel. (605) 334-1980
Exec. Dir., Rev. Delano Lind
Pres., Rev. Gayle Fischer
Treas., Mr. Leonard Swenson
Major Activities: Ecumenical Forums; Continuing Education for Clergy; Institutional Chaplaincies; Clergy Observer Corps; Church and Community Relations; Legislative Information; Peace and Justice

TENNESSEE

†Tennessee Association of Churches

112 Woodrush Ave., Knoxville 37918
Tel. (615) 688-1631
Exec. Dir., Rev. Ted. R. Witt, Sr.
Pres., Bishop J. Madison Exum
Treas., Arthur D. Brown, Sr., 1703 Villa Pl., Nashville 37212

†Regional Inter-Faith Association (RIFA)

P.O. Box 2301, Jackson 38301
Tel. (901) 427-7963
Exec. Dir., Rev. Gary Scheidt
Pres., Rev. Robert Moore
Major Activities: Cooperative Ministries; Program Development; Communication

†Association of Religious Ministries

1538 Highland Ave., Knoxville 37916
Tel. (615) 546-7811

Exec. Robert Chastain
Pres., Phil Ericson

Metropolitan Inter Faith Association (MIFA)

166-A Poplar, Memphis, TN 38103
Tel. (901) 527-0208
Dirs., Rev. Gid Smith; Mr. Robert Dempsey

TEXAS

Texas Conference of Churches

2704 Rio Grande # 9, Austin 78705
Tel. (512) 478-7491
Exec. Dir., Rev. Dr. James C. Suggs
Dir., Children and Youth Services Prog., Ms. Mary Lee Johns
Assoc. Dir., Ms. Linda B. Team
Pres., Rev. H. Richard Siciliano, 41 Oakdale, Houston 77006
Major Activities: Church and Society; Ecumenism; Education; Communication; Christian-Jewish Relations; Texas Church Women United; CROP; Children and Youth Services; Disaster Response

†Austin Area Conference of Churches

1110 Guadalupe, Austin 78701
Tel. (512) 472-7627
Jail Chaplain, Rev. Arthur R. Anderson
Ofc. Sec., Mrs. Marie Houghton
Pres., Rev. J. Carter King
Treas., Mr. A. P. Simpson
Major Activities: Church & Society; Cooperative Ministries; Education; Jail Chaplaincy; Hosp. Ministry

Greater Dallas Community of Churches

901 Ross Ave., Dallas 75202
Tel. (214) 748-5235
Exec. Dir., Dr. Paul A. Stauffer
Staff Assoc. for Urban Concerns, Mrs. Oeita Bottorff
Staff Assoc. for Interpretation and Development, Rev. F. Clark Williams
Chaplain Supervisor (Hospitals), Rev. Robert L. Davis
Chaplain, County Jail, Rev. James B. Williams
Dir. Block Partnership, Mr. David Whitenack
Dir. Pastoral Counseling and Education Center, Dr. C. Kenneth Pepper
Dir. Dallas Community College Ministry, Rev. Betsy Turecky
Dir. Life Enrichment Prog. for Older Persons, Dr. Hanno Weisbrod
Pres., Mr. John D. Miller
Treas., Thomas Unis
Major Activities: Communications and Community Relations; Pastoral Services (Counseling Center, Hospital Chaplaincy, Jail Chaplaincy); Urban Concerns (Block Partnership, Hunger, Airport Chaplaincy, Criminal Justice, Aging); Ecumenical Relations

Fort Worth Area Council of Churches

1000 Macon St., Fort Worth 76102
Tel. (817) 335-9341
Exec. Dir., ——————
Adm. Asst., ——————
Pres., Mr. Fred Woerner, 5804 Aztec Dr. 76112
Treas., Dr. Edith Heil, 6009 Wrigley Way 76133
Major Activities: Summer Recreation Prog.; Legislative Network; Lay Training Seminars; Service to the Aged; World Hunger; Special Transportation for the Handicapped

Houston Metropolitan Ministries

3217 Montrose Blvd., Ste. 200, Houston 77006
Tel. (713) 522-3955
Exec. Dir., Rev. Clifton Kirkpatrick
Exec. Asst., Rev. Arthur Pitkin
Deputy Dir., Mr. Winston John
Deputy Dir., Adm. and Fin., Rev. Garrett Wingfield
Dir. RSVP, Ms. Candy Twyman
Dir. Foster Grandparent Prog., Ms. N. Anita Sheffield
Dir., Senior Citizens Nutrition Proj., Mr. Richard Campbell
Dir. Social Action, Ms. Gail Hamilton
Dir., VISTA Proj., Rev. Roberto Flores
Dir., Meals on Wheels, Patricia Yaeger
Dir., Houston Interfaith Hunger Coalition, Sr. Pearl Ceasar
Chaplains, Rev. Edgar Seeger, Rev. George Cordova
Pres., Rev. James Tucker
Treas., Mr. Lawrence Payne
Major Activities: Opportunities for the Aging: Combatting Hunger; Community Self-Development; Criminal Justice; Interfaith Relations

United Board of Missions

648 Orange Ave., P. O. Box 3856, Port Arthur 77640
Tel (713) 982-1170
Exec. Dir., Clark Moore
Pres., Rev. Paul Bohot
Major Activities: Emergency Assistance, i.e., Food and Clothing, Rent and Utility, Medical, Dental, Transportation; Share a Toy at Christmas; Helpline; Juvenile Probation; Counseling; Back to School Clothing Assistance; Information and Referral for Elderly; Outreach, Transportation and Homemaking Aid; Hearing Aid Bank; Meals on Wheels; Scholarships

†San Antonio Community of Churches

1101 W. Woodlawn, San Antonio 78201
Tel. (512) 226-7364
Exec. Dir., Rev. Dr. C. Don Baugh
Instit. Chaplain, Rev. Christian H. Kehl; Rev. Harry Martin
Dir. Cont. Educ., Rev. Robert E. Buxbaum
Dir. of Liturgical Dances, Ms. Tinka Thruer
Chaplain, Sr. Margaret Carew
Pres., Dr. T. J. Youngblood
Sec., Rev. Robert Kownack
Treas., Rev. Wesley J. Buck
Major Activities: Christian Educ.; Missions; Social Relations; Radio-TV

San Antonio Urban Council

217 McCullough, San Antonio 78215
Tel. (512) 224-1756
Exec. Dir., Kent C. Miller
Prog. Dir., Shirley Whyte
Pres., Rev. Thomas H. Schmid
Treas., Phillip Acosta
Sec., Diana Bacon
Major Activities: Emergency Food Pantries; Residential Care for Youth; Child Care; Summer Camping; Dental Care; Senior Citizens Housing; Recreation; Community Development; Nurturing and Education Alternate Residential Care for Ex-Mental Patients

UTAH

The Solid Rock

435 E. 7th St. Brigham City, 84302
Tel. (801) 723-8276
Dir., Mr. Charles Rostkowski
Chpsn., Mr. Tom Davidson

Major Activities: Ministry With Native Americans; Elementary New Life Clubs; Community Pantry; People Who Care; Church and Community Support; Summer Youth Work/Study Camps.

Crossroads Urban Center

347 S. 4th E., Salt Lake City 84111
Tel. (801) 364-7765
Dir., Rev. Ken Fineran
Pres., Mr. Robert Archuletta, 978 Cheyenne St. 84104
Adm. Sec., Ms. Clarice Harrington
Pres., Mrs. Marilyn Wyler, 310 S. 5th E., American Fork 84003

†Utah Commission for Ministry in Higher Education

232 University St., Salt Lake City 84102
Tel. (801) 582-4357
Pres., Dr. John Lawson, 1603 S. 2100 E 84108
Interim Coord., Ms. Beth Purdie

VERMONT

Vermont Ecumenical Council and Bible Society

P.O. Box 593, 30 Elmwood Ave., Burlington 05402
Tel. (802) 864-7723
Exec. Minister, Rev. Howard Stearns
Pres., Very Rev. Donald E. Boyer
Treas., Mr. Alfred N. Drown
Major Activities: Impact; Peace; Institutional Ministry; Legislative Liaison; Christian Unity; Bible Distribution and Sales; Aging; Social Welfare; Hospice; Child and Family Justice

Vermont Religious Education Foundation

30 Elmwood Ave., P.O. Box 593, Burlington 05402
Tel. (802) 864-7723
Pres., Mrs. Julie Lepeschkin, 75 Bilodeau Ct. 05401
Treas., Rev. Howard Stearns
Major Activities: Teaching About Religion in Public Schools; Family Life Education; Teacher Training; Released Time Education

VIRGINIA

Virginia Council of Churches, Inc.

2321 Westwood Ave., Richmond 23230
Tel. (804) 353-5587
Exec. Sec., Rev. Myron S. Miller
Assoc. Exec. Rev. James A. Payne
Dir. Weekday Religious Education, Ms. Mildred Mundy, Rt. 1, Box 149, Port Republic 24471
Pres., Mrs. Y. J. Skalnik, 2643 West Ave., Falls Church 22046
Major Activities: Educational Development; Church and Society; Direct Ministries; Ecumenical Affairs; Communications

Lord Fairfax Interchurch Council

28 N. Royal Ave.
Front Royal 22630
Tel. (703) 635-3913
Exec. Dir., Rev. Jack Bellingham

WASHINGTON

Washington Association of Churches

4759 15th Ave., NE, Seattle 98105
Tel. (206) 525-1213
Exec., Min., Rev. Loren E. Arnett
Dir., Indochina American Resettlement and Job Program, Rev. John Huston, 810 18th Ave., #206, 98122. Tel. (206) 325-3277
Pres., Ms. Constance Lyle, 1462 Rainer Dr., Apt. 1, Tacoma 98466
Treas., Rev. Bruce Parker, 920 2nd Ave., Rm. 810, 98104
Major Activities: Faith and Order; Poverty Programs; Hunger Action; Legislation; Denominational-Ecumenical Coordination; Congregational Renewal; Refugee Resettlement

†Church Council of Greater Seattle

4759 15th Ave., NE, Seattle 98105
Tel. (206) 525-1213
Pres., Dir., Rev. William B. Cate
Exec. Admin., Mrs. Earl Kinnear
Dir. Friend-to Friend Prog., Mr. Joe Rust
Dir., Emerg. Feeding Prog., Rev. O. J. Moore
Coord., Racial Justice in Education Task Force, Ms. Ann Siqueland
Dir., Chilean Refugee Prog., Pat Tavan
Dir., Crossroad Theatre, Paul Sanford
Dir., Housing and Urban Development Task Force, Rev. David Bloom
Dir., Seattle Religious Peace Action Coalition, Charles Meconis
Pres., Rev. William B. Cate, 4759 15th Ave., NE 98105
Treas., Rev. Melvin Finkbeiner
Major Activities: Racial Justice; Religious Peace Action Coalition; Citizen Feed Back; Pastoral Ministry; Hunger; Religious Education; Police-Community Relations; Women in the Church; Desegregation; Housing; Employment; Mental Health; Gay Rights

†Ecumenical Metropolitan Ministry

P.O. Box 12272, Seattle 98112
Tel. (206) 324-8177
Exec. Dir., Mr. John C. Cannon
Chpsn., Rev. Thomas Fowler
Major Activities: Christian Social Action; Communications between street groups and Denominations/Church organizations: Action Training; Crisis Intervention

†Spokane Christian Coalition

E. 245-13th Ave., Spokane 99202
Tel. (509) 624-5156
Exec. Dir., Rev. John A. Olson
Pres., Mrs. Lynn Schmidt, E. 11121—22nd Ave. 99206
Treas., Rev. William Kelly, S. 324 Cedar 99204
Major Activities: Forums on Issues; Listening-Life Review Ministry with Seniors

†Associated Ministries of Tacoma-Pierce County

2520 Sixth Ave., Tacoma 98406
Tel. (206) 383-3056

Metropolitan Minister, Rev. Bruce E. Foreman
Pres., John Curran, 6464 Avondale, S.W. 98499
Treas., Victor Saathoff, 2620 Deidra Circle, N. 98407
Major Activities: Ministry with Service People; Friend to Friend (Nursing Home Visitation); FISH/Food Banks; Hunger Awareness; Tacoma Area Singles Center; Festival of Families

Associated Ministries of Thurston County

Box 895, Olympia 98507
Tel. (206) 357-7224
Exec. Adm., Nancy Hoff
Asst. Adm., Jean Heidal
Pres., Dorothy Blanchard, 321 E. 17th 98501
Treas., Ms. Joanne Mark, 3117 Wilderness 98501
Major Activities: Shared Workshops; Ecumenical Edu.; Social and Health Concerns; Legislation

WEST VIRGINIA

West Virginia Council of Churches

612 Virginia St. E., Charleston 25301
Tel. (304) 344-3141
Exec. Sec., Rev. John F. Price
Chaplain, Pipestem State Park, Gregory Blevins
Project 60/W.Va. Dir., Mr. Fred Mayer
Pres., Betty A. Roberts, 1596 Dinwiddie St. 25311
Treas., Mr. Cleek Fisher, 908 Hunt Ave. 25302
Major Activities: Christian Education; Radio-TV; Leisure Ministry; Correctional Reform; Ecumenical Events; Legislative Process and Issues; Aging; Child Abuse; Disaster Response

Greater Fairmont Council of Churches

P.O. Box 108, Fairmont 26554
Tel. (304) 366-4072
Exec. Sec., Mrs. Linda Gillett, 322 Fairmont Ave. 26554
Pres., Mrs. Eloise Beans, 832 Park Ave., Monongah 26554
Treas., Mr. Phil Sessler, 115 Avondale Rd. 26554
Major Activities: Education; Mass Media; Social Concerns; Special Services; Youth; Church Women United

The Greater Wheeling Council of Churches

110 Methodist Bldg., Wheeling 26003
Tel. (304) 232-5315
Exec. Sec., Mrs. Mabel Griffith
Hospital Notification Sec., Mrs. Ruth Fletcher
Pres., Mr. Charles Ellwood
Treas., Mr. Eric Hines, 110 Methodist Bldg. 26003
Major Activities: Christian Education; Evangelism; Vespers; Radio; Television; Institutional Ministry; Religious Film Library; Church Women United; Volunteer Pastor Care at Hospital; School of Religion; Hospital Notification

WISCONSIN

Wisconsin Conference of Churches

818 W. Badger Rd., Ste. 201, Madison 53713
Tel. (608) 257-0541
Exec. Dir., Rev. Willis J. Merriman
Adm. Asst., Mrs. Phyllis Brinkman
Program Staff, Mrs. Nancy Nack
Dir. Wisconsin-Milwaukee Religious Broadcasting Ministry, Rev. Robert P. Seater, 1442 N. Farwell, Milwaukee 53202. Tel. (414) 272-4360
Dir. Ofc. of Pastoral Services, Rev. G. Loyd Rediger, 222 N. Midvale Blvd., Madison 53705. Tel. (608) 231-1550
Pres., Mrs. Harry Hamilton
Treas., Mr. Walter Lenz
Major Activities: Church and Society; Religion and Leisure; Indian Ministry; Migrant Ministry; Pastoral Services; Broadcasting Ministry; Welfare Reform; ETN and Religious Education; World Hunger; Ecumenical Resources; Aging; IMPACT; Handicapped; Refugee Concerns; Institutional Chaplaincy

Christian Youth Council

1715—52nd St., Kenosha 53140
Tel. (414) 652-9543
Exec. Dir., Mr. Carroll K. Rikil
Industrial Chaplain, Dr. Lee Downs
Youth Coordinator, Mrs. Willa Smith
Center Mgr., Mr. David Ray
Christian Education, Rev. Mrs. Paul Mitchell
Art Consultant, Mrs. Carroll Rikli
Sports Dir., Mr. Jeff Schillinger
Club Dir., Ms. Ilda Thomas
Pres., Fr. Malcolm McClenaghan
Major Activities: Christian Education; Leisure Time Ministry; Institutional Ministries; Ecumenical Committee; Social Concerns

Greater Milwaukee Conference on Religion & Urban Affairs

1442 N. Farwell Ave., Ste. 208, 53202
Tel. (414) 276-9050
Exec. Dir., Rev. John D. Fischer
Creative Ministries Task Force, Ms. Phyllis Schiffer
Wholistic Health Care Task Force, Ms. Karen Schudson
Adm. Asst., Mrs. Charlotte Garrett
Dir., Interfaith Prog. for the Elderly, Sr. Adele Henneberry
Consultant in Communications, Rev. Robert Seater
Consultant in Planning & Research, Mrs. Fran Beverstock
Chpsn., Dr. Lance Herrick
Treas., Rev. Carl R. Simon
Major Activities: Task Forces on Education; TV Programming; Annual Clergy Luncheon; Wholistic Health Care; Pre-Transitional Training

Center for Community Concerns

1501 Villa St. Racine 53403
Exec. Dir., Rev. Jack M. Murtaugh
Assoc. Dir., Mrs. Jean Mandli
Communications Ed./Consumer Advisor for Older Adults, Rev. William S. Avery
Research and Development, Mrs. Dorothy D. Brigham
Major Activities: Advocacy; Direct Service Provider: Research; Community Consultant; Criminal Justice; Volunteerism; Public Education

CWS/Wisconsin CROP

818 W. Badger Rd., Ste. 201, Madison 53713
Tel. (608) 257-5591
Dir., William Whitcomb
Chpsn., Ardith McDowell

WYOMING

Wyoming Church Coalition

1820 Hillside Dr., Laramie 82070
Chpsn., Rev. Leland Rubesh, 511 Carey, Gillette 82001, Tel. (307) 682-7264
Treas., Mrs. Ema Bixler, 407 S. 24th St., 82070. Tel. (307) 745-5153

Exec. Sec., Rev. Shirley E. Greene, 1820 Hillside Dr. 82070 Tel. (307) 742-2583

Major Activities: Christian Education and Leadership Development; Higher Education; Impacted Areas; Christian Camping; Social Concerns; Legislative Concerns; Media

Wyoming Ministries in Higher Education

Dir., Rev. Mary Jeanette Hoover, 1115 Grand Ave., Laramie 82070

Intern Campus Minister, Rev. Lang Brownlee

Community College Facilitator, Rev. Samuel Kirk

†Board of Ministry to Impacted Areas

P.O. Box 1871, Rock Springs 82901

Coordinator, Rev. Arthur Waidmann

7. CANADIAN REGIONAL AND LOCAL ECUMENICAL AGENCIES

Most of the organizations listed below are councils of churches in which churches participate officially, whether at the parish or judicatory level.

There is one provincial body and one inter-provincial. The others operate at either the city, metropolitan area, or county level. Parish clusters within urban areas are not included.

Canadian local ecumenical bodies operate without paid staff, with the exception a few which have part-time staff. In most cases the name and address of the president or chairperson is listed. As these offices change from year to year, some of this information may be out of date by the time the Yearbook of American and **Canadian Churches** is published. However, a letter to the address listed will be forwarded. Up-to-date information may be secured from the Canadian Council of Churches, 40 St. Clair Ave., E., Toronto, Ontario M4T 1M9.

Those organizations not sending in an updated report for this edition are marked with the symbol (†)

ALBERTA

Alberta Inter-Faith Community Action Committee

Pres., Rev. Don Sjoberg, 9901-107 St., Edmonton, Alberta T5K 1G4

Calgary Inter-Faith Community Action Committee

Rabbi Lewis Ginsburg, 405-4th Ave. S.W., Calgary, Alberta T2P OJ5

Calgary Council of Churches

Pres., Rev. Canon Arthur Wilcox, 3315–35th Ave., S.W., Calgary, Alberta T3E 0Z9

Edmonton & District Council of Churches

Pres., Rev. Thomas Kroetch, 10033-84 Ave., Edmonton, Alberta T6E 2G6

ATLANTIC PROVINCES

Atlantic Ecumenical Council of Churches

Pres., Rev. Canon S.P. Davies, P. O. Box 183, Waverly, Nova Scotia B0N 2S0.

BRITISH COLUMBIA

Canadian Ecumenical Action (Formerly POEM)

Coordinator, Rev. Val Anderson, #209-1811 West 16th Ave., Vancouver, British Columbia V6J 2M3

Vancouver, Lower Mainland and Fraser Valley, Council of Christian Churches

Pres., Rev. Murray Henderson, 1708 W. 16th Ave., Vancouver, British Columbia V6J 2M1

Victoria Council of Churches

Rev. John Watson, 877 N. Park St., Victoria, British Columbia V8W 1S9

MANITOBA

Manitoba Provincial Inter-Faith Council

Chpsn., Rev. Canon W. J. G. Ayers, 1735 Corydon Ave., Winnipeg, Manitoba R3N OK4

NEW BRUNSWICK

Greater Fredericton Clergy Council

Pres., Rev. Canon H. Gordon Smith, 346 King's College Rd., Frederickton, New Brunswick E3B 2E9

Moncton Area Council of Churches

Pres., Basil Lowery, 113 Torwood Ct., Riverview, New Brunswick E1B 2K4

Nashwaak-Miramachi Inter-Church Council

Pres., Mrs. Faye Gilmore, R.R. #1, Stanley, New Brunswick E0H 1T0

Sackville Bedford Church Association

Pres., Rev. Gerad Steeves, Bedford United Baptist Church, Bedford, New Brunswick

Saint John N.B. Association of Ecumenical Churchmen

Pres., Rev. Tom Graham, 4 Second St., Saint John West, New Brunswick E2K 3L2

NOVA SCOTIA

Amherst and Area Council of Churches

Pres., Mrs. H. E. MacLean, 199 Victoria St., E. Amherst, Nova Scotia B4H 1Y8

Halifax-Dartmouth Council of Churches

Pres., Judge P.J.T. O'Hearn, 6369 Berlin St., Halifax, Nova Scotia B3L 1T4

Industrial Cape Breton Council of Churches

Pres., Rev. M. J. Findlay, P. O. Box 801, Sydney, Nova Scotia B1P 6J1

Mahone Bay Inter-Church Council

Pres., Rev. John E. Boyd, Box 373, Mahone Bay, Nova Scotia B0J 2E0

Pictou County Council of Churches

Pres., Rev. Robert Cruickshank, 195 Norma St. New Glasgow, Nova Scotia B2H 3N5

Queen's County N.S. Association of Churches

Sec., Mr. Harry Farncombe, P.O. Box 322, Liverpool, Nova Scotia B0T 1K0

Wolfeville Inter-Church Council

Pres., Mrs. Isobel Horton, Box 586, Wolfville, Nova Scotia B0P 1X0

ONTARIO

Ancaster Inter-Church Council

Chpsn., W. H. Cairney, 211 Crestview Ave., Ancaster, Ontario L9G 1E3

Brockville and District Inter-Church Council

Pres., Rev. George Clifford, 5 Wall St., Brockville, Ontario K6V 4R8

Burlington Inter-Church Council

Pres., Fred Townsend, 425 Breckonwood, Burlington, Ontario L7L 2J6

Christian Council of the Capital Area (Ottawa)

Pres., Rev. Alexandre Taché, O.M.I., 249 Main St., Ottawa, Ontario K1S 1C5

Glengarry-Prescott-Russell Christian Council

Pres., Rev. Lue Richard, 470 Main St., E., Hawkesbury, Ontario K6A 1A9

Hamilton Churches Association

Chpsn., Rev. John A. Johnston, 147 Chedoke Ave., Hamilton, Ontario L8P 4P2

Kitchener-Waterloo Council of Churches

Pres., Rev. John Griffiths, 162 Oriole St., Waterloo, Ontario N2J 2B4

London Inter-Church Council

Pres., Rev. C.L.G. Rowland, 489 Pine Tree Dr., London, Ontario N6H 3M9

Manitoulin (Western Manitoulin Inter-Church Council)

Pres., Douglas Wismer, Silver Water, Ontario P0P 1Y0

Mississauga East Community Churches for Action

Chpsn., Rev. George A. Morley, 710 Dundas St., E., Mississauga, Ontario L4Y 2B5

Oshawa Church Council

Pres., Harry Glass, 14 Westmoreland St., Oshawa, Ontario L1G 2M8

Stratford & District Council of Churches

Pres., Rev. Norman Cobson, 221 Huntingdon, Stratford, Ontario N5A 6P7

Thorold Inter-Faith Council

Sec., Mrs. Ruth Pett, 1 Dunn St., St. Catharines, Ontario L2T 1P3

PRINCE EDWARD ISLAND

Charlottetown Christian Council

Rev. J. Cameron Bigelow, 19 Tamarac Ave., Charlottetown, Prince Edward Island C1A 6T2

Summerside P.E.I. Council of Churches

Contact Person, Charles Hogan, Summerside, Prince Edward Island

QUEBÉC

Groupe de Travail des Églises de Montréal/Joint Working Group of the Montréal Churches

Pres., Pasteur Daniel Pourchot, 187 Glengarry, Town of Mount Royal, Québec H3R 1A3

SASKATCHEWAN

Saskatoon Council of Churches

Pres., Ms. Esther M. Highfield, 611 Ave., H., South Saskatoon, Saskatchewan S7M 1X1

8. THEOLOGICAL SEMINARIES IN THE UNITED STATES

The following list of theological seminaries also includes certain departments of colleges and universities in which ministerial training is given. This list has been checked with the *Education Directory* published by the U. S. Office of Education, and with other directories. The compilation is fairly complete for Protestant and Jewish institutions and for the larger Roman Catholic seminaries.

The listings follow this order: Institution, affiliation, location, head, telephone number.

Academy of the New Church (Theol. Sch.), Gen. Ch. of the New Jerusalem, 2815 Huntingdon Pike, Bryn Athyn, PA 19009, R.S. Junge. Tel. (215) WI 7-4200

American Baptist Seminary of the West, Amer. Bapt., L. Doward McBain, 2515 Hillegass, Berkeley, CA 94704. Tel. (415) 841-1905.

American Baptist Theol. Sem., Natl. Bapt., U.S.A., Inc., So. Bapt. Conv., 1800 White's Creek Pike, Nashville, TN 37207. Charles Emerson Boddie. Tel. (615) 262-3433.

Anderson School of Theology, Ch. of God, Anderson, IN 46011, Barry L. Callen. Tel. (317) 644-0951

Andover Newton Theol. Sch., Amer. Bapt., U. Ch. of Christ, 210 Herrick Rd., Newton Centre, MA 02159, Gordon M. Torgersen. Tel. (617) 964-1100

Aquinas Institute of Theology, Cath., 2570 Asbury Rd., Dubuque, IA 52001, Thomas McGonigle, Tel. (319) 556-7593

Asbury Theol. Sem., interdenom., Wilmore, KY 40390, Frank Bateman Stanger. Tel. (606) 858-3581

Ashland Theol. Sem., Breth. Ch., Ashland, OH 44805, Joseph R. Shultz. Tel. (419) 289-4004

Assemblies of God Graduate School, Assemblies of God, 1445 Boonville Ave., Springfield, MO 65802, Thomas F. Zimmerman. Tel. (417) 862-2781

Austin Presbyterian Theol. Sem., Presb. US, 100 E. 27th St., Austin, TX 78705, Jack M. Maxwell, Tel. (512) 472-6736

Azusa Pacific College, interdenom., Highway 66 at Citrus Ave., Azusa, CA 91702, Paul E. Sago. Tel. (213) 969-3434

Bangor Theol. Sem., U. Ch. of Christ, 300 Union St., Bangor, ME 04401, G. Wayne Glick. Tel. (207) 942-6781

Baptist Missionary Association Theol. Sem., Bapt. Missionary Assoc. of Amer., P. O. Box 1797, Jacksonville, TX 75766, John W. Duggar. Tel. (214) 586-2501

Berean Christian College, interdenom., P.O. Box 9268, Wichita, KS 67277. V. Charles Bachman. Tel. (316) 945-5074

Berkeley Divinity Sch. at Yale, Epis., New Haven, CT 06511, Charles H. Clark. Tel. (203) 436-3636

Berkshire Christian College, Adv. Christian Ch., Lenox, MA 01240, Vincent Taber. Tel. (413) 637-0838

Bethany Bible College, Assem. of God, 800 Bethany Dr., Santa Cruz, CA 95066, Richard Foth. Tel. (408) 438-3800

Bethany Lutheran Theol. Sem., Evang. Luth. Synod, 447 N. Division St., Mankato, MN 56001. vacant. Tel. (507) 625-2977

Bethany Theol. Sem., Ch. of Breth., Butterfield and Meyers Rd., Oak Brook, IL 60521, Warren F. Groff. Tel. (312) 620-2200

Bethel Theol. Sem., Bapt. Gen. Conf., St. Paul, MN 55112, Carl H. Lundquist. Tel. (612) 641-6230

Beulah Heights Bible College, Pentecostal, 892-906 Berne St., SE., Atlanta, GA 30316, James B. Keiller. Tel. (404) 627-2681

Biblical Theological Seminary, undenom., 200 N. Main St., P.O. Box 9, Hatfield, PA 19440, Allan A. MacRae Tel. (215) 368-5000

Boston University (Sch. of Theol.), U. Meth., 745 Commonwealth Ave., Boston, MA 02215, Richard Nesmith, Tel. (617) 353-3051

Brite Divinity Sch., Texas Christian University, Christian Ch. (Disc.), Fort Worth, TX 76129, M. Jack Suggs. Tel. (817) 921-7575

California Lutheran Bible School, Luth., 641 S. Western, Anaheim, CA 92804, Frank E. Wilcox. Tel. (714) 827-1940

Calvary Bible College, nondenom., 1111 W. 39th St., Kansas City, MO 64111, Leslie Madison. Tel. (816) 753-4511

Calvin Theol. Sem., Christian Ref., Grand Rapids, MI 49506, J. H. Kromminga. Tel. (616) 949-2494

Catholic Theological Union, Cath., 5401 S. Cornell Ave., Chicago, IL 60615. Alcuin F. Coyle. Tel. (312) 324-8000

Catholic University of America (Theol. College), 401 Michigan Ave., N.E., Washington, DC, 20017 Anthony F. Lobo. Tel. (202) 635-5900

Central Baptist Theol. Sem. in Indiana, Natl. Bapt., U.S.A., Natl. Bapt. Conv., Inc. Prog. Natl. Bapt., 1519-65 Martindale Ave., Indianapolis, IN 46202, F. Benjamin Davis. Tel. (317) 636-6622

Central Baptist Theol. Sem., Amer. Bapt., Kansas City, KS 66102, O. Dean Nelson. Tel. (913) 371-5313

Central Bible College, Assem. of God, 3000 N. Grant Ave., Springfield, MO 65802, Philip Crouch. Tel. (417) 833-2551

Central Wesleyan College, Wesleyan Ch., Wesleyan Dr., Central, SC 29630, John Newhy. Tel. (803) 639-2453

Chicago Theol. Sem., U. Ch. of Christ, 5757 University Ave., Chicago, IL 60637, Charles Shelby Rooks. Tel. (312) 752-5757

Christ Seminary-Seminex, Assn. Ev. Luth. Chs., 607 N. Grand Blvd., St. Louis, MO 63103. John H. Tietjen. Tel. (314) 534-9410

Christ the King Sem., Cath, 711 Knox Rd., P. O. Box 160, East Aurora, NY 14052, Daniel Lanahan. Tel. (716) 652-8900

Christ the Savior Sem., Am. Carpatho-Russ, Orth. Greek Cath. Ch., 225 Chandler Ave., Johnstown, PA 15906, John R. Martin, Tel. (814) 539-0116

Christian Theol. Sem., Christian Ch. (Disc.), 1000 W. 42nd St., Indianapolis, IN 46208. Thomas J. Liggett. Tel. (317) 924-1331

Church Divinity Sch. of the Pacific, Epis., 2451 Ridge Rd., Berkeley, CA 94709, Frederick H. Borsch. Tel. (415) 848-3282

Cincinnati Bible Seminary, CC/CC, 2700 Glenway Ave., Cincinnati, OH 45204, Harvey C. Bream, Jr. Tel. (513) 471-4800

Colgate Rochester Divinity School/Bexley Hall/Crozer Theological Seminary, multidenom., Rochester, NY 14620, Leon Pacala. Tel. (716) 271-1320

Columbia Bible College and Columbia Graduate School of Bible and Missions, interdenom., P.O. Box 3122, Columbia, SC 29230, J. Robertson McQuilkin. Tel. (803) 754-4100

Columbia Theol. Sem., Presb. US, Decatur, GA 30031, J. Davison Philips. Tel. (404) 378-8821

Concordia Sem., Luth. Ch.—Mo. Synod, St. Louis (Clayton), MO 63105, Ralph A. Bohlmann. Tel. (314) 721-5934

Concordia Theol. Sem., Luth. Ch.—Mo. Synod, Ft. Wayne, IN 46825, Robert Preus. Tel. (219) 482-9611

Conservative Bapt. Theol. Sem., Cons. Bapt., P. O. Box 10,000, University Park Sta., Denver, CO 80210, Haddon Robinson. Tel, (303) 761-2482

Covenant Theol. Sem., Ref. Presb., Ev. Synod, 12330 Conway Rd., St. Louis, MO 63141. William S. Barker. Tel. (314) 434-4044

Dallas Theol. Sem., undenom., 3909 Swiss Ave., Dallas, TX 75204, John F. Walvoord. Tel. (214) 824-3094

De Sales Hall School of Theology, Cath., 5001 Eastern Ave., Hyattsville, MD 20782. William J. Ruhl. Tel. (301) 559-4022

Detroit Bible College, interdenom., 35700 West Twelve Mile Rd., Farmington Hills, MI 48018, Wendell G. Johnston. Tel. (313) 553-7200

Disciples Divinity House, Univ. of Chicago, Chr. Ch. (Disc.), 1156 E. 57th St., Chicago, IL 60637, ———. Tel. (312) 643-4411

Dominican House of Studies (Pontifical Faculty of the Immaculate Conception), 487 Michigan Ave., N.E., Washington, DC 20017, Mark Heath. Tel. (202) 529-5300

Drew University (Theol. School), U. Meth., Madison, NJ 07940, James E. Kirby. Tel. (201) 377-3000

Dubuque, Univ. of (Theol. Sem.), U. Presb. Ch. USA, 2570 Asbury Rd., Dubuque, IA 52001, Walter F. Peterson. Tel. (319) 589-3222

Duke University (Divinity Sch.), U. Meth., Durham, NC 27706, Thomas A. Langford. Tel. (919) 684-3234

Earlham School of Religion, Friends (Quakers), Richmond, IN 47374, Alan L. Kolp. Tel. (317) 962-6561

Eastern Baptist Theol. Sem., Amer. Bapt., City Line and Lancaster Ave., Philadelphia, PA 19151. Daniel E. Weiss. Tel. (215) 896-5000

Eastern Mennonite Seminary, Menn. Ch. Harrisonburg, VA 22801. Myron S. Augsburger. Tel. (703) 433-2771

Eden Theol. Sem., U. Ch. of Christ, 475 E., Lockwood Ave., St. Louis, MO 63119. Robert T. Fauth. Tel. (314) 961-3627

Emory University (The Candler Sch. of Theol.), U. Meth., Atlanta, GA 30322. Jim L. Waits, Tel. (404) 329-6324

Episcopal Divinity Sch., Epis., Cambridge, MA 02138. Harvey H. Guthrie, Jr., Tel. (617) 868-3450

Episcopal Theol. Sem. of the Southwest, Epis., P. O. Box 2247, Austin, TX 78768. Gordon T. Charlton, Jr. Tel. (512) 472-4133

Erskine Theol. Sem., Assoc. Ref. Presb., P. O. Box 171, Due West, SC 29639. R. T. Ruble. Tel. (803) 379-8885

Evangelical Sch. of Theol., Evangel. Congreg. Ch., 121 S. College St., Myerstown, PA 17067, Leon O. Hynson. Tel. (717) 866-5775

Evangelical Sem. of Puerto Rico, interdenom., Ave. Ponce de Leon 776, Hato Rey, PR 00918, Luis Fidel Mercado. Tel. (809) 751-6483

Evangelical Theol. Sem., Inc., Evang. Bapt., 2302-2400 E. Ash St., Goldsboro, NC 27530. William Howard Carter. Tel. (919) 735-0831

Fort Wayne Bible College, Missionary Ch., 1025 W. Rudisill Blvd., Fort Wayne, IN 46807. Timothy M. Warner. Tel. (219) 456-2111

Franciscan Sch. of Theol. Cath., 1712 Euclid Ave., Berkeley, CA 94709, Kenan B. Osborne. Tel. (415) 848-5232

Fuller Theol. Sem., multidenom., 135 N. Oakland Ave., Pasadena, CA 91101. David A. Hubbard. Tel. (213) 449-1745

Garrett-Evangelical Theol. Sem., U. Meth., 2121 Sheridan Rd., Evanston, IL 60201, Merlyn W. Northfelt. Tel. (312) 866-3900

General Theol. Sem., Epis., 175 Ninth Ave., New York, NY 10011. James C. Fenhagen. Tel. (212) 243-5150

George Mercer, Jr., Memorial Sch. of Theol., Epis., 65-4th St., Garden City, NY 11530, George Hill. Tel. (516) 248-4800

Golden Gate Bapt. Theol. Sem., S. Bapt., Seminary Dr., Mill Valley, CA 94941. William M. Pinson, Jr. Tel. (415) 388-8080

Gordon-Conwell Theological Seminary, interdenom., South Hamilton, MA 01982, Harold John Ockenga. Tel. (617) 468-7111

Goshen Biblical Sem., Menn., 3003 Benham Ave., Elkhart, IN 46514, Marlin E. Miller. Tel. (219) 295-3726

Grace College of the Bible, interdenom., 1515 S. 10th St., Omaha, NE 68108, Robert W. Benton. Tel. (402) 342-3377

Grace Theol. Sem., Fellowship of Grace Breth. Winona Lake, IN 46590, Homer A. Kent, Jr. Tel. (219) 267-8191

Graduate Theol. Union, nondenom., 2465 Le Conte Ave., Berkeley, CA 94709, Claude Welch. Tel. (415) 841-9811

Greenville College, Free Meth., 315 E. College Ave., Greenville, IL 62246, W. Richard Stephens. Tel. (618) 664-1840

Hartford Seminary Foundation, The, interdenom., Hartford, CT 06105. John Dillenberger, Tel. (203) 232-4451

Harvard Divinity School, nondenom., 45 Francis Ave., Cambridge, MA 02138, George Rupp. Tel. (617) 495-5761

Hebrew Union College—Jewish Inst. of Religion, Jewish, 3101 Clifton Ave., Cincinnati, OH 45220; Tel. (513) 221-1875 1 W. 4th St., New York, NY 10012 Tel. (212) 674-5400; 3077 University Los Angeles, CA 90007; Tel. (213) 749-3424 13 King David St., Jerusalem, Israel, Alfred Gottschalk

Holy Cross School of Theology (Hellenic College), Greek Orthodox, 50 Goddard Ave., Brookline, MA 02146, Thomas C. Lelon. Tel. (617) 731-3500

Holy Trinity Orthodox Seminary, Russian Orthodox, Jordanville, NY 13361. Bishop Laurus (Skurla). Tel. (315) 858-1332

Howard University School of Religion, interdenom., 1240 Randolph St., NE 20017. Washington, DC. 20017. Tel. (202) 636-7277

Huntington College, School of Christian Ministries, U. B. in Christ, Huntington, IN 46750, Paul R. Fetters. Tel. (219) 356-6000

Iliff School of Theol., The, U. Meth., 2201 S. University Blvd., Denver, CO 80210, Smith Jameson Jones, Jr. Tel. (303) 744-1287

Immaculate Conception Sem., Cath., Darlington (Mahwah P. O.), NJ 07430, Edward J. Ciuba. Tel. (201) 327-0300

Interdenominational Theol. Center, 671 Beckwith St., S.W., Atlanta, GA 30314, Grant S. Shockley. Tel. (404) 522-1772

Jesuit School of Theology, Cath., 1735 Leroy Ave., Berkeley, CA 94709, Richard A. Hill. Tel. (415) 841-8804

Jewish Theol. Sem. of America, Jewish, 3080 Broadway, New York, NY 10027, Gerson D. Cohen. Tel. (212) 749-8000

Johnson Bible College, Christian Ch., Kimberlin Hts. Sta., Knoxville, TN 37920, David L. Eubanks. Tel. (615) 573-4517

Kentucky Christian College, CC/CC, Grayson, KY 41143, L. Palmer Young. Tel. (606) 474-6613

Lancaster Theol. Sem. of the U. Ch. of Christ, Lancaster, PA 17603, James D. Glasse. Tel. (717) 393-0654

THEOLOGICAL SEMINARIES IN THE UNITED STATES

Lexington Theol. Sem. (formerly College of the Bible, The), Chr. Ch. (Disc.), 631 S. Limestone, Lexington, KY 40508, Wayne H. Bell. Tel. (606) 252-0361

Lincoln Christian College and Seminary, CC/CC, Box 178, Lincoln, IL 62656, Robert E. Phillips. Tel. (217) 732-3168

Loma Linda University, Seventh-day Adv., Loma Linda Campus, Loma Linda, CA 92350. Tel. (714) 796-7311; La Sierra Campus, Riverside, CA 92515, V. N. Olsen. Tel. (714) 785-2019

Louisville Presbyterian Theol. Sem., Presb. US, U. Presb. Ch. USA, 1044 Alta Vista Rd., Louisville, KY 40205. Carl Ellis Nelson. Tel. (502) 895-3411

Luther Theological Sem., Amer. Luth. Ch., 2375 Como Ave. W., St. Paul, MN 55108, Lloyd Svendsbye. Tel. (612) 641-3456

Lutheran Brethren Seminary, Ch. of the Luth. Breth., Fergus Falls, MN 56537, C. Lloyd Bjornlie. Tel. (218) 739-3373

Lutheran Sch. of Theol. at Chicago, Luth. Ch. in Amer., 1100 E. 55th St., Chicago, IL 60615, William E. Lesher. Tel. (312) 667-3500

Lutheran Theol. Sem., Luth. Ch. in Amer., Gettysburg, PA 17325, Herman G. Stuempfle. Tel. (717) 334-6286

Lutheran Theol. Sem. at Philadelphia, Luth. Ch. in Amer., 7301 Germantown Ave., Mt. Airy, Philadelphia, PA 19119, Raymond Bost. Tel. (215) 248-4616

Lutheran Theol. Southern Sem., Luth. Ch. in Amer., Columbia, SC 29203, Hugh George Anderson. Tel. (803) 786-5150

Manhattan Christian College, Christian Churches, 14th and Anderson Sts., Manhattan, KS 66502, W. F. Lown. Tel. (913) 539-3571

Marion College (Div. of Religion and Philosophy), Wesleyan Ch., 40th and So. Washington, Marion, IN 46952, R. Duane Thompson. Tel. (317) 674-6901

Mary Immaculate Sem., Cath., Box 27, Northampton, PA 18067, John W. Gouldrick. Tel. (215) 262-7866

Maryknoll School of Theology (Cath. For. Miss. Soc. of Amer., Inc.), Cath., Maryknoll, NY 10545, John P. Meehan. Tel. (914) 941-7590

McCormick Theol. Sem., U. Presb. Ch. USA, 5555 S. Woodlawn Ave., Chicago, IL 60637. Jack L. Stotts. Tel. (312) 241-7800

Meadville/Lombard Theol. Sch., Unit. Univ., 5701 Woodlawn Ave., Chicago, IL 60637, Gene Reeves. Tel. (312) 753-3195

Memphis Theol. Sem., Cumb. Presb., 168 E. Parkway S., Memphis, TN 38104, E. Colvin Baird. Tel. (901) 458-8232

Mennonite Biblical Sem., Gen. Conf. Menn., 3003 Benham Ave., Elkhart, IN 46514, Henry Poettcker. Tel. (219) 295-3726

Mennonite Brethren Biblical Sem., Menn. Breth. Ch., 4824 E. Butler at Chestnut Ave. Fresno, CA 93727, Elmer A. Martens. Tel. (209) 251-8628

Meth. Theol. Sch. in Ohio, U. Meth., Box 630, Delaware, OH 43015, John W. Dickhaut. Tel. (614) 363-1146

Midwestern Bapt. Theol. Sem., S. Bapt., 5001 N. Oak Trafficway, Kansas City, MO 64118, Milton Ferguson. Tel. (816) 453-4600

Moody Bible Institute, interdenom., 820 N. La Salle St., Chicago, IL 60610, George Sweeting. Tel. (312) 329-4000

Moravian Theol. Sem., Morav., Bethlehem, PA 18018, William W. Matz. Tel. (215) 865-0741

Moreau Sem. (Holy Cross Fathers), Cath., Notre Dame, IN 46556, Thomas W. Smith. Tel. (219) 283-7735

Morehouse School of Religion, Amer. Bapt., Prog. Natl. Bapt. and Natl. Bapt. Conv., U.S.A., Inc. 645 Beckwith St., S.W., Atlanta, GA 30314, Bobby Joe Saucer. Tel. (404) 688-6743

Mt. Angel Sem., Cath., St. Benedict, OR 97373, James M. Ribble. Tel. (503) 845-3327

Mt. St. Alphonsus Sem., Cath., Esopus, NY 12429, Edward J. Gilbert, Tel. (914) 384-6550

Mt. St. Mary's Sem., Cath., Emmitsburg, MD 21727, Richard M. McGuiness. Tel. (301) 447-6122

Mt. St. Mary's Sem of the West, Cath., 5440 Moeller Ave., Norwood, OH 45212, Lawrence K. Breslin. Tel. (513) 731-2630

Multnomah School of the Bible, interdenom., 8435 N.E. Glisan St., Portland, OR 97220, Joseph C. Aldrich. Tel. (503) 255-0332

Nashotah House (Theol. Sem.), Epis., Nashotah, WI 53058, John S. Ruef. Tel. (414) 646-3371

Nazarene Theol. Sem., Nazarene, 1700 E. Meyer Blvd., Kansas City, MO 64131, Stephen W. Nease. Tel. (816) 333-6254

New Brunswick Theol. Sem., Ref. Amer., 17 Seminary Pl., New Brunswick, NJ 08901; Howard G. Hageman. Tel. (201) 247-5241

New Orleans Baptist Theol. Sem., S. Bapt., New Orleans, LA 70126, Landrum P. Leavell, II. Tel. (504) 282-4455

New York Theol. Sem., interdenom., 5 W. 29th St., New York, NY 10001, George W. Webber, Tel. (212) 532-4012

North American Baptist Sem., N. Amer. Bapt. Conf., 1321 West 22nd St., Sioux Falls, SD 57105, David J. Draewell. Tel. (605) 336-6588

North Park Theol. Sem., Evang. Cov. Ch., 5125 N. Spaulding Ave., Chicago, IL 60625, Arthur A. R. Nelson, actg. Tel. (312) 583-2700

Northeastern Bible College, interdenom., Essex Fells, NJ 07021, Charles W. Anderson. Tel. (201) 226-1074

Northern Bapt. Theol. Sem., Amer. Bapt. 660 E. Butterfield Rd., Lombard, IL 60148, William R. Myers. Tel. (312) 620-2101

Northwestern Lutheran Theol. Sem., Luth Ch. in Amer., 1501 Fulham St., St. Paul, MN 55108, Lloyd Svendsbye. Tel. (612) 641-3456

Notre Dame Sem., Cath., 2901 S. Carrollton Ave., New Orleans, LA 70118, J. Edgar Bruns, Tel. (504) 866-7426

Oblate College, Cath., 391 Michigan Ave., N.E., Washington, DC 20017, Richard J. Murphy. Tel. (202) 529-6544

Oblate College of the Southwest (Theol. Sem.), Cath., 285 Oblate Dr., San Antonio, TX 78216, Patrick Guidon. Tel. (512) 341-1366

Ozark Bible College, CC/CC, 1111 North Main St., Joplin, MO 64801, Ken Idleman.

Pacific Lutheran Theol. Sem., Luth. Ch. in Amer. and Am. Luth. Ch., 2770 Marin Ave., Berkeley, CA 94708, Walter M. Stuhr, Tel. (415) 524-5264

Pacific Sch. of Religion, interdenom., Berkeley, CA 94709, Neely McCarter. Tel. (415) 848-0528

Payne Theol. Sem., A.M.E., P.O. Box 474, Wilberforce, OH 45384, U.A. Hughey. Tel. (513) 376-2946

Perkins Sch. of Theol. (Southern Methodist Univ.), U. Meth., Dallas, TX 75275, Joseph D. Quillian, Jr. Tel. (214) 692-2138

Philadelphia College of Bible, nondenom., Langhorne Manor, Langhorne, PA 19047, W. Sherrill Babb. Tel. (215) 752-5800

Phillips University, The Graduate Seminary, Chr. Churches (Disc.), Enid, OK 73701, James F. Caton, actg. Tel. (405) 237-4433

Pittsburgh Theol. Sem., U. Presb. Ch. USA, Pittsburgh, PA 15206, Ronald V. Wells, interim. Tel. (412) 362-5610

Point Loma College (Div. of Graduate Studies), Nazarene, San Diego, CA 92106, Bill B. Draper. Tel. (714) 222-6474

Pontifical College Josephinum, Cath., 7625 N. High St., Columbus, OH 43085, Frank M. Mouch. Tel. (614) 885-5585

Pope John XXIII National Seminary, Cath., 558 South Ave., Weston, MA 02193, James W. Deadder. Tel. (617) 899-5500

Presbyterian School of Christian Education. Presby. U.S., 1205 Palmyra Ave., Richmond, VA 23227, John C. Otts. Tel. (804) 359-5031

Princeton Theol. Sem., U. Presb. Ch. USA, Princeton, NJ 08540, James I. McCord. Tel. (609) 921-8300

Protestant Episcopal Theol. Sem. in Virginia, Epis., Alexandria, VA 22304, G. Cecil Woods, Jr. Tel. (703) 370-6600

Rabbi Isaac Elchanan Theol. Sem. (affil. of Yeshiva Univ.), Orth. Jewish, 2540 Amsterdam Ave., New York, NY 10033, Zevulun Charlop. Tel. (212) 960-5344

Reconstructionist Rabbinical College, Jewish, 2308 North Broad St., Philadelphia, PA 19132, Ira Eisenstein. Tel. (215) 223-8121

Reformed Presbyterian Theol. Sem., Ref. Presb. Ch. in N. A., 7418 Penn Ave., Pittsburgh, PA 15208, Bruce C. Stewart. Tel. (412) 731-8690

Reformed Theol. Sem., interdenom., 5422 Clinton Blvd., Jackson, MS 39209, Luder G. Whitlock, Jr. Tel. (601) 922-4988

St. Bernard's Sem., Cath., 2260 Lake Ave., Rochester, NY 14612, Frank E. Lioi. Tel. (716) 254-1020

St. Charles Borromeo Sem., Cath., Overbrook, Philadelphia, PA 19151, Vincent L. Burns. Tel. (215) 839-3760

St. Columban's Major Sem., Cath., 1200 Brush Hill Rd., Milton, MA 02186, Charles B. Flaherty. Tel. (617) 333-0688

St. Francis Seminary School of Pastoral Ministry, Cath., 3257 S. Lake Dr., Milwaukee, WI 53207, Richard J. Sklba. Tel. (414) 744-1730

St. John's Sem., Cath., Brighton, MA 02135, Robert J. Banks. Tel. (617) 254-2610

St. John's Sem., Cath., Camarillo, CA 93010, Charles E. Miller. Tel. (805) 482-2755

St. John's University, School of Theology, Cath., Collegeville, MN 56321, Kieran P. Nolan. Tel. (612) 363-2444

St. Joseph's Sem., Cath., 201 Seminary Ave., (Dunwoodie), Yonkers, NY 10704, John J. Mescall. Tel. (914) 968-6200

St. Louis Roman Cath. Theol. Sem. (Kenrick Sem.), Cath., 7800 Kenrick Rd., St. Louis, MO 63119, A. L. Trapp. Tel. (314) 961-4320

St. Louis Univ., Dept. of Theol. Studies, Cath., 3634 Lindell Blvd., St. Louis, MO 63108, Richard L. Foley. Tel. (314) 535-3300

St. Mary-of-the-Lake Sem., Cath., Mundelein, IL 60060, James P. Keleher. Tel. (312) 566-6401

St. Mary Sem., Cath., 1227 Ansel Rd., Cleveland, OH 44108, Robert E. Bacher. Tel. (216) 721-2100

St. Mary's Sem., Cath., 9845 Memorial Dr., Houston, TX 77024, Louis J. Franz. Tel. (713) 686-4345

St. Mary's Sem. and Univ., Cath., 5400 Roland Ave., Baltimore, MD 21210, William J. Lee, Tel. (301) 323-3200

St. Meinrad School of Theology, Cath., St. Meinrad, IN 47577, Daniel Buechlein. Tel. (812) 357-6522

St. Patrick's Sem. Cath., Middlefield Rd., Menlo Park, CA 94025, ———. Tel. (415) 325-5621

St. Paul Bible College, Chr. and Miss. All., Bible College, MN 55375, Francis Grubbs. Tel. (612) 446-1411

Saint Paul Sch. of Theol., U. Meth., 5123 Truman Rd., Kansas City, MO 64127, William K. McElvaney. Tel. (816) 483-9600

St. Paul Sem., Cath., 2260 Summit Ave., St. Paul, MN 55105, William Baumgaertner. Tel. (612) 698-0323

St. Thomas Sem., Cath., Denver, CO 80210, Paul Golden. Tel. (303) 722-4687

St. Tikhon's Theol. Sem., Russian Orth., South Canaan, PA 18459, Archbishop Kiprian. Tel. (717) 937-4411

St. Vincent Sem., Cath., Latrobe, PA 15650. Demetrius R. Dumm. Tel. (412) 539-9761

St. Vladimir's Orth. Theol. Sem., Eastern Orth., 575 Scarsdale Rd., Crestwood, Tuckahoe, NY 10707, Most Rev. Metropolitan Theodosius. Tel. (914) 961-8313

SS. Cyril and Methodius Sem., Cath., Orchard Lake, MI 48033, Stanley E. Milewski. Tel. (313) 682-1885

San Francisco Theol. Sem., U. Presb. Ch. USA, San Anselmo, CA 94960, Arnold B. Come. Tel. (415) 453-2280

San Jose Bible College, CC/CC, 790 South 12th St., P.O. Box 1090, San Jose, CA 95108, Charles R. Boatman. Tel. (408) 293-9058

Savonarola Theol. Sem., Pol. Natl. Cath., 1031 Cedar Ave., Scranton, PA 18505, Thaddeus F. Zielinski. Tel. (717) 343-0100

Sch. of Theol. at Claremont, U. Meth., Christian Ch. (Disc.), Epis., Claremont, CA 91711, Richard W. Cain. Tel. (714) 626-3521

Seabury-Western Theol. Sem., Epis., 2122 Sheridan Rd. Evanston IL 60201, O. C. Edwards, Jr. Tel. (312) 328-9300

Seminary of St. Vincent De Paul, Military Trail, Box 460, Boynton Beach, FL 33435, Urban Voll. Tel. (305) 732-4424

Seminary of the Immaculate Conception, Cath., West Neck Rd., Huntington, NY 11743, Dennis M. Regan.. Tel. (516) 423-0483

Seventh-day Adventist Theol. Sem., Andrews Univ., Seventh-day Adv., Berrien Springs, MI 49104, Thomas H. Blincoe. Tel. (616) 471-3536

Seventh Day Bapt. Center on Ministry, Seventh Day Bapt. Gen. Conf., 510 Watchung Ave., Box 868 Plainfield, NJ 07061, Herbert E. Saunders. Tel. (201) 561-8700

Shaw Divinity School, Natl. Bapt., Raleigh, NC 27611, James Z. Alexander. Tel. (919) 755-4846

Southeastern Baptist Theol. Sem., S. Bapt., Wake Forest, NC 27587 W. Randall Lolley, Tel. (919) 556-3101

Southern Baptist Theol. Sem., S. Bapt., Louisville, KY 40206, Duke K. McCall. Tel. (502) 897-4011

Southwestern Baptist Theol. Sem., S. Bapt., P.O.Box 22000, Fort Worth, TX 76122, Russell H. Dilday. (Tel. (817) 923-1921

Starr King Sch. for the Ministry, Unit., Berkeley, CA 94709, Robert C. Kimball. Tel. (415) 845-6232

Swedenborg Sch. of Religion (formerly New Church Theol. Sch.), Genl. Conv. The Swedenborgian Ch., Newton, MA 02158, Robert H. Kirven, Tel. (617) 244-0504

THEOLOGICAL SEMINARIES IN THE UNITED STATES

Talbot Theol. Sem., interdenom., 13800 Biola Ave., La Mirada, CA 90639, Glenn F. O'Neal. Tel. (213) 944-0351

Theol. Sem. of the Ref. Epis. Ch., Ref. Epis., 25 S. 43rd St., Philadelphia, PA 19104, Milton C. Fisher. Tel. (215) 222-5158

Trevecca Nazarene College (Relig. Dept.), Nazarene, 333 Murfreesboro Rd., Nashville, TN 37210, H. Ray Dunning. Tel. (615) 244-6000

Trinity Evangel. Divinity Sch., Evangel. Free Ch. of Amer., 2045 Half Day Rd., Deerfield, IL 60015, Kenneth M. Meyer. Tel. (312) 945-6700

Trinity Lutheran Seminary, Am. Luth. and Luth. in Am., 2199 East Main St., Columbus, OH 43209, Fred W. Meuser. Tel. (614) 236-6407

Union Theol. Sem., undenom., Broadway and 120 St., New York, NY 10027, Donald W. Shriver, Jr. Tel. (212) 662-7100

Union Theol. Sem. in Va., Presb. US, 3401 Brook Rd., Richmond, VA 23227, Fred R. Stair, Jr. Tel. (804) 355-0671

United Theol. Sem., U. Meth., 1810 Harvard Blvd., Dayton, OH 45406, John R. Knecht, Tel. (513) 278-5817

United Theol. Sem. of the Twin Cities, U. Ch. of Christ, 3000 Fifth St., N.W., New Brighton, MN 55112, Dayton D. Hultgren. Tel. (612) 633-4311

University of Chicago (Divinity Sch.), interdenom., Swift Hall, Chicago, IL 60637, Joseph M. Kitagawa. Tel. (312) 753-4031

University of Dallas, Dept. of Theology, Cath., Irving, TX 75061, Gilbert Hardy. Tel. (214) 438-1123

University of Notre Dame, Dept. of Theology, Cath., Notre Dame, IN 46556, David Burrell. Tel. (219) 283-6312

University of St. Thomas, School of Theology, Cath., St. Mary's Campus, 9845 Memorial Dr., Houston, TX 77024, Andrew Willemsen. Tel. (713) 686-4345

University of the South (Sch. of Theol.), Epis., Sewanee, TN 37375, Urban T. Holmes, III. Tel. (615) 598-5931

Vanderbilt University (Divinity Sch.), interdenom., Nashville, TN 37240, ———. Tel. (615) 322-2776

Virginia Union University (Sch. of Theol.), Amer., Bapt., Richmond, VA 23227 Paul Nichols. Tel. (804) 359-9331

Walla Walla College (Sch. of Theol.) Seventh-day Adv., College Pl., WA 99324, Sakae Kubo. Tel. (509) 527-2195

Wartburg Theol. Sem., Amer. Luth., 333 Wartburg Pl., Dubuque, IA 52001, William H. Weiblen. Tel. (319) 556-8151

Washington Theological Union, Indep., 9001 New Hampshire Ave., Silver Spring, MD 20910, Vincent D. Cushing. Tel. (301) 439-0551

Wesley Theol. Sem., U. Meth., 4400 Massachusetts Ave., N.W., Washington, DC 20016, John L. Knight. Tel. (202) 363-2171

Western Baptist College, 5000 Deer Park Dr. S.E. Salem, OR 97302, W. Thomas Younger. Tel. (503) 581-8600

Western Conservative Baptist Sem., Cons. Bapt., 5511 S.E. Hawthorne Blvd., Portland, OR 97215, Earl D. Radmacher. Tel. (503) 233-8561

Western Evangelical Seminary, interdenom, 4200 SE Jennings Ave., Portland, OR 97222, Leo M. Thornton. Tel. (503) 654-5466

Western Theol. Sem., Ref. Ch. in Amer., Holland, MI 49423, I. John Hesselink. Tel. (616) 392-8555

Westminster Theol. Sem., Presb., Chestnut Hill, Philadelphia, PA 19118, Edmund P. Clowney. Tel. (215) 887-5511

Weston School of Theol., Cath., 3 Phillips Pl., Cambridge, MA 02138, John W. Padberg. Tel. (617) 492-1960

Winebrenner Theol. Sem., Churches of God, Gen. Conf., 701 E. Melrose Ave. Findlay, OH 45840, G. E. Weaver. Tel. (419) 422-4824

Wisconsin Lutheran Sem., Luth. (Wis.), 11831N Seminary Dr., 65W Mequon, WI 53092, Armin Schuetze. Tel. (414) 242-2644

Yale University (Divinity Sch.), undenom. , New Haven, CT 06510, Leander Keck. Tel. (203) 436-2494

9. CANADIAN THEOLOGICAL SEMINARIES AND FACULTIES, AND BIBLE SCHOOLS

The following list has been developed by direct correspondence with the institutions involved and is, therefore, a current and reasonably comprehensive list of the major Canadian theological seminaries and faculties, and Bible schools. The editor of the **Yearbook** would be grateful for knowledge of any significant omissions from this compilation.

Listings are alphabetical by name of institution and generally have the following order: Institution, affiliation, location, head, telephone number.

Acadia Divinity College, Un. Bapt. Conv. of the Atlantic Provinces, Wolfville, Nova Scotia, B0P 1X0, Harold L. Mitton. Tel. (902) 542-2285

Alberta Bible College, CC/CC, 599 Northmount Dr., N.W., Calgary, Alberta T2K 3J6, Boyd L. Lammiman. Tel. (403) 282-2994

Alberta Bible Institute, Ch. of God (And.), 4704 55th St., Camrose, Alberta T4V 2B6, Robert Hazen.

Aldersgate College, Free Meth. Ch., Box 460, Moose Jaw, Saskatchewan S6H 4P1, J. Leon Winslow. Tel. (306) 692-1816

Atlantic Baptist College, Un. Bapt. Conv. of the Atlantic Provinces, Moncton, New Brunswick, EIC 8P4, Stuart E. Murray. Tel. (506) 382-7550

Atlantic School of Theology, ecumenical (Ang. Ch. of Canada, Cath., Un. Ch. of Canada), Halifax, Nova Scotia, B3H 3B5, Lloyd J. Robertson. Tel. (902) 423-6801

Berea Bible Institute, Pent. Assem. of Canada, 1711 Henri-Bourassa, E. Montreal, Quebec, H2C 1J5, André L. Gagnon. Tel. (514) 388-1498

Berean Bible College, interdenom., Postal Bag 3900, Stn. B, Calgary, Alberta T2M 4N2, C. Hutchinson.Tel. (403) 277-5616

Bethany Bible Institute, Box 160, Hepburn, Saskatchewan SOK 1Z0, I. Bergen. Tel. (306) 947-2175

Briercrest Bible Institute, interdenom., Caronport, Saskatchewan SOH OSO, Henry H. Budd. Tel. (306) 756-2321

Canadian Mennonite Bible College, 600 Shaftesbury Blvd., Winnipeg, Manitoba R3P 0M4, George Epp. Tel. (204) 888-6781

Canadian Nazarene College, Ch. of the Nazarene, 1301 Lee Blvd., Winnipeg, Manitoba R3T 2P7, Neil E. Hightower. Tel. (204) 269-2120

Canadian Reformed Churches, Theol. College of the, Can. Ref. Chs., 374 Queen St. S., Hamilton, Ontario L8P 3T9, J. Faber. Tel. (416) 529-5569

Canadian Theological College, Chr. and Miss. All., 4400-4th Ave., Regina, Saskatchewan S4T OH8, Rexford Boda. Tel. (306) 545-1515

Central Baptist Seminary, Fell. of Evan. Bapt. Churches in Canada, 95 Jonesville Cres. Toronto, Ontario M4A 1H3, Jack Scott. Tel. (416) 752-1976

Central Pentecostal College, Pent. Assem. of Canada, 1303 Jackson Ave., Saskatoon, Saskatchewan S7H 2M9, Kenneth B. Birch. Tel. (306) 374-6655

Centre for Christian Studies, Ang. Ch. of Canada, Un. Ch. of Canada, 77 Charles St., W., Toronto, Ontario M5S 1K5, Marion G. Niven. Tel. (416) 923-1168

College Dominicain de Philosophie et de Théologie Cath., 96, avenue Empress, Ottawa, Ontario K1R 7G2, Gilles D. Mailhiot. Tel. (613) 233-5696

College of Emmanuel and St. Chad, Ang. Ch. of Canada, Saskatoon, Saskatchewan S7N 0W6, A. Gordon Baker. Tel. (306) 343-3030

Covenant Bible College, Ev. Cov. Ch. of Canada, 245-21st St., E., Prince Albert, Saskatchewan S6V 1L9, W. B. Anderson. Tel. (306) 763-2764

Eastern Pentecostal Bible College, Pent. Assem. of Canada, 780 Argyle St., Peterborough, Ontario K9H 5T2, C. George Atkinson. Tel. (705) 745-7450

Elim Bible Institute, Conf. of Menn. in Manitoba, Box 120 Altona, Manitoba R0G 0B0, Philip Bender. Tel. (204) 324-5464

Emmanuel Bible College, Miss. Ch., 100 Fergus Ave., Kitchener, Ontario N2A 2H2, E. A. Lageer. Tel. (519) 742-3572

Emmanuel College (see under **Toronto School of Theology**)

Full Gospel Bible Institute, Apost. Ch. of Pent., Box 579, Eston, Saskatchewan S0L 1A0, G. S. McLean. Tel. (306) 962-3621

Hillcrest Christian College, Ev. Ch., 2801-13th Ave., S.E., Medicine Hat, Alberta T1A 3R1, James A. Field. Tel. (403) 526-6951

Huron College, Ang. Ch. of Canada, Faculty of Theology, London, Ontario N6G 1H3, J. G. Morden, Tel. (519) 438-7224

Institute for Christian Studies, nondenom., 229 College St., Toronto, Ontario M5T 1R4, Bernard Zylstra. Tel. (416) 979-2331

Knox College (see under **Toronto School of Theology**)

Lutheran Theological Seminary, Ev. Luth. Ch. of Canada, Luth. Ch. in Am., Luth Ch. (Mo. Synod), Saskatoon, Saskatchewan, S7N 0X3, William Hordern. Tel. (306) 343-8204

Maritime Christian College, CC/CC Box 1145, 223 Kent St., Charlottetown, Prince Edward Island, C1A 7M8, Kenneth T. Norris. Tel. (902) 894-3828

McMaster Divinity College, Bapt. Conv. of Ontario and Quebec, Hamilton, Ontario L8S 4K1, Melvyn R. Hillmer. Tel. (416) 525-9140

Mennonite Brethren Bible College and College of Arts, Menn. Br., 77 Henderson Hwy., Winnipeg, Manitoba R2L 1L1, Henry G. Krahn. Tel. (204) 667-9560

Montreal Diocesan Theological College, Ang. Ch. of Canada, 3473 University St., Montreal, Quebec, H3A 2A8, A. C. Capon. Tel. (514) 849-3004

Mountain View Bible College, Miss. Ch., Box 190, Didsbury, Alberta, T0M 0W0, Edward L. Oke. Tel. (403) 335-3337.

Newman Theological College, Cath., RR8, Edmonton, Alberta T5L 4H8, C. M. McCaffery. Tel. (403) 459-6656

Nipawin Bible Institute, interdenom., Box 1986, Nipawin, Saskatchewan S0E 1E0, Jake Rempel. Tel. (306) 862-5098

North American Baptist College, N. Amer. Bapt. Conf., 11525 - 23 Ave., Edmonton, Alberta T6J 4T3, Joseph Sonnenberg. Tel. (403) 437-1960

Northwest Baptist Theological College and Seminary, B. C. Fell. Bapt., 3358 S. E. Marine Dr., Vancouver, British Columbia, V5S 3W3, Tel. (604) 433-2475

Northwest Bible College, Pent. Assem. of Canada, 11617-106 Ave., Edmonton, Alberta T5H 0S1, E. A. Francis. Tel. (403) 452-0808

Okanagan Bible Institute, interdenom. Box 407, Kelowna, British Columbia V1Y 7N8, Lawrence Wilkes. Tel. (604) 768-5183

Ontario Bible College and Theological Seminary, interdenom., 25 Ballyconner Ct., Willowdale, Ontario M2M 4B3, V. Adrian. Tel. (416) 226-6380

THEOLOGICAL SEMINARIES IN CANADA

Ontario Christian Seminary, CC/CC, 204 High Park Ave., Box 324, Sta. D, Toronto, Ontario M6P 3J9. Donald Stevenson. Tel. (416) 769-7115

Peace River Bible Institute, Box 99, Sexsmith, Alberta T0H 3C0, C. W. Johnson. Tel. (403) 568-3962

Prairie Bible Institute, nondenom., Three Hills, Alberta T0M 2A0, Paul Maxwell. Tel. (403) 443-5511

Presbyterian College, 3495 University St., Montreal, Quebec, H3A 2A8, W. J. Klempa. Tel. (514) 288-5256

Queen's Theological College, Un. Ch. of Can., Kingston, Ontario K7L 3N6. Tel. (613) 547-2787

Regis College (see under **Toronto School of Theology).**

Salvation Army Training College, Salv. Army, 2130 Bayview Ave., Toronto, Ontario M4N 3K6, Gladys McGregor. Tel. (416) 481-6133

St. Andrews College, Un. Ch. of Canada, 1121 College Dr., Saskatoon, Saskatchewan S7N 0W3. Tel. (306) 343-5145

St. Augustine Seminary (see under Toronto School of **Theology)**

St. John's College, Univ. of Manitoba, Faculty of Theology, Ang. Ch. of Canada, Winnipeg, Manitoba R3T 2M5, J. R. Brown. Tel. (204) 474-8529

St. Michael's College, Faculty of Theology (see under Toronto **School of Theology)**

St. Paul Univ., Faculty of Canon Law, Cath., 223 Main St., Ottawa, Ontario K1S 1C4, Francis G. Morrisey. Tel. (613) 235-1421

St. Peter's Seminary, Cath., 1040 Waterloo St., London, Ontario N6A 3Y1, J. J. Carrigan. Tel. (519) 432-1824

St. Stephen's College, Centre of Continuing Theological Education, Un. Ch. of Canada, University of Alberta Campus, Edmonton, Alberta T6G 2J6, Garth I. Mundle. Tel. (403) 439-7311

Steinbach Bible College, Menn., Box 1420, Steinbach, Manitoba R0A 2A0, Harvey Plett. Tel. (204) 326-6451

Swift Current Bible Institute, Menn., Box 1268, Swift Current, Saskatchewan S9H 3X4, David Ortis. Tel. (306) 773-5440

Toronto Baptist Seminary, Bapt., 337 Jarvis St., Toronto, Ontario M5B 2C7, E. T. Gurr, G. A. Adams. Tel. (416) 925-3263

Toronto School of Theology (A federation of seven theological colleges: three Roman Catholic, two Anglican, one Presbyterian, and one United Church of Canada. Affiliated with the University of Toronto. McMaster Divinity College is an associate member), 4 St. Thomas St., Toronto, Ontario M5S 2B8, C. Douglas Jay. Tel. (416) 978-4039

Emmanuel College, Un. Ch. of Canada, 75 Queen's Park Crescent, Toronto, Ontario M5S 1K7, William O. Fennell. Tel. (416) 978-3811

Knox College, Presb. Ch. in Canada, 59 St. George St., Toronto, Ontario M5S 2E6, J. C. Hay. Tel. (416) 979-2137

Regis College, Cath., 15 St. Mary St., Toronto, Ontario, M4Y 2R5, Jean-Marc Laporte. Tel. (416) 922-5474

St. Augustine's Seminary, Cath., 2661 Kingston Rd., Scarborough, Ontario M1M 1M3, Brian D. Clough. Tel. (416) 261-7207.

Trinity College, Faculty of Divinity, Ang. Ch. of Canada, Hoskin Ave., Toronto, Ontario M5S 1H8, H. W. Buchner. Tel. (416) 978-3609

University of St. Michael's College, Faculty of Theology, Cath., 81 St. Mary St., Toronto, Ontario M5S 1J4 P. J. M. Swan. Tel. (416) 921-3151

Wycliffe College, Ang. Ch. of Canada, Hoskin Ave., Toronto, Ontario M5S 1H7, R. F. Stackhouse. Tel. (416) 979-2870

Trinity College (see under **Toronto School of Theology)**

United Theological College, Un. Ch. of Can., 3521 University St., Montreal, Quebec H3A 2A9

Université de Montréal, Faculté de théologie, Cath., CP 6128, Montréal Québec H3C 3J7, Léonard Audet. Tel. (514) 343-7167

Université de Sherbrooke, Faculté de théologie, Cath., Cité Universitaire, 2500 Boulevard de l' Université, Sherbrooke, Quebec J1K 2R1, Tel. (819) 565-5913

Université Laval, Faculté de théologie, Cath., Québec 10e, Québec, G1K 7P4 Pierre Gaudette. Tel. (418) 656-7823

University of Winnipeg, Faculty of Theology, Un. Ch. of Can., Winnepeg, Manitoba R3B 2E9, A. M. Watts. Tel. (204) 786-7811

Vancouver School of Theology, ecumen., 6000 Iona Dr., Vancouver, British Columbia V6T 1L4, James P. Martin. Tel. (604) 228-9031

Waterloo Lutheran Seminary, Luth. Ch. in Am., Waterloo, Ontario N2L 3C5, Delton J. Glebe. Tel. (519) 884-1970

Western Pentecostal Bible College, Pent. Assem. of Can., Box 1000, Clayburn, British Columbia, V0X 1E0, L. Thomas Holdcroft. Tel. (604) 853-7491

Winkler Bible Institute, Menn. Breth. Box 1540, Winkler, Manitoba R0G 2X0, Victor Neufeld. Tel. (204) 325-4242

Winnipeg Bible College and Theological Seminary, Otterburne, Manitoba R0A 1G0, Kenneth G. Hanna. Tel. (204) 284-2923

Wycliffe College (see under **Toronto School of Theology)**

10. CHURCH-RELATED AND ACCREDITED COLLEGES AND UNIVERSITIES IN THE UNITED STATES

The following alphabetical listing of church-related colleges and universities is derived mainly from the *Education Directory, Colleges and Universities, 1978-79,* by Arthur Podolsky and Carolyn R. Smith, National Center for Education Statistics, Education Division, U.S. Dept. of Health, Education and Welfare, although other sources were used as well.

The listing below does not include junior colleges, teachers' colleges, and other professional schools.

Of the 653 colleges and universities listed below, approximately 80 per cent were identified as church-related in reports to the National Center for Education Statistics. The remaining 20 percent did not report it but have been identified as church-related in varying degrees.

A tabulation in the *Colleges and Universities 1978-79* cited above, indicates that in 1978-79 there were 1,962 four-year institutions of higher learning in the United States, including outlying parts. Of these, 560 were public and 1,402 private. Of the 1,402 institutions of higher education identified as private, 706 were organized independent of a religious group, 446 were Protestant, 214 Catholic, 24 Jewish and 12 others, *Colleges and Universities* notes.

Abbreviations for nationally recognized regional Accrediting Associations are as follows:

MS Middle States Association of Colleges and Secondary Schools
NC North Central Association of Colleges and Schools
NE New England Association of Schools and Colleges
NW Northwest Association of Schools and Colleges
S Southern Association of Colleges and Schools
West Western Association of Schools and Colleges

Other abbreviations are as follows:

C Co-educational
M Men
W Women
Co-Ord. Coordinate

Each item in the listing below has the following order: Name of institution, address, telephone number, head of institution, nature of student body, accrediting, denominational relationship, enrollment.

Abilene Christian University, Abilene TX 79601, Tel. (915) 677-1911. John C. Stevens, C S, Ch. of Christ, 5,003

Academy of the New Church, Byrn Athyn, PA 19009, Tel. (215) 947-4200. Alfred Acton, C MS, Ch. of New Jerusalem, 168

Adrian College, Adrian, MI 49221, Tel. (517) 265-5161. Donald S. Stanton, C NC, Un. Meth., 912

Agnes Scott College, Decatur, GA 30030, Tel. (404) 373-2571. Marvin B. Perry, W S, Presb. U.S., 551

Albertus Magnus College, New Haven, CT 06511, Tel. (203) 777-6631. Sr. Francis De Sales Heffernan, W NE. Cath., 540

Albion College, Albion, MI 49224, Tel. (517) 629-5511. Bernard T. Lomas, C NC, Un. Meth., 1,748

Albright College, Reading, PA 19604, Tel. (215) 921-2381. David G. Ruffer, C MS, Un. Meth., 1,669

Albuquerque, University of, Albuquerque, NM 87140, Tel. (505) 831-1111. Laurence Smith, C NC, Cath., 2,368

Alderson-Broaddus College, Philippi, WV 26416, Tel. (304) 457-1700. Richard E. Shearer, C NC, Am. Bapt., 971

Allegheny College, Meadville, PA 16335, Tel. (814) 724-3100. Lawrence L. Pelletier, C MS, Un. Meth., 1,912

Allentown College of Saint Francis de Sales, Center Valley, PA 18034, Tel. (215) 282-1100. Daniel G. Gambet, C MS, Cath., 695

Alma College, Alma, MI 48801, Tel. (517) 463-2141. Robert D. Swanson, C NC, U. Presb. U.S.A., 1,170

Alvernia College, Reading, PA 19607, Tel. (215) 777-5411. Sr. M. Victorine, C MS, Cath., 594

Alverno College, Milwaukee, WI 53215, Tel. (414) 671-5400. Sr. M. Joel Read, W NC, Cath., 1,101

American University, The, Washington, DC 20016, Tel. (202) 686-2000. Joseph J. Sisco, C MS, Un. Meth., 12,583

Anderson College, Anderson, IN 46011, Tel. (317) 644-0951. Robert H. Reardon, C NC, Ch. of God, (And.), 2,030

Andrews University, Berrien Springs, MI 49104, Tel. (616) 471-7771. Joseph G. Smoot, C NC, S.D.A., 2,837

Anna Maria College, Paxton, MA 01612, Tel. (617) 757-4586. Bernadette Madore, C NE, Cath., 1,193

Annhurst College, Woodstock, CT 06281, Tel. (203) 928-7773. Paul B. Buchanan, C NE, Cath., 298

Antillian College, Mayaguez, PR 00708, Tel. (809) 832-9595. Israel Recio, C MS, S.D.A., 642

Aquinas College, Grand Rapids, MI 49506, Tel. (616) 459-8281. Norbert J. Hruby, C NC, Cath., 1,684

Arkansas College, Batesville, AR 72501, Tel. (501) 793-9813. Dan C. West, C NC, Presb. U.S., 471

Ashland College, Ashland, OH 44805, Tel. (419) 289-4142. Arthur L. Schultz, C NC, Ch. Breth. (Prog.), 2,185

Assumption College, Worcester, MA 01609, Tel. (617) 752-5615. Joseph H. Hagen, C NE, Cath., 1,836

Athenaeum of Ohio, Norwood, OH 45212, Tel. (513) 731-2630. Lawrence K. Breslin, M NC, Cath., 231

Atlantic Christian College, Wilson, NC 27893, Tel. (919) 237-3161. Harold C. Doster, C S, Christian Church (Disc.), 1,647

Atlantic Union College, South Lancaster, MA 01561, Tel. (617) 365-4561. R. D. McCune, C NE, S.D.A., 662

Augsburg College, Minneapolis, MN 55454, Tel. (612) 332-5181. Oscar A. Anderson, C NC, Am. Luth., 1,751

CHURCH-RELATED COLLEGES IN THE U.S.

Augustana College, Rock Island, IL 61201, Tel. (309) 794-7000. J. Thomas Tredway, C NC, Luth. in Am., 2,342

Augustana College, Sioux Falls, SD 57102, Tel. (605) 336-0770. Charles L. Balcer, C NC, Am. Luth., 2,228

Aurora College, Aurora, IL 60507, Tel. (312) 892-6431. Alan J. Stone, C NC, Adv. Chr. Ch., 910

Austin College, Sherman, TX 75090, Tel. (214) 892-9101. John Dean Moseley, C S, Presb. U.S., 1,192

Averett College, Danville, VA 24541, Tel. (804) 793-7811. Conwell A. Anderson, C S, Bapt., 1,058

Avila College, Kansas City, MO 64145, Tel. (816) 942-8400. Sr. Olive Louise Dallavis, C NC, Cath., 1,961

Baker University, Baldwin City, KS 66006, Tel. (913) 594-6451. Vacant, C NC, Un. Meth., 999

Baldwin-Wallace College, Berea, OH 44017, Tel. (216) 826-2424. Alfred B. Bonds, Jr., C NC, Un. Meth., 3,053

Baltimore Hebrew College, Baltimore, Md 21215, Tel. (301) 466-7900. Leivy Smolar, C MS, Jewish, 161

Baptist College at Charleston, Charleston, SC 29411, Tel. (803) 797-4011. John A. Hasrick, C S, So. Bapt., 2,310

Barat College, Lake Forest, IL 60045, Tel. (312) 234-3000. Sr. Judith Cagney, W NC, Cath., 741

Barber-Scotia College, Concord, NC 28025, Tel. (704) 786-5171. Mable P. McLean, C S, Presb., U.S. and U. Presby. U.S.A., 451

Barry College, Miami, FL 33161, Tel. (305) 758-3392. Sr. M. Trinita Flood, C S, Cath., 1,845

Bartlesville Wesleyan College, Bartlesville, OK 74003, Tel. (918) 333-6151. John Snook, C NC, Wesleyan Ch., 638

Bates College, Lewiston ME 04240, Tel. (207) 782-6791. Thomas H. Reynolds, C NE, Am. Bapt., 1,366

Bayamon Central University, Bayamon, PR 00619, Tel. (809) 786-3030. Vincent A. M. Van Rooij, C MS, Cath., 2,614

Baylor University, Waco, TX 76703, Tel. (817) 755-1611. Abner V. McCall, C S, So. Bapt., 9,453

Beaver College, Glenside, PA 19038, Tel. (215) 884-3500. Edward D. Gates, C MS, U. Presb. U.S.A., 1,566

Belhaven College, Jackson, MS 39202, Tel. (601) 352-0013. Verne R. Kennedy, C S, Presb. U.S., 692

Bellarmine College, Louisville, KY 40205, Tel. (502) 452-8011. Eugene V. Petrik, C S, Cath., 1,782

Belmont Abbey College, Belmont, NC 28012, Tel. (704) 825-3711. Neil W. Tobin, C S, Cath., 626

Belmont College, Nashville, TN 37203, Tel. (615) 383-7001. Herbert C. Gabhart, C S, So. Bapt., 1,267

Beloit College, Beloit, WI 53511, Tel. (608) 365-3391. Martha Peterson, C NC, U. Ch. of Christ, 1,044

Benedict College, Columbia, SC 29204, Tel. (803) 256-4220. Henry Ponder, C S, Am. Bapt., 2,031

Benedictine College, Atchison, KS 66002. Tel. (913) 367-6110. Gerard Senecal, C NC, Cath., 905

Bennett College, Greensboro, NC 27420, Tel. (919) 273-4431. Isaac H. Miller, Jr., W S, Un. Meth. 600

Bethany College, Bethany, WV 26032, Tel. (304) 829-7000. Vacant, C NC, Christian Church (Disc.), 993

Bethany College, Lindsborg, KS 67456, Tel. (913) 227-3312. Arvin Hahn, C NC, Luth. in Am., 757

Bethany Nazarene College, Bethany, OK 73008, Tel. (405) 789-6400. John A. Knight, C NC, Naz., 1,297

Bethel College, McKenzie, TN 38201, Tel. (901) 352-5321. William L. Odom, C S, Cumb. Presb., 360

Bethel College, North Newton, KS 67117, Tel. (316) 283-2500. Harold J. Schultz, C NC, Gen. Conf. Menn. Ch., 603

Bethel College, Mishawaka, IN 46544, Tel. (219) 259-8511. Albert J. Beutler, C NC, Miss. Ch., 419

Bethel College, St. Paul, MN, 55112, Tel. (612) 641-6400. Carl H. Lundquist, C NC, Bapt. Gen'l Conf., 1,874

Bethune-Cookman College, Daytona Beach, FL 32015, Tel. (904) 255-1401. Oswald P. Bronson, C S, Un. Meth., 1,678

Birmingham-Southern College, Birmingham, AL 35204, Tel. (205) 328-5250. Neil R. Berte, C S, Un. Meth., 1,202 **Biscayne College,** Miami, FL 33054, Tel. (305) 625-6000. John J. Farrell, C S, Cath., 2,329

Bishop College, Dallas, TX 75241, Tel. (214) 372-8000. M. K. Curry, Jr., C S, Am. Bapt., 1,809

Blackburn College, Carlinville, IL 62626, Tel. (217) 854-3231. John R. Alberti, C NC, U. Presb. U.S.A., 494

Bloomfield College, Bloomfield, NJ 07003, Tel. (201) 748-9000. Merle F. Allshouse, C MS, U. Presb. U.S.A., 2,377

Blue Mountain College, Blue Mountain, MS 38610, Tel. (601) 685-5711. E. Harold Fisher, W S, So. Bapt., 329

Bluefield College, Bluefield, VA 24605, Tel. (304) 327-7137. Charles L. Tyer, C S, So. Bapt., 332

Bluffton College, Bluffton, OH 45817, Tel. (419) 358-8015. Elmer Neufeld, C NC, Menn., 641

Borromeo College of Ohio, Wickliffe, OH 44092, Tel. (216) 943-3888. Lawrence P. Cahill, M NC, Cath., 83

Boston College, Chestnut Hill, MA 02167, Tel. (617) 969-0100. J. Donald Monan, C NE, Cath., 13,943

Boston University, Boston, MA 02215, Tel. (617) 353-2000. John R. Silber, C NE, Un. Meth., 24,414

Brescia College, Owensboro, KY 42301, Tel. (502) 685-3131. Sr. George Ann Cecil, C S, Cath., 893

Briar Cliff College, Sioux City, IA 51104, Tel. (712) 279-5321. Charles J. Bensman, C NC, Cath., 1,055

Bridgewater College, Bridgewater, VA 22812, Tel. (703) 828-2501. Wayne F. Geisert, C S, Ch. Breth., 829

Brigham Young University, Provo, UT 84602 Tel. (801) 374-1211. Dallin H. Oaks, C NW, L.D.S., 28,850

Brigham Young University, Hawaii Campus, Laie Oahu, HI 96762, Tel. (808) 293-9211. Dan W. Anderson, C West, L.D.S., 1,579

Bucknell University, Lewisburg, PA 17837, Tel. (717) 523-1271. G. Dennis O'Brien, C MS, Am. Bapt., 3,240

Buena Vista College, Storm Lake, IA 50588, Tel. (712) 749-2351. Keith G. Briscoe, C NC U. Presb. U.S.A. 1,068

Butler University, Indianapolis, IN 46208, Tel. (317) 283-8000. John C. Johnson, C NC, Christian Church (Disc.), 4,025

Cabrini College, Radnor, PA 19087, Tel. (215) 687-2100. Sr. Mary Louise Sullivan, C MS, Cath., 570

Caldwell College, Caldwell, NJ 07006, Tel. (201) 228-4424. Sr. Ann John, W MS, Cath., 753

California Baptist College, Riverside, CA 92504, Tel. (714) 689-5771. James R. Staples, C. West, So. Bapt., 762

California Lutheran College, Thousand Oaks, CA 91360, Tel. (805) 492-2411. Mark A. Mathews, C West, Am Luth. and Luth. Ch. in Am., 2,489

Calumet College, Whiting, IN 46394, Tel. (219) 473-7770. James F. McCabe, C NC, Cath., 1,736

Calvin College, Grand Rapids, MI 49506, Tel. (616) 949-4000. Anthony J. Diekema, C NC, Christ. Ref., 4,075

Campbell University, Buies Creek, NC 27506, Tel. (919) 893-4111. Norman A. Wiggins, C S, So. Bapt., 2,217

Campbellsville College, Campbellsville, KY 42718, Tel. (502) 465-8158. W. R. Davenport, C S, So. Bapt., 691

Canisius College, Buffalo, NY 14208, Tel. (716) 883-7000. James M. Demske, C MS, Cath., 4,006

Capital University, Columbus, OH 43209, Tel. (614) 236-6011. Thomas H. Langevin, C NC, Am. Luth., 2,688

Cardinal Glennon College, St. Louis, MO 63119, Tel. (314) 644-0266. Francis A. Gaydos, M NC, Cath., 94

Cardinal Newman College, St. Louis, MO 63121, Tel. (314) 261-2600. A. Martial Capbern, C MS, Cath., 45

Cardinal Stritch College, Milwaukee, WI 53217, Tel. (414) 352-5400. Sr. M. Camille Kliebhahn, C NC, Cath., 1,173

Carleton College, Northfield, MN 55057, Tel. (507) 645-4431. Robert H. Edwards, C NC, U. Ch. of Christ, 1,661

Carlow College, Pittsburgh, PA 15213. Tel. (412) 578-6000. Sr. Jane Scully, W MS, Cath., 871

Carroll College, Helena, MT 59601, Tel. (406) 442-3450. Francis J. Kerins, C NW, Cath., 1,362

Carroll College, Waukesha, WI 53186, Tel. (414) 547-1211. Robert V. Cramer, C NC, U. Presb. U.S.A., 1,295

Carson-Newman College, Jefferson City, TN 37760, Tel. (615) 475-9061. J. Cordell Maddox, C S, So. Bapt., 1,562

Carthage College, Kenosha, WI 53140, Tel. (414) 551-8500. Erno J. Dahl, C NC, Luth. in Am., 1,615

Catawba College, Salisbury, NC 28144, Tel. (704) 637-4111. Martin L. Shotzberger, C S, U. Ch. of Christ, 914

Cathedral College of the Immaculate Conception, Douglaston, NY 11362, Tel. (212) 631-4600. Thomas J. Gradilone, M MS, Cath., 199

Catholic University of America, Washington, DC 20064, Tel. (202) 635-5000. Edmund D. Pellegrino, C MS, Cath., 7,237

Catholic University of Puerto Rico, Ponce, PR 00731, Tel. (809) 844-4150. Francisco J. Carreras, C MS, Cath., 11,373

Cedar Crest College, Allentown, PA 18104, Tel. (215) 437-4471. Gene S. Cesari, W MS, U. Ch. of Christ, 893

Cedarville College, Cedarville, OH 45314, Tel. (513) 766-2211. Paul H. Dixon, C NC, Bapt., 1,256

Centenary College of Louisiana, Shreveport, LA 71104, Tel. (318) 869-5104. Donald A. Webb, C. S., Un. Meth., 896

Centenary College, Hackettstown, NJ 07840. Tel. (201) 852-1400. Charles H. Dick, W MS, Un. Meth., 783

Central Methodist College, Fayette, MO 65248, Tel. (816) 248-3391. Joseph A. Howell, C NC, Un. Meth., 592

Central University of Iowa, Pella, IA 50219, Tel. (515) 628-4151 Kenneth J. Weller, C NC, Ref. in Am., 1,393

Central Wesleyan College, Central, SC 29630, Tel. (803) 639-2453. Claude R. Rickman, C S, Wesleyan Ch., 400

Centre College of Kentucky, Danville, KY 40422, Tel. (606) 236-5211. Thomas A. Spragens, C S, Presb. U.S. & U. Presb. U.S.A., 783

Chaminade College of Honolulu, Honolulu, HI 96816, Tel. (808) 732-1471. David H. Schuyler, C West, Cath., 2,581

Chapman College, Orange, CA 92666, Tel. (714) 997-6646. G. T. Smith, C West, Christian Church (Disc.), 5,680

Chestnut Hill College, Philadelphia, PA 19118, Tel. (215) 247-4212. Sr. Mary Xavier, W MS, Cath., 883

Christian Brothers College, Memphis, TN 38104, Tel. (901) 278-0100. Bro. Bernard Lococo, C S, Cath., 1,012

Claflin College, Orangeburg, SC 29115, Tel. (803) 534-2710. H. V. Manning, C S, Un. Meth., 911

Clark College, Atlanta, GA 30314, Elias Blake, Jr., C S, Un. Meth., 1,792

Clarke College, Dubuque, IA 52001, Tel. (319) 588-6300. Maneve Dunham, W NC, Cath., 643

Coe College, Cedar Rapids, IA 52402, Tel. (319) 398-1600. Leo L. Nussbaum, C NC, U. Presb. U.S.A., 1,139

Colby College, Waterville, ME 04901, Tel. (207) 873-1131. Robert E. L. Strider, II, C NE, Am. Bapt., 1,675

College Misericordia, Dallas, PA 18612, Tel. (717) 675-2181. William B. Hill, W MS, Cath., 952

College of Great Falls, Great Falls, MT 59405, Tel. (406) 761-8210. William A. Shields, C NW, Cath., 1,247

College of Idaho, Caldwell, ID 83605, Tel. (208) 459-5011. William C. Cassell, C NW, U. Presb. U.S.A., 891

College of Mt. St. Joseph-on-the-Ohio, Mt. St. Joseph, OH 45051, Tel. (513) 244-4200. Sr. Jean P. Harrington, W NC, Cath., 1,098

College of Mt. St. Vincent, Riverdale, NY 10471, Tel. (212) 549-8000. Sr. Doris Smith, C MS, Cath., 1,169

College of New Rochelle, New Rochelle, NY 10801, Tel. (914) 632-5300. Sr. Dorothy A. Kelly, C MS, Cath., 3,563

College of Notre Dame, Belmont, CA 94002, Tel. (415) 593-1601. Sr. Catherine Julie Cunningham, C West, Cath., 1,131

College of Notre Dame of Md., Baltimore, MD 21210. Tel. (301) 435-0100. Sr. Kathleen Feeley, W MS, Cath., 839

College of Our Lady of the Elms, Chicopee, MA 01013, Tel. (413) 598-8351. Edward B. D'Alessio, W NE, Cath., 442

College of St. Benedict, St. Joseph, MN 56374, Tel. (612) 363-5304. Beverly Miller, Co-Ord. NC, Cath., 1,992

College of St. Catherine, St. Paul, MN 55105, Tel. (612) 690-6000 Sr. Alberta Huber, W NC, Cath., 2,109

College of St. Elizabeth, Convent Sta., NJ 07961, Tel. (201) 539-1600. Sr. Elizabeth Ann Maloney, W MS, Cath., 681

College of St. Francis, Joliet, IL 60435, Tel. (815) 740-3360. John C. Orr, C NC, Cath., 2,927

College of St. Joseph the Provider, Rutland, VT 05701, Tel. (802) 775-0806. Sr. Mary A. Polworth, C NE, Cath., 310

College of St. Mary, Omaha, NB 68124, Tel. (402) 393-8800. John H. Richert, W NC, Cath., 540

College of St. Rose, Albany, NY 12203, Tel. (518) 471-5111. Thomas A. Manion, C MS, Cath., 2,384

College of St. Scholastica, Duluth, MN 55811, Tel. (218) 728-3631, Bruce W. Stender, C NC, Cath., 1,585

College of St. Teresa, Winona, MN 55987, Tel. (507) 452-9302. Sr. M. Joyce Rowland, W NC, Cath., 1,003

College of St. Thomas, St. Paul, MN 55105, Tel. (612) 647-5000. Terrence J. Murphy, C NC, Cath., 4,139

College of Santa Fe, Santa Fe, NM 87501, Tel. (505) 982-6011. Br. Cyprian Luke Roney, C NC, Cath., 1,272

College of Steubenville, Steubenville, OH 43952, Tel. (614) 283-3771. Michael Scanlan, C NC, Cath., 860

CHURCH-RELATED COLLEGES IN THE U.S.

College of the Holy Cross, Worcester, MA 01610, Tel. (617) 793-2011. John E. Brooks, C NE, Cath., 2,691

College of the Ozarks, Clarksville, AR 72830, Tel. (501) 754-2788. Robert L. Qualls, C NC, U. Presb. U.S.A., 582

College of Wooster, Wooster, OH 44691, Tel. (216) 264-1234. Henry J. Copeland, C NC, U. Presb. U.S.A., 1,800

Columbia College, Columbia, SC 29203, Tel. (803) 786-3012. Ralph T. Mirse, W S, Un. Meth., 910

Columbia College, Columbia, MO 65201. Tel (314) 449-0531, Bruce B. Kelley, C NC, Christian Ch. (Disc.), 2,997

Columbia Union College, Takoma Park, MD 20012, Tel. (301) 270-9200, William A. Loveless, C MS, S.D.A., 865

Conception Seminary College, Conception, MO 64433, Tel. (816) 944-2218. Isaac True, M NC, Cath., 104

Concordia College, Bronxville, NY 10708, Tel. (914) 337-9300. Ralph C. Schultz, C MS, Luth. (Mo.), 444

Concordia College, Ann Arbor, MI 48105, Tel. (313) 665-3691. Marlin S. Pohl, C NC, Luth. (Mo.), 615

Concordia College, Portland, OR 97211, Tel. (503) 288-9371. Erhardt P. Weber, C NW, Luth. (Mo.), 219

Concordia College at Moorhead, Moorhead, MN 56560, Tel. (218) 299-4321. Paul J. Dovre, C NC, Am. Luth., 2,647

Concordia College at St. Paul, St. Paul, MN 55104, Tel. (612) 641-8278. G. Will Hyatt, C NC, Luth. (Mo.), 633

Cornell College, Mt. Vernon, IA 52314, Tel. (319) 895-8811. Philip B. Secor, C NC, Un. Meth., 851

Covenant College, Lookout Mountain, TN 37350, Tel. (404) 820-1560. Martin Essenburg, C S, Ref. Presby. Ch., 553

Creighton University, Omaha, NB 68178, Tel. (402) 449-2700. Matthew E. Creighton, C NC, Cath., 4,979

Culver-Stockton College, Canton, MO 63435, Tel. (314) 288-5221. Robert W. Brown, C NC, Christian Church (Disc.), 492

Cumberland College, Williamsburg, KY 40769, Tel. (606) 549-2200. James M. Boswell, C S, So. Bapt., 1,979

Dakota Wesleyan University, Mitchell, SD 57301, Tel. (605) 996-6511. Donald E. Messer, C NC, Un. Meth., 562

Dallas Baptist College, Dallas, TX 75211, Tel. (214) 331-8311. William E. Thorn, C S, So. Bapt., 1,068

Dallas, University of, Irving, TX 75061, Tel. (214) 438-1123. John R. Summerfeldt, C S, Cath., 1,909

Dana College, Blair, NB 68008, Tel. (402) 426-4101. James G. Kallas, C NC, Am. Luth., 478

David Lipscomb College, Nashville, TN 37203, Tel. (615) 385-3855. Willard Collins, C S, Ch. of Christ, 2,172

Davidson College, Davidson, NC 28036, Tel. (704) 892-2000. Samuel R. Spencer, Jr., C S, Presb. U.S., 1,331

Davis and Elkins College, Elkins, WV 26241, Tel. (304) 636-1900. Gordon Hermanson, C NC, U. Presb. U.S.A., Presby. U.S., 970

Dayton, University of, Dayton, OH 45469, Tel. (513) 229-0123. Raymond A. Roesch, C NC, Cath., 9,620

Defiance College, Defiance, OH 43512, Tel. (419) 784-4010. Marvin Ludwig, C NC, U. Ch. of Christ, 829

Denison University, Granville, OH 43023, Tel. (614) 587-0810. Robert C. Good, C NC, Am. Bapt., 2,116

Denver, University of, Denver, CO 80210, Tel. (303) 753-1964. Ross Pritchard, C NC, Un. Meth., 7,753

DePaul University, Chicago, IL 60604, Tel. (312) 321-8000. John R. Cortelyou, C NC, Cath., 11,366

DePauw University, Greencastle, IN 46135, Tel. (317) 653-9721. Richard F. Rosser, C NC, Un. Meth., 2,421

Detroit, University of, Detroit, MI 48221, Tel. (313) 927-1000. Robert A. Mitchell, C NC, Cath., 8,363

Dickinson College, Carlisle, PA 17013, Tel. (717) 243-5121. Samuel A. Banks, C MS, Un. Meth. 1,763

Dillard University, New Orleans, LA 70122, Tel. (504) 944-8751. Samuel Dubois Cook, C S., U. Ch. of Christ, Un. Meth., 1,158

Divine Word College, Epworth, IA 52045, Tel. (319) 876-3354. Raymond Quetchenbach, M NC, Cath., 98

Doane College, Crete, NB 68333, Tel. (402) 826-2161. Philip Heckman, C NC, U. Ch. of Christ, 647

Dominican College of Blauvelt, Orangeburg, NY 10962, Tel. (914) 359-7800. Sr. Mary E. O'Brian, C MS, Cath., 1,130

Dominican College of San Rafael, San Rafael, CA 94901, Tel. (415) 457-4440. Sr. M. Samuel Conlan, C West, Cath., 688

Dordt College, Sioux Center, IA 51250, Tel. (712) 722-3771. Bernard J. Haan, C NC, Christ. Ref. Ch., 1,112

Drake University, Des Moines, IA 50311, Tel. (515) 271-2011, Wilbur C. Miller, C NC, Christian Church (Disc.), 6,732

Drew University, Madison, NJ 07940, Tel. (201) 377-3000. Paul Hardin, C MS, Un. Meth., 2,155

Drury College, Springfield, MO 65802, Tel. (417) 865-8731. John M. Bartholomy, C NC, U. Ch. of Christ, 2,250

Dubuque, University of, Dubuque, IA 52001, Tel. (319) 557-2121. Walter F. Peterson, C NC, U. Presb. U.S.A., 1,043

Duke University, Durham, NC 27706, Tel. (919) 684-8111. Terry Sanford, C S, Un. Meth., 9,402

Duns Scotus College, Southfield, MI 48075, Tel. (313) 357-3070. James Van Vurst, M NC, Cath., 56

Duquesne University, Pittsburgh, PA 15219, Tel. (412) 434-6000. Henry J. McAnulty, C MS, Cath., 7,149

D'Youville College, Buffalo, NY 14201, Tel. (716) 886-8100. Sr. Mary Charlotte Barton, C MS, Cath., 1,529

Earlham College, Richmond, IN 47374. Tel. (317) 962-6561. Franklin Wallin, C NC, Friends, 1,060

East Texas Baptist College, Marshall, TX 75670, Tel. (214) 935-7963. Jerry E. Dawson, C S. So. Bapt., 872

Eastern College, St. Davids, PA 19087, Tel. (215) 688-3300. Daniel E. Weiss, C MS, Am. Bapt., 705

Eastern Mennonite College, Harrisonburg, VA 22801, Tel. (703) 433-2771. Myron S. Augsburger, C S, Menn., 1,139

Eastern Nazarene College, Wollaston, MA 02170, Tel. (617) 773-6350. Donald Irwin, C NE, Nazarene, 810

Eckerd College, St. Petersburg, FL 33733, Tel. (813) 867-1166. Peter H. Armacost, C S, Presb. U.S., U. Presb. U.S.A. 881

Edgecliff College, Cincinnati, OH 45206, Tel. (513) 961-3770. Sr. Margaret A. Molitor, C NC, Cath., 868

Edgewood College, Madison, WI 53711, Tel. (608) 257-4861. Sr. Alice O'Rourke, C NC, Cath., 521

Elizabethtown College, Elizabethtown, PA 17022, Tel. (717) 367-1151. Mark C. Ebersole, C MS, Ch. Breth., 1,800

Elmhurst College, Elmhurst, IL 60126, Tel. (312) 279-4100. Ivan Frick, C NC, U. Ch. of Christ, 2,970

Elon College, Elon College, NC 27244, Tel. (919) 584-9711. J. Fred. Young, C S, U. Ch. of Christ, 2,225

Emmanuel College, Boston, MA 02115, Tel. (617) 277-9340. Vacant, W NE, Cath., 1,059

Emory and Henry College, Emory, VA 24327, Tel. (703) 944-3121. Thomas F. Chilcote C S, Un. Meth., 856

Emory University, Atlanta, GA 30322, Tel. (404) 329-6123. James T. Laney, C S, Un. Meth., 7,572

Erskine College, Due West, SC 29639, Tel. (803) 379-2131. M. Stanyarne Bell, C S, Asso. Ref. Presb., 708

Eureka College, Eureka, IL 61530, Tel. (309) 467-3721. Daniel D. Gilbert, C NC, Christian Church (Disc.), 431

Evangel College, Springfield, MO 65802, Tel. (417) 865-2811. Robert H. Spence, C NC, Assem. of God, 1,291

Evansville, University of, Evansville, IN 47702, Tel. (812) 477-6241, Wallace B. Graves, C NC, Un. Meth., 4,906

Fairfield University, Fairfield, CT 06430, Tel. (203) 255-5411. Thomas R. Fitzgerald C NE, Cath., 4,791

Felician College, Lodi, NJ 07644, Tel. (201) 778-1190, Sr. Hiltrude M. Koba, W MS, Cath., 697

Ferrum College, Ferrum, VA 24088, Tel. (703) 365-2121. Joseph T. Hart, C S, Un. Meth., 1,511

Findlay College, Findlay, OH 45840, Tel. (419) 422-8313. Glen R. Rasmussen, C NC, Ch. of God, Gen. Eldership, 988

Fisk University, Nashville, TN 37203, Tel. (615) 329-9111. Walter J. Leonard, C S, U. Ch. of Christ, 1,124

Florida Memorial College, Miami, FL 33054, Tel. (305) 625-4141. Willie C. Robinson, C S, Am. Bapt., 641

Florida Southern College, Lakeland, FL 33802, Tel. (813) 683-5521. Robert A. Davis, C S, Un. Meth., 2,236

Fontbonne College, St. Louis, MO 63105, Tel. (314) 862-3456. Sr. Jane Hassett, C NC, Cath., 896

Fordham University, Bronx, NY 10458, Tel. (212) 933-2233. James C. Finlay, C MS, Cath., 15,163

Fort Wright College of the Holy Names, Spokane, WA 99204. Tel. (509) 328-2970. Sr. Katherine Gray, C NW, Cath., 522

Franklin College of Indiana, Franklin, IN 46131, Tel. (317) 736-8441. Edwin A. Penn, C NC, Am. Bapt., 710

Franklin & Marshall College, Lancaster, PA 17604, Tel. (717) 291-3911. Keith Spalding, C MS, U. Ch. of Christ, 2,793

Freed-Hardeman College, Henderson, TN 38340, Tel. (901) 989-4611. E. C. Gardner, CS, Ch. of Christ, 1,401

Fresno Pacific College, Fresno, CA 93702, Tel. (209) 251-7194. Edmund Janzen, C West., Menn. Breth. Ch., 677

Friends University, Wichita, KS 67213, Tel. (316) 261-5800. Harold C. Cope, C NC, Friends, 907

Furman University, Greenville, SC 29613, Tel. (803) 294-2000. John E. Johns, C S, So. Bapt., 2,749

Gannon College, Erie, PA 16501, Tel. (814) 871-7000. Joseph P. Scottino, C MS, Cath., 3,580

Gardner-Webb College, Boiling Springs, NC 28017, Tel. (704) 434-2361. Craven E. Williams, C S, So. Bapt., 1,336

George Fox College, Newberg, OR 97132, Tel. (503) 538-8383. David C. Le Shana, C NW, Friends, 706

Georgetown College, Georgetown, KY 40324, Tel. (502) 863-8011. Ben M. Elrod, C S, So. Bapt., 989

Georgetown University, Washington, DC 20057, Tel. (202) 625-0100. Timothy S. Healy, C MS, Cath., 11,796

Georgian Court College, Lakewood, NJ 08701, Tel. (201) 364-2200. Sr. Maria Cordis Richey, W MS, Cath., 1,007

Gettysburg College, Gettysburg, PA 17325, Tel. (717) 334-3131. Charles E. Glassick, C MS, Luth. in Am., 1,938

Gonzaga University, Spokane, WA 99258, Tel. (509) 328-4220. Bernard J. Coughlin, C NW, Cath., 2,966

Gordon College, Wenham, MA 01984, Tel. (617) 927-2300. Richard F. Gross, C NE, Interdenom, 985

Goshen College, Goshen, IN 46526, Tel. (219) 533-3161. J. Lawrence Burkholder, C NC, Menn. Ch., 1,210

Grace College, Winona Lake, IN 46590, Tel. (219) 267-8191. Homer A. Kent, Jr., C NC, Breth. Ch., 727

Graceland College, Lamoni, IA 50140, Tel. (515) 784-3311. Franklin S. Hough, C NC, Reorg. L.D.S., 1,343

Grand Canyon College, Phoenix, AZ 85017, Tel. (602) 249-3300. Bill Williams, C NC, So. Bapt., 1,198

Grand Rapids Baptist College and Seminary, Grand Rapids, MI 49505, Tel. (616) 949-5300. W. W. Welch, C NC, Bapt., 1,048

Grand View College, Des Moines, IA 50316, Tel. (515) 266-2651. Karl F. Langrock, C NC, Luth. in Am., 1,144

Greensboro College, Greensboro, NC 27420, Tel. (919) 272-7102. Howard C. Wilkinson, C S, Un. Meth., 670

Greenville College, Greenville, IL 62246, Tel. (618) 664-1840. W. Richard Stephens, C NC, Free Meth., 895

Grinnell College, Grinnell, IA 50112, Tel. (515) 236-6181. A. Richard Turner, C NC, U. Ch. of Christ, 1,242

Grove City College, Grove City, PA 16127, Tel. (412) 458-6600, Charles S. MacKenzie, C MS, U, Presb. U.S.A., 2,244

Guilford College, Greensboro, NC 27410, Tel. (919) 292-5511. Grimsley T. Hobbs, C S, Friends, 1,685

Gustavus Adolphus College, St. Peter, MN 56082, Tel. (507) 931-4300. Edward A. Lindell, C NC, Luth. in Am., 2,253

Gwynedd-Mercy College, Gwynedd Valley, PA 19437, Tel. (215) 646-7300. Sr. Isabelle Keiss, C MS, Cath., 1,214

Hamline University, St. Paul, MN 55104, Tel. (612) 641-2800. Jerry E. Hudson, C NC, Un. Meth., 1,726

Hampden-Sydney College, Hampden-Sydney, VA 23943. Tel. (804) 223-4381. Josiah Bunting, III, M S, Presb. U.S., 722

Hannibal-La Grange College, Hannibal, MO 63401, Tel. (314) 221-3675. Gerald Martin, C NC, So. Bapt., 401

Hanover College, Hanover, IN 47243, Tel. (812) 866-2151. John E. Horner, C NC, U. Presb. U.S.A., 894

Hardin-Simmons University, Abilene, TX 79601, Tel. (915) 677-7281. Jesse C. Fletcher, C S, So. Bapt., 1,732

Harding College, Searcy, AR 72143, Tel. (501) 268-6161. Clifton L. Ganus, Jr., C NC, Ch. of Christ., 2,821

Hartwick College, Oneonta, NY 13820, Tel. (607) 432-4200. Philip S. Wilder, Jr., C MS, Luth. in Am., 1,514

Hastings College, Hastings, NB 68901, Tel. (402) 463-2402. Clyde Matters, C NC, U. Presb. U.S.A., 736

Haverford College, Haverford, PA 19041, Tel. (215) 649-9600. Robert B. Stevens, C MS, Friends, 900

Hawaii Loa College, Kaneohe, HI 96744. Tel. (808) 235-3641. Philip J. Bossert, C West., Interdenom., 226

Hebrew College, Brookline, MA 02146. Tel. (617) 232-8710. Eli Grad, C NE, Jewish, 116

Hebrew Union College, Main Campus, Cincinnati, OH 45220, Tel. (513) 221-1875. Alfred Gottschalk, C NC, Jewish, 141

CHURCH-RELATED COLLEGES IN THE U.S.

Hebrew Union College, California Branch, Los Angeles, CA 90007, Tel. (213) 749-3424. Lewis Barth, C West, Jewish, 205

Hebrew Union College, New York Branch, New York, NY 10023, Tel. (212) 873-0200. Paul M. Steinberg, C MS, Jewish, 181

Heidelberg College, Tiffin, OH 44883, Tel. (419) 448-2000. Leslie H. Fishel, Jr., C NC, U. Ch. of Christ, 933

Hellenic College, Brookline, MA 02146, Tel. (617) -3500. Thomas Lelon, C NE, Greek Orth., 175

Hendrix College, Conway, AR 72032, Tel. (501) 329-6811. Roy B. Schilling, Jr., C NC, Un. Meth., 959

High Point College, High Point, NC 27262, Tel. (919) 885-5101. Wendell M. Patton, C S, Un. Meth., 1,004

Hillsdale College, Hillsdale, MI 49242, Tel. (517) 437-7341. George C. Roche, III, C NC, Am. Bapt., 1,048

Hiram College, Hiram, OH 44234, Tel. (216) 569-3211. Elmer Jagow, C NC, Christian Church (Disc.), 1,193

Hobart and William Smith Colleges, Geneva, NY 14456, Tel. (315) 789-5500. Allan A. Kuusisto, Co. Ord. MS, Epis., 1,821

Holy Family College, Philadelphia, PA 19114, Tel. (215) 637-7700. Sr. M. Lillian, C MS, Cath., 1,142

Holy Family College, San Jose, CA 94538, Tel. (415) 651-1639. Sr. Jeanette Kelley, W West, Cath., 92

Holy Names College, Oakland, CA 94619. Tel. (415) 436-0111. Sr. Irene Woodward, C West, Cath., 612

Holy Redeemer College, Waterford, WI 53185, Tel. (414) 534-3191. Wm. Emmett Collins, M NC, Cath., 58

Hood College, Frederick, MD 21701, Tel. (301) 663-3131. Martha E. Church, W MS, U. Ch. of Christ, 1,655

Hope College, Holland, MI 49423, Tel. (616) 392-5111. Gordon Van Wylen, C NC, Ref. Am., 2,330

Houghton College, Houghton, NY 14744, Tel. (716) 567-2211. Daniel E. Chamberlain, C MS, Wes. Ch., 1,250

Houston Baptist University, Houston, TX 77074, Tel. (713) 774-7661. William H. Hinton, C S, So. Bapt., 1,794

Howard Payne University, Brownwood, TX 76801, Tel. (915) 646-2502. Roger L. Brooks, C S, So. Bapt., 1,406

Huntingdon College, Montgomery, AL 36106, Tel. (205) 265-0511. Allen Keith Jackson, C S, Un. Meth., 743

Huntington College, Huntington, IN 46750, Tel. (219) 356-6000. E. De Witt Baker, C NC, U. Breth., 549

Huron College, Huron, SD 57350, Tel. (605) 352-8721. Wendell L. Jahnke, C NC, U. Presb. U.S.A., 365

Huston-Tillotson College, Austin, TX 78702, Tel. (512) 476-7421. John T. King, C S, Un. Meth. and U. Ch. of Christ, 674

Illinois Benedictine College, Lisle, IL 60532, Tel. (312) 968-7270. Richard C. Becker, C NC, Cath., 1,870

Illinois College, Jacksonville, IL 62650. Tel. (217) 245-7126. Donald C. Mundinger, C NC, U. Presb. U.S.A. and U. Ch. of Christ, 740

Illinois Wesleyan University, Bloomington, IL 61701, Tel. (309) 556-3131. Robert S. Eckley, C NC, Un. Meth. 1,708

Immaculata College, Immaculata, PA 19345, Tel. (215) 647-4400. Sr. Marie Antoine, W MS, Cath., 1,171

Immaculate Heart College, Los Angeles, CA 90027, Tel. (213) 462-1301. Nancy Heer, C West, Cath., 643

Incarnate Word College, San Antonio, TX 78209. Tel. (512) 828-1261. Sr. Margaret P. Slattery, C S, Cath., 1,479

Indiana Central University, Indianapolis, IN 46227, Tel. (317) 788-3368. Gene E. Sease, C NC, Un. Meth., 3,351

Iona College, New Rochelle, NY 10801. Tel. (914) 636-2100. John G. Driscoll, C MS, Cath., 5,127

Iowa Wesleyan College, Mt. Pleasant, IA 52641, Tel. (319) 385-8021. Louis A. Haselmayer, C NC, Un. Meth., 798

Jamestown College, Jamestown, ND 58401, Tel. (701) 253-2550. J. N. Anderson, C NC, U. Presb. U.S.A., 580

Jarvis Christian College, Hawkins, TX 75765, Tel. (214) 769-2174. E. W. Rand, C S, Christian Ch. (Disc.), 664

John Carroll University, Cleveland, OH 44118, Tel. (216) 491-4911. Henry F. Birkenhauer, C NC, Cath., 3,850

Johnson C. Smith University, Charlotte, NC 28216, Tel. (704) 372-2370. Wilbert Greenfield, C S, U. Presb. U.S.A., 1,545

Judaism, University of, Los Angeles, CA 90024, Tel. (213) 879-4114. Gerson Cohen, C West, Jewish, 264

Judson College, Elgin, IL 60120, Tel. (312) 695-2500. Harm A. Weber, C NC, Am. Bapt., 412

Judson College, Marion, AL 36756, Tel. (205) 683-6161. Norman H. McCrummen, W S, So. Bapt., 406

Juniata College, Huntingdon, PA 16652, Tel. (814) 643-4310. Frederick M. Binder, C MS, Ch. Breth., 1,123

Kalamazoo College, Kalamazoo, MI 49007, Tel. (616) 383-8400, George N. Rainsford, C NC, Am. Bapt., 1,534

Kansas Newman College, Wichita, KS 67213, Tel. (316) 942-4291. Roman Galiardi, C NC, Cath., 631

Kansas Wesleyan University, Salina, KS 67401, Tel. (913) 827-5541. Daniel Bratton, C NC, Un. Meth., 441

Kendall College, Evanston, IL 60201, Tel. (312) 869-5240. Andrew N. Cothran, C NC. Un. Meth., 397

Kentucky Wesleyan College, Owensboro, KY 42301, Tel. (502) 926-3111. William E. James, C S, Un. Meth., 806

Kenyon College, Gambier, OH 43022, Tel. (614) 427-2244. Philip H. Jordan, Jr., C NC, Epis., 1,467

Keuka College, Keuka Park, NY 14478, Tel. (315) 536-4411. Elizabeth W. Shaw, W MS, Am. Bapt., 564

King College, Bristol, TN 37620, Tel. (615) 968-1187. Don R. Mitchell, C S, Presb. US., 305

King's College, Wilkes-Barre, PA 18711, Tel. (717) 824-9931. Charles D. Sherrer, C MS Cath., 2,210

Knoxville College, Knoxville, TN 37921, Tel. (615) 546-0751. Rutherford H. Adkins, C S, U. Presb. U.S.A., 735

Ladycliff College, Highland Falls, NY 10928, Tel. (914) 446-4747. Francis J. Breidenbach, Co. Ord., MS, Cath., 496

Lafayette College, Easton, PA 18042, Tel. (215) 253-6281. David W. Ellis, C MS, U. Presb. U.S.A., 2,291

LaGrange College, LaGrange, GA 30240, Tel. (404) 882-2911. Charles L. Hagood, C S, Un. Meth., 772

Lake Forest College, Lake Forest, IL 60045, Tel. (312) 234-3100. Eugene Hotchkiss, III, C NC, U. Presb. U.S.A., 1,104

Lakeland College, Sheboygan, WI 53081, Tel. (414) 565-2111. Richard E. Hill, C NC, U. Ch. of Christ, 571

Lambuth College, Jackson, TN 38301, Tel. (901) 427-6743, James S. Wilder, Jr., C S, Un. Meth., 773

Lane College, Jackson, TN 38301, Tel. (901) 424-4600 Herman Stone, Jr., C S, Chr. M.E., 673

La Roche College, Pittsburgh, PA 15237, Tel. (412) 931-4312. Sr. Mary Joan Coultas, C MS, Cath., 1,164

La Salle College, Philadelphia, PA 19141, Tel. (215) 951-1000. Br. F. Patrick Ellis, C MS, Cath., 5,850

La Verne University of, La Verne, CA 91750, Tel. (714) 593-3511. Armen Sarafian, C. West. Ch. of Breth., 3,766

Lawrence University, Appleton, WI 54911, Tel. (414) 739-3681. Thomas S. Smith, C NC, Un. Meth., 1,082

Lebanon Valley College, Annville, PA 17003, Tel. (717) 867-4411. Frederick P. Sample, C MS, Un. Meth., 1,290

Lee College, Cleveland, TN 37311, Tel. (615) 472-2111. Charles W. Conn, C S, Ch. of God, 1,31?

Le Moyne College, Syracuse, N.Y. 13214, Tel. (315) 446-2882. William J. O'Halloran, C MS, Cath., 1,874

LeMoyne-Owen College, Memphis, TN 38126, Tel. (901) 774-9090. Walter L. Walker, C S, interdenom., 1,020

Lenoir-Rhyne College, Hickory, NC 28601, Tel. (704) 328-1741. Albert B. Anderson, C S, Luth. in Am., 1,268

Lewis University, Romeoville, Il 60441, Tel. (815) 838-0500. Paul Whelan, C NC, Cath., 4,074

Lewis & Clark College, Portland, OR 97219, Tel. (503) 244-6161. John R. Howard, C NW, U. Presb. U.S.A., 3,150

Lindenwood Colleges, The, St. Charles, MO 63301, Tel. (314) 723-7152. William C. Spencer, C NC, U. Presb. U.S.A., 1,727

Linfield College, McMinnville, OR 97128, Tel. (503) 472-4121. Charles U. Walker, C NW, Amer. Bapt. 1,101

Livingstone College, Salisbury, NC 28144, Tel. (704) 633-7960 F. George Shipman, C S, A.M.E. Zion, 921

Loma Linda University, Loma Linda, CA 92354, Tel. (714) 796-7311. V. Norskov Olsen, C West, S.D.A., 5,014

Loras College, Dubuque, IA 52001, Tel. (319) 588-7100 Pasquale di Pasquale, Jr. C NC, Cath., 1,721

Loretto Heights College, Denver, CO 80236, Tel. (303) 936-8441. Adele Phelan, C NC, Cath., 852

Los Angeles Baptist College, Newhall, CA 91322, Tel. (805) 259-3540. John R. Dunkin, C West, Bapt., 377

Louisiana College, Pineville, LA 71360, Tel. (318) 487-7011. Robert L. Lynn, C S, So. Bapt., 1,430

Loyola College, Baltimore, MD 21210, Tel. (301) 323-1010. Joseph A. Sellinger, C MS, Cath., 4,774

Loyola University of Chicago, Chicago, IL 60611, Tel. (312) 670-3000. Raymond C. Baumhart, C NC, Cath., 13,219

Loyola University in New Orleans, New Orleans, LA 70118, Tel. (504) 865-2011. James C. Carter, C S. Cath., 4,212

Loyola Marymount University, Los Angeles, CA 90045, Tel. (213) 642-2700. Donald P. Merrifield, C West, Cath., 5,936

Lubbock Christian College, Lubbock, TX 79407, Tel. (806) 792-3221. Harvie M. Pruitt, C S, Ch. of Christ, 1,169

Luther College, Decorah, IA 52101, Tel. (319) 387-2000. Elwin D. Farwell, C NC, Am. Luth., 1,952

Lycoming College, Williamsport, PA 17701, Tel. (717) 326-1951. Frederick E. Blumer, C MS, Un. Meth. 1,298

Lynchburg College, Lynchburg, VA 24501, Tel. (804) 845-9071. Carey Brewer, C S, Christian Church (Disc.), 2,283

Macalester College, St. Paul, MN 55105, Tel. (612) 647-6207. John B. Davis, Jr., C NC, U. Presb. U.S.A. 1,744

MacMurray College, Jacksonville, IL 62650, Tel. (217) 245-6151. John J. Wittich, C NC, Un. Meth., 743

Madonna College, Livonia, MI 48150, Tel. (313) 591-1200. Sr. Mary Francilene, C NC, Cath., 2,521

Malone College, Canton, OH 44709, Tel. (216) 454-3011. Lon D. Randall, C NC, Friends, 850

Manchester College, North Manchester, IN 46962, Tel. (219) 982-2141. A. Blair Helman, C NC, Ch. Breth., 1,097

Manhattan College, Bronx, NY 10471, Tel. (212) 548-1400. Br. J. Stephen Sullivan, C MS, Cath., 4,590

Manhattanville College, Purchase, NY 10577, Tel. (914) 946-9600. Barbara K. Debs, C MS, Cath., 1,415

Marian College, Indianapolis, IN 46222, Tel. (317) 924-3291. Louis Gatto, C NC, Cath., 787

Marian College of Fond du Lac, Fond du Lac, WI 54935, Tel. (414) 921-3900. James M. Hanlon, C NC, Cath., 530

Marion College, Marion, IN 46952, Tel. (317) 674-6901. Robert R. Luckey, C NC, Wes. Ch., 880

Marist College, Poughkeepsie, NY 12601, Tel. (914) 471-3240. Linus R. Foy, C MS, Cath., 2,121

Marquette University, Milwaukee, WI 53233, Tel. (414) 244-7700. John P. Raynor, C NC, Cath., 10,855

Mars Hill College, Mars Hill, NC 28754, Tel. (704) 689-1111. Fred B. Bentley, C S, So. Bapt., 1,756

Mary Baldwin College, Staunton, VA 24401, Tel. (703) 885-0811. Virginia L. Lester, W S, Presb. U.S., 599

Mary College, Bismarck, ND 58501, Tel. (701) 255-4681. Sr. Thomas Welder, C NC, Cath., 911

Mary Hardin-Baylor College, Belton, TX 76513, Tel. (817) 939-5811. Bobby E. Parker, C S, So. Bapt., 1,103

Marycrest College, Davenport, IA 52804, Tel. (319) 326-9512. Ron Van Ryswyk, C NC, Cath., 1,194

Marygrove College, Detroit, MI 48221, Tel. (313) 862-8000. Raymond A. Fleck, C NC, Cath., 811

Marylhurst Education Center, Marylhurst, OR 97036, Tel. (503) 636-8141. Sr. Veronica Ann Baxter, C NW, Cath, 771

Marymount College of Kansas, Salina, KS 67401, Tel. (913) 825-2101. Sr. Mary Buser, C NC, Cath., 871

Marymount College, Tarrytown, NY 10591, Tel. (914) 631-3200. Sr. Brigid Driscoll, W MS, Cath., 1,112

Marymount College of Virginia, Arlington, VA 22207, Tel. (703) 524-2500. Sr. M. Majella Berg, W S, Cath., 822

Marymount Manhattan College, New York, NY 10021, Tel. (212) 472-3800. Sr. Colette Mahoney, W MS, Cath., 2,066

Maryville College, Maryville, TN 37801, Tel. (615) 982-6412. Wayne W. Anderson, C S, U. Presb. U.S.A., 674

Maryville College—St. Louis, St. Louis, MO 63141, Tel. (314) 434-4100. Claudius H. Pritchard, C NC, Cath., 1,264

Marywood College, Scranton, PA 18509, Tel. (717) 343-6521. Sr. M. Coleman Nee, W MS, Cath., 2,923

McKendree College, Lebanon, IL 62254, Tel. (618) 537-4481. Adolph H. Unruh, C NC, Un. Meth., 816

McMurry College, Abilene, TX 79605, Tel. (915) 692-4130. Thomas K. Kim, C S, Un. Meth., 1,225

McPherson College, McPherson, KS 67460, Tel. (316) 241-0731. Paul W. Hoffman, C NC, Ch. Breth., 515

Medaille College, Buffalo, NY 14214, Tel. (716) 884-3281. Leo R. Downey, C MS, Cath., 695

Mercer University, Macon, GA 31207, Tel. (912) 745-6811. Rufus C. Harris, C S, So. Bapt. 2,150

Mercer University in Atlanta, Atlanta, GA 30341, Tel. (404) 451-0331, Jean Hendricks, C S, So. Bapt., 1,082.

Mercy College, Dobbs Ferry, NY 10522, Tel. (914) 693-4500, Donald Grunewald, C MS, Cath., 7,054

Mercy College of Detroit, Detroit, MI 48219, Tel. (313) 531-7820. Sr. Agnes Mary Mansour, C NC, Cath., 2,226

Mercyhurst College, Erie, PA 16501, Tel. (814) 864-0681 Marion L. Shane, C MS, Cath., 1,343

Meredith College, Raleigh, NC 27611, Tel. (919) 833-6461. John E. Weems, W S, So. Bapt., 1,540

Merrimack College, North Andover, MA 01845, Tel. (617) 683-7111. John A. Coughlan, C NE, Cath., 3,183

Messiah College, Grantham, PA 17027, Tel. (717) 766-2511. D Ray Hostetter, C MS, Breth. in Christ, 1,051

Methodist College, Fayetteville, NC 28301, Tel. (919) 488-7110 Richard W. Pearce, C S, Un. Meth., 734

Mid-America Nazarene College, Olathe, KS 66061, Tel. (913) 782-3750. R. Curtis Smith, C NC, Nazarene, 1,035

Midland Lutheran College, Fremont, NB 68025, Tel. (402) 721-5480. L D. Lund, C NC, Luth. in Am., 843

Miles College, Birmingham, AL 35208, Tel. (205) 923-2771. W. C. Williams C S, CME, 2,873

Milligan College, Milligan College, TN 37682, Tel. (615) 929-0116. Jess W. Johnson, C S, CC/CC, 786

Millikin University, Decatur, IL 62522, Tel. (217) 424-6217. J. Roger Miller, C NC, U. Presb. U.S.A., 1,623

Millsaps College, Jackson, MS 39210, Tel. (601) 354-5201. George M. Harmon, Jr., C S, Un. Meth., 976

Mississippi College, Clinton, MS 39058, Tel. (601) 924-5131. Lewis Nobles, C S, So. Bapt. 3,005

Missouri Valley College, Marshall, MO 65340, Tel. (816) 886-6924. Donald C. Ziemke, C NC, Presb. U.S., 396

Mobile College, Mobile, AL 36613, Tel. (205) 675-5990. William K. Weaver, Jr., C S, So. Bapt., 946

Molloy College, Rockville Centre, NY 11570, Tel. (516) 678-5000. Sr. Janet A. Fitzgerald, W MS, Cath., 1,343

Monmouth College, Monmouth, IL 61462, Tel. (309) 457-2311. De Bow Freed, C NC, U. Presb. U.S.A., 700

Moravian College, Bethlehem, PA 18018, Tel. (215) 865-0741. Herman E. Collier, Jr., C MS, Morav, 1,657

Morehouse College, Atianta, GA 30314, Tel. (404) 681-2800. Hugh M. Gloster, M S, Am. Bapt., 1,526

Morningside College, Sioux City, IA 51106, Tel. (712) 277-5100 Miles Tommeraasen, C NC, Un. Meth., 1,521

Morris Brown College, Atlanta, GA 30314, Tel. (404) 525-7831. Robert Threatt, C S, A.M.E., 1,640

Mt. Angel Seminary, Saint Benedict, OR 97373, Tel. (503) 845-3030. Anselm Galvin, M NW, Cath., 105

Mt. Marty College, Yankton, SD 57078, Tel. (605) 668-1011. William W. Tucker, C NC, Cath., 571

Mt. Mary College, Milwaukee, WI 53222, Tel. (414) 258-4810. Sr. Mary Nora Barber, W NC, Cath., 1,102

Mt. Mercy College, Cedar Rapids, IA 52402, Tel. (319) 363-8213. Thomas R. Feld, C NC, Cath., 912

Mt. St. Mary College, Newburgh, NY 12550, Tel. (914) 561-0800. Sr. Ann V. Sakac, C MS, Cath., 1,015

Mt. St. Mary's College, Emmitsburg, MD 21727, Tel. (301) 447-6122. Robert J. Wickenheiser, C MS, Cath., 1,405

Mt. St. Mary's College, Los Angeles, CA 90049, Tel. (213) 476-2237. Sr. Magdalen Coughlin, W West, Cath., 1,034

Mount Union College, Alliance, OH 44601, Tel. (216) 821-5320. Ronald G. Weber, C NC, Un. Meth., 1,086

Mount Vernon, Nazarene College, Mount Vernon, OH 43050. Tel. (614) 397-1244. L. Guy Nees, C NC, Nazarene 935

Muhlenberg College, Allentown, PA 18104, Tel. (215) 433-3191. John H. Morey, C MS, Luth. in Am. 1,894

Mundelein College, Chicago, IL 60660, Tel. (312) 262-8100. Susan Rink, W NC, Cath., 1,516

Muskingum College, New Concord, OH 43762, Tel. (614) 826-8211. Arthur J. Dejong, C NC, U. Presb. U.S.A., 984

Nazareth College, Nazareth, MI 49074, Tel. (616) 349-7783. John S. Lore, C NC, Cath., 538

Nazareth College of Rochester, Rochester, NY 14610, Tel. (716) 586-2525. Robert A. Kidera, C MS, Cath., 2,657

Nebraska Wesleyan University, Lincoln, NB 68504, Tel. (402) 466-2371. John W. White, C NC, Un. Meth., 1,108

Newberry College, Newberry, SC 29108, Tel. (803) 276-5010. Glen E. Whitesides, C S, Luth. in Am., 831

New England, University of, Biddleford, ME 04005, C NC, Cath., 442

Niagara University, Niagara University, NY 14109, Tel. (716) 285-1212. Gerald Mahoney, C MS, Cath., 4,171

North Carolina Wesleyan College, Rocky Mount, NC 27801, Tel. (919) 442-7121 S. Bruce Patteway, C S, Un. Meth., 665

North Central College, Naperville, IL 60540, Tel. (312) 420-3400. Gael D. Swing, C NC, Un. Meth., 1,084

North Park College, Chicago IL 60625, Tel. (312) 583-2700. Lloyd H. Ahlem, C NC, Evan. Cov. Ch. of Amer., 1,361

Northland College, Ashland, WI 54806, Tel. (715) 682-4531. Malcolm McLean, C NC, U. Ch. of Christ, 731

Northwest Christian College, Eugene, OR 97401, Tel. (503) 343-1641. William E. Hays, C NW, Christian Church (Disc.), 332

Northwest College of the Assemblies of God, Kirkland, WA 98033, Tel. (206) 822-8266, D. V. Hurst, C NW, Assem. of God, 688

Northwest Nazarene College, Nampa, ID 83651, Tel. (208) 467-8011. Kenneth H. Pearsall, C NW, Nazarene, 1,242

Northwestern College, Orange City, IA 51041, Tel. (712) 737-4821. H. Virgil Rowenhorst, C NC, Ref. Am., 729

Notre Dame College, Manchester, NH 03104, Tel. (603) 669-4298 Sr. Jeannette Vezeau, W NE, Cath., 562

Notre Dame College, Cleveland, OH 44121, Tel. (216) 381-1680. Sr. Mary Marthe, W NC, Cath., 494

Notre Dame, University of, Notre Dame, IN 46556, Tel. (219) 283-6011. Theodore M. Hesburgh, C NC, Cath., 8,690

Nyack College, Nyack, NY 10960. Tel. (914) 358-1710. Thomas P. Bailey, C MS, Chr. and and Miss. All., 681

Oakland City College, Oakland City, IN 47660. Tel. (812) 749-4781. James W. Murray, C NC, Baptist, 530

Oakwood College, Huntsville, AL 35806, Tel. (205) 837-1630 Calvin B. Rock, C S, S.D.A., 1,306

Oblate College, Washington, DC 20017, Tel. (202) 529-6544. Richard J. Murphy, C MS, Cath., 32

Occidental College, Los Angeles, CA 90041, Tel. (213) 259-2974. Richard C. Gilman, C West, U. Presh. U.S.A., 1,784

Ohio Dominican College, Columbus, OH 43219, Tel. (614) 253-2741, Sr. Mary Andrew Matesich, C NC, Cath., 910

Ohio Northern University, Ada, OH 45810, Tel. (419) 634-9921. Ray B. Loeschmer, C NC, Un. Meth., 2,736

Ohio Wesleyan University, Delaware, OH 43015, Tel.

(614) 369-4431. Thomas E. Wenzlau, C NC, Un. Meth., 2,280

Oklahoma Baptist University, Shawnee, OK 74801, Tel. (405) 275-2850. E. E. Hall, C NC, So. Bapt., 1,549

Oklahoma Christian College, Oklahoma City, OK 73111, Tel. (405) 478-1661. Terry Johnson, C NC, Church of Christ 1,379

Oklahoma City University, Oklahoma City, OK 73106, Tel. (405) 521-5000. Jerald C. Walker, C NC, Un. Meth., 2,807

Olivet College, Olivet, MI 49076, Tel. (616) 749-7000. Donald A. Morris, C NC, U. Ch. of Christ, 708

Olivet Nazarene College, Kankakee, IL 60901, Tel. (815) 939-5011. Leslie W. Parrott, C NC, Nazarene, 1,862

Oral Roberts University, Tulsa, OK 74105, Tel. (918) 492-6161. G. Oral Roberts, C NC, interdenom, 3,774

Ottawa University, Ottawa, KS 66067, Tel. (913) 242-5200. Robert Shaw, C NC, Amer. Bapt., 879

Otterbein College, Westerville, OH 43081, Tel. (614) 890-3000. Thomas J. Kerr, IV, C NC, Un. Meth., 1,594

Ouachita Baptist University, Arkadelphia, AR 71923 Tel. (501) 246-4531. Daniel R. Grant, C NC, So. Bapt., 1,686

Our Lady of the Angels College, Aston, PA 19014, Tel. (215) 459-0905. Sr. Madonna Marie Cunningham, W MS, Cath., 646

Our Lady of the Holy Cross College, New Orleans, LA 70114, Tel. (504) 362-7744, Sr. Madaleine Herbert, C. S, Cath., 919

Our Lady of the Lake University of San Antonio, San Antonio, TX 78285, Tel. (512) 434-6711. Sr. Elizabeth A. Sueltenfuss, C S, Cath., 1,780

Ozarks, School of the, Point Lookout, MO 65726, Tel. (417) 334-6411. M. Graham Clark, C NC, Presby. U.S., 1,149

Pacific Christian College, Fullerton, CA 92631. Tel. (714) 879-3901. Medford H. Jones, C West, Ch. of Christ, 454

Pacific Lutheran University, Tacoma, WA 98447, Tel. (206) 531-6900. William O. Rieke, C NW, Am. Luth., 3,228

Pacific Union College, Angwin, CA 94508, Tel. (707) 965-6211. John W. Cassell, Jr., C West, S.D.A., 2,204

Pacific, University of the, Stockton, CA 95211. Tel. (209) 946-2011. Stanley E. McCaffrey, C West, Un. Meth., 6,103

Pacific University, Forest Grove, OR 97116, Tel. (503) 357-6151. James V. Miller, C NW, U. Ch. of Christ, 1,058

Palm Beach Atlantic College, West Palm Beach, FL 33401, Tel. (305) 833-8592. George R. Borders, C S, Bapt., 442

Paine College, Augusta, GA 30901, Tel. (404) 722-4471. Julius S. Scott, Jr., C S, Protestant Denoms., 843

Park College, Kansas City, MO 64152, Tel. (816) 741-2000. Harold L. Condit, C NC, Reorg. L.D.S., 2,511

Paul Quinn College, Waco, TX 76704, Tel. (817) 753-6417. William D. Watley, C S, A.M.E., 494

Pfeiffer College, Misenheimer, NC 28109, Tel. (704) 463-7343. Cameron P. West, C S, Un. Meth., 994

Philander Smith College, Little Rock, AR 72203 Tel. (501) 375-9845. Vacant, C NC, Un. Meth., 756

Phillips University, Enid, OK 73701, Tel. (405) 237-4433. Sam Curl, C NC, Christian Church (Disc.), 1,439

Pikeville College, Pikeville, KY 41501, Tel. (606) 432-3161. Jackson O. Hall, C S, Presb. U.S., 657

Point Loma College, San Diego CA 92106, Tel. (714) 222-6474. W. Vacant, C West, Nazarene, 1,905

Pontifical College Josephinum, Columbus, OH 43085, Tel. (614) 885-5585. Frank M. Mouch, C NC, Cath., 161

Portland, University of, Portland, OR 97203. Tel. (503) 283-7911, Br. Raphael Wilson, C NW, Cath., 2,540

Presbyterian College, Clinton, SC 29325, Tel. (803) 833-2820. Marc C. Weersing, C S, Presby. U.S., 822

Providence College, Providence, RI 02918, Tel. (401) 865-1000. Thomas R. Peterson, C NE, Cath., 5,930

Puget Sound, University of, Tacoma, WA 98416, Tel. (206) 756-3100. Philip M. Phibbs, C NW, Un. Meth. 3,914

Queens College, Charlotte, NC 28274, Tel. (704) 332-7121. Billy O. Wireman, W S, Presb. U.S., 591

Quincy College, Quincy, IL 62301, Tel. (217) 222-8020. Gabriel Brickman, C NC, Cath., 990

Randolph-Macon College, Ashland, VA 23005, Tel. (804) 798-8372. Luther W. White, III, C S, Un. Meth., 929

Randolph-Macon Woman's College, Lynchburg, VA 24503, Tel. (804) 846-7392. Robert A. Spivey, W S, Un. Mich., 763

Redlands, University of, Redlands, CA 92373, Tel. (714) 793-2121. Douglas R. Moore, C West, Am. Bapt., 2,965

Regis College, Denver, CO 80221, Tel. (303) 433-8471. David M. Clarke, C NC Cath., 1,082

Regis College, Weston, MA 02193, Tel. (617) 893-1820. Sr. Therese Higgins, W NE, Cath., 1,062

Richmond, University of, Richmond, VA 23173, Tel. (804) 285-6000. E. Bruce Heilman, C S, So. Bapt. 4,220

Ripon College, Ripon, WI 54971, Tel. (414) 748-8118. Bernard S. Adams, C NC, U. Ch. of Christ, 942

Rivier College, Nashua, NH 03060, Tel. (603) 888-1311 Sr. Doris Benoit, W NE, Cath., 1,675

Roanoke College, Salem, VA 24153, Tel. (703) 389-2351. Norman D. Fintel, C S, Luth. in Am., 1,280

Roberts Wesleyan College, Rochester, NY 14624, Tel. (716) 594-9471. Paul L. Adams, C MS, Free Meth., 631

Rockhurst College, Kansas City, MO 64110, Tel. (816) 363-4010. Robert F. Weiss, C NC, Cath., 3,515

Rocky Mountain College, Billings, MT 59102, Tel. (406) 245-6151. Bruce T. Alton, C NW, Un. Meth., U. Ch. of Christ, U. Presb. U.S.A., 512

Rosary College, River Forest, IL 60305, Tel. (312) 366-2490. Sr. M. Candida Lund, C NC, Cath., 1,395

Rosemont College, Rosemont, PA 19010, Tel. (215) 527-0200. Esther Sylvester, W MS, Cath., 612

Rust College, Holly Springs, MS 38635, Tel. (601) 252-4661. William A. McMillan, C S, Un. Meth., 686

Sacred Heart College, Belmont, NC 28012. Tel. (704) 825-5146. Sr. Michel Boulus, C S, Cath., 282

Sacred Heart Seminary College, Detroit, MI 48206, Tel. (313) 868-2700. Bernard J. Harrington, M NC, Cath., 280

Sacred Heart University, Bridgeport, CT 06606, Tel. (203) 374-9441. Thomas P. Melody, C NE, Cath., 2,867

Sacred Heart, University of the, Santurce, PR 00914, Tel. (809) 724-7800. Pedro Gonzalez Ramos, C MS, Cath., 5,051

St. Alphonsus College, Suffield, CT 06078, Tel. (203) 668-7393. George J. Keavewey, M NE, Cath., 70

St. Ambrose College, Davenport, IA 52803, Tel. (319) 324-1681. William Bakrow, C NC, Cath., 1,657

St. Andrews Presbyterian College, Laurinburg, NC 28352, Tel. (919) 276-3652. Alvin P. Perkinson, C S, Presb. U.S., 563

St. Anselm's College, Manchester, NH 03102, Tel. (603) 669-1030. Brendan P. Donnelly, C NE, Cath., 1,884

St. Augustine's College, Raleigh, NC 27611, Tel. (919) 828-4451. Prezell R. Robinson, C S, Epis., 1,716

St. Bonaventure University, St. Bonaventure, NY 14778, Tel. (716) 375-2000. Mathias Doyle, C MS, Cath., 2,714

St. Edward's University, Austin, TX 78704, Tel. (512) 444-2621. Stephen V. Walsh, C S, Cath., 1,968

St. Fidelis College, Herman, PA 16039, Tel. (412) 287-4794. Robert McCreary, M MS, Cath., 29

St. Francis College, Brooklyn, NY 11021, Tel. (212) 522-2300. Bro. Donald Sullivan, C MS, Cath., 3,972

St. Francis College, Fort Wayne, IN 46808, Tel. (219) 432-3551. Sr. Joellen Scheetz, C NC, Cath., 1,578

St. Francis College, Loretto, PA 15940, Tel. (814) 472-7000. Christian R. Oravec, C MS, Cath., 1,525

St. Francis de Sales College, Milwaukee, WI 53207. Tel. (414) 744-5450. William E. Puechner, M NC, Cath., 87

St. Hyacinth College, Granby, MA 01033, Tel. (413) 467-7191. David Stopyra, M NE, Cath., 54

St. John Fisher College, Rochester, NY 14616, Tel. (716) 586-4140. Charles J. Lavery, C MS, Cath., 1,956

St. John Vianney College and Seminary, Miami, FL 33165, Tel. (305) 223-4561. John J. Nevins, M S, Cath. 47

St. John's College, Camarillo, CA 93010, Tel. (805) 482-2755. James Galvin, M West, Cath., 221

St. John's Seminary, Brighton, MA 02135. Tel. (617) 254-2610. Robert J. Banks, M NE, Cath., 210

St. John's University, Collegeville, MN 56321, Tel. (612) 363-2011, Michael J. Blecker, Coord. NC, Cath., 1,943

St. John's University, Jamaica, NY 11439, Tel. (212) 969-8000. Joseph T. Cahill, C MS, Cath. 17,023

St. Joseph College, W. Hartford, CT 06117, Tel. (203) 232-4571. Sr. Mary Consolata O'Connor, W NE, Cath., 1,138

St. Joseph's College, Rensselaer, IN 47978, Tel. (219) 866-7111. Charles H. Banet, C NC, Cath., 1,034

St. Joseph's College, North Windham, ME 04062, Tel. (207) 892-6766. Bernard Currier, C NE, Cath., 517

St. Joseph's University, Philadelphia, PA 19131, Tel. (215) 879-7340. Donald I. MacLean, C MS, Cath., 5,696

St. Joseph's College, Brooklyn, NY 11205 Tel. (212) 622-4696. Sr. George A. O'Connor, C MS, Cath., 1,406

St. Joseph Seminary College, Saint Benedict, LA 70457 Tel. (504) 892-1800. James C. Boulware, C S, Cath., 103

St. Leo College, St. Leo, FL 33574, Tel. (904) 588-8200. Thomas B. Southard, C S, Cath., 1,003

St. Louis University, St. Louis, MO 63103, Tel. (314) 658-2222. Edward J. Drummond, C NC, Cath., 10,393

St. Louis University-Parks College, Cahokia, IL 62206, Tel. (618) 337-7500. Leon Z. Seltzer, C NC, Cath., 795

St. Martin's College, Lacey, WA 98503, Tel. (206) 491-4700. John Scott, C NW, Cath., 715

St. Mary College, Leavenworth, KS 66048, Tel. (913) 682-5151. Sr. Mary Janet McGilley, W NC, Cath., 817

St. Mary of the Plains College, Dodge City, KS 67801. Tel. (316) 225-4171. Michael J. McCarthy, C NC, Cath., 566

St. Mary-of-the-Woods College, St. Mary-of-the-Woods, IN 47876, Tel. (812) 535-4141. Sr. Jeanne Knoerle, W NC, Cath., 645

St. Mary's College, Notre Dame, IN 46556, Tel. (219) 232-3031. John M. Duggan, W NC, Cath., 1,751

St. Mary's College, Winona, MN 55987, Tel. (507) 452-4430. Br. Peter Clifford, C NC, Cath., 1,269

St. Mary's College, Orchard Lake, MI 48033, Tel. (313) 682-1885. Leonard F. Chrobot, C NC, Cath., 191

St. Mary's College of California, Moraga, CA 94575, Tel. (415) 376-4411. Br. Mel Anderson, C West Cath., 2,047

St. Mary's Dominican College, New Orleans, LA 70118, Tel. (504) 865-7761. Sr. Mary Gerald Shea, W S, Cath., 805

St. Mary's Seminary and College, Perryville, MO 63775, Tel. (314) 547-6533. W. Theodore Wiesner, M NC, Cath., 38

St. Mary's Seminary and University, Baltimore, MD 21210. Tel. (301) 323-3200. William J. Lee, C MS, Cath., 322

St. Mary's University of San Antonio, San Antonio, TX 78284, Tel. (512) 436-3722. James A. Young. C S, Cath., 3,274

St. Meinrad College, St. Meinrad, IN 47577, Tel. (812) 357-6611. Thomas Ostdick, M NC, Cath., 231

St. Michael's College, Winooski, VT 05404, Tel. (802) 655-2000. Edward L. Henry, C NE, Cath., 1,718

St. Norbert College, De Pere, WI 54115, Tel. (414) 337-3165. Neil J. Webb, C NC, Cath., 1,526

St. Olaf College, Northfield, MN 55057, Tel. (507) 663-2222. Sidney A. Rand, C NC, Am. Luth., 2,968

St. Patrick's College, Mountain View, CA 94042, Tel. (415) 967-9501. Gerald L. Brown, M West, Cath., 45

St. Paul's College, Lawrenceville, VA 23868, Tel. (804) 848-3111. James A. Russell, Jr. C S, Epis., 592

St. Peter's College, Jersey City, NJ 07306, Tel. (201) 333-4400. Edward R. Glynn, C MS, Cath., 4,430

St. Thomas Seminary, Denver, CO 80210, Tel. (303) 722-4687. Paul L. Golden, M NC, Cath., 151

St. Thomas, University of, Houston, TX 77006, Tel. (713) 522-7911. Patrick O. Braden, C S, Cath., 1,769

St. Thomas Aquinas College, Sparkhill, NY 10976. Tel. (914) 359-1279. Donald T. McNelis, C MS, Cath., 1,065

St. Vincent College, Latrobe, PA 15650, Tel. (412) 539-9761. Cecil G. Diethrich, M MS, Cath., 961

St. Xavier College, Chicago, IL 60655, Tel. (312) 779-3300. Sr. Irenaeus Chekouras, C NC, Cath., 1,802

Salem College, Salem, WV 26426, Tel. (304) 782-5011. James C. Stam, C NC, 7th Day Bapt., 920

Salem College, Winston-Salem, NC 27108, Tel. (919) 723-7961. Merrimon Cuninggim, W S, Morav, 609

Salve Regina The Newport College, Newport, RI 02840, Tel. (401) 847-6650, Sr. M. Lucille McKillop, C NE, Cath., 1,550

Samford University, Birmingham, AL 35209, Tel. (205) 870-2011. Leslie S. Wright, C S, So. Bapt., 3,960

San Diego, University of, San Diego, CA 92110, Tel. (714) 291-6480. Author E. Hughes, C West, Cath., 3,611

San Francisco, University of, San Francisco, CA 94117, Tel. (415) 666-0600. John J. LoSchiavo, C West, Cath., 6,392

Santa Clara, University of, Santa Clara, CA 95053, Tel. (408) 984-4242. William J. Rewak, C West, Cath., 7,295

Scarritt College, Nashville, TN 37203, Tel. (615) 327-2700. Vacant, C S, Un. Meth., 165

Scranton, University of, Scranton, PA 18510, Tel. (717) 961-7423. William J. Byron, C MS, Cath., 4,460

Seattle Pacific University, Seattle, WA 98119, Tel. (206) 281-2000. David L. McKenna, C NW, Free Meth., 2,276

Seattle University, Seattle, WA 98122, Tel. (206) 626-6200. William J. Sullivan, C NW, Cath., 3,616

Seminary of St. Pius X, Erlanger, KY 41018, Tel. (606) 371-4448. William G. Brown, M S, Cath., 93

Seton Hall University, South Orange, NJ 07079, Tel. (201) 762-9000. Lawrence T. Murphy, C MS, Cath., 9,132

Seton Hill College, Greensburg, PA 15601, Tel. (412) 834-2200. Eileen Farrell, W MS, Cath., 936

Shaw University, Raleigh, NC 27611, Tel. (919) 755-4800. Stanley H. Smith, C S, Am. Bapt., 1,378

Sheldon Jackson College, Sitka, AK 99835, Tel. (907) 747-5220. Hugh H. Holloway, C NW, U. Presb. U.S.A., 207

Shenandoah College, Winchester, VA 22601, Tel. (703) 667-8714. Robert P. Parker, C S, Un. Meth., 856

Shimer College, Mt. Caroll, Il 61053, Tel. (815) 244-2811. Don P. Moon, C NC, Epis., 103

Siena College, Loudonville, NY 12211, Tel. (518) 783-2300. Hugh Hines, C MS, Cath., 2,993

Siena Heights College, Adrian, MI 49221, Tel. (517) 263-0731. Louis C. Vaccaro, C NC, Cath., 1,070

Silver Lake College, Manitowac, WI 54220, Tel. (414) 684-6691. Sr. Anne Kennedy, C NC, Cath., 328

Simpson College, San Francisco CA 94134. Tel. (415) 334-7400. Mark W. Lee, C West, Chr. and Miss. All., 468

Simpson College, Indianola, IA 50125, Tel. (515) 961-6251. Richard Lancaster, C NC, Un. Meth., 839

Sioux Falls College, Sioux Falls, SD 57101, Tel. (605) 336-2850. Owen P. Halleen, C NC, Am. Bapt., 720

South, University of the, Sewanee, TN 37375, Tel. (615) 598-5931, Robert M. Ayres, Jr., C S, Epis., 1,093

Southern Benedictine College, St. Bernard, AL 35138. Tel. (205) 734-4110. Brian J. Egan, C S Cath., 385

Southern California College, Costa Mesa, CA 92626, Tel. (714) 556-3610. Wayne E. Kraiss, C West, Assem. of God., 638

Southern Methodist University, Dallas, TX 75275, Tel. (214) 692-2000. James H. Zumberge, C S, Un. Meth., 8,677

Southern Missionary College, Collegedale, TN 37315, Tel. (615) 396-2111. Frank A. Knittel C S, S.D.A., 1,912

Southwest Baptist College, Bolivar, MO 65613, Tel. (417) 326-5281. James L. Sells, C NC, So. Bapt., 1,469

Southwestern at Memphis, Memphis, TN 38112, Tel. (901) 274-1800. James H. Daughdrill, Jr., C S, Presb. U.S. 1,028

Southwestern College, Winfield, KS 67156, Tel. (316) 221-4150. Donald B. Ruthenberg, C NC, Un. Meth., 655

Southwestern Adventist College, Keene, TX 76059, Tel. (817) 645-3921. Donald R. McAdams, C S, S.D.A., 745

Southwestern University, Georgetown, TX 78626. Tel. (512) 863-6511. Durwood Fleming, C S, Un. Meth., 956

Spelman College, Atlanta, Ga 30314, Tel. (404) 681-3643. Donald M. Stewart, Bapt., 1,276

Spertus College Judaica, Chicago, IL 60605. Tel. (312) 922-9012. David Weinstein, C NC, Jewish, 424

Spring Arbor College, Spring Arbor, MI 49283, Tel. (517) 750-1200. Ellwood A. Voller, C NC, Free Meth., 825

Spring Hill College, Mobile, AL 36608, Tel. (205) 460-2121. Paul S. Tipton, C S, Cath., 904

Stephens College, Columbia, MO 65201, Tel. (314) 442-2211. Arland F. Christ-Janer, W NC, Am. Bapt., 1,797

Sterling College, Sterling, KS 67579, Tel. (316) 278-2173. Charles W. Schoenherr, C NC, U. Presb. U.S.A., 509

Stetson University, De Land, FL 32720, Tel. (904) 734-4121. Pope A. Duncan, C S, So. Bapt., 2,753

Stillman College, Tuscaloosa, AL 35401, Tel. (205) 752-2548. Harold N. Stinson, C S, Presb., U.S., 724

Stonehill College, North Easton, MA 02356, Tel. (617) 238-1081. Bartley Mac Phaidin, C NE, Cath., 2,334

Susquehanna University, Selinsgrove, PA 17870, Tel. (717) 374-0101, Jonathan C. Messerli, C MS, Luth. in Am., 1,592

Swarthmore College, Swarthmore, PA 19081, Tel. (215) 544-7900. Theodore W. Friend, III C MS, Friends, 1,289

Tabor College, Hillsboro, KS 67063, Tel. (316) 947-3121. Roy Just, C NC, Menn. Breth., 510

Talladega College, Talladega, AL 35160, Tel. (205) 362-2752. Joseph W. Gayles, C S, U. Ch. of Christ 586

Tarkio College, Tarkio, MO 64491, Tel. (816) 736-4131. Frank H. Bretz, C NC, U. Presb. U.S.A., 635

Tennessee Wesleyan College, Athens, TN 37303, Tel. (615) 745-9522. George E. Naff, Jr., C S, Un. Meth., 421

Texas Christian University, Fort Worth, TX 76129, Tel. (817) 921-7000. William E. Tucker, C S, Christian Church (Disc.), 6,213

Texas College, Tyler, TX 75702, Tel. (214) 593-8311. Allen C. Hancock, C S, Chr. Meth. Epis., 583

Texas Lutheran College, Seguin, TX 78155, Tel. (512) 379-4161. Charles H. Oestreich, C S, Am. Luth., 1,361

Texas Wesleyan College, Fort Worth, TX 76105, Tel. (817) 534-0251. John H. Fleming, C S, Un. Meth., 1,588

Thiel College, Greenville, PA 16125, Tel. (412) 588-7700. Louis T. Almen, C MS, Luth. in Am., 1,043

Thomas More College, Fort Mitchell, Ky 41017, Tel. (606) 341-5800. Robert J. Giroux, C S, Cath., 1,296

Tift College, Forsyth, GA 31029, Tel. (912) 994-2515. Robert W. Jackson, W S, So. Bapt., 705

Tougaloo College, Tougaloo, MS 39174, Tel. (601) 956-4941. George A. Owens, C S, U. Ch. of Christ, 1,005

Transylvania University, Lexington, KY 40508, Tel. (606) 233-8111. William W. Kelly, C S, Christian Church (Disc.), 783

Trevecca Nazarene College, Nashville, TN 37210. Tel. (615) 244-6000. Mark R. Moore, C S, Nazarene, 1,021

Trinity College, Hartford, CT 06106, Tel. (203) 527-3151. Theodore D. Lockwood, C NE, Epis., 2,114

Trinity College, Washington, DC 20017. Tel. (202) 269-2000. Sr. Rose Ann Fleming, C MS, Cath., 899

Trinity College, Deerfield, IL 60015, Tel. (312) 945-6700. Harry L. Evans, C NC, Evan. Free Ch. of Am., 900

Trinity College, Burlington, VT 05401, Tel. (802) 658-0337. Sr. Catherine T. McNamee, W NE, Cath., 434

Trinity University, San Antonio TX 78284, Tel. (512) 736-7011. M. Bruce Thomas, C S, Presb. Ch. U.S., 3,524

Tusculum College, Greeneville, TN 37743, Tel. (615) 639-2661. Earl B. Mezoff, C S, U. Presb. U.S.A., 468

Union College, Barbourville, Ky 40906, Tel. (606) 546-4151. Mahlon A. Miller, C S, Un. Meth., 1,133

Union College, Lincoln, NB 68506, Tel. (402) 488-2331. M. O. Manley, C NC, S.D.A., 923

Union University, Jackson, TN 38301, Tel. (901) 668-1818. Robert E. Craig, C S, So. Bapt., 1,141

United States International University, San Diego, CA 92131, Tel. (714) 271-4300. William C. Rust, C West, Un. Meth., 2,373

Upsala College, E. Orange, NJ 07019, Tel. (201) 266-7000. Rodney Felder, Luth. in Am., 1,675

Ursinus College, Collegeville, PA 19426, Tel. (215) 489-4111. Richard P. Richter, C MS, U. Ch. of Christ, 1,677

Ursuline College, Cleveland, OH 44124, Tel. (216) 449-4200. Sr. Mary Kenan Dulzer, W NC, Cath., 806

Valparaiso University, Valparaiso, IN 46383, Tel. (219) 464-5000. Robert V. Schnabel, C NC, Luth. (Mo.), 4,484

Villa Maria College, Erie, PA 16505, Tel. (814) 838-1966. Sr. M. Lawrence Antoun, W MS, Cath., 478

Villanova University, Villanova, PA 19085, Tel. (215) 527-2100. John M. Driscoll, C MS, Cath., 9,422

Virginia Intermont College, Bristol, VA 24201, Tel. (703) 669-6101. Floyd V. Turner, C S, So. Bapt., 677

Virginia Union University, Richmond, VA 23220, Tel. (804) 359-9331. Allix B. James, C S, Am. Bapt., 1,096

Virginia Wesleyan College, Norfolk, VA 23502, Tel. (804) 461-3232. Lambuth M. Clarke, C S, Un. Meth., 761

Viterbo College, La Crosse, WI 54601, Tel. (608) 784-0040. J. Thomas Finucan, C NC, Cath., 941

Voorhees College, Denmark, SC 29042, Tel. (803) 793-3346. George B. Thomas, C S, Epis., 954

Wadham's Hall Seminary and College, Ogdensburg, NY 13669, Tel. (315) 393-4231. Peter R. Riami, M MS, Cath. 83

Wagner College, Staten Island, NY 10301 Tel. (212) 390-3000. John Satterfield, C MS, Luth. in Am., 2,594

Wake Forest University, Winston-Salem, NC 27109, Tel. (919) 761-5000. James R. Scales, C S, So. Bapt., 4,630

Walla Walla College, College Place, WA 99324, Tel. (509) 527-2615. N. Clifford Sorenson, C NW, S.D.A., 1,886

Walsh College, Canton, OH 44720, Tel. (216) 499-7090. Br. Francis Blouin, C NC, Cath., 611

Warner Pacific College, Portland, OR 97215. Tel. (503) 775-4366. E. Joe Gilliam, C NW, Ch. of God, 480

Warren Wilson College, Swannanoa, NC 28778, Tel. (704) 298-3325. Reuben A. Holden, C S, U. Presb. U.S.A., 551

Wartburg College, Waverly, IA 50677, Tel. (319) 352-1200. William W. Jellema, C NC, Am. Luth., 1,145

Wayland Baptist College, Plainview, TX 79072, Tel. (806) 296-5521. Roy C. McClung, C S, So. Bapt., 1,148

Waynesburg College, Waynesburg, PA 15370, Tel. (412) 627-8191. Joseph F. Marsh, C MS, U. Presb. U.S.A., 772

Wesleyan College, Macon, GA 31201, Tel. (912) 477-1110. W. Earl Strickland, W S, Un. Meth., 532

West Virginia Wesleyan College, Buckhannon, WV, 26201, Tel. (304) 473-8181, Fred E. Harris, C NC, Un. Meth., 1,773

Western Baptist College, Salem, OR 97302, Tel. (503) 581-8600. W. Thomas Younger, C NC, Bapt., 430

Western Maryland College, Westminster, MD 21157, Tel. (301) 848-7000. Ralph C. John, C MS, Un. Meth., 2,080

Westmar College, Le Mars, IA 51031, Tel. (712) 546-7081. Ben F. Wade, C NC, Un. Meth., 664

Westminster College, Fulton, MO 65251, Tel. (314) 642-3361. J. Harvey L. Saunders, M NC, Presb. U.S., 638

Westminster College, New Wilmington, PA 16142, Tel. (412) 946-8761. Earland I. Carlson C MS, U. Presb. U.S.A., 1,926

Westminster College, Salt Lake City, UT 84105, Tel. (801) 484-7651. Helmut P. Hofmann, C NW, Interdenom., 1,464

Wheaton College, Wheaton, IL 60187. Tel. (312) 682-5000. Hudson Armerding, C NC, Interdenom., 2,353

Wheeling College, Wheeling, WV 26003, Tel. (304) 243-2000. Charles L. Currie, C NC, Cath., 1,031

Whittier College, Whittier, CA 90608, Tel. (213) 693-0771. W. Roy Newson C West, Friends 1,793

Whitworth College, Spokane, WA 99251, Tel. (509) 466-1000. Edward B. Lendman, C NW, U. Presb. U.S.A., 1,688

Wilberforce University, Wilberforce, OH 45384, Tel. (513) 376-2911. Charles E. Taylor, C NC, A.M.E., 1,123

Wiley College, Marshall, TX 75670. Tel. (214) 938-8341. Robert E. Hayes, C S, Un. Meth. 649

Willamette University, Salem, OR 97301, Tel. (503) 370-6300. Robert P. Lisensky, C NW, Un. Meth., 1,830

William Carey College, Hattiesburg, MS 39401, Tel. (601) 582-5051. J. Ralph Noonkester, C S, So. Bapt., 1,513

William Jewell College, Liberty, MO 64068, Tel. (816) 781-3806. Thomas S. Field, C NC, Am. Bapt. and So. Bapt., 1,730

William Penn College, Oskaloosa, IA 52577, Tel. (515) 673-8311. D. Duane Moon, C NC, Friends, 616

William Woods College, Fulton, MO 65251, Tel. (314) 642-2251. R. B. Cutlip, W NC, Christian Church (Disc.), 910

Wilmington College, Wilmington, OH 45177, Tel. (513) 382-6661. Robert E. Lucas, C NC, Friends, 857

Wilson College, Chambersburg, PA 17201, Tel. (717) 264-4141. Margaret A. Waggoner, W MS, U. Presb. U.S.A., 233

Wingate College, Wingate, NC 28174, Tel. (704) 233-4061. Thomas E. Corts, C S. So. Bapt., 1,454

Wittenberg University, Springfield, OH 45501, Tel. (513) 327-6231. William A. Kinnison, C NC, Luth. in Am., 2,308

Wofford College, Spartanburg, SC 29301, Tel. (803) 585-4821. Joab M. Lesesne C S, Un. Meth., 1,012

Xavier University, Cincinnati, OH 45207, Tel. (513) 745-3000. Robert M. Mulligan, C NC, Cath., 6,382

Xavier University of Louisiana, New Orleans, LA 70125, Tel. (504) 486-7411, Norman C. Francis, C S, Cath., 1,886

Yankton College, Yankton, SD 57078, Tel. (605) 665-3661. Orlan E. Mitchell, C NC, U Ch. of Christ, 243

Yeshiva University, New York, NY 10033, Tel. (212) 568-5400. Norman Lamm, Co. Ord. MS, Jewish, 3,985

11. RELIGIOUS PERIODICALS IN THE UNITED STATES

This list has been compiled for those who may wish to utilize a relatively large, representative group of religious periodicals. Many additional titles appear in the directories of religious bodies presented in this book. Probably the most inclusive list of religious periodicals published in the United States can be found in the 1980 *Ayer Directory of Publications* (Ayer Press, West Washington Sq., Philadelphia, PA 19106).

Each entry lists, in this order: Title of periodical, frequency of publication, religious affiliation, editor's name, address, and telephone number.

A.D. (m), U. Ch. of Christ and U. Presb. Ch. USA, J. Martin Bailey, 475 Riverside Dr., Rm. 1840, New York, NY 10027. Tel. (212) 870-3195

ADRIS Newsletter (q), non-sect., Richard F. Smith, Dept. of Theology, Fordham University, Bronx, NY 10458 Tel. (212) 933-2233

Adventist Review (w and m), Seventh-day Adv., K. H. Wood, 6856 Eastern Ave., N.W., Washington, DC 20012. Tel. (202) 723-3700

Alliance Witness, The (bi-w), The Christian & Missionary Alliance, H. Robert Cowles, P.O. Box C, Nyack, NY 10960. Tel. (914) 353-0750

America (w), Cath., Joseph A. O'Hare, 106 W. 56th St., New York, NY 10019. Tel. (212) 581-4640

American Baptist, The (m, except August), Am. Bapt., Philip E. Jenks, American Baptist Churches, U.S.A., Valley Forge, PA 19481. Tel. (215) 768-2216

American Bible Society Record (10 issues a year), undenom., Amer. Bible Society, Clifford P. Macdonald, 1865 Broadway, New York, NY. 10023,. Tel. (212) 581-7400

Arkansas Methodist, (w) U. Meth., Jerry D. Canada, P.O. Box 3547, Little Rock, AR 72203. Tel. (501) 374-4831

Banner, The (w), Chr. Ref., Andrew Kuyvenhoven, 2850 Kalamazoo Ave., S.E., Grand Rapids, MI 49560. Tel. (616) 241-1691

Baptist, The—A Monthly Magazine (m) Bapt., David N. Licorish, 18 W. 123rd St., New York, NY 10027. Tel. (212) 876-2399

Baptist and Reflector (w), S. Bapt., P.O. Box 347, Brentwood, TN 37027. Tel. (615) 373-2255

Baptist Bulletin (m), Gen. Assoc. Reg. Bapt. Chs. Merle R. Hull, 1300 N. Meacham Rd., P.O. Box 95500, Schaumburg, IL 60195

Baptist Courier (w), S. Bapt., John E. Roberts, P.O. Box 2168, Greenville, SC 29602. Tel. (803) 232-8736

Baptist Herald (m), N. A. Bapt. Conf., Reinhold J. Kerstan, 1 S. 210 Summit Ave., Oakbrook Terrace, IL 60181

Baptist History and Heritage (q), S. Bapt., Lynn E. May, Jr., 127 Ninth Ave., N., Nashville, TN 37234. Tel. (615) 251-2660

Baptist Leader (m), Am. Bapt., Vincie Alessi, Board of Educational Ministries, Valley Forge, PA 19481. Tel. (215) 768-2158

Baptist Messenger (w), S. Bapt., Jack L. Gritz, 1141 N. Robinson, Oklahoma City, OK 73103. Tel. (405) 236-4341

Baptist Record (w), S. Bapt., Donald T. McGregor, Box 530, Jackson, MS 39205. Tel. (601) 354-3704

Baptist Standard (w), S. Bapt., Presnall H. Wood, 2343 Lone Star Dr., P.O. Box 226330, Dallas TX 75266. Tel. (214) 630-4571

Biblical Recorder (w), S. Bapt., J. Marse Grant, P.O. Box 26568, Raleigh, NC 27611. Tel. (919) 832-4019

B'nai B'rith Messenger (w), Jewish, Joseph Jonah Cummins, 2510 W. 7th St., Los Angeles, CA 90057. Tel. (213) 380-5000

Brethren Journal, The (m), Unity of Brethren, Jesse E. Skrivanek, 5905 Carleen Dr., Austin, TX 78731

Catholic Chronicle (w), Cath., Daniel J. McCarthy, 1933 Spielbusch, Toledo, OH 43624. Tel. (419) 243-4178

Catholic Digest (m), Cath., Henry Lexau, P. O. Box 43090, St. Paul, MN 55164. Tel. (612) 647-5296

Catholic Herald Citizen (w), Cath., Thomas R. Leahy, 2170 N. Prospect Ave., Milwaukee, WI 53202. Tel. (414) 271-4784

Catholic Light (bi-w), Cath., Joseph P. Gilgallon, The Chancery Bldg., 300 Wyoming Ave., Scranton, PA 18503

Catholic Mind (m), Cath., Joseph A. O'Hare, 106 W. 56th St., New York, NY 10019. Tel. (212) 581-4640

Catholic Review, The (w), Cath., Robert L. Johnston, 320 Cathedral St., Baltimore, MD 21201. Tel. (301) 547-5327

Catholic Standard and Times (w), Cath., John P. Foley, 222 N. 17th St., Philadelphia, PA 19103. Tel. (215) 587-3660

Catholic Transcript, The (w), Cath., John S. Kennedy, 785 Asylum Ave., Hartford, CT 06105. Tel. (203) 527-1175

Catholic Universe Bulletin (w), Cath., Edgar V. Barmann, 1027 Superior Ave., N.E., Cleveland, OH 44114. Tel. (216) 696-6525

Catholic Worker (9/yr.), Cath., Dorothy Day, 36 E. First St., New York, NY 10003. Tel. (212) 254-1640

Celebration: A Creative Worship Service (m), Cath., Jason Petosa, P.O. Box 281, Kansas City, MO 64141. Tel. (816) 531-0538

Chaplaincy (q) and **Chaplaincy Letter** (m), interdenom., Norman G. Folkers, Ste. 310, 5100 Wisconsin Ave., N.W., Washington, DC 20016. Tel. (202) 686-1857

Chicago Catholic, The, (w), Cath., A.E.P. Wall, 155 E. Superior St., P.O. Box 11181, Chicago, IL 60611. Tel. (312) 751-8311

Christian Bookseller Magazine (m), undenom., Jane Struck, 396 E. St. Charles Rd., Wheaton, IL 60187. Tel. (312) 653-4200

Christian Century, The (44/yr.), ecumen., James M. Wall, 407 S. Dearborn St., Chicago, IL 60605. Tel. (312) 427-5380

Christian Community, The (m, except August, September and January), National Council of Community Churches, Herbert F. Freitag, 89 E. Wilson Bridge Rd., Worthington, OH 43085. Tel. (614) 888-4501

Christian Endeavor World, The (q), interdenom., Frances M. Becker, Actg., 1221 E. Broad St., P.O. Box 1110, Columbus, OH 43216. Tel. (614) 253-8541

Christian Herald (m), interdenom., David E. Kucharsky, 40 Overlook Dr., Chappaqua, NY 10514 Tel. (914) 769-9000

Christian Home, The (m), U. Meth., David I. Bradley, 201 Eighth Ave., S. Nashville, TN 37202

Christian Index, The (w), S. Bapt., Jack U. Harwell, 2930 Flowers Rd., S., Atlanta, GA 30341.Tel. (404) 455-0404

Christian Index, The (bi-w), Chr. Meth. Epis., Othal H. Lakey, P. O. Box 665, Memphis, TN 38101. Tel. (901) 947-6297

RELIGIOUS PERIODICALS IN THE U.S.

Christian Life Magazine (m), undenom., Robert Walker, 396 East St. Charles Rd., Wheaton, IL 60187. Tel. (312) 653-4200

Christian Ministry, The (formerly **The Pulpit**) (6 times a year), James M. Wall, 407 S. Dearborn St., Chicago, IL 60605. Tel. (312) 427-5380

Christian Reader, The (bi-m), non-denom., Ted Miller, 336 Gundersen Dr., Wheaton, IL 60187. Tel. (312) 668-8300

Christian Science Journal, The (m), Chr. Sc., Geoffrey J. Barratt, One Norway St., Boston, MA 02115. Tel. (617) 262-2300

Christian Science Sentinel (w), Chr. Sc., Geoffrey J. Barratt, One Norway St., Boston, MA 02115. Tel. (617) 262-2300

Christian Standard (w), Christian Churches/Churches of Christ, Sam E. Stone, 8121 Hamilton Ave., Cincinnati, OH 45231

Christianity and Crisis (bi-w), ecumen., Wayne H. Cowan, 537 W. 121st St., New York, NY 10027. Tel. (212) 662-5907

Christianity Today (semi-m), indepdt., Kenneth S. Kantzer, 465 Gunderson Dr., Carol Stream, IL 60187. Tel. (312) 682-3020

Church Advocate, The (m), Chs. of God, Gen. Conf., David E. Draper, P. O. Box 926, 2200 Jennifer Lane, Findlay, OH 45840. Tel. (419) 424-1963

Church and Society (bi-m), U. Presb. Ch. USA Presb. US, Earl K. Larson, Belle McMaster, Rm. 1244 K, 475 Riverside Dr., New York, NY 10027. Tel. (212) 870-2917

Church Herald, The (bi-w), Ref. Ch. in Am., John Stapert, 1324 Lake Dr. S.E., Grand Rapids, MI 49506 Tel. (616) 458-5156

Church History (q), undenom., Robert M. Grant, Martin E. Marty, and Jerald C. Brauer, Swift Hall, The Univ. of Chicago, Chicago, IL 60637. Tel. (312) 753-4023

Church Management: The Clergy Journal (10/yr), non-denom., Manfred Holck, Jr. 4119 Terrace La., Hopkins, MN 55343. Tel. (612) 933-6712

Churchman, The (m), interdenom., Edna Ruth Johnson, 1074 23rd Ave., N., St. Petersburg, FL 33704. Tel. (813) 894-0097

Church Woman, The (bi-m), ecumen., Church Women United, 475 Riverside Dr., New York, NY 10027. Tel. (212) 870-2346

Clarion Herald (w), Cath., Emile M. Comar, Jr., 523 Natchez St. P. O. Box 53247, New Orleans, 70153. Tel. (504) 523-7731

Columban Mission (10 times a year), Cath., Peter McPartland, St. Columbans, NB 68056

Columbia (m), Cath., Elmer Von Feldt, P. O. Drawer 1670, New Haven, CT 06507

Commonweal (bi-w), Cath., James O'Gara, 232 Madison Ave., New York, NY 10016. Tel. (212) 683-2042

Concern Magazine/Newsfold, (q and 8/yr.), U. Presb. Ch. USA, U. Presby. Women, Jane Jarrard, 475 Riverside Dr., Rm. 454, New York, NY 10027. Tel. (212) 870-2661

Congregationalist, The (q.), Congr. Chr., Natl. Assn. of, Nancy Manser, 484 E. Grand Blvd., Detroit, MI 48207.

Conservative Judaism (q), Jewish, Arthur Chiel, 3080 Broadway, New York, NY 10027. Tel. (212) 749-8000

Criterion, The (w), Cath., Thomas C. Widner, 520 Stevens St., P. O. Box 174, Indianapolis, IN 46206. Tel. (317) 635-4531

Cumberland Presbyterian, The (bi-w), Cumb. Presb., C. Ray Dobbins, 1978 Union Ave., Box 40149, Memphis, TN 38104. Tel. (901) 276-9032

Decision (m), Billy Graham Evangelistic Assn., Roger C. Palms, 1300 Harmon Pl., Minneapolis, MN 55403

Diakonia (3/yr), Cath., George A. Maloney, Fordham Univ., Bronx, NY 10458. Tel. (212) 933-2233

Disciple, The (s-m), Chr. Ch. (Disc.), James L. Merrell, Box 179, St. Louis, MO 63166. Tel. (314) 371-6900

Ecumenical Courier (q), U.S. Conference for the World Council of Churches, Bruno Kroker, Rm. 1062, 475 Riverside Dr., New York, NY 10027. Tel. (212) 870-2533

Ecumenical Review, The (q), interdenom., Philip A. Potter, World Council of Churches, 150 Route de Ferney, CH-1211 Geneva 20, Switzerland

Ecumenical Trends (m), ecum., Charles La Fontaine, Graymoor Ecumenical Institute, Garrison, NY 10524. Tel. (914) 424-3671

Emphasis On Faith and Living (s-m), Missionary Ch. Everek Storms, 336 Dumfries Ave., Kitchener, Ontario, Canada N2H 2G1

Engage/Social Action (m), U. Meth., Lee Ranck, 100 Maryland Ave., N. E., Washington, DC 20002. Tel. (202) 488-5632

Episcopal Recorder (m), Ref. Epis., Howard D. Higgins, 25 South 43rd St., Philadelphia, PA 19104. Tel. (215) 222-5158

Episcopalian, The (m), Epis., Henry L. McCorkle, 1930 Chestnut St., Philadelphia, PA 19103. Tel. (215) 564-2010

Eternity (m), interdenom., William J. Petersen, 1716 Spruce St., Philadelphia, PA 19103. Tel. (215) 546-3696

Evangelist, The (w), Cath., Kenneth J. Doyle, 39 Philip St., Albany, NY 12207. Tel. (518) 434-0107

Extension (m), Cath., George Lundy, 35 East Wacker Dr., Chicago, IL 60601. Tel. (312) 236-7240

Face-to-Face (formerly **Builders** and **Classmate**) (q), U. Meth., Eddie Robinson, 201 Eighth Ave., S., Nashville, TN 37202

Faith at Work (6/yr.), interdenom., Walden Howard, 11065 Little Patuxent Pkwy, Columbia, MD 21044

Firm Foundation (w), Chs. of Christ, Reuel Lemmons, Box 610, Austin, TX 78767

Forum Letter (m), Luth., Richard J. Neuhaus, 338 E. 19th St., New York, NY 10003. Tel. (212) 228-2832

Franciscan Herald (m), Cath., Mark Hegener, 1434 W. 51st. St., Chicago, IL 60609. Tel. (312) 254-4455

Free Will Baptist, The (w), Free Will Bapt., Tommy Manning, Free Will Baptist Press, P. O. Box 158, Ayden, NC 28513. Tel. (919) 746-6128

Friends Journal (s-m), Friends (Quakers), Ruth G. Kilpack, 152-A N. 15th St., Philadelphia, PA 19102. Tel. (215) 564-4779

Gospel Herald (w), Menn., Daniel Hertzler, Scottdale, PA 15683. Tel. (412) 887-8500

Grapevine (10/yr.), Joint Strategy and Action Committee, Ms. Dorothy Lara-Braud, 475 Riverside Dr., Rm. 1700-A, New York, NY 10027. Tel. (212) 870-3105

Herald of Christian Science, The, French, German, Portugese, and Spanish editions (m); Danish, Dutch, Greek, Indonesian, Italian, Japanese, Norwegian, Swedish and Braille editions (q), Chr. Sc., Geoffrey J. Barratt One Norway St., Boston, MA 02115. Tel. (617) 262-2300

Herald of Holiness (semi-m), Nazarene, W. E. McCumber, 6401 The Paseo, Kansas City, MO 64131. Tel. (816) 333-7000.

Historical Magazine of the Protestant Episcopal Church (q), Epis., John F. Woolverton, Seminary Post Office, Alexandria, VA 22304

Home Missions (m), S. Bapt., Walker L. Knight, 1350 Spring St., N.W., Atlanta, GA 30309. Tel. (404) 873-4041

Homiletic and Pastoral Review (m), Cath., Kenneth Baker, 86 Riverside Dr., New York, NY 10024. Tel. (212) 799-2600

International Review of Mission (q), Commission on World Mission and Evangelism, World Council of Churches, Emilio Castro, 150 Route de Ferney, P. O. Box 66, CH-1211 Geneva 20, Switzerland

Interpretation (q), Union Theol. Sem. in Va., James L. Mays, 3401 Brook Rd., Richmond, VA 23227. Tel. (804) 355-0671

Interpreter, The (m), U. Meth., Darrell R. Shamblin, 601 W. Riverview Ave., Dayton, OH 45406. Tel. (513) 222-7087

Jewish Digest, The (m), Jewish, Bernard Postal, 1363 Fairfield Ave., Bridgeport, CT 06605

Jewish Life (q), Jewish, Yaakov Jacobs, 116 E. 27th St., New York, NY 10016. Tel. (212) 725-3400

Journal of Ecumenical Studies (q), Leonard Swidler, Temple Univ., Philadelphia, PA 19122. Tel. (215) 787-7714

Journal of Pastoral Care (q), nondenom., Edward Thornton, 475 Riverside Dr., Suite 450, New York, NY 10027. Tel. (212) 870-2558

Journal of Presbyterian History (q), U. Presb. Ch. USA, James H. Smylie, 425 Lombard St., Philadelphia, PA 19147. Tel. (215) 627-1852

Journal of Religion (q), undenom., Brian Gerrish, 1025 E. 58th St., Chicago, IL 60615. Tel. (312) 753-4021

Journal of the American Academy of Religion (q), undenom., Ray L. Hart, University of Montana, Missoula, MT 59812. Tel. (406) 243-5563

Journal of the American Scientific Affiliation (q), interdenom., Richard H. Bube, Dept. of Materials Science, Stanford Univ., Stanford, CA 94305. Tel. (415) 321-5796

Judaism (q), Jewish, Robert Gordis, 15 E. 84th St., New York, NY 10028. Tel. (212) 879-4500

Liguorian (m), Cath., Norman J. Muckerman, Liguori, MO 63057. Tel. (314) 464-2500

Living Church, The (w), Epis., H. Boone Porter, 407 E. Michigan St., Milwaukee, WI 53202. Tel. (414) 276-5420

Logos Journal (bi-m), undenom., William L. Carmichael, 201 Church St., Plainfield, NJ 07060. Tel. (201) 754-0745.

Long Island Catholic, The (51/yr.), Cath., Daniel S. Hamilton, 115 Greenwich St., P. O. Box 700, Hempstead, NY 11551. Tel. (516) 538-8800

Lookout, The (w), Christian Churches/Churches of Christ, Mark Taylor, 8121 Hamilton Ave., Cincinnati, OH 45231. Tel. (513) 931-4050

Louisiana Methodist, The (w), U. Meth., L. Ray Branton, P. O. Box 4325, Shreveport, LA 71104

Lutheran, The (s-m), Luth. Ch. in America, Edgar R. Trexler, 2900 Queen Lane, Philadelphia, PA 19129. Tel. (215) 438-6580

Lutheran Forum (q), Luth., Glenn C. Stone, 155 E. 22nd St., New York, NY 10010. Tel. (212) 254-4640

Lutheran Standard (s-m), Am. Luth., Lowell G. Almen, 426 S. 5th St., Minneapolis, MN 55415. Tel. (612) 332-4561

Lutheran Witness (m), Luth., Mo, Synod, George W. Wittmer, Interim, 3558 S. Jefferson Ave., St. Louis, MO 63118. Tel. (314) 664-7000

Maryknoll (m), Cath., Darryl Hunt, Maryknoll Fathers, Maryknoll, NY 10545. Tel. (914) 941-7590

Message Magazine, The (bi-m), Seventh-day Adv., Louis B. Reynolds, P. O. Box 59, Nashville, TN 37202

Messenger (m), Ch. Breth., Kermon Thomasson, Ch. Breth., 1451 Dundee Ave., Elgin, IL 60120. Tel. (312) 742-5100

Messenger, The (formerly **New-Church Messenger**) (m), Swedenborgian, Paul B. Zacharias, Box 2642, Sta. B., Kitchener, Ontario N2H 6N2. Tel. (519) 743-3845

Methodist Christian Advocate, The (w), U. Meth., Herschel T. Hamner, 1100 Campus Circle, Birmingham, AL 35204. Tel. (205) 251-5508

Mid-Stream (q), Chr. Ch. (Disc.), Paul A. Crow, Jr., P. O. Box 1986 Indianapolis, IN 46206. Tel. (317) 353-1491

Mission Herald (bi-m), Natl. Bapt., Wm. J. Harvey, III, 701 S. 19th St., Philadelphia, PA 19146

Missionary Monthly (m), Chr. Ref. and Ref. Ch. Dick L. Van Halsema, 1869 Robinson Rd., S. E. (P.O. Box 6181), Grand Rapids, MI 49506. Tel. (616) 458-0404

Missionary Seer, The (m), A.M.E. Zion, Harold, A. L. Clement, 475 Riverside Dr., Ste. 1910 New York, NY 10027. Tel. (212) 749-2953

Mississippi United Methodist Advocate (w), U. Meth., G. Roy Lawrence P. O. Box 1093, Jackson, MS 39205. Tel. (601) 354-0515

Monitor (w), Cath., John P. Penebsky, 441 Church St., San Francisco, CA 94114. Tel. (415) 626-7200

Moody Monthly (m), interdenom., Jerry B. Jenkins, 2101 W. Howard St., Chicago, IL 60645. Tel. (312) 274-2535

Muslim World (q), undenom., Willem A. Bijlefeld, Duncan Black Macdonald Center, Hartford Seminary Foundation, 77 Sherman St., Hartford, CT 06105. Tel. (203) 232-4451

National Catholic Reporter (w, Sept.-May; bi-w, June-Aug.), Cath., Jason Petosa, P. O. Box 281, Kansas City, MO 64141. Tel. (816) 531-0538

New Catholic World (bi-m), Cath., Robert J. Heyer, 1865 Broadway, New York, NY 10023, Tel. (212) 265-8181

New Oxford Review (10/yr.), Epis., Robert S. Morse, 6013 Lawton Ave., Oakland, CA 94618. Tel. (415) 655-4951

New World Outlook (m), U. Meth., Arthur J. Moore, 475 Riverside Dr., New York, NY 10027. Tel. (212) 678-6050

North American Moravian, The (m), Morav., Bernard E. Michel, 5 W. Market St., Bethlehem, PA 18018. Tel. (215) 867-0593

North Carolina Christian Advocate (w), U. Meth., C. A. Simonton, Jr., P. O. Box 508, Greensboro, NC 27402. Tel. (919) 272-1196

Orthodox Observer, The (bi-w), Greek Orth., P. J. Gazouleas, 8 E. 79th St., New York, NY 10021. Tel. (212) 628-2590

Our Sunday Visitor (w), Cath., Albert J. Nevins, Noll Plaza, Huntington, IN 46750. Tel. (219) 356-8400

Pastoral Life (m), Cath., Victor L. Viberti, Canfield, OH 44406. Tel. (216) 533-5503

PCA Messenger, The (m), Presby. Ch. in Am., 4319-F Memorial Dr., Decatur, GA 30032. Tel. (404) 292-6102.

Pentecostal Evangel (w), Assem. of God, Robert C. Cunningham, 1445 Boonville Ave., Springfield, MO 65802. Tel. (417) 862-2781

Pilot, The (w), Cath. John J. Grant, 49 Franklin St., Boston, MA 02110. Tel. (617) 482-4316

Presbyterian Journal, The (w), indept., G. Aiken Taylor, Box 3108, Asheville, NC 28802. Tel. (704) 254-4015

Presbyterian Layman, The (10/yr.), Presbyterian Lay Committee, James J. Cochran, 1727 Delancey Pl., Philadelphia, PA 19103. Tel. (215) 545-3308

Presbyterian Outlook (w), Presb. US and U. Presb. Ch. USA, George L. Hunt, 512 E. Main St., Richmond, VA 23219. Tel. (804) 649-1371

Presbyterian Survey (m), Presb. US, William P. Lamkin, 341 Ponce de Leon Ave., N.E., Atlanta, GA 30308

Providence Visitor (w), Cath., Robert F. Baldwin, 184 Broad St., Providence, RI 02903. Tel. (401) 272-1010

Pulpit Digest, The (bi-m), interdonom., Charles L. Wallis, Keuka College, Keuka Park, NY 14478. Tel. (315) 536-6454

Quaker Life (m), Friends United Mtg., Jack Kirk, 101 Quaker Hill Dr., Richmond, IN 47374. Tel. (317) 962-7573

Quarterly Review, The (q), S. Bapt., Marguerite S. Babb, 127 Ninth Ave., N., Nashville, TN 37234. Tel. (615) 251-2044

Reform Judaism (6/yr.), Ref. Jewish, Aron Hirt-Manheimer, 838 Fifth Ave., New York, NY 10021. Tel. (212) 249-0100

Religion in Life (q), interdenom., Ronald P. Patterson, 201 8th Ave., S., Nashville, TN 37202

Religious Broadcasting (bi-m), National Religious Broadcasters, Ben Armstrong, Box 2254R, Morristown, NJ 07960. Tel. (201) 540-8500

Religious Education (bi-m), multi-faith, John H. Westerhoff, III, Duke Divinity School, Durham, NC 27706. Tel. (919) 684-4035

Resources for Youth Ministry (q), Luth., Mo. Synod, C. Leo Symmank, 500 N. Broadway, St. Louis, MO 63102. Tel. (314) 231-6969

response (m), U. Meth., Carol Marie Herb, 475 Riverside Dr., Rm. 1323, New York, NY 10027. Tel. (212) 678-6116

Restoration Herald (m), Christian Churches, Ch. of Christ, H. Sherwood Evans, 5664 Cheviot Rd., Cincinnati, OH 45239. Tel. (513) 385-0461

Review for Religious (bi-m), Cath., Daniel F. X. Meenan, 3601 Lindell Blvd., St. Louis, MO 63108

Review of Religious Research (3/yr.), The Religious Research Assoc., James D. Davidson, Dept. of Sociology and Anthropology, Purdue Univ., West Lafayette, IN 47907. Tel. (317) 749-2723

Sabbath Recorder (m), Seventh Day Bapt., John D. Bevis, 510 Watchung Ave., Plainfield, NJ 07061. Tel. (201) 561-8700

Saint Anthony Messenger (m), Cath., Jeremy Harrington, 1615 Republic St., Cincinnati, OH 45210. Tel. (513) 241-5616

Saints' Herald (semi-m), Reorg. Ch. of Jesus Christ, L.D.S., Paul A. Wellington, Drawer HH, Independence, MO 64055

Sign, The (m), Cath., Patrick McDonough, Monastery Pl., Union City, NJ 07087. Tel. (201) 867-6400

Signs of the Times (m), Seventh-day Adv., Lawrence Maxwell, Pacific Press Pub. Assn., 1350 Villa, Mountain View, CA 94042. Tel. (415) 961-2323

Social Action News Letter (bi-m except July-Aug.), Chr. Ch. (Disc.) Ian J. McCrae, 222 S. Downey Ave., Box 1986, Indianapolis, IN 46206. Tel. (317) 353-1491

Social Questions Bulletin (bi-m), Methodist Fed. for Social Action (independent), Rev. George McClain, Shalom House, 76 Clinton Ave., Staten Island, NY 10301. Tel. (212) 273-4941

South Carolina United Methodist Advocate (w), U. Meth., Maryneal Jones, 1420 Lady St., P. O. Box 11589, Columbia, SC 29211. Tel. (803) 779-9627

Southern New England United Methodist Reporter (w), U. Meth.; T. C. Whitehouse, 581 Boylston St., Boston, MA 02116. Tel. (617) 266-3900

Southwestern News (m, except Aug.), S. Bapt., John Earl Seelig, Southwestern Bapt. Theol. Sem., Box 22,000-3E, Fort Worth, TX 76122

Spirituality Today (q), Cath., Christopher Kiesling, Aquinas Institute of Theology, Dubuque, IA 52001. Tel. (319) 556-7593

Standard, The (m), Bapt. Gen. Conf., Donald E. Anderson, 1233 Central St., Evanston, IL 60201

Star of Zion (w), A.M.E. Zion, M. B. Robinson, P.O. Box 1047, Charlotte, NC 28231. Tel. (704) 377-4329

Sunday (q), interdenom., James P. Wesberry, Ste. 107, 2930 Flowers Rd., S., Atlanta, GA 30341. Tel. (404) 451-7315

Tablet, The (w), Cath., Don Zirkel, 1 Hanson Pl., Brooklyn, NY 11243. Tel. (212) 789-1500

Texas Methodist, The/United Methodist Reporter (w), U. Meth., Spurgeon M. Dunnam, III, P. O. Box 221076, Dallas, TX 75221. Tel. (214) 630-6495

Theological Education (semi-a), undenom., Jesse H. Ziegler, Association of Theological Schools in the United States and Canada, P. O. Box 130, Vandalia, OH 45377

Theology Digest (q), Cath., Wendell Langley, 3634 Lindell Blvd., St. Louis, MO 63108, Tel. (314) 658-2857

Theology Today (q), undenom., Hugh T. Kerr, P. O. Box 29, Princeton, NJ 08540

These Times (m), Seventh-day Adv., K. J. Holland, P. O. Box 59, Nashville, TN 37202

Thought (q), Cath., G. Richard Dimler, Fordham Univ., Bronx, NY 10458. Tel. (212) 933-2233, X 270

Tidings, The (w), Cath., Alphonse J. Antczak, 1530 W. Ninth St., Los Angeles, CA 90015. Tel. (213) 385-3101

Tradition (4/Yr.), Jewish (Rabbinical Council of America), W. S. Wurzburger, 1250 Broadway, Ste. 802, New York, NY 10001. Tel. (212) 594-3780

UCC Network (12/yr.), Office for Church in Society, UCC, Paul L. Kittlaus, 110 Maryland Ave. N.E., Washington, DC 20002. Tel. (202) 543-1517

Unitarian Universalist World (16/yr.), Doris L. Pullen, 25 Beacon St., Boston, MA 02108

United Evangelical, The (m), Evang. Congreg. Ch., Ronald B. Kuntz, E. C. Church Center, 100 W. Park Ave., Myerstown, PA 17067. Tel. (717) 866-2181

United Evangelical Action (q), interdenom., Harold B. Smith, 350 S. Main Pl., P. O. Box 28, Wheaton, IL 60187. Tel. (312) 665-0500

U.S. Catholic (m), Cath., Mark J. Brummel, 221 W. Madison St., Chicago, IL 60606. Tel. (312) 236-7782

Virginia Advocate (w), U. Meth., W. Hewlett Stith, 4016 W. Broad St., Rm. 208, P. O. Box 11367, Richmond, VA 23230. Tel. (804) 359-9451

Vital Christianity (bi-w), Ch. of God (Anderson, Ind.), Arlo F. Newell, Box 2499, Anderson, IN 46011. Tel. (317) 644-7721

Voice of Missions (m, except July and Aug.), Afr. Meth. Epis., John W. P. Collier, Jr., 475 Riverside Dr., Rm. 1926, New York, NY 10027. Tel. (212) 864-2471

War Cry, The (w), Salv. Army, Lt. Ralph I. Miller, 120 W. 14th St., New York, NY 10011. Tel. (212) 691-8780

Wesleyan Christian Advocate (w), U. Meth., William M. Holt, 501 Methodist Center, 159 Forrest Ave., N. E., Atlanta, GA 30308. Tel. (404) 659-7620

Western Recorder (w), S. Bapt., C. R. Daley, Box 43401, Middletown, KY 40243

White Wing Messenger, The (w), Ch. of God of Prophecy, M. A. Tomlinson, Bible Pl., Cleveland, TN 37311

Woman's Pulpit, The (q), undenom., (International Assoc. of Women Ministers), LaVonne Althouse, 5227 Castor Ave., Philadelphia, PA 19124

Word and Work (m), undenom., William Robert Heid, 2518 Portland Ave., Louisville, KY 40212

World Vision (m), undenom., David Olson, 919 W. Huntington Dr., Monrovia, CA 91016. Tel. (213) 357-1111

Worldview (m, except July/Aug. and Jan/Feb.), Council on Religion and International Affairs, James Finn, 170 E. 64th St., New York, NY 10021. Tel. (212) 838-4120

Worship (6/yr.) Cath., Aelred Tegels, St. John's Abbey, Collegeville, MN 56321. Tel. (612) 363-3765

Your Church (bi-m), undenom., Phyllis Mather Rice, 198 Allendale Rd., King of Prussia, PA 19406

Youth (m), U. Ch. of Christ, Epis. Ch., Anglican Ch. of Canada, U. Presb. Ch. USA, Amer. Luth. Ch., Moravian Ch., Luth. Ch. in Am., Presby. Ch. in the U.S., Am. Bapt. Chs. in the USA, Cumberland Presby. Ch. Christian Church (Disciples of Christ), Un. Ch. of Canada, Herman C. Ahrens, Jr., 1505 Race St., Philadelphia, PA 19102. Tel. (215) 568-3950

12. RELIGIOUS PERIODICALS IN CANADA

The religious periodicals below constitute a basic core of important newspapers and periodicals circulated in Canada. For additional publications treating religion in Canada, the reader should check the denominational directories in this **Yearbook** in the section entitled "Religious Bodies in Canada." Details on other religious periodicals circulating in Canada can also be found in the section "Religious Periodicals in the United States" in this **Yearbook.**

Each entry lists, in order: Title of periodical, frequency of publication, religious affiliation, editor's name, address, and telephone number.

Advance (bi-m), Associated Gospel Churches, Donald C. Ralph, 47 Garside Ave., N., Hamilton, Ontario L8H 7K6. Tel. (416) 549-4516

Atlantic Baptist (m), Un. Bapt. Conv. of the Atlantic Provinces, George E. Simpson, Box 756, Kentville, Nova Scotia B4N 3X9. Tel. (902) 678-6868

B.C. Ecumenical News (7/yr.), Val. J. Anderson, 1811 W. 16th Ave., Vancouver, British Columbia V6J 2M3. Tel. (604) 736-1613

B. C. Regular Baptist (m), Conv. of Reg. Bapt. Churches of B. C., Donald W. Reed 3358 S. E. Marine Dr., Vancouver, British Columbia V5S 3W3. Tel. (604) 437-5426

Berean Ambassador, The, Rev. J. R. Boyd, P. O. Box 232, Sudbury, Ontario P3E 4N5

British Columbia Catholic, The (w), Cath., 150 Robson St., Vancouver, British Columbia V6B 2A7

Calvinist-Contact (w), Reformed, Keith Knight, 99 Niagara St., St. Catharines, Ontario L2R 4L3. Tel. (416) 682-5614

Canadian Baptist, The (m), Bapt. Conv. of Ontario and Quebec and Bapt. Un. of Western Canada, William H. Jones, 217 St. George St., Toronto, Ontario M5R 2M2. Tel. (416) 922-5163

Canadian Christian Harbinger, CC/CC, Don Lewis, Box 460, Vernon, British Columbia V1T 6M4

Canadian Churchman (m), Ang. Ch. of Canada, Jerrold F. Hames, 600 Jarvis St., Toronto, Ontario M4Y 2J6. Tel. (416) 924-9192

Canadian Disciple, Chr. Ch. (Disc.) Margaret Hutchinson, 39 Arkell Rd., RR. 2, Guelph, Ontario N1H 6H8. Tel. (519) 823-5190

Canadian Free Methodist Herald, The (11 times a year), Free Methodist, Claude A. Horton, 833 D Upper James St., Hamilton, Ontario L9C 3A3

Catholic New Times (bi-w), Cath., Jack Costello, 80 Sackville St., Toronto, Ontario M5A 3E5. Tel. (416) 361-0761

Catholic Register, The (incorporating Canadian Register), (w), Cath., Larry Henderson, 67 Bond St., Toronto, Ontario M5B 1X6. Tel. (416) 362-6822

Christian Communication (6/yr). Cath., 223 Main St., Ottawa, Ontario K1S 1C4

Clarion, The Canadian Reformed Magazine (bi-w), Canadian Ref. Churches, William VanOene, Box 54, Fergus, Ontario N1M 2W7. Tel. (519) 843-1693

Credo (French m), Gérard Gautier, Église Unie du Canada, 3480, boul. Décarie, Montreál, Québec H4A 3J5. Tél. (514) 486-9213

Direction (q), Canadian and U.S. Mennonite Brethren Colleges and Seminary, Elmer Martens, 77 Henderson Hwy., Winnipeg, Manitoba R2L 1L1

Encounter (bi-m), transdenom., Robert N. Thompson, Box 100, Milton, Ontario L9T 2Y3. Tel. (416) 878-8461

Evangelical Baptist (m), Fellowship of Evan. Bapt. Churches in Canada, 74 Sheppard Ave., W., Willowdale, Ontario M2N 1M3. Tel. (416) 223-8696

Evangelical Recorder (q), nondenom., Douglas C. Percy, 25 Ballyconnor Ct., Willowdale, Ontario M2M 4B3. Tel. (416) 226-6380

Faith Today (bi-m), nondenom., Keith Neely, P. O. Box 103, Sta. D, Scarborough, Ontario M1R 4Y7. Tel. (416) 495-9644

Gospel Herald (m), Chs. of Christ, Roy D. Merritt, P. O. Box 94, Beamsville, Ontario L0R 1B0. Tel. (416) 653-7503

Gospel Standard, The (m), Fundamental, Perry F. Rockwood, P. O. Box 1660, Halifax, Nova Scotia B3J 3A1. Tel. (902) 423-5540

Gospel Witness, The (bi-w), Bapt., Eric T. Gurr, 130 Gerrard St., E., Toronto, Ontario M5A 3T4. Tel. (416) 925-3261

Guide, The (10/yr.), Organ of the Christian Labour Assoc. of Canada, Edward Vanderkloet, 1919 Weston Rd., Weston, Ontario M9N 1W7. Tel. (416) 249-3369

Mennonite, The (w), Gen. Conf. Menn., Bernie Wiebe, 600 Shaftesbury Blvd., Winnipeg, Manitoba R3P 0M4. Tel. (204) 888-6781

Mennonite Brethren Herald (fortnightly), Menn. Br., Harold Jantz, 159 Henderson Hwy., Winnipeg, Manitoba R2L 1L4. Tel. (204) 667-3560

Mennonite Reporter (bi-w), Menn., Ron Rempel, Waterloo, Ontario N2L 3G6. Tel. (519) 884-3810

Monitor, The (m), Cath., Gregory L. Hogan, P. O. Box 986, St. John's, Newfoundland, A1C 5M3. Tel. (709) 722-7700

New Freeman, The (w), Cath., Robert G. Merzetti, Box 6609, Sta. A, Saint John, New Brunswick E2L 4S1. Tel. (506) 652-3667

News of Quebec (q), Brethren, Arnold Reynolds, P. O. Box 420, Lennonxville, Quebec J1M 1Z6, Tel. (819) 562-0131

Pentecostal Testimony, The (m), Pent. Assem. of Canada, Joy E. Hansell, 10 Overlea Blvd., Toronto, Ontario M4H 1A5. Tel. (416) 425-1010

Peoples Magazine, The, Paul B. Smith, 374 Sheppard Ave., E., Toronto, Ontario M2N 3B6. Tel. (416) 222-3341

Prairie Messenger (w), Cath., Br. Bede Hubbard, Box 10, Muenster, Saskatchewan S0K 2Y0.

Prairie Overcomer, The (m), nondenom., T. S. Rendall, Prairie Bible Institute, Three Hills, Alberta T0M 2A0. Tel. (403) 443-5511

Presbyterian Record (m), Presb. Ch. in Canada, James R. Dickey, 50 Wynford Dr., Don Mills, Ontario M3C 1J7. Tel. (416) 441-1111

Relations (m), Cath., Pères de la Compagnie de Jésus, 8100 Boul. St.-Laurent, Montréal, Québec H2P 2L9

Researcher, The (q), nondenom., Rev. J. R. Boyd, P. O. Box 232, Sudbury, Ontario P3E 4N5

Shepherd, The (m), Ev. Luth Ch., Oscar Sommerfeld, 247-1st Ave. N., Saskatoon, Saskatchewan S7K 4H5. Tel. (306) 653-0133

SR (Studies in Religion/Sciences religieuses), undenom., Charles Davis, Dept. of Religious Studies, Concordia College, 7128 Ada Blvd., Edmonton, Alberta T5B 4E4. Tel. (403) 479-8481

Thrust (q), Ev. Fell. of Canada, Box 8800, Station B, Willowdale, Ontario M2K 2R6. Tel. (416) 497-4796

United Church Observer (m), Un. Ch. of Canada. Hugh McCullum, 85 St. Clair Ave., E., Toronto, Ontario M4T 1M8. Tel. (416) 925-5931

Vanguard (bi-m), undenom., Bert Witvoet, Box 1084, Sta. B, Rexdale, Ontario M9V 2B3. Tel. (416) 851-3288

La Vie Chrétienne (French m), Presby. Ch. in Canada, Jean Perret, 2302 Goyer, Montréal, Québec H3S 1G9. Tel. (514) 737-4168

War Cry (w), Salvation Army in Canada, Maj. Dudley Coles, 455 N. Service Rd., Oakville, Ontario L6L 1A5. Tel. (416) 845-9235

Western Catholic Reporter (w), Cath., V. A. Misutka, 10562-109 St., Edmonton, Alberta T5H 3B2. Tel. (403) 420-1330

13. UNITED STATES SERVICE AGENCIES: SOCIAL, CIVIC, RELIGIOUS

The Yearbook of American and Canadian Churches offers the following selected list of Service Agencies for two purposes. The first purpose is to direct attention to a number of major agencies which can provide resources of information and service to the churches. No attempt is made to produce a complete listing of such agencies. The second purpose is to illustrate the types of resources that are available. There are many agencies providing services which can be of assistance to local, regional or national church groups. It is suggested that a valuable tool in locating such service agencies is *The Encyclopedia of Associations,* Vol. I, National Organizations of the United States. The organizations are cross-referenced and the volume is in most libraries. It is published by Gale Research Co., Book Tower, Detroit, Michigan 48226.

ADRIS (Association for the Development of Religious Information Systems): Dept. of Sociology and Anthropology, Marquette Univ., Milwaukee, WI 53233. Tel. (414) 224-6838. Coordinator, Dr. David O. Moberg; Ed., Rev. Richard F. Smith, Dept. of Theology, Fordham Univ., Bronx, NY 10458. Tel. (212) 933-2233
Periodical: ADRIS Newsletter.

Adult Education Association of the U.S.A.: 810-18th St. N.W., Washington, DC 20006. Tel. (202) 347-9574. Pres., Violet Malone, Exec. Dir., Linda S. Hartsock
Periodicals: Adult Education (4/yr.); Lifelong Learning: The Adult Years (m, except July and Aug.)

American Academy of Political and Social Science, The: 3937 Chestnut St., Philadelphia, PA 19104. Tel. (215) 386-4594. Pres., Marvin E. Wolfgang
Periodical: The Annals of the American Academy of Political and Social Science (bi-m)

American Association of Bible Colleges: P. O. Box 1523, Fayetteville, AR 72701. Tel. (501) 521-8164. Exec. Dir., John Mostert

American Association of Retired Persons: 1909 K St., N.W., Washington, DC 20049. Tel. (202) 872-4700. Pres., J. Leonard Johnson Exec., Dir., Cyril F. Brickfield
Periodicals: AARP News Bulletin (m); Modern Maturity (bi-m); Dynamic Years (bi-m)

American Civil Liberties Union: 22 East 40th St., New York, NY 10016. Tel. (212) 725-1222. Chmn. of Bd., Norman Dorsen; Exec. Dir., Ira Glasser
Periodical: Civil Liberties (m).

American Council on Alcohol Problems: 119 Constitution Ave., N.E., Washington, DC 20002. Tel. (202) 543-2441. Exec. Dir., William N. Plymat. Ofc. of Exec. Dir.: 6955 University Ave., Des Moines, IA 50311

American Farm Bureau Federation: 225 Touhy Ave., Park Ridge, IL 60068. Washington office, 425 13th St., N.W., Washington, DC 20004. Pres., Allan Grant; Sec. and Admin., John C. Datt; Treas., William H. Broderick.
Periodical: Farm Bureau News(w)

American Federation of Labor and Congress of Industrial Organizations, Department of Education: AFL-CIO Bldg., 815 16th St., N.W., Washington, DC 20006; Dir., Walter G. Davis

American Friends Service Committee: 1501 Cherry St., Philadelphia, PA 19102. Tel. (215) 241-7000. Chmn., Stephen G. Cary; Exec. Sec., Louis W. Schneider
Periodical: Quaker Service Bulletin (3/yr.)

American Library Association: 50 E. Huron St., Chicago, IL 60611. Tel. (312) 944-6780. Exec Dir., Robert Wedgeworth
Periodicals: American Libraries (m except bi-m July-Aug.); Booklist (semi-m); Choice (m); College and Research Libraries (bi-m); ALA Washington Newsletter (m), Journal of Library Automation (q); Library Resources and Technical Services (q); RQ: School Media Quarterly (q); Top of the News (q)

American Medical Association: 535 N. Dearborn St., Chicago, IL 60610. Tel. (312) 751-6000. Pres., Hoyt D. Gardner, M.D.; Exec. Vice-Pres., James H. Sammons, M.D.
Periodicals: The Journal of the American Medical Association (w); The Citation (bi-w); American Medical News (w); Specialty Scientific Journals (m); Computers and Medicine (bi-m); Legislative Roundup (w); Facets (q)

American Red Cross, The: 17th & D Sts., N.W., Washington, DC 20006. Chmn., Jerome H. Holland; Pres., George M. Elsey
Periodical: The Good Neighbor (bi-m)

American Protestant Hospital Association: 1 Woodfield Pl., 1701 E. Woodfield Rd., Ste. 311, Schaumburg, IL 60195. Tel. (312) 843-2701. Pres. Charles D. Phillips.
Periodicals: Bulletin (4/yr); APHA Washington Watch (m)

American Public Health Association: 1015 18th St., N.W., Washington, DC 20036. Exec. Dir., Wiliam H. McBeath, M.D.
Periodical: American Journal of Public Health (m); Nation's Health (m)

American Public Welfare Association: 1125 15th St., N.W., Ste. 300, Washington, DC 20005. Tel. (202) 293-7550
Periodicals: Public Welfare (q); Washington Report (10/yr); W-Memo. (50-60/yr); Congressional Record Index; Directory (a)

Americans United for Separation of Church and State: 8120 Fenton St., Silver Spring, MD 20910. (Tel. (301) 589-3707. Exec. Dir., Richard G. Puckett; Ed., Edd Doerr
Periodical: Church & State (m)

Association for Clinical Pastoral Education: 475 Riverside Dr., Suite 450, New York, NY 10027. Tel. (212) 870-2558. Exec. Dir., Charles E. Hall, Jr.
Periodical: Journal of Pastoral Care (q)

Association of Jewish Chaplains of the Armed Forces: 15 E. 26th St., New York, NY 10010. Tel. (212) 532-4949. Pres., Joseph I. Weiss

Association of Regional Religious Communicators: c/o Ecumenical Communications Commission, P.O. Box 351, 105 Louisiana Ave., Perrysburg, OH 43551. Tel. (419) 874-3932. Periodical: Newsletter; The Olive Branch (q)

Association of Theological Schools in the United States and Canada: P.O. Box 130, Vandalia, OH 45377. Pres., James I. McCord, Princeton Theological Seminary, Princeton, NJ 08540. Exec. Dir., Jesse H. Ziegler; Asso. Dirs., David S. Schuller, and Marvin J. Taylor

Baptist Joint Committee on Public Affairs: 200 Maryland Ave., N.E., Washington, DC 20002. Tel. (202) 544-4226. Exec. Dir., James E. Wood, Jr.
Periodical: Report from the Capital (10/yr.)

B'nai B'rith International: B'nai B'rith Bldg., 1640 Rhode Island Ave., N. W., Washington, DC 20036. Tel. (202) 857-6600. Pres., Jack Spitzer; Exec. Vice-Pres., Daniel Thursz
Periodical: The National Jewish Monthly

Boy Scouts of America: P. O. Box 61030, Dallas/Ft. Worth

Airport, TX 75261. Pres., Downing Jenks; Chief Scout Exec., James L. Tarr
Periodicals: Scouting Magazine (8 issues a year); Boy's Life (m); Exploring Magazine (6 issues a year); Scouting Bulletin of the Catholic Committee on Scouting (q); Ner Tamid News Bulletin (a)

Boys' Clubs of America: 771 First Ave., New York, NY 10017. Tel. (212) 557-7755. Chmn. of Bd., Albert L. Cole; Pres., John L. Burns; Nat'l. Dir., William R. Bricker
Periodicals: Keynote of Boys' Club of America (q); National Directors Report (q); Accountability Update (q)

Camp Fire Girls, Inc.: 4601 Madison Ave., Kansas City, MO 64112, Tel. (816) 756-1950. Natl. Exec. Dir., Roberta van der Voort
Periodical: Camp Fire Leadership (q)

CARE (Cooperative for American Relief Everywhere, Inc.): 660 First Ave., New York, NY 10016, Tel. (212) 686-3110. Exec. Dir., Louis Samia

Center for Applied Research in the Apostolate (CARA): 3700 Oakview Terr., NE, Washington, DC 20017. Tel. (202) 832-2300. Exec. Dir., John V. O'Connor; Dir of Res., Edward M. Sullivan

Committee of Southern Churchmen, The: P.O. Box 140215, Nashville, TN 37214. Pres., Gideon Fryer; Dir., Will D. Campbell

CONTACT Teleministries USA, Inc.: 900 S. Arlington Ave., Rm. 125, Harrisburg, PA 17109. Tel. (717) 652-3410. Exec. Dir., Robert E. Larson, Jr.

Cooperative League of the U.S.A.: Pres. Glenn Anderson, 1828 L St., N.W., Washington DC 20036. Tel. (202) 872-0550. Dir. of Information, Eugene Clifford
Periodical: In League (m)

Council of the Southern Mountains, Inc.: Drawer N. Clintwood, VA 24228. Tel. (703) 926-4495
Periodical: Mountain Life and Work (m)

Council on Religion and International Affairs: 170 E. 64th St., New York, NY 10021. Tel. (212) 838-4120. Chmn., Jerald C. Brauer; Exec. Dir., Toni Greenberg; Pres., vacant
Periodicals: Worldview (m); Ethics and Foreign Policy;

Counselor Association, Inc., The: 31 Langerfeld Rd., Hillsdale, NJ 07642. Tel. (201) 664-8890. Pres., Raymond B. Knudsen, Ste. 456, 475 Riverside Dr., New York, NY 10027, Tel. (212) 749-1304

Credit Union National Association: P.O. Box 431, Madison, WI 53701. Tel. (608) 241-1211
Periodicals: Credit Union Magazine (m); Everybody's Money (q); Credit Union Executive (q); Yearbook (a)

Ecumenical Institute: 3444 Congress Pkwy., Chicago, IL 60624. Tel. (312) 769-6363. Pres., David P. Wood, Jr.; Dean, Joseph W. Mathews

Fellowship of Reconciliation, The: Box 271, Nyack, NY 10960. Tel. (914) 358-4601. Chmn., William O. Walker; Exec. Sec., Richard L. Deats
Periodicals: Fellowship (m); Local Motion (q)

Foreign Policy Association: 205 Lexington Ave., New York, NY 10016. Tel. (212) 481-8450. Chpsn., Carter L. Burgess
Periodicals: Headline Series (5/yr.); Great Decisions Book (a)

Friends Committee on National Legislation: 245 Second St., N.E., Washington, DC 20002. Tel. (202) 547-4343. Clerk, of Gen. Comm., Ralph Rudd; Exec. Sec., Edward F. Snyder
Periodical: FCNL Washington Newsletter (m)

General Federation of Women's Clubs: 1734 N St., N.W., Washington, DC 20036. Tel. (202) 347-3168. Pres., Mrs. A. M. Quint.
Periodical: General Federation Clubwoman Magazine

Girl Scouts of the U.S.A.: 830 Third Ave., New York, NY 10022. Tel. (212) 940-7500. Pres., Mrs. Orville L. Freeman; Nat'l. Exec. Dir., Mrs. Frances R. Hesselbein
Periodicals: Girl Scout Leader (7/yr); Daisy (9/yr)

Glenmary Research Center: 4606 East-West Hwy., Washington, DC 20014. Tel. (301) 654-7501. Dir., Rev. Bernard Quinn

Institute of International Education: 809 United Nations Plaza, New York, NY 10017. Tel. (212) 883-8200. Pres., Wallace B. Edgerton

Institutes of Religion and Health: 3 W. 29th St., New York, NY 10001. Tel. (212) 725-7850. Pres., Philip D. Baker.

Interreligious Foundation for Community Organization: 348 Convent Ave., New York, NY 10031. Tel. (212) 926-5757. Exec. Dir., Lucius Walker
Periodical: IFCO News (q)

Japan International Christian University Foundation, Inc., The: 475 Riverside Dr., Rm. 720, New York, NY 10027. Tel. (212) 870-2893. Pres., David H. C. Read; Chmn, Exec. Comm., Paul R. Gregory; Exec. Dir., Ruth L. Miller

John Milton Society for the Blind: A Worldwide Ministry, 29 W. 34th St., New York, NY 10001. Tel. (212) 736-4162. Gen. Sec., Chenoweth J. Watson
Periodicals (in Braille); John Milton Magazine, for Adults (m); Discovery, for Boys and Girls (m); John Milton Sunday School Quarterly (q)
Periodicals (recorded): John Milton Talking Book Magazine (bi-m); John Milton Recorded Sunday School Lessons (q). Other Recorded Publications: Memorial Talking Book Edition of New English Bible-New Testament: Paul—an Ambassador for Christ
Periodicals (in large type): John Milton Magazine-Large Type Edition (m); World Day of Prayer (a)
All publications free on request to persons who cannot see to read ordinary printed matter

LAOS, Inc.: 4920 Piney Branch Rd., N.W., Washington, DC 20011. Chpsn., Walter C. Baugh; Exec. Dir., Tom Boone
Periodicals: Conversations, Concerns and Challenges (4 times a year)

League of Women Voters of the U.S.: 1730 M St., N.W., Washington, DC 20036. Tel. (202) 296-1770. Pres., Ruth J. Hinerfeld
Periodical: The National Voter (q)

Lutheran Church Library Association: 122 West Franklin Ave., Minneapolis, MN 55404. Tel. (612) 870-3623. Exec. Dir., Wilma W. Jensen.
Periodicals: Lutheran Libraries (q)

Lutheran Resources Commission–Washington: Dupont Circle Bldg., Suite 823, 1346 Connecticut Ave., N.W., Washington, DC 20036. Tel. (202) 872-0110. Chpsn., Kenneth C. Senft, Luther. Ch. in Am.: Vice-Chpsns., Leslie F. Weber, Luth. Ch.–Mo. Synod and Dr. Melvin A. Bucka; Treas., Floyd D. Peterson. Luth. Ch. in Am.; Exec. Dir., Lloyd Foerster, Washington, DC.
(A grants consultation agency serving units of the Lutheran Church bodies, the Presbyterian Church in the U.S. and the National Benevolent Association, Christian Church (Disciples of Christ) to help develop resources for social progress.)

Mental Health Association, The: 1800 N. Kent St., Rosslyn, VA 22209.

National Association of Church Business Administrators, Inc.: Box 7181, Kansas City, MO 64113. Tel. (913) 236-9571. Exec. Dir., Floy Barnes; Pres., Victor E.

Criswell, Country Club Christian Church, 6101 Ward Pkwy., Kansas City, MO 64113

National Association of Human Rights Workers (NAHRW): Rm. 612, City Hall Annex, Philadelphia, PA 19107. Tel. (215) 686-4678. Pres., Lary Groth

National Assoc. of Pastoral Musicians: 1029 Vermont Ave., N.W., Washington, DC 20005. Tel. (202) 347-6673. Pres., Rev. Virgil C. Funk
Periodical: Pastoral Music (6/yr)

National Association of Social Workers, Inc.: Southern Bldg., 1425 H St., N.W., Washington, DC 20005. Pres., Nancy A. Humphreys; Exec. Dir., Chauncey A. Alexander

National Association for the Advancement of Colored People: 1790 Broadway, New York, NY 10019. Tel. (212) 245-2100. Pres., Dr. Montague Cobb; Exec. Dir., Benjamin L. Hooks; Chpsn. of the Bd., Margaret Bush Wilson
Periodical: Crisis (10/yr.)

National Catholic Educational Association: One Dupont Circle, N.W., Washington, DC 20036. Tel. (202) 293-5954. Pres., John F. Meyers
Periodical: Momentum

National Conference of Black Churchmen: P.O. Box 92190, Atlanta, GA 30314. Tel. (404) 524-8010. Exec. Dir., Mance Jackson

National Conference of Christians and Jews: 43 W. 57th St., New York, NY 10019. Tel. (212) 688-7530. Pres., David Hyatt

National Consumers League: 1522 K St., NW, Ste 406, Washington, DC 20005. Tel. (202) 797-7600. Pres., Erma Angevine; Exec. Vice Pres., Sandra L. Willett, Publications: Bulletin (bi-m) Newsletter

National Consultation on Financial Development, 31 Langerfeld Rd., Hillsdale, NJ 07642. Tel. (201) 664-8890. Pres., Raymond B. Knudsen, Ste. 456, 475 Riverside Dr., New York, NY 10027. Tel. (212) 749-1304.

National Council on Alcoholism: 733 Third Ave., New York, NY 10017. Tel. (212) 986-4433, Exec. Dir., George C. Dimas; Founder-Consultant, Mrs. Marty Mann.
Periodicals: Friday Letter (m).

National Council on Crime and Delinquency: 411 Hackensack Ave., Hackensack, NJ 07601. Chpsn., Arthur S. Lane; Pres., Milton G. Rector
Periodicals: Crime and Delinquency (q); Criminal Justice Newsletter (bi-w); Journal of Research in Crime and Delinquency :semi-a); Criminal Justice Abstracts (q)

National Education Association: 1201 16th St., N.W., Washington, DC 20036. Pres., Willard McGuire; Exec. Dir., Terry Herndon
Periodical: Today's Education (q)

National Farmers Union: 12025 E. 45th Ave., Denver, CO 80251. Tel. (303) 371-1760. Pres., Tony T. Dechant
Periodical: Washington Newsletter (w)

National Federation of Business and Professional Women's Clubs, Inc.: 2012 Massachusetts Ave., N.W., Washington, DC 20036. Tel. (202) 293-1100. Dir., Irma Finn Brosseau
Periodical: National Business Woman (m)

National Grange: 1616 H Street, N.W., Washington, DC 20006. Tel. (202) 628-3507. Master, John W. Scott

National Housing Conference: 1126 16th St., N.W., Washington, DC 20036. Tel. (202) 223-4844. Exec. Dir., Gene Schaefer

National Interreligious Task Force on Soviet Jewry: 1307 South Wabash Ave., #221, Chicago, IL 60605. Tel. (312) 922-1983. Exec. Dir., Sr. Ann Gillen

National PTA (National Congress of Parents and Teachers): 700 N. Rush St., Chicago, IL 60611. Tel. (312) 787-0997. Pres., Mrs. Virginia Sparling, 3271 Evergreen Point Rd., Bellevue, WA 98004

National Planning Association: 1606 New Hampshire Ave., N.W., Washington, DC 20009. Tel. (202) 265-7685. Chpsn., Walter Sterling Surrey; Pres. and Asst. Chpsn., Arthur J. R. Smith
Periodicals: Looking Ahead/Projection Highlights (q); New International Realities (q)

National Religious Broadcasters, Inc.: Box 2254 R, Morristown, NJ 07960. Tel. (201) 540-8500. Exec. Dir., Ben Armstrong

National Retired Teachers Association: 1909 K St., N.W., Washington, DC 20049. Tel. (202) 872-4700. Pres., Frank M. Hughes; Dir., Cyril F. Brickfield
Periodicals: NRTA News Bulletin (m); NRTA Journal (bi-m)

National Safety Council: 444 N. Michigan Ave., Chicago, IL 60611. Tel. (312) 527-4800. Pres., Vincent L. Tofany
Periodicals: National Safety News (m) Church in Safety Newsletter (q), Family Safety (m), Accident Facts (a), Industrial Supervisor (m)

National Urban League, Inc.: 500 E. 62nd St., New York, NY 10021. Tel. (212) 644-6500 Chmn. of Bd., Coy Ecklund; Pres., Vernon E. Jordan, Jr.

Planned Parenthood—World Population (Planned Parenthood Federation of America, Inc.): 810 Seventh Ave., New York, NY 10019. Tel. (212) 541-7800. Chpsn., Frederick C. Smith; Chpsn., Individual Rights Comm., Henry W. Foster, Jr.
Periodical: Family Planning Perspectives (bi-m); Washington Memo (20/yr.), PP News (5/yr.)

Protestant Health and Welfare Assembly: 1 Woodfield Pl., 1701 E. Woodfield Rd., Ste. 311, Schaumburg, IL 60195. Tel. (312) 843-2701. Exec. Sec., Charles D. Phillips

Protestant Radio and TV Center: 1727 Clifton Rd., N.E., Atlanta, GA 30329. Tel. (404) 634-3324. Pres., William Horlock

Public Affairs Committee: 381 Park Ave. So., New York, NY 10016. Tel. (212) 683-4331. Chmn., Maxwell Stewart; Ed. and Exec. Dir., Adele Braude
Publication: Public Affairs Pamphlets

Religious Education Association, The: 409 Prospect St., New Haven, CT 06510. Tel. (203) 865-6141. Pres., Emily V. Gibbes; Exec. Sec., Boardman W. Kathan; Chpsn. of Bd. David Wolf Silverman
Periodical: Religious Education (bi-m); Reach

Religious News Service: 43 W. 57th St., New York, NY 10019. Tel. (212) 688-7094. Ed.-in-Chief, Gerald A. Renner; Man. Ed., Gerald Fitzgerald

Religious Research Association, Inc.: P.O. Box 303, Manhattanville Station, New York, NY 10027; Pres., Dean R. Hoge; Treas., Edward A. Rauff; Sec., Constant H. Jacquet, Jr.
Periodical: Review of Religious Research (3/yr.)

Society for Values in Higher Education: 363 St. Ronan St., New Haven, CT 06511. Exec. Dir., David C. Smith

Southern Christian Leadership Conference: 334 Auburn Ave., N.E., Atlanta, GA 30312. Tel. (404) 522-1420. Pres. Joseph E. Lowery

Southern Regional Council: 3rd. Fl., 75 Marietta St., NW, Atlanta, GA 30303. Tel. (404) 522-8764. Pres., Julius L. Chambers Exec. Dir., Steve Suitts

United Ministries in Higher Education: 925 Chestnut St., 6th Fl., Philadelphia, PA 19107. Tel. (215) 546-2169. Int., Exec. Dir., A. Myrvin De Lapp

United Nations Association of the U.S.A.: 300 E. 42nd St., New York, NY 10017. Tel. (212) 697-3232. Chapters, Council of Organizations, Program consultation,

seminars, briefings. Chpsn. of the Assn., William W. Scranton; Chpsn., Bd. of Governors, Robert S. Benjamin; Pres., Robert M. Ratner
Periodicals: The Inter Dependant (m); Annual Program Manual: Reference Guide to the UN, Issues before the General Assembly (a), Fact Sheets and Program Kits on Issues

United Service Organizations, Inc.: 1146 19th St., NW, Washington, DC 20036. Tel. (202) 862-0700. Natl. Exec., Michael E. Menster

United Way of America.: 801 North Fairfax St., Alexandria, VA 22314. Tel. (703) 836-7100. Natl. Exec., William Aramony
Periodical: Community Focus (10/yr.)

Vellore Christian Medical College Board Inc.: 475 Riverside Dr., Rm. 243, New York, NY 10027. Tel. (212) 870-2642; Pres., George Varky; Exec. Dir., Herbert O. Muenstermann

Woman's Christian Temperance Union (National): 1730 Chicago Ave., Evanston, IL 60201. Tel. (312) 864-1396. Pres., Mrs. Herman Stanley
Periodicals: The Union Signal (m); The Young Crusader (m)

Women's International League for Peace and Freedom: 1213 Race St., Philadelphia, PA 19107. Tel. (215) 563-7110. Pres., Marjorie Boehm
Periodical: Peace and Freedom

World Conference on Religion and Peace: 777 United Nations Plaza, New York, NY 10017. Tel. (212) 687-2163. Sec.-Gen., Homer A, Jack. Periodical: Religion for Peace (occ.)

World Education, Inc.: 1414 Sixth Ave., New York, NY 10019. Tel. (212) 838-5255. Pres., Thomas B. Keehn; Chmn., Bd. of Trustees, Richmond Mayo-Smith
Periodicals: World Education Reports

World Peace Foundation: 22 Batterymarch St., Boston, MA 02109. Tel. (617) 482-3875. Dir., Alfred O. Hero, Jr.
Periodical: International Organization (q)

World Vision International: 919 W. Huntington Dr., Monrovia, CA 91016. Tel. (213) 357-7979. Pres., W. Stanley Mooneyham; Exec. Vice Pres., Ted W. Engstrom
Periodical: World Vision Magazine (m)

14. CANADIAN SERVICE AGENCIES: SOCIAL, CIVIC, RELIGIOUS

The following list of Canadian service agencies is offered for purposes of directing the reader's attention to a number of major Canadian agencies that can provide resources of information and service to the churches. No attempt is made to produce a complete listing of such agencies, and the reader is referred to the *Canadian Almanac and Directory for 1979* and The 1979 *Corpus Almanac of Canada* for comprehensive listings of Canadian organizations.

Listings are alphabetical by name of institution and generally have the following order: Name of institution, address, telephone number, principal officers, periodical.

Alcohol and Drug Concerns: Am. 603, 15 Gervais Dr., Don Mills, Ontario M3C 1Y8, Exec. Dir., Karl Burden. Tel. (416) 449-4933
Periodical: Concerns (q)

Alcoholics Anonymous: 272 Eglinton Ave., W., Toronto, Ontario M4R 1B2. (there are approx. 3,000 A.A. Groups in Canada). Correspondence to: Exec. Sec.

Association for the Advancement of Christian Scholarship, The: 229 College St., Toronto, Ontario M5T 1R4. Tel. (416) 979-2331. Exec. Dir., Robert VanderVennen
Periodical: Perspective Newsletter (bi-m); Anakainosis (q)

Association of Canadian Bible Colleges, The: Bethany Bible Inst. Hepburn, Saskatchewan S0K 1Z0 Sec. Treas., Isaac Bergen. Tel. (306) 947-2175
Periodical: Directory and Informational Survey of Member Schools (a)

Association of Universities and Colleges of Canada: 151 Slater, Ottawa, Ontario K1P 5N1. Tel. (613) 563-3562. Exec. Dir., Claude Thibault.
Periodicals: University Affairs (10 times a year); Directory Canadian Universities (a), Canadian Directory to Foundations and Granting Agencies

Better Business Bureau of Ottawa and Hull Inc.: Sovereign Bldg., 71 Bank St., Ottawa, Ontario, K1P 5N2. Gen. Mgr., Lorne L. Smith. Tel. (613) 237-4856

Billy Graham Evangelistic Assn. of Canada: Box 841, 402-171 Donald St., Winnipeg, Manitoba R3C 2R3. Tel. (204) 943-0529
Periodical: Decision Magazine (m)

B'nai B'rith: 15 Hove St., Ste. 200, 2nd Fl., Downsview, Ontario M3H 4Y8 Exec. Vice-Pres., Frank Dimant
Periodical: The Covenant (q)

Boy Scouts of Canada, National Council: P.O. Box 5151, Sta. F., Ottawa, Ontario K2C 3G7. Tel. (613) 224-5131. Chief Exec., J. Percy Ross
Periodicals: The Canadian Leader (m)

Boys' Brigade in Canada, The: 115 St. Andrews Rd., Scarborough, Ontario M1P 4N2. Tel. (416) 431-6052. Pres., T.C. Norwood; Nat'l Sec., C. D. Reesor
Periodicals: Hotline (m);

Boys and Girls Clubs of Canada: 3rd Fl., 620 Wilson Ave., Toronto, Ontario M3K 1Z3. Tel. (416) 635-6402. Natl. Dir., Richard L. Ryan
Periodical: Hotline (bi-m)

Canada Council The: P.O. Box 1047, Ottawa, Ontario K1P 5V8. Tel. (613) 237-3400. Dir., Charles Lussier

Canadian Association for Adult Education: 29 Prince Arthur Ave., Toronto, Ontario M5R 1B2. Exec. Dir., Ian Morrison, Tel. (416) 924-6607
Periodicals: Learning (q), Learning Resources Kit

Canadian Association for the Mentally Retarded, The: Kinsmen National Institute Bldg., York Univ. Campus, 4700 Keele St., Downsview, Ontario M3J 1P3. Tel. (416) 661-9611
Periodicals: Deficience Mentale/Mental Retardation (DM/MR) (q); The Reporter-National/Provincial Newspaper

Canadian Association in Support of the Native Peoples: 16 Spadina Rd., Ste. 201, Toronto Ontario M5R 2S7, 251 Laurier Ave., W., Ste. 904, Ottawa, Ontario K1P 5J6. Tel. (613) 236-7489. Exec. Dir., Joanne Hoople
C.A.S.N.P. Bulletin (q),
C.A.S.N.P. Newsletter (bi-m)

Canadian Association of Schools of Social Work: 151 Slater St., Rm. 909, Ottawa, Ontario K1P 5N1. Exec. Dir., M. Dennis Kimberley. Tel. (613) 563-3554

Canadian Association of Social Workers: 55 Parkdale Ave., 4th Fl., Ottawa, Ontario, K1Y 1E5. Tel. (613) 728-1865.
Periodicals: The Social Worker (q.)

Canadian Book Publishers' Council: 45 Charles St. E., Toronto, Ontario M4Y 1S2. Tel. (416) 964-7231. Exec. Dir., Jacqueline Nestmann-Hushion
Periodicals: CBPC Communique

Canadian Catholic Organization for Development and Peace/Organisation Catholique Canadienne pour le Développement et la Paix: 2111 rue Centre Montréal, Québec H3K 1J5. Tél. (514) 932-5136. Exec. Dir., Jacques Champagne; Assoc. Exec. Dir. of English Sector, Tom Johnston. English Sector Offices: 67 Bond St., Ste. 305, Toronto, Ontario M5B 1X5. Tel. (416) 868-0540. French Sector Offices: 2111 rue Centre, Montréal, Québec H3K 1J5. Tél. (514) 932-5136. Projects Offices: 2111 rue Centre, Montréal.
Periodicals (French Sector): Solidarités (newspaper)
Periodicals (English Sector): Education Notes (m), The Global Village Voice (bi-m)

Canadian Chamber of Commerce, The: 1080 Beaver Hall Hill, Ste. 710, Montreal, Quebec H2Z 1T2. Tel. (514) 866-4334. Pres., Samuel F. Hughes.

Canadian Church Growth Centre: 4400-4th Ave., Regina, Saskatchewan S4T 0H8. Tel. (306) 545-1515.
Periodical: His Dominion (q)

Canadian Civil Liberties Association: 229 Yonge St., Ste. 403, Toronto, Ontario M5B 1N9. Tel. (416) 363-0321. Gen. Counsel., A. Alan Borovoy

Canadian Committee on the Status of Women: 200 Clearview Ave., Apt. 2326, Ottawa, Ontario K1Z 8M2. Chpsn., Dorothy Flaherty. Tel. (613) 722-5364.

Canadian Co-operative Credit Society Limited: Box 800, Sta. U, Toronto, Ontario M8Z 5R2. Tel. (416) 232-1262. Chief Exec. Off., George S. May
Periodicals: World Reporter (bi-m); International Yearbook (a); Credit Union Magazine (m); Everybody's Money (q)

Canadian Council of Crisis Centers: 10 Trinity Sq., Toronto, Ontario M5G 1B1. Tel. (416) 598-0167. Chpsn., Ms. Hilda Powicke

Canadian Council on Social Development, The: 55 Parkdale Ave., Box 3505, Sta. C, Ottawa, Ontario K1Y 4G1. Tel (613) 728-1865. Exec. Dir., Pierre Bourdon
Periodicals: Perception (6/yr.); Social Development/Développment social (5/yr.); Catalogue of Publications

Canadian Education Association: 252 Bloor St. W., Toronto, Ontario M5S 1V5. Exec. Dir., Gerald Nason. Tel. (416) 924-7721
Periodicals: CEA Newsletter (9/yr.) Education Canada (q); Bulletin (9/année)

Canadian Institute of International Affairs:15 King's College Circle, Toronto, Ontario M5S 2V9. Tel. (416) 979-1851. Exec. Dir., Jacques Rastoul.
Periodicals: International Journal (q); Behind the Headlines (6/yr.); International Canada (m)

Canadian Institute of Planners: 30-46 Elgin St., Ottawa, Ontario K1P 5K6. Tel. (613) 233-2105. Exec. Officer, Mrs. K. E. Davies
Periodicals: Plan Canada (a); CIP Forum ICU (6/yr.)

Canadian Labour Congress: 2841 Riverside Dr., Ottawa, Ontario, K1V 8X7. Tel (613) 521-3400. Exec. Sec., J. F. Simonds
Periodical: Canadian Labour (q); Canadian Labour Comment (bi-w)

Canadian Medical Association, The: 1867 Alta Vista Dr., Box 8650, Ottawa, Ontario K1G 0G8. Tel. (613) 731-9331. Sec. Gen., Dr. R. G. Wilson, M.D.

Canadian Mental Health Association: 2160 Yonge St., Toronto, Ontario M4S 2Z3. Tel. (416) 484-7750. Gen. Dir., George Rohn
Periodical: Mental Health News (q)

Canadian Prisoner's Aid Societies:

The Ontario Council of Elizabeth Fry Societies, 215 Wellesley St. E., Toronto, Ontario M4X 1G1. Tel. (416) 924-3708. Exec. Dir., Mrs. Gillian Sandeman

John Howard Society of Ontario, 980 Yonge St., Ste. 407, Toronto, M4W 2J5. Tel. (416) 925-2205. Exec. Dir. Gordon C. MacFarlane
Periodical: Newsletter (2/yr.)

The St. Leonard's Society of Canada, 1787 Walker Rd., Rm. 3, Windsor, Ontario N8W 3P2. Tel. (519) 254-9430. Exec. Dir., L. A. Drouillard
Periodical: annual report

Canadian Red Cross Society: 95 Wellesley St. E. Toronto, Ontario M4Y 1H6. Tel. (416) 923-6692. Natl. Commissioner, Henri Tellier
Periodical: Service (q.)

Canadian Society of Biblical Studies: Exec. Sec., G. Peter Richardson, University College, University of Toronto, Toronto, Ontario M5S 1A1; Pres., Vernon Fawcett, Emmanuel College, University of Toronto, 75 Queens Park Cres., Toronto, Ontario M5S 1K7,
Periodical: The Bulletin of the Canadian Society of Biblical Studies (a); Newsletter for Ugaritic Studies (3/yr); Newsletter for Targumic and Cognate Studies (3/yr.)

Canadian Society of Church History: c/o J. W. Netten, Faculty of Education, Memorial University, St. John's, Newfoundland. Tel. (709) 753-1200

Canadian Urban Training Project for Christian Service: 51 Bond St., Toronto, Ontario M5B 1X1. Tel. (416) 363-8944. Exec. Dir., Edgar File

Canadian UNICEF Committee: 443 Mount Pleasant Rd., Toronto, Ontario M4S 2L8. Tel. (416) 482-4444. Exec. Dir., Harry S. Black
Periodicals: Communiqué Unicef Canada (q); UNICEF News (q)

Canadian Unitarian Council, 175 St. Clair Ave. W., Toronto, Ontario M4V 1P7. Tel. (416) 921-4506. Pres., Brian Reid; Admin. Sec., Thelma Peters

Canadian University Service Overseas: 151 Slater St. Ottawa, Ontario K1P 5H5. Tel. (613) 563-3598.
Periodicals: CUSO in the News (3/yr.)

Canadian Woman's Christian Temperance Union: 30 Gloucester St., Village Gate Apartments, Apt. 302, Toronto, Ontario M4Y 1L6. Tel. (416) 922-0757. Natl. Pres., Mrs. L. W. Mino, Box 196, Port Rowan, Ontario N0E 1M0
Periodical: Canadian White Ribbon Tidings (5 times a year)

Canadian Youth for Christ, Inc.: 50 Galaxy Blvd., Ste. 8, Rexdale, Ontario. M9W 4Y5 Tel. (416) 745-9850. P. O. Box 214, Rexdale, Ontario M9W 5L1 Pres., Brian C. Stiller

CARE Canada: 1312 Bank St., Ottawa, Ontario K1S 5H7. Tel. (613) 521-7081. Natl. Dir., Thomas Kines.
Publication: CARE Donor Newsletter (q)

Catholic Women's League of Canada, The: 2375A Ness Ave., Winnipeg, Manitoba R3J 1A5. Tel. (204) 885-4856 Exec. Sec., Miss Valerie J. Fall
Periodical: The Canadian League (q)

Christian Camping International (Canada): 745 Mount Pleasant Rd., Toronto, Ontario M4S 2N5. Tel. (416) 487-3431. Pres., John H. Wilkinson
Periodical: News and Views, Canadian Christian Camping Magazine (q)

Christian Service Brigade of Canada: 1254 Plains Rd. E., Burlington, Ontario L7S 1W6. Tel. (416) 634-1841. Gen. Dir., Tom Swan
Periodical: The Torch Runner (q)

Churches and Corporate Responsibility, Task Force on, The: 600 Jarvis St., Toronto, Ontario M4Y 2J6. Tel. (416) 923-1758. Coordinator, Bonnie Greene

Consumers' Association of Canada: 200 First Ave., Ottawa, Ontario K1S 5J3. Tel. (613) 238-4840. Natl. Pres., Yvonne Miles

Couchiching Institute on Public Affairs: 20 Eglinton Ave., E., Ste. 203, Toronto, Ontario M4P 1A9. Tel. (416) 489-9212. Exec. Dir., Michael Wilson

Evangelical Theological Society of Canada: Wycliffe College, Hoskin Ave., Toronto, Ontario M5S 1H7. Tel. (416) 979-2870. Pres., Richard N. Longenecker

Frontiers Foundation/Operation Beaver: 2328 Danforth Ave., Toronto, Ontario M4C 1K7. Tel. (416) 422-1888. Exec. Dir., Charles R. Catto
Periodical: Beaver Tales

GATT-Fly: 11 Madison Ave., Toronto, Ontario M5R 2S2. Tel. (416) 921-4615. Co-ordinator, John Dillon
Periodical: Flying Together (5/yr.)

Gideons International in Canada: 501 Imperial Rd., Guelph, Ontario N1H 7A2. Tel. (519) 823-1140. Exec. Dir., D. M. MacLeod
Periodical: Canadian Gideon Magazine (6 times a year)

Girl Guides of Canada—Guides du Canada: 50 Merton St., Toronto, Ontario M4S 1A3. Tel. (416) 487-5281. Exec. Dir., Mrs. H. F. Crosby.
Periodical: Canadian Guider (9/yr.)

Health League of Canada, The: 76 Avenue Rd., Toronto, Ontario M5R 2H1. Tel. (416) 923-8405. Exec. Dir., Miss Mabel Ferris
Periodical: Health Magazine

Inter-Church Committee on Human Rights in Latin America: 40 St. Clair Ave., E., Toronto, Ontario M4T 1M9. Tel. (416) 921-4152. Coord., Ms. Frances Arbour
Periodical: Newsletter (8/yr.)

Interfaith Committee on Chaplaincy in the Canadian Correctional Service of Canada: 40 St. Clair Ave., E., Toronto, Ontario M4T 1M9. Tel. (416) 921-4152. Sec.-Treas., M. P. Wilkinson

Interchurch Committee for World Development Education (Ten Days for World Development): 600 Jarvis St., Rm. 219, Toronto, Ontario M4Y 2J6, Nat'l Co-Ord., Robert Gardner

Liberal Party of Canada: 102 Bank St., Ottawa, Ontario K1P 5N4. Tel. (613) 237-0740.

National Inter-Faith Immigration Committee: 67 Bond St., Toronto, Ontario M5B 1X5. Tel. (416) 362-3128. Chpsn., Mrs. Dorothy Donovan

New Democratic Party: 301 Metcalfe St., Ottawa, Ontario K2P 1R9. Tel. (613) 236-3613. Sec., Robin V. Sears

Organisation Catholique Canadienne pour le Developpement et la Paix (see: Canadian Catholic Organization for Development and Peace)

Oxfam-Canada/Ontario: 175 Carlton St., Toronto, Ontario M5A 2K3. Tel. (416) 961-3935
Periodical: Inside Oxfam (2/yr.)

Pioneer Girls of Canada: Box 447, Burlington, Ontario L7R 3Y3. Tel. (416) 681-2883. Exec. Dir., Charlene de Haan
Periodical: Pioneer Girls of Canada Newspaper (5/yr.)

PLURA (Inter-Church Association to Promote Social Justice in Canada): 135 Adelaide St., E., Toronto, Ontario M5C 1L8. Tel. (416) 363-6021. Sec. A. R. Cuyler

Progressive Conservative Party: National Headquarters, 178 Queen St., Ottawa, Ontario K1P 5E1. Tel. (613) 238-6111.

Project Ploughshares: Conrad Grebel College, Waterloo, Ontario N2L 3G6. Res. Dir., Ernie Regehr; Tel. (519) 885-0220. Edu. Dir., Murray M. Thomson, Tel. (613) 224-8155. 175-75 Meadowland Dr., Ottawa, Ontario K2C 3M7
Periodical: Ploughshares Monitor (bi-m)

Save the Children (The Canadian Save the Children Fund): 720 Spadina Ave., 4th Fl., Toronto, Ontario M5S 2W3. Tel. (416) 960-3190. Natl. Dir., Gordon Ramsay
Periodical: Promises (q)

Scripture Union: 300 Steelcase Rd. W., #19, Markham, Ontario L3R 2W2. Tel. (416) 495-0890. Gen. Dir., William W. Tyler
Periodical S.U. News (q)

Shantymen's Christian Association of North America: 3251 Sheppard Ave. E., Agincourt, Ontario M1T 3K1. Tel. (416) 491-1081. Pres., M. W. Martin; Gen. Dir., Arthur C. Dixon
Periodical: The Shantyman (m)

Social Science Federation of Canada and Canadian Federation for the Humanities: 151 Slater St., Ste. 415, Ottawa, Ontario K1P 5H3. Tel. (613) 238-6112. Exec. Dir., John E. Trent (Social Science Fed. of Canada); Exec. Dir., Viviane Launay-Elbaz (Canadian Federation for the Humanities)

TELECARE Teleministries of Canada: P.O. Box 1, Weston, Ontario M9N 3M6. Tel. (416) 231-3152. Exec. Dir., Rev. J. William Lamb
Periodical: Telecare Dial-Log (8/yr.)

Unitarian Service Committee of Canada: 56 Sparks St., Ottawa, Ontario K1P 5B1. Tel. (613) 234-6827. Exec. Dir., Lotta Hitschmanova

United Nations Association in Canada: 63 Sparks St., Ottawa, Ontario K1P 5A6. Tel. (613) 232-5751. Pres., George Ignatieff; Exec. Dir., Gregory Wirick

Vanier Institute of the Family, The—L'institut Vanier de la Famille: 151 Slater St., Ste. 207, Ottawa, Ontario K1P 5H3. Tel. (613) 232-7115. Exec. Dir., William A. Dyson
Periodical: Transition (q)

Voice of Women/La Voix des Femmes: 175 Carlton St., Toronto, Ontario M5A 2K3. Tel. (416) 925-0912. Natl. Coordinator, Donna Elliott
Periodical: National Newsletter (q)

World University Service of Canada: 99, The City Centre, 880 Wellington St., Ottawa, Ontario K1R 6K7. Tel. (613) 237-7422. Exec. Dir., William W. McNeill

World Vision International of Canada: 6630 Turner Valley Rd., Mississauga, Ontario L5N 2S4. Exec. Dir., William J. Newell
Periodical: Actionews World Vision's Heartline (bi-m)

Y.M.-Y.W. Hebrew Association: 4588 Bathurst St., Willowdale, Ontario M2R 1W6, Tel. (416) 636-1880. Dir., Sid Brail

III
STATISTICAL AND HISTORICAL SECTION

This section of the **Yearbook** provides various types of statistical data and information on depositories of church history material for the U.S. and Canada. It is hoped that these materials will be useful in describing some major dimensions of religious life.

Much of the data presented here are unique, at least in form of presentation, and can be used judiciously to interpret developments in the religious life of the U.S. and Canada. Whenever necessary, qualifying statements have been made to warn the user of some of the pitfalls in the data.

Information in this section of the **Yearbook,** when compared with that of previous editions, suggests a number of interesting subjects for students, journalists, and church researchers to analyze and interpret. For the most part, generalizations on trends reflected in the data are left up to the reader.

The following information is contained in this Statistical and Historical Section.

1. **Current and Non-Current Statistical Data.** This section contains nine tables, numbered 1A-J, as follows: 1-A United States Current and Non-Current Statistics, arranged alphabetically for 222 United States religious bodies. Included is information on Number of Churches, Inclusive Membership, Full, Communicant or Confirmed Members (current data only), Number of Pastors Serving Parishes, Total Number of Clergy, Number of Sunday or Sabbath Schools (current data only), and Total enrollment (current data only). Table 1-B, Summary of United States Current and Non-Current Statistics, provides totals for 222 bodies in the above categories and compares these totals with those in the previous **Yearbook** for 1979. Table 1-C, Some Comparative United States Church Statistics, compares data mainly for 1979 with those mainly for 1978 with regard to Church Membership as a Percent of U.S. Population, Membership Gain and Percentage of Gain over Previous Year. Table 1-D, Current and Non-Current Canadian Statistics provides the same data for Canadian bodies as those described above for Table 1-A. Table 1-E provides a Summary of Canadian Current and Non-Current Statistics. Table 1-F, Number of United States Churches and of Members, by Religious Groups, is continued from the previous year with all the necessary qualifications, Table 1-G. Constituency of the National Council of the Churches of Christ in the U.S.A., is followed by Table 1-H, Church Membership Statistics, 1940-1978, for Selected U.S. Denominations. Table 1-J, Inclusive Membership, 50 Compilations, concludes this section.

2. **Church Financial Statistics and Related Data.** Complete data on contributions of members of 77 United States and Canadian religious bodies are supplied in the following categories: Total Contributions, Total Congregational Finances, and Benevolences. Per capita contributions based on both Inclusive and Full or Confirmed Membership are supplemented by Related Data consisting of several charts and tables reflecting relevant background trends relating to income and expenditures in the U.S. and Canada.

3. **Some Trends and Developments.** This part of the Statistical and Historical Section contains an article by Dr. Harold Fallding, Professor of Sociology, University of Waterloo titled "An Overview of Mainline Protestantism in Canada and the United States of America." Following this article is Trends in Seminary Enrollment: 1974-1979, and this section is concluded with the 1978 Official Catholic Data.

4. **Surveys of Religion in American Life.** Three surveys are reported in this section. The first is a report on research made by C. Kirk Hadaway, Research Associate, Research Division, Home Mission Board, Southern Baptist Convention entitled "Changing Brands: Denominational Switching and Membership Change." This is followed by the Gallup surveys on church attendance and other related matters and the U.S. Department of Commerce estimates of the value of new construction of religious buildings which are annual reports in the **Yearbook.**

5. **Main Depositories of Church History Material and Sources.** This is a listing, by denomination, of various major depositories of historical and archival materials in the United States and Canada, including a bibliographical guide to information on church archives.

1. CURRENT AND NON-CURRENT STATISTICAL DATA

Tables 1 A-J in this section, containing current and non-current data, have been compiled from questionnaires returned to the **Yearbook of American and Canadian Churches** by statisticians and other officials of religious bodies. These statistics have been checked carefully, but in no case have they been "adjusted" by the editor in any way for any purpose. What is reported here are official reports.

In Table 1-A, the religious bodies in the U.S. are listed alphabetically and current data appear in **bold face** type. Non-current data appear in the light face type. Current data are those compiled and reported in 1979 or 1978. Non-current data are those for 1977 or earlier. Table 1-A contains 111 current reports and 111 noncurrent, making a total of 222. Current reports, comprising 50.0 percent of all reports, account for 87.6 percent of reported membership.

Statistics appearing in Table 1-G, Constituency of the National Council of Churches of Christ in the U.S.A., do not show the distinction between current and non-current data, although the date of the last statistical report received is noted for each religious body. This year Table 1-D, Canadian Current and Non-Current Statistics, contains statistical reports from 78 Canadian bodies, four more than the previous edition of the **Yearbook.**

Caution should be exercised in interpreting Table 1-B, Summary of United States Current and Non-Current Statistics, which indicates the general trends that are shown by the data in the 1979 and 1980 **Yearbooks.** Since current and non-current statistics are combined for this comparison, the dangers of elaborate generalizations are obvious. The same is true for Table 1-C. Some Comparative United States Church Statistics.

Users of church statistics are referred to "A Guide for the User of Church Statistics," found at the front of this **Yearbook.** It is essential reading for all who intend to work with, and interpret, statistics contained in this volume. The Guide is placed in this prominent position to highlight its importance, and its chief function is to state candidly the many qualifications which must be taken into account when using church statistics.

TABLE 1-A: UNITED STATES CURRENT AND NON-CURRENT STATISTICS

The following table provides current and non-current statistics for United States religious bodies listed alphabetically. Current statistics are defined as those gathered and reported for 1979 and 1978. These bodies having current statistics themselves, are shown in **bold face** type. Non-current statistics are those for 1977 or earlier. They appear in light face type. No statistics for "Full, Communicant, or Confirmed members," "Number of Sunday or Sabbath Schools," and "Total Enrollment" are reported for bodies having non-current statistics.

Religious Body	Year Reported	No. of Churches	Inclusive Membership	Full, Communicant or Confirmed Members	No. of Pastors Serving Parishes	Total No. of Clergy	No. of Sunday or Sabbath Schools	Total Enrollment
Advent Christian Church	**1978**	**381**	**31,324**	**22,643**	**N.R.**	**503**	**330**	**22,872**
African Methodist Episcopal Church	**1979**	**3,050**	**1,970,000**	**1,960,000**	**3,560**	**3,938**	**2,550**	**105,250**
African Methodist Episcopal Zion Church	**1978**	**6,020**	**1,093,001**	**983,701**	**6,609**	**6,689**	**6,018**	**168,149**
African Orthodox Church	1957	24	6,000		24	50		
Albanian Orthodox Archdiocese in America	**1978**	**16**	**40,000**	**15,000**	**18**	**25**	**15**	**1,400**
Albanian Orthodox Diocese of America	**1979**	**10**	**5,250**	**475**	**2**	**4**	**2**	**130**
Amana Church Society	1970	7	735		None	None		
American Baptist Association	**1979**	**5,000**	**1,500,000**	**1,500,000**	**5,000**	**5,425**	**5,000**	**800,000**
American Baptist Churches in the U.S.A.	1977	5,815	1,316,760		4,186	7,087		
American Carpatho-Russian Orthodox Greek Catholic Church	1976	70	100,000		61	68		
The American Catholic Church, Archdiocese of New York	1975	7	700		4	7		
The American Catholic Church (Syro-Antiochian)	**1978**	**3**	**501**	**501**	**8**	**8**	**2**	**148**
The American Lutheran Church	**1978**	**4,837**	**2,377,235**	**1,773,179**	**4,334**	**6,789**	**4,544**	**625,660**
American Rescue Workers	**1978**	**15**	**2,140**	**2,140**	**32**	**43**	**18**	**2,894**
The Anglican Orthodox Church	1972	37	2,630		12	14		
The Antiochian Orthodox Christian Archdiocese of North America	1977	110	152,000		120	132		
Apostolic Christian Church (Nazarean)	1977	42	4,804		132	140		
Apostolic Christian Churches of America	1977	80	17,888		182	243		
The Apostolic Faith	**1978**	**45**	**4,100**	**4,100**	**75**	**75**	**44**	**6,800**
Apostolic Lutheran Church of America	1974	54	9,384		34	36		
Apostolic Overcoming Holy Church of God	1956	300	75,000		300	350		
Armenian Apostolic Church of America	1972	29	125,000		23	34		
Armenian Church of America, Diocese of the (including Diocese of California)	**1978**	**57**	**326,500**	**326,500**	**52**	**60**	**57**	**7,000**
Assemblies of God	**1978**	**9,410**	**1,293,394**	**932,365**	**12,391**	**14,415**	**9,410**	**1,293,394**
Associate Reformed Presbyterian Church, General Synod	**1978**	**158**	**32,139**	**28,644**	**110**	**170**	**147**	**15,566**
Baptist General Conference	**1978**	**772**	**131,000**	**131,000**	**N.R.**	**1,002**	**772**	**118,310**
Baptist Missionary Association of America	**1978**	**1,487**	**219,697**	**219,697**	**1,800**	**3,125**	**1,487**	**96,785**

TABLE 1-A: UNITED STATES CURRENT AND NON-CURRENT STATISTICS—Continued

Religious Body	Year Reported	No. of Churches	Inclusive Membership	Full, Communicant or Confirmed Members	No. of Pastors Serving Parishes	Total No. of Clergy	No. of Sunday or Sabbath Schools	Total Enrollment
Beachy Amish Mennonite Church	1978	75	4,762	4,762	N.R.	200	None	None
Berean Fundamental Church	1976	50	4,269		61	62		
Bethel Ministerial Association	1971	25	5,000		53	57		
The Bible Church of Christ, Inc.	1979	5	2,300	2,300	5	17		
Bible Protestant Church	1978	36	2,077	2,077	38	58	5	719
Bible Way Church of Our Lord Jesus Christ, World Wide, Inc.	1970	350	30,000		350	350		
Brethren Church (Ashland, Ohio)	1978	122	15,082	15,082	94	160	122	8,234
Brethren in Christ Church	1977	156	11,384		118	279		
Buddhist Churches of America	1975	60	60,000		80	108		
Bulgarian Eastern Orthodox Church (Diocese of N. & S. America and Australia)	1971	13	86,000		N.R.	11		
Christ Catholic Church	1978	7	1,365	1,279	11	12	3	98
Christadelphians	1964	850	15,800		None	None		
Christian and Missionary Alliance	1978	1,290	158,218	88,903	978	1,529	1,188	155,631
Christian Catholic Church (Evangelical-Protestant)	1979	6	2,500	2,500	12	19	6	1,325
Christian Church (Disciples of Christ)	1978	4,347	1,231,817	791,633	4,016	6,635	4,347	368,624
Christian Church of North America, General Council	1979	101	12,000	12,000	108	145	101	10,500
Christian Churches and Churches of Christ	1979	5,535	1,054,266	1,054,266	5,989	7,689	N.R.	N.R.
The Christian Congregation, Inc.	1978	1,133	81,604	81,604	1,133	1,144	1031	47,525
Christian Methodist Episcopal Church	1965	2,598	466,718		2,214	2,259		
Christian Nation Church, U.S.A.	1976	18	2,000		26	28		
Christian Reformed Church in North America	1978	623	211,302	130,613	481	950	N.R.	N.R.
Christian Union	1976	104	4,590		73	91		
Church of Christ	1972	32	2,400		169	188		
Church of Christ (Holiness) U.S.A.	1972	159	9,289		76	76		
Church of Daniel's Band	1951	4	200		4	10		
The Church of God	1978	2,035	75,890	75,890	1,910	2,737	2,025	96,500
Church of God (Anderson, Ind.)	1978	2,264	173,753	173,753	1,756	2,924	2,239	234,274
Church of God by Faith	1973	105	4,500		125	150		
Church of God (Cleveland, Tenn.)	1978	4,847	392,551	392,551	8,052	9,095	4,778	373,501
Church of God General Conference (Oregon, Ill.)	1978	132	7,550	7,550	104	119	135	9,510
The Church of God in Christ	1965	4,500	425,000		4,000	6,000		
The Church of God in Christ, International	1971	1,041	501,000		N.R.	1,502		
Church of God in Christ (Mennonite)	1978	78	7,400		N.R.	N.R.		
The Church of God of Prophecy	1975	1,791	65,801		N.R.	5,679		

TABLE 1-A: UNITED STATES CURRENT AND NON-CURRENT STATISTICS—Continued

Religious Body	Year Reported	No. of Churches	Inclusive Membership	Full, Communicant or Confirmed Members	No. of Pastors Serving Parishes	Total No. of Clergy	No. of Sunday or Sabbath Schools	Total Enrollment
The Church of God of the Mountain Assembly	1977	105	3,125		162	162		
Church of God (7th Day)	1960	7	2,000		7	9		
Church of God (Seventh Day) Denver, Colo.	1976	104	8,000		70	110		
Church of God (Which He Purchased With His Own Blood)	**1978**	**8**	**747**	**747**	**5**	**8**	**7**	**180**
The Church of Illumination	1963	14	9,000		60	60		
The Church of Jesus Christ (Bickertonites)	**1978**	**60**	**2,551**	**2,551**	**165**	**234**	**60**	**5,250**
The Church of Jesus Christ of Latter-Day Saints	**1978**	**6,272**	**2,952,000**	**2,106,000**	**18,816**	**21,536**	**6,270**	**2,380,000**
Church of Our Lord Jesus Christ of the Apostolic Faith, Inc.	1954	155	45,000		150	165		
The Church of Revelation, Inc.	1976	8	750		48	48		
Church of The Brethren	**1978**	**1,061**	**175,335**	**175,335**	**N.R.**	**N.R.**	**1,061**	**70,156**
Church of the Living God	1964	276	45,320		332	376		
Church of the Lutheran Brethren of America	**1978**	**95**	**9,192**	**5,696**	**79**	**154**	**94**	**8,586**
Church of the Lutheran Confession	**1978**	**72**	**9,316**	**N.R.**	**59**	**75**	**57**	**1,540**
Church of the Nazarene	**1978**	**4,719**	**462,724**	**462,124**	**N.R.**	**7,590**	**4,615**	**896,989**
Churches of Christ	**1978**	**17,550**	**3,000,000**	**3,000,000**	**13,000**	**16,200**	**16,000**	**1,860,000**
Churches of Christ in Christian Union	**1979**	**262**	**10,300**	**10,300**	**536**	**N.R.**	**262**	**20,900**
Churches of God, General Conference	1975	347	36,016		279	283		
Community Churches, National Council of	**1979**	**200**	**190,000**	**N.R.**	**210**	**N.R.**	**N.R.**	**N.R.**
Congregational Christian Churches, National Association of	**1978**	**382**	**95,000**	**95,000**	**375**	**554**	**N.R.**	**N.R.**
Congregational Holiness Church	1966	147	4,859		146	302		
Conservative Baptist Association of America	1977	1,114	300,000		N.R.	N.R.		
Conservative Congregational Christian Conference	**1978**	**130**	**22,750**	**22,750**	**226**	**364**	**124**	**12,333**
Coptic Orthodox Church	1976	14	40,000		12	12		
Cumberland Presbyterian Church	**1978**	**850**	**93,268**	**88,093**	**526**	**706**	**850**	**49,924**
Duck River (and Kindred) Associations of Baptists	1975	85	8,632		148	148		
Elim Fellowship	1973	70	5,000		70	128		
The Episcopal Church	**1978**	**7,009**	**2,815,359**	**1,975,234**	**7,105**	**12,310**	**N.R.**	**574,693**
The Estonian Evangelical Lutheran Church	**1978**	**25**	**8,548**	**8,548**	**20**	**28**	**N.R.**	**N.R.**
Ethical Culture Movement	**1978**	**21**	**5,000**	**4,000**	**12**	**27**	**19**	**539**
Evangelical Church of North America	**1978**	**138**	**12,210**	**12,210**	**134**	**251**	**138**	**15,398**
Evangelical Congregational Church	**1978**	**161**	**28,459**	**28,459**	**110**	**186**	**160**	**23,999**
Evangelical Covenant Church of America	**1978**	**520**	**74,678**	**74,678**	**477**	**751**	**509**	**64,577**
Evangelical Free Church in America	1977	621	100,000		N.R.	960		
Evangelical Friends Alliance	1975	257	25,531		N.R.	N.R.		
Evangelical Lutheran Church in America								

TABLE 1-A: UNITED STATES CURRENT AND NON-CURRENT STATISTICS—Continued

Religious Body	Year Reported	No. of Churches	Inclusive Membership	Full, Communicant or Confirmed Members	No. of Pastors Serving Parishes	Total No. of Clergy	No. of Sunday or Sabbath Schools	Total Enrollment
(Eielsen Synod)	1957	9	2,500		3	3		
Evangelical Lutheran Churches, the Association of	**1978**	**250**	**106,684**	**79,080**	**295**	**545**	**N.R.**	**N.R.**
Evangelical Lutheran Synod	**1978**	**108**	**19,705**	**14,833**	**77**	**92**	**100**	**3,918**
Evangelical Mennonite Brethren Conference	1977	16	2.043		17	48		
Evangelial Mennonite Church	**1978**	**21**	**3,634**	**3,634**	**21**	**37**	**21**	**4,788**
Evangelical Methodist Church	1974	139	10,502		145	218		
The Fire Baptized Holiness Church (Wesleyan)	1958	53	998		N.R.	N.R.		
Free Christian Zion Church of Christ	1956	742	22,260		321	340		
Free Lutheran Congregations, The Association of	**1979**	**132**	**14,738**	**11,085**	**60**	**91**	**119**	**5,402**
Free Methodist Church of North America	**1978**	**1,148**	**73,294**	**55,493**	**N.R.**	**1,805**	**1,118**	**119,385**
Free Will Baptists	**1978**	**2,436**	**216,831**	**216,831**	**4,302**	**4,367**	**2,436**	**187,778**
Friends General Conference	1974	233	26,184		None	None		
Friends United Meeting	**1978**	**522**	**62,080**	**53,390**	**380**	**617**	**369**	**27,041**
Full Gospel Assemblies, International	**1978**	**105**	**2,800**	**2,800**	**235**	**488**	**35**	**938**
Fundamental Methodist Church, Inc.	1976	15	745		15	19		
General Association of Regular Baptist Churches	**1979**	**1,544**	**240,000**	**240,000**	**N.R.**	**N.R.**	**N.R.**	**N.R.**
General Baptists (General Association of)	1977	867	72,000		N.R.	1,320		
General Church of the New Jerusalem	1971	33	2,143		17	31		
General Conference of Mennonite Brethren Churches	**1978**	**120**	**16,042**	**16,042**	**120**	**135**	**120**	**11,894**
General Conference of the Evangelical Baptist Church, Inc.	1952	31	2,200		22	37		
General Convention, The Swedenborgian Church	1977	47	2,640		48	51		
General Six Principle Baptists	1970	7	175		4	7		
Grace Brethren Churches, Fellowship of	**1978**	**262**	**39,605**	**39,605**	**357**	**529**	**262**	**32,776**
Grace Gospel Fellowship	**1978**	**48**	**3,500**	**2,000**	**105**	**138**	**N.R.**	**N.R.**
Greek Orthodox Archdiocese of North and South America	1977	535	1,950,000		610	655		
The Holiness Church of God, Inc.	1968	28	927		25	36		
Holy Orthodox Church in America, Eastern Catholic and Apostolic	1965	4	260		4	10		
Holy Ukrainian Autocephalic Church in Exile	1965	15	4,800		15	24		
House of God, which is the Church of the Living God, the Pillar and Ground of the Truth, Inc.	1956	107	2,350		80	120		
Hungarian Reformed Church in America	**1978**	**29**	**10,500**	**10,500**	**24**	**39**	**21**	**633**
Hutterian Brethren	1976	35	3,500		36	36		
Independent Assemblies of God, International	1962	136	N.R.		136	367		
Independent Fundamental Churches of America	**1978**	**614**	**87,582**	**87,582**	**752**	**1,252**	**N.R.**	**125,563**
International Church of the Foursquare								

TABLE 1-A: UNITED STATES CURRENT AND NON-CURRENT STATISTICS—Continued

Religious Body	Year Reported	No. of Churches	Inclusive Membership	Full, Communicant or Confirmed Members	No. of Pastors Serving Parishes	Total No. of Clergy	No. of Sunday or Sabbath Schools	Total Enrollment
Gospel	1963	714	89,215		741	2,690		
International Pentecostal Church of Christ	1977	105	11,659		130	259		
Jehovah's Witnesses	**1978**	**7,526**	**519,218**	**519,218**	**None**	**None**	**N.R.**	**N.R.**
Jewish Congregations	**1978**	**3,500**	**5,781,000**	**N.R.**	**4,000**	**5,300**	**N.R.**	**N.R.**
Kodesh Church of Immanuel	1936	9	582		N.R.	N.R.		
The Latvian Evangelical Church in America	**1978**	**56**	**12,308**	**10,727**	**56**	**70**	**24**	
Liberal Catholic Church—Province of the United States of America	1973	29	2,393		61	107		
Lutheran Church in America	**1978**	**5,778**	**2,942,002**	**2,183,666**	**4,952**	**7,822**	**5,640**	**639,306**
The Lutheran Church—Missouri Synod	**1978**	**5,669**	**2,631,374**	**1,969,279**	**4,535**	**7,161**	**5,428**	**638,074**
Mennonite Church	**1978**	**1,081**	**97,142**	**97,142**	**1,742**	**2,393**	**753**	**93,685**
Mennonite Church, The General Conference	1976	187	36,397		318	518		
Metropolitan Church Association, Inc.	1958	15	443		13	62		
Metropolitan Community Churches, Universal Fellowship of	**1978**	**118**	**25,520**	**25,520**	**N.R.**	**157**	**N.R.**	**N.R.**
The Missionary Church	1972	273	20,078		327	470		
Moravian Church—Northern Province	**1978**	**95**	**32,519**	**25,414**	**82**	**148**	**93**	**7,624**
Moravian Church—Southern Province	**1978**	**52**	**21,002**	**17,126**	**58**	**72**	**52**	**9,121**
National Baptist Convention of America	1956	11,398	2,668,799		7,598	28,574		
National Baptist Convention, U.S.A., Inc.	1958	26,000	5,500,000		26,000	27,500		
National Primitive Baptist Convention, Inc.	1975	606	250,000		460	636		
The National Spiritual Alliance of the U.S.A.	1971	34	3,230		58	N.R.		
National Spiritualist Association of Churches	1976	164	5,168		144	N.R.		
Netherlands Reformed Congregations	**1978**	**14**	**4,904**	**2,443**	**2**	**4**	**N.R.**	**N.R.**
New Apostolic Church of North America	**1978**	**362**	**26,384**	**26,384**	**501**	**579**	**362**	**9,502**
North American Baptist Conference	**1978**	**253**	**42,499**	**42,499**	**258**	**353**	**249**	**28,270**
North American Old Roman Catholic Church	**1978**	**121**	**67,314**	**67,314**	**91**	**123**	**41**	**8,504**
North American Old Roman Catholic Church (Archdiocese of New York)	**1978**	**6**	**2,500**	**2,500**	**8**	**10**	**3**	**79**
Old German Baptist Brethren	**1978**	**50**	**4,898**	**4,898**	**214**	**221**	**N.R.**	**N.R.**
Old Order Amish Church	**1978**	**513**	**33,000**	**33,000**	**1,895**	**2,007**	**N.R.**	**N.R.**
Old Order (Wisler) Mennonite Church	1972	38	8,000		60	101		
Open Bible Standard Churches, Inc.	**1979**	**280**	**60,000**	**30,000**	**496**	**781**	**N.R.**	**N.R.**
The (Original) Church of God	1971	70	20,000		50	124		
Orthodox Church in America	**1978**	**440**	**1,000,000**	**N.R.**	**457**	**531**	**N.R.**	**N.R.**
The Orthodox Presbyterian Church	**1978**	**136**	**15,806**	**10,939**	**132**	**238**	**N.R.**	**N.R.**
Pentecostal Assemblies of the World, Inc.	1960	550	4,500		450	600		
Pentecostal Church of God	1977	1,189	110,870		1,320	2,168		
Pentecostal Fire-Baptized Holiness Church	1969	41	545		80	80		

TABLE 1-A: UNITED STATES CURRENT AND NON-CURRENT STATISTICS—Continued

Religious Body	Year Reported	No. of Churches	Inclusive Membership	Full, Communicant or Confirmed Members	No. of Pastors Serving Parishes	Total No. of Clergy	No. of Sunday or Sabbath Schools	Total Enrollment
The Pentecostal Free-Will Baptist Church, Inc.	**1978**	**128**	**12,272**	**12,272**	**120**	**195**	**128**	**12,272**
Pentecostal Holiness Church	1977	2,340	86,103		1,329	2,899		
Pillar of Fire	1949	61	5,100		N.R.	N.R.		
Plymouth Brethren	**1978**	**800**	**74,000**	**42,000**	**N.R.**	**380**	**N.R.**	**N.R.**
Polish National Catholic Church of America	1960	162	282,411		151	141		
Presbyterian Church in America	**1978**	**440**	**82,095**	**73,665**	**419**	**584**	**440**	**40,595**
Presbyterian Church in the United States	**1978**	**4,007**	**862,416**	**862,416**	**3,019**	**5,254**	**4,000**	**405,926**
Primitive Advent Christian Church	**1978**	**10**	**550**	**550**	**10**	**10**	**9**	**568**
Primitive Baptists	1960	1,000	72,000		N.R.	N.R.		
Primitive Methodist Church, U.S.A.	**1978**	**88**	**10,222**	**9,376**	**68**	**91**	**82**	**6,639**
Progressive National Baptist Convention, Inc.	1967	655	521,692		N.R.	863		
The Protestant Conference (Lutheran)	1977	7	2,635		9	13		
Protestant Reformed Churches in America	**1978**	**21**	**4,040**	**2,266**	**21**	**25**	**16**	**669**
Reformed Baptists	**1979**	**250**	**5,000**	**3,000**	**300**	**350**	**N.R.**	**N.R.**
Reformed Church in America	**1978**	**898**	**348,080**	**212,631**	**824**	**1,418**	**898**	**108,540**
Reformed Church in the United States	1977	26	3,790		22	31		
Reformed Episcopal Church	1977	68	6,211		N.R.	91		
Reformed Mennonite Church	1970	12	500		18	21		
Reformed Methodist Union Episcopal Church	1976	17	3,800		17	26		
Reformed Presbyterian Church, Evangelical Synod	1977	145	25,448		255	385		
Reformed Presbyterian Church of North America	1977	68	4,878		51	86		
Reformed Zion Union Apostolic Church	1965	50	16,000		23	N.R.		
Religious Society of Friends (Conservative)	1976	27	1,728		None	None		
Religious Society of Friends (Unaffiliated Meetings)	1975	87	5,696		None	None		
Reorganized Church of Jesus Christ of Latter Day Saints	**1978**	**1,048**	**185,636**	**185,636**	**16,039**	**16,039**	**N.R.**	**N.R.**
The Roman Catholic Church	**1978**	**25,542**	**49,602,035**	**N.R.**	**N.R.**	**58,856**	**10,513**	**8,527,253**
The Romanian Orthodox Episcopate of America	**1978**	**34**	**40,000**	**40,000**	**34**	**55**	**34**	**1,600**
Russian Orthodox Church in the U.S.A., Patriarchal Parishes of the	1975	41	51,500		55	60		
The Russian Orthodox Church Outside Russia	1955	81	55,000		92	168		
The Salvation Army	**1978**	**1,117**	**414,035**	**110,700**	**2,321**	**5,104**	**1,067**	**107,549**
The Schwenkfelder Church	1977	5	2,748		6	9		
Second Cumberland Presbyterian Church in the US	1959	121	30,000		121	125		

TABLE 1-A: UNITED STATES CURRENT AND NON-CURRENT STATISTICS—Continued

Religious Body	Year Reported	No. of Churches	Inclusive Membership	Full, Communicant or Confirmed Members	No. of Pastors Serving Parishes	Total No. of Clergy	No. of Sunday or Sabbath Schools	Total Enrollment
Separate Baptists in Christ	1972	84	7,496		65	106		
Serbian Eastern Orthodox Church for the U.S.A. and Canada	1967	52	65,000		56	64		
Seventh-Day Adventists	**1978**	**3,591**	**535,705**	**535,705**	**1,885**	**4,016**	**3,673**	**477,208**
Seventh Day Baptist General Conference	**1978**	**60**	**5,181**	**5,181**	**45**	**76**	**53**	**1,790**
Social Brethren	1975	30	1,784		47	47		
Southern Baptist Convention	**1978**	**35,357**	**13,191,394**	**13,191,394**	**33,500**	**56,000**	**34,450**	**7,331,954**
Southern Methodist Church	1977	169	11,000		113	127		
Syrian Orthodox Church of Antioch (Archdiocese of the U.S.A. and Canada)	**1978**	**13**	**30,000**	**N.R.**	**14**	**18**	**N.R.**	**335**
Triumph the Church and Kingdom of God in Christ (International)	1972	475	54,307		860	1,375		
Ukrainian Orthodox Church in the U.S.A.	1966	107	87,745		107	131		
Ukrainian Orthodox Church of America (Ecumenical Patriarchate)	1977	28	25,000		32	35		
Unitarian Universalist Association	**1978**	**936**	**136,207**	**136,207**	**550**	**898**	**N.R.**	**37,783**
United Brethren in Christ	1976	281	28,035		165	290		
United Christian Church	1976	11	430		5	11		
United Church of Christ	**1979**	**6,491**	**1,769,104**	**1,769,104**	**5,003**	**9,704**	**N.R.**	**508,964**
United Free Will Baptist Church	1952	836	100,000		784	915		
United Holy Church of America	1960	470	28,980		379	400		
The United Methodist Church	**1978**	**36,682**	**9,731,779**	**9,731,779**	**20,357**	**35,939**	**36,485**	**4,410,471**
United Pentecostal Church, International	**1979**	**2,830**	**450,000**	**300,000**	**2,655**	**5,881**	**N.R**	**N.R.**
The United Presbyterian Church in the United States of America	**1978**	**8,567**	**2,520,367**	**2,520,367**	**7,522**	**13,871**	**8,567**	**886,100**
United Zion Church	**1978**	**13**	**952**	**952**	**16**	**24**	**13**	**1,294**
Unity of the Brethren	1964	32	6,142		13	13		
Vendanta Society	**1978**	**12**	**1,000**	**1,000**	**1**	**1**	**N.R.**	**N.R.**
Volunteers of America	**1978**	**607**	**36,634**	**36,634**	**704**	**704**	**102**	**8,590**
The Wesleyan Church	**1978**	**1,714**	**99,016**	**86,064**	**1,439**	**2,367**	**1,714**	**201,238**
Wisconsin Evangelical Lutheran Synod	**1978**	**1,116**	**402,972**	**303,924**	**928**	**1,241**	**1,045**	**47,862**

Table 1-B: SUMMARY OF UNITED STATES CURRENT AND NON—CURRENT STATISTICS

Current statistics are those reported for the year 1979 or 1978. Non-current statistics are those for the years 1977 and earlier. Only current totals are provided in the categories: Full Communicant, or Confirmed Members; Number of Sunday or Sabbath Schools: Total Enrollment.

	Year Reported	No. of Churches	Inclusive Membership	Full, Communicant or Confirmed Members	No. of Pastors Serving Parishes	Total No. of Clergy	No. of Sunday or Sabbath Schools	Total Enrollment
1980 **Yearbook**								
Current	111	259,193	117,179,426	57,575,568	224,507	393,884	196,237	35,639,778
Non-Current	111	73,777	16,569,350	N.R.	57,994	103,417	N.R.	N.R.
Totals	222	332,970	133,748,776		282,501	497,301		
1979 **Yearbook**								
Current	115	270,468	120,094,411	59,318,400	220,028	400,419	189,924	33,959,508
Non-Current	107	62,707	12,718,059	N.R.	51,428	89,941	N.R.	N.R.
Totals	222	333,175	132,812,470		271,456	490,360		

TABLE 1-C: SOME COMPARATIVE UNITED STATES CHURCH STATISTICS

	1978	**1979**
Church Membership as a Percent of U.S. Population	60.8	60.7
Membership Gain or Loss over Previous Year	914,931	936,306
Percentage of Gain of Loss over Previous Year	0.7	0.7

TABLE 1-D: CANADIAN CURRENT AND NON-CURRENT STATISTICS

The following table provides current and non-current statistics for Canadian denominations listed alphabetically. Current statistics, defined as those gathered and reported for 1979 and 1978 are shown in **bold face** type. Non-current statistics are those for 1977 and earlier, and appear in light face.

Religious Body	Year Reported	No. of Churches	Inclusive Membership	Full, Communicant or Confirmed Members	No. of Pastors Serving Parishes	Total No. of Clergy	No. of Sunday or Sabbath Schools	Total Enrollment
The Anglican Church of Canada	**1978**	**3,030**	**961,952**	**581,040**	**1,393**	**2,832**	**2,049**	**107,505**
The Antiochian Orthodox Christian Archdiocese of North America	1972	4	25,000		4	4		
Apostolic Christian Church (Nazarean)	1977	13	1,237		39	40		
Apostolic Church of Pentecost of Canada	**1978**	**120**	**N.R.**	**N.R.**	**135**	**209**	**N.R.**	**N.R.**
Armenian Church of North America, Diocese of Canada	**1978**	**4**	**23,500**	**1,500**	**5**	**5**	**4**	**500**
Associated Gospel Churches	1977	102	11,558		76	174		
Baptist Federation of Canada	**1978**	**1,117**	**128,391**	**118,791**	**600**	**1,032**	**896**	**56,305**
Baptist General Conference	**1978**	**69**	**5,288**	**5,288**	**69**	**87**	**69**	**7,345**
Bible Holiness Movement	**1979**	**26**	**372**	**211**	**10**	**16**	**N.R.**	**N.R.**
Brethren in Christ Church, Canadian Conference	1976	26	1,835		18	39		
British Methodist Episcopal Church	**1978**	**13**	**2,000**	**700**	**9**	**9**	**N.R.**	**N.R.**
Buddhist Churches of Canada	**1978**	**15**	**2,600**	**2,600**	**10**	**10**	**10**	**330**
Canadian Baptist Conference	1977	35	2,858		29	37		
Canadian Jewish Conference	1977	N.R.	305,000		N.R.	N.R.		
Canadian Yearly Meeting of the Religious Society of Friends	**1978**	**27**	**1,075**	**1,075**	**None**	**None**	**N.R.**	**N.R.**
The Christian and Missionary Alliance in Canada	**1978**	**224**	**32,900**	**16,966**	**103**	**251**	**213**	**33,483**
Christian Church (Disciples of Christ)	**1978**	**39**	**4,753**	**2,693**	**20**	**49**	**39**	**824**
Christian Churches and Churches of Christ in Canada	**1978**	**69**	**4,871**	**4,871**	**68**	**110**	**N.R.**	**N.R.**
The Christian Congregation	**1978**	**26**	**2,650**	**2,650**	**26**	**26**	**26**	**1,751**
Christian Reformed Church in North America	**1978**	**191**	**77,709**	**38,932**	**161**	**192**	**N.R.**	**N.R.**
Church of God (Anderson, Ind.)	**1978**	**46**	**2,529**	**2,529**	**33**	**44**	**44**	**3,408**
Church of God (Cleveland Tenn.)	**1978**	**55**	**2,067**	**2,067**	**100**	**108**	**57**	**3,038**
The Church of God of Prophecy of Canada	**1979**	**26**	**1,215**	**1,215**	**24**	**29**	**28**	**1,962**
The Church of Jesus Christ of Latter-day Saints in Canada	**1978**	**269**	**74,900**	**61,400**	**807**	**927**	**270**	**70,100**
Church of the Foursquare Gospel of Western Canada	**1978**	**27**	**2,025**	**2,025**	**70**	**75**	**23**	**1,794**
Church of the Lutheran Brethren of America	**1978**	**11**	**1,430**	**1,040**	**8**	**9**	**10**	**522**
Church of the Nazarene	**1978**	**138**	**8,537**	**8,502**	**N.R.**	**193**	**136**	**18,860**
Conference of Mennonites in Canada	**1978**	**133**	**25,818**	**25,818**	**333**	**447**	**1,624**	**18,122**
The Coptic Church in Canada	1977	5	2,200		5	6		
The Estonian Evangelical Lutheran Church	**1978**	**15**	**8,889**	**N.R.**	**9**	**14**	**N.R.**	**N.R.**

TABLE 1-D: CANADIAN CURRENT AND NON-CURRENT STATISTICS—Continued

Religious Body	Year Reported	No. of Churches	Inclusive Membership	Full, Communicant or Confirmed Members	No. of Pastors Serving Parishes	Total No. of Clergy	No. of Sunday or Sabbath Schools	Total Enrollment
Evangelical Baptist Churches of Canada, The Fellowship of	1974	370	44,000		375	420		
The Evangelical Church in Canada	1977	45	3,673		34	58		
The Evangelical Covenant Church of Canada	**1978**	**24**	**1,127**	**1,127**	**14**	**22**	**22**	**1,803**
The Evangelical Lutheran Church of Canada	**1978**	**317**	**82,065**	**57,961**	**193**	**284**	**237**	**16,294**
Evangelical Mennonite Conference	**1978**	**45**	**4,680**	**4,680**	**72**	**80**	**N.R.**	**N.R.**
Evangelical Mennonite Brethren Conference	1977	17	1,924		16	20		
Evangelical Mennonite Mission Conference	1977	31	3,385		43	48		
Free Methodist Church in Canada	**1978**	**125**	**5,951**	**4,600**	**97**	**191**	**N.R.**	**11,088**
Greek Orthodox Diocese of Toronto	1977	41	220,000		41	41		
Independent Assemblies of God—Canada	1967	45	4,500		125	165		
Independent Holiness Church	1971	12	N.R.		12	13		
The Italian Pentecostal Church of Canada	1976	16	2,755		12	12		
Jehovah's Witnesses	**1978**	**1,035**	**61,836**	**61,836**	**None**	**None**	**N.R.**	**N.R.**
The Latvian Evangelical Lutheran Church in America	**1978**	**11**	**4,275**	**3,737**	**11**	**17**	**2**	**72**
Lutheran Church—Canada	**1978**	**354**	**92,939**	**66,732**	**188**	**275**	**273**	**18,977**
Lutheran Church in America—Canada Section	**1978**	**325**	**121,693**	**88,182**	**202**	**344**	**302**	**19,888**
Mennonite Brethren Churches of North America, Canadian Conference of the	**1978**	**131**	**20,900**	**20,900**	**152**	**152**	**16,366**	**18,926**
Mennonite Church (Canada)	**1978**	**113**	**9,819**	**9,819**	**165**	**226**	**75**	**9,947**
The Missionary Church—Canada	1972	75	4,468		81	130		
Moravian Church in America—Northern Province, Canadian District of the	**1978**	**9**	**1,684**	**1,137**	**7**	**10**	**8**	**594**
North American Baptist Conference	**1978**	**102**	**14,742**	**14,742**	**99**	**144**	**102**	**9,018**
The Old Catholic Church of Canada	1976	2	350		7	8		
The Pentecostal Assemblies of Canada	**1978**	**868**	**200,000**	**100,000**	**N.R.**	**997**	**579**	**131,344**
Pentecostal Assemblies of Newfoundland	**1978**	**152**	**30,000**	**30,000**	**N.R.**	**165**	**152**	**16,500**
Plymouth Brethren (Also known as Christian Brethren)	1976	395	34,700		N.R.	177		
Polish National Catholic Church	1977	11	6,000		11	12		
The Presbyterian Church in Canada	1977	1,067	168,502		725	945		
Primitive Baptist Convention of New Brunswick	1977	15	1,050		8	9		
Reformed Church in America—Ontario Classis	**1978**	**19**	**5,541**	**2,753**	**17**	**23**	**19**	**1,252**
Reformed Doukhobors, Christian Community and Brotherhood of	**1979**	**1**	**3,075**	**2,575**	**1**	**1**	**1**	**308**
Reformed Presbyterian Church, Evangelical Synod	1976	6	271		6	6		
Reinland Mennonite Church	**1978**	**7**	**780**	**780**	**12**	**13**	**5**	**216**
Reorganized Church of Jesus Christ of Latter Day Saints	**1978**	**86**	**10,152**	**10,152**	**988**	**988**	**N.R.**	**N.R.**

TABLE 1-D: CANADIAN CURRENT AND NON-CURRENT STATISTICS—Continued

Religious Body	Year Reported	No. of Churches	Inclusive Membership	Full, Communicant or Confirmed Members	No. of Pastors Serving Parishes	Total No. of Clergy	No. of Sunday or Sabbath Schools	Total Enrollment
The Roman Catholic Church in Canada	**1978**	**5,880**	**10,082,341**	**N.R.**	**7,885**	**13,374**	**N.R.**	**N.R.**
The Romanian Orthodox Church in America (Canadian Parishes)	1972	19	16,000		19	19		
The Romanian Orthodox Episcopate of America (Jackson, Mich.)	**1978**	**13**	**8,000**	**8,000**	**8**	**9**	**10**	**535**
Russian Orthodox Church in Canada (Patriarchal Parishes)	**1978**	**24**	**4,000**	**4,000**	**6**	**7**	**3**	**56**
Serbian Orthodox Church in America and Canada, Diocese of Eastern America and Canada	**1978**	**8**	**10,036**	**10,036**	**10**	**10**	**6**	**315**
Seventh-Day Adventist Church in Canada	**1978**	**252**	**29,258**	**29,258**	**130**	**218**	**293**	**23,851**
Ukrainian Greek Orthodox Church of Canada	1970	118	140,000		N.R.	75		
Union of Spiritual Communities of Christ (Orthodox Doukhobors in Canada)	1972	25	21,300		None	None		
Unitarian Universalist Association	**1978**	**43**	**4,858**	**4,858**	**20**	**30**	**N.R.**	**N.R.**
United Brethren in Christ, Ontario Conference	1978	11	841		9	14		
The United Church of Canada	**1978**	**4,271**	**2,087,313**	**916,651**	**1,986**	**3,688**	**3,543**	**225,388**
United Pentecostal Church in Canada	**1979**	**131**	**21,250**	**13,750**	**150**	**N.R.**	**N.R.**	**N.R.**
The Wesleyan Church	**1979**	**76**	**4,750**	**4,203**	**69**	**110**	**76**	**13,925**
Wisconsin Evangelical Lutheran Synod	**1978**	**7**	**938**	**733**	**5**	**6**	**7**	**161**

TABLE 1-E: SUMMARY OF CANADIAN CURRENT AND NON-CURRENT STATISTICS

Current statistics are those reported for the year 1979 or 1978. Non-current statistics are those for the years 1977 and earlier. Only current totals are provided in the categories: Full Communicant, or Confirmed Members; Number of Sunday or Sabbath Schools: Total Enrollment.

	Year Reported	No. of Churches	Inclusive Membership	Full, Communicant or Confirmed Members	No. of Pastors Serving Parishes	Total No. of Clergy	No. of Sunday or Sabbath Schools	Total Enrollment
1980 **Yearbook**								
Current	52	20,119	14,299,474	2,355,115	16,470	28,058	27,579	846,307
Non-Current	26	2,506	1,009,007	N.R.	1,695	2,472	N.R.	N.R.
Totals	78	22,625	15,308,481		18,165	30,530		
1979 **Yearbook**								
Current	57	20,369	14,622,993	2,853,011	18,272	29,248	11,113	920,429
Non-Current	17	1,303	581,620	N.R.	736	1,174	N.R.	N.R.
Totals	74	21,672	15,204,613		19,008	30,422		

TABLE 1-F: NUMBER OF UNITED STATES CHURCHES, AND OF MEMBERS, BY RELIGIOUS GROUPS

The 222 U.S. religious bodies reporting in this edition of the **Yearbook** may be classified somewhat arbitrarily, into seven major categories.

It should be reiterated that comparisons of statistics of the various religious groups tabulated below are not meaningful because definitions of membership vary greatly from one religious body to another. For example, Roman Catholics count all baptized individuals, including infant members, as do many Protestant bodies. Some Protestant bodies, however, count as members those who have been received into the church at baptism, which usually takes place at around age 13, thereby leaving out of official counts of membership many millions of children. Jewish statistics are estimates of the number of individuals in households in which one or more Jews reside and, therefore, include non-Jews living in such households as the result of intermarriage. The total number of persons in Jewish households is estimated to be 8 percent larger than the number of Jewish persons residing in these households.

The definition of membership in each case is of necessity left up to the religious body itself, and the statistics reported by various religious bodies are not adjusted by the editor of the **Yearbook.**

	Number Bodies Reporting	Number of Churches	Number of Members
Buddhists	1	60	60,000
Eastern Churches	17	1,583	3,632,555
Jews*	1	3,500	5,781,000
Old Catholic, Polish National Catholic, Armenian Churches	9	421	808,684
Protestants**	186	300,676	73,704,162
Roman Catholic	1	25,542	49,602,035
Miscellaneous***	7	1,188	160,340
Totals	222	332,970	133,748,776

*Including Orthodox, Conservative, and Reformed branches.

**Some bodies included here are, strictly speaking, not "Protestant" in the usual sense, such as various Latter-Day Saints groups and Jehovah's Witnesses.

***This is a grouping of bodies officially non-Christian, including those such as Spiritualists, Ethical Culture Movement, and Unitarian-Universalists.

TABLE 1-G: CONSTITUENCY OF THE NATIONAL COUNCIL OF THE CHURCHES OF CHRIST IN THE U.S.A.

A separate tabulation has been made of the constituent bodies of the National Council of Churches of Christ in the U.S.A. and is given below:

Religious Body	Year	Number of Churches	Inclusive Membership	Pastors Serving Parishes
African Methodist Episcopal Church	1979	3,050	1,970,000	3,560
African Methodist Episcopal Zion Church	1978	6,020	1,093,001	6,609
American Baptist Churches in the U.S.A.	1977	5,815	1,316,760	4,186
The Antiochian Orthodox Christian Archdiocese of North America	1977	110	152,000	120
Armenian Church of America, Diocese of the (including Diocese of California)	1978	57	326,500	52
Christian Church (Disciples of Christ)	1978	4,347	1,231,817	4,016
Christian Methodist Episcopal Church	1965	2,598	466,718	2,214
Church of the Brethren	1978	1,061	175,335	N.R.
Community Churches, National Council of	1979	200	190,000	210
Coptic Orthodox Church	1976	14	40,000	12
The Episcopal Church	1978	7,009	2,815,359	7,105
Friends United Meeting	1978	522	62,080	380
General Convention, the Swedenborgian Church	1977	47	2,640	48
Greek Orthodox Archdiocese of North and South America	1977	535	1,950,000	610
Hungarian Reformed Church in America	1978	29	10,500	24
Lutheran Church in America	1978	5,778	2,942,002	4,952
Moravian Church in America				
Northern Province	1978	95	32,519	82
Southern Province	1978	52	21,002	58
National Baptist Convention of America	1956	11,398	2,668,799	7,598
National Baptist Convention, U.S.A., Inc.	1958	26,000	5,500,000	26,000
Orthodox Church in America	1978	440	1,000,000	457
Philadelphia Yearly Meeting of the Religious Society of Friends	1967	202	(1965) 16,965	(1965) 23
Polish National Catholic Church of America	1960	162	282,411	151
The Presbyterian Church in the United States	1978	4,007	862,416	3,019
Progressive National Baptist Convention, Inc.	1967	655	521,692	N.R.
Reformed Church in America	1978	898	348,080	824
Russian Orthodox Church in the U.S.A., Patriarchal Parishes of the	1975	41	51,500	55
Serbian Eastern Orthodox Church for the U.S.A. and Canada	1967	52	65,000	56
Syrian Orthodox Church of Antioch (Archdiocese of the U.S.A. and Canada)	1978	13	30,000	14
Ukrainian Orthodox Church of America (Ecumenical Patriarchate)	1977	28	25,000	32
United Church of Christ	1979	6,491	1,769,104	5,003
The United Methodist Church	1978	38,682	9,731,779	20,357
The United Presbyterian Church in the United States of America	1978	8,567	2,520,367	7,522
Total (32) bodies		134,975	40,191,346	105,349

TABLE 1-H: CHURCH MEMBERSHIP STATISTICS, 1940-1978

Compiled by Constant H. Jacquet Jr., Editor.

The following statistical time series for 30 U.S. denominations is presented in this edition of the **Yearbook of American and Canadian Churches** as a response to a number of requests for such a tabulation. The denominations selected represent a cross-section of theological orientations, ecclesiastical structures, and geographical foci. Reliability and completeness in statistical reporting were the criteria used in selecting the bodies. Many conclusions can be drawn from the material presented below but interpretations are left to the user of the statistics. The reader is referred to the qualifications relating to statistical data stated throughout this statistical and historical section and in "A Guide for the User of Church Statistics" on page iv.

Denomination	1940	1947*	1950	1955
American Lutheran Church	(1,129,349)	N.A.	(1,587,152)	(1,911,641)
Assemblies of God(b)	198,834	241,782	318,478	400,047
Baptist General Conference	N.A.	N.A.	48,647(c)	54,000
Christian and Missionary Alliance**	22,832(d)	N.A.	58,347	57,109(e)
Christian Church (Disciples of Christ)	1,658,966	1,889,066	1,767,964	1,897,736
Church of God (Anderson, Ind.)	74,497	95,325	107,094	123,523
Church of God (Cleveland, Tenn.)	63,216	N.A.	121,706(f)	142,668
Church of Jesus Christ of Latter-day Saints	724,401(d)	911,279	1,111,314	1,230,021
Church of the Brethren	176,908	182,497	186,201	195,609
Church of the Nazarene	165,532	201,487(g)	226,684	270,576
Cumberland Presbyterian Church	73,357	75,427	81,806	84,990
Episcopal Church	1,996,434	2,155,514	2,417,464	2,852,965(h)
Evangelical Covenant Church of America	45,634	N.A.	51,850	55,311
Free Methodist Church of North America	45,890	46,783(g)	48,574	51,437
Jehovah's Witnesses	N.A.	N.A.	N.A.	187,120
Lutheran Church in America	(1,988,277)	N.A.	(2,395,356)	(2,760,442)
Lutheran Church—Missouri Synod	1,277,097	1,422,513	1,674,901	2,004,110
Mennonite Church	51,304	52,596	56,480	70,283
North American Baptist Conference	N.A.	N.A.	41,560	47,319
Presbyterian Church in the U.S.	532,135	596,037	678,206	810,917
Reformed Church in America	255,107	274,455	284,504	319,593
Reorganized Church of Jesus Christ of Latter-Day Saints	106,554	116,888	124,925	137,856
Roman Catholic Church	21,284,455	24,402,124	28,634,878	33,396,647
Salvation Army	238,357	205,881	209,341	249,641
Seventh-day Adventists	176,218	208,030	237,168	277,162
Southern Baptist Convention	4,949,174	6,079,305	7,079,889	8,467,439
United Church of Christ	(1,708,146)	(1,835,853)	(1,977,418)	(2,116,322)
United Methodist Church	(8,043,454)	(9,135,248)	(9,653,178)	(10,029,535)
United Presbyterian Church in the U.S.A.	(2,158,834)	(2,373,345)	(2,532,429)	(2,890,718)
Wisconsin Evangelical Lutheran Synod	256,007(d)	259,097	307,216	328,969

*Reported in the **Christian Herald,** June, 1947. Only bodies of 50,000 or more reported.

(a) Data for 1966
(b) Assemblies of God statistics for 1971 and later are full membership statistics.
(c) Data for 1952
(d) Data for 1939
(e) Data for 1954
(f) Data for 1951
(g) Data for 1945
(h) Data for 1956
(j) Data for 1961

**A change in the basis of reporting occurred in this body and statistics for 1970-1977 are inclusive statistics as opposed to those reported earlier.

FOR SELECTED U.S. DENOMINATIONS

Yearbook of American and Canadian Churches

(Note: Statistics contained in parentheses are composite totals for the denominations listed prior to merger of the several component bodies. The symbol NA means "Not Available." Most recent titles are used in the case of denominations listed. For information concerning dates and circumstances of merger, see the historical sketches for these denominations in Directory 3, "Religious Bodies in the United States" in this edition.)

1960	1965	1970	1975	1976	1977	1978
2,242,259	2,541,546	2,543,293	2,415,687	2,402,261	2,390,076	2,377,235
508,602	572,123	625,027	785,348	898,711	939,312	932,365
72,056	86,719	103,955	115,340	117,973	120,222	131,00
59,657	64,586	112,519	145,833	150,492	152,841	158,218
1,801,821	1,918,471	1,424,479	1,302,164	1,278,734	1,256,849	1,231,817
142,796	143,231	150,198	166,257	170,285	171,947	173,753
170,261	205,465	272,278	343,249	365,124	377,765	392,551
1,486,887	1,789,175	2,073,146	2,336,715	2,391,892	2,486,261	2,592,000
199,947	194,815	182,614	179,336	178,157	177,534	175,335
307,629	343,380	383,284	441,093	449,205	455,648	462,724
88,452	78,917	92,095	94,050	92,995	93,200	93,268
3,269,325	3,429,153(a)	3,285,826	2,857,513	2,882,064	2,818,830	2,815,359
60,090	65,780	67,441	71,808	73,458	74,060	74,678
55,338	59,415	64,901	67,043	68,180	69,134	73,294
250,000	330,358	388,920	560,897	577,362	554,018	519,218
(3,053,243)	3,142,752	3,106,844	2,986,078	2,974,749	2,967,168	2,942,002
2,391,195	2,692,889	2,788,536	2,763,545	2,757,271	2,673,321	2,631,374
73,125	80,087	88,522	94,209	96,092	96,609	97,142
50,646	53,711	55,080	42,122	42,277	42,724	42,499
902,849	950,139	958,195	878,126	877,664	869,693	862,416
354,621	385,754	367,606	355,052	350,734	351,438	348,080
155,291	168,355	152,670	157,762	185,839	186,414	185,636
42,104,900	46,246,175	48,214,729	48,881,872	49,325,752	49,836,176	49,602,035
254,141	287,991	326,934	384,817	380,618	396,238	414,035
317,852	364,666	420,419	495,699	509,792	522,317	535,705
9,731,591	10,770,573	11,628,032	12,733,124	12,917,992	13,078,239	13,191,394
(2,241,134)	2,070,413	1,960,608	1,818,762	1,801,241	1,785,652	1,769,104
(10,641,310)	(11,067,497)	10,671,774	9,957,710	9,861,028	9,785,534	9,731,779
3,259,011	3,034,321	3,087,213	2,657,699	2,607,321	2,561,234	2,520,367
348,184(i)	358,466	381,321	395,440	399,114	401,489	402,972

TABLE 1-I: INCLUSIVE MEMBERSHIP, 50 COMPILATIONS

The following are the figures reported on inclusive membership in religious bodies in the U.S. in 50 compilations, between 1890 and 1978 as reported in the Census of Religious Bodies, as indicated, and by private publications. For years omitted, no compilations were made.

Year	Membership	Source
1890	41,699,342	(CRB)[1]
1906	35,068,058	(CRB)
1916	41,926,852	(CRB)
1926	54,576,346	(CRB)
1931	59,268,764	(CH)[2]
1932	60,157,392	(CH)
1933	60,812,624	(CH)
1934	62,007,376	(CH)
1935	62,678,177	(CH)
1936	55,807,366	(CRB)
1936	63,221,996	(CH)
1937	63,848,094	(CH)
1938	64,156,895	(YBAC)[3]
1940	64,501,594	(YBAC)
1942	68,501,186	(YBAC)
1944	72,492,699	(YBAC)
1945	71,700,142*	(CH)
1946	73,673,182*	(CH)
1947	77,386,188	(CH)
1948	79,435,605	(CH)
1949	81,862,328	(CH)
1950	86,830,490	(YBAC)
1951	88,673,005	(YBAC)
1952	92,277,129	(YBAC)
1953	94,842,845	(YBAC)
1954	97,482,611	(YBAC)
1955	100,162,529	(YBAC)
1956	103,224,954	(YBAC)
1957	104,189,678	(YBAC)
1958	109,557,741	(YBAC)
1959	112,226,905	(YBAC)
1960	114,449,217	(YBAC)
1961	116,109,929	(YBAC)
1962	117,946,002	(YBAC)
1963	120,965,238	(YBAC)
1964	123,307,449	(YBAC)
1965	124,682,422	(YBAC)
1966	125,778,656	(YBAC)
1967	126,445,110	(YBAC)
1968	128,469,636	(YBAC)
1969	128,505,084	(YBAC)
1970	131,045,053	(YBAC)
1971	131,389,642	(YBAC)
1972	131,424,564	(YBAC)
1973	131,245,139	(YBACC)[4]
1974	131,871,743	(YBACC)
1975	131,012,953	(YBACC)
1976	131,897,539	(YBACC)
1977	132,812,470	(YBACC)
1978	133,748,776	(YBACC)

Note: For certain other years *Christian Herald*, New York, published compilations of "communicant" or adult membership only. These totals are not included in the table because they are not comparable with the inclusive figures here noted.

[1] CRB—*Census of Religious Bodies*, Bureau of the Census, Washington.

[2] CH—*The Christian Herald*, New York.

[3] YBAC—*Yearbook of American Churches*, New York.

[4] YBACC—*Yearbook of American and Canadian Churches*, New York.

*Including only bodies with over 50,000 members.

2. CHURCH FINANCIAL STATISTICS AND RELATED DATA, UNITED STATES AND CANADA

For this edition of the **Yearbook of American and Canadian Churches,** complete financial data were supplied by 42 United States communions. The results are presented in the table entitled "Some Statistics of Church Finances—United States Churches." The data are complete for each communion in the three major categories of reporting. It will be noted that Total Contributions are the sum total of Total Congregational Finances and Total Benevolences.

Similarly, data were supplied by 25 Canadian church bodies. The information is included in the table "Some Statistics of Church Finances—Canadian Churches." Both the U.S. and Canadian data are current, and incomplete information submitted by denominations has been excluded from the tables.

A third table, "Summary Statistics of Church Finances," provides totals for the U.S. and Canadian bodies. The 42 U.S. bodies report total contributions of $7,454,316,525 and the 25 Canadian groups $357,633,159. It must be remembered however, that many of the Canadian groups are not wholly Canadian denominations but, rather, sections of denominations existing and headquartered in the U.S. Only 8 of the 25 bodies listed in the table "Some Statistics of Church Finances—Canadian Churches" are strictly Canadian denominations. Per capita contributions for full membership of U.S. communions amounted to $176.37 and for the Canadian bodies, $181.80. Benevolences as a percentage of total contributions amounted to 19.9 percent for the U.S. bodies and 25.4 percent for the Canadian.

Readers of the tables should be aware of the fact that the Canadian and U.S. financial data appearing in this section are only a significant part of total contributions from members of all communions. Not all bodies in the U.S. and Canada gather church financial data centrally, and some have information but do not reveal it publicly. Additionally, little is known about other major segments of church financial income such as earned income, interest from investments, and bequests.

Comparisons between this year's aggregate financial data and those in previous editions of the **Yearbook** should not be made, since the same bodies do not report financial data each year. However, for an individual denomination, or groups of denominations, reporting annually over time, comparisons can be made.

Comparative data for ten major Protestant denominations in the U.S. among the 42 listed in this section show a total 1978 membership of 24,893,417 or 580,716 less than the same churches' total for 1977. Yet these fewer members increased total giving in the ten denominations by 8.5 percent. When this is compared with an 9.0 percent rate of inflation in the U.S. in 1978, the total effect is decreased real income for these denominations. For Canada, comparative statistics for ten communions indicate a decrease in membersip from 1977 to 1978 of 7,400 to a total of 1,283,533 and an increase in giving of $23,701,790 to a total of $247,358,423. Assuming an inflation rate in Canada of 8.4 percent for 1978, the total contributions of these ten communions show a real increase, after inflation, of $2,923,683.

The other statistical charts and tables as well as the textual and bibliographical materials in the section present useful background information for interpreting church finances. The data are completely new and come from both Canadian and U.S. sources.

SOME STATISTICS OF CHURCH FINANCE

COMMUNION	Year	Full or* Confirmed Membership	Inclusive** Membership	TOTAL CONTRIBUTIONS		
				Total Contributions	Per Capita Full or Confirmed Membership	Per Capita Inclusive Membership
African Methodist Episcopal Zion Church	1978	983,701	1,093,001	$ 49,309,967	$ 50.13	$ 45.11
American Baptist Churches in the U.S.A.	1977	1,316,760	1,316,760	222,884,570	169.27	169.27
The American Lutheran Church	1978	1,773,179	2,377,235	313,517,665	176.81	131.88
Associate Reformed Presbyterian Church, General Synod	1978	28,644	32,139	7,392,977	258.10	230.03
Christian Church (Disciples of Christ	1978	791,633	1,231,817	192,039,822	242.59	155.90
Church of God (Anderson, Indiana)	1978	173,753	173,753	68,845,378	396.23	396.23
Church of God General Conference (Oregon, Illinois)	1978	7,550	7,550	1,245,000	164.90	164.90
Church of the Brethren	1978	175,335	175,335	34,873,751	198.90	198.90
Church of the Nazarene	1978	462,124	462,724	178,455,549	386.16	385.66
Conservative Congregational Christian Conference	1978	22,750	22,750	5,954,312	261.73	261.73
Cumberland Presbyterian Church	1978	88,093	93,268	15,794,637	179.30	169.35
The Episcopal Church	1978	1,975,234	2,815,359	430,116,564	217.76	152.77
Evangelical Church of North America	1978	12,210	12,210	6,513,165	533.43	533.43
Evangelical Congregational Church	1979	28,459	28,459	6,969,660	244.90	244.90
The Evangelical Covenant Church of America	1978	74,678	74,678	34,218,331	458.21	458.21
Evangelical Lutheran Synod	1978	14,833	19,705	3,468,851	233.86	176.03
Evangelical Mennonite Church	1978	3,634	3,634	2,076,657	571.45	571.45
Free Methodist Church of North America	1978	55,493	73,294	34,033,258	613.29	464.34
Free Will Baptists, National Association of	1978	216,831	216,831	33,671,826	155.29	155.29
Friends United Meeting	1978	53,390	62,080	10,141,221	189.95	163.36
Grace Brethren Churches, Fellowship of	1978	39,605	39,605	23,087,997	582.96	582.96
Independent Fundamental Churches of America	1979	120,499	266,450	79,308,185	658.16	297.65
Lutheran Church in America	1978	2,183,666	2,942,002	349,612,711	160.11	118.84
Lutheran Church—Missouri Synod	1978	1,969,279	2,631,374	388,164,990	197.11	147.51
Mennonite Brethren Churches	1978	16,042	16,042	5,272,969	328.70	328.70
Mennonite Church	1978	97,142	97,142	36,993,174	380.82	380,82
Moravian Church in America, Northern Province	1978	24,854	31,765	5,067,286	203.88	159.52
Moravian Church in America, Southern Province	1978	17,126	21,002	3,145,887	183.69	149.79
North American Baptist Conference	1978	42,499	42,499	15,189,292	357.41	357.41
Orthodox Presbyterian Church	1978	10,939	15,806	5,243,093	479.30	331.71
Presbyterian Church in America	1978	73,665	82,095	32,633,691	443.00	397.52
Presbyterian Church in the United States	1978	862,416	862,416	243,010,389	281.77	281.77
The Primitive Methodist Church, U.S.A.	1978	9,376	10,222	2,636,904	281.24	257.96
Reformed Church in America	1978	212,631	348,080	76,034,078	357.58	218.43
Seventh-day Adventists	1978	535,705	535,705	330,737,725	617.39	617.39
Seventh Day Baptist General Conference	1978	5,181	5,181	1,164,426	224.75	224.75
Southern Baptist Convention	1978	13,191,394	13,191,394	1,984,583,145	150.45	150.45
United Church of Christ	1978	1,769,104	1,769,104	270,382,991	152.84	152.84
The United Methodist Church	1977	9,731,779	9,731,779	1,264,191,548	129.90	129.90
The United Presbyterian Church in the U.S.A.	1978	2,520,367	2,520,367	578,057,376	229.35	229.35
The Wesleyan Church	1978	86,064	99,016	45,059,083	523.55	455.07
Wisconsin Evangelical Lutheran Synod	1978	303,944	402,972	63,216,424	207,98	156.87

*Full or Confirmed Membership refers to those with full, communicant, or confirmed status.

CONGREGATIONAL FINANCES			BENEVOLENCES			
Total Congregational Contributions	Per Capita Full or Confirmed Membership	Per Capita Inclusive Membership	Total Benevolences	Per Capita Full or Confirmed Membership	Per Capita Inclusive Membership	Benevolences as a Percentage of Total Contributions
$ 45,853,898	$ 46.61	$ 41.95	$ 3,456,069	$ 3.52	$ 3.16	7.0%
191,458,544	145.40	145.40	31,426,026	23.87	23.87	14.1
256,371,804	144.58	107.84	57,145,861	32.23	24.04	18.2
5,865,416	204.77	182.50	1,527,561	53.33	47.53	20.7
166,249,455	210.01	134.96	25,790,367	32.58	20.94	13.4
57,630,848	331,68	331.68	11,214,530	64.55	64.55	16.3
1,135,000	150.33	150.33	110,000	14.57	14.57	8.8
25,397,531	144.85	144.85	9,476,220	54.05	54.05	27.2
153,943,138	333.12	332.69	24,512,411	53.04	52.97	13.7
4,343,900	190.94	190.94	1,610,412	70.79	70.79	27.0
13,657,931	155.04	146.44	2,136,706	24.26	22.91	13.5
365,885,454	185.24	129.96	64,231,110	32.52	22.81	14.9
5,253,975	430.30	430.30	1,259,190	103.13	103.13	19.3
5,514,834	193.78	193.78	1,454,826	51.12	51.12	20.9
26,200,708	350.85	350.85	8,017,623	107.36	107.36	23.4
2,629,719	177.29	133.45	839,132	56.57	42.58	24.2
1,281,761	352.71	352.71	794,896	218.74	218.74	38.3
23,911,458	430.89	326.24	10,121,800	182.40	138.10	29.7
27,973,595	129.01	129.01	5,698,231	26.28	26.28	16.9
8,172,337	153.07	131.64	1,968,884	36.88	31.72	19.4
20,009,221	505.22	505.22	3,078,776	77.74	77.74	13.3
64,736,216	537.23	242.96	14,571,969	120.93	54.69	18.4
277,186,563	126.94	94.22	72,426,148	33.17	24.62	20.7
329,134,237	167.13	125.08	59,030,753	29.98	22.43	15.2
3,285,242	204.79	204.79	1,987,727	123.91	123.91	37.7
22,922,417	235.97	235.97	14,070,757	144.85	144.85	38.0
4,441,750	178.71	139.52	625,536	25.17	19.69	12.3
2,297,156	134.13	109.38	848,731	49.56	40.41	27.0
11,629,309	273.64	273.64	3,559,983	83.77	83.77	23.4
4,107,705	375.51	259.88	1,135,388	103.79	71.83	21.7
24,446,721	331.86	297.79	8,186,970	111.14	99.73	25.1
194,685,709	225.74	225.74	48,324,680	56.03	56.03	19.9
2,138,541	228.09	209.21	498,363	53.15	48.75	18.9
60,494,317	284.50	173.79	15,539,761	73.08	44.64	20.4
104,044,989	194.22	194.22	226,692,736	423.17	423.17	68.5
877,769	169.42	169.42	286,657	55.33	55.33	24.6
668,120,760	126.46	126.46	316,462,385	23.99	23.99	15.9
232,593,033	131.48	131.48	37,789,958	21.36	21.36	14.0
972,038,703	99.88	99.88	292,152,845	30.02	30.02	23.1
498,187,102	197.66	197.66	79,870,274	31.69	31.69	13.8
36,819,228	427.81	371.85	8,239,855	95.74	83.22	18.3
50,255,539	165.34	124.71	12,960,885	42.64	32.16	20.5

clusvie Membership refers to those who are full, communicant, or confirmed members, plus other members listed as baptized, confirmed, or noncummunicant.

SOME STATISTICS OF CHURCH FINANCES

COMMUNION	Year	Full or* Confirmed Membership	Inclusive** Membership	TOTAL CONTRIBUTIONS: Total Contributions	Per Capita Full or Confirmed Membership	Per Capita Inclusive Membership
The Anglican Church of Canada	1977	599,903	1,001,927	$ 73,120,061	$121.88	$ 72.98
Baptist Convention of Ontario and Quebec	1978	38,000	47,600	12,780,043	336.32	268.49
Baptist General Conference	1978	5,288	5,288	3,363,603	636.09	636.09
Baptist Union of Western Canada	1978	19,020	19,020	6,527,681	343.20	343.20
The Bible Holiness Movement	1979	211	372	29,946	141.92	80.50
Christian Church (Disciples of Christ)	1978	2,693	4,753	934,200	346.90	196.55
Church of the Foursquare Gospel of Western Canada	1978	2,025	2,025	926,063	457.32	457.32
Church of the Nazarene	1978	8,502	8,537	3,763,473	442.66	440.84
The Evangelical Covenant Church of Canada	1978	1,127	1,127	782,522	694.34	694.34
The Evangelical Lutheran Church of Canada	1978	57,961	82,065	9,198,119	158.70	112.08
The Free Methodist Church in Canada	1978	4,600	5,951	3,387,955	736.52	569.30
Lutheran Church—Canada	1978	66,732	92,939	10,931,456	163.81	117.62
Lutheran Church in America—Canada Section	1978	88,182	121,693	13,022,741	147.68	107.02
Mennonite Brethren Churches of North America, Canadian Conference of	1978	20,900	20,900	11,413,901	546.12	546.12
Mennonite Church	1978	9,819	9,819	3,294,624	335.54	335.54
Mennonites in Canada, Conference of	1978	25,818	25,818	8,594,532	332.89	332.89
Moravian Church in America, Northern Province, Canadian District of the	1978	1,137	1,684	322,168	283.35	191.31
North American Baptist Conference	1978	14,742	14,742	6,697,265	454.30	454.30
Presbyterian Church in Canada	1978	166,920	166,920	31,576,561	189.18	189.18
Reformed Church in America—Ontario Classis	1978	2,753	5,541	911,805	331.21	164.56
Seventh-day Adventist Church in Canada	1978	29,258	29,258	22,138,711	756.67	756.67
United Baptist Convention of the Atlantic Provinces	1978	61,130	61,130	12,276,468	200.83	200.83
The United Church of Canada	1978	735,430	2,087,313	117,492,742	159.76	56.29
The Wesleyan Church	1978	4,203	4,750	3,972,200	945.08	836.25
Wisconsin Evangelical Lutheran Synod	1978	733	938	174,319	237.82	185.84

*Full or Confirmed Membership refers to those with full, communicant, or confirmed status.

**Inclusive Membership refers to those who are full, communicant, or confirmed members, plus other members listed as bap nonconfirmed, or noncommunicant.

†Although most denominations reported Canadian dollars for this table, certain denominations reported U.S. dollars. In order to standardize these amounts, U.S. dollars were multiplied by 1.156, a factor which represents the average differential in exchange rates over the four quarters of 1978. Thus the totals are all expressed in Canadian dollar amounts.

SUMMARY STATISTIC

	Total Bodies	Full or* Confirmed Membership	Inclusive** Membership	TOTAL CONTRIBUTIONS: Total Contributions	Per Capita Full or Confirmed Membership	Per Capi Inclusiv Membersh
United States Communions	42	42,265,227	45,954,600	$ 7,454,316,525	$176.37	$162.2
Canadian Communions†	25	1,967,087	3,822,110	357,633,159	181.80	93.5

*Full or Confirmed Membership refers to those with full, communicant, or confirmed status.

**Inclusive Membership refers to those who are full, communicant, or confirmed members, plus other members listed as baptized nonconfirmed, or noncommunicant.

†Shown in Canadian dollars

—CANADIAN CHURCHES†

CONGREGATIONAL FINANCES			BENEVOLENCES			
Total Congregational Contributions	Per Capita Full or Confirmed Membership	Per Capita Inclusive Membership	Total Benevolences	Per Capita Full or Confirmed Membership	Per Capita Inclusive Membership	Benevolences As a Percentage of Total Contributions
$ 56,158,484	$ 93.61	$ 56.05	$16,961,577	$ 28.27	$ 16.93	23.2%
10,716,683	282.02	225.14	2,063,360	54.30	43.35	16.1
2,709,768	512.44	512.44	653,835	123.65	123.65	19.4
5,074,902	266.82	266.82	1,452,779	76.38	76.38	22.3
8,506	40.31	22.87	21,440	101.61	57.63	71.6
811,628	301.38	170.76	122,572	45.52	25.79	13.1
858,361	423.88	423.88	67,702	33.44	33.44	7.3
3,267,486	384.32	382.74	495,987	58.34	58.10	13.2
597,291	529.98	529.98	185,231	164.36	164.36	23.7
7,491,927	129.26	91.29	1,706,192	29.44	20.79	18.5
2,526,347	549.21	424.52	861,608	187.31	144.78	25.4
8,413,941	126.08	90.53	2,517,515	37.73	27.09	23.0
10,264,550	116.40	84.35	2,758,191	31.28	22.67	21.2
5,948,252	284.61	284.61	5,465,649	261.51	261.51	47.9
1,888,292	192.31	192.31	1,406,332	143.23	143.23	42.7
4,491,215	173.96	173.96	4,103,317	158.93	158.93	47.7
255,602	224.80	151.78	66,566	58.55	39.53	20.7
4,807,597	326.12	326.12	1,889,668	128.28	128.28	28.2
27,083,865	162.26	162.26	4,492,696	26.92	26.92	14.2
757,208	275.05	136.66	154,597	56.16	27.90	17.0
5,948,947	203.33	203.33	16,189,764	553.34	553.34	73.1
10,516,727	172.04	172.04	1,759,741	28.79	28.79	14.3
93,420,817	127.03	44.76	24,071,925	32.73	11.53	20.5
2,643,364	628.92	556.50	1,328,836	316.16	279.75	33.5
123,154	168.01	131.29	51,165	69.80	54.55	29.4

F CHURCH FINANCES

CONGREGATIONAL FINANCES			BENEVOLENCES			
Total Congregational Contributions	Per Capita Full or Confirmed Membership	Per Capita Inclusive Membership	Total Benevolences	Per Capita Full or Confirmed Membership	Per Capita Inclusive Membership	Benevolences As a Percentage of Total Contributions
$ 5,973,183,533	$141.33	$129.98	$1,481,132,992	$35.04	$32.23	19.9%
266,784,914	135.62	69.80	90,848,245	46.18	23.77	25.4

TOTAL GIVING IN 1978, CONTRIBUTIONS AND DISTRIBUTIONS (In Billions)

Contributions		Percent of Total
Individuals	$32.80	82.9%
Bequests	2.60	6.6
Foundations	2.16	5.5
Corporations	2.00	5.0

Distributions		Percent of Total
Religion	$18.40	46.5%
Health and Hospitals	5.45	13.8
Education	5.52	14.0
Social Welfare	3.99	10.0
Arts & Humanities	2.49	6.3
Civic & Public	1.14	2.9
Other	2.57	6.5

Total giving in 1978 is estimated at $39.56 billion, an increase of 9.4 percent over the $36.15 billion in 1977 according to *Giving USA: 1979 Annual Report,* published by the American Association of Fund-Raising Counsel, New York.

"Religion" as a category received an estimated $18.40 billion in 1978, or 46.5 percent of total giving.

The greatest amount of contributions came from living donors, a total of $32.80 billion, or 82.9 percent of the total. If that is combined with bequest giving of $2.60 billion it equals 89.5 percent of all giving in 1978.

AVERAGE INCOME WITH AVERAGE CHARITABLE DONATIONS, IN DOLLARS, AND AS A PERCENTAGE OF AVERAGE INCOME, BY AGE AND SEX, CANADA, 1976

Age	Sex	Average Income	Average Donations	Donations as % of Income
20 and under	Male	$ 6,791.28	$ 4.70	0.07%
	Female	5,644.71	5.72	0.10
20 to 29	Male	11,528.95	18.28	0.16
	Female	8,475.51	12.27	0.14
30 to 39	Male	16,847.17	57.09	0.34
	Female	10,130.83	20.66	0.20
40 to 49	Male	18,787.22	103.20	0.55
	Female	10,091.03	38.90	0.39
50 to 59	Male	17,888.43	123.03	0.69
	Female	10,315.06	75.40	0.73
60 to 64	Male	16,054.09	143.88	0.90
	Female	10,553.19	96.78	0.92
65 and over	Male	15,694.61	234.68	1.50
	Female	12,279.68	196.91	1.60
Total Taxpayers	Male	15,303.87	75.01	0.49
	Female	9,479.45	39.57	0.42

Source: *Taxation Statistics, 1978 Edition* (1976 information)
Ottawa: Department of National Revenue, Taxation. Pages 52 to 59

INDIVIDUAL GIVING AS A PERCENTAGE OF PERSONAL INCOME AND DISPOSABLE PERSONAL INCOME 1965-1978
(In Billions of Dollars)

Year	Personal Income	Individual Giving	As % of Personal Income	Disposable Personal Income	As % of Disposable Personal Income
1965	$537.0	9.28	1.72	$ 472.2	1.96
1966	584.9	10.53	1.80	510.4	2.06
1967	626.6	11.14	1.77	544.5	2.04
1968	685.2	12.60	1.83	588.1	2.14
1969	745.8	13.60	1.82	630.4	2.15
1970	801.3	14.40	1.79	685.9	2.09
1971	859.1	15.40	1.79	742.8	2.07
1972	942.5	16.84	1.78	801.3	2.10
1973	1,054.3	18.36	1.74	903.1	2.03
1974	1,154.7	19.80	1.71	983.6	2.01
1975	1,246.0	21.47	1.72	1,076.8	1.99
1976	1,375.3	26.26	1.91	1,181.7	2.22
1977	1,536.7	29.45	1.91	1,309.0	2.25
1978	1,707.6	32.80	1.92	1,451.4	2.26

Source: *Giving USA: 1979 Annual Report.* New York: American Association of Fund-Raising Counsel, 1979, p. 10.

RECIPIENTS OF GIVING 1968-1978
(In Billions of Dollars)

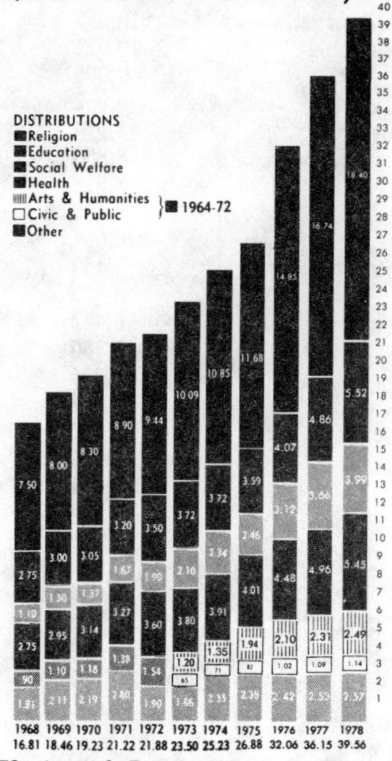

Source: *Giving USA: 1979 Annual Report,* New York, American Association of Fund-Raising Counsel, p. 23.

CANADIAN PER CAPITA PERSONAL DISPOSABLE INCOME IN DOLLARS, 1978 ESTIMATES, WITH 1980 PROJECTIONS (IN BRACKETS), BY PROVINCES

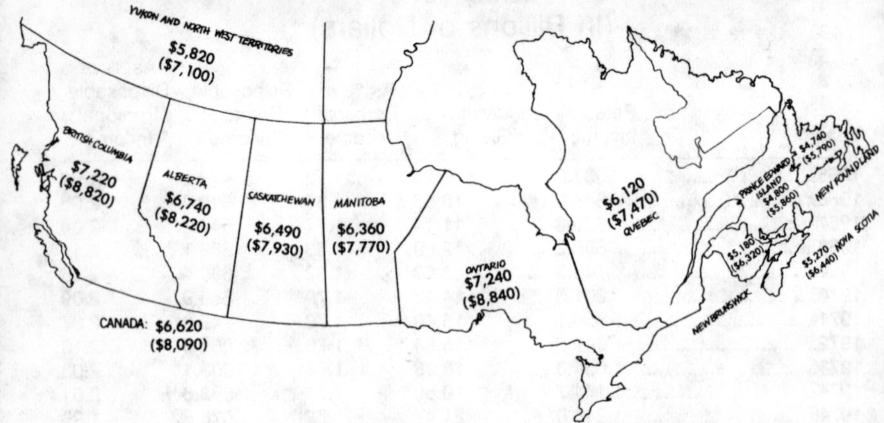

Source: *The Financial Post Survey of Markets, 1979.* Toronto: Maclean-Hunter Ltd., 1978.

UNITED STATES PER CAPITA PERSONAL INCOME 1978, BY STATES, AND PERCENTAGE OF CHANGE FROM 1977

Rank	State	Per Capita Personal Income[1]	% Change 1977-1978
1	Alaska	$10,851	3.4%
2	Dist. of Columbia	10,022	11.6
3	Wyoming	9,096	21.0
4	Nevada	9,032	13.2
5	Connecticut	8,914	10.7
6	California	8,850	11.9
7	New Jersey	8,818	10.7
8	Illinois	8,745	10.0
9	Delaware	8,604	11.4
10	Washington	8,450	11.7
11	Utah	8,450	11.7
12	Michigan	8,442	11.0
13	Hawaii	8,380	8.8
14	Maryland	8,306	9.7
15	New York	8,267	9.9
16	Massachusetts	8,063	11.0
17	Colorado	8,001	11.7
18	Kansas	8,001	12.0
19	Iowa	7,873	14.3
20	Minnesota	7,847	10.2
21	Oregon	7,839	11.8
22	Ohio	7,812	10.2
	UNITED STATES	7,810	11.2
23	Pennsylvania	7,733	10.5
24	Texas	7,697	12.7
25	Indiana	7,696	11.2
26	Virginia	7,624	11.4
27	Wisconsin	7,597	10.7
28	Rhode Island	7,526	11.1

Rank	State	Per Capita Personal Income[1]	% Change 1977-1978
29	Florida	7,505	12.1%
30	North Dakota	7,478	27.4
31	Nebraska	7,391	10.7
32	Arizona	7,374	13.1
33	Missouri	7,342	10.2
34	New Hampshire	7,277	10.6
35	Montana	7,051	15.7
36	Oklahoma	6,951	10.9
37	South Dakota	6,841	14.9
38	Idaho	6,813	13.6
39	Georgia	6,700	11.6
40	Louisiana	6,640	12.4
41	Kentucky	6,615	10.5
42	North Carolina	6,607	11.7
43	Vermont	6,541	12.3
44	New Mexico	6,505	11.3
45	Tennessee	6,489	11.9
46	West Virginia	6,456	7.6
47	Maine	6,333	10.1
48	Alabama	6,247	10.9
49	South Carolina	6,242	10.7
50	Arkansas	6,183	12.0
51	Mississippi	5,736	14.1

[1]Preliminary.

Source: U.S. Department of Commerce, Bureau of Economic Analysis, *Survey of Current Business,* April, 1979, Adapted from Table 1, p. 20.

FAMILIES AND UNRELATED INDIVIDUALS BY TOTAL MONEY INCOME IN 1977 (Families and unrelated individuals as of March, 1978)

Total money income	Families		Unrelated Individuals	
	Number (thousands)	Percent distribution	Number (thousands)	Percent distribution
Total	57,215	100.0	23,110	100.0
$2,000-4,999	5,343	9.4	9,959	43.2
$5,000-8,999	8,358	14.6	5,589	24.2
$9,000-13,999	10,475	18.2	4,087	17.7
$14,000-17,999	8,414	14.7	1,808	7.9
$18,000-24,999	11,817	20.6	1,042	4.5
$25,000 and over	12,808	22.4	626	2.7
Median Income	$16,009		$5,907	
Mean Income	$18,264		$7,981	

Source: Adapted from U.S. Bureau of the Census, *Current Population Reports,* Series P-60, No. 118, "Money Income in 1977 of Families and Persons in the United States," U.S. Government Printing Office, Washington, D.C., 1979, Table A, p. 2.

"White families had a median income of $16,740 in 1977, which represented a marginal increase (1 percent) over their 1976 median in real terms. The 1977 median income of Black families ($9,560) and Spanish families ($11,420) did not differ significantly from their respective 1976 median incomes after adjusting for inflation."

PRETAX INCOME IN 1979 NECESSARY TO EQUAL 1960 PURCHASING POWER

1960 Pretax Income	$3,000	$ 5,000	$10,000	$15,000	$25,000	$ 50,000	$100,000
Less: Federal income tax	36	380	1,218	2,213	4,719	14,043	39,894
Less: Social security tax	90	144	144	144	144	144	144
Equals: Income after taxes	2,874	4,476	8,638	12,643	20,137	35,813	59,962
1979 Necessary Pretax Income	$6,960	$12,113	$25,043	$37,531	$64,628	$129,978	$236,094
Less: Federal income tax	(304)	722	3,089	6,049	15,318	43,375	92,040
Less: social security tax	427	743	1,404	1,404	1,404	1,404	1,404
Less: Amount to cover inflation since 1960	3,963	6,172	11,912	17,435	27,769	49,386	82,688
Equals: Income after taxes in 1960 dollars	2,874	4,476	8,638	12,643	20,137	35,813	59,962

Source: *Economic Road Maps,* Nos. 1852-1853, April, 1978. New York, The Conference Board, 1978.

"Federal income and social security taxes are computed for married couples, only one of whom works, with two children. No allowances are made for any other taxes."

The above data indicate, among other things, that to obtain an income after taxes of $12,643 (in 1960 dollars) in 1979, an income of $37,531 would be necessary, whereas in 1960 it took an income of $15,000. The amount to cover inflation since 1960 amounts to $17,435.

UNITED STATES PERSONAL CONSUMPTION BY TYPE OF EXPENDITURES 1974 and 1977 (In Billions of Dollars)

	1974	1977	% Increase or Decrease
Food and Tobacco[1]	203.7	261.8	28.5%
Clothing, Assessories and Jewelry	76.3	95.6	25.3
Personal Care	13.5	16.7	23.7
Housing	136.5	184.6	35.2
Household Operation	130.6	176.9	35.4
Medical Care Expenses	76.9	118.0	53.5
Personal Business	45.5	60.4	32.7
Transportation	115.1	172.1	49.6
Recreation	60.9	81.2	33.3
Private Education and Research	13.8	18.8	36.2
Religious and Welfare Activities	11.6	15.4	32.8
Foreign Travel and Other, Net	5.3	5.1	-3.8
Total	889.7	1,206.6	35.6

[1]Expenditures for Alcoholic Beverages, included in this total, amounted to $23.0 billion in 1974 and $28.2 billion in 1977, an increase of 22.6%. Tobacco Product expenditures over the four-year period 1974-77 rose from $13.8 billion to $16.5 billion, an increase of 19.6%.

Source: Adapted from U.S. Department of Commerce, Bureau of Economic Analysis, *Survey of Current Business,* July, 1978, Table 2.6—Personal Consumption Expenditures by Type of Expenditures, p. 37.

SELECTED AVERAGE CANADIAN URBAN FAMILY EXPENDITURES IN SELECTED MAJOR CITIES, AS PERCENTAGE OF TOTAL EXPENDITURES, 1976 (ALL FAMILIES AND UNATTACHED INDIVIDUALS)

	St. John's	Halifax	Montreal	Ottawa	Toronto	Winnipeg	Edmonton	Vancouver
Total Expenditures	$16,964	$16,913	$16,499	$20,679	$19,124	$14,994	$17,943	$18,840
Selected Expenditures:								
Food	17.6%	14.2%	18.2%	13.8%	15.1%	16.9%	15.2%	15.0%
Shelter	15.1	15.8	14.7	15.9	16.5	15.5	15.0	16.1
Travel and Transportation	13.0	13.8	12.1	12.1	11.8	12.9	14.3	12.5
Clothing	7.2	6.9	7.6	6.5	7.0	7.1	7.2	5.9
Security (e.g. Savings, Insurance)	5.3	6.0	4.6	6.4	5.1	5.7	4.7	5.4
Recreation	3.0	4.4	3.5	4.2	3,8	4.1	4.2	4.1
Alcoholic Beverages	2.2	1.9	1.9	1.8	2.0	1.9	1.8	2.0
Cigarettes and Tobacco	1.8	1.4	1.8	1.2	1.1	1.4	1.0	0.9
Education (excluding Taxes)	.7	1.0	.6	1.0	.7	.7	.8	.6
Reading	.5	.6	.7	.6	.5	.5	.5	.5
Charitable Gifts: Religious Organizations	.6	.5	.1	.3	.4	.5	.6	.4
Charitable Gifts: Other Organizations	.1	.2	.1	1.4	.2	.2	.2	.2

Source: *Urban Family Expenditure, 1976.* Ottawa: Statistics Canada, 1979. Catalogue No. 62-547, Table 21

EFFECTS OF INFLATION ON PER CAPITA GIVING 1961-1978

Constant H. Jacquet, Jr.
Office of Research, Evaluation and Planning
National Council of Churches

Somewhere between 38 and 52 religious bodies have been able to supply annually complete financial data on total contributions received. Total contributions are the sum of all benevolences plus all congregational finances. Representing roughly 20 percent of the total number of U.S. denominations and 30 percent of total U.S. membership reported to the *Yearbook of American and Canadian Churches*, giving to these bodies is approximately 40 percent of total church contributions in the U.S. in any given year.

At least four reasons why more denominations do not supply statistical data on church finances are: 1) the desire to keep the information confidential, 2) a belief that there are biblical restrictions against this type of accounting, 3) a lack of adequate statistical programs in denominations to report accurate membership and financial data, and 4) denominational polities that do not require full reporting to a central office.

The fragmentary information currently received, however, provides a good "sample" that helps to determine what is happening in the area of U.S. church contributions. It should be remembered that these are aggregate data and the experiences of individual denominations may vary from what is presented here.

Organized religion, like other privately financed agencies, is on the whole, struggling with powerful forces of inflation in the U.S. Although the dollar amounts of giving have increased from $69.00 per capita full member in 1961 to $176.37 in 1978, an increase of 156 percent, in constant 1967 dollars the increase is only from $77.01 in 1961 to $90.31 in 1978, an increase in real terms of only 17 percent. Therefore, much education and action in the area of stewardship has been necessary to defend the financial structure of organized religion.

Though it is generally known that benevolences average roughly 20 percent of contributions from year to year, there is some evidence available, at least for certain large mainline Protestant bodies, that the pattern of distribution of benevolence money has shifted somewhat to local and regional agencies and away from national agencies. This trend is having a considerable effect on the structures and staffing of national denominational agencies in some communions.

DENOMINATIONAL PER CAPITA FULL MEMBER CONTRIBUTIONS, AND ADJUSTED TO 1967 DOLLARS, 1961–1978

Year	No. of Denoms.	Per Capita Full Member	Constant 1967 Dollars	Year	No. of Denoms.	Per Capita Full Member	Constant 1967 Dollars
1961	46	$69.00	$77.01	1970	45	$ 96.84	$83.27
1962	42	68.76	75.89	1971	42	103.94	85.69
1963	41	69.87	76.19	1972	39	110.29	88.02
1964	41	72.04	77.55	1973	40	118.16	88.77
1965	38	77.75	82.38	1974	44	127.16	86.09
1966		(Not Reported)		1975	43	138.54	85.94
1967		(Not Reported)		1976	43	149.07	87.43
1968	52	95.31	91.47	1977	45	159.33	87.78
1969	48	99.68	90.78	1978	42	176.37	90.31

3. SOME TRENDS AND DEVELOPMENTS

This year, this section contains information on three surveys. The first is "An Overview of Mainline Protestantism in Canada and the United States of America," by Harold Fallding, Professor of Sociology, University of Waterloo, Waterloo, Ontario. Dr. Fallding presents many interesting similarities and differences in religious organization and in the impact of religious institutions on the theological and social climate in both Canada and the U.S.

This article is followed by two reports appearing yearly in this section of the **Yearbook**—"The 1978 Official Catholic Data" and "Trends in Seminary Enrollment: 1974-1979," prepared by the Association of Theological Schools in the U.S. and Canada.

AN OVERVIEW OF MAINLINE PROTESTANTISM IN CANADA AND THE UNITED STATES OF AMERICA*

By
Harold Fallding
Professor of Sociology, University of Waterloo
Waterloo, Ontario

When we attend to both likenesses and differences in comparing American and Canadian Protestantism, a striking fact emerges. The differences appear more clearly in the impact made by Protestantism on the society. The likenesses stand out when we look at the way Protestantism goes about pursuing its own goals in the two countries. Let us, then, divide this analysis into two parts. First, Protestantism's impact on society will be examined, and in two aspects: (1) its role in nation-making, and (2) it's efforts to secure religious liberty. Then its internal life will be examined by considering the adaptations it has made in three major areas: (1) social teachings, (2) evangelistic and pastoral ministry, and (3) doctrinal instruction.

Protestantism's Impact on the Society

Much of the difference in the religion of the two nations is the only to be expected result of their difference in scale. For, to the nearest million, America's population stood at 203 million in 1970, Canada's at 22 million in 1971. Its numbers have allowed the United States an elaboration of life and culture that makes it recognizably its own civilization, but I doubt that this could be claimed for Canada. It is to this difference that we can attribute, for instance, the lower level of theological productivity in Canada. For Canada has no Reinhold Niebuhrs or Paul Tillichs to offer us. Rather, the religious leaders Canada celebrates—men like Laval, Strachan, Ryerson, Aberhart, Coady, and Vanier—have been men of action devising forms of organization to implement received ideas. To this difference of scale we can also attribute, at least in part, the greater proliferation of new religious movements in the United States and the greater sectarian diversity.

1. *Protestantism's role in nation-making*

The two nations' different ideas of national mission have, however, had the same determining importance as scale. For, from

* This article is a direct abridgment of 'Mainline Protestantism in Canada and the United States of America: an overview,' *Canadian Journal of Sociology*, 3(2) 1978, and is reproduced in this form by permission of the editors. For reasons of space bibliographical references are omitted from the abridgment, but may be obtained by referring to the original paper.

the first, but especially from the time of the Revolutionary War, the United States has been dedicated to distinctive nationhood, and it came in time to include world leadership under that mission. This has made it essentially innovating culturally. Canada, by contrast, is essentially a colonial development—although I mean colonial in the best sense: the extension, missionizing sense of taking a metropolitan culture to some new place. I do not believe Canada has ever found reason to repudiate this colonial character, even though it repudiated dependent colonial status. Canada remains a traditional society dedicated to consolidating in North America the British and French cultural traditions and, to a lesser extent, some other European traditions as well.

Canada struggled zealously for political independence from the parent authority, but this was a matter of achieving independence in the copy. The more faithful the copy they could make in North America of British and French institutions, the greater was the proof that Canadians could manage on their own. The more faithful this copy, likewise, the greater resistance they would offer to conquest by or absorption into the American political system; a concern that Canadians developed quite early. The Canadian idea was to live off a cultural inheritance.

But not only did the United States set distinctive nationhood before it, a religious component was integral with that self-conception. There is a sense in which it could be said that the nation was founded for religion's sake, and even for Protestantism's sake. For the settlers were seeking religious freedom, and yet not only that. They also sought to establish an economy and polity, a science, technology, and learning that would give expression to their Protestant belief. That they succeeded in taking leadership in these spheres and maintaining it, is sufficiently evidenced in the research of people like the Beards, Handlin, Merton, Baltzell, and Lenski. This religiously motivated public participation generated its own religious expression, and it became sufficiently autonomous for Bellah to consider it a religious system in its own right now—he calls it "civil religion." This civil religion expressed the conviction that in public and cultural affairs men and women are pursuing the will of God. Because of that, Bellah claims, this civil religion is more distinctively Protestant than it is distinctively Christian even.

Canada's own variety of civil religion is different. It consists in the religious legitimation of sovereignty, a practice which it has inherited from Britain. The American civil religion sanctifies the future to be built, whereas the Canadian civil religion upholds the authority established. The American civil religion is practiced apart from the churches, not in opposition to them, but as a kind of religious supplement. The civil religion of Canada is sponsored by the churches, but mainly today by the Anglican, Presbyterian, and United churches, which perpetuate the nationality loyalty of the formerly established church in Britain. It is mainly a matter of supporting government and offering prayers for its success in securing order and justice. Since the ruling monarch is charged with defending the Christian faith and is made head of the Church of England, the nation thus declares itself officially Christian and under Christ.

But Protestantism made more than this formal contribution to nationhood. The Anglican, Presbyterian, and Methodist churches probably contributed as much to the consolidation of national unity in Canada as any other force operating immediately before and after Confederation. Because their memberships reached into all sections of society and all regions of the country, they had an interest in securing that unity, as Gwynne-Timothy has pointed out. Furthermore, as he also shows, the Anglicans' and Methodists' political concerns were translated fairly directly into the formation and policies of the Conservative and Liberal parties respectively. It seems that Protestantism also assisted by offering the leadership for Canada's industrial development. At least it is the prevalent view that this was so, and in Quebec especially. If greater wealth allows greater social influence, Protestants may also have had greater influence because of this. Census tract data on median incomes in five widely separated Canadian cities showed higher incomes to be associated with Protestantism. Thus we have evidence in Canada, just as in the United States, of Protestants' public leadership, stemming from their activist understanding of religion.

2. *The measures taken to secure religious liberty*

The innovating orientation of the United States is further evident in the way Protestantism went about securing religious liberty, thereby opening a door to sectarianism. The people were freed to experiment with a variety of religious movements that are quite distinctively American in character—even though they might prove to be exportable in the long run. Mormonism, Christian Science, Seventh-day Adventism, Disciples of Christ, Assemblies of God, Jehovah's Witnesses, and the American variety of Baptists—these are truly indigenous. Yet America's great religious diversity is mainly due to the welcome its religious freedom sounded to sects arising elsewhere—and not only to sects, for traditionalists like Catholics and Jews also responded. Elmer Clark counted over 400 sects in the United States a quarter of a century ago. The *1976 Yearbook of American and Canadian Churches* gives membership counts for 223 distinct religious bodies in the United States, as against only 63 in Canada. Yet we do have to get this perspective. Most of the current American church membership is concentrated in a smaller number of these denominations, Westhues' tabulation showing that 87 percent of it falls in 21 of them. Canada seems to have been just as willing as the United States to admit sects from elsewhere, although it cannot claim responsibility for starting a great many. But in Canada the church membership is even more concentrated than in the States, Westhues' tabulation on this showing that 87 percent of it falls within three denominations.

In both countries the Roman Catholics are the largest single body. In Canada they make between 40 and 50 percent of all churched people, in the United States between 30 and 40 percent. They are only outnumbered if the non-Roman Catholics are aggregated. As figures 1 and 2 show, the very composition of mainline Protestantism is quite different for the two countries. In Canada it means the United Church predominantly and then the Anglican church, with the Presbyterians, various Lutherans, and various Baptists supplying a rather trailing tail. In the United States mainline Protestantism means the various Baptists overwhelmingly. (Twenty-four separate Baptist bodies contribute to the Baptist membership totaled from the *Yearbook).* Then come the Methodists and various Lutherans, each of whom is less than half as numerous as the Baptists; and a trailing tail is supplied by the Presbyterians and Episcopalians.

Figure 1.

Scale diagram of the composition of mainline Protestantism in the United States.

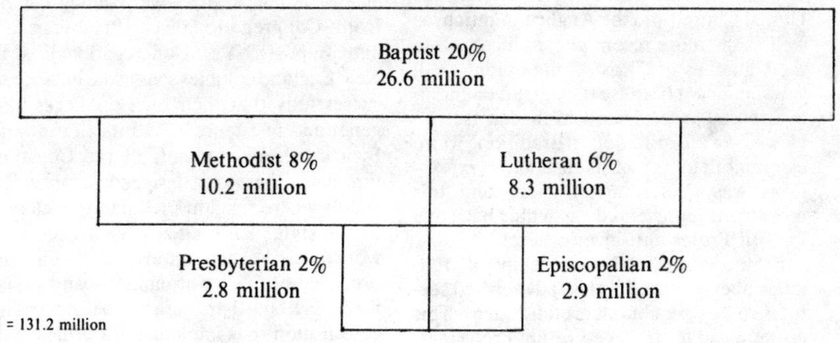

Figure 2.

Scale diagram of the composition of mainline Protestantism in Canada.

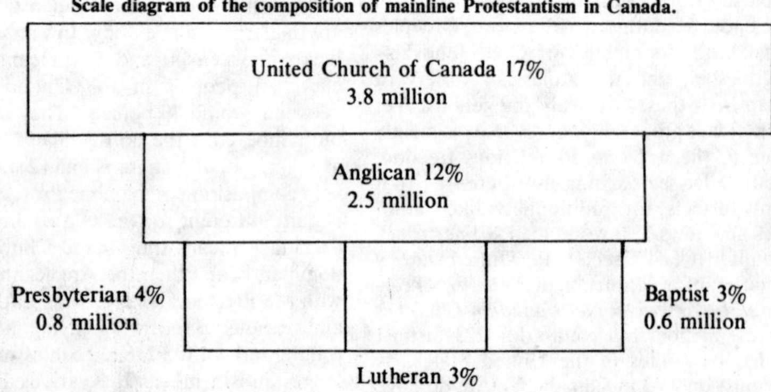

Membership numbers are rounded to the nearest hundred thousand, percentages to the nearest one percent. The percentage figure (and box volumes) are rough ways of comparing the distribution of adherence to a core of religious denominations in the two countries. They are, however, calculated on different bases. Those for the U.S.A. in Fig. 1 are percentages of the total of all church memberships reported in the *1975 Yearbook of American and Canadian Churches*. Those for Canada in Fig. 2 are percentages of the religious affiliations reported to the 1971 Census of Canada.

To me it seems significant that the important Protestant initiative in Canada took a different direction from sect formation—virtually an opposite one. I refer to the amalgamation into one United Church of Canada, of Methodists, Presbyterians, Congregationalists, and Evangelical United Brethren, and the serious contemplation over thirty years of a merger between this United Church and the Anglican Church, as well as the more recent plan to incorporate the Churches of Christ in the union. I call this significant because the pursuit of union, as opposed to sectarian schism, can itself be viewed as a distillation of tradition. More essential than any of its distinctive expressions was Protestantism itself, and this movement represented a reaching back to a kind of Protestantism in general.

Protestantism's championship of religious liberty caused its less advantaged sections to oppose church establishment. This crusade had to be waged within Protestantism on occasion, since Protestant churches have themselves enjoyed establishment. In both Canada and the United States the anti-establishment movement won successes, but it is interesting to compare the different reasons for this and the different means taken and results achieved. Discussion of this question always suffers from the imprecision in the very notion of establishment. Let us say it obtains when one or more religious organizations receives privileges from the state that are not enjoyed by the others.

In the United States the struggle was raised to the constitutional level, this being the culmination of persistent protests against Anglican privilege, coming mainly from Congregationalists, Presbyterians, and Baptists. Yet Congregationalists in New England colonies swung the balance so successfully that their own privileges also generated resistance. The First, Fifth, and Fourteenth amendments of the Constitution were therefore designed to prescribe legally where religion shall stand in relation to the state. Each citizen has freedom to worship as he may choose, and religious organizations are autonomous and equal with one another before the law. The constitution thus implements a principle of separation rather than one of mutually exclusive jurisdictions for church and state. Church and state shall be separately organized expressions of community solidarity, each finding its separate legitimation in the kind of public support it is able to win.

Canada's resolution of the issue was more *ad hoc* and piecemeal. It was in Ontario—

then Upper Canada—that the character of Canada's dominant Protestantism was forged, and it was there that the question of church establishment was decisively resolved. Anglicanism had come into Canada enjoying the establishment it had enjoyed in England, yet this was continuously eroded. On the other hand, the Quebec Act of 1774 established the Roman Catholic Church among the French Canadians of Quebec, whose Catholic parish is recognized in law, and in that *fait accompli* Canadian Protestantism has virtually acquiesced.

The established status accorded to Anglicanism in Nova Scotia was extended through the Maritime Provinces and into Lower and Upper Canada. But in Upper Canada it was resisted and defeated. The main privileges that provoked resistance were the Anglicans' control of education and the lands set aside to endow the established church known as the Clergy Reserves. There were two distinct groups of Methodists in Upper Canada. They derived from Britain and the United States respectively, the latter being much the more numerous and influential—and they were under suspicion of disloyalty to the Crown. But it was these who sponsored the successful movement to abolish establishment for the Anglicans.

Probably the most interesting outcome in Canada of all the interchurch jostling to exclude one another from privilege is the arrangement reached in five of the provinces for financing church schools. The situation in Quebec, Ontario, Newfoundland, Alberta, and Saskatchewan comes near to establishment for the Roman Catholic Church, since it is only that church that makes provision for separate education on a large scale. Since, under the arrangement, property-holders *must* pay education taxes to the local authority but *may choose* to designate it for the support of church schools, you have in effect a public collection of money for the support of nonpublic schools.

The Internal Life of Protestantism

Protestantism's internal life is to be examined by noting the adaptations made in three areas. In assigning these adaptations to historic phases I want to make clear how I see periodization to operate. To speak of a later phase means to recognize the introduction of some important new influence. But this does not necessarily mean that forces operating previously are extinguished. In a later phase the activity in a society can simply be more layered, since earlier practices may continue side by side with the newer ones. Figure 3 summarizes the adaptations noted in the following discussion and shows how I name the periods in which they occur.

Figure 3.

Adaptations in four periods in the internal life of Protestantism.

Period		*Adaptation*
Settlement	*Social teaching*	Classical Protestant ethic or life-calling and social responsibility.
	Ministry	Revivalism.
	Doctrine	Classical Reformation teaching.
1865		
Industrial expansion	*Social teaching*	Social gospel.
	Ministry	Professional ministry attempted. Missionary expansion. Ecumenicalism launched.
	Doctrine	Liberal theology ("modernism").
1915		
Eclipsed national isolation	*Social teaching*	Compromise ethic.
	Ministry	Highly professionalized ministry achieved, with paralysis of the laity. Further missionary expansion. Further ecumenicalism.
	Doctrine	Counter-attack of fundamentalism and neo-orthodoxy.
1960		
Secularization	*Social teaching*	Situationalism.
	Ministry	Innovation, spontaneity, charismatics. Repudiation of officialdom and professionalism. Grass roots ecumenicalism.
	Doctrine	Reconstruction theology.

1. *Social teachings*
Protestant social teachings seem to have continued in the tradition of the original reformers and the Puritans till around the time of the American Civil War—shall we say 1865. (The corresponding and almost coinciding turning point for Canada is Confederation, which occurred in 1867). These traditional teachings encompassed the stress on a life-calling and social responsibility in general that led to the economic, political, and cultural initiative already noted. The era was the one marked by great frontier activity, and may therefore be called the era of settlement.

After the Civil War a new ingredient was added to Protestant social teachings by the social gospel movement, a movement that peaked in the decade before World War I. The phase of social development then in train was really the great industrial expansion, and the social gospel movement partook of the evolutionary optimism inherent in that. It expressed a belief that social institutions can be what we choose to make them, and that Christian initiative must therefore be consciously applied there. In particular, since industrialism was entailing great social injustice, inequality, suffering, and want; the economy should be controlled to serve human welfare. It seems that the social gospel in the United States did not radically challenge the capitalist system but asked mainly for planning within it. It was in Canada that the more collectivist note was struck.

This same social gospel movement spread through Canada and also peaked there before World War I. Yet its long-lasting outcomes were two delayed reverberations. During the depression years of the thirties, William Aberhart's Baptist fundamentalism in Alberta drew inspiration from the social gospel, and it led him to establish right-wing Social Credit. About the same time in Saskatchewan, the Baptist minister Tommy Douglas, similarly inspired by the social gospel, led the Cooperative Commonwealth Federation to conspicuous success. This was a socialist movement that was to be the precursor of the New Democratic Party.

The great general change of mood that followed the eclipse of the prewar optimism brought a new emphasis in Protestant social teaching. It was epitomized, I would guess, in the writings of Reinhold Niebuhr. Two world wars, a devasting economic depression, Nazism—such developments were stinging reminders of the persistence of sin, and it seemed that a realistic social teaching would be one that did not expect too much in view of that. Rather, it should make the Christian task one of limiting or containing social evils, this to be done by practice in the art of choosing the least evil of all the alternatives present. We may call this the compromise ethic. The phase of social development marked by this compromise social teaching might be taken to extend from around 1915 to the end of the 1950s—and perhaps we could characterize this as the era of eclipsed isolation. For both the economic and military upheavals of that era showed that the nations of the world are locked in interdependence and cannot hope to build society alone and apart.

With the 1960s something else again hit us. How shall we name this phase of social development? It is the era of everybody's bid for power—student power, black power, women power, gay power. The era of instant protest and instant remedies expected. The era of draft-dodging and war-resisting. The era of doing your own thing. The era of minding your own business—for a sphere of private decisions and judgments is jealously enclosed. The era of everything made new—the new math., the new morality, the new theology. The era of revolutions declared accomplished—the sex revolution, the fitness revolution, the Quebec revolution, Vatican II, and the aggiornamento. The era of affluence—or at least it was that at first—and it is affluence, I would guess, that helped to get it launched. And, notwithstanding the desperate reassertion of the suffocating individual, it is the era of encroaching bureaucracy. Both assured wealth and bureaucratic omniprovidence have lifted people's feet off the ground and made them feel floated. Although its champions might not admit it, as an observer I would add that it is the era of acute unhappiness. This is partly the result of the expectation of instant satisfactions, whereas in fact, gratifications only come to us as the products of cooperation over time. We live more happily if we are socialized to expect the delay and find satisfaction in the striving. The unhappiness also results from living too exclusively in one's personal time and place, from severing the wider loyalties that lift us out of ourselves. As a result, for all its urgency and activism, it is the era of inconsequentiality. For the gains made, arrive out of any context that would make them meaningful.

What ethic has Protestantism proposed for this time of empty, impassioned restlessness? The ethic of situationalism. What was right for another time and place is not necessarily right for now. Perhaps this current ethic is short on naming the general principles that are to be applied, however differently, to all situations. Perhaps it is also too much infected by the sickness it is supposed to help. For its atomizing of personal biography and human history into a series of situations neglects the distinctively religious vision of all situations cohering in a total situation in which, above all, the religions say, we must strive to locate ourselves. Possibly "secularization" is the correct word by which to characterize this era, using the term in the sociological sense of the fragmentation that results from rational differentiation during the interlude before the elements have been drawn into a coherence again.

2. *Evangelistic and pastoral ministry*

The salient adaptation here is the revivalism of the first period. The American Great Awakening of the eighteenth century, Moberg claims, fixed the pattern of frontier religion. S. D. Clark notes that an evangelistic Methodism, expressed in love-feasts and camp meetings, became the dominant religious force in Upper Canada in the early part of the nineteenth century. These developments might be explained by the needs peculiar to an uprooted, largely frontier population. When conventional moral supports have been stripped away, there is a need for intensified social solidarity, spiritual experience, and moral strictness.

The industrialization and eclipsed isolation periods were marked by attempts to consolidate an ever more qualified and professionalized ministry. Advocated and attempted in the industrializing period, a high degree of it was achieved in the period that followed. Enthusiasm gave way to formalism as charisma was routinized. This went to such an extreme toward the end that Protestant ministers were often bothered by dilemmas over the allocation of their time between very diverse demands. For a member of the clergy had to be a preacher, educator, administrator, group leader, counsellor, organizor, prophet, and priest—and there seemed to be no limit to the training that could be obtained for doing any one aspect better. This professionalization of the ministry tended to confine the work of spiritual ministry to the appointed pastor, even though this is not directly in line with much Protestant theology. The laity of mainline Protestantism was paralyzed as a result.

Routinizations of charisma other than professionalized ministry followed the eighteenth-century revivalism. A zeal for missions was born from this same revivalism. Missionary efforts gathered such momentum throughout the nineteenth century that Latourette was able to call it the great century of Christian expansion. But it was an expansion that continued till the middle of the twentieth century. Thus missionary extension coincided with industrial expansion at home and the breakdown of national isolation. Of this latter it was virtually a progenitor, of course.

So also was ecumenicalism—and it was partly missions that made it so. The word "ecumenical" did not take on its current usage till after the World Missionary Conference in Edinburgh in 1910. But the ecumenical movement was well away in the nineteenth century with its interdenominational and international missions, its Sunday school movement, tract societies and American Bible Society, with the formation of the world's Y.M.C.A. in 1878 and the World's Student Christian Federation in 1895.

In some ways, the organizational ecumenicalism to which this movement succumbed is a dreary, doctrinaire thing, and it has to be distinguished from the more spontaneous grassroots growth of interchurch cooperation. We noticed how Canada witnessed an exceptional development of the latter in the formation of its United Church. But it would be a mistake to ignore the fact that the United States has had its own expressions of grassroots ecumenicalism, the tendency toward sectarian division notwithstanding. Many mergers have occurred there.

Our fourth period—the secularization period—is marked by innovation in ministry. Countless novelties have been tried in worship and outreach and preaching and teaching to communicate meaningfully with a population getting ever more submerged in meaninglessness. In a general way, a greater spontaneity has been sought in worship, and it has brought a revival of charismatic expressions in some places. The ordination of women has been accepted. There is also a by-passing of church officialdom and professionalism to some extent, in that lay people are once again prepared to act more on their own initiative and authority. They have, for instance, given direct support to independent publishers, new missions, and innovating service groups like World Vision and Bread for the World. Informal house meetings seem to have become commoner, and as often as not have crossed denominational barriers.

3. *Doctrinal instruction*

The important time to pinpoint in this area is the entry into the churches of liberal theology, or what is also often simply called "modernism." What developed, seemingly as a new thing, in liberal theology had its roots in the enlightenment view that biblical sources must be critically sifted, and that one should try to piece together a doctrine of the nature of Christ by giving greatest weight to the documents that seemed to have the greatest historical validity. Strauss' *Life of Jesus* in 1835 and Renan's *Life of Jesus* in 1863 were the precursors of an eventual ferment of thought of the same kind, and it occurred during what we have identified as the period of industrial expansion. It accompanied the adoption of the evolutionary perspective of that era as well as the more general perspectives of science. Thus, the liberal theology era, coinciding largely with the social gospel ethic, peaked just before the First World War.

From then on the liberal theology was

worn down, both by the resistance presented by the fundamentalist movement and from within *avant-garde* theology itself. The controversy between fundamentalism and modernism reached its height in the 1920's. Many of the sects outside mainline Protestantism supplied the fundamentalist resistance, but much came from within it. This fundamentalism was essentially an expression of populist culture: its leadership came from the less professionalized pastors and training centers and was concentrated in rural areas. The tendency in *avant-garde* theology worked in the same direction, even though it opposed what it identified as extreme fundamentalism. For, what eventually became known as "form criticism" showed that it was futile to seek some pure picture of Jesus apart from the way he appears in the Gospels, and that he must be accepted as already "interpreted" through the various forms of thought and expression the writers employed. This return to the Bible, from both left and right as you might say, ushered in the phase in Protestant theology that can be called neo-orthodox. German in origin, neo-orthodoxy's impact was most vividly felt in North America in the twenties and thirties.

A decisive transcending of this kind of doctrine came with the sixties. The new theology was marked by the same relativism as marked the new morality. Dietrich Bonhoeffer's advocacy of a "religionless" or "secular" Christianity came into its own. Harvey Cox found the "secular city" where we dwell the fitting scene for its implementation. This Christianity had to be so secular and religionless that some announced that God was "dead." These various startling expressions were clumsy and terribly misleading. I think they were wanting to say that earlier formulations of faith lost their validity with the passage of time—that all things human pass, even human images of the changeless. Not that the living God was dead, but that our images of God had faded beyond recognition. These images must be continually reconstituted on the platform to which we have come at the time. This is a muted theology that seems embarrassed even to refer to God. Yet I think it is not an embarrassment over God but over language. It arises from the feeling that language is so situation-bound that referring to God is any language, save the one the moment breeds, is a stultification. Possibly the best name to give it is "reconstruction theology."

Critical Conclusion

All the transformations we have followed in the second part of this paper, were evident in both Canada and the United States. Possibly there was a lag, in that these transformations had their first North American realization in the United States. It seems significant that we have no ready instance of the diffusion going the other way.

But what, in conclusion, are we to make of this chameleon Protestantism, this creature that changes with every changing time? Some would say that Protestantism is too adaptive, too vacillating to be an authentic Christian expression even. Does mainline Protestantism lack the kind of stabilizing that would keep it witnessing to an unchanging truth through changing times? Or is it, alternatively, endowed with the flexibility that allows it to keep that truth relevant by highlighting different elements in it according to the need of the day?

This is altogether too large a question to settle in so sketchy a paper as this. But my own inclination is to say that mainline Protestantism is not adaptive at the expense of stability. As I view it, the dynamism of modern culture is to some extent Protestantism's own creation, and Protestantism has then continually to minister to people at the *avant-garde* positions into which it has propelled them. The propensity for adaptations we noted in the second part of the paper is all one with the Protestant nation-making, sectarianism, and disestablishment that we noted in the first. In these developments Protestantism shows itself emboldened to be experimental in religious culture, just as it is experimental in the scientific, technological, economic, and political spheres. In the experimental approach, often, one does not know how far to go till he has gone too far. Some self-correction is involved. Protestantism is apparently unabashed by this fallibility in religion if, through allowing it, it can come closer to where people are. Fallibility in religion is only to be expected, it seems to assume, since, as it also assumes, infallibility belongs to God alone.

TRENDS IN SEMINARY ENROLLMENT 1974-1979

The Association of Theological Schools in the United States and Canada

Despite the fact that enrollments in North American Colleges have stabilized in the last few years, theological school registrants have continued to rise—even though more slowly recently. The Fall 1974 increase was + 8.1%; 1975 up + 11.0%; 1976 up + 5.2%; 1977 up + 5.1%; in 1978 the increase fell to + 2.7%; but rose again in 1979 to + 4.2%. Table 1 contains these details. It should be noted that the number of institutions reporting varies slightly from year to year; hence the parallels are not quite precise. Note also that the *rate of increase* in Canadian schools is much greater than in the United States. For first time this year graduate enrollment (chiefly academic doctorates) showed a sharp increase also.

TABLE 1
AUTUMN ENROLLMENTS IN ATS MEMBER SCHOOLS

	1974	*1975*	*1976*	*1977*	*1978*	*1979*
Number of Schools	191	192	193	191	193	193
Total Enrollment	36,830	40,895	43,023	45,222	46,460	48,433
By Nation						
Canada	1,746	1,965	1,880	2,100	2,288	2,707
United States	35,084	38,930	41,143	43,122	44,172	45,726
By Membership						
Accredited	31,519	34,681	38,234	41,303	42,839	44,654
Associate	5,311	6,214	4,789	3,919	3,621	3,779
Professional Pgms.	33,189	37,179	39,291	41,665	42,823	44,374
% Total	90.1%	90.9%	91.3%	92.1%	92.2%	91.6%
Graduate Pgms.	3,641	3,716	3,732	3,557	3,637	4,059
% of Total	9.9%	9.1%	8.7%	7.9%	7.8%	8.4%

Women in Theological Schools

In the past seven years the number of women in theological schools has more than tripled, even though total enrollment has increased only 68.2% since 1972. Or to state the facts more sharply, women's participation has risen +203.9%. In contrast male enrollment rose only +28.8%. Table 2 provides the details.

TABLE 2
WOMEN THEOLOGICAL STUDENTS

	Number of Women	% Annual Increase	% Total Enrollment
1972	3,358		10.2%
1973	4,021	+ 19.7%	11.8
1974	5,255	+ 30.7	14.3
1975	6,505	+ 23.8	15.9
1976	7,349	+ 13.0	17.1
1977	8,371	+ 13.9	18.5
1978	8,972	+ 7.2	19.3
1979	10,208	+ 13.8	21.1

Black Seminarians

Racial data regarding black student enrollment has been collected for ten years; since 1970. Each year produces a small increase, far below the proportion that blacks represent in the total population of the two nations. The rate of increase tends to fluctuate considerably, although it has been larger than the total increase in every year except two during the decade, 1974 and 1975. Details are found in Table 3.

TABLE 3
BLACK THEOLOGICAL STUDENTS

	Number of Black Students	% Annual Increase	% Total Enrollment
1970	808		2.6%
1971	908	+12.4%	2.8
1972	1,061	+16.9	3.2
1973	1,210	+14.0	3.6
1974	1,246	+ 3.0	3.4
1975	1,365	+ 9.6	3.3
1976	1,524	+11.6	3.5
1977	1,759	+15.4	3.9
1978	1,919	+ 9.1	4.1
1979	2,043	+ 6.5	4.2

Hispanic Students

ATS first sought Hispanic enrollment data in 1972. Proportionately the increase since then has been substantial, up + 211.4%. Yet Hispanics constitute only 1.7% of total enrollment. See Table 4.

TABLE 4
HISPANIC STUDENT ENROLLMENT

	Number of Hispanic Students	% Annual Increase	% Total Enrollment
1972	264		0.8%
1973	387	+46.8%	1.1
1974	448	+15.8	1.2
1975	524	+17.0	1.3
1976	541	+ 3.2	1.3
1977	601	+11.1	1.3
1978	681	+13.3	1.5
1979	822	+20.7	1.7

PACIFIC/ASIAN AMERICAN STUDENTS

The Fall 1979 data were the third year this information has been solicited. Table 5 indicates the changes

TABLE 5

	Number of Pacific/Asian Students	% Annual Increase	% Total Enrollment
1977	494		1.1%
1978	499	+ 1.0%	1.1
1979	577	+15.6	1.2

THE 1978 OFFICIAL CATHOLIC DATA

Catholics in the 50 States, including all families of the defense forces both at home and abroad, and diplomatic and other services abroad, now number 49,602,035, according to **The Official Catholic Directory** for 1979, issued by P. J. Kenedy & Sons, New York. The new total represents a decrease over last year of 234,141.

The Official Catholic Directory, 1979, 1541 pages, sells for $49.50.

Archdioceses and Dioceses

There are now 32 archdioceses in the United States, with a Catholic population of 21,367,376, and 138 dioceses recording a Catholic population of 28,234,659—for a total Catholic population of 49,602,035.

The 32 archdioceses reported a loss of 360,518, and the 138 dioceses increased by 126,377. Chicago remains the largest archdiocese with a Catholic population of 2,415,354, followed by Boston, 2,016,272. Over one million are Los Angeles, 1,964,000; New York, 1,825,090; Newark, 1,400,727; Philadelphia, 1,377,258; and Detroit, 1,187,382. Brooklyn continues as the largest diocese, with a Catholic population of 1,458,951, followed by Rockville Centre, reporting 1,038,505. In addition, nine archdioceses and five dioceses reported Catholic populations of over one-half million.

Ten Dioceses reported no change in Catholic populations, and 55 reflected decreases. Advances were reported by 104 sees. The largest increases have been noted in Brooklyn, 43,289; Miami, 27,800; Fresno, 25,296; and Galveston-Houston, 25,000. The largest decreases were noted in Detroit, 404,068; Military Ordinariate, 50,000; Syracuse, 35,104; Hartford, 33,455; and Newark, 26,121. Statistical information is available for the first time on the new Diocese of San Bernardino, which was formed on November 6, 1978, when the Diocese of San Diego was split.

Hierarchy and Clergy

The 1979 **Directory** lists 345 members of the hierarchy—an increase of four over the 341 listed a year ago.

A decrease of 55, brings the total of ordained priests to 58,430; there are now 35,472, or 294 fewer diocesan or secular priests, and 22,958 religious order priests, an increase of 239. Permanent deacons, numbering 798, were added during the past year to the 2,498 recorded in 1978, to bring the current total to 3,296, for a total of 61,726 clergy. Professed religious personnel include 7,965 brothers, a decrease of 495, and 128,378 sisters, representing a decrease of 1,013.

	1959	1969	1979
Priests	52,689	59,620	58,430
Deacons	—	—	3,296
Brothers	9,709	11,755	7,965
Sisters	164,922	167,167	128,378

The **Directory** reports 17,968 parishes with resident pastors, an increase of 30, and 727 parishes without resident clergy, an increase of 40, for a record total of 18,695 Catholic parishes in the 50 States—up 70. Also listed are 4,025 missions—down 63; 1,822 stations—up 67; and 9,485 chapels—down 250.

Educational Institutions

There are a total of 10,373 separate educational institutions—112 fewer than reported in 1978. Included are 92 diocesan seminaries; 258 religious order seminaries or novitiates and scholasticates; 241 colleges and universities; 905 diocesan and parish high schools; 637 private high schools; 7,929 parish elementary schools; and 311 private elementary schools. There are, in addition, 140 protective institutions, with 10,082 youths in attendance.

Teachers

Full-time teaching staffs of all educational institutions under Catholic auspices, have decreased by 1,888, to a total of 169,149, comprising 5,800 priests; 162 scholastics; 3,179 brothers; 43,713 sisters; and 116,295 lay teachers. There are 602 fewer priests; 46 fewer scholastics; 340 fewer brothers; 2,957 fewer sisters; and 2,107 more lay teachers than a year ago.

In 1944, when first recorded, lay teachers numbered 7,633 (8.25 percent). Their number continually increased through 1971, when 106,844 outnumbered religious teachers for the first time. Today, lay teachers represent 68.7 percent of all teachers in Catholic schools (66.7 percent in 1978).

	1944	1950	1960	1970	1979
Priests	4,647	7,436	10,890	9,958	5,800
Scholastics	—	405	802	596	162
Brothers	3,233	3,411	4,778	5,297	3,179
Sisters	76,908	82,048	98,471	85,616	43,713
TOTAL RELIGIOUS	84,788	93,300	114,941	101,467	52,854
Lay Teachers	7,633	13,477	45,506	98,001	116,295
GRAND TOTAL	92,421	106,777	160,447	199,468	169,149

Seminaries and Seminarians

During 1978, there were in operation 6 fewer diocesan and 20 fewer religious order seminaries. The 92 diocesan seminaries report enrollments of 8,694 seminarians, a decrease of 866, while the 258 novitiates and scholasticates of the religious orders have 5,266 students, or 172 fewer, indicating a total of 13,960 candidates for the priesthood, 20,030 fewer than the 33,990 seminarians reported ten years ago in 1969.

Colleges and Students

There are currently 241 Catholic colleges and universities, up three from the 238 reported in 1978, showing an enrollment of 483,760—up 26,262.

Children in Catholic Schools

The number of full-time pupils in Catholic elementary and high schools decreased 38,624 during the past year. The 905 parish and diocesan high schools, 33 fewer, report 512,413 pupils, a decrease of 28,420 over 1978; the 637 private high schools, 3 more, with 341,193, show an increase of 12,758 in one year. Pupils in 7,929 parish elementary schools, down 30, now number 2,313,110, or 26,555 fewer, while students in the 311 private elementary schools now total 66,706, an increase of 3,593.

Youths Under Religious Instruction

Religious instruction to children under released time, in religious vacation schools and other classes, indicates in the 1979 reports 1,086,150 high school pupils (up 76,511), and 3,699,879 in elementary grades (up 58,122), for a total of 4,786,029 public school children receiving religious instruction, a year's increase of 134,633 pupils. There is an aggregate, (including dependent children) of 8,527,353 American youth of all grades, under Catholic instruction—an increase of 122,784 over comparable figures for 1978.

Hospitals

Nine fewer general and one more special hospital bring the number of Catholic hospitals to 720; bed capacity decreased by 623, to 171,785. General hospitals number 634, with 164,967 beds, and 86 special hospitals accommodate 6,818. Patients treated increased by 745,717, to a record high of 34,171,565.

Current enrollments of 20,136 student nurses in the 121 Catholic training schools decreased by 519, in 3 fewer schools. Children in the 206 orphanages and infant asylums decreased by 751, to a total of 14,505; while 15,006 children are cared for in foster homes. The total of 29,571 dependent children reflect a decrease of 620. Homes for invalids and aged increased by 12 and now number 498, with facilities for 62,903 guests, an increase of 3,128.

Baptisms, Converts, Marriages

The 896,151 baptisms recorded is an increase of 5,474 over 1978. The number of converts decreased by 1,393, to a total of 77,205.

Marriages recorded decreased by 840 to 340,489; during the same period, 407,102 Catholics died in the U.S., 2,939 more deaths than in the previous year.

4. SURVEYS OF RELIGION IN AMERICAN LIFE

In this section, the results of three surveys related to religion in American life are presented.

The first, "Changing Brands: Denominational Switching and Membership Change," by C. Kirk Hadaway of the Home Mission Board, Southern Baptist Convention, describes how national survey data on denominational switching relates to membership trends. This is followed by some survey data on church attendance and other matters selected from the Gallup Poll's survey of religion as presented in *Religion in America, 1979–1980,* published by the Princeton Religious Research Center, 53 Bank St., Princeton, NJ 08540. The third report is on "Value on New Construction of Religious Buildings," which contains estimates on this subject prepared by the U.S. Department of Commerce.

CHANGING BRANDS: DENOMINATIONAL SWITCHING AND MEMBERSHIP CHANGE*

By

C. Kirk Hadaway

Home Mission Board, Southern Baptist Convention

Unlike most nations, the United States lacks a dominant religious organization. Ours is a religiously pluralistic society where a profusion of religious groups exist and more or less tolerate one another. Some of these religious bodies are composed of many individual congregations, such as the United Methodist Church, which has 38,000, while others are made up of only one independent local church. Not only is there a large number of different "denominations" in the United States, there is also a broad range of types. American churches include everything from the snake-handlers in West Virginia, to Roman Catholics in Boston, Southern Baptists in Texas, and homosexual churches in California.

Despite the obvious differences that exist among American religious bodies, there are also great similarities. Congregationalists, Episcopalians, Baptists, Disciples of Christ, Presbyterians, Methodists, Lutherans, and most other Protestant denominations share basically similar styles of worship and a common history of mutual toleration. Also important is the fact that among Protestants, religious identity no longer closely coincides with ethnic identity, as it still does among the Jews and certain other groups. So becoming a Methodist would not mean rejecting an ethnic or cultural heritage for someone who had been raised in a Presbyterian home.

Because of this similarity and toleration there is a relatively high degree of "brand changing" or switching among Protestant bodies in the United States. In fact, studies have shown that around 40 percent of American Protestants indicate a different denominational preference than they had when growing up. There are various ways of looking at this changing of religious brands. For instance, we could ask what social characteristics of life-changing events prompt the decision to switch; and important research has been conducted in these and other areas (see Roof and Hadaway, 1977, 1979; Newport, 1979; Hadaway and

*Data for this research were made available through the Roper Public Opinion Research Center and the Survey Archive for the Social Sciences at the University of Massachusetts. Certain portions of this paper appeared earlier in *Sociological Analysis* 39: 321-337.

Roof, 1979; Alston, 1971).* But the present concern is with the possible *impact of switching on denominational membership change*.

Switching is not usually considered a source of denominational growth or decline, yet if people systematically leave one denomination for another and are not replaced by people switching *in* at the same rate, decline should result. Likewise, if people are switching into one denomination faster than others are switching out, this would tend to produce growth. No denomination is able to retain all those who are reared members, but some are more stable than others. All denominations attract former members of other religious bodies, but some are more aggressive in their "sheep-stealing," and others are simply more "attractive" to would-be switchers. As a result, switching is not a process of equal shuffling of members. Some denominations gain and others lose in the process, and this paper attempts to show how these changes occur.

Sources of Information About Switching

Most denominations keep relatively poor records on the previous denominational affiliation of those who switch in. In many cases such individuals are counted as "other additions" to separate them from those reared in the denomination. Also, there is the problem of churches not being aware of those who leave. Some people are left on the rolls who are now members of other denominations.

Because of this lack of accurate information from denominational statistics, studies of switching have almost universally employed national survey data. Employing modern sampling techniques, surveys such as those conducted by the National Opinion Research Center, the Center for Political Studies, and the Gallup Organization produce national samples that are representative of the adult United States population. This allows one to generalize from switching patterns found in such samples to the total population. Questions asking for one's religious preference are routine in national surveys. Less prevalent are questions which ask for the respondent's religious preference at some previous time. But if *both* questions are asked it is possible to deal with denominational switching by comparing the respondent's present and previous denominational preference. Fortunately, in 1973 the National Opinion Research Center began including the items necessary to deal with switching in its annual *General Social Survey*. To obtain a sample large enough to look at switching in detail the 1973-1977 versions of the survey were merged. This resulted in a sample of approximately 7,500 persons.

*References will be found at the end of this article.

Switching and Current Membership Trends

It is well known that since the mid-1960s most of the large, mainline Protestant denominations have been declining while the Southern Baptists, Assemblies of God, Church of Christ, and many other theologically conservative religious bodies have continued to grow, or at least have remained largely stable. Given these denominational membership trends, it should be expected that switching patterns would favor those denominations that are currently growing, if switching is truly a source of denominational growth or decline.

Previous studies of switching have tended to stress only one aspect of its relationship to membership trends. However, there are apparently at least *three* ways in which switching influences growth and decline. These include: (1) patterns of net gains and losses; (2) the stability of a denomination; and (3) the "quality" of those gained.

Patterns of Net Gains

One possible source of denominational growth through switching is the pattern of net gains. To determine how a denomination fares in the process of in and out migration among religious bodies, we subtract the number who are raised in a denomination from the number who currently identify with it. So out of 100 persons in the survey that were raised in a denomination, if 60 remain and 40 switch to other groups, but 45 switch in, that denomination would have a 5 percent net gain through switching. Obviously, the size of a denomination's net gain is determined by its stability (or the percent it retains) and its attractiveness (or the number who switch in). Thus, very stable religious organizations do not need to attract many persons in order to show a net gain, but denominations who lose many of their members must attract large numbers if they are to avoid losses through switching.

TABLE 1

THE SWITCHING OF RELIGIOUS IDENTIFICATION BY DENOMINATIONAL PREFERENCE[a]

	Denominational Preference							
	Episcopal (N=185)	U.C.C.[b] (N=92)	Presby-terian (N=394)	Disciples (N=100)	Methodist (N=1063)	Lutheran (N=649)	Baptist (N=1766)	Sect (N=339)
Stayers	60%	55%	56%	52%	61%	74%	73%	59%
Switchers to Other Faiths	29	39	36	43	34	22	22	36
Switchers to "None"	11	6	8	5	5	4	5	5
	100%	100%	100%	100%	100%	100%	100%	100%
Net % Gain or Loss	+12%	+21%	−11%	−1%	−14%	−6%	−12%	+32%

[a]Data source is a merged file composed of the 1973–1977 NORC General Social Surveys. The Ns in the table refer to the number of respondents who stated that this was their religious preference when they were growing up.
[b]United Church of Christ.

The bottom row of table 1 gives the percent net gain or loss for each of eight denominational clusters. These groups are ranked according to theological conservatism, with those on the right being the most conservative and those on the left being the least conservative.[1] As can be seen, rather than the growing conservative denominations exhibiting net increases, it is the most extreme groups on either end of the scale that gain. The sects[2] show a large 32 percent increase and the liberal "mainline" denominations, as the Episcopalians and United Church of Christ can be termed, increase by 12 percent and 21 percent respectively. Obviously, these net gains and losses do not directly translate into denominational growth since both of the liberal groups that experience net *gains* through switching are also suffering serious membership *declines*. Instead, the pattern of net gains and losses represents only one aspect of the relationship switching to membership trends. The entire picture must be seen before the relationship becomes apparent.

Patterns of Stability

As was noted above, a denomination's level of stability influences whether or not it has a net gain or loss through switching. But there is another way in which the retention of members is important to the growth of a denomination. Stability means that those who grow up in a religious body tend to stay in it throughout their lives. The more stable the denomination, the more it will add the children of its members. Members also die, of course, but so long as the birth rate exceeds the death rate a very stable denomination can grow even without increases through switching. This is what church growth writers call biological growth. The stability levels of U.S. denominations are shown in the first row of table 1. The Baptists and the Lutherans are clearly the most stable of the Protestant clusters, as over 70 percent of those raised within each remain adherents. All the other groups cluster between 55 percent and 61 percent, with the Disciples of Christ being slightly less stable at 52 percent. Although the

Lutherans and Baptists are fairly conservative, the possible relationship between conservatism and stability falls through among sects. The cluster of small religious bodies is more conservative than either Lutherans or Baptists, yet is rather unstable. Around 41 percent of those raised in a sectarian group now identify with a nonsectarian religious body. And the percentage who have switched would be even higher if it included those who switch from one sect to another.

This aspect of the relationship between switching and growth reveals a clearly different pattern than did net gains. Here Baptists, who are growing, and Lutherans, who are fairly stable, have the advantage, but sects who are also growing are at a disadvantage with respect to stability. To clear up the confusion it is necessary to look at a third aspect of the relationship of switching to membership trends.

Quality of Converts

Even though denominations like the Episcopal Church and the United Church of Christ experience net gains through switching, there is some question about how these gains translate into actual membership. It is important to note that the NORC surveys ask for a *religious preference,* not whether one is a *member* of a particular denomination. For this reason we do not know how many of those who switch to a denomination actually bother to become members. Perhaps a large number of persons simply mentally affiliate after attending a few times, but do not join or give to their new church.

Given the lower levels of church attendance among those who identify with liberal denominations like the United Church of Christ and the Episcopal Church (see Stark and Glock, 1968), it may well be that their converts are less likely to attend church and become members than those who switch into growing conservative denominations. If true, this might explain why the two most liberal Protestant denominations experience net gains through switching but also manage to decline in membership.

TABLE 2

PERCENT HIGH[a] IN CHURCH ATTENDANCE AMONG SWITCHING CATEGORIES BY DENOMINATIONAL TYPE

	Denominational Type		
	Liberal	Moderate	Conservative
Switching Status:			
Stayers	23.3%	29.8%	39.4%
N	(40)[b]	(465)	(642)
Switchers in	33.1%	38.3%	55.6%
N	(49)	(160)	(215)
Switchers out	31.1%	38.0%	31.3%
N	(32)	(245)	(149)

[a]Those attending church nearly every week or more.
[b]Data set is the merged 1973–1977 NORC sample.

In table 2 we compare three groups of denominations with respect to the percent who attend church nearly every week or more, within categories of stayers and switchers. The liberals are composed of the Episcopalians and the United Church of Christ; the moderates include the Presbyterians, Disciples of Christ, Methodists, and Lutherans; and the conservative category is made up of the Baptists and sect members. The primary reason for combining denominations in this manner was to avoid problems of meaningless fluctuation in the percentages—due to minute numbers of switchers among smaller bodies like the Episcopalians, Congregationalists, and Disciples of Christ.

Looking along the first row, it can be seen that as we move from liberals to conservatives the percent who attend church frequently increases. Conservative stayers tend to be more religious than liberal stayers. It is the second row, however, that deals with the quality of converts. As expected, liberal and moderate converts are much less likely to attend church often than conservative converts. Further, it is only in the conservative cluster that both the stayers and converts are *more* likely to attend church than those who leave this group. The conservatives gain the most committed converts, retain the most committed members, and lose those who are least likely to attend.

Is There a Relationship?

If anything, the relationship of switching patterns to denominational growth is not simple. Neither the Baptists nor the sects have the advantage in all aspects of switching, even though both are composed of growing denominations. The sects lack stability; and as we have seen, the Episcopal Church and the United Church of Christ have net gains through switching, while the Baptists experience net losses. So rather than either net gains, stability, or quality of converts *directly* translating into membership growth or decline, each aspect is either a *plus* or a *minus* working for or against a denomination. By considering how denominations fare on all three aspects, insights can be gained into the functioning and major sources of growth in each religious body.

Looking first at the conservative denominations, *sects* are unstable, growing, exhibit a large net gain through the switching process, and attract very committed converts. Their *mode of functioning,* so to speak, is to mobilize the unchurched and to aggressively evangelize, while at the same time suffering a serious attrition of those who were raised in sects. Organizational instability, a loss of upwardly mobile members, and a somewhat deviant status in the larger society all contribute to a high rate of switching out. Sects seem to be prime examples of religious bodies that increase through *expansion*—evangelism and rapid new church development—and they *must* continue this activity so that they will not lose ground.

Apparently, the growth of Baptists and the minor losses of the Lutherans have somewhat different roots than the growth of the sects. Rather than net gains through switching, both Baptists and Lutherans experience moderate net losses. However, they also lose a very small percentage of their members and attract fairly committed converts. So their health in terms of growth comes from holding onto their members, and effectively incorporating the children of members into the denomination. Because of size and regional concentration, they are no longer effective in attracting many new members from the outside, and so their losses as a result of switching outweigh their gains. Those who are attracted tend to be committed, but converts apparently are not the major source of growth among Baptists and Lutherans. Stability is their key.

The Presbyterians, Disciples of Christ, and Methodists are all less stable than the Lutherans and Baptists, and have small to moderate levels of net losses through switching. These denominations apparently have become less stable than they were in the past. The growth that once came through effectively holding onto their members and to the children of members is now lost because of the relatively large percent who switch out. And to make matters worse, they lose many of their *best* members to other denominations. Their mode of functioning is similar to that of the Lutherans and Baptists, yet it has become inefficient. Having lost their stability these denominations are at a disadvantage in *all* aspects of switching, and their recent membership declines are just one result.

An entirely different type of functioning is represented by the Episcopal Church and the United Church of Christ. They can be called *unstable destination denominations* because of the high percentage of switching out and the fact that they exhibit net *gains* through switching *without emphasizing evangelism.* They appear to be destinations for those rising in social status. Thus, the upwardly mobile Baptist may become an Episcopalian as an "adjustment" to a new, higher socio-economic status. Still, these net gains have not translated into membership growth, which may suggest that it takes a very large net switching increase and very committed converts to overshadow instability.

Switching to "None"

A final aspect of switching, which is not a source of growth, but is rather a source of loss for all denominations, is called switching to none. Persons who select this option have left institutionalized religion altogether, and when asked their current religious preference they reply they have none. Much has been said in recent years about these drop-outs and most of the views are consistent; such persons tend to be young, liberal in social values, and are part of a "gradual but growing trend on the part of Americans to identify themselves in non-institutional religious terms" (Roof and Hadaway, 1979).

Even though an increase in the drop-out rate fits most of our preconceptions concerning religious change during the 1960s and 1970s, such an increase is hard to document without good time-series data. Luckily, in the case of switching to none, three surveys[3] at different intervals (1960, 1965, and 1978) asked identical questions which make a comparison possible. These surveys clearly show that from 1960 to 1965 and from 1965 to 1978 *there were increases in the percent switching to none.*

As with all aspects of switching, some religious bodies are affected more than others. It is no surprise that switchers to none, being more liberal in social values, tend to switch disproportionately from the Episcopal Church, the United Church of Christ, and from Presbyterian bodies among Protestants. Jews and Catholics also lose substantially to the ranks of the drop-outs. Since this switching occurs predominantly among younger respondents, it raises the possibility that the more liberal bodies are losing the very members that would normally be expected to produce the next generation of liberal Protestants. Such denominations already have a higher median age and low birth rates, so the loss of younger members will aggravate an already serious problem.

Conclusions

Despite complexities, it is possible to show with national survey data that switching patterns do relate to denominational membership trends. Three facets of switching were considered which act as either sources of growth or sources of decline: (1) the pattern of net gains or losses; (2) levels of stability; and (3) the quality of converts. In addition, a fourth aspect, switching to "none," was introduced as a source of decline among all religious bodies.

Each facet of switching that we have reviewed sheds some light on denominational membership trends, and it is necessary to consider *all* aspects in order to understand how a denomination functions and thus why it has either grown or declined. For instance, the pattern of net gains alone would give a misleading picture of how switching patterns affect denominations like the Episcopal Church and the United Church of Christ. These religious groups have an advantage in net gains, but they still decline in membership because of instability, uncommitted converts, and losses to the "none" category.

Another insight gained by considering switching patterns is that conservative denominations and conservative sects apparently do not receive the majority of their growth from the same sources, as Kelley's (1977) theory seems to indicate. The constituent religious bodies that make up these clusters can be seen to have different modes of functioning, reflecting their institutional structure, their posture towards the world, their size, methods of outreach, internal group pressures, and so on. Growth results in each case, but the predominant source is different. Sects grow through aggressive expansion, while the growth of conservative denominations results primarily from their stability.

Finally, a certain degree of caution should be exercised in abstracting from this kind of survey data. It has been noted that such surveys deal with religious preference, not membership; and even if a membership question was asked there would be no way of distinguishing true church members from those who only thought they were members.[4] Another consideration is that we do not know *when* individuals in the survey switched. In the 1940s and 1950s the prestige of one's church was somewhat more important to social standing in the community than it apparently is now. Thus, as has been suggested by Benton Johnson (1978), the net gains of the liberal denominations may result from upward switching *during the post-war years* on the part of those rising in social status.

As can be seen, problems do exist in bridging between switching data and membership trends. Progress has been made, but all the answers have not been found.

Notes

1. Theological conservatism was measured by two questions included in the Anti-Semitism in the United States Survey, conducted in 1964 by the National Opinion Research Center. The items asked about belief in the Devil and if it is necessary to accept Jesus to be saved.
2. The sect category is composed of numerous religious bodies that are typically called sects in sociological literature. Among others the Assemblies of God, Holiness, Church of God, Nazarene, Seventh-day Adventist, and Pentecostal churches were included.
3. The surveys included the SRC 1960 American National Election Study, a 1965 NORC survey, and the Gallup Unchurched American Survey. Each of these surveys included father's religious preference (when the respondent was growing up) and respondent's present religious preference. With these items nearly identical measures of inter-generational switching are obtained.
4. It was also necessary to use denominational clusters rather than actual denominations because surveys are usually not discriminating enough to distinguish between, say, Southern Baptists and American Baptists. This clustering acts to reduce differences between groups and should not alter any of our conclusions.

References

Alston, Jon
1971 "Religious mobility and socio-economic status." *Sociological Analysis* 32: 140-48.

Hadaway, C. Kirk
1978 "Denominational switching and membership growth: in search of a relationship." *Sociological Analysis* 39: 321-37.

Hadaway, C. Kirk and Wade Clark Roof
1979 "Those who stay religious 'nones' and those who don't: a research note." *Journal for the Scientific Study of Religion* 18: 194-200.

Johnson, Benton
1978 "Summary of some main trends affecting church growth and decline in the U.S.A." (Unpublished).

Kelley, Dean
1977 *Why Conservative Churches Are Growing*. New York: Harper.

Newport, Frank
1979 "The religious switcher in the United States." *American Sociological Review* 44: 528-52.

Roof, Wade Clark and C. Kirk Hadaway
1977 "Shifts in religious preference—the mid-seventies." *Journal for the Scientific Study of Religion* 16: 409-12.
1979 "Denominational switching in the seventies: going beyond Stark and Glock." *Journal for the Scientific Study of Religion* (forthcoming).

CHURCH ATTENDANCE POLLS AND RELATED MATTERS

In 1978, 41 percent of adults 18 years of age or older said they attended church or synagogue in a typical week. This is the same percentage as in 1977, according to the Gallup Poll. The 1978 percentage was derived from five sample surveys taken during 1978, involving more than 7,500 adults 18 years of age or older, in more than 300 scientifically selected sampling locations.

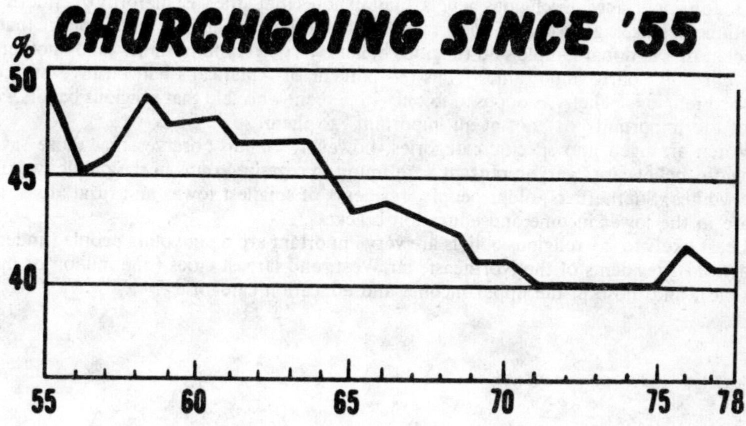

Church and synagogue attendance reached an all time high of 49 percent in 1955 and again in 1958 and then declined slowly and steadily until it reached 40 percent during the period 1971–75. An increase to 42 percent was recorded in 1976, which declined to 41 percent in both 1977 and 1978.

Among the large amount of survey data on church attendance gathered by Gallup, we find that Catholics attend more regularly than Protestants (52 percent as compared with 40 percent); that women attend more frequently than men (45 percent to 36); that non-whites are better attenders than whites (43 percent to 40). People in the South and Midwest attend more frequently (44 percent) than those in the East (41) and West (30). The older a person is the more likely he or she is to attend church. Those 50 and older have an attendance rate of 48 percent; those 30 to 49, 42 percent; and those under 30, 29 percent.

INFLUENCE OF RELIGION ON AMERICAN LIFE

A somewhat larger percentage of Americans see religion decreasing its influence (48 percent) than increasing (37 percent) according to the latest survey of the Gallup Poll in 1978. This, however, is a more favorable situation than in 1970 when some 75 percent felt that religion was decreasing in influence.

PUBLIC CONFIDENCE IN ORGANIZED RELIGION

In terms of public confidence is ten key institutions in our society, however, the church or organized religion has consistently ranked highest over a six-year period. The 1978 data shows that 65 percent of the public expressed a "great deal" or "quite a lot" of confidence in the church or organized religion. Other institutions scored as follows: banks and banking—60 percent; military—54; public schools—53; newspapers—51; U.S. Supreme Court—45; television—38; organized labor—36; congress—34; and big business—32 percent.

IMPORTANCE OF RELIGIOUS BELIEFS

On the importance of religious beliefs, Gallup notes that "the vast majority of Americans continue to place a good deal of importance on their religious beliefs." Data indicate that 57 percent of a national sample said religious beliefs were "very important," and another 27 percent said "fairly important." Thus, 84 percent of Americans had positive attitudes toward religious beliefs, as opposed to only 15 percent who said that religious beliefs were "not too important" or "not at all important" to them.

When arranged into specific categories, however, Gallup observes that those saying religious beliefs are "very important" are found in certain groups in the public: women, non-whites, Southerners, older people, residents of smallest towns and rural areas, and those in the lower income and education brackets.

Least likely to say religious beliefs are very important are men, young people (under 30 years old), residents of the Northeast, far West, and largest cities (one million or more people), and those in the upper income and education categories.

VALUE OF NEW CONSTRUCTION OF RELIGIOUS BUILDINGS IN CURRENT AND 1972 DOLLARS (In Millions of Dollars)

Year	Current Dollars	1972 Dollars
1970	$ 931	$1,056
1971	813	859
1972	844	845
1973	814	754
1974	918	711
1975	867	627
1976	956	689
1977	1,046	708
1978	1,244	749

Source: U. S. Department of Commerce, Bureau of the Census, "Value of New Construction Put in Place," *Construction Reports,* April, 1979, Table 2, p. 4 and Table 3, p. 6 and U.S. Department of Commerce, *Construction Review,* Vol. 24, No. 8, December, 1978, p.3.

In constant dollar terms, estimates of the value of new church building continued to decline in the decade of the '70's but showed a slight upturn for the years 1976—1978. New construction of religious buildings reached its peak in the early 1960's and since then has declined steadily until the slight upturn which began in 1976. It is estimated that new religious construction was valued in real terms at two and one half times as much in 1962 as in 1978 and nearly one and one half times as much in 1970 as in 1978.

This general decline parallels the decline in the growth of church membership and birth rates and the rapid increase in building costs associated with the 1970's.

5. MAIN DEPOSITORIES OF CHURCH HISTORY MATERIAL AND SOURCES IN THE UNITED STATES

The directory which follows was recently updated and revised by the Rev. Aug. R. Suelflow, D.D., Director of the Concordia Historical Institute of the Lutheran Church—Missouri Synod. Dr. Suelflow also has served as chairman of the religious archives committee on the Society of American Archivists.

Many denominations have established central archival-manuscript depositories and, in addition, are dealing with regional, diocesan, synodical, or provincial subdivisions. Communions functioning through this type of structure especially are the Roman Catholic, Episcopal, Baptists, Lutheran, and Methodist.

Some denominations with headquarters in the United States also have churches in Canada. Historical material on Canadian sections of these denominations will occasionally be found at the various locations cited below. The reader is also referred to the section "Main Depositories of Church History Material in Canada," which follows.

Adventists:

Adventual Library, Aurora College, Aurora, IL 60507 (Advent Christian Church)

Dr. Linden J. Carter Library, Berkshire Christian College, Lenox, MA 01240

Andrews University, Berrien Springs, MI 49104

General Conference of Seventh-day Adventists, 6840 Eastern Ave. NW, Washington, DC 20012

Baptists

American Baptist Historical Society (including Samuel Colgate Baptist Historical Collection), 1100 South Goodman St., Rochester, NY 14620

Andover Newton Theological School (including Backus Historical Society), Newton Centre, MA 02159

Bethel Seminary (Swedish Baptist material), 3949 Bethel Dr., St. Paul, MN 55112

Historical Commission, Southern Baptist Convention, 127 9th Ave., N., Nashville TN 37234

Seventh Day Baptist Historical Society, 510 Watchung Ave., P.O. Box 868, Plainfield, NJ 07061

Brethren in Christ Church:

Archives of the Brethren in Christ Church, Messiah College, Grantham, PA 17027

Church of the Brethren:

Bethany Theological Seminary, Butterfield and Meyers Roads, Oak Brook, IL 60521

Historical Library, 1451 Dundee Ave., Elgin, IL 60120

Juniata College, Huntingdon, PA 16652

Congregationalists:

(See United Church of Christ)

Disciples:

The Disciples of Christ Historical Society, 1101 Nineteenth Ave., S., Nashville, TN 37212

Christian Theological Seminary, Indianapolis, IN 46208

Lexington Theological Seminary, Lexington, KY 40508

The Disciples Divinity House, University of Chicago, Chicago, IL 60637

Texas Christian University, Fort Worth, TX 76219

Culver-Stockton College, Canton, MO 63435

Episcopalians:

National Council, Protestant Episcopal Church, 815 2nd Ave., New York, NY 10017

Library and Archives of the Church Historical Society, 606 Rathervue Pl., Austin, TX 78767

Berkeley Divinity School at Yale, New Haven, CT 06510

General Theological Seminary, 175 Ninth Ave., New York, NY 10011

Evangelical United Brethren:

(see United Methodist Church)

Evangelical Congregational Church:

Historical Society of the Evangelical Congregational Church, 121 S. College St., Myerstown, PA 17067

Friends:

Friends' Historical Library, Swarthmore College, Swarthmore, PA 19081

Haverford College, Quaker Collection, Magill Library, Haverford, PA 19041

Jewish:

American Jewish Archives, 3101 Clifton Ave., Cincinnati, OH 45220

Yiddish Scientific Institute—YIVO, 1048 Fifth Ave., New York, NY 10028

American Jewish Historical Society, 2 Thornton Rd., Waltham, MA 02154

Latter Day Saints:

Historian's Office, Church Archives, Historical Department, 50 East North Temple St., Salt Lake City, UT 84150

The Genealogical Society, 50 E. North Temple, Salt Lake City, UT 84150

Lutherans:

Concordia Historical Institute, Dept. of Archives and History. The Lutheran Church-Missouri Synod, Historical Library, Archives and Museum on Lutheranism, 801 De Mun Ave., St. Louis, MO 63105.

Archives of American Lutheran Church, Wartburg Theological Seminary, 333 Wartburg Place, Dubuque, IA 52001

Archives of the Lutheran Church in America, Lutheran School of Theology at Chicago, 1100 East 55th St., Chicago, IL 60615

Luther College, Decorah, IA 52101

Lutheran Archives Center at Philadelphia, 7301 Germantown Ave., Philadelphia, PA 19119

Lutheran Theological Seminary, Gettysburg, PA 17325

Concordia Theological Seminary, St. Louis, MO 63105

Finnish-American Historical Archives, Hancock, MI 49930

St. Olaf College (Norwegian), Northfield, MN 55057

Archives of Cooperative Lutheranism, Library of the Lutheran Council in the U.S.A., 315 Park Ave. S., New York, NY 10010

Lutheran Theological Southern Seminary, 4201 N. Main St., Columbia, SC 29203

Mennonites:

Bethel College, Historical Library, N. Newton, KS 67117

The Archives of the Mennonite Church, 1700 South Main, Goshen, IN 46526

Menno Simons Historical Library and Archives, Eastern Mennonite College, Harrisonburg, VA 22801

Mennonite Historical Library, Bluffton College, Bluffton, OH 45817

Methodists:

Commission on Archives and History of the United Methodist Church, Box 488, Lake Junaluska, NC 28745

Archives of De Pauw University and Indiana Methodism, Greencastle, IN 46135
Drew Theological Seminary, Madison, NJ 07940
Garrett Biblical Institute, Evanston, IL 60201
Duke University, Durham, NC 27706
United Methodist Publishing House Library, 201 Eighth Ave. S., Nashville, TN 37202
New England Methodist Historical Society Library, Boston University, School of Theology, 745 Commonwealth Ave., Boston, MA 02215
Emory University Library, Atlanta, GA 30322
Perkins School of Theology, Bridwell Library, Southern Methodist University, Dallas, TX 75222
The Upper Room Library and Museum, 1908 Grand Ave., Nashville, TN 37203
World Methodist Council material: The World Methodist Building, Lake Junaluska, NC 28745
Historical Society, 1810 Harvard Bldg., Dayton, OH 45406 (E.U.B.)

Moravians:
The Archives of the Moravian Church, 1228 Main St., Bethlehem, PA 18018
Moravian Archives, Southern Province of the Moravian Church, Drawer M., Salem Station, Winston-Salem, NC 27108

Pentecostals:
Oral Roberts University Library, 7777 South Lewis, Tulsa, OK 74105

Presbyterians:
Presbyterian Historical Society and Department of History, United Presbyterian Church in the U.S.A., 425 Lombard St., Philadelphia, PA 19147
Historical Foundation Montreat, NC 28757
Princeton Theological Seminary, Speer Library, Princeton, NJ 08540
McCormack Theological Seminary, 800 West Belden Ave., Chicago, IL 60614

Reformed:
Calvin College, Grand Rapids, MI 49056 (Christian Reformed)
Commission on History, Reformed Church in America, New Brunswick Theological Seminary, New Brunswick, NJ 08901
Evangelical and Reformed Historical Society, Lancaster Theological Seminary, Lancaster, PA 17603. (Reformed in the U.S., Evangelical and Reformed)

Roman Catholics:
Archives of the American Catholic Historical Society of Philadelphia, St. Charles Boromeo Seminary, Overbrook, Philadelphia, PA 19151
Department of Archives and Manuscripts, Catholic University of America, Washington, DC 20017
University of Notre Dame Archives, Box 513, Notre Dame, IN 46556
St. Mary's Sem. & Univ., Roland Park, Baltimore, MD 21210
Georgetown University, Washington, DC 20007
St. Louis University, St. Louis, MO 63103

Salvation Army:
The Salvation Army (Eastern Territory), 120 W. 14th St., New York, NY 10011

Schwenkfelder:
Schwenkfelder Library, Seminary Ave., Pennsburg, PA 18073

Shakers:
Western Reserve Historical Society, Cleveland, OH 44106
Ohio Historical Society, Division of Archives & Manuscripts, Columbus, OH 43211

Swendenborgian:
Academy of the New Church Library, Bryn Athyn, PA 19009

Unitarians and Universalists:
Harvard Divinity School Library, 45 Francis Ave., Cambridge, MA 02138
Rhode Island Historical Society, Providence, RI
Meadville Theological School, 5701 S. Woodlawn Ave., Chicago, IL 60637
Archives of the Unitarian-Universalist Association, 25 Beacon St., Boston, MA 02108

The United Church of Christ:
Archives of the United Church of Christ, 555 W. James St., Lancaster, PA 17603
Congregational Library, 14 Beacon St., Boston, MA 02108
Chicago Theological Seminary, 5757 University Ave., Chicago, IL 60637
Divinity Library, and University Library, Yale University, New Haven, CT 06520
Library of Hartford Theological Seminary, Hartford, CT 06105
Harvard Divinity School Library, Cambridge, MA 02138
Eden Archives, 475 E. Lockwood Ave., Webster Groves, MO 63119. (Evangelical and Reformed)

STANDARD GUIDES TO CHURCH ARCHIVES

William Henry Allison, **Inventory of Unpublished Material for American Religious History in Protestant Church Archives and other Depositories** (Washington, D. C., Carnegie Institution of Washington, 1910, 254 pp.).
John Graves Barrow, **A Bibliography of Bibliographies in Religion** (Ann Arbor, Mich., 1955), pp. 185-198.
Edmund L. Binsfield, "Church Archives in the United States and Canada: a Bibliography," in **American Archivist**, V. 21, No. 3 (July 1958) pp. 311-332, 219 entries.
Nelson R. Burr, "Sources for the Study of American Church History in the Library of Congress," 1953. 13 pp. Reprinted from **Church History**, Vol. XXII, No. 3 (Sept. 1953).
Church Records Symposium, **American Archivist**, Vol. 24, October 1961, pp. 387-456.
Mable Deutrich, "Supplement to Church Archives in the United States and Canada, a Bibliography," Washington, DC: 1964.
E. Kay Kirkham, **A Survey of American Church Records, for the Period Before The Civil War, East of the Mississippi River** (Salt Lake City, 1959-60, 2 vols.). Includes the depositories and bibliographies.
Peter G. Mode, **Source Book and Bibliographical Guide for American Church History** (Menasha, Wisc., George Banta Publishing Co., 1921, 735 pp.).
Society of American Archivists. **American Archivist**, 1936/37 (continuing). Has articles on church records and depositories.

STATISTICAL AND HISTORICAL SECTION

Aug. R. Suelflow, **A Preliminary Guide to Church Records Repositories,** Society of American Archivists, Church Archives Committee, 1969. Lists more than 500 historical-archival depositories with denominational and religious history in America.

United States, Library of Congress, Division of Manuscripts, **Manuscripts in Public and Private Collections in the United States** (Washington, D.C., 1924).

U. S. Library of Congress, Washington, D. C.: **The National Union Catalog of Manuscript Collections,** A59—16 vols. see below. Based on reports from American repositories of manuscripts.

Vol. 1, 1959—reports 1959-61 with index, 1959-61
Vol. 2, 1962—2 parts, with cumulative index 1959-62
Vol. 3, 1963—1964, new index
Vol. 4, 1965—cumulative index for 1963-65
Vol. 5, 1966—with index from 1963-1966
Vol. 6, 1967—with index for 1967
Vol. 7, 1968—with index for 1967-68
Vol. 8, 1969—with index for 1967-69
Vol. 9, 1970—with index for 1970
Vol. 10, 1971—with index for 1970-71
Vol. 11, 1972—with index for 1970-72
Vol. 12, 1973-74—with index for 1970-74
Vol. 13, 1975—reports
Vol. 14, 1975—index
Vol. 15, 1976—reports
Vol. 16, 1975-76—index

Contains many entries for collections of church archives. This series is continuing. Extremely valuable collection. Researchers must consult the cumulative indexes.

Notes

The Libraries of the University of Chicago, Chicago; Union Theological Seminary, New York; and Yale Divinity School, New Haven, have large collections.

The Archives of the National Council of the Churches of Christ in the U.S.A., and predecessor agencies, have been transferred to the Presbyterian Historical Society, 425 Lombard St., Philadelphia, PA 19147

The Missionary Research Library, 3041 Broadway, New York, NY 10027, has a large collection of interdenominational material.

The Library of the American Bible Society, Broadway at 61st St., New York, NY 10023, has material on the history of transmission of the Bible text, Bible translation, etc.

Zion Research Library, Boston University, 771 Commonwealth Ave., Boston, MA 02215 has a noteworthy archival collection.

"Specialized Research Libraries in Missions" are described by Frank W. Price in **Library Trends,** Oct, 1960, V. 9, No 2, University of Illinois Graduate School of Library Science, Urbana, IL 61801.

MAIN DEPOSITORIES OF CHURCH HISTORY MATERIAL IN CANADA

The list of depositories of church history material which follows was reviewed recently by the Rev. C. Glenn Lucas, Archivist-historian of the United Church of Canada, to whom the editor is grateful.

A few small Canadian religious bodies have headquarters in the United States, and therefore the reader is advised to consult "Main Depositories of Church History Material and Sources in the United States," which immediately precedes this section for possible sources of information on Canadian religious groups.

Anglican:

General Synod Archives, 600 Jarvis St., Toronto, Ontario M4Y 2J6. Archivist: ———. Also Diocesan Archives.

Baptists:

Canadian Baptist Archives, McMaster Divinity College, Hamilton, Ontario L8S 4K1.

Evangelical Baptist Historical Library, 74 Sheppard Ave., W. Willowdale, Ontario M2N 1M3

Baptist Historical Collection, Acadia University, Wolfville, Nova Scotia B0P 1X0

Congregational:

Congregational Christian Church Collection, Victoria College, Toronto, Ontario M5S 2C4

Disciples of Christ:

Canadian Disciples Archives, 39 Arkell Rd., R.R. 2, Guelph, Ontario N1H 6H8. Archivist: James A. Whitehead

Reuben Butchart Collection, Victoria, College, Toronto, Ontario M5S 2C4

Jewish:

Jewish Historical Society of Western Canada, Ste. 403, 322 Donald St., Winnipeg, Manitoba R3B 2H3. Archivist: L. Hershfeld

Canadian Jewish Congress (Central Region) Archives, 150 Beverley St., Toronto, Ontario M5T 1Y6. Archivist: Stephen A. Speisman

Lutheran:

Lutheran Council in Canada, 500-365 Hargrave St., Winnipeg, Manitoba R3B 2K3. Archivist: Rev. N. J. Threinen

Evangelical Lutheran Church in Canada, 247—1st Ave., N., Saskatoon, Saskatchewan S7K 4H5. Archivist: Dr. G. O. Evenson.

Lutheran Church—Canada, Ontario District, 149 Queen St., S., Kitchener, Ontario N2G 1W2. Archivist: Rev. W. W. Wentzlaff; Manitoba-Saskatchewan District, 1927 Grant Dr., Regina, Saskatchewan, S4S 4V6. Archivist: Rev. P. G. Becker; Alberta-British Columbia District, 205-10645 Jasper Ave., Edmonton, Alberta T5J 1Z8. Archivist: Rev. N. J. Threinen.

Lutheran Church in America, Eastern Canada Synod Archives, Wilfred Laurier University, Waterloo, Ontario N2L 3C5. Archivist: Rev. E. R. W. Schultz; Central Canada Synod Archives, Lutheran Theological Seminary, 114 Seminary Cres., Saskatoon, Saskatchewan S7N 0X3. Archivist: Mr. D. K. Hande;

Western Canada Synod, 9901—107 St., Edmonton, Alberta T5K 1G4. Archivist: Dr. W. H. Freitag.

Mennonites:

Conrad Grebel College, Archives Centre, Waterloo, Ontario N2L 3G6. Archivist: Sam Steiner

Mennonite Brethren Bible College, Center for Mennonite Brethren Studies in Canada, 77 Henderson Hwy., Winnipeg, Manitoba R2L 1L1, Archivist: Herbert Giesbrecht

Canadian Mennonite Bible College. Archives of the General Conference of Mennonites (Church), 600 Shaftesbury Blvd., Winnipeg, Manitoba R3P 0M4. Archivist: Lawrence Klippenstein

Free Methodist:

Mr. John Seigsworth, Chmn., Historical Committee, 300 Humber Ave., Oshawa, Ontario L1J 2T2

Pentecostal:

The Pentecostal Assemblies of Canada, 10 Overlea Blvd., Toronto, Ontario M4H 1A5.

Presbyterian:

Presbyterian Archives, Knox College, University of Toronto, Toronto, Ontario M5S 2E6. Archivist: Dr. John Meir

Roman Catholic:

Centre for Canadian Catholic Church History, St. Paul's College, University of Ottawa, Ottawa, Ontario. (Also: Archdiocesan archives in Montreal, Quebec City, Halifax, Ottawa, St. Boniface, Manitoba, and Vancouver)

United Church of Canada:

Central Archives, Victoria University, Toronto, Ontario M5S 2C4. Archivest-Historian: Rev. G. Glenn Lucas. Also Regional Conference Archives.

A GUIDE TO CANADIAN CHURCH ARCHIVES

Edmund L. Binsfield, "Church Archives in the United States and Canada. A Bibliography," in American Archivist, V. 21, No. 3 (July 1958), pp. 311-332, 219 entries.

IV: INDEX

INDEX

INDEX